The Boundary Commissions

MANCHESTER
UNIVERSITY PRESS

The Boundary Commissions

Redrawing the UK's map
of parliamentary constituencies

D. J. Rossiter, R. J. Johnston
and C. J. Pattie

Manchester University Press

Manchester and New York

distributed exclusively in the USA by St. Martin's Press

Published by Manchester University Press
Oxford Road, Manchester M13 9NR, UK
and Room 400, 175 Fifth Avenue, New York, NY 10010, USA
http://www.man.ac.uk/mup

Distributed exclusively in the USA by
St. Martin's Press, Inc., 175 Fifth Avenue, New York,
NY 10010, USA

Distributed exclusively in Canada by
UBC Press, University of British Columbia, 6344 Memorial Road,
Vancouver, BC, Canada V6T 1Z2

British Library Cataloguing-in-Publication Data
A catalogue record for this book is available from the British Library

Library of Congress Cataloging-in-Publication Data applied for

ISBN 0 7190 5083 9 *hardback*

First published 1999

06 05 04 03 02 01 00 99   10 9 8 7 6 5 4 3 2 1

Typeset in Times
by Northern Phototypesetting Co. Ltd, Bolton
Printed in Great Britain
by Bookcraft (Bath) Ltd, Midsomer Norton

Contents

List of figures

List of tables

List of boxes

Acknowledgements

The research reported here would not have been possible without the assistance of a wide range of bodies and individuals. Much of it was undertaken with a two-year (1995–97) research grant from the Leverhulme Trust, part of which was used to employ David Rossiter; we are extremely grateful to the Trust for its support and for its sympathetic consideration of our various requests.

Most of the work reported in Chapters 5–7 could not have been undertaken without the full co-operation of the four Boundary Commissions and their staffs. We are deeply indebted to all four sets of Commissioners for acceding to our requests for access to a wide range of documents, to the Assistant Commissioners who agreed to be interviewed during their busy schedules, and to the Commissions' staffs for their unfailing helpfulness. We are particularly indebted to the Commissions' Secretaries, Bob McLeod (England and Wales), David Jeffrey (Scotland) and John Fisher (Northern Ireland), for their support in a great variety of ways. All of the copies of documentation provided to us by the Commissions have been deposited in the Special Collections of the University of Essex Library, where they are available to be consulted by other researchers: we are grateful to the Librarian, Robert Butler, for his willing assistance with this.

Many people are involved in the redistribution process in various capacities, and those we have approached have been very generous with their help. The political parties throughout the United Kingdom have been forthcoming with materials and willingness to be interviewed regarding the events of 1991–95: we are especially grateful to David Gardner, Rob Hayward, Chris Rennard and Dame Angela Rumbold. A large number of MPs responded to our questionnaire, as also did many local government officers. We are extremely grateful to Rob Hayward and Dame Angela for reading and commenting on the manuscript.

Other researchers have been of considerable assistance, too. Just after our research started in 1995 we were fortunate to attend a two-day seminar at Nuffield College organised by Iain McLean and David Butler, where we not only met many of the main actors involved in the redistribution process but were able to test our initial ideas. Philip Cowley, John Curtice, David Denver, Danny Dorling, Iain

McLean, Colin Rallings, Andrew Russell and Michael Thrasher have provided particular assistance at various stages; Pippa Norris provided us with some valuable data from the Candidates Study which she conducted with Joni Lovenduski; and David Butler very kindly agreed to write a Foreword to this book. Simon Godden, of the School of Geographical Sciences at the University of Bristol, produced the excellent maps and diagrams.

We are also indebted to JANET (the Joint Academic Network operated by British Universities) for facilitating the flow of material between us. The project started with one of us in Colchester, one in Sheffield and one in Oxford, but soon after our geography became more complicated, with one living and working in Oxford, one working in Sheffield and living in Ely, and the third working in Bristol and living in Salisbury. Without the network joining us together, and the staff in our various institutions who made sure it worked for us, the research would have been much more tedious (and demanding of paper).

Foreword by David Butler

The political map of the United Kingdom has been redrawn eight times since the 1832 Reform Bill. At first there was substantial political interference with the findings of the Boundary Commissioners but gradually their autonomy was established. Yet the Commissioners, independent and honourable as they have been, have to work under statutory rules which have evolved incrementally over the years and which are in some ways confusing and contradictory. The Home Office, the legislative draftsmen and Parliament itself do not come well out of the story.

'If it ain't broke, don't fix it'. There has been no great scandal in the history of boundary-drawing - only a lot of muddle and incomprehension. This book chronicles the confusions: the attempt to set up permanent machinery in 1944 and its cumbrous modification in 1946 and 1958; the controversial suspension of redistribution in 1969; the misguided attempt to bring in the courts in 1982; the arbitrary changes to the timetable in 1992. It also records the long-drawn-out hypocrisies involved in Local Inquiries and the conflicting considerations that have guided Assistant Commissioners in their verdicts. It is a story that has never been fully told before. At a time when so many parts of the United Kingdom's electoral arrangements are under scrutiny this book should be read as an object lesson in the legislative and administrative process.

Underlying this book there is a moral. In the 1950s the rules led the Commissioners to draw boundaries that favoured the Conservatives; in 1951 they won a clear Parliamentary majority although they secured one per cent less of the UK vote than the Labour party. But in 1997 an equally objective redistribution of seats produced a situation when, if the votes had been more equal, Labour would have won 82 more seats than the Conservatives. There is no way in which even the most honest and efficient drawing of compact contiguous districts with equal population can permanently guarantee equity between the parties. But while we retain the first-past-the-post voting those who administer it need to read this book.

Introduction

On five occasions since the Second World War, the independent Boundary Commissions established in 1944 for that purpose alone have conducted comprehensive reviews of all of the constituencies from which MPs are elected to the House of Commons. Four of those reviews have recommended changes to at least three-quarters of the existing constituencies. Approximately once every decade, therefore, MPs face the possibility of some disruption to their occupancy of a Parliamentary seat. At the very worst, their constituencies may be abolished, and their Parliamentary careers ended, unless another can be found where their party will adopt them as candidates and they can then win the succeeding electoral contest. Most constituencies remain in place, but for many their boundaries will be changed and their population compositions (and thus political complexions) altered. Some of those changes may be beneficial, making it easier for the incumbent to hold the seat at the next election, but others may be damaging to her or his electoral prospects: in any case, uncertainty will be introduced. That uncertainty is the eventual outcome of a procedure that may take a year or more for any one constituency, during which the incumbent MP will be nervously awaiting the Commission's deliberations and hoping to influence them, within the legal constraints set.

The deliberations over each individual constituency cause uncertainty for the incumbent MP plus her or his party organisation and other supporters. For the political parties nationally, the entire period of the Commissions' work is full of uncertainties, as they evaluate what the likely consequences for them are in terms of the number of seats they can expect to win at the next election, and the amount of local party reorganisation that may be necessary to promote victory then. They too will be seeking to influence the Commissions' deliberations, both to assist their incumbent MPs in at least sustaining their re-election chances and also to ensure an overall system of constituencies which best meets their partisan interests.

If such change to the map of Parliamentary constituencies is so nerve-racking, why is it done, why are there such frequent redistributions (the American term is redistrictings)? The answer is to be found in political theory, particularly the theory underpinning representation in liberal democracies. This is extremely over-simplified in the slogan 'one person, one vote: one vote, one value'. A voter in a constituency with 100,000 electors will have much less influence over the outcome of an election there, if just one MP is to be elected, than a voter in a constituency with only 50,000, which can be presented as inequitable: each voter should have the same (potential) influence. Thus one cannot have a fixed set of constituencies for a long period of time if the geography of electors is changing; to do so will almost certainly lead to anomalies, with some large and some small constituencies whose electors have unequal influence over election outcomes.

This potential for inequality was widely recognised in the United Kingdom during the nineteenth century as franchise reform was pursued and a growing proportion of the adult male population was granted the right to vote. Three redistributions were undertaken in concert with the three Reform Acts which changed the franchise and the geography of those entitled to vote. But those redistributions were extremely political activities, with constituency boundaries drawn up, wherever possible, within *ad hoc* general rules determined by Parliament to promote the majority party's electoral interests. By the twentieth century, there was an increasing acceptance that such biased redistributions were contrary to democratic ideals, and arguments were advanced that they should be undertaken regularly, and not just when a government decided they were desirable; that they should be conducted in the context of clear rules; and that the work should be done by Commissions which were independent of Parliament and the political parties. These were generally accepted, and the *House of Commons (Redistribution of Seats) Act 1944* was the first piece of legislation to implement them.

Since then the four Commissions (one for each of England, Northern Ireland, Scotland and Wales) established in 1944 have operated independently of Parliament, with their terms of reference occasionally altered. But they have not operated entirely outside the political arena, because parties can make representations on the Commissions' provisional recommendations, which may then be revised in the light of those representations before being transmitted to Parliament for action: unlike the situation in some countries, the Commissions do not implement their recommendations, which is a decision reserved to Parliament. The Parliamentary arena can thus be used to try and influence not only what the Commissions do (by rewriting the rules to which they work) but also the acceptance or otherwise of their recommendations. This has been the case on several occasions during the last fifty years. When the Commissions delivered their Initial Reports in 1947, for example, this was followed by a government request that they reconsider the situation in some English urban areas with relatively large recommended constituencies, which was challenged by the opposition as blatant gerrymandering. Seven years later, when the Commissions' reports on their First Periodical Reviews were delivered, many MPs complained that changes were being made too soon after the previous ones, and that the Commissions had not justified their actions in many cases (or been prepared to hear submissions against their recommendations): the law was changed in 1958 to take all three of these concerns into account.

The next Periodical Review reports were delivered in 1969. The government believed that they would be damaging to its re-election chances, and tried to avoid bringing them before Parliament. It was forced to do so, but achieved its goal by instructing its MPs to vote against acceptance of the Commissions' recommendations, so ensuring that the next election (which it lost!) was fought in the old rather than the new constituencies. Twenty-three years later, the opposite occurred, when an incumbent government believed that it would benefit electorally from the introduction of new constituencies before the next election, and so legislated to bring forward the timing of the Fourth Periodic Review. Thus only the Third Periodic Review went through without some Parliamentary concern, but this was preceded by a Court case brought by members of the opposition who sought a ruling that the English Commission had, in effect, disobeyed the rules; its goal was either to delay the next general election or to ensure that it was fought in the old rather than the new constituencies.

The definition of Parliamentary constituencies is thus an issue of considerable political import and debate. There is no standard treatment of the current system, however, of how it has evolved and how it is operated. David Butler's (1958 and 1963) pioneering book on *The Electoral System in Britain since 1918* covers only part of the period and deals with a much wider canvass than just redistribution: the origins of the current system were outside its remit and there have been considerable changes to the system since the 1960s. The only other substantial treatment was in Roger Mortimore's (1992) Oxford D. Phil. thesis, from which unfortunately virtually nothing has been published. The current book has been prepared to fill the gap in our understanding of the current situation. Its main focus is the period since 1944; it reports on not only the debates about redistribution and the outcomes of the five undertaken since then but also much original research into the procedures of all four Commissions during their Fourth Periodic Review which ended in 1995. The absence of any detailed previous treatment of nineteenth-century redistributions – with very few exceptions historians have focused on the franchise reforms – has been tackled by research into what happened then, based on secondary sources, to provide a foundation on which an appreciation of twentieth century developments can be built.

The book is in two main parts. The first provides a general overview of the relevant democratic theory of representation (Chapter 1), of redistributions before 1944 (Chapter 2), of the changing legal framework since then (Chapter 3) and of the outcome of the five reviews conducted since 1944 (Chapter 4). The second half reports in detail on our research into the Fourth Periodic Review (1991–95), with three chapters (Chapters 5–7) on the Commissions' work and two on the political and electoral implications (Chapters 8–9).

Electoral reform is a continuing topic of political debate in the United Kingdom, with occasional peaks of interest, usually after a general election whose result is seen by some as 'unfair'. The debate may focus on reforming the current system, with a new set of rules to guide the Commissions, for example, or it may be more widely based in discussions about replacing the current method of electing the UK's Parliament by one which is perceived as 'fairer'. We are currently experiencing much debate of the latter type, some of which has already led to political action, though not with regard to elections to the House of Commons. Alternative (proportional) electoral systems are to be used in the 1999 elections to the European Parliament and for the first elections to the Scottish Parliament and the Welsh Assembly (also in 1999). Furthermore, a Commission has been established to make a recommendation on an alternative, more proportional system for elections to the House of Commons, which will then be placed before the electorate at a referendum. All of those systems employ constituencies – spatially-defined divisions of the national territory – as the basic units which elected members will represent. We do not address those issues in detail here, but our detailed discussion of the current method of defining constituencies offers a base against which to evaluate proposed alternatives. (See Johnston, Pattie and Rossiter, 1998b, 1998c for our suggestions regarding appropriate rules to guide the work of Boundary Commissions under different electoral systems.)

Part I

Redistribution
in the United Kingdom

1

The theory of representation and the 'British compromise'

The nature of representation and of representative government are frequent topics of concern for political theorists, whereas for practitioners the main issues are how to make agreed representation principles work. Resolution of the issues involved has produced a great variety of political systems (ranging from New Zealand's unicameral sovereign Parliament, for example, through the tripartite separation of powers at federal and state levels in the USA, to Switzerland's decentralised decision-making procedures) and, within them, of electoral systems. The latter differ not only on major subjects – such as whether constituencies should be single- or multi-member and how those members should be elected – but also on details, such as how constituencies should be defined (IDEA, 1997). Whereas many countries have superficial similarities in their electoral organisation, very few indeed are directly comparable in all aspects. Even those whose democratic structures are based on the Westminster system differ considerably; Australia, Canada and New Zealand, for example, all differ from the United Kingdom and from one another in the procedure for constituency definition, on which this book focuses.

A fundamental tension which has continually faced the designers and redesigners of the UK's electoral system is between models of the MP as a representative of people and those of the MP as a representative of communities – a tension which was characterised by an MP in the debates on the 1947 *Redistribution of Seats Act* as between the mathematic and the organic. (The difference was first introduced by the then Home Secretary, J. Chuter Ede, in 1946 – *Hansard*, vol. 431, 13 December 1946, col. 1559–1560 – and it was further emphasised by C. Pickthorn in the 1954 debate on the Boundary Commissions' reports on their First Periodic Reviews – *Hansard*, vol. 535, 12 October 1954, cols. 1806–1809.) This book explores the resolution of that tension in the definition of Parliamentary constituencies, focusing especially on the period since 1947 and with particular reference to the Fourth Periodic Review of constituencies undertaken by the Boundary Commissions in the early 1990s.

The organic v. mathematic strain is not the only tension to influence constituency definition, however. It involves two 'fairness principles' – fairness to people (the mathematic requirement) and fairness to communities (the organic). A further such principle is fairness to parties. With their predominance in the House of Commons and most other aspects of political life, it is not surprising that the political parties want an electoral system, including a procedure for defining and redefining Parliamentary constituencies, which is at least fair to them. (Each party, of course, would like a system which is more than fair to it, and less fair to its rivals, but since all cannot succeed in such a zero-sum game they are likely to settle for a procedure which is fair to all.) Hence, this further tension has to be added to the mathematic v. organic: electoral systems have to be designed to be fair to people, to communities, and to parties. Achieving all three is extremely difficult, as this book documents.

The development of political representation in the UK

Representation is a familiar concept with a variety of interpretations. Birch (1971, 13) has identified three major distinct usages of the term: (1) representatives as agents or spokespersons, acting on behalf of others; (2) representatives as samples, reflecting the characteristics and interests of the populations from which they are drawn; and (3) representatives as symbols. The first two are widely employed in discussions of political representation, and are frequently confounded. Indeed, UK MPs are apparently asked to play both roles, and the two are often in conflict. This is clarified on certain occasions when MPs vote in the House of Commons: are they delegates, required to vote according to the instructions of their principals (i.e. their constituency electors), or are they merely a selection drawn from the wider population who act as they see fit? This question over the representative's degrees of freedom may be complicated by a tension between the wishes of the electorate and those of the party, on whose policy platform the MP was elected: parties may demand a vote that is contrary to either or both of the MP's interpretation of constituents' wishes and his or her own personal views.

The development of representative government in the UK stemmed not from popular agitation for greater involvement in decision-making but rather from successive monarchs' needs for legitimation of and support for their actions, especially those which depended on levies or taxes being raised on the general population. Their initial gatherings of representatives had no decision-making powers, but as the English monarchs' demands grew and the need for legitimation expanded, so such ritual assemblies were slowly transformed into deliberative bodies, whose members then sometimes demanded that their powers be enshrined in legislation or similar written agreements – as with the contract between the barons and King John signed in 1215 (the Magna Carta).

As this system of Parliamentary sustenance for the monarchy grew, the first elements of a system of political representation were put in place. It was based on the two main components of the country's territorial organisation (Reeve and Ware, 1992): the counties and the boroughs. The counties, or shires, were England's ancient administrative units, within which the landowners were enfranchised. Initially, all barons were entitled to attend on the monarch in Parliament, but in 1254 each county was invited to send two representatives who had been elected in the relevant County Court as persons who could speak for their constituents and would deliver local support for the policies agreed in Parliament: in effect, as Birch (1971, 27) notes, they were delegates whose assent to the monarch's requests was interpreted as conveying the consent of those they represented. The same was true of the borough representatives from the urban settlements which had been incorporated as towns and given privileges with regard to the conduct of trade. They, too, were entitled to two representatives, but whereas the franchise for the counties was externally defined (as freeholders with land worth above a specified value) in the boroughs it was locally determined, producing wide variations in the extent of the franchise. (This remained in place until the 1832 Great Reform Act, as illustrated in Chapter 2; see also Reeve and Ware, 1992, 46.)

Over the following 600 years, the structure of Parliament remained largely that instituted in the thirteenth century, though there were some changes in who was represented (such as representation for the Universities; Reeve and Ware, 1992, 47) and the widening of the territorial coverage with expansion of the United Kingdom following the incorporation of Wales (conquered in 1282 and annexed by the English in 1536), Scotland (Act of Union, 1707) and Ireland (Act of Union, 1800). There was considerable debate about the nature of the representation involved, however, especially in the seventeenth and eighteenth centuries as Parliament's power was enhanced relative to the monarch's. The view which came to dominate was crystallised by Edmund Burke's classic 1774 speech to the electors of Bristol, in which he contended that Parliament is a deliberative assembly which acts in the interests of the nation as a whole, so that once elected MPs are independent of those who voted for them: they do not act as agents for the narrow interests of their particular constituents (though they may consult them to learn of their views), nor are they to be considered as a representative sample, acting for that portion of the population whose interests they are closest to. Rather they are elected representatives, who govern as they see fit, having been authorised to by the election process (Birch, 1971, 40).

Birch (1971, 48) argues that by the nineteenth century two major concepts of political representation had emerged.

1 Sovereignty rests with the people, and not with a hereditary ruler, so that power is granted popularly and ultimately rests with the people: MPs are elected to exercise that power on their behalf.

2 MPs are independent makers of national policies, who are empowered to do so by the electoral process. Parliament is a representative assembly 'whose power derives its legitimacy from the fact that its members have gone through a process of election, even though they have no obligation to take instructions from their electors'. (Indeed, the concept of Parliamentary privilege as operated in the House of Commons allows electors to make requests of their MPs, but not to give them instructions backed by threatened sanctions – though the

threat always exists, since MPs have to return to their constituents regularly to seek re-election.)

Implementing those concepts became increasingly contentious during that century, however, when reforms of the franchise and other aspects of the electoral system were pressed as the nature of British society changed irrevocably following the industrial revolution. Who should representatives be elected by, and on what criteria?

Nineteenth-century developments

Population growth and, even more so, its redistribution through urban-industrialisation created challenges to the established status quo of Parliamentary representation during the nineteenth century. The creation of the large industrial conurbations not only saw the growth of a substantial number of urban settlements whose populations were substantially under-represented (on an arithmetic basis) relative to those of the older – 'rotten' – boroughs, many of which had declined in size and some of which were almost entirely depopulated, such as Old Sarum, where elections were never contested and the number of electors, all 'owned' by Earl Caledon, was 11 in 1831 (see Chapter 2); it also saw the establishment of major cities outside that ancient structure of urban communities, which had no separate Parliamentary representation but were included within wider, largely rural, constituencies – Birmingham, Manchester and Sheffield were the classic exemplars.

For those who contended that if the House of Commons was to be an assembly acting in the national interest then its composition should reflect the canvass of that interest, this uneven representation was contrary to the democratic principles on which Parliament had been founded. A redistribution of seats was needed. This argument was supported by some who saw MPs as agents, delegated to represent their constituents' interests, because some of those interests were not being argued. Against those views, others promoted what Birch terms the concept of *virtual representation*: as long as some industrial cities are represented, then it doesn't matter that Sheffield is not, because its interests will be presented by MPs elected from similar places, so that the national interest will always incorporate the requisite variety.

That last argument was increasingly criticised by those who contended that more equitable representation was needed, which could not be guaranteed by a Parliament dominated by representatives elected from among the wealthy in the small boroughs and the shires (Reeve and Ware, 1992, 48). Joseph Priestley, drawing from Rousseau, argued in the late eighteenth century that civil government created by a sovereign people was in effect

> a social contract in which men surrendered part of their natural freedom in return for a certain degree of influence on government decisions. All citizens were therefore entitled to political representation, and could not be obliged to obey the laws unless it was granted to them. (Birch, 1971, 52)

This was an argument for both extension of the franchise ('no taxation without representation') and more equitable representation. The latter case was increasingly accepted by the country's legislators, and when the franchise was extended by the century's three Reform Acts (1832, 1867 and 1885) there was an accompanying geographical redistribution of seats to promote equitable representation of people.

The tension between the mathematic and the organic – between the representation of people and of communities/places – was resolved in the nineteenth century by a shifting emphasis towards the mathematic, although, as we discuss below, the adopted system was a compromise between the two. Before dealing with that, however, two additional features of the British political system must be introduced, each of which became part of that compromise.

Expansion of the UK and Parliamentary representation

The system just described evolved largely in England and for England, but over the intervening centuries between the thirteenth and the nineteenth it had to incorporate the three separate countries which were joined to England – Wales, Scotland, and Ireland – and granted representation in its Parliament.

Each country was allocated a number of seats in the House of Commons when it joined what eventually became the United Kingdom. Scotland, for example, was allocated 45 by the Act of Union of the English and Scottish Parliaments in 1707 (McLean, 1995), and this was raised to 53 in 1832, 72 in 1885 and 74 in 1918 (the Scottish Universities obtained representation in 1868; Reeve and Ware, 1992, 47). Ireland was allocated 100 seats by the Act of Union in 1800: this was increased to 105 in 1832 but reduced to 103 in 1885; when the Irish Free State left the UK, 12 were retained for Northern Ireland, which was a less than proportionate number relative to either population or electors because a separate Assembly was established for Northern Ireland (on this decision, see French, 1978). Wales initially had 24 seats: including Monmouthshire, it had 27 before the 1832 Reform Act and 31 after, and the number was increased to 33 in 1868, 34 in 1885 and 37 in 1918.

In terms of proportional representation, McLean shows that Scotland was under-represented (relative to its share of the UK's population) until 1885, proportionately represented from then until 1917, and over-represented after that redistribution. Wales was over-represented until 1918.

The Speaker's Conference of 1917, which heralded the first reform of constituencies in the twentieth century, gave target populations of 70,000 per constituency in each of England, Scotland and Wales, but the number of seats for Ireland was unchanged (suggesting that the 1921 treaty was anticipated): after 1921, when the size of the House of Commons was reduced from 707 to 622, Scotland became significantly over-represented with 74 seats whereas Wales (including Monmouthshire), with 37, was proportionately represented.

The further Speaker's Conference of 1944, which presaged that year's *Repre-*

sentation of the People Act and *House of Commons (Redistribution of Seats) Act*, guaranteed significant over-representation for both Scotland and Wales. The case for it, as advanced for Scotland, rested on three contentions (McLean, 1995, 261):

1 The need for substantial representation of a separate nation, if necessary over-and-above that entitled by strict application of arithmetic rules;
2 A case that areas of population decline, as a result of economic decay, should not be penalised, when the reasons for that decay were outwith local control; and
3 An argument (which McLean shows had no factual basis) that Scotland was guaranteed a certain level of representation by the Act of Union.

Those arguments were successful, and the Conference Minutes record a strong argument that 'it would be very desirable, on political grounds, to state from the outset that the number of Scottish and Welsh seats should not be diminished' (McLean, 1995, 262–3); the number in Northern Ireland was similarly not cut. (In 1977, when Northern Ireland's representation was discussed following abolition of its separate Assembly at Stormont, similar arguments were made for over-representation to the Speaker's Conference on electoral law, notably by the Unionist parties, but were rejected.)

These recommendations were enacted in the *House of Commons (Redistribution of Seats) Act 1944*, and the guaranteed minimum numbers of seats for Scotland and Wales were not disputed during the Parliamentary debates on the Bill. The *1949 House of Commons (Redistribution of Seats) Act* consolidated the position in the first clause in its Rules for Redistribution of Seats. Although the detailed wording was altered in the *Parliamentary Constituencies Act 1986*, the numerical contents were not, so that over-representation for Scotland and Wales continued to be guaranteed (and, as in 1944, MPs were not prepared to face the political consequences of tackling that when the issue was raised in 1986 in the considerations of the Home Affairs Select Committee; see Chapter 3). Northern Ireland is a special case: it was under-represented while the Stormont Assembly was in existence, but allocated between four and six more seats in 1977, which gives it proportionate representation relative to England. The over-representation of Wales was extended by its Boundary Commission's Fourth Periodic Review in 1995, when Northern Ireland too was allocated an extra seat (see Chapter 4).

The growth of the party system

The nineteenth century saw the inauguration of a further major trend in British political life, paralleled in most comparable democracies, with the growing importance of political parties, both in Parliament and in the country's life generally. This has been substantially extended during the twentieth century.

Political parties are perceived as necessary to the functioning of modern Parliamentary democracies for two main reasons:

1 They provide a focus for the mobilisation of sectional interests around which individual voters will cluster. Those who join the party, are active in it and cam-

paign for it are likely to be committed voters who accept its policy stances and general positions, and their support does not have to be continually reactivated; the same will be true of those who identify with the party, even if they do not join it and participate in its activities (hence the importance of the concept of party identification in many analyses of voter mobilisation stemming from the seminal work of Campbell *et al.*, 1956).

2 They provide a body within Parliament whose members are committed to vote in agreed ways and, if the party becomes part of a government, to implement an agreed legislative programme.

In each case, the party guarantees support (subject to individuals deciding to with-draw it) in both the electorate and Parliament. Parties provide the continuity for democratic government.

The evolution of political parties in Western Europe has been crystallised in a classic model formulated by Lipset and Rokkan (1967). They identified two main events in the continent's history that were fundamental to the development of political parties: each is associated with the development of two electoral cleav-ages, divisions within society exploited by political parties which mobilise sup-port on different sides of the divide.

I   *The national revolution*: this is associated with the growing importance of the nation-state and of centralised power, which stimulated two cleavages within many of the societies involved.

1 *Subject v. dominant culture (or core-periphery)*. In many European coun-tries the emerging state apparatus sought domination over the territories of more than one national culture, and the centralised bureaucracy was usually associated with one of those cultures only. The outcome may have been con-flict between the dominant culture and the other(s), which was exploited by different political parties. To the extent that the cultures occupied different parts of the state territory, this was a spatial cleavage between the national core area (the dominant culture area) and the periphery.

2 *Church(es) v. government*. Until the emergence of the nation-state the church(es) were extremely powerful within Europe, and the growth of the state apparatus was a major threat to that established power base. The chal-lenge was reflected in some places by a developing political cleavage between those who wished to sustain church power through political parties based on religious principles and those who supported secular organisa-tions.

II *The industrial revolution* stimulated conflicts within societies, as new modes of organising production, distribution and exchange took root. As with the national revolution, two major cleavages were generated.

3 *Primary v. secondary economy (or town v. country)*. The growth of manu-facturing industry saw the emergence of a new class of capitalists whose trading concerns were very different from those of the traditional landed interests. Whereas the former backed the principles of free trade so that they could sell their products world-wide, the latter sought protection through

tariffs against imports from other countries. The difference was thus largely between urban-based interests on the one hand and those based in the countryside on the other.

4 *Workers v. employers (the class cleavage)*. The growth of manufacturing industry created a new class of employees, concentrated in the combined job and housing markets of the factory towns, where conflicts focused on working conditions and wages. The workers were increasingly mobilised by political parties allied to trades unions, whereas the interests of employers were reflected by parties based in the emerging urban middle classes.

All four did not emerge within each society, depending on the nature of conditions there. Lipset and Rokkan argued that the extension of the franchise through the nineteenth and twentieth centuries provided a near-universal context within Western Europe for the evolution of the class cleavage, which was overlain on the existing pattern created by the other three and to a greater or lesser extent supplanted them.

The British party system is generally presented as dominated by the class cleavage. Divisions based on the two cleavages associated with the national revolution have only rarely been strong, especially after the Irish Free State left the UK in 1921; nationalist parties representing Scottish and Welsh interests have come to the fore only in the last three decades; and the church–state divide has been typical of Northern Ireland only (though it is reflected in the politics of cities with large Irish immigrant populations, notably Glasgow and Liverpool). Thus, British politics for most of the twentieth century have been polarised around the class divide, with a minor urban–rural divide largely incorporated within it. The promotion of a 'central party' in recent decades sought to break that mould but, despite winning the support or about one-quarter of all voters in the 1980s, failed to see this translated into a substantial Parliamentary presence (Crewe and King, 1995) because of the nature of the electoral system, in part because of the implicit 'partisan gerrymandering' which is implicit to constituency-based electoral systems when minority parties have spatially dispersed rather than areally concentrated support (Gudgin and Taylor, 1979; Taylor and Johnston, 1979; Taagepera and Shugart, 1989).

Representation and the 'British compromise'

The British system of representation has thus had to accommodate three separate requirements: representation of people, of communities, and of parties. The first involves calls for all electors to be represented equally, which is operationally interpreted in most countries as requiring a constant ratio of MPs to electors across constituencies (within limits and with exceptions for 'special geographical considerations'). Each MP then has the task of representing (or being an agent for) the entire population of her or his constituency irrespective of who they voted for, and even if they did not vote at all (including those ineligible to vote). The second requires constituencies to be defined so that they mesh, as far as is practicable, with communities having clearly defined separate interests, so that their MPs are a representative sample of the 'national whole'. (This was made clear in the instructions to the 1885 Boundary Commissioners, who were asked to 'fix boundaries according to the pursuits of the population'; Chadwick, 1976, 677.) At one scale within the UK this involves determining how many constituencies should be allocated to the three 'minority countries' of Scotland, Wales and Northern Ireland in order to ensure that their separate interests are properly represented in the House of Commons. At a finer-grained scale, it involves determining what the local communities are within each country and how their separate interests (to the extent that they exist) can be represented.

These requirements call for decisions over the relative importance of two criteria – the mathematic and the organic. Different weights have been given to them in various countries which employ the first-past-the-post electoral system with single-member constituencies. In New Zealand, for example, equality of electorates was the paramount decision-criterion in redistricting procedures prior to the adoption of a new electoral system in 1993. That has also been the case in the USA since the Supreme Court's malapportionment decisions of the 1960s, although attempts were made to introduce racial composition as an important criterion through the various Voting Rights Acts; that has now been thrown into doubt by a 1994 Supreme Court decision (see Congressional Quarterly, 1994; Forrest, 1997). In Fiji, a complex system of six overlapping sets of single-member constituencies, with each elector having four separate votes, was created to meet the community representation criterion (Leonard and Natkiel, 1987). In the UK, however, a typically 'British compromise' has been reached, with both criteria included in the Rules scheduled for the independent Boundary Commissions and with, according to a 1982 court decision (as discussed in Chapter 3), no clear priority between them.

The third requirement, fairness in representation for the political parties, is formally excluded from the British redistricting process and the independent Commissions act in a 'blind' manner when drawing constituency boundaries – they are not aware of the likely electoral consequences of their proposals; the political parties are consulted by the Commissions on general principles of redistricting, however, and can make representations during the obligatory public consultations on the Commissions' recommendations. The entire electoral system is well known for its propensity to produced biased outcomes, with bias defined as the difference between a party's percentages of the votes cast and of the seats won (Rossiter *et al.*, 1997b). Furthermore, the extent of that bias is subject to manipulation, as demonstrated in computer simulations which show that very different allocations of seats between the parties are possible within individual cities, depending on the particular solution to the redistricting issue recommended by the Commissions (Johnston and Rossiter, 1983; see also Chapter 8). The political parties are well aware of this, and exploit their opportunities to make representations to the Commissions regarding proposed constituencies and to argue for alternatives – in written statements and at public Local Inquiries – in order to promote their own electoral interests, without at any stage explicitly referring to them.

The 'British compromise' to the issues raised by the difficulties of meeting the various requirements for representing separate interests within the chosen electoral system is, therefore, just that, a compromise. It expresses two of the main requirements – equal representation of people and separate representation of communities – in its redistricting rules which, as this book demonstrates, are ambiguous and unclear with regard to the relative priority of the various criteria. With regard to the third – the representation of party interests – it allows the parties to seek influence over the redistricting procedures, within the context of the other, ambiguous, criteria. This book is about the evolution and operation of those procedures, with particular reference to the most recent redistricting of Parliamentary constituencies.

2

The evolution of the
'British compromise': 1832–1944

The Rules under which the current Boundary Commissions operate when reviewing Parliamentary constituencies evolved over more than a century, as the franchise was extended and theories of representation were modified and put into
practice. The process of change was far from gradual, however (Butler, 1963, 2–3):

> Even during the period when electoral reform was one of the most important of
> political issues, interest in the subject fluctuated and change came in stages. There
> are five major heads under which electoral legislation can be classified: systems of
> voting; redistribution; suffrage; corrupt practices; and administrative machinery.
> The simple plurality system of election has hardly been tampered with since the
> Middle Ages, but the other four questions have tended always to be dealt with col-
> lectively. Indeed it might be said that there are only five dates in the evolution of
> the electoral system – 1832, 1867, 1883–85, 1918 and 1948. Apart from the Ballot
> Act in 1872, the Equal Franchise Act in 1928, the Representation of the People Act
> in 1945, and, perhaps, one or two Corrupt Practices Acts in the nineteenth century,
> there has been no other legislation which in any way approached major importance.

This chapter focuses on one of those heads only, redistribution, and its links to
changes in the suffrage, as an introduction to the legislation which inaugurated
the current system – the *House of Commons (Redistribution of Seats) Act 1944*.

The changes that occurred during this period, and especially during the nineteenth century, involved a total revolution in the nature of the electoral system, especially as it refers to representation. Under the current legislation, all constituencies
return a single MP, local government boundaries provide the template within which
constituencies are defined, and equality of electorates is a key criterion to be applied
by the independent Boundary Commissions when undertaking redistributions. At
the beginning of the nineteenth century, there were only five single-member constituencies in England (out of 489) and 32 (out of 100) in Ireland, although all Scottish and Welsh MPs (45 and 24 respectively) were elected as a constituency's sole
representative (Brock, 1973). The local government map provided the template for
the allocation of seats (apart from the University representation), but although the
County boundaries were well defined those of many of the Boroughs were not (and

Boroughs accounted for 465 of the 658 seats in the 'unreformed' House of Commons of 1830). Thus, when redistributions occurred in the nineteenth century, although the decisions on where seats should be allocated were political, and taken by Parliament, the boundaries of the new Borough seats had then to be defined by (politically) appointed Boundary Commissioners. The key decisions were, thus, explicitly political, taken by Parliament on recommendations produced by the government – and thus liable to manipulation for electoral gain.

The nineteenth-century Reform Acts

The major focus of the nineteenth-century reforms was extension to the franchise, plus the related introduction of secret ballots and the elimination of corrupt practices involved in electioneering by candidates. At the beginning of the century, as Seymour (1915, 2) notes:

> the power of selecting the members of the House of Commons lay practically with a small group of influential persons. In many of the electoral constituencies the number of voters was trifling and their choice of a representative was dictated by the peer or wealthy commoner whose influence in the community was supreme.

By the century's end, the Reform Acts of 1832, 1867 and 1885 had 'increased the electorate so that from a small and unevenly distributed number of voters it grew to include all but a comparatively slight portion of the adult male population' (Seymour, 1915, 3). Redistribution was a consequence of these changes.

The redistributions, however, were very substantial, especially those associated with the 1867 and 1885 Acts. Table 2.1 compares the composition of the 'unreformed' House of 1830 with that which convened after each of the century's Reform Acts. Before the reforms began, whereas England predominantly returned MPs from two-member constituencies (both Borough and County), the representation from Scotland and Wales was entirely from single-member constituencies and Ireland occupied an intermediate position, with its County members coming from two-member constituencies while its Boroughs returned single MPs. Borough (i.e. urban) representation dominated (465 of the 658 seats). The great majority of Boroughs had very small electorates, as Brock's (1973, 20) figures for England indicate:

Number of electors	Number of Boroughs
more than 5000	7
1001 – 5000	36
601 – 1000	22
302 – 600	24
101 – 300	36
51 – 100	21
51 – 100	21
less than 50	56

Many of these, and especially the smallest, were what were known as 'pocket boroughs', with very small numbers of electors who, in a public balloting system, were in effect 'owned' by one or two major landlords (these were known as 'rotten boroughs'). Wiltshire, for example, had sixteen Boroughs returning two MPs each prior to the 1832 Act, most of which had been represented in Parliament since 1295. Several of these had not had a single recorded contested election (at least in 'living memory' in 1830: Philbin, 1965). They included Old Sarum (which returned Pitt the Younger to the House of Commons during his Parliamentary career): its population in 1831 was 15; it had 11 qualified electors, but never had a contested election; and its MPs were nominated by the sole landowner, the Earl Caledon. Elsewhere, the relatively small numbers of electors were either the Borough corporation or the holders of burgage tenements, and both groups' votes were in effect 'owned' by the Borough's patron(s), as with the Earl of Radnor at Downton (1831 population, 450; electors 100) and Sir William Ashe A'Court at Heytesbury (population, 81; electorate 26 burgage holders). Only Cricklade had a large electorate, with 1600 enfranchised householders. Even in the larger settlements, however, the possibilities of corruption were great. Philbin (1965) refers to Wootton Bassett as a classic example of a 'rotten borough': most of its 309 eligible voters worked for either the Earl of Clarendon or Viscount Bolingbroke, but many of their votes were 'bought' by Joseph Pitt (who also 'owned' other Boroughs) for £22,000, and individual votes were 'for sale' at between 20 and 45 guineas. Only five of those Boroughs retained their two MPs after the 1832 legislation, with four others being reduced to a single seat.

The Reform Act, 1832

Although it is often known as the 'Great Reform Act', the Act of 1832 was more important symbolically than arithmetically: it introduced only relatively modest increases to the franchise, but initiated the processes of change which the later Acts built upon substantially. In 1831, the electorate of England and Wales was 435,391; in 1833 it was 652,777 – an increase of 49 per cent – but this was in a country with an adult male population, according to the 1831 Census, of nearly 14 million (the figures are from Seymour, 1915, 533); Scotland and Ireland had 2.4 and 7.8 million respectively. Franchise extension was strongly contested, with the main pressure being for more voters in the burgeoning urban areas, where the Whig party had its main support. The extension granted was complex, but the main features benefited town and country alike.

These extensions increased both Borough and County electorates by 49 per cent (some 123,000 additional voters in the Counties and 94,000 in the Boroughs). This apparent even-handedness across the two main sectional interests was countered by the redistribution of seats, however, which removed representation, in part if not in its entirety, from many small Boroughs (most of them in the agricultural regions of the south such as Wiltshire – see above) and allocated seats to the rapidly growing industrial towns, most of which were in the north. It certainly did not achieve parity of representation, however, as Seymour (1915, 45) notes:

Table 2.1 *The changing composition of representation to the House of Commons during the nineteenth and early twentieth centuries*

	England	Scotland	Wales	Ireland	Total
The 'unreformed' House, 1830					
Boroughs					
Four-member	2	0	0	0	2
Two-member	195	0	0	2	197
Single-member[a]	5	15	12	31	63
Counties					
Four-member	1	0	0	0	1
Two-member	39	0	0	32	71
Single-member[b]	0	33	12	0	45
Universities					
Two-member	2	0	0	0	2
Single-member	0	0	0	1	1
Total	244	48	24	66	382
Seats	(489)	(45)	(24)	(100)	(658)
After the 1832 Act					
Boroughs					
Four-member	1	0	0	0	1
Two-member	133	2	0	6	141
Single-member	54	19	13	27	113
Counties					
Six-member	1	0	0	0	1
Four-member[c]	26	0	0	0	26
Three-member	7	0	0	0	7
Two-member	6	0	3	32	41
Single-member[d]	1	30	9	0	40
Universities					
Two-member	2	0	0	1	3
Total	229	51	28	66	374
Seats	(470)	(53)	(32)	(105)	(660)
After the 1867 Act					
Boroughs					
Four-member	1	0	0	0	1
Three-member	4	1	0	0	5
Two-member	89	2	1	6	98
Single-member	91	19	14	27	151
Counties					
Ten-member[c]	1	0	0	0	1
Eight-member[c]	1	0	0	0	1
Six-member[c]	10	0	0	0	10
Four-member[c]	15	0	0	0	15
Three-member	7	0	0	0	7
Two-member	5	3	4	32	44
Single-member[d]	1	26	9	0	36
Universities					
Two-member	2	0	0	1	3
One-member[e]	1	2	0	0	3
Total	228	53	28	66	375
Seats	(460)	(60)	(33)	(105)	(658)

	England	Scotland	Wales	Ireland	Total
After the 1885 Act					
Boroughs					
Two-member	21	1	1	1	24
One-member	183	29	10	14	236
Counties					
One-member	231	39	22	85	377
Universities					
Two-member	2	0	0	1	3
One-member	1	2	0	0	3
Total	438	71	33	101	634
Seats	(461)	(72)	(34)	(103)	(670)
After the 1917 Act[f]					
Boroughs					
Two-member	11	1	0	0	12
One-member	233	31	11	4	279
Counties					
Two-member	0	0	0	3	3
One-member	230	38	24	2	294
Universities					
Three-member	0	1	0	0	1
Two-member	3	0	0	0	3
One-member	1	0	1	1	3
Total	478	71	36	10	595
Seats	(492)	(74)	(36)	(13)	(615)

Notes:
a   In Scotland and Wales many boroughs and burghs were combined into single-member constituencies
b   In Scotland, six Counties returned members for alternate Parliaments only (i.e. three at each election)
c   Each of these Counties was divided into two-member constituencies
d   In Scotland three of these involved the pairing of Counties
e   In Scotland, Edinburgh and St Andrew's together elected one member, as did Glasgow and Aberdeen
f   The data for Ireland refer only to the six counties which remained in the United Kingdom after 1922

Source: for 1830 and 1832 Brock (1973: 19-20, 310-311), 1867 Hanham (1978), 1885 and 1917 Craig (1989)

Figure 2.1 *The regions used by Seymour in his analyses of the nineteenth-century redistributions*

The redistribution was certainly tentative and incomplete, leaving the industrial sections of the country inadequately represented; but, as the first assault upon the electoral predominance of the small boroughs, and thus upon aristocratic influence, it may be regarded as a significant factor in the democratization of representative institutions.

The Counties lost no seats: English Counties retained at least their two representatives each, and the Welsh Counties one, and 65 additional seats were allocated (Table 2.2). The main shifts involved the Boroughs (36 Boroughs had registered electorates less than 25 and a further 115 had less than 200): 143 Borough seats were withdrawn, 69 of them from the southwestern Counties (monarchs had been especially partial to granting Borough status for small Cornish and Wiltshire towns), and 65 new ones were allocated. The Act had five sched- ules, the first of which completely disenfranchised 56 Boroughs (i.e. removed both of their representatives), whereas the others reduced the representation of 30 Boroughs to one MP each, allocated two MPs to 22 towns, allocated one MP to a further 21 towns, and allocated 65 new representatives to County divisions. In addition, Scotland gained eight new seats and Ireland five. All of Scotland's new seats were in the Boroughs (Edinburgh's representation was increased from one to two, Glasgow was allocated two seats, and Aberdeen, Dundee, Greenock, Paisley and Perth were each allocated one). In Ireland, four new two-seat Bor- oughs were determined (joining Cork and Dublin) and the number of single-mem- ber Boroughs decreased from 31 to 27.

In terms of the geography of representation, the main losses were from Bor- oughs in the southern regions (a map of Seymour's regions is given as Figure 2.1). One part of Cornwall, now represented by a single MP, had contained nine Boroughs which returned two representatives each in 1830, for example, but the 'rotten boroughs' were not confined to that part of England: in the Vale of York the small town of Boroughbridge and the adjacent village of Aldborough (both in the same ecclesiastical parish) each returned two MPs prior to 1832. Although the southwest and southeast were the main losers, however, with a net loss of some 81 seats, and the main gains were in the north of England (33 seats in the northern and northwestern regions alone; see Table 2.2), the geography of population and set- tlement emerging from the industrial revolution was far from fully reflected in the redistribution.

Compared to the issue of extending the franchise, the redistribution of seats was a much more important political issue; according to Seymour (1915, 52) '[t]he saving or winning of seats was the vital issue'. The Tories argued that seats once allocated could not be withdrawn from Boroughs, and that many of the small ones offered nomination opportunities for young talented politicians who would otherwise not readily gain access to Parliament. (They also claimed that some of the Boroughs – Bridgwater, Bristol, Cricklade, Hythe, Malmes- bury, Old Sarum, Rochester and Sandwich – in effect provided MPs for the colonies, since they were 'owned' by the East India Company!) To counter the Whigs' case for enfranchising the northern industrial cities (led by Macaulay's rhetoric) the Tories fought many individual cases, whilst arguing that the gov- ernment was denuding England in favour of increased representation for Scot- land and Ireland. The Bill, comprising five complex Schedules, was eventually passed after many compromises. (In Schedule A, for example, the decision on which Boroughs would lose both seats was not determined by their population alone. Instead, each Borough's importance was assessed by a system which (1) divided its number of houses by the average for 100 Boroughs and (2) divided its assessed taxes by the average for those Boroughs. The two results were summed, points were awarded, and those with fewest points lost their seats; Seymour, 1915, 58.) Despite the many changes, therefore, control of Parliament

Table 2.2 *The impact of the nineteenth-century Reform Acts on the geography of representation*

	1832					1868					1885				
	C		B			C		B			C		B		
	–	+	–	+	Net	–	+	–	+	Net	–	+	–	+	Net
Region															
Metropolitan	0	0	0	10	+10	0	0	0	4	+4	0	5	2	39	+42
Southeastern	0	9	36	3	–24	0	4	8	1	–3	0	5	20	1	–14
South Midland	0	6	9	0	–3	0	0	5	0	–5	0	1	12	0	–11
Eastern	0	9	10	0	–1	0	6	8	0	–2	1	5	18	4	–10
Southwestern	0	9	69	3	–57	0	4	17	0	–13	0	7	33	0	–26
West Midland	0	7	5	5	+7	0	0	6	0	–6	1	4	16	2	–11
Midland	0	10	0	7	+17	0	4	1	2	+5	0	1	12	9	–2
Northwestern	0	6	3	17	+20	0	7	5	7	+9	0	30	8	18	+40
Northern	0	6	11	18	+13	0	0	2	4	+2	0	6	12	0	–6
South Wales	0	2	0	2	+4	0	0	0	1	+1	0	3	4	1	0
North Wales	0	1	0	0	+1	0	0	0	0	0	0	1	1	0	0
Scotland					+8					+5					+12
Ireland					+4					0					–2
Universities					+1					+3					0
Total	0	65	143	65	0	0	25	52	19	0	2	68	138	74	+8

Key: C – Counties; B – Boroughs; – seats lost; + seats gained
Source: Seymour (1915, 535–7)

remained with the urban middle classes, especially those in the country's market towns rather than its industrial centres. And those market towns remained over-represented. Harwich and Totnes, for example, had 214 and 217 registered electors respectively after the Act, compared to 11,600 and 11,300 in Westminster and Liverpool (Brock, 1973, 312). Similarly in Ireland, whereas Dublin (returning two MPs) had 7000 voters, Lisburn, the smallest Borough separately represented, had just 90 and Carrickfergus, the largest, had only 1000 (Brock, 1973, 312–13).

The details of the new constituencies were determined by specially appointed Boundary Commissioners. When the Act was initially drafted, it was assumed that the new constituencies would be coterminous with the Borough boundaries, but many of these were 'outdated and artificial' (Brock, 1973, 157), and some indeed were unknown with any degree of certainty. In addition, the latest Census did not record the population of every Borough, using ecclesiastical parishes instead as its reporting units. Thus the Commissioners were given the task, once the outline of the Act's schedules was known, to determine the boundaries of the relevant Boroughs and, where necessary, determine the boundaries of newly created constituencies within the Counties.

With regard to the Boroughs, the government collected information from the relevant authorities on their populations, property values and electors. It appointed Lt. T. Drummond RE to supervise the work of determining Borough boundaries, giving him a list of twenty people considered suitable to act as Commissioners. These were expected to validate the data, and Drummond's circular letter to them stated that (reprinted in Parliamentary Representation, 1831):

> It is scarcely necessary to state that the information you furnish must be such as will stand the test of the strictest examination ... it will be borne in mind that the information you obtain is intended to be laid before the government.

For small Boroughs, the particular concern was whether they contained at least 300 households whose properties had an annual value of at least £10, which in many cases would require extending the boundaries (where known) well beyond those currently used to define them. If extension was deemed necessary, then the Commissioners were enjoined (Parliamentary Representation, 1831) that:

> in fixing such boundaries it will be proper, as far as possible, to take the known limits of parishes, wards, townships or chapelries, or other known denominations.

As far as possible, the Borough constituencies were to be groups of administrative areas. The Commissioners could not recommend detaching sections from the existing Borough areas, were asked to make their recommended areas compact, if possible, and not to extend more than seven miles from the Borough boundary (which might require subdividing an administrative unit, to be undertaken only when 'manifest advantage results from establishing new boundaries'). The new boundaries should be either streams, roads or straight lines between conspicuous objects in the landscape, and must be described so that they can be followed on the ground. The Commissioners should pay attention to the direction in which the town was growing, or likely to grow, and:

> The employment of the surrounding population, their connection with the town or with the country, their municipal or rural character, may become proper objects of inquiry and consideration.

For larger Boroughs, where extension was not necessary to meet the 300 household threshold, the Commissioners were not expected to recommend extensions of more than one mile, and they were given greater freedom to divide parishes and other administrative areas. In effect, theirs was a power of remedy only in such cases.

When it had received the Commissioners' reports and recommendations (accompanied by superb coloured maps produced by the Ordnance Survey), the government (on 24 November 1831, only three months after the Commissioners had been appointed) asked a group of three (Drummond plus E. J. Littleton MP and Capt. F. Beaufort RN) to consider them and determine whether they were 'suitable to the places'. They were entirely satisfied.[1] On the larger Boroughs, for example, they reported that the 'utmost attention appears to have been bestowed by the Commissioners in examining the peculiarities of each' and on the two new constituencies for industrial districts (based on Stoke and Stroud) 'the boundaries which they propose appear to be in every respect appropriate'. They concluded that:

> Having gone through these reports with great care, and given them the best consideration in our power, we feel justified in expressing our opinion, that the boundaries proposed appear to have been in all cases carefully – and in those of difficulty and importance, judiciously and skilfully selected – that they are distinctly described and may, with the aid of the plans which accompany them, be easily traced on the ground – that they are conformable to the instructions of the government, and suitable to the places for which they are recommended.

The Commissioners' task regarding Boroughs was thus to separate the urban built-up areas from the countryside as a means of defining constituencies (many of which returned more than one MP). A smaller, parallel task was the definition of constituencies as divisions of the Counties identified in the Act. This was undertaken by a single Commissioner who reported on 23 English Counties returning two MPs each that:

> I wished to divide each County into two parts, equal in extent, equal in population, and equal in number of voters. I soon found that I could not do this without altogether breaking through the established divisions of Counties into parishes and hundreds, and without separate districts and places which, from their community of interest and feeling, manifestly ought to be placed in the same division of their County. As far, however, as I have found it compatible with a due regard to these considerations, I have endeavoured to approach towards each of these equalities …

Only in a few cases were hundreds divided between divisions (constituencies). In some already-divided Counties new divisions were suggested (as in Suffolk, where the populations of the previous divisions were 93,047 and 157,081 and those of the recommended new ones were 138,637 and 112,211); in others, he also sought to identify communities of interest, as in Cumberland where 'all the manufacturing and trading part of the County lies within the two Allerdale wards [creating a division with a population of 55,535], and the remaining three are almost all purely agricultural [their population was 70,337]'.

The work of these Commissioners and those overseeing them initiated what became the accepted method of determining constituencies during the nineteenth century. Parliament decided, in a draft Bill, where the seats would be allocated (which Boroughs would be represented, and by how many MPs, and how many MPs would be returned by each County). Commissioners were then appointed to do the detailed work of defining those areas on the ground, making recommendations as to the Borough boundaries and those of the separate single-member County constituencies. The brief was a very constrained one, therefore, with the government (through Parliament) having made the major decisions regarding the geography of representation.

Comparison of the outcome with the pre-reform situation (Table 2.1) shows that the main features of the changes were:
- a small redistribution of seats away from England;
- a substantial reduction in the number of two-member Boroughs in England, with a compensating growth in the number of single-member Boroughs; and
- major increases in the number of seats for a majority of English Counties.

Single-member constituencies remained very much in the minority, however, returning 152 of the 658 MPs, although England returned only one-third of these.

The Reform Act, 1867

Although it made a dent into the massive malapportionment that characterised the British electoral system at the start of the nineteenth century, the 1832 Act achieved relatively little in either extending the franchise or redistributing Parliamentary representation in line with the population distribution. According to Seymour (1915, 196–7):

> So long as a majority of the House of Commons was returned by the proprietors, a general and widespread system of corruption was unnecessary and accordingly not practised. The aristocracy held their boroughs as part of their estates and returned their members with as little effort as they presented church benefices to their protégés. ... Nomination had lost the supremacy of its control, but electoral power was not yet in the hands even of that class to which it apparently been assigned by the act of 1832.

Thus agitation for reform continued, focusing on the demand for universal (or at least universal male) suffrage, as advanced by the Chartist movement, but bringing in its wake the need for consequent redistribution of seats. As Gladstone put it in one of the debates (quoted in Smith, 1966, 27), 'every man who is not presumably incapacitated by some consideration of personal unfitness or of political danger is morally entitled to come within the pale of the Constitution'.

The pressure for reform suffered several setbacks, but was eventually met by the 1867 Reform Act, which almost doubled the number of enfranchised Parliamentary electors. The 1866 electorate of England and Wales was a little under 1.1 million; in 1869 it was almost exactly 2 million, an increase of 88 per cent (the largest yielded by any of the century's three Reform Acts). Furthermore most of that growth was in the Boroughs: the County electorates increased by 45 per cent, compared to 134 per cent for the Boroughs. The main beneficiaries were Borough householders who had occupied a home for at least two years, and who paid rates for the relief of the local poor, but the changes were tied to reforms of the local rating systems which remained spatially very variable. (Enfranchisement of the urban working class was not in the Tories' interests: Seymour, 1915, 275 claims that the explanation of government acquiescence to this 'remains yet to be discovered'.)

The debates over the consequent Redistribution Bill introduced in 1866, both between the main parties and within the Liberal government, focused on the likely political implications of proposed changes. The government, led by Russell, wanted to reduce the number of seats for small Boroughs (despite the loss of some Liberal MPs that this would produce, and who might therefore vote with the opposition against the plan in Parliament), in order to release seats to be real-located to the expanding towns and Counties. Expanding the House was rejected by the Cabinet, many of whose members believed that 'the House was already overcrowded and the nation was already over-represented' (Smith, 1966, 92), so disenfranchisement of small Boroughs seemed the only way unless, as was ini-tially proposed but later dropped because of the difficult negotiations that would have been involved, small Boroughs (with less than 8000 residents) were grouped together to share MPs. The proposals for pairing included Honiton and Bridport, which are 21 miles apart, and Cirencester and Evesham, which were separated not only by 25 miles but also by a four-and-a-half-hour rail journey (Smith, 1966, 95). Interestingly, groups of non-contiguous Boroughs forming separate con-stituencies were common in Scotland and Wales in the nineteenth century (eight of the ten single-member Welsh Borough constituencies comprised such groups after the Third Reform Act, for example, as did 13 of the 39 in Scotland; six of the 30 Scottish Burgh seats were for such groups after the 1918 Act). The Con-servatives wanted Borough boundaries extended (most were underbounded), thereby taking suburban 'Liberal-voting villa dwellers' into the towns and leav-ing a Conservative hegemony in the Counties (Halifax had 40,000 suburban res-idents beyond the Borough boundaries, for example; Smith, 1966, 96).

The debates over these issues, and a variety of others, led to defeat for the Bill introduced in 1866 by the Liberals, and the government subsequently resigned. It was replaced by a Conservative administration led by Disraeli, which intro-duced a further Bill in 1867 'devised to give the minimum of offence to the small borough men' (Smith, 1966, 215). During the course of the debates, Disraeli 'humiliated and outmanoeuvred his rival' (Gladstone) with great ease (Bradford, 1996, 271), as well as 'privately charming rebels' from within his own party (Smith, 1966, 218). The final form of the Bill was designed to favour the Con-servatives – Disraeli's biographer, Blake (1960, 396) refers to the matter being viewed by him 'first and foremost in the light of party expediency' – because the reallocation of seats was linked to the redrawing of Borough boundaries by (Brad-ford, 1996, 271):

> a Commission packed with Conservatives [which] effected the transference of arti-
> san suburban voters from the counties to the boroughs, the object being that poten-
> tially Liberal votes would be attached to Liberal constituencies, while the counties
> remained undilutedly Conservative.

Disraeli had initially proposed that it be heavily weighted with Conservative-favouring members, but was forced to change the balance somewhat (Cowling, 1967). The Commissioners had 'wide-ranging and indefinite powers' according to Cowling (1967, 231; see below). Not only did they interpret the instructions very liberally (by, for example, recommending incorporation of separate villages within a Borough because it appeared that they might develop into suburbs, as around Manchester) but they also reported in secret to a Cabinet sub-committee which in turn consulted Tory agents about the proposals. The result was that, save in the case of the West Riding, the Commission's final recommendations were 'blatantly one-sided'; nevertheless, although 'the Conservative agents were content ... the country gentlemen were far from convinced that the counties had been sufficiently scoured' of potential Liberal voters (Smith, 1966, 220).

The Commission's recommended extensions to the boundaries of 81 Boroughs were opposed not only by the Liberals but also by some Tories. Its report was referred to a Select Committee, as a sop to both groups, though it had only a small time to consider and report because of an impending dissolution. It recommended returning to the status quo situation in some cases (including Birmingham, Liverpool and Manchester) and a reduction in the proposed extensions to others (including Bristol and Nottingham), and these were adopted when the Select Committee's report was voted on in the House. In all, fifteen of the Commission's crucial recommendations were either rejected or reduced, thereby destroying 'the crucial part of the Conservative's redistribution' (Smith, 1966, 224); 58 English Boroughs were enlarged in the final Bill passed in 1868, however, as were 10 groups of Welsh Boroughs – all of them transferring Liberal voters from the County to the Borough constituencies (Cowling, 1967). Smith argues that the 'traditional ruling interests' were, therefore, favoured by the redistribution, not only because of the continued malapportionment discussed below but also because of the anomalous situation whereby urban but not rural labourers were enfranchised.

The Commissioners' appointment and terms of reference were set out on the 48th section of the 1867 Act, as follows:

> They shall immediately after the passing of this Act, proceed, by themselves or by Assistant Commissioners appointed by them, to inquire into the temporary boundaries of every Borough constituted by this Act, with power to suggest such alterations therein as they may deem expedient.
>
> They shall also inquire into the boundaries of every other Borough in England and Wales, except such Boroughs as are wholly disenfranchised by this Act, with a view to ascertain whether the boundaries should be enlarged, so as to include within the limits of the Borough all premises which ought, due regard being had to situation or other local circumstances, to be included therein ...
>
> They shall also inquire into the Divisions of Counties as constituted by this Act ... with a view to ascertain whether, having regard to the natural and legal divisions of each County, and the distribution of population therein, any and what alterations should be made in such Divisions or places.

They were required to hold advertised Local Inquiries and report 'with all practicable despatch'. (The statement of their duties and a copy of the Commissioners' full report is reproduced in every County and Borough report: Boundary Commission, 1868.) The five Commissioners conducted none of the Local Inquiries themselves. Instead, they divided England and Wales into 18 Districts, to each of which they appointed 'two Assistant Commissioners, namely, a Barrister-at-Law and an officer of the Royal Artillery or Royal Engineers, in order to secure a combination of the special professional qualifications required for receiving and weighing evidence, and for inspecting and describing existing and proposed boundaries'. A total of 265 Inquiries was held, and the reports were delivered on 5 February 1868, less than six months after the Act received the Royal Assent (15 August 1867) – the Commissioners were appointed on 16 August. The instructions to the Assistant Commissioners were sent out on 26 August (and they were asked to provide a weekly report on progress). Regarding Boroughs these included the requirements that:

- If the current boundaries were to be extended (contraction was only allowed for newly created Boroughs), these should be based on the outcome of their inquiries into whether 'there are any considerable number of houses beyond the existing Borough boundaries the occupiers of which, from community of interests with the Borough or from other local circumstances, may be considered as forming part of the Town population;
- attention should be paid to 'the directions in which a town is increasing';
- when extensions are proposed, they should 'ascertain and report whether the alterations are consistent with well-known limits, such as parochial and other boundaries'.

For County Divisions, they were required to report on 'the convenient character of the Divisions themselves' and whether alterations were necessary, in the context of the statement that:

> [i]t appears to have been the object of the Legislature to equalize, as far as practicable, the population of each Division, and to render the Division as compact as possible with regard to geographical position, without disturbing the old-established and well-understood boundaries of Hundreds. Where, however, probably owing to a scattered subdivision of the Hundreds, this has not been found practicable, the modern arrangement of Petty Sessional Divisions has been adopted.

The Commissioners reported that proposals for extending Borough boundaries were not popular. Indeed:

> We found that there was a general indisposition on the part of persons residing in the immediate neighbourhood of Boroughs to their premises being included within the Parliamentary Boundary; but that in almost every case this indisposition was attributable to the fear that an extension of Parliamentary Boundaries would be followed by a corresponding extension of Municipal area, and that consequently they would become liable to the payment of Borough Rates.

The great 'diversity of character and circumstances' meant that they found it 'impossible to lay down one general rule which would be applicable to all cases' and so each had to be dealt with 'according to its own special circumstances'. Of the 197 Boroughs existing before the Act, extensions were recommended for 81; of the ten new ones, extensions were proposed for three, contractions for four, and both extensions and contractions for two others.

Thirteen Counties had their representation altered. In recommending their division, the Commissioners 'adhered as far as practicable to the old and well established divisions of Hundreds' but in Somerset this was not practicable and so they used 'the more modern arrangement of Petty Sessional Divisions'. In most cases, they were very successful at grouping Hundreds into Divisions with relatively equal populations: the three divisions of Cheshire had 100,929, 119,417 and 122,483 residents, for example, the divisions of Norfolk were 112,852, 113,600 and 113,902, but those of the West Riding of Yorkshire were 527,592, 574,695 and 614, 829.

As in 1832, therefore, the Commission's main task was separating town from country for the purpose of Parliamentary representation by recommending new boundaries for the Boroughs; defining separate constituencies within an area was a much smaller task. Nevertheless, experience of defining boundaries was being accumulated, which would be drawn on in later redistributions and to a considerable extent set their parameters. The constraints on their freedom of action were very similar to those in place in 1832, and in addition their reports were only recommendations which, as noted above, were altered by Parliament in almost one-third of cases. The definition of constituencies remained very closely controlled by the politicians who would either benefit from or be disadvantaged by proposed changes.

Disraeli had also promised immediate reform for Scotland and Ireland. The Irish Bill was first delayed and then postponed indefinitely (because Irish supporters had indicated that their votes on the English, Welsh and Scottish Bills were contingent on there being no change in Ireland); it was later introduced, but its main proposal to increase County representation was opposed by the Liberals, and the Bill was withdrawn in 1868. For Scotland, Disraeli offered a further seven seats, including two to be shared by the country's four Universities. The Liberals claimed that an increase of 22 was necessary to give Scotland equality of representation with England and Wales, and the Bill was withdrawn. It was reintroduced in 1868, only slightly changed and still pro-Conservative; it survived, but only at the price of the seven additional seats coming from the smallest English Boroughs, rather than expand the House of Commons any further.

Before the Act, the Counties, with some 542,000 electors from a total population of 11.5 million, were somewhat under-represented relative to the Boroughs, which had 514,000 electors for 8.6 million people (ratios of 21.3 and 16.9 respectively). In 1869, the comparable ratios were 14.6 and 7.2, which meant that the Act had substantially skewed representation in favour of the urban areas. As Smith (1966, 6) rather over-states it:

> The Act ... hastened the development of the boroughs into preserves of the commercial interest and tipped the balance of representation in the Commons to the towns ... [it] broke the age-old rural bias of Parliament and brought the representative system into conformity with the realities of the nineteenth century.

If the distribution of seats had remained unchanged, however, there would have been very substantial inequities of representation within each group: Oxford had one elector per nine persons, for example, and Lincoln one per 11, whereas Warrington and Oldham had ratios of 1:34 and 1:40 respectively. The southern Boroughs were again the major losers from the redistribution (Table 2.2) and the northern towns the main gainers: 35 Boroughs each lost one of their two seats, six Boroughs lost both of their seats, and five others lost their sole seat. Countering this, 10 Counties had their representation increased: Lancashire and Yorkshire received five more seats for their various Ridings (which had substantial urban populations outside the incorporated Boroughs), and six major urban centres (Birmingham, Leeds, Liverpool, Manchester, Merthyr Tydfil – the largest town in Wales – and Salford) received an additional seat each. There was no other change in Wales, and none at all in Ireland. In Scotland, the Counties of Peebles and Selkirk were merged for this purpose, and so lost one seat; three Counties gained an additional seat (with each being divided into two separate constituencies); one new Burgh seat was created (Hawick); Glasgow and Dundee were each allocated an extra seat; and two University seats were created, one for Edinburgh and St. Andrew's, the other for Glasgow and Aberdeen.

Even after the Second Reform Act the British electoral system continued to favour the small Boroughs over the Shires, however (Table 2.3). In most regions, whereas the ratio of electors to population in the Boroughs more than halved between 1866 and 1869, in the Counties the reduction rarely exceeded one-third; furthermore, the ratios in the former areas were generally no more than half those in the latter. Regarding the ratio of population to MPs, on the other hand, although this increased slightly in the Boroughs, it decreased in the Counties of most regions: the rural areas retained much of their relative strength in the House of Commons.

The Act did reduce inter-regional disparities, especially with regard to the ratio of population to MPs, however, with one major exception: the under-representation of the metropolitan Counties (Middlesex and the London Boroughs), and to a lesser extent of the northwestern Counties (Cheshire, Lancashire and the West Riding of Yorkshire, according to Seymour's classification). These were the country's main urban-industrial centres, and they were very significantly under-represented in the House of Commons as well as, in London's case, having many fewer enfranchised citizens.

Thus, the 1867 Act carried forward the process of reform initiated in 1832, but nowhere near completed it; as Seymour (1915, 295) argues:

> [it] did much to wipe out the numerical anomalies which existed between borough and borough as well as between county and county. But to the more democratic reformers the measure was nevertheless unsatisfactory because of the partiality shown to boroughs.

Those still deprived of the vote were predominantly small traders in towns, artisans and labourers, especially those resident in mining districts, plus rural residents without substantial land-holdings; a movement to extend household suffrage

Table 2.3 *The ratios of electors to population and of MPs to population before and after the Second and Third Reform Acts in England and Wales*

| | Second Act | | | | Third Act | | | |
| | 1866 | | 1869 | | 1884 | | 1886 | |
Region	E:P	P:MP	E:P	P:MP	E:P	P:MP	E:P	P:MP
Boroughs								
Metropolitan	15.1	137,000	10.0	124,000	9.6	157,000	8.0	65,000
Southeastern	14.3	13,000	7.9	16,000	7.9	21,000	7.0	42,000
South Midland	13.6	8,000	6.3	10,000	6.8	14,000	6.2	30,000
Eastern	14.5	12,000	5.9	14,000	6.1	22,000	6.5	39,000
Southwestern	16.8	8,000	8.7	11,000	7.5	12,000	7.5	28,000
West Midland	16.0	19,000	6.6	18,000	7.0	25,000	8.7	48,000
Midland	17.5	32,000	6.1	34,000	6.3	47,000	5.9	56,000
Northwestern	20.4	49,000	7.0	48,000	7.2	67,000	6.8	58,000
Northern	16.6	17,000	6.3	20,000	6.0	30,000	5.5	46,000
South Wales	25.1	28,000	6.6	25,000	7.2	37,000	6.2	49,000
North Wales	9.7	18,000	6.6	18,000	6.6	22,000	6.5	23,000
Counties								
Metropolitan	24.9	184,000	14.6	184,000	10.2	197,000	5.5	53,000
Southeastern	23.0	72,000	13.7	59,000	13.1	84,000	5.6	57,000
South Midland	22.5	47,000	16.6	47,000	16.6	50,000	5.5	52,000
Eastern	20.9	66,000	15.0	53,000	15.1	60,000	4.6	44,000
Southwestern	20.3	68,000	15.3	56,000	13.8	56,000	5.5	50,000
West Midland	17.2	51,000	12.8	51,000	13.8	59,000	5.3	53,000
Midland	19.8	63,000	13.9	52,000	13.5	59,000	5.0	52,000
Northwestern	25.2	171,000	15.7	111,000	15.7	152,000	5.7	57,000
Northern	16.5	57,000	13.5	57,000	13.5	70,000	5.4	54,000
South Wales	18.6	53,000	11.5	54,000	13.2	63,000	5.3	47,000
North Wales	19.9	48,000	11.9	48,000	11.7	53,000	5.2	48,000

Key: E:P ratio of electors to population; P:MP – ratio of population to MPs
Source: Seymour (1915, 541–2)

to the rural areas developed. At the same time, it was recognised that although the 1832 and 1867 Acts had reduced the electoral power of the southern small towns and rural districts, they had by no means eliminated it: 'the power of the landowners was in reality but slightly reduced by the redistribution of 1867' (Seymour, 1915, 338). These differences were continually accentuated as population shifted to the burgeoning urban centres; by 1884, for example, South Lancashire had one MP per 193,277 residents, compared to one per 39,274 in Buckinghamshire, and whereas many small towns (such as Bodmin, Bridport, Chippenham, Devizes, Malmesbury, Tavistock, Wareham and Westbury) had one MP per 6–7000 residents, Birmingham had one per 133,586, Leeds one per 103,042, Liverpool one per 184,082, Manchester one per 131,225, Sheffield one per 142,205 and Wolverhampton one per 153,254. It remained the case that 'the upper classes profited greatly by the number of small boroughs and by the electoral disadvantage of the industrial constituencies' (Seymour, 1915, 349–50).

The Reform Act 1885

Table 2.4 indicates the situation in Great Britain and Ireland a decade after the 1867 Act. Two very clear patterns stand out:
1 The Borough populations were much better represented than the Counties'.
2 The larger the unit of local government, whether Borough or County, the poorer the representation.
The first of these was the most important, and reflected the greater enfranchisement of urban as against rural populations, as shown in the final column of Table 2.4: Boroughs had, on average, eight residents to every elector, whereas Counties had twice as many. These ratios were consistent across the size ranges, however. At the extremes, the smallest Boroughs averaged one MP per 5928 residents (one per only 736 electors) whereas the largest had the average MP representing over 150,000 people (and 17,000 electors). Even to bring the largest Boroughs alone down to the Borough average of an MP to every 41,142 people would have required allocating them another 120 seats, whereas to achieve the same ratio for the largest Counties (in the northern industrial areas for the most part) would have required 125. If there were to be no overall increase in the size of the House of Commons, this would involve removing separate representation from a majority of Boroughs and Counties – redistribution on a scale that was undoubtedly both practically and politically inconceivable.

Smith's (1966, 238) figures starkly illustrate the political issues. The electorates of the six largest Boroughs (Birmingham, Finsbury, Leeds, Liverpool, Manchester and Sheffield) grew from 98,363 in 1866 to 316,400 in 1877, but their representation remained at 16 seats; they returned twelve Liberals and four Conservatives in 1868 and ten Liberals and six Conservatives in 1874. Six of the smallest Boroughs, on the other hand (Andover, Knaresborough, Midhurst, Northallerton, Petersfield and St Ives) had a total electorate of only 2060 in 1866 and 5470 in 1877 (an increase of 166 per cent, compared to 222 per cent for the

Table 2.4 *Constituency size variations in Great Britain and Ireland, 1881*

Size	Population	Electors	C	MPs	P:MP	Ratios E:MP	P:E
Counties							
50,000>	609,235	39,116	19	21	29,011	1,863	15.58
50,000–74,999	1,762,134	110,121	28	43	40,980	2,561	16.00
75,000–99,999	1,947,490	140,902	22	41	47,499	3,436	13.82
100,000–124,999	2,631,433	167,287	23	47	55,988	3,559	15.73
125,000–149,999	3,554,281	202,706	27	54	65,820	3,755	17.53
150,000–199,999	2,427,399	136,835	15	29	83,703	4,718	17.73
200,000<	7,105,149	400,680	25	48	148,024	8,347	17.73
Total	20,037,121	1,197,647	159	283	70,803	4,232	16.73
Boroughs							
7,000>	248,990	30,913	42	42	5,928	736	8.05
7,000–9,999	250,317	33,662	30	30	8,344	1,122	7.43
10,000–19,999	713,137	91,826	48	72	9,904	1,275	7.77
20,000–29,999	569,963	74,265	22	32	17,811	2,320	7.67
30,000–49,999	1,543,466	207,721	38	55	28,063	3,776	7.43
50,000–99,999	2,309,614	334,961	34	53	43,577	6,320	6.90
100,000–199,999	2,430,047	340,340	18	33	73,637	10,313	7.14
200,000<	6,745,594	736,789	19	43	156,874	17,134	9.16
Total	14,811,118	1,850,477	251	360	41,142	5,140	8.00

Key: C – number of constituencies; P:MP – population per MP; E:MP – electors per MP; P:E – population per elector
Source: Hanham (1978, 403–4)

largest six) and returned six MPs; two of these were Conservatives in 1868, as were all six in 1874. As Smith puts it: 'in 1874, the members [from] six small boroughs neutralized the Liberal representation of six other boroughs with over 300,000 more electors', which was a very substantial pro-Conservative bias built-in to the electoral system. He called it a 'capricious system', and in the mid-1880s a further attempt was made to reform it, by a Liberal government strongly divided between its Whig (the old landed element) and Radical (largely urban) compo-

nents, after a decade in which legislative attention had focused on corrupt practices, electoral expenditure and voter registration.

There was agitation on behalf of the unenfranchised miners, urban tradesmen
and rural householders, for example, as well as against the residential requirement which prevented those mobile within the labour and housing markets from
registering as voters; at the extreme were those who campaigned for full adult
suffrage. The major anomaly remaining after the 1867 Act was the separate treatment of Borough and County artisans: whether you were enfranchised or not
depended on where you lived and where your job was. As pointed out by a Scottish trade unionist in 1884 (quoted in Jones, 1972, 1):

> In the districts of Govan and Partick there were 94,000 inhabitants, the majority
> of whom were skilled mechanics. Of this population, 19,442 persons exercised
> the municipal franchise; but only 3426 persons had a voice in the political affairs
> of the country. That was through no fault of their own, but was due to the shift-
> ing character of their employment, occasioned by the removal of large firms to
> cheaper land.

In effect, you could 'improve' your personal position in the labour market by
moving from an 'urban' to a 'rural' local government area, but lose the vote as
a consequence.

Under considerable pressure from his party's Radical wing, Gladstone proposed
in 1884 to extend the current Borough provisions to County areas. The 67 per cent
increase in the electorate which resulted (from 2.6 million in 1883 to 4.4 million
in 1886) involved a 162 per cent increase in the County electorate compared with
only 11 per cent in the Boroughs. This, according to Seymour (1915, 488)

> went far ... towards completing the transfer of predominant political power from
> the aristocracy and middle classes to the nation as a whole. So far as the electoral
> aspect of the question was concerned, the process only demanded for its comple-
> tion along broad lines, a redistribution of seats. This was accomplished in 1885.

In order to get his Franchise Bill through, especially in the face of the Conservative majority in the House of Lords, Gladstone proposed to make the subsequent
Redistribution Bill 'the subject of friendly communication with the leaders of the
Opposition' (Jones, 1972, 8), and the following extensive inter-party discussions
the Redistribution Bill produced by far the most wide-ranging changes of all three
nineteenth-century reforms. According to Jones (1972, 8-9):

> Ninety-one boroughs with less than 15,000 population, the 6 agricultural boroughs,
> and Sandwich and Macclesfield (corrupt beyond all redemption) were merged into
> their respective counties. Thirty-five boroughs and 2 counties, with a population
> between 15,000 and 50,000, were docked of one Member. The City of London lost
> 2 of its 4. Haverfordwest and Pembroke were to be treated as one. Seats liberated
> by want of population went where population demanded, by application of a uni-
> form rule – to the metropolis and to the great or new industrial and manufacturing
> areas, whether borough or county, English, Welsh, Scottish or Irish. Though, curi-
> ously and suspiciously, the net result was that no country filched from another –

Ireland maintained its Union total, and an increase of 12 in the numbers of the House met Scotland's need. ... Perhaps, however, greater novelty lay in adoption of the system of single-member districts, save only for the Universities, the City and those 23 boroughs which were to retain their two members.

The need for this redistribution consequent on the franchise reform was indicated by the new ratios of voters to MPs in the Boroughs and Counties: England and Wales's 187 County MPs represented an average of 73,200 people each, whereas their 297 Borough counterparts averaged only 41,400 each, though there were very substantial variations about each figure (among the Boroughs, for example, Liverpool had one MP per 185,000 people whereas Calne had one per 5000). These differences produced major discrepancies in the representation of the Liberal and Conservative parties, because of the spatial concentration of their votes in town and country respectively.

Resolving malapportionment thus meant tackling not only sectional but also partisan interests, as recognised by Disraeli when he opposed a suggestion for regular redistributions (Seymour, 1915, 493):

It was impossible, he contended, to obviate anomalies in distribution without inaugurating a commission of Parliamentary revision and a periodical redistribution; this he objected to on various grounds, but chiefly because it would afford frequent opportunities for gerrymandering. The distribution of political power after all, said he, was not a matter of abstract right, but of expediency. That twenty thousand votes were necessary in one constituency for election of a member, while three hundred and fifty were sufficient in another, was perhaps an offence to the principles of symmetry; but it was preferable to a system of equal electoral districts which would involve continual organic change.

Nevertheless, extension of the franchise generated widespread realisation of the need for a redistribution, and attention focused on its detail – though some argued strongly that the results of the 1874 and 1880 general elections indicated the need for change to a system of proportional representation. The use of single-member versus two-member and, in some cases, three-member constituencies was a particular bone of contention, with the Conservatives favouring single-member districts in the hope that this would prevent substantial minorities failing to achieve representation, whereas the Whigs wanted them retained to assist their contests with the Radical wing for strength within the Liberal party.

Before the Bill was passed and the redistribution completed, the Conservative leader – Lord Salisbury – published an article in *The National Review*, aimed largely at his own party, backing the proposed redistribution using statistics to show that 'if the proportion of Conservative and Liberals among [British householders] could be exactly reproduced at Westminster, [they] would elect a House of Commons much more favourable to us that that which sits there now' (Salisbury, 1884, 10: the Liberals had a majority of 128 after the 1880 election). Achievement of his goal meant that he opposed what he termed 'equal electoral districts' because (Salisbury, 1884, 146):

They proceed exclusively on the system of direct territorial representation, to the exclusion of virtual representation altogether; and I doubt very much whether any mechanism can be found to give anything like an exact copy in Parliament of the wishes of the people which does not make use of the principle of virtual representation.

For him, virtual representation meant a redistribution which 'reproduce[s] with fidelity the balance of opinion in the country' (i.e. 'fairness to parties': see p. 8 above), and he provided illustrations of how constituencies with equal electorates could be constructed to ensure that this did not happen. His data suggested that 45 per cent of Borough voters in Great Britain were Conservatives, as were 51 per cent of County voters and he concluded that (Salisbury, 1884, 156):

If we believe the county householders to be as Liberal as the householders of the towns, we are weaker now in Parliament by thirty-five votes than we should be with a true distribution and the proposed enfranchisement. If we believe the county householders to be as Conservative as the present county electors, we are now weaker by eighty-nine votes than we should be with a true distribution and the proposed enfranchisement.

Achievement of that goal required his concept of 'virtual representation' to be implemented. He accepted that this would be difficult, though claimed that 'the effort has never really been made' (Salisbury, 1884, 157). At this time, agricultural interests were 'suffering a serious wrong', but Conservatives need not fear the proposed franchise extension 'if it be coupled with a redistribution which is even moderately just towards interests which, by the existing arrangement, are submerged' (Salisbury, 1884, 158).

Salisbury's purpose was not only to generate support for his agreement to a redistribution but also backing for his claim that its method had to be 'fair' to his party. Thus his

figures … show the momentous significance of the question whether we are to have a redistribution or not; and whether, if we have one, it is to be fair. They show that whatever the influence of the Conservative Party may be, whatever measure of success or failure awaits them, a just solution of the question of redistribution means to them a difference in their favour of some hundred votes in the House of Commons. (Salisbury, 1884, 159–60)

He argued that a 'system of distribution' must 'give to the minority a representation corresponding to its actual weight', contrasting that with the Radical's position 'whose doctrine is essentially despotic. In their language freedom means little more than the right of the majority to choose an absolute ruler' (Salisbury, 1884, 160).

The Bill introduced in December 1884 proposed that all Boroughs with less than 15,000 residents should lose their separate representation and be merged with their surrounding Counties, with Boroughs having 15,000–50,000 residents being reduced to one MP only. The consequence, in Seymour's (1915, 508) words, was 'to liberate' 136 seats in England and Wales; 72 Boroughs, formerly returning 79 MPs, were absorbed into the Counties, and another 36 lost one of their members (the great majority of these were in the southern regions; see Table 2.2).

A total of 142 seats was released for redistribution (six had been released earlier when corrupt practices were identified in some Boroughs) and these were allocated approximately equally between the Boroughs and Counties. The largest single allocation was of 39 seats to the metropolitan Boroughs in London, with a further 18 to the large manufacturing centres (Birmingham, Liverpool, Manchester and Sheffield got from three to six additional seats each). In the County areas, too, it was the industrialised regions that benefited most, with 15 new constituencies in Lancashire and 13 in Yorkshire's West Riding. All of these were single-member constituencies so that, for example, Liverpool finished with nine constituencies and Tower Hamlets with seven, and the goal was for them to have equal populations (though the outcome saw some constituencies with twice the populations of others within the same Borough).

Once the allocation of seats had been agreed, the detailed work, as before, was done by specially appointed Boundary Commissions, whose recommendations were incorporated in the final version of the Bill, passed in June 1885. The remit for those Commissions was agreed between Dilke and Salisbury, 'strongly directing them, in settling the single-member districts, to separate as far as possible, the urban from the rural' (Hayes, 1987, 251–2). The Chairman and Vice-Chairman of all three Commissions (England & Wales, Scotland, Ireland) were senior civil servants (see below). Each Commission also had two other members (for England & Wales these were two Local Government Board Inspectors: one known to be a Conservative and the other a Liberal), plus army officers from the Ordnance Survey to provide maps. Their instructions (extracts of which are given in Box 2.1) required them to ensure that the division (i.e. constituency) populations within each County and Borough 'be proximately equalised', to include all suburbs within one division, and to produce compact divisions using Petty Session Divisions as the building-blocks. In Boroughs, wards should be used as the building-blocks. In both 'special regard shall be had to the pursuits of the population', a phrase which clearly reflects Salisbury's goal (see above) to ensure that the redistribution was 'fair' to his party.

The Commissions were assisted in their work by Assistant Commissioners: there were three for England and Wales (two Army officers and one barrister). Both the Commissioners and the Assistant Commissioners held well-advertised Local Inquiries to assess opinion regarding the recommendations – according to Chadwick (1976, 681) most acted in areas for which they had local knowledge. According to the Commission's report (Boundary Commission for England and Wales, 1885, 5–6):

> The Inquiries have been numerously attended; many of the most influential persons in the County have been present and have taken part in the proceedings, and the different political associations have almost always been represented by their agents.

(Interestingly, they also report that the main topic of concern at many of the Inquiries was the constituency names, and in the detailed reports for each County and Borough all of the names are justified.) In the Boroughs they met with the Town Council and representatives of the political parties prior to the Inquiries, at which they were 'subject to attempts … to influence their decisions' (Chadwick, 1976, 681).

Their Instructions required them to obtain copies of 'any schemes for divisions prepared by the Borough authorities or any local association' (Boundary Commission for England and Wales, 1885, 7). Chadwick (1976, 681) states that 'most borough boundaries were decided by Dilke and Salisbury. If the delicate political question of the extension of boroughs to include the suburbs had been left to the Commissions and discussed at Inquiries, not only would their work have taken longer, but would probably not have received such general approval'. There were lengthy discussions of the recommendations in Parliament at the Committee stage, but the party leaderships stood firmly behind the Commissions' recommendations and no major alterations were made. It was recognised that these had been produced in a 'non-partisan spirit' (Chadwick, 1976, 682), especially by the Assistant Commissioners, and were considered an 'equitable end result' (Hayes, 1987, 263).

The Commissions worked extremely fast. The English and Welsh Commission was appointed on 29 October 1884 and reported on 10 February 1885; the 81 Local Inquiries were held between 11 November and 5 February, with up to six being held on a single day. (There were eleven Inquiries in Scotland, held on nine days between 22 December and 21 January, including one on 24 December.) In the Counties, they noted that although Hundreds had been used as the building blocks in the 1832 and 1868 redistributions, these were now obsolete, were not all composed of contiguous areas, and many of their boundaries were unknown (although they couldn't be changed except by Act of Parliament). Hence their use of Petty Sessional Divisions (PSDs) as the basic building blocks, which nested within Counties and within which parishes nested. Many PSDs had to be split, however, because of the 'proximate equality' and 'communities engaged in similar pursuits' requirements (Boundary Commission for England and Wales, 1885, 5). In almost every County they were able to meet the 'proximate equality' requirement extremely well: in Cambridgeshire, for example, the three recommended divisions had populations of 48,650, 48,958 and 47,108; in Suffolk, the populations of the five recommended constituencies were 56,503, 56,877, 56,328, 56,018 and 55,502; and in Derbyshire the seven divisions had populations of 53,357, 53,908, 54,927, 55,514, 53,298, 54,542 and 55,209.[2] (They were equally successful in Scotland: the two recommended constituencies in Perth, for example, had populations of 46,933 and 48,111.) Major recommended deviations from equality were justified: in Bedfordshire, for example, the two divisions ensured that 'the straw-plait industries of the County ... will be brought within the same electoral area'; in Cheshire, the Commissioners felt 'obliged to ... constitute a separate division which should embrace in the main the population engaged in the special and important industry of the County – salt manufacture'; in Durham they were 'able to group the populous and important districts on the south of the Tyne in one compact division'; in Hampshire, Basingstoke division was substantially larger than all others because it included the large military population at Aldershot; and in Somerset 'in order to group, as far as practicable, populations with similar pursuits, the Commission have allowed a somewhat larger margin of inequality than they would otherwise have done'. In particular cases, relatively small constituencies were recommended to reflect areas with well-defined separate characters, such as Holderness and the Isle of Thanet, and in Cumberland 'considerable inequality ... was inevitable from the mountainous character of the County'. Finally, in the Boroughs the Commissioners found 'a strong desire in every Borough that the wards should if possible be preserved intact, and in deference to this feeling we have allowed a larger disparity in the population of several of the divisions than we should otherwise have recommended' (Boundary Commission for England and Wales, 1885, 8).

The 1885 Boundary Commissions were the first of those appointed in the nineteenth century whose work was dominated by the task of defining constituency boundaries for single-member constituencies; their two predecessors had concentrated almost exclusively on delimiting the Parliamentary Boroughs, a much smaller task in 1885. The criteria which they were required to apply – population equality, reflection of communities of interest (separation of urban from rural and the 'pursuits of the population'; see Table 2.5), and use of local government areas as the template and building blocks – reflected the main theories of representation (Chapter 1), whereas the procedures that had to apply, involving public consultations, indicated the importance placed on winning local acceptability. All developed from the work of the two earlier Commissions and formed the foundations of the criteria employed when their twentieth-century successors were established. But there was strong partisan involvement too, not only in the role that Parliament and the parties played in the detailed deliberations but also in the partisan nature of the appointments to the Commissions.

Politically, the 1885 redistribution was a major success for one member of Gladstone's Cabinet, a Radical destined for high office but denied it as a result of a 'sex scandal' in which, long after the event, it seems that he was entirely innocent (Jenkins, 1965). Sir Charles Dilke was given the task of overseeing the Redistribution Bill once franchise reform had been achieved, and rapidly produced schemes during the summer of 1884 with the assistance of the Permanent Secretary of the Local Government Board, Sir John Lambert. (Lambert chaired the 1885 Commission: according to Chadwick (1976, 679) he had 'avowed Liberal sentiments' and these were balanced by the appointment of a 'keen Conservative' as his deputy.) He drew up a scheme designed to reflect both Gladstone's 'conservatism' (University representation and plural voting were not affected: Jenkins, 1965, 190 argues that Gladstone 'believed in the theory of popular democracy, but thought that it should be accomplished within the framework of an electoral map as similar as possible to that which he had known in his youth') and the Whig's fear of being overwhelmed by the Radicals within the Liberal party: the Whigs preferred two-member constituencies in areas of Liberal strength, which allowed one Whig and one Radical to be elected. Dilke's mastery of the details allowed him to advance his scheme (he made little reference to the Cabinet committee to which he was supposed to report). Nevertheless, the Tories made significant gains in the inter-party discussions, especially with regard to two-member Boroughs, as a result of Salisbury's negotiations – on which see Jones (1972, 210) who claims that Dilke was 'bamboozled into the belief that Salisbury did not know his subject' and that he declared his 'bottom line' too readily as a consequence. These were all to be subdivided into single-member constituencies, as were the Counties and, as Jenkins (1995, 498) claims: 'This was the real gain for the Tories. It laid the foundation of 'villa Conservatism' and the safe Tory seats of the Home

Table 2.5 *The overall impact of the nineteenth-century Reform Acts on the geography of representation in England and Wales*

Region	Counties		Boroughs		Net Change
	Losses	Gains	Losses	Gains	
Metropolitan	0	5	2	53	+56
Southeastern	0	18	64	5	−41
South Midland	0	7	26	0	−19
Eastern	1	20	32	4	−9
Southwestern	0	20	119	3	−96
West Midland	1	11	27	7	−10
Midland	0	15	13	18	+20
Northwestern	0	43	16	42	+69
Northern	0	12	25	22	+9
South Wales	0	5	4	4	+5
North Wales	0	2	1	0	+1
Total	2	158	329	158	−15

Source: derived from Seymour (1915, 535–7)

Counties and the prosperous suburbs in and around the big provincial cities'. The main losers were the Whigs. Piloting the Bill through Parliament was difficult, despite the support of both front benches, and all stages were eventually completed only after a Conservative government had been elected in 1885.

Of the three nineteenth-century redistributions, this last was also the most extensive, providing the foundation for the modern system, though still leaving the details the subject of partisan political manoeuvring. Thus, according to Jenkins (1965, 193):

> [Dilke] had decisively re-drawn the electoral map of Britain. Despite the subsequent changes of 1918, 1950 and 1955, today's pattern is recognisably based on that of 1884, and on no earlier arrangement. The modern county constituency and the modern divided borough are both Dilke's creations.

More generally, Cannadine (1996, 36) saw the 1885 Act as ending the landed aristocracy's hegemony of political power:

> The Reform measures of 1832 and 1867 had simply altered and adapted the old rural, oligarchic and proprietary system. But the Third Reform Act created a new and very different representational structure for the whole of Great Britain and Ireland, in which the cities and the suburbs were pre-eminent, and in which a working-class electorate possessed the dominant voice.

This final major redistribution of the nineteenth century produced approximately equal representation, both across regions and between the Boroughs and Counties. In terms of the ratio of electors to population, under-representation of the Counties was removed, and the redistribution eliminated the gross anomalies in terms of the ratio of MPs to population (Table 2.3). Among the Boroughs, however, the main centres of population (London, the Midlands and the Northwest) remained under-represented relative to the areas of traditional power – the small Boroughs of the southeast and southwest; nevertheless the ratio between the largest and the smallest constituency had been reduced from 250:1 to 8:1 (Chadwick, 1976, 683). Furthermore, as Seymour notes (1915, 515), glaring anomalies remained within regions – 'By comparing individual constituencies it can be seen at a glance that the principle of exact proportion to population was by no means followed out to its completion': York, for example, was smaller than Middlesbrough but had two MPs to the latter's one. And so he summarised a century of major changes (Table 2.5) by concluding that much remained to be done, which would require establishing a new system for redistributions:

> the survivals of the old system protected many numerical anomalies. The redress of industry's disadvantage was not niggardly, the very small boroughs were eliminated, and something like a regular proportion of representation was established, especially in the county divisions; but a completely democratic system was not introduced. And the advance toward uniformity of representation in 1885 could not continue, nor indeed be maintained, without provisions for a periodical redistribution. Inevitably the anomalies then preserved must become greater, and new ones spring up, with the growth of population in certain districts and the rise of new industries and interests.

Into the twentieth century: two wartime reforms

The nineteenth-century Reform Acts changed the map of representation in Great Britain very significantly, therefore, but did not end the movement towards universal suffrage (indeed, they did not even deliver universal male suffrage). Nor did they establish either principles or mechanisms for the redistribution of constituencies consequent on either or both of franchise changes and population movements (both absolute and relative); such decisions were all made *ad hoc*, with very strong political, and thus partisan, involvement.

After a lull following the 1885 Act, various aspects of electoral reform returned to the political agenda during the early years of the twentieth century. The initial concerns were plural voting and female suffrage: attempts in 1906, 1912 and 1913 to resolve the first in the House of Commons were blocked by the House of Lords, whereas legislation for the latter was not even introduced. Other concerns, such as proportional representation, were also regularly aired, leading to what Butler (1963, 6-7) calls a 'notable but mysterious event', the establishment of a Royal Commission on Electoral Systems in 1909 which reported in the next year but 'neither its appointment nor its report was the subject of debate in Parliament or of editorial comment in *The Times*': it did not advocate adoption of proportional representation but did commend a shift from plurality voting in single-member constituencies (the 'first-past-the-post' system which is still employed) to the alternative vote system later adopted by the Commonwealth of Australia.

As both Butler (1963) and Pugh (1978) note, these issues were overshadowed by other political issues of the day, notably the struggles between the Houses of Commons and Lords (exemplified by the failures to abolish plural voting). The Liberal government, elected in 1906 on a manifesto which included constitutional reform, failed to alter a situation in which four out of every ten 'Englishmen [sic]' were deprived of Parliamentary suffrage (Pugh, 1978, 29).

Early in the century, however, there had been growing concern about disparities in constituency size, and by 1905 it was believed that the Conservative government was intending to propose a redistribution. To that end, a Cabinet Minister – the President of the Local Government Board – produced a paper for the government (without the prior knowledge of Parliament) which proposed rules for a redistribution (which Butler, 1963, 213, called 'hardly very radical'): these were laid before Parliament, though not debated, in July 1905.[3] In the introduction, it was pointed out that (Local Government Board, 1905, 3):

> Prior to 1832, population as a determining element in representation was practically ignored. The Reform Acts of 1832 and of 1868 did much to remove the gross anomalies (as they appear from a modern point of view) which had accumulated … but these Acts did not follow any rule or method capable of exact expression. It was the Act of 1885 which for the first time proceeded on a more or less definite numerical plan. This principle, once introduced, is not likely to be abandoned in any succeeding schemes of redistribution.

The rules on which the 1885 redistribution was based were not formulated in a Resolution or Bill presented to Parliament, however, and had to be identified by collecting together 'statements made in Parliament while the subject was under discussion'. The rules proposed in 1905 are very similar but, because of population growth, the desire for little or no expansion in the size of the House of Commons, and the anomalies by then apparent,[4] the thresholds were raised.

The proposed Rules are set out in Box 2.2. They incorporate a clear arithmetic requirement for the allocation of *new* seats to Counties and urban areas (Boroughs and Urban Districts) – one MP per 65,000 – which both requires that greater equality of representation should ensue and seeks to fit constituency boundaries within the new local government template established in 1888. Rule 2 substantially impedes achievement of the equality goal, however, by proposing that separate representation should only be removed from Boroughs with a population of less than a third of that norm – 18,500. As a result, 59 Boroughs with populations less than 60,000 would be separately represented in the House of Commons, including two with populations below 20,000 (Whitehaven and the St Andrews District of Burghs), a further sixteen with populations between 20,000 and 29,999, and seventeen with 30,000–39,999. Small towns would still be very substantially over-represented.

Box 2.2 *Proposed Rules for the Redistribution of Seats, 1905*

The Scheme of Redistribution embodied in the Resolution of which notice has been given, is based on the following general rules:

1 The number of Members of the House of Commons shall not be materially altered.
2 A Municipal Borough or Urban District with a population exceeding 65,000, not at present separately represented, shall become a separate constituency.
3 A County or Borough with a population exceeding 65,000 multiplied by the number of its Members shall have an additional member for every complete 65,000 of the excess.
4 A Borough with a population of less than 18,500 shall cease to exist as a separate constituency.
5 A County or Borough with two Members and a population of less than 75,000 shall (except in the case of the City of London) lose one Member.
6 A County or Borough with more than two Members and a population of less than 65,000 multiplied by its number of Members shall have one less Member for every complete 65,000 of the deficiency.
7 The County and the Borough shall, as far as practicable, be made coextensive with the Administrative County and the Municipal Borough respectively, but the boundaries of a Borough shall not be curtailed except when the population affected is inconsiderable.
8 In London each Metropolitan Borough shall be treated as if it were a Borough returning the number of Members returned by the present Boroughs or Divisions to which it most nearly corresponds.

Rule 1 lays down the governing condition of the scheme – namely, that the number of the Members of the House of Commons is not to be materially altered.

Rules 2 to 6 determine the relations to be established in various cases between population and representation.

Rules 7 and 8 deal with the question of boundaries.

Source: Local Government Board (1905, 1)

This statement of the principles followed an undertaking given by the then Prime Minister (Balfour), in response to a question from the Liberal leader of the Opposition, that 'the Government do intend to proceed with the Resolution' for a redistribution (*Hansard*, vol. 148, 3 July 1905, col. 789). This raised many concerns among members, not least because the outcome identified in the Local Government Board report would be a net loss of 22 seats from Ireland, countered by gains of 17 for England, 4 for Scotland and 1 for Wales. Members were also concerned about the procedure to be adopted: the Local Government Board paper recommended the appointment of Boundary Commissioners who would (Local Government Board, 1905, 6):

> not ... [be] empowered to report in favour of changes in the boundaries of Counties or Boroughs except in accordance with the Rules. For instance they would not ... be authorized to recommend that the Boundaries of a Borough should be extended so as to include part of a division of a County not already included within the municipal area. Their principal function would be to report on the readjustment of divisions within the limits of a County or Borough where such a readjustment is rendered necessary or desirable in consequence either of a change in the number of its Members or of an important increment of population in one of its divisions compared with another.

The framework had already been established, and the Commissioners' main task would have been to define boundaries for new constituencies *within* Boroughs and Counties.

The Resolution was withdrawn, however, partly because of the lack of Parliamentary time for its debate, and Balfour promised a Bill for the next session (*Hansard*, vol. 148, 20 July.1905, col. 1079). As to procedure, he agreed that (col. 1080):

> any Committee [presumably used as a synonym for Commission, which was the term used throughout the discussion] which we may appoint shall start with a general knowledge of the views by which the Government have reached the proposals which they have submitted to the House. Whether those views will suffer any change in the course of the investigation by the Committee is a thing which it is impossible to foresee at the present moment.

Furthermore, such a Commission (he reverted to that term in later debates) would have advisory powers only and 'it must ultimately rest with the House of Commons to decide what shall be adopted'. Balfour later agreed that recommendations for revised Rules would be published and in August established a Committee, operating within the Local Government Board, 'to inquire and report on certain questions connected with a proposed redistribution of seats at Parliamentary elections' (Local Government Board, 1906, 9). The Committee was chaired by an ex-Director-General of the Ordnance Survey, and comprised with him a senior lawyer and a Principal Clerk of the Local Government Board. It was given the following task (Local Government Board, 1906, 9):

> It will be the duty of the Committee to inquire and report:
> (a) As to the changes of boundaries which would be necessary or advisable for the purpose of giving effect to the principles of a Scheme of Redistribution based on the general Rules set out in the Memorandum ... dated the 10th July 1905; and
> (b) Whether any division or re-division of any County or Borough is necessary or advisable for that purpose or for the purpose or remedying any considerable disparity in the population of the divisions of that County or Borough.

The instructions also included a clause that:

> The governing condition of the Scheme is that the number of Members of the House of Commons is not to be materially altered. Subject to this, it is intended that the Com-

mittee should not interpret the Rules too rigidly, but should consider and report upon
any case which may appear to them to come within the spirit of a particular Rule.

In addition, the Committee was asked to consider cases where local government
boundaries were not coterminous with those of Parliamentary constituencies
(notably for Boroughs), to consider 'special circumstances' (population growth
and decline are the only issues cited), and the grouping of adjacent Boroughs and
urban districts (though if at all possible only grouping whole parishes): no alterations of the new Parliamentary Boroughs in London were to be proposed. In
addition (Local Government Board, 1906, 10):

> It will be observed that under Rule 4 [see Box 2.2] the population which would
> cause a Borough to cease to be a separate Constituency is 18,500. It may be found
> expedient to raise the minimum limit of population above this number, as regards
> both Counties and Boroughs, to 20,000 or upwards. It is desired that the Commit-
> tee should investigate the circumstances of all cases where the population of a
> County or Borough is less than 25,000, and report whether in the case of a County
> it might properly be added to another County or, in the case of a Borough, whether
> it could properly be enlarged, and if so to what extent, without destroying its urban
> character.

A general revision of boundaries was not called for, save where there are considerable disparities between the populations of constituencies within a County
or Borough, or where a Borough is to be divided for the first time (multi-member Boroughs were not advocated). Finally (Local Government Board, 106, 11):

> Each Division [i.e. constituency] should be as compact as possible with respect to
> geographical position, and should be based upon such existing areas as may be
> found most appropriate for the purpose. The divisional boundaries of a County
> should in no case intersect a Parish, and in the case of a Borough which is divided
> into wards for the purpose of municipal elections, the Parliamentary Divisions
> should, as far as possible, be based upon them.

The Committee was given a year in which to report (it did so within seven
months). It was not required to hold Local Inquiries but could seek information
locally (perhaps visiting a location if necessary) and consider any representations
received (45 were), 'but it will be understood that they are not in a position to
decide what is to be done, and that they are merely to obtain information for the
guidance of the Government' (note that it says Government and not Parliament).
The Committee was specifically directed to Ordnance Survey maps plus material held by the Board of Agriculture and Fisheries, the Local Government Board,
and the Registrar General and was told that 'As regards the divisions of Counties and Boroughs, the Committee should not extend their labours beyond England and Wales without further instructions'.

In its report the Committee listed fifteen Parliamentary Boroughs whose areas
should be extended either by incorporation of adjacent Urban Districts or by extension to the current County Borough boundaries, and nine Boroughs whose boundaries should be redrawn to make them consistent with the new local government

template (the maximum population affected was 6,571 in Monmouth); these changes had consequences for a number of Counties, but in only one (Glamorgan) was there a movement of more than 10,000 people between County and Boroughs.

To address the issues regarding small Boroughs and Counties plus disparities within Boroughs and Counties, the Committee – 'with your verbal approval' (Local Government Board, 1906, 3) – produced six different Schemes, one of which was 'worked out in detail for England and Wales'. Most were only slight variants on the original proposal, however, and in each the main changes were in England and Ireland, with the former a net gainer of some 20 seats and the latter losing about the same number.

With regard to the division of Counties and Boroughs into constituencies, the Committee 're-divided' 29 Counties in England and Wales (Lancashire was treated as four separate Counties and Yorkshire as three), seventeen Boroughs and fifteen London Boroughs. A Supplementary Report detailed similar work on Scotland and Ireland, complete (as was the case for England and Wales) with very detailed statistical tables. The goal when dividing Boroughs was to produce constituencies as groups of undivided wards but in some cases this was not practicable if 'reasonable equality of population' was to be achieved (Local Government Board, 1906, 40) and in addition:

> In the cases of Dublin and Belfast we have found it necessary to divide the Wards more freely than in some other cases, in order to secure a fairer grouping of areas in accordance with the general character of their populations than appears to have been observed in the formation of the Municipal Wards.

No redistribution was proposed before the government fell in 1906, however, and the replacement Liberal administration did not proceed with the matter. Thus, two reports and the Rules which they operated did not produce what would have been the first attempt at a transparent, to a considerable extent non-political, attempt at redistribution which incorporated both the organic and the mathematic criteria which dominated debates on the issue from the 1940s on. But the Rules used in 1917 were clearly based on this foundation laid by Balfour's government.

The 1918 Representation of the People Act

Moves towards change began during the First World War: 'War, so often the midwife of reform, led to the most comprehensive Representation of the People Act that had yet been seen' (Butler, 1963, 7). The conduct of elections is especially difficult during wartime, when many residents are away from their homes, and in 1916 the Home Secretary suggested that an all-party committee investigate the issues raised by the problems of compiling a register and conducting a general election before the war ended (Parliament's term was due to expire). One Bill was passed to delay the forthcoming election but a second, which tackled the issue of representation, foundered. For the government 'it became vital to employ an alternative expedient if the Bill were not to be withdrawn' (Pugh, 1978, 67), and so a committee was established (with a clear Conservative majority: Butler, 1963, 118) in order to sustain the government. The Speaker agreed to chair it, so establishing the practice of important constitutional matters being considered by a Speaker's Conference.

The Conference was established in August 1916, began its work in the following October, and reported in January 1917. Although chaired by the Speaker, the driving force behind its work was the Home Secretary, W. H. Long, a Conservative intent on major electoral reform. Its proposals were largely unanimous: the Speaker reported to the Prime Minister that up to mid-December, only four of its 24 resolutions were contentious, with three being passed with a single dissenting vote only and the other, relating to the Alternative Vote, being carried by 11 to 8 (Pugh, 1978, 77). In its final report, Butler notes (1963, 7):

> a surprising measure of agreement; its members were divided on only one recommendation, women's suffrage; on new methods of registration, on plural voting, on university representation, on redistribution, and, astonishingly, on proportional representation complete unanimity was achieved.

(See, however, Pugh, 1978, 78–9 on the contrived compromise over the franchise.) The government's *Representation of the People Bill* incorporated these proposals, with many sections, including redistribution, largely uncontroversial: the franchise (i.e. women's suffrage) and proportional representation were the foci of debate, on which the government allowed free votes.

Redistribution was needed for the reasons identified by Seymour, and also because of the universal male suffrage based on residence which the Bill proposed, with very little plural voting (only in the University seats and for occupants of business premises worth £10 annually). It was to be undertaken by three Boundary Commissions (one each for England and Wales, Scotland, and Ireland), whose warrants of appointment directed the Commissioners to execute their duties in accordance with certain Instructions. The Instructions for England and Wales are reproduced in Box 2.3. The Scottish Commissioners were given similar Instructions, with different wording to reflect the local government terminology there (e.g. Burgh for Borough); in addition Rule 8 was omitted and the subsequent rules renumbered, save that an additional Rule 14 was added to cover the Scottish practice of grouping non-contiguous Burghs into constituencies:

> Where districts of burghs comprise burghs in different counties, or where under the foregoing rules a constituency which is a district of burghs would lose representation, the Commissioners shall consider the desirability of re-grouping the burghs or adding neighbouring burghs in the same county, regard shall be had to their size, to a proper representation of the urban and rural population, and to the distribution and pursuits of such population, provided that the representation of the county is not thereby affected.

The Irish Commissioners, who were appointed some six months after the others, were given much briefer Instructions, however, no doubt reflecting ongoing discussions rewarding the political future of the island:

In determining the number of members to be assigned to any county or borough and the boundaries of any county or borough and of any divisions thereof the Commissioners will proceed in accordance with the following general rules:

1　The total number of members of the House of Commons for counties and boroughs in Ireland shall remain unchanged.
2　In assigning members regard shall be had to the population and size of the constituencies.
3　Existing constituencies and the boundaries thereof shall not be altered except so far as appears to the Commissions to be necessary or desirable for the purpose of these instructions.

This procedure clearly reflected a major shift in policy towards redistributions. The government decided that one was necessary. It then laid down general rules to be followed and passed the task to independent Commissions, which were instructed to consult local opinion. All three Commissions were chaired by the Speaker and had a common Secretary, who was also a member of each. The England & Wales and the Scotland Commission had three additional members each, one of whom was on both, and the Ireland Commission had one additional member. Of the eleven Assistant Commissioners appointed to assist the England and Wales Commission with its Local Inquiries, four were barristers and three had the qualification M.Inst.C.E.; no indication of the others' occupations was given: of the eleven appointed to assist the Scotland Commission, nine held the position of Sheriff Substitute and two were Sheriffs.[5] The Ireland Commission held eight Local Inquiries and seven Assistant Commissioners were appointed; one had the qualification M.Inst.C.E., and no indication of the others' occupations is given.

The instructions were sent out in mid May 1917, as a result of which Parliament, having already passed the *Representation of the People Act 1917*, reopened its discussion of the redistribution issue. As a consequence, the relevant Secretaries of State sent letters to the Commissions (dated 22 June 1917 in the case of England and Wales and 3 July 1917 in the case of Scotland) amending the Instructions accordingly (Box 2.4). These changes gave the Commissions greater flexibility, and introduced what later became known as 'special geographical considerations' as well as inviting the Commissions to consider the ratio of population to electors (once universal adult franchise was introduced in 1928, this was no longer necessary).[6]

Having been appointed in May 1917, the Commissions undertook their substantial tasks very speedily: the England and Wales Commission reported on 27 September, and the Scottish Commission on the following day. (The Irish report is undated, other than the year – 1917.) The first two Commissions operated very similar procedures. (There is no discussion of the work of the Irish Commission in its report.) Provisional allocations and constituency boundaries were determined for each County and Borough and these were extensively advertised in the local press. Representations were invited, and many were received; as a consequence many Local Inquiries were held – 120 in England and Wales, dealing with 465 constituencies, and an unstated number in Scotland, covering 56 constituencies. (The Local Inquiries were conducted by Assistant Commissioners, appointed

Box 2.3 *The Instructions given to the Boundary Commission for England and Wales, and for Scotland in 1917*

1 The number of members of the House of Commons for Great Britain shall remain substantially as at present.
2 A county or borough (other than the City of London) with a population of less than 50,000 shall cease to have separate representation.
3 A county or borough with a population of 50,000 but less than 70,000 shall continue to have separate representation.
4 A municipal borough or urban district with a population of not less than 70,000 shall become a separate parliamentary borough.
5 A county or borough at present returning two members shall not lose a member if the population is not less than 120,000.
6 A member shall be given for a population of 70,000 and for every multiple of 70,000 and an additional member for any remainder which is not less than 50,000.
7 The boundaries of parliamentary constituencies shall, as far as practicable, coincide with the boundaries of administrative areas.
8 The City of London shall continue to return two members.
9 A Parliamentary Borough which would be entitled on the basis of population to return three or more members shall be a single constituency: provided that a constituency entitled to return more than five members shall be divided into two or more constituencies each returning not less than three nor more than five members. For the purpose of this rule the Metropolis (excluding the City of London) shall be treated as a single area, and divided into constituencies returning not less than three nor more than five members.
10 Where there are contiguous boroughs which if formed into a single

by the relevant Secretary of State at the Commission's request, 'with a view to the proper fulfilment of our duties'; Boundary Commission (Scotland), 1917, 3.) They were 'in some cases very numerously attended' (Boundary Commission (England & Wales), 1917, 8) and the Scottish Commission reported that (Boundary Commission (Scotland), 1917, 3):

> Great interest appears to have been shown in these local Inquiries by local authorities, by political and labour associations, and by private persons. They have proved of the utmost value in eliciting the expression of local opinion, and have enabled us in a number of cases to effect improvements on our original proposals.

The England and Wales Commission introduced its discussion of how it had undertaken its task by noting the requirement in Rule 7 and stating that (Boundary Commission (England & Wales), 1917, 8):

> It is generally recognised that at the present time much confusion and inconvenience are caused by overlapping boundaries, and we have endeavoured to give, as far as might be consistent with our other Instructions, the fullest effect possible to this rule.

constituency would be entitled to return not less than three nor more than five members such boroughs shall be united in a single constituency.

11 The foregoing Rules 9 and 10 shall only have effect in the event of Proportional Representation being adopted. Otherwise all boroughs returning two or more members shall be divided into single member constituencies except that any borough at present undivided and returning two members which will under Rules 5 and 8 be entitled to continue to return two members shall remain undivided.

12 Counties entitled to return two or more members shall be divided and in the formation of such divisions the Commissioners should endeavour after ascertaining local opinion to segregate as far as possible adjacent industrial and rural areas.

13 Where a borough loses its right to separate representation in Parliament the Commissioners may after ascertaining local opinion on the subject, combine such borough with any other such borough or boroughs lying within the county or with any borough in the same county having separate representation instead of merging it in the county or county division.

14 Where an ancient Parliamentary borough loses its representation the county division in which the borough becomes merged shall be named after the merged borough.

15 For the purpose of the foregoing rules 'population' shall mean the population as estimated by the Registrar-General for the middle of the year 1914, due allowance, as estimated by the Registrar-General, being made as regards the population of any area which has been transferred from one administrative area to another.

Source: Boundary Commission (England and Wales) 1917; Boundary Commission (Scotland) 1917

This involved:
1 adhering wherever possible to the boundaries of administrative Counties;
2 ensuring that the boundaries of Parliamentary Boroughs are coterminous with the relevant Municipal or London Borough boundaries;
3 where necessary, uniting two or more adjacent Boroughs, and in some cases adding an adjacent urban district to a Borough or Boroughs;
4 within Counties, using the urban and rural districts as the 'building blocks' which would not be divided if possible – it reported that 78 out of 662 rural districts were divided (in which case the parishes were used as the building blocks: only one parish was subdivided); none of the 1156 urban districts (including Municipal Boroughs) was divided between constituencies; and
5 within urban areas, wards were used as the 'building blocks' where possible.
The Scottish Commission adopted a similar policy, except in Glasgow where a new set of 37 wards had been enacted in 1912 but never implemented. The Commission decided to adopt a set of constituencies presented to it by the City Corporation, which involved detailed topographic descriptions of the boundaries and areas,

> **Box 2.4** *The Letter from the Secretary of State amending the Instructions to the Boundary Commission for England and Wales, 1917*
>
> I desire to draw the attention of the Commissioners to the Resolution which was passed by the House of Commons on Monday, the 18th June, as follows:
>
> > 'That this House approves of the Instructions appended to the warrants appointing Commissioners to determine for the purposes of the Representation of the People Bill, the number of members to be assigned to the several counties and boroughs in England and Wales, and in Scotland respectively, and the boundaries of such counties and boroughs and divisions thereof.
> >
> > 'Provided that the Commissioners may depart from the strict application of these Instructions in any case where it would result in the formation of constituencies inconvenient in size or character, or where the narrowness of margin between the figure representing the estimated population of any area and the figure required for any of the purposes of these Instructions seem to them to justify such a departure.
> >
> > 'Provided also that it be an Instruction to the Boundary Commissioners to have regard to electorate rather than population where it appears that the proportion of electorate to population is abnormal.
> >
> > 'Provided also that, in carrying out these Instructions, the Commissioners shall act on the assumption that proportional representation is not adopted.
> >
> > 'Provided also that the Commissioners shall have power when re-grouping boroughs to extend such grouping to boroughs in contiguous counties.'
> >
> The provisos to this Resolution should be deemed to be incorporated in the Instructions to the Boundary Commissioners for England and Wales which were attached to the Warrant of their appointment; and I beg to request the Commissioners in making their determination to act on these Instructions as amended by the provisos to the resolution.
>
> Source: Boundary Commission (England and Wales) 1917; Boundary Commission (Scotland) 1917

but the Commission noted that (Boundary Commission (Scotland), 1917, 4):

> It was stated that these Divisions would conveniently and satisfactorily lend themselves to sub-division into the 37 new Municipal wards, and, on the evidence submitted at the local Inquiry, it appeared that the proposals of the Corporation were generally accepted.

Of the 99 County districts in Scotland, only four were divided.

In the allocation of constituencies to Counties and Boroughs, the England and Wales Commission applied three considerations in deciding whether to deviate from the clear instructions linking seats to electorate, in particular with regard to

the 'narrowness of margin' referred to in the additional Instructions:
1 The elasticity between the 'standard unit of 70,000' and the minimum of 50,000 in some cases;
2 The requirement that the size of the House of Commons should not be increased; and
3 '... a wide departure from the general rules would tend to increase the disparity between the populations of different constituencies, which must inevitably be produced, in a greater or less degree, under any scheme of redistribution founded on an arithmetic basis coupled with the maintenance of a territorial system of representation. (Boundary Commission (England & Wales), 1917, 9)

As a result, it decided to add an additional constituency, above the entitlement, to four Counties and three Boroughs. In addition, 13 Counties received an additional seat 'where a strict application of our Instructions would result in the formation of constituencies inconvenient in size or character'. On this last point, the Scottish Commission indicated that (Boundary Commission (Scotland), 1917, 5):

> The remoteness and inaccessibility of some of the Highland and Island constituencies, coupled with their great extent, seemed to us to fulfil precisely the conditions envisaged by the proviso; and be a reasonable exercise of the discretion given to us we have as regards those areas, and others, been able, as we hope, to secure for them a fairer Parliamentary representation than would otherwise have been possible.

Seven additional constituencies were created, including three for Counties that otherwise would not have justified a single MP.

Regarding the ratio of electors to population, the England and Wales Commission reported that (Boundary Commission (England & Wales, 1917, 10):

> in the counties the average number of electors per cent. of the population ... is about 20, and we were unable to find any such variation from the average as would justify either an increase or a decrease in the representation to which the county would be entitled under the general rules.

In Boroughs the average was 16.8 in England and 17.7 in Wales, but ranged from 11 to 21.5. Five divisions of Tower Hamlets had an average of 8.8, however, a situation ascribed to 'the presence of a large alien population': all were in the metropolitan Borough of Stepney, whose representation was reduced from four to three (and one of them – Whitechapel – was much larger, with 112,519 residents, than the other two with 73,627 and 93,658). The Scottish Commission reported average percentages of 19 in the Counties and 17 in the burghs, and no variations which would justify changing the number of seats allocated from the theoretical entitlement.

Finally, with regard to the creation of constituencies within local government areas, the Commissions sought 'to secure that the populations of the several divisions should be approximately equal' (Boundary Commission (England & Wales), 1917, 11): no evaluation of how successful they were is provided.

The Ireland Commission had much weaker instructions than the other two, merely requiring it to 'have regard to' constituency size and population within a fixed number of seats for the Counties and Boroughs. It decided that to operate within these, and to 'give effect as far as practicable to the principle of "one vote, one value"' (Boundary Commission (Ireland), 1917, 3), it should adopt 'a standard unit of population'. No 1914 population estimates were available, so it operated with the 1911 Census figures, which gave an average electorate per MP of 43,000. To give itself flexibility around that figure, it adopted 30,000 as the electorate which should entitle a Borough or County to retain separate representation. Counties or Boroughs with 73,000 (30,000 + 43,000) should retain or be entitled to two members, with one more for every further multiple of 43,000. (It noted that the 'ratio of 43,000 and 30,000 corresponds very nearly to the ratio between the units of 70,000 and 50,000 laid down in the general rules ... adopted for Great Britain'; Boundary Commission (Ireland), 1917, 4.) The Commission found that applying these guidelines would mean three more seats for Dublin and five more for Belfast (each previously had four). In each, it 'found it possible to adhere generally to the boundaries of the Municipal Wards' (Boundary Commission (Ireland), 1917, 7), and in the Counties wherever possible the Rural Districts were used as the building blocks. Two of the Belfast constituencies comprised a single ward only, and five contained two wards each. One ward was divided between the remaining two constituencies, each of which also contained one entire ward. The constituencies, like the wards, are organised on a sectoral basis (Figure 2.2). Unionists won eight of the nine seats in 1918; in the ninth – the Falls division, which was the smallest – the nationalist candidate defeated Eamonn de Valera, the future President of Ireland, who was standing for Sinn Fein. The wards had been defined in 1896, and Catholic pressure ensured that two (which later comprised the Falls constituency) were Catholic-dominated (Budge and O'Leary, 1973, 116–19; see also the quote from the Local Government Board on p. 49 above), hence introducing a division of the city into constituencies on religio-political grounds.[7]

Once proposals for introducing election by proportional representation fell in the 1917 House of Commons debates (by only eight votes, 149–141, on the first occasion, but later by 238–141; Butler, 1963, 10) the Commissions' work was required, whether or not the other potential change to the electoral system, adoption of the Alternative Vote, was to be adopted. (The House of Commons twice supported this, by 127–126 and then by 195–194, but it was opposed in the House of Lords and finally abandoned in a compromise between the two Houses.) The Commissions did not start from scratch, however, since the directions basically required them only to deal with cases where constituencies did not conform to the prescribed limits (Butler, 1963, 214).

The outcome was a set of recommendations which would increase the size of the House of Commons by 34 seats – to which the House of Lords added one more with an amendment granting representation to the University of Wales (Morris, 1921, 178). In England, London received three more seats, taking its representation to 62 (there were strong claims for four more on the basis of population, but these were resisted); the other Boroughs received 27 more; and the Counties lost one: in addition, two more University seats were created. The Welsh Boroughs

Figure 2.2 *The constituencies used for the 1918 general election in Belfast, and the wards with which they were built*
Source: Boundary Commission (Ireland), 1917

gained one seat and the Counties two, while in Scotland two more Burgh seats were countered by one less for the Counties: each country also gained a further University seat. Ireland also gained two seats, both for the Universities (Morris, 1921, 198). Overall, England, Scotland and Wales were allocated 492, 74 and 36 seats respectively.

Within this general pattern of redistribution, the main gains went to the largest Boroughs: Birmingham's representation, for example, increased from five to twelve; Bradford's, Hull's and Nottingham's from one to four each; Bristol's from one to five; Liverpool's from two to eleven; Manchester's from four to ten; and Sheffield's from two to seven. Several of the smaller Boroughs lost representation, however, including County towns such as Canterbury, Colchester, Peterborough, Shrewsbury and Warwick. For the first time, the country's major industrial conurbations (Greater London, Birmingham, Glasgow, Lancashire,

Northeast England and the West Riding of Yorkshire) would provide a majority of Great Britain's MPs, although not of the UK's, because Ireland (on which the Commission's recommendations were not debated because of a prior compromise among the parties) had 105 in a House of 707 members. When the recommendations came before the House of Commons 183 amendments were tabled (of which Mortimore, 1992 categorised 113 as 'purely consequential' and a further 31 dealt only with names). There were few divisions and one of the few controversial issues was whether London should have been treated as a whole for the allocation of seats or separately, on a Borough-by-Borough basis: the Commission's use of the latter was upheld although, according to Mortimore (1992, 129), this meant that London was under-represented by four seats.

The impact of these changes is summarised in Table 2.1. Single-member constituencies now predominated, with only twelve two-member Borough constituencies (eleven of them in England) and three two-member County constituencies (all in Northern Ireland: in 1917, of course, the whole of Ireland remained part of the United Kingdom and returned Westminster MPs, but the data in Table 2.1 refer only to the six Counties which became Northern Ireland in 1922). Each of the Commissions provided a table at the end of its report indicating average electorates for each type of seat: there was no commentary, but the England and Wales Commission thought it 'may be of interest' (Boundary Commission (England & Wales), 1917, 13). These suggest some equalisation in the averages, and a redistribution from urban to rural areas, so that County electorates were smaller than the Borough figures after 1917 but larger beforehand (Table 2.6). No indication of variation around those averages was given, however.

Table 2.6 *Average constituency populations after the 1917 redistribution*

	Previous Constituencies		Recommended Constituencies	
	Members	Average Population	Members	Average Population
England				
Counties	231	77,708	230	68,287
London Boroughs	59	76,773	62	72,871
Other Boroughs	166	67,294	193	73,644
Wales (including Monmouthshire)				
Counties	22	75,608	24	71,604
Boroughs	12	63,013	11	73,177
Scotland				
Counties	39	68,807	31	67,015
Burghs	38	62,925	33	71,394

Note: the previous constituency averages relate to the 1911 Census figures; the recommended constituency averages relate to the Registrar Generals' estimates for 1914.
Source: Boundary Commission (England & Wales) 1917; Boundary Commission (Scotland) 1917

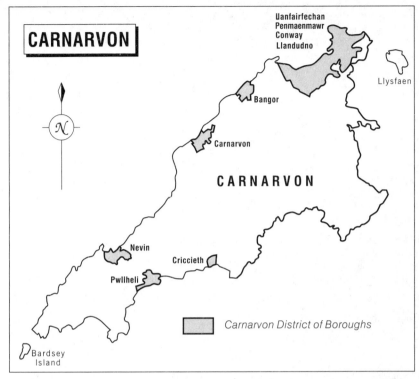

Figure 2.3 *The Carnarvon District of Boroughs constituency, as defined in 1917*
Source: Boundary Commission (England and Wales), 1917

Those variations are shown in Table 2.7 which also separates out the Districts of Borough (Burgh) seats in Wales and Scotland from the other urban constituencies: in Scotland, those groups of non-contiguous towns had electorates little different from County constituencies, and averaging 10,000 less electors than the other Burgh seats, whereas in the one Welsh case the District of Boroughs constituency had more than 20,000 fewer voters than the average urban seat. The decision regarding that case is presented in some detail. The pre-existing Carnarvon District of Boroughs seat had an estimated population of 30,757 and the Commission decided to abolish it and merge the Boroughs with the County which was entitled to two MPs; a division of the County was then proposed. However, at the Local Inquiry a strong case was made to keep a separate District of Boroughs seats because this separated the urban-industrial and rural areas and so secured 'a fairer Parliamentary representation' (Boundary Commission (England & Wales), 1917, 12): the Commission accepted this, and by adding four urban districts and a civil parish to the four Municipal Boroughs, it created a constituency with 50,550 residents (24,000 less than the rural seat surrounding them). The District of Boroughs constituency is in six separate parts, some 40 miles apart (Figure 2.3). Of the six Districts of Burghs seats in Scotland, only

The Boundary Commissions

Table 2.7 *Frequency distributions of the number of constituencies, by population size, after the 1917 redistribution*

	England			Scotland		
	C	B	L	C	B	DB
Size of population						
<39,999	0	0	2	0	0	0
40,000 – 44,999	2	0	0	2	0	0
45,000 – 49,999	3	2	1	5	0	0
50,000 – 54,999	12	12	1	4	1	1
55,000 – 59,999	35	7	5	2	2	1
60,000 – 64,999	40	31	11	5	1	0
65,000 – 69,999	38	38	6	9	6	4
70,000 – 74,999	47	36	9	9	5	0
75,000 – 79,999	23	23	9	1	6	0
80,000 – 89,999	26	28	11	1	5	0
90,000 – 99,999	4	9	3	0	1	0
100,000 – 109,999	0	3	2	0	0	0
110,000<	0	4	2	0	0	0

	Wales			Northern Ireland	
	C	B	DB	C	B
Size of population					
<39,999	0	0	0	7	3
40,000 – 44,999	1	0	0	3	4
45,000 – 49,999	0	0	0	6	2
50,000 – 54,999	2	1	1	3	1
55,000 – 59,999	1	1	0	0	0
60,000 – 64,999	5	2	0	0	0
65,000 – 69,999	1	0	0	0	0
70,000 – 74,999	6	1	0	0	0
75,000 – 79,999	1	1	0	0	0
80,000 – 89,999	4	3	0	0	0
90,000 – 99,999	3	1	0	0	0
100,000 – 109,999	0	0	0	0	0
110,000<	0	0	0	0	0

Key: C – county constituencies; B – borough (burgh) constituencies; L – London borough constituencies; DB – district of borough (burgh) constituencies

one (Montrose) is similarly punctiform and dispersed: the remainder comprise groups of towns which are near neighbours.

In all four countries, the figures in Table 2.7 indicate considerable variation about the means, although much less so in Northern Ireland than in Great Britain. (Constituencies were on average very much smaller in Northern Ireland, too.) The implication to be drawn from Table 2.7 is of substantial variations in constituency size within each of the four countries, with the partial exception of Northern Ireland. Very few seats in England, Scotland and Wales fell below the government's minimum of 50,000, and virtually all of those were County constituencies in rural areas. Many were much larger than the 70,000 'norm', however, especially in the English Boroughs, which had six with populations of 110,000 or more. In part this was a consequence of the rules, which indicated that allocations should increase by multiples of 70,000, with an additional seat if the remaining population is more than 50,000 (so that a Borough with a population between 120,000 and 190,000 would be entitled to two). There was also considerable variation within individual Counties and Boroughs, however, presumably reflecting the Commissions' difficulties in assembling the building blocks to produce equal-sized constituencies. Within Lancashire, for example, the eighteen County constituencies had an average population of 69,640 with a standard deviation of 8,255: the largest (Mossley) had 83,224, and the smallest (Lonsdale) 53,085. The 48 Borough seats included 24 in undivided Boroughs, ranging in size from 109,131 for Burnley to 53,531 for Ashton-under-Lyne,[8] and 24 in the divided Boroughs of Liverpool, Manchester and Salford. (Liverpool's eleven seats ranged in size from 79,095 to 57,638 and Manchester's ten from 85,886 to 49,964). Substantial equality was achieved in most of the divided London Boroughs, but Glasgow's fifteen constituencies ranged between 54,000 and 90,500. Similar variations were recorded from some of the Counties with only small numbers of constituencies: the four in East Sussex, for example, had populations of 77,430, 71,026, 60,325 and 50,538.

In summary, therefore, although the 1917 redistribution was the first for which population norms were set (with the same norms applying across the whole of Great Britain) consistency between the map of constituencies and that of local government areas was the dominant criterion to be observed. Thus, although at least one of the Commissions explicitly referred to "one vote, one value" as an indicator of the desirability of achieving electoral equality, the outcome was very considerable variation in constituency sizes, within as well as between the major local government units. (Again, Northern Ireland was a considerable exception to this.)

The 1918 Act, through the warrant issued to the Boundary Commissioners, continued and extended the four main principles applied in the 1885 redistribution:

- the use of administrative (i.e. local government) boundaries as the template within which constituencies were to be allocated;
- the desirability of equality of population between constituencies;
- the desirability of segregating different communities into separate constituencies;[9] and
- the use of Commissions to undertake the task of redistricting.

The major extension was in the degrees of freedom given to the Commissioners:

in 1885, the Boroughs which should be separately represented and the number of seats for each Borough and County were determined by Parliament before the Commissions were given the task of determining Borough and Constituency boundaries; in 1917 the prior decisions which constrained the Commissioners were considerably weaker, especially after the amending letter was issued (Box 2.4) and were phrased as general formulae without reference to specific places (except the City of London). This established the 'British compromise' in legislation, with the separate representation of communities and equal representation of people as the main goals of a redistribution. On the issue of community representation, however, the 1917 Instructions (Box 2.3) were more prescriptive than those introduced later: the Commissions were asked to segregate adjacent urban and industrial areas (in 1885 the instruction had been to achieve segregation according to the 'pursuits of the population'), an injunction which was not repeated in the 1944 Act.

Towards the eventual resolution

During the decade after passage of the 1918 Act the only major concern regarding the electoral system was with women's universal suffrage, eventually achieved by the *Equal Franchise Act 1928*. The registered electorate increased substantially (Table 2.8) – first when women aged 30 and over were enfranchised in 1918 and then when all adult women were in 1928 – but as constituencies were defined by population and not (as now) by registered electors, this stimulated no need for a redistribution as the male:female ratio varied little across the country. Systems of voting were frequently discussed, and came to the fore after the 1929 general election, when the Liberals won 25 per cent of the votes cast but were elected in less than 10 per cent of the seats. A Speaker's Conference was established, but reached no sensible agreement; indeed, its four votes indicated irreconcilable difficulties (as reported in Butler, 1963, 60). Labour was prepared to introduce an electoral reform bill, however, in order to sustain Liberal support for its minority government (Labour had 288 MPs, Conservative 260 and Liberal 59); this included no formal alterations to the electoral system, but a willingness to shift to the Alternative Vote was indicated. In the event, the Bill, which was subjected to protracted debates over many of its provisions, was abandoned when the Labour government fell in August 1931.

Table 2.8 *Early twentieth century changes in the electorate*

Year	Population	Adults	Electorate	Percentage
1910	44,900,000	26,100,000	7,700,000	29.5
1919	44,600,000	27,300,000	21,800,000	79.9
1929	46,700,000	31,700,000	28,900,000	91.1
1939	47,800,000	32,900,000	32,400,000	98.5

Note: final column refers to electorate as a percentage of the adult population (aged 21 and over).
Source: Butler and Butler (1994)

The following decade saw very little debate on electoral issues, although the problem of a small number of very large constituencies was identified in a ten-minute Private Member's Bill proposing to divide the Romford constituency into three. The main exception was another Private Member's Bill – *Representation of the People (Redistribution of Seats)* – introduced in March 1934 by Mr (later Sir) Herbert Williams, which the government declined to 'provide facilities for' (i.e. allocate time to its debate: *Hansard*, vol. 287, 26 March 1934, col. 1634); interestingly, no reply was given to a follow-up question which inquired whether 'It is not a fact that this question is being considered by another body in another way'. The Bill was very prescient with regard to what was to be agreed a decade later, however. The main clauses would have established a standing Electoral Commission, required to review all constituencies (other than those for Universities and the City of London) once every decade, and the recommendations from that review would have to be published and subject to consultation and possible amendment (Box 2.5). The First Schedule (not reproduced here) stated that the Commission should have six members, none of whom were MPs, and that they should be salaried and provided with secretarial and other support. The Second Schedule included eight clauses (2-9) setting out the criteria to be applied in determining constituency boundaries, of which the most important were:

- a common electoral quota for the entire UK, obtained by dividing the total electorate by 650;
- all constituencies to be single-member;
- constituencies to be allocated separately to County Boroughs and administrative Counties;
- grouping of County Boroughs and/or Counties whose electorates were less than half of the electoral quota;
- the allocation of constituencies to County Boroughs and administrative Counties to be based on dividing their electorates by the electoral quota, with rounding-up and rounding-down at either side of 0.5;
- the use of wards in County Boroughs and districts in administrative Counties for the determination of constituency boundaries (County rural districts were not warded at the time); and
- all constituencies, 'so far as may be reasonably practicable', should have the same number of electors – 'save in thinly populated areas'.

The Commission's provisional recommendations had to be published, with representations invited, and where it deemed necessary a Local Inquiry should be held before final recommendations were produced.

The main difference between these proposals and those which emerged in 1944 concerned the treatment of the four countries of the United Kingdom: Mr Williams and his colleagues opted for a UK-wide system whereas the 1944 Speaker's Conference made specific recommendations for the representation of Scotland, Wales and Northern Ireland. But the framework of constituencies with equal electorates, set within the local government template, and subject to local consultation, was adopted as the method for determining constituency boundaries

Box 2.5 *The 1934 Representation of the People
(Redistribution of Seats) Bill*

The four clauses

1 (1) For the purposes of this Act there shall be constituted a commission
to be called the Electoral Distribution Commission and hereinafter
referred to as the Commission ...

 (2) The function of the Commission shall be to determine from time to
time, in accordance with the provisions of this Act, the number of
members, other than those representing universities and the city of
London, to be elected to Parliament, together with the boundaries of
the constituencies to elect such members to Parliament.

2 As soon as may be after the passing of this Act and every ten years there-
after the Commission shall, in accordance with the provisions of the Second Schedule to this Act prepare and publish a draft scheme.

3 (1) Within not more than six months after the publication of a draft scheme
the Commission shall prepare and publish a final scheme.

 (2) A scheme shall come into operation on a day to be appointed by His
Majesty in Council and shall remain in operation until the date
appointed for the next final scheme prepared under the provisions of
this Act:
Provided that the day to be appointed shall be such time before the
qualifying date for the next register of electors as may be necessary to
enable that register to be prepared in accordance with the scheme.

4 This Act may be cited as the representation of the People (Redistribution
of Seats) Act, 1934.

The Second Schedule

1 In preparing a draft scheme the Commission shall take account of paragraphs 2 to 9 of this Schedule.

2 The quantum shall be the number of registered electors of the United Kingdom of Great Britain and Northern Ireland, other than those of the City of
London and the universities, divided by six hundred and fifty.

3 Each administrative county and each county borough the number of registered electors of which exceeds one-half of the quantum shall elect at least
one member of Parliament.

4 The number of members to be elected to Parliament by each administrative county and each county borough shall be equal to the number ascertained by dividing their respective numbers of registered electors by the

quantum. When the remainder after so dividing exceeds one-half the quantum there shall be one additional member.

5 No constituency shall return more than one member of Parliament.

6 In determining the boundaries of the constituencies in a county borough returning more than one member to Parliament regard shall be had to the boundaries of the wards into which the county borough is divided for the purpose of municipal elections and to geographical and administrative considerations.

7 In determining the boundaries of the constituencies in an administrative county returning more than one member of Parliament regard shall be had to the boundaries of boroughs and districts within the county and to geographical and administrative considerations.

8 Where the number of registered electors of a county borough or administrative county is less than one-half the quantum, it shall be grouped with the whole or part of an adjacent county borough or county, so as to form part of a constituency with a population as near as may be to the quantum.

9 So far as may be reasonably practicable the boundaries of all constituencies shall be determined so as to provide that the number of electors shall be as near as may be the same, save in thinly populated areas where on geographical and administrative grounds the number may be less, always provided that the population is not less than half the quantum.

10 In determining a final scheme the Commission shall not include any provisions not in accord with paragraphs 2 to 9 inclusive of this schedule.

11 The parts of a draft scheme affecting each county borough and administrative county shall be published by the Commission in such manner as they think best adapted for informing all persons affected, together with notice of the fact and the place where copies of the whole or parts of the scheme may be obtained, and of the time, which shall be not less than six weeks nor more than three months, within which any objection made with respect to the draft scheme by or on behalf of persons affected, must be sent to them.

12 Every objection shall be in writing and shall state the portions of the draft scheme which are objected to, the specific grounds of objection, and the omissions, additions or modifications asked for.

13 The Commission shall consider any objection made by or on behalf of any person appearing to them to be affected which is sent to them within the required time.

14 Where it appears to be desirable to the Commission that a local inquiry should be held to consider any objections, the Commission or any members thereof, or any persons appointed by them, may hold such an inquiry to be conducted in accordance with a procedure to be presented by the Commission.

15 The Commission shall give at least fourteen days' notice of any such inquiry to the persons whose objections will be considered at the inquiry.

for the second half of the twentieth century. (Sir Herbert Williams served on the 1944 Speaker's Conference on Electoral Reform and Redistribution of Seats.)

Two years later, Sir John Train introduced a motion (*Hansard*, vol. 308, 5 February 1936, col. 283):

> That, in view of the changing distribution of the electorate, the question of redistribution of seats should receive the careful attention of His Majesty's Government.

He noted that since 1918 there had been both a major extension to the franchise (votes for all adult women in 1928) and substantial shifts in the distributions of population and industry; constituency electorates now varied from 30,000 to 150,000 as a consequence. A number of MPs supported him, but in responding for the government, G. Lloyd (an Under-Secretary at the Home Office), while welcoming the motion and accepting the anomalies, asked (col. 306):

> Ought we to be carried away completely by a number of striking anomalies or ought we not to consider the broad question as it affects the country as a whole?

The average constituency had 50,000 voters – which one member had claimed was the 'ideal' – and only 38 constituencies in England and Wales deviated by more than 50 per cent from that figure. Thus, for him, the '1918 Act ... has stood the test of years and of changes very well but ... there are certain striking anomalies'.

The government could not even consider rectifying those anomalies at that time, however, because it was reviewing local government boundaries (col. 307):

> Having regard to the fact that under previous redistributions great care has always been taken to preserve local communities and not to interfere with administrative boundaries, the fact that this process [reviewing County districts] is still going on precludes redistribution being undertaken. It cannot be undertaken until that process is finished.

(Very similar arguments were used 33 years later: see p. 102.)

Electoral issues were revisited at the outbreak of the Second World War, however, when legislation was introduced to suspend electoral registration and general elections: none were to be held during the war and the electoral registers were not to be updated, with the register compiled in 1939 remaining in force for by-elections. In 1942, however, the government started preparations for post-war elections by establishing a committee on the electoral machinery, chaired by the Registrar-General (Sir Sylvanus Vivian) and containing MPs, the parties' agents and official experts. Its report (Vivian Committee, 1942), according to Butler (1963, 88), not only 'served as a basis for the interim arrangements on registration' but also provided the basis for 'the permanent solution of the redistribution problem'.

The Vivian Committee report

The Vivian Committee's terms of reference with respect to redistribution were

> to examine the technical problems involved in any scheme of redistribution of Parliamentary seats by way of preparation for consideration of the principles on which any scheme should be based.

Paragraphs 63–138 of its report dealt with these issues. It began with a clear statement of the problem (Vivian Committee, 1942, #64, 14):

> The fundamental considerations giving rise to a need for the redistribution of seats, though elementary, are so important that we make no apology for recapitulating them. The essential basis of representative Government in this country is that the main representative body of the legislature should consist of persons elected under conditions which confer upon them an *equal representative status*. It is also a fundamental principle of our Parliamentary system that representation (with the exception of University constituencies) should be *territorial*. Both these features appear to us to be of the greatest importance. It follows from them that seats must be assigned to a series of local areas or communities each of which contains as equal as may be a share of the total number of persons to be represented.

Hence the two main aspects of representation salient in the emerging 'British compromise' are established as principles: MPs should be elected to represent separate territorially-based communities, which are equal in their populations. Furthermore, because 'population is at all times in motion' (#65) under- and over-representation will emerge over time, calling for revisions to the constituency map.

In setting out how such revisions should be conducted, the Committee reported extensively on the instructions to and procedures adopted by the 1918 Commission. Within the principle of equal representation it identified six features that influence the progress of a redistribution:

1 The need for a *quota*, or 'average of the number of persons to be represented per member' (#77) which will serve as a standard for both evaluating the pre-existing situation and creating new constituencies.
2 The extent of the *limits of toleration*, recognising that 'trifling' departures (#79) from the quota should not trigger a redistribution and arguing that no clear rule can be formulated – 'What degree of departure is to be accepted is in fact determined by the formulation of such limits [as in the 1918 rules]. But in the application of both the quota and the limits of toleration rigid or artificial precision is not necessary or invariably possible' (#79), which is why the Boundary Commission was given discretionary powers in 1918.
3 The need for *continuity of constituencies* – 'we believe to be the general opinion that, other things being equal, the continuity of constituencies is a good thing' (#80). Change should only be proposed where necessary, and even then continuity should if possible be maintained by minor adjustments only, for 'changes in any particular constituency can rarely fail to affect other adjoining constituencies; and the adjustment of even a single constituency may be found to react upon the surrounding constituencies over a gradually widening radius like the ripples from a stone thrown into a pond'.
4 The requirement to *conform to local government boundaries* is justified because these are 'the only defined, ascertained and recognised local boundaries which can be used for the demarcation of Parliamentary constituencies' (#83); because such boundaries are frequently changed, however, this will

almost certainly require substantial redistributions of Parliamentary seats, if such events are undertaken at long time intervals.

5 The *assignment of seats* to the separate parts of the United Kingdom was left to 'the fluid working of the quota and the limits of toleration' (#85) in 1918, within a prescribed maximum, although the number for each separate part could be prescribed: if it is not, then 'it is imperative, of course, that the quota and the rules for its operation should operate uniformly throughout the whole area covered' (#87): the Committee identified disagreement over interpretation of the phrase 'the total of the persons to be represented', however, which could refer to either total population or qualified electorate. With a universal franchise the difference between the two should be slight, except for areas with large proportions of their population under the minimum voting age (then 21), but they claim that the choice between the two definitions 'may have some small effect upon the allocation of seats as between England and Wales and Scotland' (#87), and

6 How the issues of *two-member constituencies and the grouping of Boroughs in adjacent Counties* into constituencies (both permitted in 1918) are to be dealt with.

Having identified these issues, the Committee then addressed what it identified as the main problem before it – how to operationalise the principles enacted in 1918, which it very largely accepted. It pointed out that redistributions had occurred only infrequently during the preceding hundred years and that as a general conclusion very often (#91):

> the whole subject remains and may continue to remain indefinitely in abeyance until the mal-distribution of seats is so extreme and notorious that something must be done.

Because no statutory provisions exist to ensure that it is, it then becomes a subject of legislation, and hence a political matter as (#93):

> In both [1867 and 1885] … redistribution was to some extent consequential upon revision of the franchise. The records of the proceedings indicate that on both occasions there was some Parliamentary manoeuvring to secure that the concurrent redistribution proposals should be tabled before assent was given to the franchise amendments themselves. It might perhaps be inferred that this tendency arose out of the disposition of Parties and individual Members to ascertain to what extent the redistribution would affect their interests before finally giving support to the franchise amendments.

This was undesirable and unnecessary, and the Committee concluded that the procedure for redistributions should be 'the subject of standing machinery' (#95), which needed three main components (#96):

- legislation to set out matters of principle and policy, such as establishing the quota and determining the limits of toleration;
- statutory Rules which would indicate how those principles were to be applied; and
- the administrative procedures to be employed.

This legislation should establish an administrative body empowered to act without Parliamentary initiative, and so it recommended creation of a statutory Commission.

The Committee also commented on the timetable which such a Commission should operate to, arguing from first principles that it should review the situation frequently (#98):

> The proper adjustment of constituencies in conformity to the principle of equal representation is a consideration affecting every General Election; and in normal circumstances the statutory life of a Parliament determines that a General Election will take place at not more than quinquennial intervals ... we recommend [that] a review of the state of constituencies coupled with redistribution proposals, where necessary, is to be forthcoming during the life of every Parliament.

Such a Commission must be both independent and linked to Parliament, with the latter being non-Party in character, hence the recommendation that the Speaker be *ex officio* the Commission chair, although the day-to-day task of chairing meetings would be delegated to a nominated vice-chair. The Commission would include representatives of various related government departments, such as the Home Office and the Registrar General, and because the various functions are differently allocated in the separate parts of the UK this meant that four separate Commissions would be needed for England, Scotland, Wales and Northern Ireland (#105).

Regarding the Commissions' procedures, the Committee was brief (#110):

> At a suitable stage, public notice of proposals provisionally framed would need to be given; and it will probably be thought necessary that local hearings should be arranged to enable representations or suggestions to be made respecting the provisional lay-out of any adjusted constituencies.

The phrase 'it will probably be thought necessary' with regard to local hearings is intriguing, given the large number held at the time of the previous redistribution (1917; see p. 51 above) and the practice of inviting local comments adopted by the Commissioners appointed to implement the details of the nineteenth-century redistributions. In addition, the Committee thought it desirable for each Commission to meet the chief national officers of the various political parties 'with regard to the provisional proposals' (#111) which 'might be of advantage by withdrawing from the hearings any representations arising out of Party interests'. And then, once final proposals had been agreed by the Commissions they would be 'submitted to Parliament through the appropriate Minister in the form of an Order embodying the report of the full Commission' (#112), with the implication that Parliament could accept or reject, but not modify, the recommendations.

The Committee commented on the current malapportionment (using 1939 data). It applied '30 per cent below' and '70 per cent above' limits of toleration around the quotas established for each country, and showed that 119 constituencies did not have 'an equal share of representation in the House of Commons' (#116): 87 no longer justified their present level of representation, and the other

32 were much too large. All of the constituencies above the 70 per cent limit returned only 9 MPs per million electors whereas the 30 per cent or more below the quotas returned 30 MPs per million. This led to the mild conclusion that 'we think it probable that in the light of the particulars given the Government and the country will take the view that redistribution is essential' (#119).

The Committee doubted that this could be done in time for the first post-war general election (in part because of the need for reliable electoral registration figures, which had not been collected since 1939), however, but suggested that a partial redistribution might be undertaken for those areas where malapportionment was most acute. It made no firm recommendation, however, and the Committee's three Labour MPs presented a written reservation (Vivian Committee, 1942, 32), arguing that a partial redistribution would largely affect London, which had undergone massive temporary population movements during the war so that the changes could be temporary only, and whose local government boundaries were obsolete. (They failed to point out, of course, that many parts of London were Labour strongholds!)

Butler (1963, 89) notes that the Committee's report attracted little attention and the government announced Bills in 1943 to arrange for a new register and to establish Boundary Commissions. Under pressure to cover more issues, however, it instead established a Speaker's Conference of 32 members (29 MPs and three members of the House of Lords), whose terms of reference were:

> To examine and, if possible, submit agreed resolutions on the following matters:
> (a) Redistribution of seats;
> (b) Reform of franchise (both Parliamentary and local government);
> (c) Conduct and costs of Parliamentary elections, and expenses falling on candidates and Members of Parliament;
> (d) Methods of election.

Although asked by the Prime Minister to report as soon as possible on the first two issues (his letter is reproduced in Speaker, 1944), the Conference decided that it could not deal with the first before the fourth. It determined by a large majority (24–5) to recommend neither proportional representation (not even on an experimental basis) nor the alternative vote, and then moved to the issue of redistribution. It recommended the immediate creation of new constituencies, by a Boundary Commission which would split constituencies that in 1939 had more than 190 per cent of the average population, and then set out the rules and procedures under which Boundary Commissions would normally operate.

The Conference also made recommendations regarding Rules and Machinery for redistribution, which are listed in Box 2.6. These both displayed considerable continuity with what had gone before and made certain more radical suggestions, in line with Sir Herbert Williams' Bill of 1934. Thus the local government map remained the template within which seats were to be allocated, all seats were to return a single member (except where local opinion favoured retention of existing two-member seats) and the basis for redistribution was to be the registered electorate rather than the population; equality across electorates was to be achieved by application of a national quota and tolerance limits (albeit broad, though see Chapter 3 on debates in the 1950s). The task should be undertaken by Boundary Commissions which would consult political parties after they had produced provisional recommendations and, after the first redistribution, implementation was to be by Order in Council not by Bill, so that Parliament could accept or reject, but not amend, what was recommended. (The relevant Secretary of State was to have the power to recommend changes in that Order, however.)

The decision to have separate Boundary Commissions for each of the four countries (which in effect meant having a separate one for Wales, since Scotland and Ireland had their own Commissions at each preceding redistribution) followed the one to guarantee minimum representation for Scotland and Wales. McLean (1995, 262) reports that the Conference Secretariat produced a briefing paper, 'at the direction of the Speaker', which stated that 'it is clearly out of the question to instruct the Boundary Commissioners to apply only a strict mathematical test' in Scotland and Wales, for which only the problem of sparse population in the Highlands was offered as a reason. This view clearly prevailed, and McLean quotes the relevant Minute of the Speaker's Conference that:

> It was pointed out that a strict application of the quota for the whole of Great Britain would result in a considerable decrease in the existing number of Scottish and Welsh seats, but that in practice, in view of the proposal that the Boundary Commissioners should be permitted to pay special consideration to geographical considerations, it was ... unlikely that there would be any substantial reduction. It was strongly urged that ... it would be very desirable, on political grounds, to state from the outset quite clearly that the number of Scottish and Welsh seats should not be diminished. The absence of any such assurance might give rise to a good deal of political feeling and would lend support to the separatist movements in both countries.

Given that the great majority of the Scottish and Welsh populations live in their countries' urban-industrial areas, the use of 'geographic considerations' to ensure a continuation of their substantial over-representation to avoid a potential political backlash is somewhat dubious, but the result was that redistribution in the UK involves, in effect, four separate operations. More importantly, the politically-inspired decision to guarantee a minimum number of seats to Scotland and Wales went against the principle established in 1917 that common rules for redistribution should apply across the whole of Great Britain, and created the 'Celtic preference' in the distribution of constituencies which no subsequent Parliament or government was prepared to tackle (Rawlings, 1988).[10]

A Bill to deal with both the immediate proposals and the longer-term procedures was presented to Parliament in 1944. It attracted little debate on its core provisions, much of the discussion focusing on representation for (1) the Universities and (2) the City of London. It provided the foundation for the current system, and is the starting-point for our discussion in the next chapter.

Box 2.6 *Main recommendations of the 1944 Speaker's Conference*

Rules

Total number of MPs
The total number of Members of the House of Commons for Great Britain shall remain substantially as at present (i.e. 591, excluding University seats).

Special provision for Scotland and Wales
There shall be no reduction in the present number of Members of the House of Commons for Scotland or for Wales and Monmouthshire.

Redistribution basis
Redistribution shall be effected on the basis of the qualified electorate.

Quota
The standard unit of electorate for each Member of the House of Commons for Great Britain shall be a quota ascertained by dividing the total electorate in Great Britain by the total number of seats in Great Britain (other than University seats) existing at the time the Boundary Commissioners report.

Limits of toleration
The Boundary Commissioners shall not be required to modify an existing constituency if its electorate falls short of or exceeds the quota by not more than approximately 25 per cent.

Double-member constituencies
Constituencies at present returning two Members shall be abolished, except where after local inquiry by the Boundary Commissioners it is found in any particular case that abolition is undesirable.

The local government template
The boundaries of Parliamentary constituencies shall, where convenient, coincide with the boundaries of local government administrative areas.

City of London
The City of London shall continue, as at present, to return two Members. (This Resolution was passed by a majority – Ayes 15; Noes 13.)

Northern Ireland
It shall be an Instruction to the Boundary Commissioners for Northern Ireland, in applying the foregoing rules, that there shall be no change in the present number of Members of the House of Commons for Northern Ireland, and that the quota for Northern Ireland shall be ascertained by dividing the total electorate by twelve (that is, the number of Northern Ireland seats, other than the University seat).

Discretionary Powers for the Boundary Commissioners
The Boundary Commissioners may depart from the strict application of these rules if special geographical considerations (including the area, shape

In summary

In just over a century, therefore, the UK moved from a malapportioned and gerrymandered electoral system, in which power lay very firmly in the hands of the

and accessibility of a constituency) appear to them to render such a course desirable.

University constituencies

Nothing in the foregoing rules shall apply to University constituencies.

Machinery

Separate Commissions

There should be four separate Boundary Commissions: one for England; one for Scotland; one for Wales and Monmouthshire; and one for Northern Ireland.

Chairman of the Commissions

The Speaker should be ex-officio Chairman of all four Commissions.

Deputy-Chairman

The Speaker should nominate one of the members of each Commission as Deputy-Chairman of the Commission.

Party representations

Each separate Boundary Commission should sit (its Deputy-Chairman presiding) to hear any representations from the Chief or National Officers of the Party organisations with respect to the Commission's provisional proposals for redistribution.

Periodic reviews

Each Boundary Commission should be required to undertake, at intervals of not less than three years and not more than seven years, a general review of the representation in the House of Commons of that part of the United Kingdom with which it is concerned.

Special reports

The Boundary Commissions should, in addition, have authority to submit special reports at any time recommending changes in respect of any particular constituency or group of constituencies.

Action

The reports of the Boundary Commissions should be submitted to the Secretary of State concerned, and the Secretary of State should be required to lay every such report before Parliament, together with an Order in Council giving effect to any recommendations (with or without modification) for redistributions, and providing for any consequential or incidental matters. Any such draft Order should be subject to affirmative resolutions.

There should, however, be a special provision that when the Boundary Commissions have made their first general reports with respect to the whole of the United Kingdom, effect should be given to this first comprehensive scheme by Bill, and not by Order in Council.

landed interests and its political representatives (who were elected by a very small proportion of the population), to a universal franchise with single-member constituencies of broadly similar size. It became recognised that the legitimacy of the first-past-the-post electoral system to which most of its politicians were wedded required regular reviews of constituency electorates and, if necessary, redistributions in order that the principle of equality of representation be adhered to. That was not the only key principle, however: it was also widely accepted that communities should be separately represented, as reflected by local government administrative areas and the different socio-economic interests of major groups within the population, and so the two principles had to be operated in tandem. Nevertheless, the 1944 Act and all subsequent legislation makes no reference to constituencies representing separate interests, which had characterised all instructions to Boundary Commissioners up to and including the 1917 redistribution: from 1958 on, these were referred to only through the vague term 'local ties', as discussed in the next chapters.

It was further recognised by the end of this process that redistribution should not be undertaken (or even driven) by politicians, who would be likely to promote their sectional interests, but instead allocated to an independent body – a Boundary Commission – with strong links to Parliament. Legislation would enact the principles that such a body must operate and indicate the procedures that it should follow, but it would have freedom to act within those constraints. Those principles, most of which emerged from the instructions given to the nineteenth-century Commissions, should cover not only the two concepts of representation, equality and communities, but also the desirability of continuity in the map of constituencies, separate treatment for the four countries which make up the United Kingdom, and regular reviews in order that the map kept pace with the changing distribution of population. These were all enacted in 1944 and form the foundation of the current system.

Notes

1 The government's original intention had been to give final power of decision on constituency boundaries to the Boundary Commissioners (who would report directly to the King) but this caused much concern in both Houses and was amended so that Parliament made the final decisions and MPs determined their own fates (Mortimore, 1992, 19–20).

2 Equality in population did not, of course, necessarily also mean equality in electors.

3 This episode is not referred to in Mortimore's (1992) historical survey of redistributions in the UK, nor is the 1934 Bill referred to later in his chapter.

4 The report presented data to show that the population ratio of the largest to the smallest constituency after the 1885 redistribution was 5.9 (the smallest constituency had 15,278 residents then, and the largest 89,573) whereas by 1905 it was 16.5 (217,085 to 13,137). If the report's proposals were accepted, the latter would be reduced to 6.3 (127,495 to 20,185) (Local Government Board, 1905, 5).

5 This is the first appearance of a difference between the Scottish and all other Commissions in the choice of Assistant Commissioners (ACs): the Scottish Commission continues to employ Sheriffs who work in the area they are considering, whereas the English Commission selects ACs who do not know the area concerned.

6 Mortimore (1992, 128) claims that the debate on this issue in 1917 was 'perhaps the

only effective Parliamentary discussion of the form that the instructions to the Commissioners should take'. He notes that reference was made to the *South Africa Act 1909*, in which Boundary Commissioners were required to take into account: (1) community or diversity of interests, (2) means of communication, (3) physical features, (4) existing electoral boundaries and (5) sparsity or density of population. These could be used to argue for deviations from the electoral quota when recommending constituencies, but not by more than 15 per cent from that quota. In the debate, many MPs sought to protect rural areas, one arguing for a maximum permissible area for any constituency, and this led to the phrase 'an inconvenient size or character', which Mortimore sees as the precursor to Rule 6 in the current legislation.

7 We are grateful to Prof. Cornelius O'Leary for further information on this case.

8 Four boroughs returned two members from a single constituency, and their populations have been halved for this exercise.

9 Attempts to have area as well as population included in the criteria, thereby protecting rural interests, were resisted (Morris, 1921, 178).

10 Though in the draft *Scotland Bill*, introduced in December 1997 to create the Scottish Parliament approved by referendum in the previous September, the Boundary Commission for Scotland is instructed to use the electoral quota for England for the Fifth Periodic Review only.

3

The current legislative framework

Until the Second World War, electoral distributions were undertaken on an *ad hoc* basis, with no established machinery for determining constituencies let alone a procedure for regular review. The Vivian Committee (1942) proposals envisaged major changes to this situation, with establishment of a machinery incorporating clear rules and guidelines and operated outside Parliament, though the latter had the ultimate power of veto. Those proposals, amended slightly by the subsequent Speaker's Conference, formed the basis for legislation over the next fifty years, and provide the context within which Parliamentary constituencies are currently determined.

The 1944 Act

Following the Speaker's letter to the Prime Minister in 1944, a Bill was rapidly prepared to put its recommendations and suggestions into operation, with regard to both the immediate issue of creating new constituencies to rectify the anomalies of under-representation in some of the largest Boroughs and to provide a framework for the continued work of the Boundary Commissions. As Butler (1963, 96) reports, although some of those recommendations became the focus of considerable conflict four years later, in 1944 'they created little stir'.

Only two components of the *House of Commons (Redistribution of Seats) Act 1944* received substantial Parliamentary attention at the Committee stage – the representation of the Universities and of the City of London. On the former, Labour concerns about the quality of the University MPs in the past were the cause of some debate but the relevant clause excluding the University constituencies from the conditions of the Act was accepted by 152 votes to 16. Regarding the City of London, the Rules set out under point 7 in the Third Schedule to the Act stated that:

> Nothing in rules 2 to 6 of these rules shall apply to the City of London, but that
> City as constituted at the commencement of this Act shall continue to be a separate

constituency, and shall return either two member or a single member as may be provided by the Act giving effect (whether with or without modifications) to the recommendations contained in the reports submitted by the Boundary Commissions under section three of this Act.

Thus the Commission, rather than the government, was to advise on the City's representation; a Labour member's amendment to remove separate representation for the City was defeated by 163 to 31. With those decisions, 'The Bill then passed its remaining stages in both Houses with almost no further discussion' (Butler, 1963, 98).

The first section of the Act established the four Boundary Commissions, and determined that 'For the purposes of this Act the administrative county of Monmouth shall be taken to be part of Wales and not part of England'. The second section gave the Commissions the immediate task of creating new constituencies to replace the twenty defined as 'abnormally large' (i.e. all had electorates of at least 100,000, and so were 190 per cent or more above the average): all were in England, so only the English Commission was involved. A quota of 50,000 was to be applied, single-member seats were to be defined, and the Commission was given discretion to include adjacent constituencies in its review and recommendations, if this were deemed necessary, in particular in order to achieve conformity with the then-current local government boundaries. Its report, laid before Parliament within six months (Boundary Commission for England, 1945), recommended the creation of 25 new constituencies, which was accepted by Parliament. The Commission (1945, #4) indicated that it saw the task as an entirely temporary one, undertaken to allow conduct of the first European post-war election; however:

> A consequence of the narrow circumscription of our task and powers has been that in some difficult cases we have been obliged to make recommendations which do not give us full satisfaction. In these cases we have preferred, where the issue arises, to take a course which facilitates the next ensuing stage of a general redistribution of seats…, rather than to recommend an arrangement which, though somewhat more satisfactory according to short-term standards, would have to be completely recast later.

Three such cases were cited: Manchester and the adjacent County of Cheshire, Birmingham and Warwickshire, and an area overlapping Kent and Surrey.

The third section required all four Commissions to undertake a full review of all constituencies, applying the rules set out in Schedule III to the Act. The fourth section set the calendar for subsequent reviews – which became known as periodical reviews. The first should occur within 3–7 years of the passing of the Act giving effect to the recommendations of the Initial Review (unless the latter proposed no changes, in which case six years was set as the maximum period), and from then on the period was to be set at 3–7 years. The Commissions were required to announce the establishment of a periodical review publicly, and the relevant Secretary of State was obligated to lay their recommendations before Parliament (with or without modification) 'as soon as after may be'. Under the fifth section the Commissions were to recommend whether each constituency should be a Parliamentary County (or division thereof) or a Parliamentary Borough (or division thereof): this requirement arose because the related *Representation of the People Act* regarding candidates' election expenses allowed more to be spent per elector in County (i.e. rural) areas than in Borough (i.e. urban) areas.

The First Schedule to the Act established the (nominal) role of the Speaker as the chairman of each Commission. Membership of the Commissions (in addition to the Speaker) varied slightly (reflecting the different situations in the various countries noted by the Vivian Committee):

> *England*: The Registrar-General for England; the Director-General of the Ordnance Survey; and two others, one appointed by the Secretary of State [commonly known as the Home Secretary] and one by the Minister of Health.
> *Scotland*: The Registrar-General for Scotland; the Director-General of the Ordnance Survey; and two others appointed by the Secretary of State [for Scotland].
> *Wales*: As for England.
> *Northern Ireland*: The Registrar-General for Northern Ireland; the Commissioner of Valuation for Northern Ireland; and two others appointed by the Secretary of State [for Northern Ireland].

Provision was made for the Speaker to nominate one member of each Commission as Deputy Chairman. The Secretary of State was also empowered to (First Schedule, Part II, #1 (1)):

> at the request of any Commission, appoint one or more assistant Commissioners to inquire into and report to the Commission upon, such matters as the Commission think fit.

This allowed the Commissioners to distance themselves from the detailed consideration of particular schemes at the consultation stage (see below), but the main reason for employing Assistant Commissioners, as at nineteenth-century redistributions, was the workload involved in exploring public opinion.

Part III of the First Schedule to the Act set out procedural requirements (Box 3.1). The first clause set the quorum for a Commission meeting as two members, even if there were a vacancy, and the second empowered the Commission to hold joint meetings, 'for the purpose of considering any matter of common concern'. The next two clauses introduced the crucial element of public consultation: the Speaker's Conference only suggested consultations with the national officers of the political parties 'to hear any representations ... with respect to the Commission's provisional proposals for redistribution' (Speaker, 1944, #20), but those drafting the Bill decided to widen the consultation process, along the lines adopted in 1917 (see p. 51 above) and recommended by Vivian. The following clause indicated that such Inquiries should apply the rules for attendance of witnesses set out in the relevant Local Government Acts, and then clause 6 gave the Commissions wide powers to regulate their own procedures regarding public consultation. Finally, the Third Schedule set out the 'Rules for Distribution of Seats', reproduced in full as Box 3.2.

Box 3.1 *Aspects of the procedure to be adopted by the Boundary Commissions, set out in Part III of the First Schedule to the* House of Commons (Redistribution of Seats) Act 1944

3 Where a Commission have provisionally determined to make recommendations affecting any constituency, they shall publish in at least one newspaper circulating in the constituency a notice stating –

   (a) the effect of the proposed recommendations and (except in a case where they propose to recommend that no alteration be made in respect of the constituency) that a copy of the recommendations is open to inspection at a specified place within the constituency; and

   (b) that representations with respect to the proposed recommendations may be made to the Commission within one month after the publication of the notice;

   And the Commission shall take into consideration any representations duly made in accordance with any such notice.

4 A Commission may, if they think fit, cause a local inquiry to be held in respect of any constituency or constituencies.

   …

6 Subject to the foregoing provisions of this Schedule, each of the Commissions shall have power to regulate their own procedure.

These Rules show that Parliament had not tackled a number of issues which remained controversial, and which were to become more so after the election of a Labour government in 1945: two-member constituencies, separate representation for the Universities and for the City of London, and plural voting (i.e. the 'business vote', whereby those owning and operating a business in a constituency had a vote there, as well as at their domestic residence). These are almost entirely outside the focus of this book, however, except insofar as they impact upon the other rules (e.g. in defining the electorate from which the electoral quota is derived). Those issues aside, the Rules set the framework for the current procedure used in defining constituencies, though not without considerable debate and some significant modifications.

Four key features of those Rules stand out:

- The establishment of representation minima for Scotland and Wales, within an overall maximum for Great Britain, thereby precluding growth in representation for England (on the assumption that the English population continued to grow more rapidly that that of either of the other two countries) – although the phrase 'not substantially greater or less than 591' in Rule 1 is (presumably deliberately) vague enough to give the Commissions (and eventually Parliament) some flexibility.
- A clear statement of limits to the variation in constituency electorates, though apparently set generously at 25 per cent plus or minus and within the context of the phrase 'so far as is practicable'.

Box 3.2 *Rules for the Distribution of Seats, set out in the Third Schedule to the* House of Commons (Redistribution of Seats) Act 1944 *and as amended in 1947*

1   The number of constituencies in the several parts of the United Kingdom set out in the first column of the following table shall be as stated respectively in the second column of that table-

Part of the United Kingdom		*No. of Constituencies*
Great Britain	...	Not substantially greater or less than 591
Scotland	...	Not less than 71
Wales	...	Not less than 35
Northern Ireland	...	12

2   (1) A two-member constituency within the meaning of the next following rule which is not divided or required to return a single member as therein provided shall, subject to any adjustment of its boundaries made in accordance with that rule, continue to return two members.

(2) Every other constituency shall return a single member.

3   (1) Any two-member constituency, the electorate whereof is less than approximately thirty-seven twentieths of the electoral quota or more than approximately two and a half times that quota, shall be divided into or among two or more other constituencies:

provided that, where the electorate of the constituency is less than approximately one and a quarter times the electoral quota, the constituency may, instead of being divided as aforesaid, be required to return a single member.

(2) Any other two-member constituency shall be divided as aforesaid unless the Boundary Commission concerned, after causing a Local Inquiry to be held, are satisfied, having regard to any particular circumstances affecting the constituency, that it is undesirable so to divide it.

(3) Where the boundaries of a borough as last defined for the purpose of ascertaining the boundaries of a two-member constituency –

(a) do not include an area which is included within the boundaries of the borough as defined for local government purposes on the enumeration date; or

(b) include an area which is not included within the boundaries of the borough as so defined for local government purposes;

then-

(i) in reckoning the electorate of the constituency for the purpose of paragraph (1) of this rule, that area shall be included on or excluded from the constituency, as the case may be; and

(ii) if it is determined under paragraph (2) of this rule that the constituency shall not be divided as aforesaid, the boundaries of the borough shall be redefined, for the purposes of ascertaining the boundaries of the constituency, so as to include or exclude that area, as the case may be.

(4) In the last foregoing paragraph, for references to a borough there shall be substituted, in its application to Scotland, references to a county of a city and, in its application to Northern Ireland, references to a county.

(5) In this rule the expression 'two-member constituency' means a constituency returning two members on the enumeration date.

*4 So far as is practicable having regard to rule 1 of these rules, the electorate of any constituency returning a single member shall not be greater or less than the electoral quota by more than approximately one quarter of the electoral quota.

5 (1) So far as is practicable having regard to the foregoing rules–
  (a) in England and Wales,–
    (i) no county or any part thereof shall be included in a constituency which includes the whole or part of any other county or part of a county borough or metropolitan borough;
    (ii) no county borough or any part thereof shall be included in a constituency which includes the whole or part of any other county borough or the whole or part of a metropolitan borough;
    (iii) no metropolitan borough or any part thereof shall be included in a constituency which includes the whole or part of any other metropolitan borough;
    (iv) no county district shall be included partly in one constituency and partly in another.
  (b) in Scotland,–
    (i) no county or burgh shall be included partly in one parliamentary county and partly in another, or partly in a parliamentary county and partly in a parliamentary burgh;
    (ii) no burgh other than a county of a city shall be included partly in one constituency and partly in another.
  (c) In Northern Ireland, no county district shall be included partly in one constituency and partly in another.
(2) In paragraph (1) of this rule the following expressions have the following meanings, that is to say:–
'county' means, in sub-paragraph (a), an administrative county other than the county of London, and, in sub-paragraph (b) a county exclusive of any burgh situate therein;
'county borough' has the same meaning as in the Local Government Act, 1933;
'county district' has, in sub-paragraph (a) the same meaning as in the Local Government Act, 1933, and, in sub-paragraph (c), the same meaning as in the Local Government (Ireland) Act, 1898.
**

6 A Boundary Commission may depart from the strict application of the last two foregoing rules if special geographical considerations, including in particular the size, shape and accessibility of a constituency, appear to them to render a departure desirable.

7 Nothing in rules 2 to 6 of these rules shall apply to the City of London, but that City as constituted at the commencement of this Act shall continue to be a separate constituency, and shall return either two members or a single member as may be provided by the Act giving effect (whether with or without modifications) to the recommendations contained in the reports submitted by the Boundary Commissions under section three of this Act.

8 (1) For the purposes of these rules—
        (a) the expression 'electoral quota' means–
             (i) in the application of these rules to a constituency in Great Britain, a
                  number obtained by dividing the electorate for Great Britain by the
                  number of constituencies in Great Britain existing on the enumera-
                  tion date, or, in applying these rules for the purposes of section three
                  of this Act, by the number of such constituencies existing at the com-
                  mencement of this Act, namely five hundred and ninety-one; and
             (ii) in the application of these rules to a constituency in Northern Ireland,
                  a number obtained by dividing the electorate for Northern Ireland by
                  the number of constituencies in Northern Ireland existing on the enu-
                  meration date.
        (b) the expression 'electorate', in relation to any constituency or any part
             thereof, means—
             (i) in a case where the enumeration date falls before the expiration of
                  the Parliamentary Electors (War-Time Registration) Act, 1943, the
                  number of persons whose names appear in the lists of persons qual-
                  ified to be registered in the civilian residence, business premises and
                  service registers for the constituency, or that part thereof, published
                  on or last before that date in pursuance of regulations made under
                  subsection (3) of section twelve of that Act; and
             (ii) in a case where the enumeration date falls after the expiration of the
                  said Act, the number of persons whose names appear on the parlia-
                  mentary register of electors for the constituency, or that part thereof,
                  in force on that date under the Representation of the People Act, 1918;
             and, in relation to Great Britain or Northern Ireland, means the aggregate
             electorates as hereinbefore defined of all the constituencies therein.
    (2) In reckoning for the purpose of these rules the number of constituencies in
         any part of the United Kingdom, a constituency returning two members shall
         be reckoned as two constituencies.

Notes:
* removed by the 1947 act
** the following rule 5A was added by the 1947 Act

5A (1) The electorate of any constituency shall be as near the electoral quota as is practicable
        having regard to the foregoing rules: and a Boundary Commission may depart from
        the strict application of the last foregoing rule if it appears to them that a departure is
        desirable to avoid an excessive disparity between the electorate of any constituency
        and the electoral quota, or between the electorate thereof and that of neighbouring
        constituencies in the part of the United Kingdom with which they are concerned.

    (2) For the purposes of this rule a constituency returning two members shall be treated as
         two constituencies.

- Clear guidelines that the major areas of local government – County Boroughs, Metropolitan Boroughs, Burghs (in Scotland), and County Districts (i.e. Rural Districts Urban Districts, and Municipal Boroughs) – should not be divided and their parts included in constituencies including parts of other local government areas.
- The caveat that the Boundary Commissions could depart from the rules regarding the quota and local government areas if 'special geographical considerations' (defined as size – presumably area – shape and accessibility) deemed it desirable.

In terms of the 'organic vs. mathematic' conflict, therefore, the Commissions were expected to consider both, with the wording of Rules 4 and 5 indicating that electoral equality (Rule 4) had precedence over community integrity (Rule 5) – to the extent that this equates with local government boundaries – though equality was broadly interpreted as within a 25 per cent tolerance limit.

The Initial Review and the 1947 Act

When undertaking their Initial Review of all constituencies, the Boundary Commissions found the conflict between Rules 4 and 5 too constraining and the Speaker, as Chairman of all four Commissions, asked the Home Secretary to amend the law by removing Rule 4. The nature of the problems that the Commissions faced is set out in the reports to their Initial Reviews. According to the English Commission (Boundary Commission for England, 1947, #8, 4):

> The difficulties we encountered during our review of constituencies under the provisions of the Act of 1944 arose in the main from the fact that Rule 4 prescribed that the electorate of a constituency should not be greater or less than the electoral quota by more than approximately one quarter. We found that it was not practicable to give effect to this rule, having regard to the limiting provisions of Rule 1, without disturbing the unity of local government areas [*], and in a number of instances, e.g. where the electorate or a borough was too large for a single member but too small to justify two members, we found it necessary to detach part of the borough and add it to an adjoining area.

The Welsh Commission's report contained exactly the same words up to [*] in the above quotation (Boundary Commission for Wales, 1947, #8, 4), perhaps not surprisingly since the two Commissions, as now, shared a Secretariat who not only service the Commissions but do all the necessary preliminary research involved in preparing redistribution schemes: the Commissions deliberate over options presented to them by their Secretariats.

A proposed amendment was introduced to Parliament in November 1946, when the Home Secretary informed the House of Commons that:

> in endeavouring to keep all constituencies within 25 per cent of the quota the Boundary Commissions had been forced to recommend the complete dismemberment for

> Parliamentary purposes of many unified communities; the rules guiding the Com-
> missioners would, therefore, have to be relaxed to allow them to preserve localities
> intact, although they would, of course, still aim to maintain approximate numerical
> equality. (Butler, 1963, 103)

This produced an Opposition charge that the changes were being proposed for
party political (i.e. Labour) gain, but the Speaker intervened to indicate that he
had asked for the relaxation, as Chairman of the Commissions. (His words were
'I do not say that I advised but, having been consulted, I approved, the steps
which had been taken': *Hansard*, vol. 430, 13 November 1946, col. 79.[1]) Despite
the claims of gerrymandering pressed by Winston Churchill, *The Times* claimed
that the (belated in its view) decision to allow the Commissions 'to give greater
weight in their recommendations to local considerations will be widely popular'
(quoted in Butler, 1963, 104), and met all-party demands.

A Bill introduced later in 1946 and passed in 1947 effected the change by giving the 'organic' requirement precedence over the 'mathematic' – which is what
one MP claimed had been the intention of the 1944 Speaker's Conference. In
introducing it, the Home Secretary, Chuter Ede, stated that 'We desire that the
principle of community of interest, of local government boundaries, shall be made
superior to mere mathematics' (*Hansard*, vol. 431, 13 December 1946, col. 1560);
in presenting the 1944 Act, Herbert Morrison had stated that 'The object to be
aimed at is not exact mathematical equality but a reasonable approximation to
equality. Substantial margins of toleration are necessary. If we run the doctrine
of electoral equality too far, we shall find ourselves divorced from reality'
Hansard, vol. 403, 10 October 1944, col. 1611). Rule 4 was removed, and a new
Rule 5A added (see Box 3.2). This re-ordering made electoral equality a secondary consideration – after both community integrity (as reflected in local government boundaries) and the overall size of the House of Commons.

The Commissions were well advanced in their work when this change was
introduced (they all reported in the autumn of 1947). The English, Scottish and
Welsh Commissions reported that it had made their work easier, even though they
had to reconsider some decisions already made (Boundary Commission for Scotland, 1947, #3, 3). According to the English Commission, in words almost exactly
those of the Welsh (Boundary Commission for England, 1947, #8, 4; Boundary
Commission for Wales, 1947, #8, 4):

> The amended rules of the Act of 1947 by removing Rule 4 and giving greater promi-
> nence to the principle of local unity have enabled us to avoid many of the difficul-
> ties which were an inevitable result of the rigid terms of the Act of 1944.

It should be stressed, however, that the Commissions did not say that they could
not produce a map of constituencies within the 25 per cent bands of the quota,
only that they could not do so while *both* respecting most local government
boundaries *and* not increasing the size of the House of Commons: the implication is that they could have done so, but with many constituencies crossing local
government boundaries and with many close to the limits plus or minus 25 per
cent. The changes that they made after the amendment were consistent with the

evidence that they were receiving from the interested parties: 'Such alterations had in the main been decided on as desirable in view of representations which had been received following publication of our earlier proposals' (Boundary Commission for Wales, 1947, #8, 4).

Two aspects of the Commissions' adopted procedures are of particular interest. The first relates to the 1944 Act's stipulation regarding public consultation. The Commissions took the requirement to advertise their provisional recommendations seriously, and reported that they did more than the minimum required in many cases (i.e. one press notice in a local newspaper per constituency), and the Scottish Commission also issued 'Press notices explaining the broad effect of the proposals' (Boundary Commission for Scotland, 1947, #5, 3). The response was not overwhelming. The English and Welsh Commissions both reported that in a substantial proportion of cases no representations at all were received; the Scottish Commission noted that the lack of representations was especially common where no change to the current constituencies was proposed. As a consequence, Local Inquiries were few: the Scots held three and the Welsh just one; the English held 21, but these referred to just 70 constituencies out of the total of 489. Substantial public involvement – in effect, local involvement by the political parties – was the exception rather than the rule, therefore, which may reflect a number of issues: more pressing concerns nationally and locally; the continuation of many existing constituencies, with which the parties were largely satisfied; the lack of detailed data on which to challenge the Commissions' recommendations and produce viable alternatives; and the newness of the system. Whatever the reasons, Butler (1963, 107) claims that the Commissions' reports were 'welcomed as providing a just and workmanlike solution of a pressing problem'.

The second issue concerned the spatial units to be employed when local government areas were to be divided into two or more constituencies, on which the 1944 Act is entirely silent – although the Williams' Bill of 1934 specifically referred to wards as the units for constituency-building in Boroughs. Urban authorities (County Boroughs, Metropolitan Boroughs, Burghs, Urban Districts and Municipal Districts) were divided for electoral purposes into wards and rural authorities (Rural Districts) into civil parishes, and these are the units employed by the local government authorities for reporting on the number of electors. The Commissions clearly decided to adopt these as their 'building blocks', for pragmatic reasons if for no other, although this is implicit rather than explicit in the report from the Boundary Commission for England (1947, #16, 5) that:

> In no case have we had to divide a civil parish. In the formation of Parliamentary Boroughs we have had occasion to intersect the boundaries of only 16 boroughs while in only two cases have we found it necessary to split a ward.

The Welsh Commission included a similar statement: its proposals intersected only one Borough boundary and divided only one ward (Boundary Commission for Wales, 1947, #12, 4). (The English Commission did note that this sometimes created a problem because of disparities between wards in their electorates – an issue tackled by the Local Government Commission established in the mid-1990s, which sets a 10 per cent tolerance band around average ward electorates. Thus, 'it would ease the future labours of the Commission if, when local authorities redistribute their wards, they would give some weight to the possibility of grouping them into Parliamentary constituencies'; Boundary Commission for England, 1947, #21, 6.) The Scottish Commission reported that it 'endeavoured to reduce to a minimum the cases where our proposed constituencies involve the splitting of municipal wards', and in Edinburgh it determined to use the new wards then being promulgated by the City Council rather than those existing at the time that they started their review (Boundary Commission for Scotland, 1947, #12-13, 5).

The 1944 Act gave Parliament the opportunity to debate and vote on the details of the Commissions' recommendations, as well giving the Secretary of State powers to modify those recommendations. This happened when the Commissions' reports were tabled in 1948 prior to enactment in the *Representation of the People Act, 1948*. In the initial exchanges, several members referred to the variations between electorates in their constituencies – which Ede claimed reflected the Commissions endeavouring 'to deal with the constituencies as communities rather than mere mathematical aggregations' (*Hansard,* vol. 447, 16 February 1948, col. 841). Hugh Dalton claimed that the gap was too wide, and involved a bias against blitzed cities (col. 939) and Churchill argued that 'one vote, one value' had not been achieved, despite movement towards that goal (col. 858).

A 'leaked report', however, indicated that the government had asked the Commissions 'how the eight seats with more than 80,000 electors should be divided in two and how the boundaries in nine of the largest English Boroughs should be redrawn in order to give each of them one more member' (Butler, 1963, 127), which was interpreted by Churchill as undermining the Commissions' independent status and, in effect, handing redistribution to the Home Secretary; it was 'a plot to give extra seats to the Labour party' (Butler, 1963, 129). (So virulent was the debate, and so aggrieved were the Conservative MPs, that they proposed an amendment to the Act's title, changing it from the 'Representation of the People Act' to the 'Representation of the Labour Party Act'!) The Home Secretary subsequently reported that the Boundary Commission for England had sent him a letter fifteen days before members signed their report, indicating misgivings about the situation in several large Boroughs and, as a consequence, the government was modifying the recommendations to add a further 17 seats, by recommending divisions of the seats for those Boroughs. Churchill's response was that the government didn't like what had been recommended, claimed that the treatment of the 17 'would merely serve to reduce slightly the gap between the lowest and the highest electorates' (*Hansard*, vol. 448, 24 March 1948, col. 3013) and concluded that (col. 3014):

> For party advantage, and party advantage alone, they are to make seats which will be in the neighbourhood of 40,000, smaller than in many cases is thought right in regard to sparsely populated agricultural and mountainous areas.

But the government prevailed. Proposals for the new constituencies were brought to the House in April 1948, and produced what Butler (1963, 131) refers to as 'a host of amendments, mostly from members indulging in special pleading for their own constituencies', although the Home Secretary himself introduced 17 as well as accepting 12 of 41 proposed by other MPs. Second seats were allocated to eight single-member Boroughs with electorates in excess of 80,000 (Battersea, Blackburn, East Ham, Gateshead, Hammersmith, Norwich, Paddington and Reading) and there were additional seats for nine others which already had more than one (Birmingham, Bradford, Bristol, Leeds, Leicester, Liverpool, Manchester, Nottingham and Sheffield). The Act was eventually passed by a large majority, however, though not without further invective from Churchill claiming that its redistribution provisions were a partisan move.

The 1949 Acts

Having established the Commissions with rules that were generally workable and procedures that seemed acceptable, the government then proceeded to produce a new Redistribution of Seats Bill, introduced to the House of Commons within a year of the Commissions' initial reports. This was part of a larger exercise of electoral reform, which focused on the associated comprehensive *Representation of the People Act 1949* (it has 197 pages); the broad outline established in the 1944 *Redistribution of Seats Act* was retained, though with important changes relating to plural voting (abolition), University representation (abolition) and representation of the City of London (largely abolished). Much of Parliament's debating time focused on these rather than the rules and procedures for redistribution. In addition, the terms Parliamentary Boroughs and Counties were abolished and replaced by the simple term 'Parliamentary constituencies'.

Parliamentary and public debate over the proposed *Representation of the People Act* was substantial and virulent because, according to Butler (1963, 111), it tackled six issues which had 'excited' the 1944 Speaker's Conference, on which the parties had taken opposing views, and on which there had been no clear recommendations. As a consequence, these had so far not been incorporated in legislative proposals, all of which 'tended to be desired by Labour and all would undoubtedly serve their narrow party advantage; all by the same token would hurt the Conservatives'. Of the six, only the last explicitly affected the redistribution process, though others had indirect implications through their impact on the size of the registered electorate in different local government areas and the freeing of some the University and City seats for 'reallocation':

- the assimilation of the local government and Parliamentary franchises
- abolition of the business vote
- abolition of University representation
- treatment of the City of London as an ordinary constituency
- limits on the use of cars on polling days, and

Box 3.3 *Rules for the Redistribution of Seats set out in the Second Schedule to the* House of Commons (Redistribution of Seats) Act, 1949

1 The number of constituencies in the several parts of the United Kingdom set out in the first column of the following table shall be as stated respectively in the second column of that table–

Part of the United Kingdom	*No. of Constituencies*
Great Britain	... Not substantially greater or less than 613
Scotland	... Not less than 71
Wales	... Not less than 35
Northern Ireland	... 12

2 Every constituency shall return a single member.
3 There shall continue to be a constituency which shall include the whole of the City of London and the name of which shall refer to the City of London.
4 (1) So far as is practicable having regard to the foregoing rules–
    (a) in England and Wales,—
        (i) no county or any part thereof shall be included in a constituency which includes the whole or part of any other county or part of a county borough or metropolitan borough;
        (ii) no county borough or any part thereof shall be included in a constituency which includes the whole or part of any other county borough or the whole or part of a metropolitan borough;
        (iii) no metropolitan borough or any part thereof shall be included in a constituency which includes the whole or part of any other metropolitan borough;
        (iv) no county district shall be included partly in one constituency and partly in another.
    (b) in Scotland, no burgh other than a county of a city shall be included partly in one constituency and partly in another;
    (c) In Northern Ireland, no county district shall be included partly in one constituency and partly in another.
    (2) In paragraph (1) of this rule the following expressions have the following meanings, that is to say:–
    'county' means an administrative county other than the county of London;

- the indefinite postponement of redistribution.

The Conservatives argued that the proposed changes went against the 'inter-party bargain' agreed after the 1944 Conference with regard to changes to the franchise (on which see the discussion in Butler, 1963, 111–22).

The only changes between the 1944 and 1949 *House of Commons (Redistribution of Seats) Acts* are in the Schedule relating to the Rules for Redistribution (called the Rules for Distribution in 1944); no changes were recommended to that part of the First Schedule dealing with the Commissions' procedure. The Second

'county borough' has the same meaning as in the Local Government Act, 1933;

'county district' has, in sub-paragraph (a) the same meaning as in the Local Government Act, 1933, and, in sub-paragraph (c), the same meaning as in the Local Government (Ireland) Act, 1898.

5 The electorate of any constituency shall be as near the electoral quota as is practicable having regard to the foregoing rules: and a Boundary Commission may depart from the strict application of the last foregoing rule if it appears to them that a departure is desirable to avoid an excessive disparity between the electorate of any constituency and the electoral quota, or between the electorate thereof and that of neighbouring constituencies in the part of the United Kingdom with which they are concerned.

6 A Boundary Commission may depart from the strict application of the last two foregoing rules if special geographical considerations, including in particular the size, shape and accessibility of a constituency, appear to them to render a departure desirable.

7 For the purposes of these rules–
(a) the expression 'electoral quota' means—
   (i) in the application of these rules to a constituency in Great Britain, a number obtained by dividing the electorate for Great Britain by the number of constituencies in Great Britain existing on the enumeration date;
   (ii) in the application of these rules to a constituency in Northern Ireland, a number obtained by dividing the electorate for Northern Ireland by the number of constituencies in Northern Ireland existing on the enumeration date.
(b) the expression 'electorate' means—
   (i) in relation to a constituency, the number of persons whose names appear on the register of parliamentary electors in force on the enumeration date under the Representation of the People Acts for the constituency; and
   (ii) in relation to Great Britain or Northern Ireland, the aggregate electorates as hereinbefore defined of all the constituencies therein;
(c) the expression 'enumeration date' means, in relation to any report of a Boundary Commission under this Act, the date on which the notice with respect to that report is published in accordance with section two of this Act.

Schedule is reproduced in Box 3.3. The separate status of the City is much reduced in the new Rule 3; Rules 4, 5 and 6, which govern the process of redistribution, remain unchanged (though reflecting the new order of priorities introduced by the 1947 Act); and Rule 1 increases the number of seats overall for Great Britain (because of the loss of University and City seats), giving the Commissions, especially the English Commission, greater flexibility.

The First Periodical Review and the 1958 Act

The Boundary Commissions were required to conduct periodical reviews of all constituencies within 3–7 years of the passing of the 1949 *Representation of the People Act*: the Scottish Commission announced the start of that review on 31 July 1953, the English and Welsh Commissions followed suit on 28 August 1953, and the Northern Ireland Commission commenced work in January 1954. All four reports were presented to Parliament in November 1954.

The Commissions proceeded very largely as they had done in 1946–47. Much of their work proved uncontentious, and they were able to finish it in little more than a year. The Northern Ireland and Wales Commissions apparently had the easiest tasks. The former reported that 'we came to the general conclusion that, at the present time, it is not necessary to make any changes in the existing boundaries of the constituencies' (Boundary Commission for Northern Ireland, 1954, #3, 2). This stimulated only one representation, from the Northern Ireland Labour Party, regarding the boundaries of Belfast's four constituencies; it proposed splitting three of the City's wards, in order to nest constituencies for Northern Ireland's Assembly at Stormont within those for the House of Commons, but this was rejected by the Commission, without a Local Inquiry. The Welsh Commission decided to recommend no change in 30 of its 36 constituencies, and found none of the representations made regarding the other six of sufficient substance to justify a Local Inquiry (Boundary Commission for Wales, 1954).

The Scottish Commission's provisional recommendations were for no change in 44 of the country's 71 constituencies; it received only two representations regarding these, and both were rejected (Boundary Commission for Scotland, 1954, #6–7, 3–4). Few of its recommended changes produced substantial representations either, and most of those received were rejected. The main exception was in Midlothian and the Borders area. Objections were received from both Labour and Liberal parties and these apparently led to separate meetings (e.g. 'In correspondence and at subsequent meetings in Edinburgh representatives of these associations made us fully aware of the precise nature of their objections to the proposals. The Labour Party deputation had no alternative suggestion to offer…'; Boundary Commission for Scotland, 1954, #9B, 5). The Labour party requested a Local Inquiry, but 'we did not see our way to accede to this request because we were convinced that our examination of this problem in all its aspects and our meetings with the representatives of the objectors had elicited all the facts necessary to enable us to make up our minds'.

The Boundary Commission for England had by far the largest of the tasks. It provisionally recommended no change to 324 of the 506 existing constituencies and very minor modifications to 30 of the others, in order to bring their boundaries in line with altered local government boundaries. It reported that 'In general, little objection was received where we had provisionally recommended that no alteration was required to be made, but a lively interest was shown in the effects of the changes we proposed. Many of the representations submitted to us gave evidence of a careful appreciation of the problems confronting us and contained suggestions which we found helpful in framing our final recommendations' (Boundary Commission for England, 1954, #7, 2). Only seven Local Inquiries were held.

Conducted relatively soon after the Initial Review, although population mobility and change had been insufficient over the intervening seven years to generate many substantial disparities, nevertheless this First Periodical Review generated some concerns as it proceeded. The English Commission was concerned about the need to recommend some change so soon after the changes of 1948, and commented accordingly (Boundary Commission for England, 1954, #20, 4):

> The provisions of the Act of 1949 require that our next periodical report must be submitted not less than three or more than seven years from the date of submission of this report. Considerable comment has been made in the Press and elsewhere to the effect that the general review of constituencies now concluded and the changes recommended as a result of that review have come too soon after the very considerable changes brought about by the Representation of the People Act, 1948. It was clear from representations submitted to us that the changes recommended, even where they included proposals for additional representation, were not wholly welcome because of the disturbance they would inevitably cause both to the electorate and to their representatives in Parliament. The provisions of the Act of 1949 left us no alternative but to proceed with the review and to make such recommendations as we considered necessary and desirable. Nevertheless we have been impressed by the arguments put forward against reviews at comparatively short intervals and we think that consideration should be given to lengthening the minimum and maximum periods between reviews. Provision exists in Section 2(3) of the Act for periodical reviews of a particular constituency or constituencies and the powers given to the Commissions under this Section should, we think, suffice to deal with any local abnormalities requiring adjustment between reviews.

None of the other Commissions made this point, nor did they raise another which the Boundary Commission for England (1954, #20, 4–5) clearly also wanted Parliament to consider:

> The terms of Rule 6 gave us discretion to depart from the strict application of Rules 4 and 5 if in our view departure was desirable to meet special geographical considerations. We have used this discretion as widely as circumstances appeared to us to justify it. In many areas no special geographical considerations exist which would justify the use of this discretion but the terms of Rule 5 left us no alternative to making provisional recommendations designed to bring electorates into closer conformity with the electoral quota. Among constituencies so treated were those contained wholly within borough boundaries. In representations received by us there has been unanimity among all political parties in voicing objections, on grounds substantially similar to those referred to in paragraph 19 [quoted earlier in this paragraph], to our proposals to give effect to Rule 5. In a number of cases we have felt able to modify our original proposals and to recommend that no alteration should be made although on a strict view of Rule 5 some adjustment of boundary would be justified. It would ease the future labours of the Commission and remove much

local irritation if Rule 5 were to be so amended as to allow us to make recommendations preserving the status quo in any area where such a course appeared to be desirable and not inconsistent with the broad intention of the Rules.

In other words, the parties had convinced the Commission that it would be to their (i.e. the parties') interests if reviews were less frequent and if preservation of the status quo, wherever practicable, should be one of the criteria applied in such reviews.

Members of Parliament were clearly concerned about the amount of change being recommended so soon, and part of this was linked – in a partisan manner – by the Home Secretary (Gwillym Lloyd George) to the decision to create additional seats in 1948: he argued that the 'present review is a completion of the review of 1947 and restores the balance which was upset in 1948' (*Hansard*, vol. 535, 15 December 1954, col. 1790). The frequency of change was a common theme: the member for Chelmsford (Hubert Ashton), noting that Essex had been allocated two additional seats, necessitating considerable changes, argued that 'I cannot believe that it is anybody's interest to have this constant chopping and changing' (col. 1801), and Kenneth Pickthorn, (who was a member of the 1944 Speaker's Conference) claimed that 'Since 1944, we have already legislated four times and we do not want redistributions very often' (col. 1807). Frequent change created three problems, according to Arthur Skeffington (col. 1825):

1 Voters were moved around 'merely to fit a mathematical equation'
2 MPs didn't get to know their constituency and constituents (another MP – Rt. Hon. A. Woodburn, col. 1849 – remarked that 'if the constituencies are to be involved in a general scrabble every few years, no member can get down to the continuity of work or representation') , and
3 The dislocations caused 'chaos and confusion' for the parties.

The Commissions were blamed for much of this – according to Skeffington because their very existence as permanent Commissions made them believe that they had to 'do things' (col. 1034) – and Michael Foot concluded that every three or four years MPs are 'going to have their positions undermined or destroyed by the arbitrary decisions of a Boundary Commission' (col. 1867). (He cited a case in the later debate on the particular orders for Plymouth, claiming that the Commission, in order to achieve a net shift of 5,000 voters between constituencies had moved 30,000 voters in five wards, when the movement of just one ward could have had the same effect: col. 2038.) Skeffington argued that the Commissions handled the consultation process very badly, claiming that many of those who had made representations had not been told whether there was to be a Local Inquiry, and if so when and where. Only seven Inquiries had been held in England and he claimed that this was because there was (col. 1034):

> so much criticism of the arbitrary way in which the Commission was proposing changes for Surrey [at the Local Inquiry there] that I think the Commission decided to hold as few inquiries as it could.

MPs wanted greater continuity in the areas that they represented, so that they could appreciate local problems and develop working relationships with local authorities and interest groups. As the member for Liverpool, Walton, Kenneth Thompson, expressed it, not only did a redistribution undermine party structures since they may move a party worker out of the constituency whose organisation she had contributed to 'and hived [her] off to what is to her a foreign land, where there are a lot of people who do not speak her language' (*Hansard*, vol. 535, 15 December 1954, col. 1839) but also broke links with 'ordinary people who live in the streets and villages of our constituencies':

> Time goes on, and they may not like us very much, they may tolerate us but they do get to know us as their Member or candidate. Something happens in their lives, big or little, ... and they think in the first place of their Member of Parliament. If he has done his job reasonably well over the passage of years, it is not difficult for them to recall his name or his face ... Then the Boundary Commission draws a line, and out of their lives completely goes this man or woman.

Related to that point, Skeffington pointed out (col. 1532) that one ward in Kent had been in four different constituencies within a span of only nine years (1945–54).

The former Home Secretary, Chuter Ede, congratulated the Scottish Commission on giving reasons for its recommendations (col. 1792) – by implication criticising the others for not – and reported that many local authorities had tried to lobby the current Home Secretary about their concerns, but had received no response: he suggested that a Local Inquiry should be obligatory in all cases where representations had been made (col. 1796). Anthony Greenwood pointed to the major disparities in electorates which were being recommended for adjacent London Boroughs (41,298 in Walthamstow West, for example, but 76,457 in Leyton and 72,984 in Edmonton), in contrast to the situation in Reading South where a constituency having 41,624 electors had been abolished (col. 1812). The under-representation of England was also remarked upon and several MPs returned to the earlier discussions about organic and mathematic principles, stressing the importance of the former in most cases. Kenneth Pickthorn, for example, claimed that the revised Act still 'gave the mathematical factor more importance than the House had wished' and argued that the Commissions had 'paid insufficient attention to the factor of local organic unity' (col. 1807); he concluded that 'I am quite certain that what the House wanted was that the mathematical factor should be inferior to the organic factor' (col. 1809), which Thompson rephrased as the Boundary Commission regarding its task as 'entirely a business of lines on ... maps, considering figures, not electors' (col. 1835).

Following the general debate about 'principles and practice', the Commissions' recommendations for each local government area were then laid before the House in a series of separate Orders. Of the 43 separate Orders concerning changes to English and Welsh constituencies, 31 were debated, some at considerable length, in two all-night sittings on 16 December 1954 and 26 January 1955. In fifteen cases, MPs in the areas affected pressed for a vote; in each, the Order was passed, but never by a large majority (the largest was 47 and the smallest 25). This was the last time that separate Orders were placed before the House;

after each of the subsequent Reviews there was a single vote on an Order implementing all of a Commission's recommendations.[2]

Before the detailed Order to implement the recommendations for the Manchester area were laid before Parliament, there was a Court case which sought an
injunction to prevent the Order for Manchester, Oldham and Ashton under Lyne
being presented, on the grounds that the Boundary Commission for England had
acted in a way that was inconsistent with the rules. The case was brought by the
Conservative Lord Mayor of Manchester and a City Councillor. The Commission's recommendations were not to their party's satisfaction, and they sought to
get them changed by using a general issue – in *Harper and another v .Secretary
of State for the Home Department.*

In their report, paragraph 8 (Boundary Commission for England, 1954, 2) outlined a major element of the procedure adopted:

> Rule 1 of our instructions provides that the number of constituencies in Great Britain
> shall not be substantially greater or less than 613 of which the number of con-
> stituencies in Scotland shall be not less than 71 and the number of constituencies in
> Wales shall be not less than 35. At an early stage in our proceedings we were advised
> that it was unlikely that the Boundary Commissions for Scotland and Wales would
> find it necessary to allocate more than the existing number of seats, viz. 71 in Scot-
> land and 36 in Wales. We thus proceeded on the basis that the number of con-
> stituencies available for distribution in England was to be not substantially greater
> or less than 506 and we allocated seats provisionally to administrative Counties with
> their associated County Boroughs on the basis of one seat for each complete unit of
> electors, the unit representing the average electorate in England, namely 57,122,
> determined by dividing the total English electorate viz. 28,904,108 by 506.

This led, in the next paragraph, to the statement that (#9):

> Our aim was to create 506 constituencies each of which would be at or near the
> electoral quota without cutting across local government boundaries.

Their final recommendations were for 511. The plaintiffs claimed that the Commission had 'misdirected' itself, because this was not the procedure set out in
Rule 7, which defines the electoral quota as the electorate divided by the current
number of constituencies (Box 3.3). If the calculation had been done on this basis,
then the aim would have been for 519 seats, not 506.

The injunction was initially granted on the grounds that there was *prima facie*
evidence of the Commission having acted outside the rules,[3] but that was overturned in the Court of Appeal, on the grounds that (332 *All England Law Reports*
1, Chapter 238, 1955).

> on the true construction of the Act of 1949, in so far as the discretion over the divi-
> sion of England into Parliamentary constituencies … was not the discretion of the
> Boundary Commission for England, on whom it was primarily conferred, the exer-
> cise of the discretion was a matter for Parliament, and it was not competent for the
> court to determine whether a particular line of approach, which commended itself
> to the commission, was the best.

The Commission was established to advise Parliament, and the final determination as to constituencies was Parliament's alone. The Master of the Rolls (Sir Raymond Evershed) found it 'impossible to believe that Parliament contemplated that on any of the occasions when these reports were presented it would be competent for the court to determine and pronounce on' an approach which a Commission might take (p. 338); he quoted approvingly from the judge in another case – *Hammersmith Borough Council v. Boundary Commission for England* (heard in December 1954, but whose full judgement was not publicly reported) – who said that 'the machinery set up under this Act does not leave any room which makes it appropriate for the court to intervene either at this or any other stage'.

Despite that ruling, however, the Court did pass judgement on the merits of the case, and found against the plaintiffs: 'the recommendations of the commission were not manifestly at variance with the Act of 1949 ... and the injunction should not have been granted' (p. 332). Sir Raymond reviewed all of the rules, and summarised them as conferring on the Commission 'a measure of latitude or of discretion' (p. 336). With reference to paragraph 8 of the Commission's report, he concluded that 'it seems impossible to suggest that the Boundary Commissions have done anything ... to which anybody could take the slightest exception'. The Commission had given precedence to Rule 1, which was within its discretion to do, and he disagreed with the judge in the lower court who granted the initial injunction and who claimed that 626 (which would have been the outcome if 519 constituencies had been recommended for England) was not 'substantially greater than 613'. If the Commission had misdirected itself, then its report could be considered 'no report at all', in which case the courts may have the power to intervene. But in his judgement – agreed by the other Lord Justices sitting with him – the plaintiffs had failed to make the case of misdirection, and so the injunction was removed.

Rawlings (1988, 33) points out that the Court of Appeal was wrong in its judgement, stating that the Commission 'clearly misinterpreted and misapplied the rules' (one consequence of which was to exacerbate the Celtic [i.e. Scottish and Welsh] preference, because England was under-represented relative to expectations under Rule 7). More importantly, however, he shows – as does Blackburn (1995) – that the potential for challenging a Commission's recommendations through the courts is relatively small – a point emphasised two decades later in the *Foot et al.* case (see p. 113 below). The Commissions have very considerable discretion in how they operate and recommend, and the decision-making powers lie with Parliament, whose decisions are only very rarely subject to scrutiny by the courts.

Butler (1963, 218–19) summarised the concerns raised by MPs and in the Court cases as follows (the first two refer more to the Court case than to the MPs' deliberations):

1 There was no administrative procedure for appeal from the Commissioners' revised recommendations.
2 The English Boundary Commissioners (unlike the others) failed to explain their decisions.

3 The redistribution took place too soon. There were few gross anomalies, but the rigorous pursuit of mathematical equality meant that, after only 5 years, 170 constituencies had their boundaries altered, often drastically.
4 There was no real possibility of Parliament or the Government altering the Commissioners' recommendations, so that the debates on them became farcical.
5 In several major respects, the rules laid down for the Boundary Commission were ambiguous, contradictory or inadequate:
   (a) the Commissioners were instructed to allocate seats on the basis of a quota for Great Britain, yet they were also to leave Scotland and Wales with at least 106 seats and they were not to increase substantially the total number of seats. In practice, therefore, they had either to sanction an increase of 13 seats (which they decided was too substantial) or they had to disobey the instruction to distribute English seats according to the quota for Great Britain.
   (b) The Commissioners were given no clear guidance on how far they should take imminent population changes into account (they did in practice do so to a small extent – in contrast to 1947).
   (c) The Commissioners had difficulty in interpreting what was involved in respecting local government boundaries 'as far as practicable'.
   (d) The Commissioners had no clear guidance on how strictly to adhere to the quota; an excessive devotion to numerical equality could produce seemingly gratuitous upheavals.
   (e) The Commissioners' mandate to depart from the quota if 'special geographical considerations' rendered it desirable did not make clear whether it was intended in general to give county seats a lower quota than borough seats.

Many of these points were accepted by all political parties and led to a new Bill being brought forward in 1958. Although some parts of it stimulated debate (over England's representation, for example, and the possibility of a 'rural weighting') it was passed easily.

The *House of Commons (Redistribution of Seats) Act 1958,* which was an amendment of the 1949 Act rather than a new piece of primary legislation, addressed many of Butler's points (Box 3.4):

• The time-lag between periodical reviews was extended.
• Separate electoral quotas for the four countries were introduced.
• The criteria to be met for a mandatory Local Inquiry were set out, as were procedures to be followed if the provisional recommendations were altered.
• The strict criteria regarding electoral equality in Rule 5, but not those relating to conformity with the local government template, were relaxed, to allow the Commissions to take account of both 'the inconveniences' caused by changes to constituency boundaries and the breaking of local ties.

(The concept of 'local ties' was undefined, however, and it was left to the Commissions to interpret what Parliament meant by the phrase.) The procedures were both tightened and made more transparent, therefore, and MPs' concerns about

Box 3.4 The House of Commons (Redistribution of Seats) Act 1958

1 (1) The deputy chairman of each Boundary Commission under the House of Commons (Redistribution of Seats) Act, 1949 ..., shall be a judge who–

(a) in the case of the Commission for England shall be a judge of the High Court appointed by the Lord Chancellor,

(b) in the case of the Commission for Scotland shall be a judge of the Court of Session appointed by the Lord President of the Court of Session ...,

(c) in the case of the Commission for Wales shall be a judge of the High Court appointed by the Lord Chancellor,

(d) in the case of the Commission for Northern Ireland shall be a judge of the High Court in Northern Ireland appointed by the Lord Chief Justice of Northern Ireland.

...

(2) The officers of each Commission shall include two assessors who shall be –

(a) in the case of the Commission for England, the Registrar General for England and Wales and the Director General of Ordnance Survey

(b) in the case of the Commission for Scotland, the Registrar General of Births, Deaths and Marriages in Scotland and the Director General of Ordnance Survey

(c) in the case of the Commission for Wales, the Registrar General for England and Wales and the Director General of Ordnance Survey

(d) in the case of the Commission for Northern Ireland, the Registrar General of Births, Deaths and Marriages for Northern Ireland and the Commissioner of Valuation for Northern Ireland,

and those persons shall cease to be members of the Commissions.

2 (1) After the coming into force of this Act a Boundary Commission's report under subsection (1) of section two of the principal Act shall be submitted not less than ten or more than fifteen years from the date of submission of the Commission's last report under that subsection; and subsection (2) of that section (which in general requires reports to be made not less than three or more than seven years from the date of the submission of the Commission's last report) shall cease to have effect.

(2) It shall not be the duty of a Boundary Commission, in discharging their functions under the said section two, to aim at giving full effect in all circumstances to the rules set out in the Second Schedule to the principal Act, but they shall take account, so far as they reasonably can, of the inconveniences attendant on alterations of constituencies other than alterations made for the purposes of rule 4 of those rules, and of any local ties which would be broken by such alterations; and references ...

3 The application of rule 5 of the rules set out in the Second Schedule to the principal Act (under which the electorate of a constituency is to be brought as near the electoral quota as is practicable having regard to the other rules in that Schedule) to a constituency in any of the several parts of the United Kingdom for which there is a Boundary Commission, the expression 'electoral quota' shall mean a

number obtained by dividing the electorate for that part of the United Kingdom by the number of constituencies in it existing on the enumeration date (and not, as at present in Great Britain, a number obtained by reference to Great Britain as a whole).

4 (1) Where a Boundary Commission revise any proposed recommendations after publishing a notice of them under paragraph 3 of Part III of the First Schedule to the principal Act, the Commission shall comply again with that paragraph in relation to the revised recommendations, as if no earlier notice had been published.

(2) Where, on the publication of the notice under the said paragraph 3 of a recommendation of a Boundary Commission for the alteration of any constituencies, the Commission receive any representation objecting to the proposed recommendation from an interested authority or from a body of electors numbering one hundred or more, the Commission shall not make the recommendation unless, since the publication of the said notice, a Local Inquiry has been held in respect of the constituencies under paragraph 4 of the said Part III:

Provided that, where a local inquiry was held in respect of the constituencies before the publication of the said notice, this subsection shall not apply if the Commission, after considering the matters discussed at the local inquiry, the nature of the representations received on the publication of the said notice and any other relevant circumstances, are of the opinion that a further local inquiry would not be justified.

(3) In the last foregoing subsection, 'interested authority' and 'elector' respectively mean, in relation to any recommendation, a local authority whose area is wholly or partly comprised in the constituencies affected by the recommendation, and a parliamentary elector for any of these constituencies; and for this purpose 'local authority' means the council of any county, or any borough (including a metropolitan borough) or of any urban or rural district.

(4) In the application of the last foregoing subsection to Scotland, for the reference to a borough there shall be substituted a reference to a burgh, and for a reference to an urban or ...

frequent change were handled in two ways: reviews were to be less frequent; and Clause 2(2) introduced what the Home Secretary (R. A. Butler) referred to as a 'presumption against making changes unless there is a very strong case for them' (*Hansard*, vol. 582, 11 February 1958, col. 230), while recognising the primacy of the original Rule 4 that 'there must be compliance' with local government boundaries. The enlarged need for Local Inquiries was welcomed, with Lucas-Tooth suggesting that they 'will do nothing but good, even if they are not, perhaps, really necessary to enable the Commission to make up its mind' and 'the Commission ought to set out quite clearly what considerations it has borne in mind and how it has come to its conclusions' (col. 246).

One issue not discussed much in Parliament was the decision to have separate electoral quotas for each of the three countries in Great Britain (Northern Ireland being separately treated in the 1949 Act): compare Clause 7 (a) (i) in Box 3.3 with Clause 3 in Box 3.4. This meant that in subsequent reviews the Scottish and Welsh Commissions would have to consider whether to increase representation there above the minima established in the 1949 Act, which did not happen previously, given that the Great Britain quota was unlikely to suggest that each was allocated more than its minimum (Rossiter *et al.*, 1997c). As outlined in Chapter 4, this has been one of the reasons why Scottish and Welsh representation has increased in size since 1958, paralleling what was occurring in England (the latter of which experienced more substantial electorate expansion).

The issue of the rules being 'ambiguous, contradictory or inadequate' was not fully addressed, however. Indeed, introduction of the new Clause 2(2) regarding the status quo, inconvenience and local ties made the rules if anything more ambiguous – because it was not incorporated within the rules themselves. (It was added as a *General and Supplementary* section to the rules when the Act was replaced in 1986.) Butler (1963, 219–20) concluded that 'There is no doubt that these amendments should smooth the process of redistribution' but also noted, however, that although the Commissions' neutrality is 'beyond question':

> There is always a chance that there will be some correlation between movements of population and social class – and, therefore, with party sympathy ... It is not, of course, within the Boundary Commissioners' powers to eliminate all biases in the distribution of seats. They can ensure the approximate equality of electoral districts, but there is no way in which they can counter the geographical chance which may lead to the strength of one party being more favourably distributed for the winning of seats than that of its rivals.

In the House, however, the call for even further clarification of the rules was countered by a statement from an Under-Secretary of State for Scotland (Niall Macpherson) that (*Hansard*, vol. 582, 11 February 1958, col. 293):

> we all agree ... that this is desirable and that they should be as clear as possible. In studying the rules, I cannot fail to observe that, whilst it is possible to make them clearer, it does not seem to be possible to draft them in such a way that they may not contradict each other in certain cases. Therefore, a discretion must be left to the Boundary Commissions, to deal with specific cases.

One of those specific cases, apparently, was whether urban constituencies should, on average, have more electors than their rural counterparts, as issue which Butler was prepared to 'leave to the good sense of the Boundary Commissions' (col. 231).

The Second Periodical Review

The Commissions were required to submit the reports of their Second Periodical Reviews between 1964 and 1969; they did so in 1969, having begun the task in February 1965. The English Commission had to take account of changes to the government of Greater London in 1962: the County's boundaries had been extended very substantially (leading to the elimination of all of Middlesex and the transfer of substantial parts of Essex, Kent and Surrey plus a small section of Hertfordshire to the new authority), and a new set of 32 Metropolitan Boroughs had been defined. Major changes to local government throughout the rest of the country were being considered by Royal Commissions, but no final reports had been submitted to the government, let alone acted upon, before the due date for the Commissions' reports.

The reports were produced in the context of the 1958 Act's requirements regarding Local Inquiries. This involved much more work than previously: the English Commission reported receiving 1,200 written representations, for example, holding 70 Local Inquiries (including seven 'second or re-opened inquiries'), and as a result publishing revised recommendations in 40 of the 70 cases (Boundary Commission for England, 1969, #16–22, 3). Its report also has very substantially more textual defence of its decisions than previous volumes, plus associated statistical material. The Welsh Commission was required to hold only one Inquiry, however – in Glamorgan (Boundary Commission for Wales, 1969, #10, 4); the Scottish Commission held five (Boundary Commission for Scotland, 1969, #9, 6); and there was one in Northern Ireland (Boundary Commission for Northern Ireland, 1969, #16, 6).

In the light of the earlier discussions about the need to justify their recommendations, and in the context of the new 'procedures' set out in the 1958 Act, each Commission provided a commentary on its work. The English Commission began by noting that (Boundary Commission for England, 1969, #27, 5):

> The Rules embrace two principles of representative government, equal representation (Rule 5) and territorial representation (Rule 4), which are often difficult to reconcile. The more equality in constituency electorates is sought, the greater the likelihood of disrupting local government units. Conversely, the more the preservation of local government units is pursued, the greater is disparity in electorates.

It noted that the political parties had been unanimous at the time of the Second Periodical Review that changes to meet these two conflicting criteria often produced much local inconvenience and welcomed the new section 2(2) of the 1958 Act. It then continued:

> The debates on the Redistribution Bill in 1958 showed, moreover, a broad measure of agreement that local ties were of greater importance than strict mathematical equality … 'The effect of the Bill', said the Home Secretary, 'is to bring in a presumption against making changes unless there is a very strong case for them'.

It had clearly tried to operate as Parliament and the parties wished (#28, 5):

> We therefore began the review with the intention of avoiding, where possible, proposals that would change constituency boundaries for the sake of adjustments in the size of electorates. We also considered it reasonable to assume that each existing constituency normally represents a community with its own distinct character, problems and traditions. Ties of many sorts may exist within this local community

and we believe it to be proper for these ties, whatever they may be, to be taken fully into account before a constituency is disturbed. We were, however, not inclined to accept the argument put forward at some inquiries that 'local ties' could refer only to the specific ties of political life that would be broken by redistribution.

The Welsh Commission, which shared a Secretariat with the English Commission, reported similarly (Boundary Commission for Wales, 1969, #16, 5):

We considered that in applying the Rules we should do our best to avoid departing from local government boundaries and from breaking local ties, and that we should recommend changes only where there was good reason for them. Above all, we should refrain from recommending changes simply to make small adjustments in the size of electorates.

The Scottish Commission merely noted that 'The terms of Rule 4(1)(b) of Schedule 2 to the 1949 Act and the principle that the Commission would always wish to follow, that local government and constituency boundaries should wherever possible conform' (Boundary Commission for Scotland, 1969, #17, 80). The Northern Ireland Commission made no reference either.

A general topic was raised by the English Commission, relating to the 'building blocks' issue. It reported that (Boundary Commission for England, 1969, 5):

30 For administrative purposes we decided to use ward boundaries for the division of boroughs into constituencies. In some boroughs we were urged to draw constituency boundaries through wards in order to eliminate polling difficulties such as those caused where wards were divided by busy thoroughfares, or where blocks of flats had been built across existing ward boundaries. Some borough councils assured us that in this type of case they would be prepared to re-draw their ward boundaries to follow any new constituency boundary which adopted a more natural line.

31 We took the view, however, that we ought not to depart from existing ward boundaries. Where polling difficulties existed, it was for local authorities to resolve them by ward reviews. If these were not resolved during the course of our general review, it would be open to us to bring constituency boundaries into line with altered ward boundaries by the procedure under section 2(3) of the 1949 Act which authorises us to submit from time to time recommendations for particular constituencies.

The *ad hoc* decision of the 1940s to use ward boundaries (following the lead set by Williams' 1934 Bill) was clearly becoming enshrined in the Commissions' practice, as illustrated by the Scottish Commission's comment that in Edinburgh and Glasgow, where there was considerable, lengthy conflict over ward boundaries (Boundary Commission for Scotland, 1969, #49, 16):

The co-ordination of constituency and ward boundary changes would appear to be practicable only in these cases where the ward boundary changes can be agreed ... in the case of both Edinburgh and Glasgow ... we were finally placed in the position of having to devise considerably altered constituencies on the basis of the existing out-of-date wards. It would be beyond our remit to suggest a solution to this problem and we raise it only to suggest that it is one which could, with advantage, be looked at on the next occasion when the legislative arrangements for fixing local government electoral areas are reviewed.

A final, substantial point regarding the outcome of the Second Periodical Review was the government's attempt to prevent its implementation. It was widely accepted that if the new constituencies were used at the next general election this would be to the disadvantage of the incumbent Labour party, whose Home Secretary (James Callaghan) sought to delay bringing the Commissions' recommendations to the House. On 19 June 1969 his opposition shadow, Quintin Hogg, tabled a motion (*Hansard*, vol. 785, 19 June 1969, col. 729) 'That this House calls upon the Secretaries of State for the Home Department and Scotland to implement in full, and without further delay, the recommendations of the Parliamentary Boundary Commissions'.

The government had hoped to justify not implementing the full redistribution (they feared they might lose up to 30 of their seats; Crossman, 1976, 318 and 1978, 506), by arguing that the forthcoming proposals for local government reform would make the new constituencies obsolete in the context of Rule 4. Callaghan's response was that 'Constituencies are not merely areas bounded by a line on a map; they are living communities with a unity, a history and a personality of their own' (*Hansard*, vol. 785, 19 June 1969, col. 742) and so once new constituencies are created their residents should be guaranteed a subsequent period free from change, a guarantee that he could not give because of the upcoming legislation to implement the recommendations of the Royal Commission on Local Government in England (the Redcliffe-Maud Commission: the government had not then received the parallel Wheatley Commission report on Scotland). There would need to be drastic changes to the constituency map very soon (*Hansard*, 19 June 1969, col.743)

> When I compare the Redcliffe-Maud Report with the Boundary Commission maps, I see that between 90 and 100 of the constituencies proposed by the Boundary Commission would be divided between two or more of the recommended main local government units. Outside Greater London [not being considered by the Maud Committee] there would be no more than two units out of the total number proposed where constituency boundaries and local government boundaries were coterminous.
>
> A similar situation occurs in Wales … Nineteen of the proposed constituencies there would contain a part of more than one county district.
>
> About one in four, certainly one in five, of the total number of constituencies in England outside Greater London, and one half of those in Wales, would be directly affected. But that is by no means the end. It would then become necessary to fit the remaining parts of these constituencies into new constituencies. So a second wave would be affected, and beyond that a third wave. It is quite clear that nothing short of a further general review of constituencies involving yet another major upheaval – not a minor upheaval – of the political map would follow within a few years, and nothing less than that would do.

Callaghan indicated that legislation would be introduced the next day to give effect to the Commission's recommendations for Greater London, and to request the

Boundary Commission for England to make recommendations for dealing with 'those abnormally large constituencies outside London' (col. 747). In addition 'the Boundary Commission ... will be asked to make a further general review as soon as it is clear that the prospect for local government reorganisation will not make it premature' (col. 748); Hogg's motion was then put and lost, and the House received Callaghan's promised Bill on 20 June 1969. (As an aside, it is interesting to note that some Ministers were not convinced that Labour would lose substantially from the new constituencies – George Brown (1972, 256) said that 'There was no way of knowing whether the calculations were right or wrong. Somehow they became an accepted doctrine', and Harold Wilson (1974, 854) said that he agreed with his party's national organiser that only 6-8 seats were at risk; furthermore, Steed (1969) questioned Callaghan's claim regarding overlapping boundaries.)

The government's compromise – the *House of Commons (Redistribution of Seats) (No. 2) Bill* – would:

- mean that no action would be taken on the reports recently submitted by the Commissions;
- require the Commissions to make no further reports until their next periodi-cal review was due, unless the Secretary of State at the Home Office decided to accelerate that review, by placing an Order in Council before Parliament;
- implement the Boundary Commission for England's recommendations for Greater London, which was not affected by the local government reviews; and
- require the Boundary Commission for England to suggest new constituencies for (a) the four pairs of adjacent constituencies each having in excess of 90,000 electors (Billericay and South East Essex; Portsmouth, Langstone and Gosport & Fareham; Hitchin and South Bedfordshire; and Horsham and Arundel & Shoreham) and (b) the one constituency (Cheadle) with an electorate exceed-ing 100,000.

Richard Crossman (1978, 506), claimed that this had long been the government's intention but also notes dissension in Cabinet, however, because the Scottish Sec-retary (Ross) claimed introduction of the new constituencies would 'save the Labour Party in Scotland, whereas we reckon that in England it will lose us fif-teen to seventeen seats'.

The issue was developed by the media into a minor constitutional crisis, and Crossman (1978, 558) accepted that the government's case for delay and, in effect, for asking the Boundary Commissions to do their work all over again, 'hasn't been very well put'. (He described the Tory case as 'we are simply disregarding the Boundary Commission and just bloody well cheating to try to cling to power', and referred to it elsewhere as a 'murky issue, which has gradually become more and more unsuccessful' and which most Cabinet members didn't want to 'be thought to be immersed in'; Crossman, 1978, 591.) There was a fear that Callaghan's Bill would be defeated in the House of Lords, and so the Cabinet was discussing an alternative tactic 'for the Home Secretary to lay the Orders [i.e. implementing the Commissions' recommendations], as he was statutorily required to do, but to ensure that the Whips instructed the Government's own backbenchers to vote against them' (Crossman, 1978, 559). This was the eventual outcome. The House of Lords sent the Bill back to the Commons on 23 July, and when it was returned to the Lords on 16 October unchanged it was lost by 78 votes to 229. In November, therefore, the Home Secretary laid the Commissions' reports before the House of Commons and moved that they 'be not approved' (*Hansard*, vol. 790, 12 November 1969, col. 428). In defending that he claimed (col. 430) that:

> [the] government were ready and anxious to see that the Greater London seats were redistributed in accordance with the Boundary Commission proposals. The other place has used its power to prevent this happening.

The opposition, he argued, by pressing for full implementation of the Commissions' recommendations (col. 442) want:

> to introduce changes now which will affect 346 constituencies, most of them in a major way, and are asking that Parliament should do this knowing full well that the task will have to be embarked on again, from the beginning, in three years' time.

Against opposition charges of gerrymandering (by Edward Heath; col. 462) his proposal was carried by 303 votes to 250. (Crossman – 1978, 683 – described it as a 'great achievement and it has come out right because of the skilled work between Callaghan and Wilson'.) Thus the 1970 general election, which Labour lost, was fought in the old constituencies. The new Conservative government reintroduced the Commissions' reports in October 1970, with the same motion as that proposed by Callaghan in 1969 except that the word 'not' was omitted. The Home Secretary (Reginald Maudling) indicated the necessity for changing the constituencies then because (*Hansard,* vol. 805, 28 October 1970, col. 245):

> we do not intend to hold back on local government reform. We intend in due course to put comprehensive proposals before the House. But they will take a long time to work out. They will take a long time to pass this House … It is not right to await that process.

If they did await the outcome of the local government reforms, it was very likely that the next general election would be fought in the constituencies defined in 1954, with many glaring disparities in electorates. Despite lengthy debates over procedural matters and details regarding individual constituencies, the Orders passed easily, with only a hard core of some 55–60 Labour MPs voting against. The promised major local government reforms, implemented in 1974, were very different from those recommended by Maud and provided the context for the Commissions' Third Periodic Reviews, which began in 1976.

The Third Periodic Review and its aftermath

No direct change in the law relating to the Commissions was proposed between the Second and the Third Periodic Reviews, except in Northern Ireland, which was allocated additional seats consequent upon the loss of its separate Assembly, and during a period when the minority Labour government was dependent on the support of some Northern Ireland MPs for its survival.[4] The wording of the legislation – the *House of Commons (Redistribution of Seats) Act 1979* – was somewhat odd, however. The entitlement to twelve seats in Rule 1 of the existing Act was changed to 'Not greater than 18 or less than 16', and the next clause stated that:

> in discharging their functions under section 2 of the principal Act, the Boundary Commission for Northern Ireland shall read Rule 1 as if it required the number of constituencies in Northern Ireland to be 17, unless it appears to the Commission that Northern Ireland should for the time being be divided into 16 or (as the case may be) into 18 constituencies.

A subsequent clause defined the 'electoral quota' at the time of the next periodic review as Northern Ireland's electorate divided by 17. This posed no problems for the Northern Ireland Commission during the Third Periodic Review – 17 constituencies were defined – but it did at the Fourth (see below).

The change in Northern Ireland's representation was the outcome of a Speaker's Conference, as established for such constitutional initiatives earlier in the century. On 19 July 1977 the Prime Minister requested that the Speaker chair a Conference with the following terms of reference 'to consider, and make recommendations on, the number of Parliamentary constituencies that there should be in Northern Ireland'. This resolved, by 18 votes to 4, that there should be an increase in representation; it then voted, by 22 votes to 1, that Northern Ireland should have 17 seats or more, and by the same majority agreed to the following final recommendation (Speaker, 1978, 1):

> That the number of Parliamentary constituencies in Northern Ireland should be 17 but that the Boundary Commission should be given power to vary that number, subject to a minimum of 16 and a maximum of 18.

The Conference published both its Minutes of Evidence and the written submissions received. Among the latter, the Unionist parties argued for an increase in representation, claiming a number of seats equivalent to that currently allocated to Scotland rather than to England or Wales (i.e. at least 20, rather than 16 or 18 respectively). The Vanguard Unionist Party, for example, argued that this was justified on three grounds: (1) historical discrimination against the province, (2) geographical location (i.e. isolation from London), and (3) lack of representation in a major Westminster party (Speaker, 1978, 7). The Ulster Unionist Council and the Alliance Party also argued for 20, whereas the (British) Conservative and Unionist party agreed with the Kilbrandon Commission (Royal Commission on the Constitution, 1973, #1338, 402) that it should be increased 'from twelve to seventeen or thereabouts'. The Labour party concurred, with the Lord President of the Council (Michael Foot), nevertheless stating in oral evidence that although the government offered no view on what the Conference should determine, (Speaker's Conference, 1977, 22, #115):

> Assuming the Conference accept the case for an increase, the major question before the Conference we believe will be how many more seats. On the basis of electoral quotas 16 seats would give Northern Ireland parity with the rest of the United Kingdom. I am not saying that that should be the figure, although clearly it could be the figure, but the Government is not making a recommendation to the Conference about the specific number of seats, I am merely indicating that; I am sure that the figure is already well in your minds.

When it was pointed out to him that 18 would give parity with Wales he responded by suggesting the flexibility that was finally recommended (Speakers's Conference, 1977, 24, #122):

> I think there would be an argument for this Conference suggesting a certain degree of degree of tolerance to give flexibility to the Boundary Commission so that they could follow their terms of reference more efficiently. May I illustrate what I mean? If, for example, they were given an upper and a lower limit – I will not name the figures – would you agree that would enable them to give better weight to geographical considerations which they are obliged to regard?

Against the Unionist parties' views, and also the general tenor of political opinion in Great Britain, the 'nationalist' Social Democratic and Labour Party argued that the Conference should recommend no increase in Northern Ireland's representation (Speaker's Conference, 1977, 17). It claimed that to consider this issue outside that of an overall settlement of the Northern Ireland issue was wrong, and that an increase in representation 'would undeniably ... seriously, if not totally, undermine the possibility of an acceptable solution'. Part at least of the reason for this view was expressed in Gerry Fitt's questioning of Michael Foot (Gerry Fitt was the only SDLP MP at the time). He pointed out that most of Northern Ireland's population lived within 30 miles of Belfast where one 'political viewpoint' (i.e. Unionism) predominated; additional seats would undoubtedly be placed there, with a change in the balance of Unionist and Nationalist representation,[5] that could only be countered by the introduction of proportional representation (Speaker's Conference, 1977, 28,# 145):

> It is the policy of the present Government, the Opposition and all parties in the House of Commons, to try and bring about consensus politics in Northern Ireland, to create structures which will bring the two communities together without giving favour to one as opposed to the other. If the extra seats to be created were to be taken by members of one particular party almost in their entirety, that would seem to be coming down very heavily in favour of one community, would it not?

Michael Foot responded that 'if that were to occur I think there would be many people who would draw those conclusions'

Mr. Fitt was in a minority, however, and the recommendation for an increase was taken to the House of Commons by the Northern Ireland Secretary (Roy

Mason), who commended it on three grounds: (1) equity (later expanded to 'equity, fairness, justice and equality'; *Hansard*, vol. 959, 28 November 1978, col. 243), (2), problems of access for Northern Ireland MPs because of the size of their constituencies, and (3) the unfair burden on the current number of MPs. The SDLP continued its opposition, while Unionists argued for more seats – Ian Paisley (leader of the Democratic Unionist Party) claimed that the tolerance should be 21–24, not 16–18.

Although the altered representation for Northern Ireland was the only direct change to the *House of Commons (Redistribution of Seats) Act*, there was also a set of indirect changes that were introduced as part of the very significant restructuring of local government that was completed in the early 1970s. Throughout Great Britain, the division between a single-tier, unitary structure for the main cities and towns (the County Boroughs), and a two-tier structure for the remainder of the country (Counties subdivided into Rural Districts, Urban Districts, Municipal Boroughs and Burghs), was replaced by a two-tier structure throughout. (Greater London had already had its government reformed in the mid 1960s, with an overarching County Council and 32 London Boroughs.) Furthermore, in England six Metropolitan Counties were established for the main conurbations (Greater Manchester, Merseyside, South Yorkshire, Tyne and Wear, West Midlands, West Yorkshire), with each divided into Metropolitan Districts. This altered the detailed template within which constituency definition was set, as illustrated by the new wordings of Rule 4 in Box 3.5.

Those changes went further than necessary in order to conform to the new local government template, however, as illustrated by clauses which were repealed by the various Local Government Acts:
1 In England and Wales, repeal of rule 4(1)(a)(iv) removed the requirement not to subdivide County Districts ('so far as is practicable').
2 In Scotland, the Commission is simply required to 'have regard' to local government boundaries (presumably all, both Regional and District).
3 In Northern Ireland, District Council boundaries receive no mention at all, and only ward boundaries are not to be crossed. (The Counties lost all of their roles, and so Districts, most of which were relatively small, became the sole local government units.[6])

The main reason for these changes was that the government, having created the new template, did not want the consequent disruption to constituency boundaries to be too great, bearing in mind the House of Commons debates in 1954 and 1958. In effect, therefore, these changes meant a very substantial relaxation of the constraints on the Commission's activities posed by the local government template and, by implication, the importance of respecting communities as reflected by the local government map, long held as a cardinal feature of Parliamentary representation in the United Kingdom.

In England, for example, at the time of its next review the Commission noted that after the 1972 Act over 1,200 local authorities outside Greater London were replaced by just 378 (Boundary Commission for England, 1983, #8, 2); under the

---

Box 3.5 *Rule 4 of the* House of Commons (Redistribution of Seats) Act
after the amendments introduced by local government reforms of the 1970s

(1) So far as is practicable having regard to the foregoing rules–
  (c) in England and Wales–
    (i)   no county or any part thereof shall be included in a constituency which includes the whole or part of any other county or the whole or part of a London borough;
    (ii) (Repealed by Local Government Act 1972)
    (iii) no London borough or any part thereof shall be included in a constituency which includes the whole or part of any other London borough;
    (iv) (Repealed by Local Government Act 1972)
  (d) in Scotland, regard shall be had to the boundaries of local government areas;
  (e) in Northern Ireland, no ward shall be included partly in one constituency and partly in another.
(2) In paragraph (1) of this rule the following expressions have the following meanings, that is to say–
  'county' means an administrative county.
  'area' and 'local authority' have the same meaning as in the Local Government (Scotland) Act 1973.

Source: reproduced from Boundary Commission for England (1983, 149)

---

new structure, 49 existing constituencies crossed County boundaries and 'only 61 of the 296 non-Metropolitan Districts … each formed a single constituency'. The changed local government template meant that major changes in the constituency boundaries must be undertaken, given the precedence of Rule 4. The greater freedom that repeal of rule 4(1)(a)(iv) appeared to imply was perhaps more apparent than real, however. The Commission recorded (Boundary Commission for England, 1983, #15, 8) that although 'the Local Government Act 1972 repealed the provision relating to county boroughs (which were being abolished) and also the provision that no county district should be divided between constituencies' and 'the Act of 1972 did not substitute any requirement that the districts constituted by the Act were to be subject to any special consideration' nevertheless:

when the amendment to Rule 4 was debated in Standing Committee on 20 March, 1972, the (then) Minister of State (Home Office), said:
  'It is almost certain that a proportion of constituencies will have to straddle district boundaries because in many cases districts will be too large to make one constituency and too small to make two. Therefore we are proposing that the rule should be amended to give the Boundary Commission rather more discretion than they have at the moment, but at the same time advice will be given to them that

they should take district boundaries into account, though that guidance will be slightly more informal that that given in the rules at present. ... The alternative to what we are here proposing was to put down a much more complex Amendment stating the kind of proportion which the Boundary Commission should regard as acceptable in drawing up constituency boundaries where these were bound to overlap district boundaries'.

This was followed by that 'informal advice':

A letter from the Home Office which drew the Commission's attention to this part of the debate explained that, in making this statement, the Minister of State had it in mind that the Commission would in any case be bound to take account of district boundaries, and that it would be appropriate to bring the relevant extracts from the Official Report formally to the Commission's attention before we started on our next general review.

The Commission acted in the context of this advice, noting (Boundary Commission for England, 1983, #16, 8):

There were important advantages in having coterminous constituency and district boundaries, but this could not often be achieved. The electorates of districts ranged between 20,000 and 766,000. There were often large differences between electorates of districts in the same county and it was sometimes necessary to divide a district of near-average constituency electorate to accommodate adjoining districts of very large or very small electorates. Multi-division of a district was obviously undesirable, especially if it had a small electorate. Equality of representation in numerical terms between districts was often difficult, if not impossible, to reconcile with local government boundaries. ... We were very conscious, however, of the emerging sense of identity of the new districts and of the resentment that disruption of that identity could create. Although we were convinced that it was not desirable to make minor changes to otherwise satisfactory constituencies merely for the sake of some fine-tuning to produce electorates nearer the electoral quota, we were equally convinced that we should not leave unaltered constituencies of high electorates solely because each was contained in one district.

This clearly implies that the equal electorates requirement of Rule 5 became somewhat more prominent in the Commission's mind, though not enough so for some later objectors (see below, p. 113). The Local Government Acts of the early 1970s thus marked a key development in the evolving redistribution mechanism in the United Kingdom, though through consequential amendments to other legislation rather than by direct debate of the criteria that should govern redistributions.

The situation in Wales was somewhat different, as expressed by its Commission (Boundary Commission for Wales, 1983, #9, 3):

The reorganisation of local government had a major effect on one of the criteria we have to apply. A number of the former Counties are now districts, while Rule 4(1) requires that we should recommend, so far as is practicable, constituencies which are contained within county boundaries. In effect, therefore, many of the former counties in Wales are no longer entitled to be considered separately for the allocation of constituencies. The removal of this entitlement has mean that our prime con-

sideration for the areas of those former counties must now be their equal representation with the electorates of other areas

Nevertheless it, too, received a letter from the Home Office advising it to 'take
district boundaries into account whenever possible ... and we have always borne
it in mind when formulating our recommendations, especially in view of the
change in relevance of Rule 4 to areas which were formerly counties and are now
districts' (Boundary Commission for Wales, 1983, #10, 3).

The Scottish Commission was given even greater flexibility than the Welsh
and the English by the wording of the new Rule 4(1)(b), which made no specific
reference to the boundaries of the superior local government areas, the Regions
(Counties were abolished by the *Local Government (Scotland) Act 1973*). The
draft Bill originally stated that 'no region or part thereof shall be included in a
constituency which includes the whole or part of any other region'. The Scottish
Grand Committee (on 20 March 1973) expressed great concern about this, however, because the proposed Regional structure cut across many existing, long-
established constituencies (including that held by the then Secretary of State –
Moray and Nairn) and Labour introduced an amendment to reduce the requirement: this was withdrawn when the government agreed to table its own, with the
current wording.[7] Nevertheless, the Commission reported that (Boundary Commission for Scotland, 1983, #24, 10):

> we resolved to avoid making recommendations for constituencies which would
> cross regional boundaries except in most exceptional circumstances where special
> geographical considerations made this desirable.

Although not required to, they would use the major components of the local government template if at all possible; no commitment was made regarding District
boundaries.

Both the English and the Welsh Commission indicated continued adherence
to their previous operating procedure that District Council wards should not be
divided. The English Commission stated that (Boundary Commission for England, 1983, #18, 8):

> Subject to the constraints imposed by the desirability of respecting district bound-
> aries we were, therefore, no longer limited to the use of such large areas as districts
> as building blocks for the constituencies we proposed.

It then made the use of wards as the 'subsidiary' building-blocks more explicit than
ever before, based on a case which linked local ties to party political interests:

> In general the local political party organisations were based on the district wards
> and these wards frequently represented a community with interests in common. Any
> division of wards between constituencies was likely to break local ties, disrupt polit-
> ical party organisation and be confusing to electors. The boundaries of wards were
> legally defined and would cause no problems when defining constituency bound-
> aries. Nor would there be any difficulty in preparing electoral registers for Parlia-
> mentary elections. We decided therefore, like our predecessors in 1965, that we

should adopt the practice of not dividing district or London borough wards between constituencies.

In that context, the Commission decided to use the latest revisions of ward boundaries, and so its work depended on the pace at which the Local Government Boundary Commission acted. The latter only completed its work in 1981 (having been delayed for eight months by litigation over the London Borough of Enfield), five years after the Boundary Commission for England started its Third Periodic Review.

The Welsh Commission also clarified its use of wards as building-blocks, in the context of the necessity of dividing many District Council areas between constituencies (Boundary Commission for Wales, 1983, #17, 5):

> Obviously it is less confusing to electors and all those concerned with elections if these divisions are related to other legally-defined areas which are well-known. Most local party political organisations use district wards as the basis for their activities and these wards usually provide a good indication of areas of common interest. We considered that any division of district wards would disrupt local affinities and, therefore, that when it was necessary to divide a district between constituencies, the boundary of the constituencies should follow the ward boundaries rather than divide them. Thus the district wards became the building blocks for the constituencies we were to recommend.

Like the English Commission, therefore, the Welsh Commission decided to use the District Council wards as building-blocks, rather than the somewhat larger County Council electoral divisions. The Scottish Commission operated differently, however, choosing the latter rather than the former (Boundary Commission for Scotland, 1983, #24, 10):

> Our aim was, wherever possible, to propose constituencies which would lie wholly within one district or comprise whole districts, but it was clear that the electorates of many districts were not of a suitable size to facilitate the achievement of this aim. It appeared to us that any division of the basic local government electoral area (say into polling districts) between constituencies would be likely to break local ties, disrupt political party organisation and be confusing to the electorate. We accordingly decided to adhere to the regional electoral division basis, or exceptionally the district ward basis, for forming constituencies where districts had to be divided.

This decision to use the larger divisions appears somewhat illogical, and also constraining on the Commission, although it could, if it wished, split a division, because the District wards nest within them:[8] this is not the case in England and Wales, where District wards do not always nest within County wards.

Finally, in Northern Ireland the Commission was faced with a major task consequent upon the increase in the number of constituencies from 12 to 17, with the possibility of either 16 or 18 providing a 'degree of flexibility to overcome practical difficulties' (Speaker, 1978): as the Commission noted (Boundary Commission for Northern Ireland, 1982, #1.4, 2), this gave it for the first time 'power to make recommendations not only as to the boundaries of Parliamentary constituencies ... but also as to the total number'. The Commission recommended 17 seats; representations received from Unionist interests argued for more, on three grounds (Boundary Commission for Northern Ireland, 1982, #3.2, 5):

1 The remoteness of Northern Ireland from Westminster, and hence its relative inaccessibility,
2 The 'density, distribution and increasing size' of Northern Ireland's electorate, and
3 A requirement for parity with other parts of the UK.

(The SDLP continued to argue for retaining only 12 constituencies.) The Commission argued that Parliament had endorsed the allocation of 17 seats as 'the fair and proper' number of seats for Northern Ireland, but that flexibility had been allowed the Commission to overcome 'practical difficulties': as it had experienced no such difficulties it perceived no need to depart from the requirement to allocate 17 seats: if Parliament wished Northern Ireland to have more seats because of either remoteness or parity with other parts of the UK that was for Parliament to decide, not the Commission.

The Northern Ireland Commission was also released by the amendments to the *House of Commons (Redistribution of Seats) Act* from the requirement to use District Council boundaries as its template: it was only constrained not to cross District Council ward boundaries, as far as is practicable. Nevertheless, the Commission itself imposed the District Council map as a template within which it should work (Boundary Commission for Northern Ireland, 1982, #1.8, 3): 'We also attached considerable importance to ensuring maximum compatibility between local government and Parliamentary representation'.

Between the Second and Third Periodic Reviews, Northern Ireland's local government system had been substantially restructured:

1 The six Counties had lost all administrative status.
2 A new system of 26 all-purpose District Councils ('unitary authorities' in current parlance) had been introduced in 1971.
3 The former differentiation between Rural and Urban District Councils was removed, but the former Boroughs retained their charters.
4 Each of these Districts is comprised of a number of district electoral wards.
5 Because membership of those Councils is determined by the STV electoral system using multi-member constituencies and preferential voting, those district wards are grouped into district electoral areas (DEAs).

The DEAs are thus the basic electoral units, given the electoral system, and the wards are not used in the electoral process; nevertheless, the Act refers to the wards and not the DEAs, which can be subdivided. In effect, the map of DEAs proved too severe a constraint to the Commission, which reported that (Boundary Commission for Northern Ireland, 1982, #1.8, 5):

It was our aim that as far as possible we should avoid splitting district council areas between two or more constituencies but given that there are 26 councils and 17 Parliamentary constituencies it was inevitable that some of the former be divided between two or more Parliamentary constituencies. Where we found it necessary to divide a district council area we wished to avoid hiving off small areas into other constituencies and consequently our original intention was to split off 3 or more wards which might ultimately form a district electoral area.

Their final recommendations, outside the City of Belfast (which was divided between four constituencies, one of which incorporated wards from an adjacent District), involved crossing only six District Council boundaries and 'in only one case did we reluctantly decide to recommend that a single ward from one district council area should be part of a Parliamentary constituency thus leaving the remainder of the wards from the area in an adjoining constituency or constituencies' (Boundary Commission for Northern Ireland, 1982, #4.2, 13): no ward was to be split.

The Foot et al. *case*

The local government changes ensured that the Third Periodic Reports recommended much wider-ranging alterations to the UK's map of constituencies than had been the case with either of their predecessors. Each of the Commissions provided a much fuller justification of its recommendations than previously, plus a summary of their main characteristics. All four included data which showed how well they had been able to meet the criterion of Rule 5. The English Commission, for example, included a table showing that 75 per cent of the new constituencies had 1976 electorates (the data used because that was when the review started) within 10 per cent of the electoral quota, and nearly 97 per cent were within 20 per cent; 'If accepted this will represent a very much closer approach to electoral equality than exists at present' (Boundary Commission for England, 1983, #4, 147). This clearly shows that its earlier inability to meet the 25 per cent criterion (see above, p. 84) was because of the constraint posed by the local government template, not the inability to produce electoral equality per se. The Welsh Commission reported that 33 of its 38 recommended constituencies were within 15 per cent of the quota, with two of the exceptions being the consequence of special geographical considerations (Boundary Commission for Wales, 1983, #208, 53); it also claimed that this was a substantial improvement on the current situation. The Scottish Commission similarly showed that 57 per cent of its recommended constituencies were within 10 per cent of the quota and 90 per cent were within a 20 per cent band (Boundary Commission for Scotland, 1983, #277, 98).

Despite these outcomes, the recommendations *for England alone* were subject to legal challenge on the grounds that the disparities were greater than necessary, so that the Boundary Commission for England had, in legal terminology, misdirected itself. The case was brought in August 1982, after the Commission had completed its work but before its final report had been delivered to the Secretary of State; it was finally resolved in February 1983 when the House of Lords refused permission to appeal to it after the plaintiffs lost in the Court of Appeal. The decision is of importance because of the interpretation that was placed on aspects of the Act by the judges on the Queen's Bench and in the Court of Appeal.

The case was brought by four senior members of the Labour party – Michael Foot, the Leader; Michael Cocks, the Chief Whip; James Mortimer, the General Secretary; and David Hughes, the National Agent – though it was stressed throughout that they were acting as individuals not for the Party, which was making no contribution to the costs (which it is believed were met by Robert Maxwell, a publisher and former Labour MP). The work for it was done by Edmund Marshall, then MP for Goole, and Gerry Bermingham, a Sheffield City Councillor and Parliamentary candidate for St Helens South. There was little doubt that the case was brought for partisan electoral purposes, either to delay the next general election or to ensure that it was held using the existing constituencies. It was widely believed that, as with the previous redistribution, the Labour party would be disadvantaged by introduction of the new constituencies – Waller (1983) suggested that the Conservative advantage when the 1983 election was held on the new constituencies was 30 seats – and so a strategy which forced the Boundary Commission to reconsider its recommendations (presumably involving the long process of public consultation) could, if successful, have substantially enhanced Labour's prospects at the next election (due to be held by May 1984).

Their claim, in brief, was that the Commission's recommendations involved substantial disparities, both nationally and between neighbouring constituencies, that were inconsistent with the Act, and that a set of constituencies with much reduced inequality could be produced, using available computer methods (on which see Johnston *et al.*, 1984; Johnston and Rossiter, 1983). Thus, for example, they pointed to electorates varying from 57,082 to 75,369 among Hampshire's 15 constituencies and from 51,602 to 76,180 among Staffordshire's 11; to the difference between 46,493 and 84,401 within Greater London; and to the disparity of 28,280 between the electorates of two neighbouring constituencies there – Barnet, Hendon South and Haringey, Hornsey & Wood Green.

Many of the issues considered by the Queen's Bench and the Court of Appeal – standing, timing and jurisdiction – are of little relevance here (see Johnston, 1983; Rawlings, 1988; Rallings and Thrasher, 1994; Blackburn, 1995), but two aspects of the judgements are of substantial importance. The first relates to the Commissions' flexibility, and on this the courts were clear in deeming that the *House of Commons (Redistribution of Seats) Act* provides a framework within which the Commissions have a great many degrees of freedom. Rawlings (1988, 61), for example, cites Justice Oliver's observation that the trend of legislation since 1944 has been to give the Commissions increasingly wide discretion, such that 'the scope of discretionary powers which have been allocated renders it unlikely in the extreme that a court will feel able to hold either that the rules ("guidelines") have been misconstrued such as to justify judicial intervention, or that the discretionary powers have been used unreasonably'. In the Court of Appeal, Sir John Donaldson stated that (1983 2 *W.L.R.*, 484):

It is important to realise that Parliament did not tell the Boundary Commission to do an exercise in accountancy – to count heads, divide by a number and then draw a series of lines around each resulting group. It told it to engage in a more far-reaching and sophisticated undertaking, involving striking a balance between many factors which can point in different directions. This calls for judgement, not scientific precision. That being so, strict compliance with Parliament's instructions could result in several different answers. Indeed it must surely be the fact that it is possible to come up with many different answers to the problem of where constituency boundaries shall be drawn, all of which would be sensible, that has led Parliament to seek advice from the Commission. This is not to say that it is impossible for the Commission to come up with a wrong answer, in the sense that it is one which could not possibly be given in the light of Parliament's instructions, properly understood. But it does mean that mere demonstration that there is an alternative answer, which also could be put forward consistently with those instructions, tells us nothing. There being more than one answer, Parliament has asked the Commission to advise on which, in their judgement, should be adopted.

Furthermore, the Commission had consulted widely, and the plaintiffs, among others, had had the chance to make their case to the Commission. (In this context, the courts noted that the four plaintiffs were arguing for constituencies that crossed London Borough boundaries, something that the Labour party had opposed when invited to comment on that issue; Boundary Commission for England, 1983, #5, 12.) Rawlings (1988, 61) summarised these judgements in the following terms:

> in the effective absence of Parliamentary control over the redistribution process … [the] position we reach is that the Boundary Commissions are effectively free of any serious external restraint in presenting their recommendations, and that this central element in our system of representative government is dependent in large part for its effective working on the administrative integrity of a relatively small number of officials acting under the general direction of part-time Commissioners. To this we should add the important role of the Assistant Commissioners who conduct local inquiries (without any statutory rules of procedure), since their conclusions are treated with the greatest respect and incorporated into a Commission's final recommendations unless there is very good reason not to do so. Seen in this light, the edifice of Parliamentary government in Britain appears to rest upon somewhat insubstantial foundations.

The second issue relates to the priority of the various criteria set out in the Rules. The plaintiffs sought priority for equal electorates under Rule 5, whereas Sir John Donaldson ruled that both this and Rule 4 were subsidiary to the new 'rule' introduced in the 1958 Act (Rule 7 in the *Parliamentary Constituencies Act 1986)* and stated that:

> It shall not be the duty of a Boundary Commission to aim at giving full effect in all circumstances to the above rules, *but* [our emphasis] they shall take account, so far as they reasonably can,
> (a) of the inconveniences attendant on alterations of constituencies other than alterations made for the purpose of rule 4, and
> (b) of any local ties which would be broken by such alterations.

According to Sir John the dispensation given by the 'first limb' of that rule (i.e. up to the italicised word *but*) is not merely, as was stated in the Queen's Bench opinion, to allow the Commission to reduce its focus on the preceding rules in the context of the inconveniences set out in the following subclauses (a) and (b) but, even more extensively (1983 2 *W.L.R.*, 472):

> We consider that the function of the first limb is to do just what it says, viz. To relieve Boundary Commissions from the duty to give effect in all circumstances to the rules, with the result that, although plainly Boundary Commissions must have regard to the rules, they are not strictly bound to give full effect to them in all circumstances. The word 'but' has a role to play because it points the contrast between the dispensation in the first part limb of the subsection, and the mandatory requirement in the second limb, that Boundary Commissions shall nevertheless take account of the matters specified in the second limb.

He then went further (473):

> The second limb ... requires Boundary Commissions to take account of the specified matters, and this must mean that they are required to take account of them when making ... recommendations [and so] the practical effect is that a strict application of the rules ceases to be mandatory so that the rules, while remaining very important indeed, are reduced to the status of guidelines.

This Rawlings (1988, 60) found incorrect, at least in the cases of Rules 2 and 3 which are explicit requirements regarding single-member constituencies and the status of the City of London (Box 3.4). Lord Davidson, Deputy Chairman of the Boundary Commission for Scotland, when this interpretation was presented to him at a Home Affairs Committee hearing, stated that: 'Subject to anything Parliament may say and the courts may say, we do not subscribe to that view' (Home Affairs Committee, 1986–87, 49).

The *Foot et al* case was heard by the courts at the same time as another brought by two Borough Councils in the Metropolitan County of Tyne & Wear (Gateshead and Newcastle upon Tyne, supported by North Tyneside Borough Council), plus the County Council. This claimed that the Boundary Commission for England should have allocated 14 seats to the County, not 13: the Commission's report (Boundary Commission for England, 1983, #162, 60) indicated that its theoretical entitlement was 13.48; it justified allocating 13 – the harmonic mean rule, which its Deputy Chairman discussed in the report, would have allocated 14 – on the grounds that if 14 seats were allocated, there would be substantial differences between adjacent Boroughs in the average constituency size, and any attempt to counter that would 'cause severe disruption of local ties'. (On the harmonic mean rule, see the discussion in Chapter 4, p. 184.) The argument for 14 seats had been made at the Local Inquiry, and dismissed by the Assistant Commissioner who concluded that the Commission 'had ... been correct to allocate only 13 constituencies to the county' (Boundary Commission for England, 1983,#171, 61). Part of the plaintiff's argument at the Inquiry and to the courts had been that the Commission did not take account of the substantial population growth since 1976 in the Washington New Town area of Sunderland Borough, which the Commission claimed, in a statement read at the Local Inquiry by the Assistant Commissioner, that it was precluded from doing by the statute (1983 2 *W.L.R* 484). The Assistant Commissioner's report to the Commission included a lengthy consideration of the legal issues, and concluded that the decision to allocate 13 seats was 'well within their [i.e. the Commission's] discretion to make'.

Lord Donaldson's judgement in the Court of Appeal stated that the Assistant Commissioner's report was 'confused and confusing' (1983 2 *W.L.R.,* 491), implying both that the Commission was precluded from allocating 14 seats and yet agreeing that the decision not to was within the Commission's discretion. After the plaintiffs had begun their legal proceedings, the Commission's Deputy Chairman swore an affidavit that the Commission had 'never regarded themselves as prohibited from allocating more than 13 seats' (1983 2 *W.L.R.,* 492), but that there was insufficient justification for doing that, within the statutory provisions. As a consequence, the plaintiff's case was shifted to an argument that the Local Inquiry was 'unfair' because the Assistant Commissioner 'made an error in law' which may have coloured his other judgements and recommendations. The Court of Appeal concluded, however, that (1983 2 *W.L.R.*, 493):

> we think that the assistant commissioner did express himself in unfortunately ambiguous terms, which were at least capable of being misunderstood. ... Nevertheless, even assuming that he was under such a misapprehension, we see no reason to suppose, from a reading of his report as a whole or from any other evidence, that this caused him to refrain from giving full and proper consideration to the applicants' counter-proposals for 14 constituencies on their merits. Having done so and having indicated ... some sympathy in principle with a proposal for 14 constituencies, he then made clear his ultimate conclusion ... that these particular counter-proposals were unacceptable to him on their merits. We can see no sufficient grounds for thinking that, even if he misdirected himself as to the law, this ... affected this ultimate conclusion in any way.

The Commission considered that report properly, and there is no evidence that it was unaware of the errors. The report fully outlined the arguments for and against 14 seats and the Commission recommended against the case for 14 'on its merits' (p. 494). Thus there was no case that the Commission operated improperly, again within the very substantial discretion allowed to it by the Act.

The Home Affairs Committee

The work of the Boundary Commissions came under Parliamentary scrutiny during the 1986–87 session though its Home Affairs Committee, which sat subsequent to the passing of the *Parliamentary Constituencies Act 1986* (see p. 121). The Committee's particular concern was with the continued growth in the size of the House of Commons, which it noted was the consequence of a 'fundamental defect' in the 1949 Act (Home Affairs Committee, 1986–87, #6, iv). Such enlargement is 'almost inevitable', according to Butler and McLean (1996a, 25), for four connected reasons:

1 The denominator used for calculating the electoral quota is the number of already-existing constituencies, so that, given population mobility, entitlements will probably increase even if the total electorate stays the same.
2 Additional seats allocated because of 'special geographical considerations' are included in that denominator, thereby reducing the quota.
3 As seats are allocated to local government units (at least in England and Wales), the rounding-up involved in the allocation of integer numbers almost certainly leads to the creation of more seats (see p. 184), and
4 The presumption of no change under the (new in 1986) Rule 7 means that areas of declining population tend not to lose seats.

The Home Affairs Committee argued that this in-built growth tendency should be halted by the provision of fixed divisors, with the four electoral quotas 'obtained by dividing the electorate for England by 515, for Scotland by 66, for Wales by 36 and for Northern Ireland by 17' (Home Affairs Committee, 1986–87, #13, vi). As a result, Rule 1 could then be rewritten so that the number of constituencies in each country would be:

England	not substantially more than 523
Scotland	not substantially more than 72
Wales	not substantially more than 38
Northern Ireland	not more than 18

A Commission might then recommend an additional constituency at one Review, for special geographical reasons, but this would not then be automatically incorporated into the procedure for determining the number of constituencies at future Reviews.

In its response to the Committee, the government indicated that, although sympathetic to the goal, it (Government Reply, 1988, #2, 1):

> does not, however, accept the Select Committee's intention to stabilise the size of the House of Commons at its present level would be satisfactorily achieved by the use of fixed divisors as they recommended. This White Paper discussed the use of the fixed divisor, and concludes that the disadvantages of fixed divisors outweigh their potential advantages.

This was because although the fixed divisor would prevent the incremental growth in the size of the House of Commons it would increase uncertainty over the number of constituencies after any particular Periodic Review, because of the implications of applying any new divisor within the constraints provided by the other rules. Statistical simulations had suggested 'that the desired result, i.e. the status quo, would only be achieved in less than half of the years for which calculations were done' (Government Reply, 1988, #1.5, 3). Since (Government Reply, 1988, #1.6, 3):

> The outcome of any review is dependent upon the independent exercise of their discretion by the Parliamentary Boundary Commissions and some exact stipulations in the Rules. The interplay between any level of fixed divisor and the remainder of

the Rules would produce an unacceptable level of uncertainty. ... The Government considers that the uncertainty engendered by the fixed divisor would be a most unwelcome addition to our electoral law, and that the disadvantages of the fixed divisor, in producing a variable number of seats at each review, would outweigh its advantages in preventing the incremental growth in the number of seats.

Such incremental growth, it must be assumed, was preferred by the government to slight variation in the number of seats in the House around a fixed norm. (An alternative interpretation is that it did not want to introduce and allocate time to a measure which might be divisive, especially between the four countries of the United Kingdom.) In sum, the government avoided the issue on a minor technicality.

The government did accept some administrative suggestions (to do with the time period for making representations, etc.) and promised to incorporate them in future legislation: it had not done so by the time of the Fourth Periodic Review. More generally, and in the context of the *Foot et al.* case as well as the Committee's discussions, it concluded (Government Reply, 1988, #2.8, 6):

The Government appreciates the work of the Boundary Commissions, and the scrupulous fairness and impartiality which they bring to their work: that independence must be cherished and protected. The Government is confident that the Boundary Commissions will continue to carry out their duties impartially and that they will, within the limits of their discretion, take due account of the developing problems to which the Select Committee has drawn attention.

If a (Labour) minority on the Committee had been successful in some of its proposals, the list of 'developing problems' that the government had to address might have been much longer. For example, they sought to remove the protection for London Borough boundaries by deleting Rule 4(1)(a)(ii), but the final report states that (Government Reply, 1988,#17, 7):

It is true that a much closer approach could be made to electoral parity if counties or parts of counties were combined to form review areas. We doubt, however, whether the desirability of electoral parity is great enough to justify the disruption to local ties which that course would produce. ... [Furthermore] the English Boundary Commission ... pointed out to us that if they were required to make recommendations without the structure of counties to limit areas under consideration their task would be almost impossible.

The Committee also rejected suggestions that all entitlements for Counties and London Boroughs should be rounded up to the nearest integer, that 'modern communications' render the 'special geographical considerations' criterion of Rule 6 obsolete, and that a common electoral quota should be introduced to end the 'over-representation' of Scotland and Wales; the latter decision was made solely on the argument that it was 'not ... feasible on political grounds, because it would be successfully resisted by MPs from those two countries' (see also McLean, 1995).

The last point was relevant to a concern raised in both 1979 and 1997 when Labour governments proposed devolution to Wales and, especially, Scotland. The 'over-representation' of those two countries was seen by many as even more indefensible if many of the House of Commons' powers regarding those two countries were to be devolved, and yet Scottish and Welsh MPs would be able to vote on legislation affecting only England (particularly if the incumbent government at Westminster was dependent on Scottish and/or Welsh MPs for its majority there; Rossiter *et al.*, 1997c). The devolution proposals fell in 1979 (and their defeat then initiated the procedures which led to the fall of the Labour government) but when new measures were presented in 1997, no proposals for dealing with the 'over-representation' were made when these were before the Scottish and Welsh electorates for ratification in referendums. Subsequent to their passage, the draft *Scotland Bill* (1997) included sections to amend 'Rules for the Redistribution of Seats' in the *Parliamentary Constituencies Act 1986*. These, if enacted, will: (1) delete the minimum guarantee of 71 seats for Scotland, (2) ensure that the Orkney and Shetland Islands are not combined with any other local government area in the creation of a Parliamentary constituency; and (3) add a new requirement which states that:

> In applying rule 5 (electoral quotas for each part of the United Kingdom) to Scotland for the purposes of the first report of the Boundary Commission for Scotland to be submitted ... [after passage of this Act], 'electoral quota' means the number which, on the enumeration date in relation to that report, is the electoral quota for England.

By using the English quota on one occasion, Scotland is brought into line with England, and so when it reverts to its own quota afterwards the differences between the two should be minor only (depending on the application of Rules 6 and 7 by the Scottish Commission). From then on, however, the Boundary Commission will revert to using a Scottish denominator and, unless it is as firm in the future as it was in the Fourth Review with regard to the growth in the number of seats, Scottish representation will undoubtedly increase again, for the reasons set out by McLean and Mortimore (1992).

No comparable amendments to the *Parliamentary Constituencies Act* were included in the 1997 *Government of Wales Act*, however, presumably on the grounds that as the proposed Welsh Assembly has many fewer powers compared to the Scottish Parliament, there are no grounds for reducing Welsh representation at Westminster. The overall result of these two Acts, therefore, will be a temporary (though relatively long-term – perhaps fifty years) removal of Scottish over-representation but a continuation of the current situation for Wales. The impact on Scotland will not happen until its Boundary Commission's Fifth Periodic Review, however, which is due to be reported between 2002 and 2006 according to the *Boundary Commissions Act 1992*. The next general election in the United Kingdom is due by mid-2002 so that Scottish 'over-representation' will continue for at least several years after inauguration of the Scottish Parliament in the year 2000, and it may be (if either the Boundary Commission reports very late within the defined period or at least one of the next two general elections is called before the Parliament has served a full term) that two further UK Parliaments will be elected before Scottish over-representation is removed.

The 1986 Act, the 1992 Act and the Fourth Periodic Review

In 1986 the government introduced a *Parliamentary Constituencies Act*, whose main purpose was to consolidate the 1949–1979 *House of Commons (Redistribution of Seats) Acts*, all of which were repealed. This was very largely uncontroversial: it was presented to the House of Commons by the Solicitor-General as 'pure consolidation. No change in the present law will be effected' (*Hansard*, vol. 162, 24 October 1986, col. 1445) and accepted as such by the Labour spokesman who saw 'no reason at all why the passage of this Bill should be delayed'. The rules set out in the Second Schedule (Box 3.6) contained few differences from those in their predecessor, except that the key clause from 1958, regarding inconveniences attendant on changes, was incorporated as, in effect, Rule 7 (note that it comes under a section entitled *General and supplementary* after *The rules*). This did not alter the Commissions' procedures in any significant way at all, and they accordingly embarked upon their Fourth Periodic Reviews in the early 1990s, albeit aware of the opinions expressed during the *Foot et al.* case regarding the importance of equality (albeit by a very small number of members of the Labour party associated with the case) and those of Parliament, as expressed in the Home Affairs Committee, regarding the growth of the House of Commons.

The second of these two issues clearly engaged the Commissioners. The Boundary Commission for England (1995, #1.8-1.11, 2) noted that:

> During the debate on the third periodical report in 1983 there was considerable criticism of the manner in which that review had been conducted. The Home Affairs … Committee's main area of concern was the cumulative increase in the number of constituencies. … The Government was sympathetic to the Committee's view that the Commons should be stabilised at its present level but it rejected the fixed divisor method (because it would not always produce the same number of seats) and did not propose an alternative of its own.

The Commission determined, however, not 'to set a target number of constituencies … but to concentrate upon recommending constituencies with electorates as close to the electoral quota as practicable whilst at the same time keeping in mind the requirements of Rule 1' (Boundary Commission for England, 1995, #2.10, 7), and it took specific steps to promote this (see Chapter 4).

Immediately prior to making this decision, however, the Commission had increased the number of seats in England by its interim review of parts of Buckinghamshire. The 1986 Act and its predecessors make provision for such Reviews,[9] but with this one exception that has only been used to modify constituency boundaries slightly following changes to local government boundaries. In December 1988, however, the Commission announced its intention to review the constituencies of Buckingham and Milton Keynes. The latter was by then the largest constituency in the UK, with 103,239 electors, and the Borough (which contains a rapidly-growing new town) contained 119,568. Local government

Box 3.6 *Rules for the Redistribution of Seats, as set out in the Second Schedule to the* Parliamentary Constituencies Act, 1986

RULES FOR REDISTRIBUTION OF SEATS

The rules

1   (1) The number of constituencies in Great Britain shall not be substantially greater or less than 613.
(2) The number of constituencies in Scotland shall not be less than 71.
(3) The number of constituencies in Wales shall not be less than 35.
(4) The number of constituencies in Northern Ireland shall not be greater than 18 or less than 16, and shall be 17 unless it appears to the Boundary Commission for Northern Ireland that Northern Ireland should for the time being be divided into 16 or (as the case may be) into 18 constituencies.

2   Every constituency shall return a single member.

3   There shall continue to be a constituency which shall include the whole of the City of London and the name of which shall refer to the City of London.

4   (1) So far as is practicable having regard to rules 1 to 3 –
(a) in England and Wales,–
(i) no county or any part thereof shall be included in a constituency which includes the whole or part of any other county or the whole or part of a London borough,
(ii) no London borough or any part of a London borough shall be included in a constituency which includes the whole or part of any other London borough,
(b) in Scotland, regard shall be had to the boundaries of local authority areas;
(c) in Northern Ireland, no ward shall be included partly in one constituency and partly in another.
(2) In sub-paragraph (1)(b) above 'area' and 'local authority' have the same meanings as in the Local Government (Scotland) Act 1973.

5   The electorate of any constituency shall be as near the electoral quota as is practicable having regard to rules 1 to 4: and a Boundary Commission

boundary changes required a 'normal' interim review and the Commission took the opportunity to consider a wider remit (Boundary Commission for England, 1990, 4, #5):

> We concluded that, because of the large size and the rapid growth of the electorate of the Milton Keynes constituency and borough, an interim review should also provide fairer representation in Parliament for the electors of the area.

The normal procedures were followed and provisional recommendations pub-

may depart form the strict application of rule 4 if it appears to them that a departure is desirable to avoid an excessive disparity between the electorate of any constituency and the electoral quota, or between the electorate thereof and that of neighbouring constituencies in the part of the United Kingdom with which they are concerned.

6   A Boundary Commission may depart from the strict application of rules 4 and 5 if special geographical considerations, including in particular the size, shape and accessibility of a constituency, appear to them to render a departure desirable.

General and supplementary

7   It shall not be the duty of a Boundary Commission to aim at giving full effect in all circumstances to the above rules, but they shall take account, so far as they reasonably can–
(a) of the inconveniences attendant on alterations of constituencies other than alterations made for the purposes of rule 4, and
(b) of any local ties which would be broken by such alterations.

8   In the application of rule 5 to each part of the United Kingdom for which there is a Boundary Commission -
(a) the expression 'electoral quota' means a number obtained by dividing the electorate for that part of the United Kingdom by the number of constituencies in it existing on the enumeration date,
(b) the expression 'electorate' means–
(i) in relation to a constituency, the number of persons whose names appear on the register of parliamentary electors in force on the enumeration date under the Representation of the People Acts for the constituency; and
(ii) in relation to the part of the United Kingdom, the aggregate electorates as defined in sub-paragraph (i) above of all the constituencies in that part,
(c) the expression 'enumeration date' means, in relation to any report of a Boundary Commission under this Act, the date on which the notice with respect to that report is published in accordance with section 5(1) of this Act.

9   In this Schedule, a reference to a rule followed by a number is a reference to the rule set out in the correspondingly numbered paragraph of this Schedule.

lished which recommended dividing Milton Keynes Borough into two constituencies, with one of them including three of the Borough's wards formerly included in the adjoining Buckingham constituency: the two constituencies with electorates of 72,252 (Buckingham) and 103,239 (Milton Keynes) were to be replaced by three – Buckingham (55,923), Milton Keynes East (58,895) and Milton Keynes West (60,673) – and the Commission described the two in Milton Keynes as having 'very equal electorates' (#7; one was 3 per cent larger than the other). Of the three, only Buckingham was changed in the Fourth Review, with several wards from the former Aylesbury constituency added: the two Milton Keynes electorates had increased over the three years between the two qualifying dates (December 1988 and February 1991) to 61,057 and 65,788, 12 and 5 per cent below the electoral quota respectively.

The Scottish Commission was much more determined to respond to Parliament's concerns about growth in the number of MPs (Boundary Commission for Scotland, 1995, #5, 13):

> We addressed the question of the total number of constituencies in Scotland as an issue of fundamental importance at the outset of this review. ... We decided to settle on a target number of seats which we considered would be sustainable for the duration of the review, though we recognised the possibility of matters coming to light which might cause us to reconsider that objective. The target we set was 72 seats. ... Having determined on this objective before examining proposals for any part of Scotland, we prepared a memorandum ... setting out our reasons for doing so and explaining the manner in which we intended to pursue this target. In the course of the review we did not encounter any reason to re-consider this policy, nor was any representation made to us that the total number of seats in Scotland should be altered.

The Welsh Commission, like the English, noted the Home Affairs Committee discussions, but decided that there was 'no viable alternative' open to it but to recommend an increase in the number of seats from 38 to 40 (Boundary Commission for Wales, 1995, #189, 47) and called for legislation to stop the continued growth in the number of MPs, noting that under the current legislation Wales would almost certainly be allocated a further seat in each of the Fifth and Sixth Periodic Reviews (#190, 47). Finally, the Northern Ireland Commission, after provisionally recommending 17 constituencies, and in the light of legal advice, finally recommended 18 in order 'to reduce or alleviate difficulties in applying the Rules for Redistribution of Seats on the basis of 17 constituencies ... it not having been possible to devise an acceptable scheme for 16 constituencies' (Boundary Commission for Northern Ireland, 1995, #3-4, 17; see below, p. 187 and also Rossiter *et al.*, 1998).

As on previous occasions, however, the Commissions' work (except in Northern Ireland) was potentially affected by the government's decision to restructure local government in Great Britain during the early 1990s. Its hope was to replace the two-tier structure of Counties (Regions in Scotland) and Districts by a system of unitary authorities. This had already been partly achieved in 1987 by the abolition of the Greater London Council and the six Metropolitan County Councils in England; the 32 London Boroughs were joined by the 36 Unitary Metropolitan Boroughs. In Wales and Scotland it was achieved by legislative fiat – a new structure was imposed by legislation in 1993 (see Johnston and Pattie, 1996c; Johnston *et al.*, 1997). But in England a Local Government Commission was appointed with the task of consulting the general public over the proposed changes: the government expected a move to unitary authorities, but did not insist on it, and the Commission failed to deliver what was expected, save in a small number of cases (Chisholm, 1995; Johnston and Pattie, 1996a, 1996b). In any case, no changes had been enacted within the time limit set by the 1992 Act requiring that they be taken into consideration (June 1994: see below).

The Boundary Commissions Act 1992

In November 1992 Parliament passed a new Act, whose preamble indicates its concern with Boundary Commission membership, the timing of reports, and local government boundaries. Its background lay in the 'conventional wisdom' that the Conservative party tends to benefit from a redistribution, relative to Labour, and its small margin of victory (21 seats over all other parties) at the 1992 general election. It was generally assumed after the 1987 general election that the next redistricting would give the Conservatives approximately 20 additional seats. (This was claimed by a Conservative MP – Rob Hayward, who later worked for the party on aspects of the review in 1992 and 1993 – in an article in the *Daily Telegraph*.) Although he reduced this by about half in 1992 after observing the likely impact of the ongoing work on the Fourth Review (see Chapter 6, p. 251; the Westminster Communications Group, 1993, also produced some, not very accurate, estimates), the government decided that it wished to reap that benefit at the next general election. This was due to be held not later than June 1997, but the reports on the Fourth Periodic Reviews need not have been delivered until 1998. The *Boundary Commissions Act 1992* was conceived as a means of ensuring that the next general election would be held on the new set of constituencies. The then Home Secretary, Chris Patten (who was Conservative Party Chairman between 1990 and 1992), thought that bringing the date for submitting reports forward was a good way of ensuring that the Conservatives reaped any benefit from the Fourth Review, given the closeness of the 1992 general election result, and so the Act was hurried through early in the new Parliament.

Section 2 of the Act brought the submission date forward, and shortened the inter-Review period for the future, on the grounds that rapid changes in the distribution of population require more frequent attention if maldistribution is not to result; the new subsection (2A) allows late submission, however. Introducing the Second Reading, the Home Secretary (Kenneth Clarke) indicated that there were already considerable discrepancies between constituency electorates, and that the next election could be conducted using constituencies that were twenty years out-of-date (the Third Review used 1976 electorate data for England; 1978 data were used for Scotland and Northern Ireland, and 1981 data for Wales). He argued that (*Hansard*, vol. 209, 15 June 1992, col. 671):

> The procedures via which the Boundary Commissions arrive at their conclusions are an essential part of our democratic system. There is no compelling need for any changes in the rules

and rejected a case that the over-representation of Scotland and Wales should be removed by noting that this was a long-standing element of representation in the

House of Commons, that it would need separate primary legislation, and the government view was that 'a proposal that solely determined the number of seats in Scotland and Wales would not be useful' (col. 670). Opposition spokespeople claimed that there had been no prior inter-party consultations, let alone a Speaker's Conference, as on previous occasions when such constitutional changes were under consideration, to which Clarke responded that there was need for a speedy decision. Others used the occasion, and the subsequent discussion in Committee, to air a range of issues related to the work of the Boundary Commissions (David Trimble, later to be elected leader of the Ulster Unionist party, argued that the use of wards in Northern Ireland should be replaced by DEAs – see above, p. 112, *Hansard*, vol. 209, 22 June 1992, col. 191) but all of these were rejected by Ministers as outside the scope of the Bill.

The Commissions had indicated to the government that the requirement to submit their reports by the end of December 1994 would create difficulties for them, and referred to these in their final reports (all but one – the Scottish – were late). The English Commission reported that, despite additional resources being made available, it 'found it impossible to produce this report by the due date' (Boundary Commission for England, 1995, #1.14, 2) and provided an illustration of how the public consultation procedure made this so; the Scottish Commission referred on several occasions to 'the limited time available to us' and its impacts on the local government template employed (see below); the Welsh Commission indicated that the change would have created no problem, other than one potentially created by Section 3(2) of the 1992 Act (see below); and the Northern Ireland Commission told the Secretary of State that 'they could not commit themselves to completing their review by the end of 1994 in view of the procedural obligations placed on them by the 1986 Act', in particular with regard to any representations that might be received after publication of revised recommendations (Boundary Commission for Northern Ireland, 1995, #5, 2). In the event, the Scottish and Welsh reports were laid before Parliament in February 1995 (when the relevant Orders in Council were adopted without debate), the English report was tabled and debated on 6 June, and the Northern Ireland report was tabled in October.

The purpose of the rather difficult-to-understand wording of Clause 3 of the 1992 Act (Box 3.7) was to require the Commissions to take account of any local government reorganisation which had been put in place by 1 June 1994. Clause 3(3) makes special provision for Wales, stating that the boundaries used need not be in operation so long as they are specified in an Act passed before 1 June 1994, irrespective of whether it had since come into force; the government's intention to reorganise Welsh local government and introduce a unitary, single-tier structure was known, and a House of Commons Library Division Research Note (Gay, 1992, 31) indicates that:

> The provisional proposals of the Secretary of State for 23 unitary authorities, set out on 3 March [1992], use districts as building blocks, and do not cross existing county boundaries.

No similar provision was made for Scotland in the *Boundary Commissions Act*, however, although a similar intention to create a unitary system of local government had been announced in June 1991. The 1986 Act only requires the Boundary Commission for Scotland to 'have regard to the boundaries of local government areas', however, and it would therefore be less constrained by any changes.

This requirement caused considerable consternation for the Commissions, given that only seven months were allowed between the date on which the relevant boundaries should be in place and that for delivery of the final reports. This was made clear by the Boundary Commission for Wales (1995, #11, 3):

> The imposition of a deadline of 31 December 1994 would have caused us no particular difficulty had it not been for the amendment to the 1986 Act ... which directed that for the purposes of application of the Rules in paragraph 4 of Schedule 2 to the 1986 Act ... a report of a Boundary Commission shall take account only of those boundaries (in the case of Wales, County boundaries) which are in operation on 1 June 1994. Our difficulty was that we could not be certain what the county boundaries in Wales would be on 1 June 1994 because certain changes were envisaged in the Local Government (Wales) Bill ... , which was published on 30 November 1993. Not only was there uncertainty about the county boundaries, but within those boundaries we would have preferred to try where possible to make constituencies co-terminous with the districts or the new unitary authorities. ... In an attempt to avoid wasted work, we asked to be notified by the Welsh Office once it was known when the Bill was likely to receive Royal Assent. Quite simply, if Royal Assent was to be achieved by 1 June 1994, we would produce recommendations based on the new preserved county boundaries, and within them take into account the proposed unitary authority boundaries. If Royal Assent was achieved after 1 June 1994, we could only make recommendations based on existing county boundaries.

The Commission further noted that Section 3(3)(b) allowed it to proceed with the new boundaries if the Bill had received its second reading in the House of Commons by 1 June 1994, but felt it could not risk waiting until then. Royal Assent was not given until 5 July 1994, which the Commission saw as vindicating its decision to begin the review in November 1993, using the then-existing County boundaries (although it delayed holding its public inquiries until March 1994, in case it had to restart the operation; Boundary Commision for Wales, 1996, #13, 5).

Reference to 'the new preserved county boundaries' in the above quotation introduces a further aspect of the local government template introduced to the legislation, which applies to Wales only. Having been made aware of the Secretary of State's proposals for local government reorganisation, the Boundary Commission pointed out that this would create difficulties for it. The proposed 21 new unitary authorities had populations at the time ranging from 66,700 to 295,400, with 15 of them having less than 150,000. Future constituency maps would probably involve many boundaries crossing those of local authorities, and the Commission suggested that a new class of local authority – 'preserved counties' – be

> **Box 3.7** *Extracts from the* Boundary Commissions Act 1992
>
> 2 (2) The first mandatory report of each Boundary Commission which falls to be made after the passing of this Act shall be submitted to the Secretary of State not later than 31st December 1994, instead of fifteen years from the date of submission of the Commission's last mandatory report.
>
> (3) Except as respects a report to which subsection (2) above applies, subsection (2) of section 3 of the 1986 Act shall have effect with the substitution for the words 'not less than ten or more than fifteen years' of the words 'not less than eight or more than twelve years'.
>
> (4) After subsection (2) of section 3 of the 1986 Act there shall be inserted the following subsection—
>
> '(2A) A failure by a Boundary Commission to submit a report within the time limit which is appropriate to that report shall not be regarded as invalidating the report for the purposes of any enactment.'
>
> 3 (1) Subject to subsections (2) and (3) below, at the end of section 3 of the 1986 Act there shall be added the following subsections—
>
> '(7) For the purposes of the application of the rules in paragraph 4 of schedule 2 to this Act (relationship between constituencies and certain local government boundaries) a report of a Boundary Commission under subsection (1) above shall take account only of those boundaries (whether of counties, London boroughs, local authority areas in Scotland or wards in Northern Ireland) which are in operation at whichever is the earlier of–
>
> (a) the date of the report; and

created as the units which would form the template for the operation of Rule 4 of the *Parliamentary Constituencies Act 1986*. This was agreed, and the *Local Government (Wales) Act 1994* created eight such Counties, with the country's Local Government Commission required to ensure compatibility between their boundaries and those of the new unitary authorities. The English Commission made similar representations to the Department of the Environment (responsible for local government in England), but problems were encountered with the status of the new unitary authorities, so no provision has been made there to facilitate the Commission's future work (Rossiter, Johnston and Pattie, 1996; Johnston, Rossiter and Pattie, 1997).[10]

The work of the Local Government Commission in England was proceeding slowly, and no changes were enacted by 1 June 1994; the Boundary Commission for England's work was delayed, however, both by its timetable and by Parliamentary consideration of proposals for ward and other boundary changes from the Local Government Boundary Commission (Boundary Commission for England, 1995, #1.6, 2). The Scottish Commission suffered even more from a similar problem. The Local Government Boundary Commission for Scotland was in the process of re-warding the country, and although new Regional Electoral Divi-

(b) the tenth anniversary of the date of the submission of the most recent report of the Commission under subsection (1) above;

but nothing in this subsection shall prevent a Boundary Commission publishing proposed recommendations which take account of boundaries which at the time of publication are prospective only.

(8) For the purposes of subsection (7) above, a boundary shall be regarded as prospective at any time if, at that time, it is specified in a provision of an Act, Measure of the Northern Ireland Assembly, statutory instrument or statutory rule but the boundary has not yet come into operation.'

(2) In its application to a report to which subsection (2) of section 2 above applies, subsection (7) of section 3 of the 1986 Act (as set out in subsection (1) above) shall have effect as if for paragraph (b) there were substituted–

(b) 1st June 1994'.

(3) For the purposes of the application of subsection (7) of section 3 of the 1986 Act (as set out in subsection (1) above) to that report of the Boundary Commission for Wales which is a report to which subsection (2) of section 2 above applies–

(a) a boundary which, apart from this subsection, would not be regarded as in operation on a particular date shall be so regarded if it is specified in an Act passed on or before that date, whether or not the Act (or any provision of it) is in force on that date; and

(b) a boundary which has not yet come into operation on a particular date and which, apart from this subsection, would not be regarded as prospective on that date shall be so regarded if it is specified in a Bill which, on or before that date, has been read a second time by the House of Commons.

sions (REDs) had all been gazetted by 7 October 1993 no new wards had been produced for the District Councils. (The District Council wards contain approximately half the number of electors as the Regional Electoral Divisions.) The Commission wrote that it was obliged to wait for the new REDs (Boundary Commission for Scotland, 1995, #10-11, 8):

We took the view that it would not be appropriate to ignore the structure of local electoral arrangements, instead placing Parliamentary constituency boundaries wherever we chose. There was no precedent for this. We recognised also, that there were many practical difficulties involved in ignoring local government electoral arrangements. Not only would this put the deadline at risk; but the new regional electoral divisions represented community groupings which had been put in place as a result of a recent review by an independent body which had engaged in extensive local consultation. In addition, the effective administration of Parliamentary elections, both for the local authorities which were charged with this duty and the political parties which had to organise themselves for the contest, meant that it would be better to ensure that Parliamentary constituency boundaries were based on territorial areas which fitted in with these local structures. We decided that there was no practical alternative to proceeding with the issue of provisional proposals based on the new regional electoral divisions.

> We would have been prepared to follow the example set by our predecessors of using district wards to sub-divide regional electoral divisions, in appropriate cases, had the new district wards been available to us. This did not prove possible [not least because in February 1994 the Commission learned that the Secretary of State did not intend to confirm the new district wards statutorily – like the REDs, they would never be used because of the local government restructuring about to take place; Boundary Commission for Scotland, 1995, #8, 14]. ... We very much regret that we were unable to make use of district wards as there are a number of instances in various parts of the country where we believe that we could have improved our recommendations in a manner which would have commanded greater public support.

The existing wards could not be used as building-blocks because they did not nest within the new REDs in many cases, and so the Commission proceeded using REDs alone, recognising that this could produce greater disparities from the quota than would have been the case with District wards (Boundary Commission for Scotland, 1995, #8, 14). The combination of the changed timetable plus the impending local government reorganisation made its task particularly difficult.

This was not the case in Northern Ireland, where the 1986 Act defines the District wards as the building-blocks for constituency formation. Its Boundary Commission noted that problems had been created soon after the Third Periodic Review, when a re-warding exercise conducted by the Local Government Boundaries Commissioner resulted in many new wards being divided between constituencies, an outcome criticised as 'irrational and unnecessary' by the Standing Advisory Committee on Human Rights (Boundary Commission for Northern Ireland, 1995, #4, 1). To avoid any repetition of that, a sensible timetable was operated, and the Commission could report that it was:

> grateful that the Local Government Boundaries Commissioner (Northern Ireland) Order 1990 enabled the last local government review to be completed in June 1992 which was earlier than would otherwise have been possible.

Although the *Boundaries Commission Act 1992* proposed only small amendments to the *Parliamentary Constituencies Act 1986*, therefore, its requirement for an earlier reporting date, combined with the ongoing local government changes in three of the four constituent parts of the UK, significantly impacted upon the work of the Commissions. At the same time, these had all determined to promote wider public participation in their work: their provisional and final recommendations were widely advertised and interested parties were encouraged to make their views known, both negative and positive.

Conclusions

The 'modern' procedure of conducting redistributions in the UK dates from the *House of Commons (Redistribution of Seats) Act 1944*, which enacted most of the recommendations of the Vivian Committee and the subsequent Speaker's Conference. It followed a series of earlier attempts to increase the importance of equality in constituency size and make the procedures both transparent and independent of political interference. The bases of that foundation have been retained since, with the redistricting undertaken by independent bodies acting within Rules laid down by Parliament, and consulting the political parties and the general public over their recommendations. There has been considerable change over the ensuing half-century; however, much of it has reflected the desire of political parties in general and governments in particular to influence the outcome of the Commissions' recommendations, without directly affecting what the Commissions do. Hence the many amendments to the 1944 Act discussed in this chapter, and the changes consequent on other legislation, notably that concerned with local government.

Over the fifty-year period, undoubtedly the main change has been the gradual shift in emphasis away from the representation of communities (the 'organic principle') and towards the equal representation of people (the 'mathematic principle'). To a considerable extent this has been necessitated by the reorganisations of local government that have been undertaken to reflect the greater scale and mobility of modern society; since local government areas were taken as the main indicators of local communities, the replacement of the late-nineteenth-century mosaic of small units by fewer, larger bodies ended the concentration on place rather than people. Intriguingly, equal representation of people was given priority over the representation of communities in 1944, but the Commissions argued that the two were incompatible, and if community representation were to be important equality should be a secondary consideration. Over time, however, this secondary consideration has regained a pre-eminent position, even though there has been no direct change in the law. Community ties remain an important criterion for challenges to the Commissions' recommendations, as illustrated in Chapters 5–7, but the shift has been substantial.[11]

Notes

1 Inspection of the papers in the Public Record Office (HO45/24248; 8G2153/38) suggests that consideration of this issue was indeed initiated by the goverment for political reasons. The Prime Minister's office raised it with the Home Secretary, who transmitted those concerns to the Commission.

2 This change did not result from legislation but an administrative decision by the Home Secretary: as Mortimore (1992, 70) observes, this was suggested by David Butler in his paper.

3 That decision was described by the MP for Oldham West (C. L. Hale) as 'the most serious constitutional crisis which has occured since the reign of Queen Anne' (*Hansard*, vol. 535, 16 December 1954, col. 2247).

4 A biography of Enoch Powell, a former senior Conservative MP who joined the Ulster Unionist (UU) party in 1974, claims that he had 'done more than anybody to ensure' the establishment of the Speaker's Conference (Shepherd, 1997, 488). Powell and the

UU leader (James Molyneaux) met the Prime Minister (Callaghan) in March 1977 after the Labour Government lost its majority in the House of Commons to discuss whether minority parties would support the government. In response to three demands that the two made for their support Callaghan gave an 'unconditional offer ... to refer their demand for equal representation at Westminster' to a Speaker's Conference 'irrespective of whether or not the Unionists supported the Government in the confidence vote' that was held in that month (Shepherd, 1997, 471). In his memoirs, Callaghan (1987, 542–5) mentions only meeting Molyneaux (on 21 March 1997) to whom he made an unconditional offer of a Speaker's Conference, on the advice of Michael Foot.

5 He was subsequently proved wrong, however, and additional seats in the Third and Fourth Periodic Reviews did not favour the Greater Belfast area over the west (see Rossiter, Johnston and Pattie, 1998).

6 Some Districts overlap the traditional County boundaries; see Rossiter, Johnston and Pattie (1998).

7 Interestingly, in the Fourth Periodic Review the Commision used that wording to justify crossing regional boundaries and disrupt existing constituencies (see p. 158), when the purpose of the 1973 amendment was to minimise such disruption. Moray and Nairn constituency straddled the boundary between the new Grampian and Highland Regions, for example, and was split into two new ones on either side of that divide.

8 The ratio between the populations of District wards and Regional Electoral Divisions was approximately 1:2 in the more rural parts of Scotland (such as the Highlands and Grampian) and 1:4 in the heavily urbanised areas (such as Strathclyde: Glasgow District's Regional Electoral Divisions had electorates of about 20,000).

9 Clause 3 (3) of the *Parliamentary Constituencies Act* states that 'Any Boundary Commission may also from time to time submit to the Secretary of State reports with respect to the areas comprised in any particular constituency or constituencies'.

10 The new unitary authorities in England have the status of Counties – as indicated by their listing in the draft *European Parliamentary Elections Bill* of November 1997.

11 It is of interest to note the continued stress on community representation, using terms such as 'the cohesiveness of a constituency', 'a community of interest' and 'social and economic homogeneity' in contributions to the debates on the 1992 Act.

4

The Reviews and
their outcomes

The preceding two chapters have outlined developments in the law and practice with regard to redistribution in the United Kingdom, focusing on the tensions between the mathematic and organic views of representation. We turn now to an evaluation of that practice since 1944 through analyses of the outcomes of the Initial Reviews and four Periodic Reviews conducted by the Boundary Commissions,[1] before a more detailed analysis of the conduct of the Fourth Periodic Review, which occupies the second half of this book.

The Rules which the Commissions operate have been criticised by a number of academic commentators, and even by Commission staff. Butler and McLean (1996a, 6), for example, stated that the English and Welsh Commissions 'operate under strict but confusing statutory rules' and that 'the Scottish Commission has looser, but still confusing rules'. McLeod (1996a, 96), who was Secretary of the English and Welsh Commissions during their Fourth Periodic Reviews, referred to 'the current unsatisfactory Rules'. He also expressed an 'expectation that there will be changes to the Rules before the commencement of the next general reviews'. A review of the Rules was promised by the Secretary of State in the House of Commons debate on the Boundary Commission for England's recommendations in June 1995, but no announcement had been made two years later. These comments were not new. As early as 1954, in the House of Commons debate on the reports of the Boundary Commissions' First Periodical Reviews, Christopher Hollis, a Conservative MP, observed that (*Hansard*, vol. 535, 15 December 1954, col. 1823):

> the instructions of Parliament are very unclear, [so] that it would be very difficult to follow the contradiction in the two obligations which have been placed upon [the Commissions].

When the 1958 Act was being debated, the Under-Secretary of State for Scotland (N. MacPherson – *Hansard*, vol. 582, 11 February 1958, col. 293) claimed that although clarification of the rules is desirable:

> I cannot fail to observe that, whilst it is possible to make them clearer, it does not seem to be possible to draft them in such a way that they may not contradict each

other in certain cases. Therefore, a discretion must be left to the Boundary Commissions, to deal with specific cases.

That is how it has been, throughout the five decades since the 1944 Act.

Butler and McLean's (1996a, 6) critical comment referred to the organic and mathematic principles only, however, claiming that the English and Welsh Commissions:

> must 'so far as is practicable' not cross county or London Borough boundaries, and make constituencies 'as near the electoral quota as is practicable'. These two principles repeatedly conflict, and the commissioners have never had a consistent policy in deciding between them.

Their later discussion of 'six specific problems' with the current Rules and procedures covers the frequency of reviews, the relative levels of representation for England, Scotland, Wales and Northern Ireland, growth of the House of Commons, fairness to the political parties, and administrative reforms, as well as the conflict between the two principles. The problem of the ever-enlarging House of Commons is, as they show, a function of both the vaguely worded Rule 1 (Box 3.6) and the operation of Rules 4 and 5 (see below). In addition, Rules 6 (special geographical considerations) and, especially, 7 (on the inconveniences caused by altering constituency boundaries) further complicate the Commissions' task. These compound the difficulties on which they focus, and more than sustain their conclusion that redistribution in the United Kingdom is undertaken in the context of 'ill-drawn legislation embodying conflicting principles' (Butler and McLean, 1996b, 271). Furthermore, their claim that 'Different priorities have prevailed at different times' is a partial representation only; as we show in the rest of this book, different priorities have also prevailed at the same time both between Commissions and in the work of individual Commissions, especially that charged with the largest task, the Boundary Commission for England.

In this chapter, we evaluate the statistical outcome of the reviews in the light of all of the Rules, building on our earlier analyses of the Third and Fourth Periodic Reviews only (Johnston, Rossiter and Pattie, 1996a, 1996b). We focus on each rule in turn, but start with the current Rules 4 and 5 and finish with Rule 1, the number of seats, since the final number emerges from the interaction of the others.

The procedure

In approaching their task of implementing these 'unsatisfactory rules' the English, Welsh and Scottish Commissions have evolved a largely common procedure over the Four Periodic Reviews conducted to date: commonality between the English and Welsh Commissions is not surprising as they share a Secretariat; the Scottish Commission differs from them slightly because of a variation in the wording as it applies to Scotland. Because the Northern Ireland Commission has had much less flexibility on one count – a fixed number of seats until 1979 – and more on another – no reference to local government District boundaries – it operates in a somewhat different manner, a situation also necessary because of the particular political situation there.

The English, Scottish and Welsh Commissions now work in the following general way:

1 Having decided to conduct a Review, the electoral quota is determined.
2 This quota is then applied to each local government unit covered by the Rules, to determine its 'theoretical entitlement' in terms of number of seats.[2]
3 If considered necessary, local government units are then combined to make for more equitable seat allocations.
4 Provisional recommendations are determined for the composition of each constituency in each local government area, using local government electoral divisions as the building blocks, in the light of the criteria set out in the Rules and, as discussed below, government advice regarding their interpretation – not crossing local government boundaries, achieving electoral equality across constituencies, recognising special geographical considerations and paying heed to the disruption that can follow changes and the undesirability of breaking local community ties.
5 Representations are called for – both positive and negative – and, if necessary, a Local Inquiry is held to hear further evidence, conducted by an Assistant Commissioner.
6 The provisional recommendations are reconsidered in the light of the Assistant Commissioner's report, and revised recommendations may be published: if they are, further representations are invited and a second Local Inquiry may be necessary; and
7 Final recommendations are drawn up and submitted to the relevant Secretary of State for presentation to Parliament.

The Northern Ireland Commission does not have to undertake the second and third steps; rather it has to decide how may constituencies should be recommended, and then it moves straight to the fourth step. It may, as may the other three, decide to change the number of constituencies recommended in the light of representations received and Assistant Commissioners' reports.

Within this general framework, there are differences both between Commissions and in the practice adopted by the same Commission at different reviews. For example, although each Commission has always determined that it would not, save in exceptional circumstances, subdivide a local government electoral ward, on the grounds that these are basic units of local political organisation so that 'Any division of wards between constituencies was likely to break local ties, disrupt political party organisation and be confusing to the electors' (Boundary Commission for England, 1983, p.8, #18) and also 'frequently represented a community with interests in common', no such wards were available to the Scottish Commission at the time of its Fourth Periodic Review, and in order to meet the timetable set in the *Boundary Commissions Act 1992* it was obliged to use the much larger and less flexible Regional Electoral Divisions (see Chapter 3).

Table 4.1 *Criteria used in the production of provisional recommendations mentioned by the Boundary Commission for England in the Assistant Commissioners' statements prepared for the Local Inquiries held during the Fourth Periodic Review (the criteria mentioned are shown by a *)*

	Electoral Equality	Local Ties	Minimising Disturbance	Special Geographical
A Nonmetropolitan Counties				
Avon	*		*	
Bedfordshire	*	*		*
Berkshire	*			*
Buckinghamshire	*		*	
Cambridgeshire	*		*	
Cheshire	*	*		
Cleveland	*	*	*	
Cornwall		no inquiry		
Cumbria	*	*		*
Derbyshire	*	*	*	
Devon	*	*	*	
Dorset	*	*	*	
Durham	*		*	
East Sussex	*	*	*	
Essex	*	*		*
Gloucestershire	*	*		
Hampshire	*	*	*	
Hereford and Worcester	*	*		
Hertfordshire	*	*		*
Humberside	*		*	
Isle of Wight		no inquiry		
Kent	*		*	
Lancashire	*	*	*	
Leicestershire	*		*	
Lincolnshire	*	*	*	
Norfolk	*	*	*	
Northamptonshire	*		*	
Northumberland		no inquiry		
North Yorkshire	*	*	*	
Nottinghamshire	*		*	
Oxfordshire	*	*	*	
Shropshire		*	*	
Somerset		none given		
Staffordshire	*	*	*	
Suffolk	*	*	*	
Surrey	*		*	
Warwickshire	*		*	
West Sussex	*	*	*	
Wiltshire	*			
Total	34	22	26	5
B Metropolitan Counties				
Greater Manchester				
Bolton	*		*	
Bury, Rochdale, Oldham, Tameside and Stockport	*	*		
Manchester and Trafford	*	*	*	
Salford and Wigan	*		*	

	Electoral Equality	Local Ties	Minimising Disturbance	Special Geographical
Merseyside				
Knowsley and Sefton	*		*	
Liverpool	*		*	
Wirral	*			
St Helens	*			
South Yorkshire				
Barnsley and Doncaster	*		*	
Rotherham		no inquiry		
Sheffield	*		*	
Tyne and Wear				
Entire county	*		*	
West Midlands				
Birmingham	*		*	
Coventry	*		*	
Dudley and Sandwell	*		*	
Solihull		no inquiry		
Walsall		no inquiry		
Wolverhampton	*		*	
West Yorkshire				
Bradford		no inquiry		
Calderdale		no inquiry		
Kirklees and Wakefield	*	*	*	
Leeds	*	*	*	
Total	17	4	14	0
C London Boroughs				
Barking and Dagenham		no inquiry		
Barnet		*		*
Brent		*		
Bromley	*		*	
Camden	*		*	
Croydon	*		*	
Enfield		no inquiry		
Hackney		no inquiry		
Haringey		no inquiry		
Harrow		no inquiry		
Havering	*		*	
Hillingdon	*			
Hounslow	*			
Islington		no inquiry		
Lewisham		no inquiry		
Sutton		no inquiry		
Merton		*		*
Wandsworth		no inquiry		
Bexley and Greenwich	*	*		
Ealing, Hammersmith and Fulham	*		*	*
Kensington & Chelsea and Westminster				
Kingston and Richmond	*			*
Lambeth and Lewisham & Southwark	*			
Newham and Tower Hamlets	*			*
Redbridge and Waltham Forest	*	*		
Total	12	5	5	5

Regarding the relative priority to be given to the various criteria set out in the Rules for Redistribution the Secretaries of the English and Welsh Commissions during the Third and Fourth Reviews respectively published a list in a 1989 article which, although no priority ordering is explicit, gives a clear indication of their views (Barnes and McLeod, 1989, 34):

1 the theoretical entitlement for each constituent area (i.e. County and London Borough);
2 'minimising disparity';
3 no detached parts to any constituency;
4 constituencies should be as unchanged as possible;
5 constituency and District boundaries should be coterminous wherever possible;
6 avoid fragmentation of constituencies across Districts;
7 avoid fragmentation of Districts across constituencies;
8 avoid dividing towns, taking account of;
9 local ties; and
10 geographical features.

The fifth, sixth and seventh of these bring the Home Office advice of 1972 into prominence (see p. 109): although District Council boundaries are not mentioned in the legislation they are important because, according to Barnes and McLeod (1989,32), 'it is better that districts are not subdivided between several constituencies, so that the district councils do not have to brief several MPs on local matters'.

The English Commission's priorities during the Fourth Periodic Review are illustrated by the number of times it mentioned each of the criteria in its statements prepared for the Local Inquiries (Table 4.1). In the Nonmetropolitan Counties electoral equality was mentioned in all but two cases: and in Shropshire a reference that 'allowance is made for continuing growth in The Wrekin District since 1991 and its continuation' is undoubtedly an indirect reference to that criterion. It was also mentioned in 29 of the 32 cases relating to London Boroughs and Metropolitan Districts. Minimising disturbance was also mentioned very frequently – and was undoubtedly a major concern in those areas for which no Inquiry was deemed necessary. Local ties were less frequently referred to, notably in the urban areas, however, and special geographical considerations occurred only rarely – as in Essex with the reference to the difficulties created by the unbridged estuaries in the long coastline.

One major change over the half-century of operation has been in the amount of public involvement, as measured by the number of representations received and Local Inquiries held. The Commissions have always been required to publicise their recommendations and to hold Local Inquiries where relevant; the 1958 Act makes Inquiries obligatory if representations are received from either an interested local authority or 100 electors. The Third and the Fourth Periodic Reviews saw the Commissions take steps to promote such public participation. Each published an information booklet at the start of each review, and each issued occasional *Newsletters* during the Fourth Review. The number of representations made to the Commissions increased substantially, especially at the Fourth Review, the

English Commission recording that (Boundary Commission for England, 1995a, 11, #2.50):

> The report of the third general review records that over 8,000 representations and petitions were received. The equivalent figure for this review is 40,000. The petitions alone contained an approximate total of 75,000 signatures giving an overall participation of about 115,000. Although a substantial number of representations supported our proposals, the majority contained objections. These figures suggest that the policy of expanding the information available to the public has been successful.

The political parties have also become much more active and sophisticated in seeking to influence the Commissions' recommendations, for their own electoral gain, as we detail in the following chapters.

The consequence of this greater public and political participation has been a substantial increase in the number of Local Inquiries held (Table 4.2). Provisional recommendations for no change stimulate relatively few representations in most cases, and the likelihood of an Inquiry being necessary is low. (The Welsh Commission received only five objections to the provisional recommendations in its First Periodical Review, when it recommended no change to 30 of the 36 existing constituencies; Boundary Commission for Wales, 1954, 1, #7.) The largest number of such Inquiries was held during the Third Periodic Review,[3] which followed the major restructuring of the local government template in the 1970s and stimulated many more recommendations for change than the previous reviews.

Table 4.2 *The number of Local Inquiries held*

	*England**	*Scotland*	*Wales*	*Northern Ireland*
Initial Review	21	3	1	0
Periodic Reviews				
First	7	0	0	0
Second	70	5	1	1
Third	95	11	7	4
Fourth	68	8	3	5

*In addition three second inquiries were held in England during the Third Periodic Review and two during the Fourth

At these Inquiries, local ties dominate the discussions, in many cases as a 'cover' for the parties' arguments which are structured for electoral gain but cannot refer to that. This brings Rule 7 of the current rules to the fore, to a greater extent than in the Commissions' own representations – in part because it relies on local knowledge which is not available to them. Hence the operation of the various rules takes different priorities in different fora: the Commissions are most concerned with the formal, more mechanical, requirements regarding fixed local government boundaries and electoral equality, whereas the public participation focuses more on communities and their interests – in a sense the Commissions pays more attention to the mathematic requirement and the public to the organic.

The local government template

The requirement that constituencies fit into the local government template, as far as practicable, has been consistent throughout the period under review, although with the changes to that template in the 1960s and 1970s the Rules have become less demanding. Nevertheless, the Commissions have always seen it as important to avoid splitting local government units whenever possible, presenting them as primary identifiers of the local communities which are to be separately represented under the organic principle.

The first three redistributions

The Rules applied at the Initial Review required the Commissions to respect all local government boundaries while Rule 4 prescribed an allowed tolerance around the electoral quota: the latter was removed before the Commissions reported (Box 3.2). The English Commission wrote favourably that 'the amended rules of the Act of 1947 by removing Rule 4 and giving greater prominence to the principle of local unity have enabled us to avoid many of the difficulties' relating to local government boundaries, thereby facilitating its 'general aim [which] was the creation of constituencies as near to the electoral quota as practicable consistent with the preservation of local unities' (Boundary Commission for England, 1947, 4, #8, 10). This form of words was also employed by the Welsh Commission, which found it necessary to cross the boundaries of only one Borough. It also divided four Rural Districts, but only where 'we deemed a division necessary or desirable to give effect to Rule 6 [special geographical considerations] or with a view to meeting local objections' (Boundary Commission for Wales, 1947, 4, #12). The Scottish Commission could claim, in slightly tortuous language, that (Boundary Commission for Scotland, 1947, 4, #10):

> In accordance with the requirements of rule 5 our recommendations do not involve the inclusion of a county, as defined in the rule, or of a burgh partly in one Parliamentary county and partly in another or partly in a Parliamentary county and partly in a burgh; nor do they involve the inclusion of a burgh other than a county of a city partly in one Parliamentary constituency and partly in another.

Although the Rules gave the boundaries of County Boroughs the same status as both Counties and Metropolitan Boroughs, the former were much more likely to be crossed than the latter, in part because the Commissions (especially the English and Welsh) treated them as part of their encompassing 'Shire' Counties for determining the number of seats to which areas were entitled, the English Commission recording after the Second Review that (Boundary Commission for England, 1969, 7, #45):

> Our predecessors in 1954 found it convenient at the outset of their review to allocate seats provisionally to areas comprising administrative counties and their associated county boroughs (that is, the geographical counties) on the basis of one seat for each complete unit of electors, the unit representing the electoral quota. We also came to the conclusion that this was the best method of setting about our task. It guaranteed fair and consistent treatment of one area as compared with another, and ensured that our recommendations for each area would always be made with the eventual total number of seats in mind.

They sought to keep County Boroughs intact, but were unable to in some cases: the most extreme failure was with Reading at the First Periodical Review, when eleven of its wards comprised the Reading constituency with the other two allocated to the Newbury and Wokingham constituencies respectively. Alternatively, adjacent suburban districts were added to County Borough-based constituencies: Manchester Gorton, for example, included two Manchester wards plus the adjoining districts of Audenshaw and Denton after the First Review, and nearby Manchester Openshaw incorporated three Manchester wards plus Failsworth Urban District. This practice came under particular criticism during the Parliamentary debates on the 1958 Act (Boundary Commission for England, 1969, 5, #27).

Overall, the Commissions successfully separated County Boroughs from other administrative areas when defining constituencies in the Initial and the First and Second Periodical Reviews. At each, no more than one quarter of the constituencies involving part of an English County Borough crossed that Borough's boundaries. In Scotland, only one constituency included an area outwith the relevant County Borough, and this was also the case in Wales on the first two occasions (in the Second Review, none of its eight County Borough constituencies crossed a boundary). Only in Northern Ireland was there an exception to this generalisation, and then only at the Second Review, when four of its five County Borough constituencies crossed a boundary.

In England as a whole, over half (257) of the 489 constituencies recommended in the Initial Review involved no division of a local government unit, and just 13 incorporated parts only from two Districts; four of the latter were in Cornwall, where the Kerrier, St. Austell, Wadebridge, and West Penwith Rural Districts were all divided between two constituencies each. Three others were in Hampshire, one of which involved the inclusion of a single civil parish in the Romsey and Stockbridge Rural District with ten wards of Southampton County Borough to form the Southampton Test constituency. Few constituencies represented a single community, as defined by local government status, however; in only 69 of the 489 cases were the boundaries of a local government District or Borough (invariably an urban area) coterminous with those of a constituency, although there were five cases of whole Counties constituting single constituencies (Isle of Ely, Huntingdon, Lincolnshire (Holland), Westmorland, and Isle of Wight); in addition, the entire County of Rutland was incorporated with parts of Lincolnshire (Kesteven) in a single constituency, as was all of Cambridgeshire outwith the Municipal Borough of Cambridge. East and West Suffolk were separate administrative bodies but considered together for the reviews, as were Northamptonshire and the Soke of Peterborough (Boundary Commission for England, 1954, 5, #15). Finally, of the 219 constituencies which contained part of one District only, well over half (133) contained no other Districts at all: these were the divided Boroughs. There was a substantial number of cases, however, in which between one and nine whole Districts were joined with part of one other in order to produce what the Commission identified as an acceptable electorate.

The Commission drew particular attention to one group of cases, comprising five Metropolitan Boroughs with electorates of 40,000 or less (Chelsea, Finsbury, Holborn, Shoreditch and Stoke Newington). Finsbury and Shoreditch were adjacent, and so were joined to form a single constituency with 56,764 electors (the London average was 59,507). Holborn was joined with four wards from neighbouring St Pancras, whose remaining wards made another seat (their electorates were 54,978 and 65,545 respectively), and the same strategy was applied by linking Stoke Newington with Hackney (electorates of 77,540 and 74,019). Chelsea was linked to Westminster – 'with some reluctance'; Chelsea's electorate of 39,177 was considered too small for the Borough to retain separate representation (although Bermondsey, with 41,735 and Bethnal Green with 42,451 did), and Westminster's 77,411 was too small for it to be awarded two seats.

Very similar patterns emerge from an analysis of the First and Second Periodical Reviews. In the First, 390 of the 489 constituencies comprised either one or more Districts, but no parts of any District only, so that boundaries were crossed in just 20 per cent of all constituencies. The comparable figures for the next two Reviews were 22 and 20 per cent, so Rule 5(a) was observed in over three-quarters of all constituencies.

Scotland and Wales both had large numbers of small towns and Rural Districts within their local government structures at that time, and in each a majority of the constituencies recommended in the Initial Review involved either groups of entire local government areas or subdivisions of large cities: Wales had two constituencies (Denbigh and Wrexham) involving parts of more than one District, but Scotland had none. At each of the Reviews, Rule 5 was applied in 60 of the 71 constituencies recommended for Scotland, although only 27 of them involved either all or part of just one District: the comparable figure for Wales was 29 of the 36 constituencies conforming with the Rule in the first two Reviews and 28 at the other, though again only a small number (8) involved either all or part of just one District.

In three cases, the Scottish Commission continued the practice of previous redistributions of grouping together Burghs which were not contiguous – two of those constituencies were in Fife (Dunfermline, Cowdenbeath, Inverkeithing, and Lochgelly; Kirkcaldy, Buckhaven and Methil, Burntisland, and Kinghorn) and the third comprised Stirling, Falkirk and Grangemouth at the head of the Firth of Forth. Three other such groupings (one involving Burghs from adjacent Counties) were not retained, however, the Commission noting that (Boundary Commission for Scotland, 1947, 6, #17):

> It is not clear on what grounds, other than those of tradition and historic continuity, some burghs which are not large enough to be entitled to separate Parliamentary representation have been grouped with others to form districts of burghs. ...
> We have been anxious not to recommend more changes in constituencies than are in our view desirable to give effect to the rules laid down for us, but we feel that there is much to be said for associating such burghs with the surrounding landward areas in county divisions.

Similarly, the Welsh Commission decided against retaining the Carnarvon District of Boroughs as a separate constituency (it comprised 'four boroughs or parts of boroughs, four Urban Districts or parts of Urban Districts, and part of a civil parish': Boundary Commission for Wales, 1947, 4, #11; see also Figure 2.3), arguing – apparently without any representations to the contrary – that the character of its constituent areas 'is not such as to justify the continuance of the special treatment hitherto accorded to them'.

Northern Ireland differed from the other three parts of the United Kingdom in the construction of its constituencies, in large part because they were on average much larger. Eight of its twelve constituencies contained part only of at least one local government area: four of these were in Belfast. The others were in the more rural areas, three of which (Antrim, Down, and Fermanagh and Tyrone) had previously been two-member constituencies. Even dividing each of those areas produced large constituencies in area (Boundary Commission for Northern Ireland, 1947, 5, #12):

> The length from east to west of the proposed new constituency of Fermanagh and South Tyrone is some 67 miles. Other examples, not much less striking, could be given. No recommendations which we could make could avoid producing constituencies which are unwieldy in size and sometimes uncouth in shape. The best we can hope to achieve is to distribute the inevitable burden of size and distance and administrative inconvenience as fairly and as evenly as may be, in accordance with the Rules.

The Northern Ireland Commission was unable to create additional constituencies for 'special geographical reasons', as in other parts of the United Kingdom, because it was constrained to a fixed number of seats. It could, like the other Commissions (see below), have recommended smaller constituencies in rural areas (by number of electors) by creating much larger seats in Belfast. There is no evidence that this was considered, however; indeed, the four Belfast constituencies were not changed, the Commission reporting that 'We were of the opinion that there were no special factors which required that any of these ... should be altered. No representations of any sort were received with respect to them, and we therefore had no difficulty in deciding to adhere to our proposed recommendations that no change should be made' (Boundary Commission for Northern Ireland, 1947, 3, #5).

The First Periodical Review reports were delivered only seven years after completion of the Initial Reviews, and they involved little change, save in England, where an additional 22 constituencies were created. The Scottish Commission recommended changes to just 27 of the 71 constituencies, and the Welsh Commission recommended altering only 6 of its 36; in Northern Ireland, all 12 existing constituencies were retained unaltered.

Only England experienced substantial change to the fit between constituencies and local government districts, therefore, and in general terms it became slightly weaker. The major change, however, was the increase of 16 in the number of constituencies comprising part of a single district (usually a County Borough) only; the Commission recorded that it subdivided only 44 Rural Districts (compared to 41 in the Initial Review), and that it recommended constituencies crossing the boundaries of 28 Boroughs and one Urban District, almost twice as many as previously (Boundary Commission for England, 1954, 5, #14). For the first time, a constituency (Eastleigh) was created which contained parts of three separate Districts around its core (the Municipal Borough of Eastleigh).

In London, the union of Chelsea and Westminster was ended, and replaced by one linking the Borough of Chelsea to one Kensington ward. (This was a change from the Initial Review recommendations, but not those implemented after the government added further constituencies in 1949; see p. 86) The groupings of Finsbury with Shoreditch and of Holborn with St Pancras were retained, and the Borough of Bethnal Green was added to the grouping of Hackney with Stoke Newington. As a consequence of the last decision, nine of Hackney's wards comprised the Hackney Central constituency (electorate 67,733), three others were in a constituency also including Bethnal Green (63,536), and four were joined with Stoke Newington (66,456). Finally, the declining electorates of Fulham and Hammersmith led to their merger for this purpose, with the new constituency of Baron's Court containing wards from each Borough.

There were more changes between the First and Second Reviews, notably in England where a considerable number was stimulated by the reorganisation of local government in London. A new Greater London County Council was created in 1965, containing within it an entirely new structure of 32 London Boroughs, plus the City of London. These changes removed any need for combining Boroughs, the Commission recording that 'Not only did we respect the Rules but it also seemed desirable, both for political organisation and for electoral administration, that constituencies in Greater London should conform with borough boundaries. Our discussions with the chief officers of the political parties confirmed this' (Boundary Commission for England, 1969, 10, #53). The smaller number of larger Boroughs meant that more were subdivided into two or more constituencies, however, generating much of the increase from 149 to 206 in the number of constituencies comprising part of a single local authority only.

There were relatively few changes in either Scotland or Wales but several in Northern Ireland where the electorates of the four Belfast constituencies had declined and those of the adjacent areas of Antrim and Down increased. To counter this, three of the four Belfast constituencies were extended beyond the

City boundaries, with one – Belfast South – containing District Electoral Divisions from two Rural Districts.

The Third and Fourth Periodic Reviews

The restructuring of local government throughout Great Britain in the 1970s had very substantial impacts on the Boundary Commissions. The very substantial decrease in the number of districts in each country (Table 4.3) very significantly reduced the Commissioners' degrees of freedom to group together whole districts, as recognised in the changes to the *House of Commons (Redistribution of Seats) Act,* certain sections of which were repealed by the relevant *Local Government Acts* of the 1970s. The English and Welsh Commissions were no longer required to avoid splitting districts, as far as is practicable; the Scottish Commission was only required to 'have regard to' local authority boundaries; and the sole direction to the Northern Ireland Commission on this issue referred to the undesirability of dividing District Council wards (Box 3.5).

Table 4.3 *The changing local government structure of the United Kingdom in the 1970s, outside Greater London*

Before			After	
England				
County Boroughs	76		Metropolitan Counties	6
Counties	44		Districts	36
Boroughs		218		
Urban Districts		444	Nonmetropolitan Counties	39
Rural Districts		271	Districts	296
Scotland				
Cities	4		Regions	9
Counties	32		Districts	56
Large Burghs		21		
Small Burghs		174	Islands areas	3
Districts		200		
Wales				
County Boroughs	4		Counties	8
Counties	13		Districts	37
Boroughs		32		
Urban Districts		73		
Rural Districts		59		
Northern Ireland				
County Boroughs	2		Districts	26
Counties	6			
Boroughs		10		
Urban Districts		26		
Rural Districts		29		

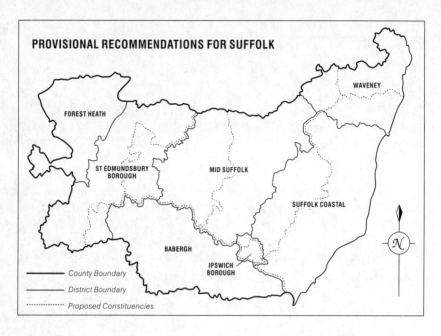

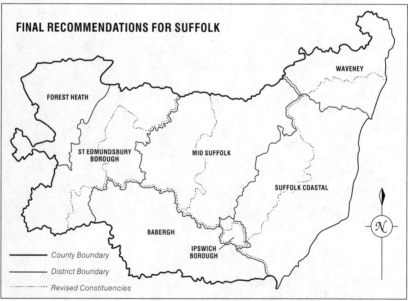

Figure 4.1 *The Boundary Commission's provisional and final recommendations for constituencies in Suffolk in the Fourth Periodic Review, showing constituency and district boundaries.*

Source: based on the Ordnance Survey map with the permission of The Controller of Her Majesty's Stationery Office © Crown Copyright

Although the legal requirement to respect local government district boundaries wherever practicable was removed, nevertheless the government made it clear to the Commissions that they should all 'have regard to' those district boundaries. As recorded in Chapter 3 (p. 108 above), the Commissions took this advice when undertaking their Third Periodic Reviews. The new structure created problems for them, however, as illustrated by the case of Suffolk at the Fourth Review (Figure 4.1). Moving west to east across the northern part of the County, there were four Districts with electorates of 33,767 (Forest Heath), 70,025 (St Edmundsbury), 61,120 (Mid Suffolk) and 79,339 (Suffolk Coastal). Because the westernmost District was small the Commission was bound to recommend amalgamating it with about half of its only neighbour to create one constituency in its provisional recommendations (West Suffolk); some wards in the remainder of St Edmundsbury District were in turn linked with part of Mid Suffolk District to form the Bury St Edmunds constituency, and the remainder were joined with Babergh District to form the South Suffolk constituency. Only two of the Districts were undivided in the provisional recommendations. After the Local Inquiry the fragmentation was reduced slightly, but St Edmundsbury remained split between three constituencies in the final recommendations as an almost inevitable consequence of the County's administrative geography.

There was only one transgression of the amended Rule 4 in the Third Periodic Review: the English Commission, of necessity, continued its practice of merging the Isles of Scilly (electorate in 1976: 1,463) with the County of Cornwall, from which they are formally separate. Six constituencies were created that crossed Metropolitan District boundaries, however. At the Fourth Review, this number more than doubled, and the English Commission also produced eight constituencies crossing London Borough boundaries; in addition, the Scottish Commission paired two adjacent Regions in two parts of the country. But, as stressed earlier, the emphasis on the organic requirement in the 1986 Act is much weaker than in its predecessors, making the Commissions' task much easier. Nevertheless, as exemplified by Suffolk, their task of fitting constituencies with the 'communities' defined by the new local government Districts was much harder.

The Metropolitan Counties
Creation of the six Metropolitan Counties in England in 1972 (they became operational in 1974) provided a further complication. Most of their constituent Metropolitan Districts had electorates larger than the London Boroughs, whose boundaries were still 'protected'. (The average electorate of a London Borough in 1976 was just over 164,000, whereas for a Metropolitan District it was nearly 235,200; the former would have been entitled to 2.5 constituencies and the latter 3.6.) Nevertheless, the Commission reported that (Boundary Commission for England, 1983, 39, #3):

Early in our review we decided that because of the importance, large electorates, history and sense of identity of most metropolitan districts we should endeavour to avoid recommending the crossing of their boundaries. This was in accordance with the tenor of the Home Office advice … and clearly it would be possible in the case of such districts to take their boundaries into account to a much greater extent than would be possible with the non-metropolitan districts with their smaller electorates. When we discussed the matter with representatives of the political parties there was no dissent from this approach.

This was somewhat tempered in the following paragraph, however:

Nonetheless, because we were at liberty to cross district boundaries and because of the need for avoiding disparities between constituencies generally, we decided that we should formulate our original, revised and modified recommendations for the whole of each metropolitan county at the same time, so that the possibility of crossing metropolitan boundaries would always be considered.

By the time of the next Review, the Metropolitan County Councils had been abolished, with the Metropolitan Districts remaining as unitary authorities; the Commission recorded, however, that 'the counties remain for the purposes, inter alia, of the redistribution of Parliamentary constituencies' (Boundary Commission for England, 1995a, 75, #4.1). The 1972 advice to respect district boundaries where possible was again noted, however (using almost exactly the same words), and it 'sought to recommend constituencies contained within those boundaries'.

One of the cross-District constituencies created by the Third Review was in Tyne and Wear – Tyne Bridge: it involved crossing not only a Borough boundary (that separating Newcastle upon Tyne from Gateshead) but also the Tyne River, a major divide between separate communities. The two Boroughs' theoretical entitlements were 3.42 and 2.52 respectively, and North Tyneside – immediately to the east of Newcastle – was entitled to a further 2.31. The Commission noted that if it followed its normal rules for allocating seats to Districts individually, whereas Gateshead would have three seats with average electorates of 55,181 the three seats each for Newcastle and for North Tyneside would produce averages of 74,887 and 75,896 respectively; such disparities were clearly out of line with that part of Rule 5 which allows the Commission 'to depart from the strict application' of Rule 4 'if it appears to them that a departure is desirable to avoid an excessive disparity between the electorate of any constituency and the electoral quota [65,951], or between the electorate thereof and that of neighbouring constituencies'. It reported that (Boundary Commission for England, 1983, 60, #163):

Schemes which joined all three districts in a common area reduced the disparities between the new constituencies, and from the electoral quota, but seemed likely to cause severe disruption of local ties. We noted, however, that schemes which amalgamated Gateshead and Newcastle upon Tyne produced seats with electorates close to the average for that area and appeared, for the most part, to reflect local affinities.

Local opinion on this was clearly divided in the representations received, but after the Local Inquiry (Boundary Commission for England, 61, #172):

The assistant Commissioner concluded that there was, on balance, more community of interest between those living north and south of the Tyne than those opposing any cross-river seat would have him believe and that … our recommendations constituted the most practicable, equitable, convenient and generally acceptable solution to the problems of providing the county with its own Parliamentary representation for the first time in its history.

West Yorkshire Metropolitan County also had a constituency which crossed District boundaries (Leeds and Wakefield), but in this case the recommendation came not from the Commission itself but from a counter-proposal put in representations against the provisional recommendations and debated extensively at the Local Inquiry. (The same Assistant Commissioner conducted both inquiries for those Districts: Boundary Commission for England, 1983, 41, #12.) The County was entitled to 22.92 seats, generating an expectation that 23 would be recommended. The individual District entitlements were: Bradford, 5.00; Calderdale, 2.16; Kirklees, 4.13; Leeds, 8.24; and Wakefield, 3.38. On this basis, the Commission allocated 22, arguing that 'we treated each district separately, because we thought that local opinion would prefer that arrangement'. Local opinion expressed at the Wakefield Inquiry was that West Yorkshire should receive its full entitlement of 23 seats, however, and (Boundary Commission for England, 1983, 74, #279):

The assistant Commissioner considered that the need to achieve fairness and adequate representation in West Yorkshire made the case for a 23rd seat overwhelming. He also agreed with the arguments presented that the additional seat should be contained 'predominantly or entirely within the City of Wakefield because, by reason of the large electorate, the extent to which it had increased in recent years and the likely increase still to come, that area had by far, the strongest claim to the extra seat'.

His recommendation was for a constituency (Normanton) comprising four Wakefield wards, one Leeds ward, and parts from two other Leeds wards, but the Commission declined to split wards. The result was that whereas in the provisional recommendations Leeds was to have eight seats with an average electorate of 67,762 and Wakefield three averaging 74,015, the final recommendations produced twelve constituencies averaging 63,679 electors each.

Metropolitan Districts were also paired in Greater Manchester. The County's entitlement was 29.69 seats, and if each of its Districts had been allocated its entitlement the total would have been 30. (The harmonic mean applied in two of these cases – Oldham and Tameside; see below, p. 184.) But, the Commission noted, 'there would have been anomalies' (Boundary Commission for England, 1983, 41, #13), with seven of the ten Districts entitled to three seats each even though their electorates varied by 61,000. After investigating a number of options, the Commission recommended two pairings of adjacent Boroughs. Among the objections to the pairing strategy was a claim that 'a Member of Parliament's difficulties were lessened and his efficiency increased if the whole of his constituency lay within one district council's area' (Boundary Commission for England, 1983, 47, #48) but to counter this the Commission reported that 'the assistant Commissioner [for the Inquiry covering four Districts] noted ... that a substantial body of opinion ... considered that the problems were not too great and should not be allowed to outweigh the requirement to have constituencies that were reasonably close to one another and to the electoral quota. He accordingly concluded that our approach to the problem was the most logical and practical one and that the most natural and satisfactory pairs of Districts were Manchester and Trafford, and Salford and Wigan': the provisional recommendations for four constituencies crossing District boundaries were upheld.

In the Fourth Review, the Commission increased the number of cross-District constituencies to thirteen, which it justified as necessary in order to meet the requirements of Rule 5 (Boundary Commission for England, 1995a, #2.25); this involved 21 of the 36 Districts and all six of the Counties. In five of the six cases, introduction of the cross-boundary constituencies made no difference to the overall allocation: only in Tyne and Wear did consideration of the entire County result in more seats being allocated (one) than if each District had received a separate allocation. Reduction in the disparity of electorates was the prime consideration, with the final recommendations resulting in reductions from: 21,320 to 14,690 in Greater Manchester; 34,412 to 15,277 in Merseyside; 22,404 to 5,450 in South Yorkshire; 26,598 to 6,610 in Tyne and Wear; 38,365 to 24,600 in West Midlands; and 20,844 to 13,614 in West Yorkshire.

The largest of the six exercises occurred in the smallest of the Counties, Tyne and Wear, where all five Districts have at least one cross-District constituency; Newcastle upon Tyne has two and Gateshead three (Figure 4.2). This involved retaining the seat which crossed the Tyne, otherwise there would have been very substantial disparities between the County's two halves: with twelve seats the average electorates would have been 73,262 and 72,946, but these were considered too large relative to the electoral quota (Boundary Commission for England, 1995a, 111, #6): with thirteen, and eight of them on the south bank, they would have been 73,262 and 63,828. Retention of Tyne Bridge created difficulties on both sides of the river unless both Gateshead and Newcastle upon Tyne were linked to their other neighbours. The representations to the provisional recommendations largely accepted the general principle, although the Tyne Bridge constituency continued to be challenged on the grounds that 'there was no historical or political justification for its retention, that it had proved to be unpopular with the electorate and the two local authorities involved, and that its abolition would allow a reduction to 12 seats' (Boundary Commission for England, 1995a, 112, #17(e); the last point was made by the Liberal Democrats, but received no support from the local authorities concerned). There were many claims that the proposed constituencies would break well-established local community ties, but the Commission made revised recommendations only with respect to the City of Sunderland.

In Greater Manchester, the Commission originally considered three groupings of Districts, leaving only Bolton and Stockport unpaired. Bury, Oldham, Rochdale, Stockport and Tameside were considered together at the Local Inquiry stage, however. The Assistant Commissioner recommended that Bury be removed from the grouping, and commended an alternative scheme for the other Districts which involved: one constituency crossing the Oldham–Rochdale boundary (including eight Oldham wards and one from Rochdale); one crossing the Old-ham–Tameside boundary; and one crossing Stockport and Tameside's (Figure 4.3). The Commission concluded that this 'was clearly the best overall solution to a series of difficult problems, and had received a good degree of local support ... [which] respected local ties [in several areas where they had been over-ridden previously]' (Boundary Commission for England, 1995a, 83, #38).

In the West Midlands, the Commission argued that if Dudley and Sandwell were not linked (124, #68):

> major disruption and breaking of established local ties would result, because we would be bound to increase the allocation of seats to Dudley from three to four, and to reduce the allocation to Sandwell from four to three. We further noted that there would be a wide disparity between the seven seats.

Figure 4.2 *The Boundary Commission's final recommendations for Tyne and Wear County in the Fourth Periodic Review, showing constituency and district boundaries*
Source: based on the Ordnance Survey map with the permission of The Controller of Her Majesty's Stationery Office © Crown Copyright

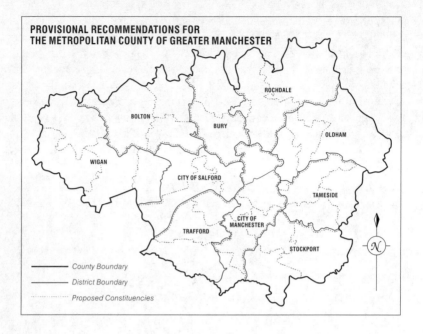

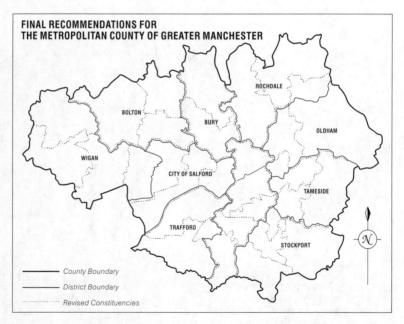

Figure 4.3 *The Boundary Commission's recommendations for Greater Manchester*
County in the Fourth Periodic Review, showing constituency and district boundaries
Source: based on the Ordnance Survey map with the permission of The Controller of
Her Majesty's Stationery Office © Crown Copyright

This produced a scheme which involved the minimum of change overall. The pairing decision was 'universally accepted' (125, #73), and only the detailed composition of the constituencies was contested.

The London Boroughs

The London Boroughs (previously known as the Metropolitan Boroughs) have always been identified separately in (what is now) Rule 4. As discussed above, they were almost invariably provided with separate representation in the Initial, First Periodical and Second Periodical Reviews, and this was continued in the Third. By then, however, only two of the 32 Boroughs were entitled to four seats, and fourteen were entitled to only two. The English Commission recognised that 'if none of the constituencies was to cross a London Borough boundary, there would be some Boroughs which even with quite small differences between their electorates would be entitled to different numbers of constituencies' with consequences for their number of electors (Boundary Commission for England, 1983, 7, #13), but it accepted that proposals to cross any Borough boundaries would generate 'serious repercussions' (12, #2), not only breaking local ties but also potentially stimulating demands for similar developments elsewhere 'which might involve virtually all boroughs being to some extent fragmented'. As a consequence, it 'tentatively decided to follow the existing pattern' (#3) but 'as an exercise in discovering whether our approach to the breaking of local ties would receive support from those more directly in touch with feeling in the various constituencies, we decided to consult the national representatives of the political parties' (#4). These were 'unanimously of the opinion that none of the London borough boundaries should be crossed' even though this would result in 'disparities in the representation' of Boroughs (#5), and it proceeded accordingly. The expected differences emerged: the four constituencies in Barnet had average electorates of 56,766, for example, compared to 71,337 in adjacent Camden. (This was part of the basis for the *Foot et al.* case; see p. 113.)

By the time of the Fourth Periodic Review the problem was even more acute. At the Third Review, only eight of the 32 Boroughs had fractional entitlements of 0.4, 0.5 or 0.6, compared to fifteen twelve years later (Table 4.4). The Commission was aware of this and stressed, in the introductory booklet that it published and distributed widely at the start of the review process, that it had the flexibility to cross London Borough boundaries, if it deemed necessary (Parliamentary Boundary Commission for England, 1991; see also Rossiter, Johnston and Pattie, 1992). By 1993, the Commission determined that some grouping of Boroughs and cross-boundary constituencies would be necessary, both to avoid excessive disparities and to limit the growth in the size of the House of Commons: it presented its strategy for this at a meeting with the political parties (the Minutes of which are reproduced in Boundary Commission for England, 1995b, 116–18) and announced it more generally in its Summer 1993 *Newsletter*.

The procedure for determining which Boroughs would be paired was undertaken within the constraint of a 'flexible guideline' (Boundary Commission for

Table 4.4 *The distribution of fractional entitlements to constituencies for London Boroughs at the Third and Fourth Periodic Reviews*

	Third	Fourth
0.0	1	0
0.1	4	3
0.2	3	2
0.3	3	3
0.4	1	7
0.5	4	3
0.6	3	5
0.7	6	2
0.8	3	5
0.9	4	2
Total	32	32

England, 1995a, 14, #3.9) which limited consideration only to the nine Boroughs whose average number of electors per seat was more than 12,500 above or below the quota (69,281). Further constraints were that: (1) the number of seats allocated to a pair of Boroughs should not exceed the total to which they were separately entitled (this would have been the case if Newham were paired with Waltham Forest, for example); (2) that the result would reduce the deviations of the Borough average from the quota in both cases; (3) that there was a 'continuous residential area or some community of interest across the relevant boundaries' (Boundary Commission for England, 1995a, 16, #3.11; see also the discussion of a proposal for crossing a Borough boundary where there were 'marked contrasts' in the land use on either side – 42, #37); and (4) no Boroughs on opposite banks of the River Thames below Richmond would be paired. Nineteen possible pairings were identified which met these criteria, and seven were selected, involving eight constituencies which straddled one boundary between two Boroughs only; this resulted in an allocation of 74 seats instead of the 77 which was the total of the individual Borough entitlements (Figure 4.4). All of the pairings were contested, with alternatives being suggested (including one to pair a London Borough – Kingston upon Thames – with another County – Surrey, which interestingly has its administrative headquarters in Kingston and not in Surrey); these were major issues at the relevant Local Inquiries, but all of the pairings were sustained following receipt of the Assistant Commissioners' reports.

Wales
Crossing County boundaries was a contentious issue during the Welsh Third Review, where the Commission's provisional recommendations were to combine

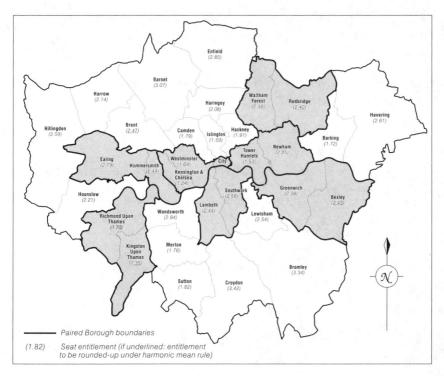

Figure 4.4 *The London Boroughs, showing their theoretical entitlements to seats at the Fourth Periodic Review and the pairings recommended by the Boundary Commission*

the Counties of Gwent and Powys. 'Theoretical entitlements' to seats were obtained by dividing County electorates by the electoral quota.

> This theoretical entitlement we rounded up or down to the nearest whole number; with one exception this produced an average electorate nearest to the electoral quota. The exception was Powys, which posed a special problem. Powys was theoretically entitled to 1.4 seats and we were therefore faced with the dilemma of having to allocate either one constituency with over 84,000 electors or two constituencies with an average of about 42,000 electors. Our preliminary decision was that we would not be justified in allocating two constituencies and that the allocation of one would be absurd in view of the size of the county. In the past, consideration had been given to the amalgamation of Merioneth and Montgomery to form one constituency. We concluded that we should not propose such an arrangement because of the physical barriers between these areas. After studying the alternatives we concluded that there were far less barriers in the south of the county to amalgamation with Gwent. (Boundary Commission for Wales, 1983, 9, #34)

Gwent's entitlement was 5.6 seats, so a combination of the two Counties would produce a joint entitlement of 7.01. (The County of Powys comprises the former Counties of Brecknock, Radnor and Montgomery, which are arranged south–north along

the Welsh border with England; Gwent lies to the south and east of Brecknock; Meri-
oneth is to the west of Montgomery, on the western side of the main divide.)

The Commission's provisional recommendations were for a Powys North constituency wholly within Powys, having an electorate of 57,877, and for another
called Abergavenny and Brecon which crossed the County boundary, combining
the industrial areas around the former town with the rural areas to the north. Amal-
gamation of the two Counties was the main issue addressed at the Local Inquiry,
and the Assistant Commissioner concluded that it should be abandoned: instead
Powys should have two constituencies and Gwent six.

> We accepted that we had underrated the disadvantages of our provisional scheme
> combining the two counties and that there were very strong reasons advanced at the
> inquiry and contained in the assistant Commissioner's report for separating Gwent
> from Powys. If Powys were to be separate it seemed obvious that it should be allo-
> cated two constituencies. We noted that with such an allocation the average of each
> seat would be nearer the electoral quota than if one seat were allocated by round-
> ing down the theoretical entitlement [see below on the harmonic mean]. Geo-
> graphical considerations were the deciding factor: with two constituencies our
> proposals could pay much better regard to the shape and accessibility of the county,
> and the area of the largest constituency we had proposed would be reduced.

As a result, the number of seats allocated in Wales was increased. By the time of
the Fourth Review, Gwent was entitled to 5.75 seats and Powys 1.62 and so they
retained their Third Review complements.

Scotland
The issue of crossing Regional boundaries was raised in Scotland during the public consultation period of the Third Review. The Commission had decided during its preliminary discussion of general principles that the number of
constituencies there should be kept at 71, in the light of its predecessor's statement that 'an increase in Scottish representation was not necessary nor could it
reasonably be justified having regard to the position in Great Britain as a whole'
(Boundary Commission for Scotland, 1969, 6, #10) and the slower rate of growth
of the Scottish electorate since, relative to both England and Wales (Boundary
Commission for Scotland, 1983, 10, #23). It noted, however, that (11, #28):

> A number of theoretical entitlements were near the midway point between two
> whole numbers. In these cases we took into account whether or not there were spe-
> cial geographical considerations (as in Borders and Highland Regions) or other fac-
> tors in deciding whether to allocate the higher or lower number of seats. Not all
> theoretical entitlements could be rounded up given our conclusion at the initial stage
> that the number of seats should remain at 71.

The Commission was unwilling to tackle this problem by recommending constituencies that crossed Regional boundaries. It presented its interpretation of the
new Rule 4 that in Scotland 'regard shall be had to the boundaries of local authority areas' with the clause 'i.e. the boundaries of regions, islands, areas and dis-

tricts' (Boundary Commisssion for Scotland, 1983, 10, #24) and continued:

> In pursuance of Rule 4 we resolved to avoid making recommendations for constituencies which would cross regional boundaries except in the most exceptional circumstances where special geographical considerations made this desirable.

Three Regions 'suffered' from this in the provisional recommendations – Lothian, Strathclyde and Tayside: Lothian's entitlement of 10.60 was rounded-down to 10; Tayside's 5.51 was reduced to 5; and for Strathclyde the Commission provisionally recommended 32 against the entitlement of 33.29.

The Commission justified its provisional recommendations for Lothian, Strathclyde and Tayside thus: 'There are no special geographical considerations which would justify the inclusion in any constituency of a part of any other region' (Boundary Commission for Scotland, 1983, 43, #127(b); 57, #169(b); and 88, #253(b)). The issue was apparently not raised in the representations received with regard to the Lothian Region, nor at either of the two Local Inquiries held there but in Tayside the Commission stated that, in addition to the general statement regarding special geographical considerations, 'Given our resolve not to cross regional boundaries we saw no way of avoiding the formation of one geographically large constituency, i.e. North Tayside' (88, #253(e)). The City of Aberdeen District Council argued that the north-east of Scotland was generally under-represented in the provisional recommendations: Grampian Region's entitlement of 6.38 had been rounded-down to 6 and Tayside's of 5.51 to 5; jointly they were entitled to 11.89, and a constituency crossing the District boundary would enable 12 to be allocated. (Part of the rationale for this argument was to allow the City of Aberdeen to be allocated three seats rather than the two provisionally recommended; six of the City's 25 Regional Electoral Divisions were placed in two constituencies that included a majority of Districts outwith the City boundaries.)

In considering this case, the Assistant Commissioner who conducted the Local Inquiry in Grampian Region is recorded as stating that Rules 5 and 6 allow for Rule 4 to be set aside only in exceptional circumstances. Rule 5, for example, uses the words 'strict application' in referring to Rule 4's requirement that regard shall be had to local authority area boundaries. The issue for him, therefore, was identified as asking (Boundary Commission for Scotland, 1983, 29, #81):

> whether it is practicable to adhere to that boundary and whether departure from that boundary is desirable to avoid excessive disparity of the types mentioned in Rule 5, or for geographical considerations as mentioned in Rule 6. The assistant Commissioner added that a regional boundary appeared to be of a more fundamental character in terms of local administration than a District boundary.

(Rule 7 also allows rules other than Rule 4 to be over-ridden in the context of breaking community ties and the consequences of change, but could not be applied in this situation because of the new local government template.) He concluded that Rule 6 could not be used to justify a cross-boundary constituency and, in the context of Rule 5, that 'it is not the case that it is impracticable to have regard to, and use, the boundary between the two regions for Parliamentary constituency purposes'. He also argued that '"hiving off" parts of the City of Aberdeen District … is not so objectionable in principle that some other course of action is to be preferred' (Boundary Commission for Scotland, 1983, 30, #81) and reached a final conclusion that 'there are not factors of sufficient weight to make it desirable to depart from the regional boundary'. The Assistant Commissioner who chaired the Tayside Local Inquiry considered the same arguments and reached a similar conclusion.

By the time of its Fourth Periodic Review, the Scottish Commission was even firmer in its view that no increase in the number of seats could be justified. It decided 'to settle on a target number of seats which we considered would be sustainable for the duration of the review' (Boundary Commission for Scotland, 1995, 13, #5) and published a memorandum in March 1993 (reprinted as Appendix D to its Report, pp.167–9), which included the following paragraph (169, #7):

> In view of the experience of the previous Review, the Commission has decided to explore the possibility of grouping regions together in order to provide a means of achieving a total number of constituencies not greater than 72 in circumstances whereby the number of seats allocated to any amalgamated area is not less than that which the electorate of the area justifies.

It reports that it encountered no reason to reconsider its policy during the Review and received no representations that Scotland's representation be increased (13, #5). Crossing Regional boundaries, for reasons other than 'special geographical considerations', was presented as a necessary corollary of the policy on the number of seats (14, #6); the Commission argued that the requirement that it have regard to local authority area boundaries is a positive one that does not prohibit cross-boundary constituencies being proposed (#7), and contended that the relative weakness of Rule 4(b) for Scotland means that Rule 5 'does not apply so strongly' there (15, #10): the latter, in particular, facilitated its argument that the 'theoretical entitlements' calculated by dividing each Region's electorate by the electoral quota, 'have a certain illustrative and practical value [but] they have no status in law' (16, #14). Thus it was decided that, given the importance of Rule 6 in parts of Scotland, 'if it was necessary to give effect to other aspects of the Rules, particularly Rule 5 which seeks to minimise disparity in electorates, we should make proposals which cross regional boundaries' (17, #15).

The 'most practical pairings' identified (Boundary Commssion for Scotland, 1995, 18, #16) were Borders and Lothian Regions and Central and Tayside Regions. The separate entitlements of the former pair were 1.54 and 10.83, giving a rounded-up total of 13; together they were entitled to 12.37, which was rounded-down to 12. It was noted that prior to the Third Periodic Review parts of the Borders Region had been linked with areas now in Lothian and it was decided to recommend two cross-boundary constituencies, linking Berwickshire with East Lothian and Tweeddale with Midlothian. These were opposed locally in the Borders Region, where the status quo was preferred and it was claimed that the Commission had elevated Rule 5 above Rule 4; in any case, the electorates of the exist-ing constituencies were growing and coming closer to the Scottish quota. The Assistant Commissioner reported that he 'was impressed by the sheer number of objections from both Borders and Lothian (but particularly the former) which saw no case for these 2 areas to share Parliamentary representation' (30, #15), but there were conflicting representations regarding both the desirability of equality in elec-torates and links between the areas within the proposed cross-boundary con-stituencies. He 'was persuaded by the arguments for making minimal changes to the existing 4 county constituencies' (i.e. outside Edinburgh; 32, #24) and also considered that the Commission's approach was open to legal challenge in the light of the *Foot et al.* judgement (p. 113). The Commission rejected the latter point, claiming that Rule 4 was less strict in its application to Scotland than to England, but accepted that his alternative recommendations for the four non-Edin-burgh constituencies reflected both 'greater adherence to local ties and regional and district boundaries' (34, #32). The revised recommendations thus included only one constituency which crossed the Regional boundary, rather than two, and no new evidence was presented which led to further modifications.

The Central and Tayside Regions also both had theoretical entitlements which implied 'rounding-up' to a total of ten seats, but their joint electorates justified only 9 (rounded down from 9.47); one cross-boundary constituency was provisionally recommended as a consequence, which also had the benefit of allowing minimum disruption to boundaries elsewhere in the Regions (Boundary Commission for Scot-land, 1996, 45, #4-5). The cross-boundary Ochil constituency was the focus of much of the local concern, though largely for reasons other than its cross-boundary nature: only its detailed composition was altered in the revised recommendations, therefore.

Other district boundaries

Although the requirement to respect local government District boundaries was removed from the *House of Commons (Redistribution of Seats) Act* by the *Local Government Acts* of the early 1970s, the government indicated that it expected the Commissions to 'have regard to' the new boundaries implemented. The greater size of the smaller number of such Districts made conformity between District and constituency boundaries more difficult, as illustrated above, but the Commissions clearly made substantial efforts to follow the government's advice.

The Welsh Commission has reported fully on its achievements. Its report on the Third Periodic Review included (Boundary Commission for Wales, 1983, 55, #211–12):

211 Seven constituencies would be coterminous with district boundaries and twelve more would not be divided between districts. Eighteen would be divided between two districts and one (Clwyd South West) would include the whole of one and parts of two other districts.
212 Conversely, eighteen districts would not be divided between constituencies, sixteen would be divided between two constituencies, two (Swansea and Wrex-ham Maelor) would be divided between three constituencies and one (Cardiff) would be divided between four constituencies.

Twelve years later it claimed an improved performance (Boundary Commission for Wales, 1995, 49, #193–4 ,):

193 Eleven of our recommended constituencies are co-terminous with districts and thirteen more are not divided between districts. Fourteen are divided between two districts and one (Vale of Clwyd) includes the whole of one and parts of two other districts, while Monmouth includes parts of three districts.

194 Conversely, nineteen districts will not be divided between constituencies, fifteen will be divided between two constituencies, two (Glyndwr and Swansea) will be divided between three constituencies, and one (Cardiff) will be divided between four constituencies. In the case of the cities of Cardiff and Swansea this is not surprising because of the size of their respective populations.

The English Commission made slightly less of its achievements, simply reporting in 1995 that 159 of its recommended constituencies crossed non-Metropolitan District boundaries, compared to 167 in the Third Periodic Review (Boundary Commission for England, 1995a, 9, #2.25). The Scottish Commission reported in 1983 that (Boundary Commission for Scotland, 1983, 97, #276):

Ten constituencies … consist of a complete district, and one constituency … consists of a complete islands area. Three constituencies … each consist of two complete districts, and one … consists of two complete islands areas. Two complete districts … are divided into two constituencies each. Thirty-three constituencies consist of part of one district only, and 16 consist of one district and part of another, or parts of two districts. Two constituencies … consist of two districts and part of one other, and one … consists of one district and parts of two others. One constituency … consists of three districts and part of one other.

In 1982 the Northern Ireland Commission reported that, outside Belfast, its final recommendations 'involved the splitting of 6 district council areas [out of 25]. This has understandably attracted criticism from the areas involved but it seems to us the best compromise upon the relevant considerations' (Boundary Commission for Northern Ireland, 1982, 13, #4.2). Thirteen years later, its successor reported that Belfast and eight other local government Districts were divided in its provisional recommendations (Boundary Commission for Northern Ireland, 1995, 62, #26), which was justified as offering 'the minimum disruption to the framework of local government consistent with other constraints'. No summary is offered for the final recommendations: only four of the 18 constituencies did not contain part only of at least one District, and only 17 of the 26 Districts were undivided. Tables 4.5 and 4.6 summarise the outcomes of the Third and Fourth Periodic Reviews. The first shows the number of Districts (part or whole) in each constituency, and indicates that the English and Welsh Commissions achieved a slightly better fit at the second of the reviews, whereas the Scottish and Northern Irish 'performance' deteriorated somewhat – substantially so in the latter case. Apart from Northern Ireland, where Districts are on average much smaller, each Commission was able to achieve a modal allocation of only one District per constituency.

Table 4.5 *The number of local government districts by constituency at the Third and Fourth Periodic Reviews*

	Districts per Constituency				
	1	2	3	4	5
England (Nonmetropolitan Counties only)					
Third Review	140	146	23	0	0
Fourth Review	156	144	29	2	0
Scotland					
Third Review	51	16	2	3	0
Fourth Review	49	15	7	1	0
Wales					
Third Review	19	18	1	0	0
Fourth Review	24	14	2	0	0
Northern Ireland					
Third Review	3	9	4	1	0
Fourth Review	1	12	5	0	0

Table 4.6 *The number of constituencies by local government district at the Third and Fourth Periodic Reviews*

	Constituencies per District				
	1	2	3	4	5
England (Nonmetropolitan Counties only)					
Third Review	130	136	24	5	1
Fourth Review	101	147	42	5	2
Scotland (excluding Edinburgh and Glasgow)					
Third Review	34	15	2	3	0
Fourth Review	27	20	6	1	0
Wales					
Third Review	18	16	2	1	0
Fourth Review	19	15	2	1	0
Northern Ireland					
Third Review	19	5	0	2	0
Fourth Review	17	5	3	1	0

'Doughnuts' and 'sandwiches'

An issue which generated much discussion during these reviews in England concerned the policy to be followed when a District containing an urban area was to be divided into two constituencies: should the urban component be separated from the surrounding rural area – producing a 'doughnut' effect – or should the town be split so that each constituency was part-urban and part-rural – the so-called 'sandwich'? This came to prominence during the Third Review with the case of Colchester in Essex, which up until then had a separate constituency for the urban area.

(Colchester's separate local authority had a much smaller area prior to the 1972 restructuring than the current one.) The Commission's provisional recommendations proposed a 'doughnut' which was likely to benefit the Labour party (in a 'sandwich' solution the Conservatives were likely to win both seats; with a 'doughnut' Labour had a good chance of winning the urban seat), and this was the focus of many representations. The Assistant Commissioner recommended change to the 'sandwich' solution after representations from the Conservative-dominated Borough Council, however, and this was implemented. As the Boundary Commission later noted (Parliamentary Boundary Commission for England, 1991, 34):

> The argument for this arrangement was that the shopping, recreational and educational activities of the rural areas were centred upon the town, and that as far as possible they should be included in the same constituencies.

It further noted, however, that this solution 'proved to be no more popular locally than the original proposal; which seemed to suggest that many people who approved the Commission's original recommendations had presumed that these would not be revised and they therefore did not bother to notify their support'.[4]

The issue recurred in the Fourth Review's provisional recommendation that Colchester's 'sandwich' be retained. This was strongly, and successfully, countered by the local authority (by then under Liberal Democrat control) and many others, part of whose case was that the 'doughnut' solution was widely used in other Counties, and that Colchester (as Great Britain's oldest recorded town) should be treated similarly.[5] As it reported the issue (Boundary Commission for England, 1995a, 190 # 16,):

> One political party [Conservative] supported a town divided on substantially existing lines. They stated that the combination of rural and urban interests within the seats worked well and reflected the perspective of the majority of the local people. The two serving MPs said that the division gave rise to no disadvantages.

Against this, the other political parties argued that (#17):

> [Colchester's] size did not render a division essential; it had no natural division and had only been divided since 1983; the division was opposed by a large number of residents; the rural communities in the town's hinterland had more in common with each other than with the town; and affinity felt by the rural communities was with the town as a whole, not any particular part of it; and one of the town's most distinctive features, the garrison, was split between two seats.

The Assistant Commissioner 'could see merit in the arguments on both sides' (#18) but 'was persuaded that re-unification of the town in a single seat would better respect local ties and receive more support than any division of the town'. At the same time, he accepted linked counter-proposals presented by that consortium of local authorities which reduced both the number of constituencies crossing District boundaries and the amount of change from the existing constituencies (Figure 4.5), but in so-doing created problems in producing acceptable constituencies for the nearby Chelmsford urban area.

Figure 4.5 *The Boundary Commission's provisional and final recommendations for Essex County in the Fourth Periodic Review, showing constituency and district boundaries*
Source: based on the Ordnance Survey map with the permission of The Controller of
Her Majesty's Stationery Office © Crown Copyright

The issue of 'doughnut' versus 'sandwich' was raised in a number of examples, and led the Commission to devote three paragraphs to it in the general section of its final report (Boundary Commission for England, 1995a, 9–10 #2.32-2.34,). It stressed that 'We had no single formula or policy for choosing between the alternatives but tried to find the best scheme for each town, within the overall consideration of the county' (#2.33), but its final recommendations included many more 'doughnuts' than 'sandwiches', which meant greater separation of the two main parties' supporters than might otherwise have been the case (and which therefore almost certainly benefited the Labour party at the subsequent general election of 1997).

Electoral equality

Set against the organic requirement of respecting and/or having regard to the local government map the Commissions also have to implement the mathematic requirement of equal-sized constituency electorates, as far as is practicable. From the outset of the period this has been considered a primary requirement by the Commissions, and one which it has been difficult to meet, especially before the local government reforms of the 1970s, because of the apparently greater importance of fitting constituencies into the local government template.

Concern over Rule 5 was expressed in the English Commission's Initial Report, which set out the criteria that it applied with regard to electoral equality; 'Our general aim was the creation of constituencies as near the electoral quota as practicable consistent with the preservation of local unities' (Boundary Commission for England, 1947, 4, #10) but it also set itself tolerance limits, albeit weaker than those in the original 1944 Bill of a maximum deviation of 25 per cent (#11):

> As a general guide to the formulation of our provisional recommendations we adopted a rough working rule under which electorates within a range 50,000 to 70,000 were treated as normal [the electoral quota was 59,312]; electorates of under 50,000 and over 70,000 were treated as exceptional and subject to special consideration, while no constituency should be created with an electorate of less than 40,000 or more than 90,000.

It reported that of the 489 constituencies recommended, 73 per cent fell within the normal range, and 27 per cent within the special range; none had an electorate of less than 40,000 or more than 87,100.

Within this general context, however, the Commission indicated that it applied separate guidelines to urban and rural areas, having accepted 'the view that in general urban constituencies could more conveniently support large electorates than rural constituencies' (Boundary Commission for England, 1947, 5, #14). Many large urban areas had electorates exceeding 70,000 and it was 'impressed by the advantages of accessibility they enjoy over widely scattered rural areas'; this led to the conclusion that urban constituencies could sustain larger electorates than their rural counterparts 'and would in a majority of cases prefer to do so rather than suffer severance of local unity for Parliamentary purposes' (#12; it argued that strict application of the 25 per cent deviation rule in the 1944 Act would have required many large towns to be divided). In effect, the Commission was implicitly applying Rule 6 regarding special geographical considerations somewhat generously,[6] by arguing that the 'difficulties and disadvantages attendant upon the creation of large rural constituencies' (#14) justified treating a departure 'from close approximation to the electoral quota' for all rural areas under the rubric for special geographical considerations – 'size, shape and accessibility'. This issue was not raised by any of the other Commissions then; there was a single British electoral quota at the time which, if applied in Scotland and Wales, would have prevented them allocating the minimum number of seats guaranteed to each country by Rule 1.

The English Commission returned to the urban–rural issue in its First Periodical Report because its policy had in part been over-ridden by Parliament which had required the creation of additional constituencies in several of the Boroughs with recommended electorates above 80,000. The Commission saw 'no reason to recede from the view expressed in our initial report' that 'in general, urban constituencies could more conveniently support large electorates than rural constituencies' (Boundary Commission for England, 1954, 5, #14), but accepted that Parliament wished a greater balance between the two than it had recommended in 1947. The Commission undoubtedly felt it had achieved that by recommending that 410 of the 511 constituencies (80 per cent) have electorates between 45,000 and 65,000 (the quota was 55,670), with none either below 40,000 or above 80,000. Once again, this issue was not addressed by the Scottish and Welsh Commissions in their reports, both of which recommended no change to a majority of constituencies (see below); the Northern Ireland Commission recommended no change to any of its twelve constituencies, two of which deviated from the electoral quota by 17 per cent, on the grounds that in Belfast at least 'The figures are fluctuating, and will continue for some time to do so, owing to building developments' (Boundary Commission for Northern Ireland, 1954, 3, #5(b)).

Fifteen years later, the English Commission dropped the concept of an urban–rural difference in the redistribution process, noting the considerable shift of population outside the cities and towns since the previous review. Whereas in 1953 the average Borough constituency had 57,883 electors and the average County constituency 56,093, by 1965, without any changes to constituency boundaries, the respective figures were 56,208 and 62,081 (Boundary Commission for England, 1969, 6, #34). The Commission considered whether 'we should give some weighting in favour of rural constituencies' (#36), although there was nothing in the rules allowing for such a distinction, and eventually rejected it (#37):

> It can be argued that extensive rural constituencies with possibly poor communications present problems for the Member of Parliament in representing his [or her] constituency, for the public in meeting their member, and for local political party organisations. These problems, however, may not be so great today as in the past.

On the contrary, it has been argued that a member representing a borough constituency, more accessible as he is to the electorate, may be faced with more community problems than a Member for a county constituency. Our discussions with
the chief officers of the political parties led us to the view that the arguments were
evenly balanced and that there was no obvious case for deliberately seeking to create constituencies with smaller electorates in the rural areas. We did, however, take
account of Rule 6 (special geographical considerations) in certain exceptional areas.

As a result, the Commission should have been even better able to concentrate
constituencies within the 50,000-70,000 electors band, which was its stated aim
(#32): it placed 75 per cent of constituencies there, with a further 24 per cent
within the broader limits of 40,000-80,000, but with four constituencies having
recommended electorates below 40,000 (68, #70). Interestingly, although two of
these – Berwick-upon-Tweed and Leominster – were in relatively remote rural
areas the others – Thanet West and Norwich North – were not; with the former
the Commission felt it necessary to treat the Isle of Thanet as separated from the
rest of Kent – Thanet East had an electorate of 41,521 (Boundary Commission
for England, 1969, 45) – and the two Norwich seats were small because of a decision not to cross the County Borough boundaries.

Changes in attitudes to a claim for separate treatment for rural areas over the
period of the first three Reviews interestingly follow changes in political power
in the country. On receipt of the English Commission's Initial Report in 1947 the
Labour government determined that the 'rural weighting' applied by the Commission should be removed by requiring that several of the largest urban constituencies be subdivided (p. 86 above). It thus over-ruled the Commission's view,
but the latter persevered with it in its First Periodical Report, as described above,
and this was accepted by the Conservative government. There was a Labour government in place when the Commission was deliberating over policy for its Second Periodical Review, however, and at this stage it abandoned the implicit 'rural
weighting'.

Although the changes that they recommended achieved greater electoral equality among constituencies, neither the Scottish nor the Welsh Commission made
any general reference in their Second Periodical Review reports to a policy on
this issue, nor did they provide summary data on constituency size. The Northern Ireland Commission did make the issue explicit, however, including a table
which showed that the 1965 electorates of the current constituencies ranged from
47 per cent above to 24 per cent below the electoral quota (Boundary Commission for Northern Ireland, 1969, 3, #3). Its goal was to bring those 'several electorates closer to the electoral quota' (4, #6), and a further table showed that its
final recommendations reduced the variation to 16 per cent above and 17 per cent
below (7, #18).

The greater detail provided by the English Commission in its Second Periodical Report was an innovation taken up by the others at the time of the next review,
with more justification of their decisions and more analysis of the outcome. Somewhat paradoxically, the English Commission was less precise in presenting its

strategy then, noting that between 1965 and 1976 (the enumeration dates for the Second and Third Reviews) England's electorate had increased by nearly four million, and the electoral quota by some 7,000. The changes were unevenly distributed, however, in part because of population movements and in part because of the enfranchisement of young people (the minimum voting age was reduced to 18 in 1968). Nevertheless, the Commission 'preferred not to adopt such wide limits for constituency electorates' as had been the case with the two previous reviews (Boundary Commission for England, 1983, 7, #11), but if it had adopted guidelines these were not published – it merely referred to 'a need to redress the existing imbalance of representation and to avoid excessive disparities between the electorates of neighbouring constituencies. However, we thought we would have to allow some flexibility in order to meet any exceptional circumstances'. Twelve years later, its Report on the Fourth Periodic Review contained no discussion at all of variation around the quota in its chapter on 'General Principles', other than the statement that 'We aim to recommend seats which are as close as practicable to the county or London borough average and thereby to the electoral quota' (Boundary Commission for England, 1995a,8, #2.12).

The Scottish Commission used similar words in its reference to the issue when reporting on the Third Periodic Review: 'we saw it as the primary objective of the review to recommend, where practicable, a constituency with a near-average electorate' (Boundary Commission for Scotland, 1969, 10–11, #26). In its next report, it implied that Rule 5 had a greater import for Scotland than for England or Wales because of the weaker wording of Rule 4 relating to Scottish local government boundaries; the choice of words to describe its policy was, however exactly those quoted above for the previous review. The Welsh Commission recorded that with the changes in local government boundaries prior to the Third Periodic Review, and in particular the reduction in the number of Counties from fourteen to eight, 'our prime consideration for the areas of these former Counties must now be their equal representation with the electorates of other areas, whereas in previous reviews there was strong justification for keeping the boundaries of constituencies within those county boundaries even though this created high disparities' (Boundary Commission for Wales, 1969, 3, #9). Only the Northern Ireland Commission set itself strict guidelines: in 1982 it reported that 'we adopted the established objective of having all constituencies within a tolerance of 10 per cent (above or below) of the quota of 61,206' (Boundary Commission for Northern Ireland, 1982, 2, #1.7), a criterion which was hardened thirteen years later, when 'the Commission constructed a set of principles on which to base their decisions' (Boundary Commission for Northern Ireland, 1995, 3, #5), that included 'to promote electoral equality by aiming, in the first instance, to restrict constituency electorates to within a tolerance of 7 per cent above or below the electoral quota'

The Commissions' commitment to promoting electoral equality within the changed local government context is illustrated by their inclusion of summary tables in the reports of their Third and Fourth Periodic Reviews to show the distribution of constituency sizes as deviations from the relevant electoral quota. Their main purpose was to show that a major consequence of the review has been a significant reduction in those deviations, by comparing the existing and recommended constituencies. They also allowed the Commissions to indicate how successful they had been so that, for example: in England 75 per cent of recommendations were within 10 per cent of the Third Review quota, as were 84 per cent in the Fourth; in Scotland, 57 per cent were within 10 per cent of the Third Review quota, with a further 33 per cent within 20 per cent, and at the Fourth Review the Scottish Commission reported 36 per cent within 5 per cent of the quota and a further 33 per cent within 10 per cent; in Wales, the Commission claimed that 33 of its 38 proposed Third Review constituencies were within 15 per cent of the quota, as were 37 of the 40 at the next Review.

The Third Periodic Review marked a major shift in the outcome of the Commissions' reviews with regard to this criterion, therefore, somewhat surprisingly given the change of emphasis suggested by the 1958 amendments to the Act (Box 3.4), and their interpretation. In its report on the Second Periodic Review, for example, the English Commission stated that (Boundary Commission for England, 1969, 5, #27–8):

> The debates on the Redistribution Bill in 1958 showed, moreover, a broad measure of agreement that local ties were of greater importance than strict mathematical equality. … 'The effect of the Bill', said the Home Secretary, 'is to bring in a presumption against making changes unless there is a very strong case for them'.

> We therefore began the review with the intention, of avoiding, where possible, proposals that would change constituency boundaries for the sake of adjustments in the size of electorates. We also considered it reasonable to assume that each existing constituency normally represents a community with its own distinct community problems and traditions. Ties of many sorts may exist within this local community and we believe it to be proper for these ties, whatever they may be, to be taken fully into account before a constituency is disturbed.

Nevertheless, although this apparently influenced their decisions then, by the time of the Third Review the salience of electoral equality had apparently increased.

This conclusion is illustrated by the deviations of each constituency's electorate from the relevant electoral quota. (After 1958 there was a separate quota for each country; before that, the single British quota really only applied in England because in the other three parts of the country its application was precluded by the minimum number of seats to which each was entitled.) The difference between each constituency's electorate and the electoral quota is expressed as a percentage of the latter sum, so that, for example, in a constituency with an electorate of 50,000 when the quota was 55,000 the deviation would be −9.09 per cent [((50,000–55,000)/55,000) * 100]. The summary statistics for these deviations are in Table 4.7.

These data support two main conclusions. The first is that the Commissions have become increasingly efficient at narrowing the range of constituency elec-

Table 4.7 *Deviations from the electoral quota as percentages of that quota: summary statistics (the means are calculated irrespective of sign)*

	Minimum	Maximum	Mean	SD	±10%*
England					
Initial	−30.7	46.7	11.9	9.0	53.9
First	−29.2	36.2	10.5	8.0	56.2
Second	−34.1	35.6	11.2	8.5	51.4
Third	−21.4	34.5	7.3	6.7	74.7
Fourth	−21.4	46.9	5.8	4.7	87.0
Scotland					
Initial	−47.4	33.7	12.3	11.7	57.8
First	−47.3	38.5	13.5	11.5	48.0
Second	−53.8	25.5	14.0	12.7	47.8
Third	−57.7	20.2	10.3	9.7	57.0
Fourth	−57.8	22.8	8.9	8.9	73.7
Wales					
Initial	−46.7	40.7	15.3	11.8	39.2
First	−44.4	45.7	16.1	11.9	42.0
Second	−48.5	44.5	17.4	12.5	36.4
Third	−48.2	14.0	9.3	9.6	68.4
Fourth	−43.8	14.7	8.1	8.0	75.0
Northern Ireland					
Initial	−12.3	14.6	5.1	4.6	83.0
First	−17.0	16.8	8.8	5.4	66.4
Second	−15.6	18.1	6.8	6.1	74.7
Third	−7.1	8.0	4.6	3.3	100.0
Fourth	−16.4	5.0	7.1	6.0	77.8

* The percentage of constituencies within 10 percentage points of the mean

torates relative to the electoral quotas, especially so since the local government restructuring that preceded the Third Periodic Review. Prior to that the ranges and standard deviations (SDs) were large (Table 4.7), and the mean deviations high – with the exception of Northern Ireland. At both the Third and the Fourth Reviews, however, the means and standard deviations were reduced very substantially (except for Northern Ireland at the Fourth Review, when the late decision to add an eighteenth seat produced greater deviations from an electoral quota based on seventeen). The ranges remain substantial, notably in Scotland and Wales which each have a small number of small constituencies because of special geographical considerations, but the increased concentration of constituencies with deviations of less than +/−10 per cent is considerable. Very large constituencies relative to the electoral quota are now extremely rare – with only one more than 30 per cent above the quota in the Fourth Review: the Isle of Wight (see below, p. 175) – as are those more than 20 per cent below, save the special geographical cases in Scotland and Wales.

Within each local government unit to which constituencies are allocated (Counties and London Boroughs in England, Counties in Wales, Regions in Scotland), the average electorate is likely to vary from the electoral quota because few units qualify for exact integer allocations. For the Third and Fourth Reviews, we have calculated the percentage deviations from both the electoral quota and the local average constituency electorate. In addition, for those reviews the Commissions published their full provisional as well as final recommendations (the English and Welsh Commissions did so for the Second Review, too), which allows us to compare their initial and their final recommendations on this key indicator.

Comparing deviations around the electoral quotas and local averages (Table 4.8) shows that each Commission produced more compact outcomes at the Fourth than at the Third Review against both norms, at both the provisional and final recommendations stage, with two exceptions:

1 As discussed elsewhere (p. 155), the Welsh Commission's decision at the final recommendation stage to keep Gwent and Powys separate in the Third Review was sustained in its provisional recommendations for the Fourth, hence the much larger deviations then (considerations of electoral equality led to the provisional recommendation to merge the two Counties in the Third Review).

2 Similarly, the decision of the Northern Ireland Commission to create an eighteenth constituency there after receiving representations on its provisional recommendations meant greater variability around the quota (see p. 187), and also the local average at the final stage of the Fourth compared to the Third Review.

With those two exceptions, the means are smaller, indicating closer conformity to the quota or local average overall, and the standard deviations are smaller too, indicating more compressed distributions.

Comparison of the provisional and final recommendations shows that in most cases the pattern of deviations was smaller at the first than at the second stage, especially with regard to deviations around the local average. At the Fourth Review, for example, the average constituency deviated by only 3.62 per cent from the average electorate for all seats in that local government unit in the English Commission's provisional recommendations, but by 4.22 per cent in its final recommendations. The implication is clearly that electoral equality was of less concern to those who made successful representations than were other criteria, notably local community ties, on which many of their cases were made, albeit usually to promote partisan electoral interests (see p. 302). The Commissions' responses to these cases led to more variability. In Nottinghamshire at the Fourth Review, for example, the Commission's provisional recommendations for eleven constituencies, six of which were unchanged from those adopted after the Third Review, showed a mean deviation from the electoral quota of 3.09 per cent, and from the local average of 1.90 (the standard deviations were 1.99 and 1.55 respectively). Those appearing at the Local Inquiry convinced the Assistant Commissioner that none of the eleven existing constituencies should be changed and his advice to this effect was adopted for the final recommendations; the mean deviations were then 3.53 per cent from the electoral quota and 3.40 from the local average (standard deviations 3.20 and 1.46). Public participation led to some increase in the variation among constituencies in their electorates, as local issues were introduced to counter the general principles applied by the Commission prior to its consultation phase.

Table 4.8 *Deviations from the electoral quota and the local average at the Third and Fourth Periodic Reviews, provisional and final recommendations: summary statistics*

	Electoral Quota				Local Average			
	Third		Fourth		Third		Fourth	
	Mean	SD	Mean	SD	Mean	SD	Mean	SD
England								
Provisional	6.94	6.46	5.24	4.23	5.06	5.37	3.62	3.08
Final	7.31	6.68	4.77	4.68	5.68	5.62	4.22	3.22
Scotland								
Provisional	11.06	9.88	8.33	8.63	7.13	6.50	6.52	5.26
Final	10.33	9.74	8.86	8.89	6.88	6.81	7.22	5.68
Wales								
Provisional	4.43	3.07	8.00	7.99	3.32	2.36	5.88	5.88
Final	9.29	9.59	8.12	7.98	7.06	6.57	6.01	5.89
Northern Ireland								
Provisional	3.61	2.38	3.35	2.10	3.61	2.38	3.22	2.07
Final	4.56	3.33	7.12	6.01	4.56	3.33	5.78	3.97
Within England								
	Mean	SD	Mean	SD	Mean	SD	Mean	SD
Non-Metropolitan Counties								
Provisional	6.07	6.77	4.54	3.55	4.90	5.97	3.28	2.60
Final	6.55	6.95	6.53	4.37	5.50	6.17	4.10	2.86
Metropolitan Counties								
Provisional	7.08	5.00	5.36	4.24	6.73	4.67	5.29	4.11
Final	7.27	5.40	5.47	4.27	7.14	5.11	5.35	4.22
Greater London								
Provisional	9.95	6.30	8.16	5.56	3.14	2.45	2.34	1.55
Final	10.27	6.62	8.28	5.74	4.06	3.06	2.86	1.91

The Commissions' ability to meet the requirements of Rule 5 is easier in some areas than others because of the size of the wards that they use as building blocks. Urban areas generally have larger wards than their rural counterparts, as illustrated for England by Table 4.9 in which average ward electorates in 1991 are given by three local District types – Nonmetropolitan and Metropolitan Counties and London Boroughs – with two of them subdivided: the Nonmetropolitan Counties are divided into urban and rural (the former are Avon and Cleveland, which are dominated by the Bristol and Teesside conurbations respectively); and the London Boroughs are divided into those which were and were not paired for the Fourth Periodic Review. The urban areas had the largest wards, especially in the Metropolitan Counties, which reflects the rules applied by the Local Government Commission for electoral arrangements. Each Metropolitan District should have a Council comprising no more than 99 elected members, and each ward must return three members. As a consequence the largest cities have large wards; the largest, Birmingham, had an electorate of 737,310 in 1991, for example, and its 39 wards averaged 18,905 electors. (Even so, its number of councillors exceeds the 'ideal' set by the Local Government Boundary Commission.)

Table 4.9 *Average ward electorate by local government type in England, 1991*

	Mean	SD
Nonmetropolitan		
Rural	3,229	626
Urban	4,189	566
Metropolitan District	10,231	1,875
London Borough		
Unpaired	6,814	1,574
Paired	6,166	1,217

The smaller the number of wards relative to the number of constituencies the greater the potential problems for the Commissions. Their task involves selecting that grouping of adjacent wards into constituencies which best meets the criteria set out in the Rules, and the fewer the wards the greater the constraints. (The nature of this combinatorial problem in urban areas was discussed in the context of the Third Periodic Review in Johnston and Rossiter, 1982, 1983.) Birmingham was allocated eleven constituencies, and the Commission recommended six containing four wards each with average electorates of 72,559 plus five (average electorates 60,390) with three wards each – the largest three were combined in the Sutton Coldfield seat, with an electorate of 72,487. (With ten constituencies, each could have contained four wards, with average electorates of 73,731; see p. 279.)

For this reason, the Metropolitan Counties had much larger deviations around the local averages than either their Nonmetropolitan counterparts or the London Boroughs, at both the Third and the Fourth Reviews (Table 4.8), although the variation was considerably reduced at the latter Review compared to the former. Interestingly, the smallest variations around the local average, though not the electoral quota, are recorded for Greater London. The large deviations around the quota reflect the problem of allocating an integer number of seats to relatively small local authorities, none of which was entitled to more than four constituencies at either review; the reduction in the variation from Third to Fourth Reviews reflects the decision to pair some Boroughs. Within each Borough, or pair of Boroughs in the Fourth Review, however, the Commission achieved very substantial equality, significantly more so than in the Nonmetropolitan Counties where there are many more, and much smaller, wards. The problems that the Commission faces in the latter – of the differences between town and country, the many local ties that have to be reflected (both those represented by District boundaries and those claimed by the inhabitants), the strong pressures for no change, and the 'geographical impediments' to grouping (such as unbridged estuaries in coastal Counties) – are rarely matched in London Boroughs, where the Commission is better able to tackle the combinatorial problem of amalgamating wards to produce equal-sized constituencies with few other constraints. Most London Boroughs have between 8 and 12 wards per constituency, providing the Commission with considerable freedom of action in meeting Rule 5.

Special geographical considerations

Rule 6 gives the Commissions greater flexibility in particular circumstances, and although the term 'geographical' has been interpreted by some to incorporate social concerns (such as the concentration of people of non-British origin, and thus not registered electors, in some inner city areas) the subsequent clause, referring to 'in particular the size, shape and accessibility of a constituency', implies that the intention is to allow special provision to be made in relatively isolated areas of low population density. (The Boundary Commission for England – 1995a, 9, #2.29 – states that 'we do not consider that, in all the circumstances, human or social geography are relevant considerations'. The issue was raised regarding proposals for the City of Westminster, where it was claimed that two wards should be in the same constituency because they contained England's largest Moroccan community; 43, #55. Elsewhere the Commission wrote that – Parliamentary Boundary Commission for England, 1991, 19 – 'The Commission are of the opinion that the "special geographical considerations" justifying departures from rules 4 and 5 occur mainly in Scotland and Wales and rarely in England'.) Although, as outlined above, the English Commission for some time interpreted this as justifying smaller constituencies (in terms of their numbers of electors) in rural than urban areas, the Rule has generally been applied very sparingly.

The English Commission made no reference to Rule 6 in the commentary on its Initial Report, although seven Counties, all rural, were allocated one more seat than their theoretical entitlement. The Welsh Commission noted that it had only divided a Rural District 'where we deemed a division necessary or desirable in order to give effect to Rule 6 or with a view to meeting local objections' (Boundary Commission for Wales, 1947, 4, #12), but the only Counties allocated more seats than their entitlement – Glamorgan and Monmouth – were the most urbanised then, as now, and no mention is made as to where Rule 6 was applied. The Scottish Commission, on the other hand, referred to six constituencies with recommended electorates below 36,000, in all of which cases it considered over-riding Rule 5 was justified by Rule 6 (Boundary Commission for Scotland, 1947, 5, #14). Finally, the Northern Ireland Commission cited Rule 6 to justify dividing the Larne Rural District between two constituencies, as not to have done so 'would have resulted not only in giving to one or other … a fantastic shape, but also an electorate greatly in excess of the electoral quota' (Boundary Commission for Northern Ireland, 1947, 6, #15).

The English Commission was again enigmatic in 1954, reporting that it had used the discretion provided by Rule 6 'as widely as circumstances appeared to us to justify it' (Boundary Commission for England, 1954, 6, #20) but giving no examples: five Counties received more seats than their entitlement, however, so we assume that they were employing it to justify the rural weighting discussed above. The Welsh Commission, even more enigmatically, started a paragraph by referring to the discretion provided by Rule 6 which led to it feeling 'justified in recommending that no alteration is required to be made to the boundaries of 30 of the 36 constituencies' (Boundary Commission for Wales, 1954, 2, #9). The Northern Ireland Commission recommended no change to any of its twelve constituencies, but without any reference to Rule 6, and the only changes recommended by the Scottish Commission had no impact on the northern and western regions.

In its Second Periodical Report the English Commission again referred to taking account of Rule 6 in 'certain exceptional areas' (Boundary Commission for England, 1969, 6, #37). Cornwall, Cumberland, Lancashire and Northumberland were all allocated one seat additional to their theoretical entitlements, but special geographical considerations were only specifically referred to in the case of Northumberland. The Commission noted that the urban areas (now in Tyne and Wear County) fully justified their allocation; the rural areas were entitled to 2.37 constituencies, but these 'would each contain about 615,000 acres and it was our provisional view that it would be undesirable to propose constituencies with such high electorates and acreages in this area' (Boundary Commission for England, 1969, 57). No mention is made of a similar case for an additional seat in Lancashire, and in both Cornwall and Cumberland the Commission provisionally recommended a reduction in their entitlement to four and three seats respectively. Local representations pressed for more; the Assistant Commissioner recommended that Cornwall should retain five seats 'on geographical grounds' (Boundary Commission for England, 1969, 33), and for Cumberland the Commissioner recommended that the four existing constituencies should remain unaltered, with the rules requiring separate representation for Carlisle County Borough. (In both of these last two cases, the Commission delayed acting on the Assistant Commissioners' reports until all of them had been received, since it did not want to allocate more seats. At a late stage, however, it decided to remove one seat each from West Yorkshire and Greater London because of population declines since the enumeration date, and this allowed it to increase the representation of both Cornwall and Cumberland, 'on geographical grounds' (8, #48), as well as Oxfordshire, where the population was growing rapidly.) The Welsh Commission had no particular need to refer to Rule 6, as it proposed changes in only the two most urbanised Counties – Glamorgan and Monmouth. The Scottish Commission recommended no changes in those areas where special geographical considerations had previously applied, however, and referred to them again in justifying its recommendations (Boundary Commission for Scotland, 1969, 7, #12-13).

The Commissions were much more explicit in their use of Rule 6 in their Third and Fourth Periodic Reviews, and also increasingly sparing with it, recommending seven additional seats on these grounds in the Third but only two in the Fourth, though special geographical considerations were cited for variations in constituency electorates within areas at the latter, in both England and Scotland. In reporting on its Third Review, the English Commission noted that the special discretion allowed by Rule 6 'would seldom apply to the constituencies in England' (Boundary Commission for England, 1983, 9, #20), but it awarded three additional seats by applying this rule – to Cumbria, Lancashire and Northumberland – because of 'large areas … , the geographical location of the centres of population and the lines of communication within the county' (i.e. Cumbria; 93, #109), 'sparsely populated fell areas' where, without an additional seat, there would have to be 'constituencies with excessively large areas and equally high electorates' (i.e. Lancashire; 120, #285), and 'large areas of sparsely populated country' (i.e. Northumberland; 128, #345). Twelve years later, however, it recorded that no extra seats had been allocated under this rule: 'the counties of Cumbria and Northumberland had a theoretical entitlement to the "extra seat" and, in our opinion, the reasons why Lancashire was given an extra seat no longer apply' (Boundary Commission for England, 1995a, 9, #2.30). In fact, the Commission allocated one seat less than necessary for 'special geographical considerations'. The Isle of Wight's entitlement to 1.47 seats justified allocating two on the harmonic mean rule (see below) but the Commission identified three reasons why it should not be allocated (219, #2):

1 The island is divided into two districts for local government purposes, but to use these as the bases for constituencies would produce a disparity of 12,212 between them, with one 35 per cent below the electoral quota.
2 No other suitable division was obvious; and
3 To place part of the island in a constituency with parts of Hampshire would create confusion and loss of identity and make the task of representing such a seat very difficult for its MP.

In Wales, as in England, one of the areas previously allocated an additional seat (Powys) now justified it on its electorate (Powys was entitled to two in 1983 on the harmonic mean rule, but this was not applied then), which left just one additional seat being recommended, in Gwynedd, where 'the geography of the county makes communication relatively difficult' (Boundary Commission for Wales,

1995, 31, #124). Similarly in Scotland, the Commission continued to recommend a very small constituency (23,015 electors) for the Western Isles on these grounds, but the combined electorates of Orkney and Shetland justified one seat there, and so reduced the number of special allocations to one.

Minimising change

This additional criterion, introduced in the 1958 Act and later incorporated as Rule 7 in the *Parliamentary Constituencies Act 1986*, states that the Commissions need not give full effect to the preceding rules but 'shall take account, so far as they reasonably can … of the inconveniences attendant on alterations of constituencies other than alterations made for the purposes of Rule 4'. Within a constant local government template, therefore, the assumption is that continuity rather than change is the norm, and that any recommendations for change have to be fully justified. As indicated in Chapter 3, many MPs were critical of the number of changes to constituencies when the reports of the First Periodical Reviews were presented to the House of Commons (*Hansard*, vol. 535, 15 December 1954) so the new rule and the longer period between reviews were incorporated in the 1958 Act in order, in the Home Secretary's words, to introduce both 'a presumption against making changes unless there is a very strong case for them' and to provide 'a reasonable period of stability' while ensuring that 'gross differences or discrepancies' do not become established (*Hansard*, vol. 582, 11 February 1958, cols. 229–230).

There is a clear implication that the First Periodical Review had involved a major redrawing of the country's constituency map, which MPs and their parties wished to prevent recurring. In effect, continuity rather than change was the major feature of that redistribution, as Table 4.10 shows. Of the 625 constituencies existing at the start of that review, the Commissions recommended no change to 402 (64 per cent; note that although the English Commission recommended only 489 seats in its Initial Review, this was later increased to 506 – see p. 86). Wales had the highest percentage of unchanged seats (83), followed by England (64), Scotland (62) and Northern Ireland (42).

Table 4.10 *Number of unchanged constituencies at each of the four Periodic Reviews*

	First	Second	Third	Fourth
England	323	165	68	159
Scotland	44	25	3	12
Wales	30	25	4	29
Northern Ireland	5	12	0	3

At the following review, fifteen years later, and in the context of the alterations introduced by the 1958 Act, the number of 'no change' constituencies was much smaller, at only 227 (36 per cent of the pre-existing seats): Northern Ireland's twelve constituencies were all untouched, as were 69 per cent of those in Wales, but population movements in England and Scotland, plus the restructuring of local government in Greater London, created the need for much more change there (see above, p. 100). This was followed by even more comprehensive changes to the entire map in the Third Periodic Review fourteen years further on, when only 75 of the 635 constituencies remained unscathed, most of them in England. Continued population movement was undoubtedly a significant contributor to this, but the main cause was the wholesale restructuring of the local government template outside Greater London, and Rule 7 cannot be used to over-ride Rule 4: new constituencies had to be recommended which fitted into the restructured local government map. The English Commission noted that it had received many representations arguing against its proposals to change existing constituencies, citing Section 2(2) – now Rule 7 – of the 1958 Act. Its response was (Boundary Commission for England, 1983, 10, #26):

> It was clearly not the intention that we should depart from Rules 1, 2 and 3 solely to preserve the existing constituency boundaries. Although Rule 4 (observance of local government boundaries) is not inflexible, being qualified by Rules 5 and 6, the provisions of section 2(2) expressly exclude alterations made for the purpose of Rule 4. We noted that although section 2(2) had widened the scope of consideration, it had not amended Rule 6 which provides the conditions for departing from Rule 4 and Rule 5 (special geographical considerations).
>
> It appeared, therefore, that the primary purpose of section 2(2) was to remove the former requirement in Rule 5 to recommend changes that produced greater arithmetical equality of electorate in constituencies, even though no great abnormality existed. Only in these circumstances did we have the positive duty to take in account the inconveniences caused and the ties broken by alterations.

The Welsh and Scottish Commissions similarly recorded the impact of Section 2(2), with the former also noting the effect of population movements (Boundary Commission for Wales, 1983, 3, #12):

> Many constituencies had remained unaltered for a long time (13 for over 60 years) and it was inevitable that there would have to be a great number of changes to the present constituencies at this review.

For the Northern Ireland Commission, the increase in its number of seats from 12 to 17, with an unaltered electoral quota, made change to all of the existing seats inevitable.

After this major shift stimulated by external factors, the Fourth Periodic Review saw the Commissions return to a very similar outcome overall from that produced in the Second Review – 203 of the 650 constituencies (31 per cent) created by the Third Review remained intact. The only part of the United Kingdom unaffected by the local government changes introduced between the Second and Third Periodic Reviews was Greater London. Of the 92 seats created there by the Second Review, 21 (23 per cent) were unchanged by the Third Review, despite the number of constituencies for the County overall being reduced by eight. And then at the Fourth Review, the number of seats for Greater London as a whole was reduced from 84 to 74 but 26 of the 84 (31 per cent) remained unchanged.

Most changes are unpopular with the political parties, which do not want their organisations unnecessarily disturbed, and this is recognised by the Commissions; indeed, even before the 1958 Act was passed it was standard practice for all of the Commissions to categorise separately their recommendations for constituencies with no change recommended, constituencies with minor changes only (usually adjustments to take account of changes in local government District and ward boundaries), and constituencies for which major changes were proposed. The current general approach was summarised in the Assistant Commissioner's opening statement (see p. 136 above) to the Local Inquiry at Knowsley and Sefton in January 1994, which referred to the task as being 'to reduce disparity with minimum change', and where change is considered necessary it is often introduced somewhat apologetically – 'Although the previous general review had resulted in major changes to most of the constituencies in Hampshire, it was clear that extensive alterations were again required' (Boundary Commission for England, 1983, 107, #202). In some cases, the Commissions have recommended more change than local opinion can accept, and they have been persuaded to return to the status quo, even if this means less strict application of Rule 5.

The clear implication of Section 2(2) of the 1958 Act is that seats which are not changed will deviate more on average from the electoral quota and the local average than is the case with recommendations for 'new' constituencies, and this is what the Commissions did. (The Boundary Commission for Scotland – 1995, 16, #12 – noted that where change was deemed necessary it 'saw it as the primary objective of the review to recommend, where practicable, a constituency with an electorate much nearer to the quota'.) Table 4.11 shows the mean and SD for the deviations from the electoral quota for the three categories of seat identified by the Commissions at the First and Second Periodical Reviews (note that there were no 'minor changes' in either Scotland or Northern Ireland at the First Review and no changes at all in Northern Ireland at the Second). With a few exceptions, usually involving small numbers of seats, both the mean and the SD are smaller for the 'major change' constituencies than for those recommended for 'no change': where they made major changes, the Commission paid close attention to Rule 5, with much less variation around the average than was the case where they proposed to retain the existing seats.

Although the Commissions continued to operate the 'no change' rule at the Third and, especially, the Fourth Periodic Reviews, they no longer categorised their recommendations in the way done in their previous reports, although the number of 'no change' seats is readily identifiable. For both the Third and the Fourth Periodic Reviews, however, researchers have calculated an 'Index of Constituency Change' (ICC) as part of their procedure for estimating the impact of the changes on the standing of the political parties. (They use local government electoral data to estimate what the result of the previous election would have been if it had been fought in the new constituencies; BBC/ITN, 1983; Rallings and Thrasher, 1995). Their formula is

$$ICC = \left(\frac{DBC+ABC}{EBC}\right) \times 100$$

where

BC   is the base constituency, the constituency in the previous Review which forms the largest part of the new constituency;

DBC is the number of electors removed from that base constituency to another;

ABC is the number of electors added to that base constituency from another; and

EBC is the electorate of the base constituency.

An ICC value of 0.0 indicates no change, and the larger the value (as a percentage of EBC), the greater the change.

Table 4.11 *Deviations from the electoral quota by degree of change to constituencies at the first two periodical reviews*

	Amount of change		
	None	*Minor*	*Major*
First Periodical Review			
England			
Mean	11.7	8.3	8.3
SD	8.6	7.3	6.3
Scotland			
Mean	14.6	n.a.	11.7
SD	11.7	n.a.	8.5
Wales			
Mean	15.3	20.0	n.a.
SD	11.0	15.9	n.a.
Northern Ireland			
Mean	7.3	n.a.	3.5
SD	6.1	n.a.	3.5
Second Periodical Review			
England			
Mean	12.1	10.7	10.9
SD	8.6	9.2	8.2
Scotland			
Mean	22.2	14.2	8.3
SD	15.9	10.2	6.5
Wales			
Mean	16.5	24.1	16.8
SD	12.9	13.9	10.9

Table 4.12 shows the mean and standard deviation (SD) values for this index at the last two Periodic Reviews, both for all constituencies and just for those for which change was recommended. All of the means are much smaller at the

latter review, as are most of the standard deviations. This is only to be expected for the figures for all seats, since there was a much larger number of zero values after the Fourth than the Third Review. More interestingly, they are also smaller when the calculations refer only to those seats where change is involved. The Fourth Review was not influenced by a major restructuring of local government, and so when they were operating within a consistent template, the Commissions were able to achieve the needed changes with less overall disruption to constituencies than was the case when the template was much altered.

The number of seats

Rule 1 is by far the vaguest of the seven in Schedule 2 of the *Parliamentary Constituencies Act 1986,* in that it:
1 sets minimum representation for Scotland and Wales;
2 sets both a minimum and a maximum figure for Northern Ireland; and
3 sets a general target only for Great Britain, which includes the imprecise term 'substantially greater or less than'.
England's representation can therefore be influenced by the decisions of the Scottish and Welsh Commissions (on which see McLean, 1995), within the constraints of that vague phrase, although in practice the English Commission has always made its recommendations independently of what the other two are likely to recommend. Nevertheless, with a relatively fixed overall number of seats, and minima for three of the four constituent areas, the likelihood is that England, by far the largest in terms of its electorate (36.3 million in 1991, compared to 3.9 million in Scotland, 2.2 million in Wales and 1.2 million in Northern Ireland), will be under-represented.

The consequence of this criterion is that the average English constituency has had many more electors than its Scottish and Welsh counterparts after every review (see Table 4.13: the figures refer to the electorate in the year for which the electoral quota was derived, divided by the number of seats allocated by the relevant review). Furthermore, the disparity between England on the one hand and Scotland and Wales on the other has widened, as illustrated by the percentage change in the average constituency electorate in each country, which has occurred because England's electorate has grown more rapidly than the number of seats allocated.

A major reason for this growing disparity between England on the one hand and Scotland and Wales on the other is that the latter pair have a guaranteed minimum number of seats, whereas the number for England has not grown commensurate with its increased electorate. England's representation increased considerably between the Initial and First Periodic Reviews, largely because of the creation of additional seats by subdividing several large ones in 1947 (see p. 81). Between the First and the Fourth Periodic Reviews the number increased by only 3.5 per cent, however, whilst the average electorate per constituency increased by 21.3 per cent. England has become increasingly under-represented, if the ratio of seats to electors is used as the measure.

The issue of Scottish and Welsh 'over-representation' has frequently concerned MPs, especially those representing large English constituencies. A common belief that Scotland and Wales were in the past guaranteed minimum representation which has now become over-representation is not accurate, as pointed out by Sir Herbert Williams (*Hansard*, vol. 396, 1 February 1944., col. 1174):

> As far as I know, there are no binding treaties as to the relative share in this Chamber of the four countries which make up the United Kingdom.

Table 4.12 *Values of the Index of Constituency Change at the Third and Fourth Periodic Reviews: summary statistics*

	Third		Fourth	
	Mean	*SD*	*Mean*	*SD*
England				
All	37.5	34.0	24.2	29.1
Change only	42.5	33.1	32.4	29.5
Scotland				
All	48.8	33.8	27.8	29.8
Change only	51.0	32.9	31.8	29.8
Wales				
All	38.2	28.9	12.5	25.6
Change only	42.9	27.1	35.7	35.3
Northern Ireland				
All	50.1	24.8	26.7	26.1
Change only	50.1	24.8	30.0	25.8
Total				
All	39.1	33.6	23.9	29.1
Change only	43.8	32.6	32.3	29.0

One member of the Conference however (Parker: *Hansard*, vol. 582, 11 February 1958, col. 266) said that:

> we tried to do two things which have not worked out in practice. We accepted the fact that Scotland and Wales should have a larger representation than their population entitles them to. This was partly due to the Act of Union and partly because we considered that the two smaller nations should have a larger representation because they were smaller [but] It was assumed that, roughly speaking, a constituency in Glasgow would have an electorate of about the same size as a constituency in Newcastle, Birmingham or London. I cannot see that there should be a much larger representation given to Glasgow in comparison with other industrial centres. It was the intention of the Speaker's Conference to see that justice was done in these matters.

Table 4.13 *The relative representation of the four parts of the United Kingdom: the average number of electors per constituency excluding University constituencies.*

	Initial	First	Second	Third	Fourth
England	58,734	56,562	58,192	64,873	68,626
		(–3.7)	(+2.9)	(+11.5)	(+5.8)
Scotland	49,620	47,990	47,670	52,904	54,569
		(–3.3)	(–0.7)	(+11.0)	(+3.1)
Wales	51,641	50,363	50,366	55,660	55,559
		(–2.5)	(+0.0)	(+10.5)	(–0.0)
Northern Ireland	71,457	72,913	76,405	61,206	64,082
		(+2.0)	(+4.8)	(–19.9)	(+4.8)

Note: the figures in brackets indicate the percentage change in the number of electors per constituency.

The current situation is a consequence of the wording of the 1944 Act (see McLean, 1995; Rossiter, Johnston and Pattie, 1997c), which derived from the preceding Speaker's Conference deliberations. In 1948, Herbert Morrison (who had been Home Secretary at the time of the 1944 Speaker's Conference) stated that (*Hansard*, vol. 448, 17 February 1948, col. 1114):

> my Scottish and Welsh friends were pressing [the Conference] for an undertaking that this guaranteed minimum of theirs in their representation should be conceded to them for all time. I said 'No, this time; not for all time'.

The argument was put on several occasions, however, that the Scots and Welsh were minorities within the United Kingdom and should get some preference on that account (e.g. Lucas-Tooth: *Hansard*, vol. 582, 11 February 1958, col. 243), as well as the special geographical considerations of some constituencies 'containing within [them] places as far apart as London and York' (Taylor: col. 263). Where the injustice of the discrepancy was conceded, however, as by Jo Grimond ('the Act of Union … was never intended to result in such unjustly large English constituencies'; col. 273) the usual suggestion was to increase English representation: e.g. Mitchison – who was leading in the 1958 debate for Labour – suggested a further 15–20 extra seats for England (col. 235–6); Maitland argued, however, that 'we, in Scotland, could probably take on another ten, twenty, thirty, forty or fifty English members without noticing very much difference' (col. 274). But no major changes were made, and the issue of English under-representation remained (see Chapter 3, p. 119); the introduction of separate national quotas in the 1958 Act exacerbated the situation, however, because it provided a rationale for increasing the number of Scottish and Welsh seats which was formerly absent.

The issue of 'over-representation' for Wales and, especially, Scotland was a focus of considerable debate in the late 1970s when the Labour government proposed to establish devolved Assemblies for those countries. Much of this centred on the so-called 'West Lothian question', after the then-member for that constituency, Tam Dalyell, who argued that Scottish MPs would be able to vote on

English legislation at Westminster but English MPs could not vote on Scottish legislation which would be determined in Edinburgh. Scottish and Welsh 'over-representation' at Westminster were not integral to this issue (it would have existed without the 'over-representation') but clearly exacerbated it, particularly so since it seemed that Labour was unable to win a majority at Westminster without the 'Celtic preference' (Rossiter, Johnston and Pattie, 1997c). The devolution Bills were lost in 1979 and the issue was removed from the political agenda, although several English Conservative MPs complained about the 'over-representation' in the House of Commons debate on the Boundary Commission for England's Fourth Periodic Review recommendations (see *Hansard,* vol. 261, 14 June 1995).

Devolution returned to the political agenda in the mid-1990s with the Labour party's proposals for a devolved Scottish Parliament and a Welsh Assembly (the former was to have more powers than the latter, including those of tax-varying if approved by the electorate at a referendum). The 'West Lothian question' was resurrected,[7] as was the wider issue of Welsh and, especially, Scottish 'over-representation'. The government's response, with regard to Scotland, was to propose an amendment to the *Parliamentary Constituencies Act 1986* in its draft *Scotland Bill* (published in December 1997; see Chapter 3, p. 120).This should lead to Scottish over-representation being largely removed (save for any application of Rule 6), but not until the Fifth Periodic Review, which has to be reported between 2003 and 2007 according to the *Boundary Commissions Act 1992,* which could mean that Scottish 'over-representation' at Westminster remains for the next, and perhaps the next two, UK Parliaments even though the Scottish Parliament is due to be inaugurated in 2000. (The next general elections are due to be held in 2002 and 2007, if the present and the next Parliament both run a full term of five years.) No comparable amendment was proposed in the parallel *Government of Wales Bill (1997),* however, and that country will remain substantially 'over-represented'.

Concern has also grown over recent decades with the apparently ever-expanding House of Commons (from 615 to 659 seats between 1944 and 1997; 7.2 per cent), which the current legislation encourages and which Parliament has not been prepared to amend.[8] Butler and McLean (1996a, 25–8) demonstrate that this 'ratchet effect' operates through the interaction of four factors:

1 Since enactment of the *House of Commons (Redistribution of Seats) Act 1958,* the Commissions are required to calculate their electoral quotas using the number of constituencies authorised at the previous redistribution as the denominator.
2 The Commissions are able, under the current Rule 6 (Box 3.6), to allocate additional seats if justified by 'special geographical considerations', and these are then included in the denominator for calculating the electoral quota for the next Review. The quota is thus lower than it would otherwise be, and if 'special geographical considerations' are again invoked, then these are in effect being incorporated twice.

3 The English and Welsh Commissions are required to allocate constituencies
   within the local government template, so far as is practicable, and the Scottish Commission (since the 1972 Amendment to the Act) is required to have
   regard to local government boundaries. Because most local authorities are entitled to a small number of constituencies only (rarely more than ten) this means
   that there is a rounding effect to take account of the fractional entitlements.
   Furthermore, such rounding is rarely neutral (with the number of local government areas whose allocation is less than the full entitlement balanced by
   the number which gain more), because rounding-up should occur not at the
   arithmetic mean between two integer numbers but rather at the harmonic mean,
   which is always less than half-way between those two numbers; it is an asymp-
   totic relationship stabilising at 0.48. (The harmonic mean is treated in fuller
   detail by Balinski and Young, 1982, and by McLean and Mortimore, 1992; it
   was 'discovered' by the Commissions at the time of their Third Periodic
   Reviews, with the Deputy Chairman of the English Commission providing an
   appendix to its report on it: Boundary Commission for England, 1983, 153.)
      This can be illustrated by a simple example. If the electoral quota is 50,000,
   then a local government area with 74,000 electors is entitled to 1.48 constituencies. Using the arithmetic mean, this would be rounded-down to 1, giving a single constituency having 74,000 electors, 48 per cent above the quota. If two
   constituencies were allocated, however, each, with 37,000 electors, would be 26
   per cent below the quota, so two seats would produce a better fit to the Act's
   requirement that seats have electorates as close to the electoral quota as is practicable. Table 4.14 shows the 'break-points' for the harmonic mean, and illustrates the point that rounding-up is more likely to occur than rounding-down if
   most local government areas have an entitlement of less than ten constituencies.
4 Rule 7 requires the Commissions to take account of the inconveniences that
   can be caused by change, and so creates a presumption against change, which
   can protect areas with declining populations from losing seats.

All four of these together produce a strong tendency for growth in the number of
constituencies (except, of course, in Northern Ireland, where there was a fixed
number until 1979 and a narrow prescribed range only from then onwards). The
growth has not been as great as it might have been, however, because the Commissions have been aware of the politicians' concern and have taken steps to limit
the increase, especially during the Fourth Periodic Review.

An example of the 'creeping growth' is provided by the Boundary Commission
for Scotland's treatment of the Strathclyde Region during its Third Periodic Review.
The Region contained almost half of Scotland's electorate. Its largest District was
the City of Glasgow, with a 1978 electorate of 610,500, giving a theoretical entitlement to 11.38 seats. The Commission's provisional recommendation was that it
be allocated only ten, however, with none of them straddling the District boundary; the main reason justifying this was that the City's electorate was declining (it
was 595,600 in 1981) 'and [given] the expectation that it would continue at about
the same rate (i.e. about 5,000 a year) we considered that an allocation of 10 seats

Table 4.14 *The 'break-points' for 'rounding-up' rather than 'rounding-down' with the arithmetic and harmonic means*

Number of Seats	Arithmetic Mean	Harmonic Mean
1		
	1.5	1.333
2		
	2.5	2.400
3		
	3.5	3.429
4		
	4.5	4.444
5		
	5.5	5.455
6		
	6.5	6.462
7		
	7.5	7.467
8		
	8.5	8.471
9		
	9.5	9.474
10		
	10.5	10.476
11		

would be appropriate' (Boundary Commission for Scotland, 1983, 58, #170(c)). It was further justified by comparing Glasgow with the country's other main cities: with 11 constituencies its average 1978 electorate would have been 55,000 which 'while closer to the electoral quota, would be well below the average' proposed for the others (Aberdeen, 59,400; Dundee, 64,000; Edinburgh, 58,100: #170(d)). This was strongly opposed by many of the objectors, including various arms of the Labour party, the Liberal party and the Scottish National party, though not by the Conservatives and the SDP. As fully reported by the Commission, the Local Inquiry held to consider the City of Glasgow alone, which took four days, covered a wide range of matters, but the Assistant Commissioner focused in his final recommendations on whether some areas should be under-represented in order to compensate for over-representation elsewhere. His conclusions included the following statements (Boundary Commission for Scotland, 1983, 67):

(i) Apart from Rule 1, there is no basis in the rules for departing from the quota in order to compensate for the effects of Rule 6: to do so would be to depart from quota in favour of average (or total number) as the criterion under the rules.

(ii) Apart from Rule 1, there is no basis in the rules for departing from the quota in Strathclyde Region or Glasgow District in order to compensate for the effects of applying Rule 4(b) *elsewhere* in Scotland; ...

(v) ... The submissions made to me ... did not in my view provide any support for a view that a major departure from the quota in Glasgow, entailing ten seats rather than eleven, could be regarded as equitable unless the alternatives all involve substantial inroads upon the equitable treatment of other areas in Great Britain as a whole.

This led to his recommendation that:

(A) Unless the Commission has concluded that Rule 1 requires a restriction of Scottish seats to a total of 71, in order to comply with the limit upon constituencies in Great Britain to a total not substantially greater than 613, I recommend that the draft proposals be replaced by a proposal for eleven constituencies.

He also found that no satisfactory ten-constituency solution could be identified for the City. The Commission accepted his arguments in full; it was 'satisfied that a seat could not be saved elsewhere in Scotland' and so increased the total number of recommended seats from 71 to 72 (Boundary Commission for Scotland, 1983, 81, #235).

The Scottish Commission was determined that there should be no repeat of this outcome during its Fourth Periodic Review, at the outset of which it published a statement (reproduced in full in its final report; Boundary Commission for Scotland, 1995, 167–9) indicating its conclusion that the number of seats in Scotland 'should remain at 72' (167, #1). It was also 'not minded to recommend a reduction' to 71, however, although that would have been entirely consistent with the Rules and trends in the relative distribution of electors between Scotland and England (see Table 4.13). Drawing on the experience with Glasgow in the previous review, it announced that it had 'decided to explore the possibility of grouping regions together in order to provide a means of achieving a total number of constituencies not greater than 72' (169,#7).

The Commission stuck to that over-riding goal. At the same Review, however, the Welsh Commission recommended creating two additional seats, consistent with the growth in the Welsh electorate from 2,115,093 in 1981 (the enumeration date for the Third Periodic Review) to 2,295,294 in 1993. Together with two additional seats at the previous Review, Welsh representation in the House of Commons thus increased by 11 per cent between 1969 and 1995, compared to 3.8 per cent for the entire UK and only 2.7 per cent for England, whose electorate had increased by 20.9 per cent over the intervening period compared to only 8.5 per cent for Wales. In each case, the Welsh Commission allocated two more seats than its total population suggested was the entitlement, one because of special geographical considerations and one because there was more rounding-up than rounding-down in the allocation to Counties. The Commission recognised that its recommendations were contrary to Parliament's expressed concern about the growth of the House of Commons, but argued that expansion of Welsh representation was inevitable under the existing rules. Thus its summary of the Third Periodic Review justified using special geographical considerations to allocate additional seats to Gwynedd and Powys, and concluded that Rule 5 did not allow it to recommend reducing the representation of any other County (Boundary Commission for Wales, 1983, 53, #205): having had to overturn its provisional recommendation for combining Gwent and Powys after the Local Inquiry, it was clearly not prepared to countenance other amalgamations at that stage, and there is no evidence that it had done so earlier. (The Scottish Commission had interpreted Rule 5 differently, of course, because of its weaker wording for their case.) Similarly at the end of its Fourth Periodic Review it argued that the 'special geographical considerations' justifying an extra seat in Gwynedd remained and as a consequence concluded that 'we see no viable alternative but to recommend a total of 40 seats' (Boundary Commission for Wales, 1995, 47, #189). It followed this with a case for legislative changes to prevent a recurrence of the issue at the Fifth Review – 'we have calculated that even if the number of electors at the next (fifth) review were to remain the same as for this (fourth) review, and with the same distribution by County, the allocation of 40 seats we have proposed in this review would, upon a strict application of Rule 5, result in the allocation of an extra, 41st, seat' (#190).

The Northern Ireland Commission also increased its representation after the Fourth Review, from 17 to 18. The Act stipulates that:

> The number of constituencies in Northern Ireland shall not be greater than 18 or less than 16, and shall be 17 unless it appears to the Boundary Commission for Northern Ireland that Northern Ireland should for the time being be divided into 16 or (as the case may be) into 18 constituencies.

The Commission started its work by assuming that it should again be recommending 17 seats, having (Boundary Commission for Northern Ireland, 1995, 3, #4):

> sought legal opinion as to the number of constituencies which they might recommend. They concluded, on the advice of Senior Crown Counsel, that they would be justified in recommending a number of constituencies other than 17 only to reduce or alleviate difficulties experienced in applying the Rules on the basis of 17 constituencies.

In producing its provisional recommendations, however, the Commission experienced considerable difficulties because of population decline in Belfast, which led to proposals for only three constituencies there, which was opposed by most of the political parties and others who made representations. Because the Commission is not required to have regard to local authority boundaries (other than District wards), it has no template within which to determine theoretical entitlements or to hold Local Inquiries, and its decision to hold five of these dealing with particular seats exacerbated its difficulties, since the Assistant Commissioners did not have a fixed area within which to work and make recommendations. When the five reports had been received, the Commission realised that a major restructuring of its proposals was necessary, and it reported that (Boundary Commisssion for Northern Ireland, 1995, 17, #4):

> In examining the options for Revised Recommendations, the Commission sought to draw up proposals for 17 constituencies which would give effect to the substance of the reports and recommendations of the five assistant Commissioners. They found it impossible to do so without causing an excessive disparity between the electorates of constituencies and the electoral quota or between the electorates of neighbouring constituencies. The Commission therefore considered that they were entitled, in accordance with the opinion of Senior Crown Counsel, to put forward Revised Recommendations on the basis of 18 constituencies, it not having been possible to devise an acceptable scheme for 16 constituencies.

Even so, this involved increasing the tolerance around the average constituency electorate from the stated initial target of 7 per cent to 11 per cent. Following publication of the revised recommendations, the Commission concluded that 'none of the representations received persuaded the Commission that there might be another, preferable scheme for 18 constituencies which would give better effect to the Statutory Rules for the Redistribution of Seats' (29, #22; for further details on this issue, see Rossiter, Johnston and Pattie, 1998).

Whereas the Scottish Commission made a clear commitment to no growth in the number of constituencies at the Fourth Review, and then kept that commitment, the Welsh and Northern Ireland Commissions saw no alternative but to propose expansion. The same occurred with the English Commission, which was operating with less clear guidance from the Rules and much more demand generated by growth in the electorate. This is reflected in its statement that (Boundary Commission for England, 1995a, 7, #2.9):

> The 1986 Act has a requirement, in Rule 1, that Great Britain should have a number of constituencies, not substantially greater or less than 613, but provides no mechanism for reducing the number of seats in one part of Great Britain if another increases its allocation. Exactly what number would be substantially greater than 613 is also obscure and the increase in the number of seats to 651 [after the Third Review and the addition of a further seat in Milton Keynes by an Interim Review in 1990] has made this an increasingly relevant problem.

In that context (#2.10)

> Faced with this dilemma, we decided not to set a target number of constituencies for the review but to concentrate upon recommending constituencies with electorates as close to the electoral quota as practicable whilst at the same time keeping in mind the requirements of Rule 1. As we said in our booklet (Parliamentary Boundary Commission for England, 1991, p.16):
>
> > 'The Commission take the view that, where it is necessary to do so in order to give effect to Rule 1, it would be proper for them in the exercise of the discretion given to them in Rules 5, 6 and 7 to limit any further increase in the number of seats'.

This was done in two ways: (1) by recommending seats which cross London Borough boundaries (see p. 154 above); and (2) by not applying the harmonic mean rule for rounding up in a number of cases.

Although the Boundary Commission for England 'discovered' the harmonic mean rule during its Third Periodic Review, there were only two cases then – Buckinghamshire and the Isle of Wight – in which the entitlement according to the harmonic mean differed from that using the arithmetic mean: Buckinghamshire was allocated the larger figure as its 'entitlement' (Boundary Commission for England, 1983, 85, #52), but for the Isle of Wight the arithmetic rather than the harmonic rounding rule was applied, for 'special geographical considerations' (see p. 175). In the Fourth Review, on the other hand, there were seven cases in which the harmonic mean entitlement was greater than the arithmetic, but the former was allocated in only two of the cases – Brent and Northumberland: the others were Avon, Derbyshire, Isle of Wight, Norfolk and Warwickshire. Northumberland presented a particular problem: its entitlement in the Third Review was only 3.30 but a fourth seat was allocated using Rule 6 (see p. 175). Its entitlement twelve years later was 3.43, and 'a strict application of Rule 5 alone supports a continued allocation of four seats and there is no longer any need to rely on special geographical considerations under Rule 6 to justify retention of the fourth seat' (Boundary Commission for England, 1995a, 243, #2). With Brent, the Commission was unable, in the light of its own criteria (see p. 154), to recommend pairing it with a neighbouring Borough without causing 'undue disruption' to local ties (28, #3) and was 'satisfied that the allocation of three seats.., to which it was entitled, was to be preferred to any possible linkage ... with a neighbouring borough' (#6). The provisionally recommended three seats stimulated only fourteen representations, which included two proposing that Brent be paired with either Ealing or Harrow and one (from a Liberal Democrat Borough Councillor there) that Brent be allocated only two seats.[9] On the latter point (29, #20):

> The Assistant Commissioner considered that it was necessary, to give effect to rule 5, for the electorate of any constituency to be as near the electoral quota as possible. An allocation of three seats would better achieve this than an allocation of two seats.

This advice was accepted by the Commission.

Apart from the special case of the Isle of Wight, in each of the other Counties involved (Avon, Derbyshire, Norfolk and Warwickshire) application of the harmonic mean rather than the arithmetic mean rule would have involved increasing the County's representation from its Third Review allocation, and in each case the Commission argued that because the insertion of an additional seat would break local ties, the further allocation should not be made. In Derbyshire, for example, with an entitlement of 10.49 seats (Boundary Commission for England, 1995a, 166, #3):

> We considered that the very slight numerical advantage of allocating 11 seats was outweighed by the very considerable amount of change which would be necessary, and by the fragmentation of districts which would result from the allocation of the extra seat. In contrast, the allocation of 10 seats would mean little change to the

composition of the existing seats, in order to reduce the disparity between constituencies … we therefore decided that Derbyshire should continue to be allocated
10 seats.

Very similar statements were made with regard to Avon (141, #2), Norfolk (238,
#3) and Warwickshire (271, #3). This provisional recommendation was not chal-
lenged in any of the representations received in the case of Derbyshire, and a
constituency Labour party counter-proposal that Warwickshire be allocated six
seats was withdrawn prior to the Local Inquiry, where it was not addressed (271,
#9). In Norfolk, a case for nine seats – pressed by 'one of the political parties
[Labour], three local councils who submitted a joint proposal, and one from a
political analyst and academic' (239, #8) – attracted many counter-arguments and
was a major issue addressed at the Local Inquiry. However, 'The Assistant Commissioner was not persuaded that there was a compelling need for nine seats and
stated that the need would have to be very great to justify the upheaval involved'
(#11); the Commission accepted that advice (#13) and was not prepared to reopen the issue when it was raised again in representations stimulated by the
revised recommendations.

The number of seats was also the major issue to concern the Local Inquiry in
Avon, with the proponents of an eleven-seat allocation arguing that it would allow
disparities within the County to be reduced substantially while producing constituencies either coterminous with or wholly contained within local authority
areas. Against this, the majority of the representations favoured the provisionally
recommended ten-seat option, arguing that the arithmetic gains from allocating
eleven seats were small and would severely disrupt the continuity represented by
the Commission's proposals. 'The Assistant Commissioner weighed the evidence
submitted at the inquiry but felt unable to recommend an 11 seat option' (Boundary Commission for England, 1995a, 143, #14, 144, #25):

> We accepted the Assistant Commissioner's recommendations in full. He had heard
> the evidence, weighed up the arguments, and where in doubt had visited the areas
> of contention. His conclusions were not reached lightly and appeared to us to be
> both practical and logical solutions. He had opted wherever possible for no change
> so as to ensure continuity, and we accepted this.

In all of these cases, therefore, the Commission applied Rule 7 to promote its
goal of not increasing the size of England's Parliamentary representation too
much. Disruption was given greater priority than electoral equality – as it also
was, however, in the decision not to reduce Brent's allocation! In this it was
assisted in each case by at least one of the main political parties realising that
continuity rather than change was in its electoral interests, and arguing accordingly. This led to somewhat contradictory recommendations from Assistant Commissioners, with the adherence to Rule 5 in Brent standing out against the
emphasis on Rule 7 elsewhere. (Brent, of course, would have had its number of
seats reduced if the Commission had been consistent, whereas all of the others
would have received an additional constituency.)

A new geography of representation?

This chapter has charted a major shift in the foundation of representation in the United Kingdom over the half-century in which the statutory Boundary Commissions have been operating. The mathematic has become much more important as the major principle on which redistributions have been based, and the organic much less so. To a considerable extent, this has happened against Parliament's wishes, as the quotations from debates in this and the previous chapter have illustrated: MPs want to represent communities, not mere population aggregates, and do not want those communities' boundaries to be changed unless it is really necessary because of either or both changes to the local government map and changes in the distribution of electors. (Of course, their main desire as individuals is to ensure their re-election, and their parties want to maximise their representation, and arguments for these ends are often contradictory!) But as the local government map has been changed, with fewer and larger units, so the link with communities defined by their separate local government status has become weaker and the Commissions, while remaining aware of the need to meet the organic requirement, have placed greater stress (albeit usually implicit only) on the arithmetic requirement: constituencies are much more equal in their electorates now than has ever been the case.

A major consequence of this, and the trend towards it, has been a substantial change in the geography of representation. This is illustrated in Table 4.15, which shows the number of seats in each of the current (1998) government regions after each of the major reviews of all constituencies (the regions are indicated in Figure 4.6).[10] As shown by the final row, the main changes in the geography of representation occurred in the nineteenth century, especially in 1832 and 1885. Apart from the removal of representation from southern Ireland in 1922, changes in the twentieth century have been much smaller – and generated at least in part at the final two reviews by the growth in the size of the House of Commons.

The nineteenth century started with the two southern regions of England (excluding Greater London) returning 40 per cent of the country's MPs, which was reduced to 15 per cent by the 1885 reform, and now stands at 20 per cent. The Southwest saw its representation fall by some two-thirds during the nineteenth century, a position regained in 1995 after further falls early in the current century. The main gainers were Greater London, whose representation increased nearly sevenfold between 1831 and 1885, the Northeast and Northwest of England (an increase from 40 to 104) and Scotland. London's representation continued to increase until 1945, after which population decentralisation has seen it decline substantially again (from 115 to 74); indeed, London has been the focus of change in the geography of representation since 1945, its declining share of the national number of MPs being balanced by growth in the two regions surrounding the capital (Eastern and Southeast).

In sum, the nineteenth-century and early-twentieth-century redistributions (most of them accompanying a franchise change) brought the distribution of MPs

Table 4.15 *The changing regional division of representation: the distribution of constituencies since the beginning of the nineteenth century*[a]

Region[b]	U	1832	1868	1885	1918	1922	1945	IN	R1	R2	R3	R4
England												
NE	12	21	25	26	31	31	31	31	31	31	30	30
NW	28	48	57	78	86	86	88	84	83	82	79	76
YH	34	38	40	52	56	56	56	57	55	55	54	56
EM	35	41	44	38	37	37	37	39	39	39	42	44
WM	45	59	58	47	47	47	50	52	54	56	58	59
E	56	54	45	39	34	34	36	39	41	45	51	56
GL	11	23	30	74	100	100	115	100	102	92	84	74
SE	111	83	74	50	50	50	53	59	61	70	77	83
SW	150	97	82	52	44	44	44	45	45	46	48	51
England (*total*)	482	464	455	456	485	485	510	506	511	516	523	529
Wales	27	32	33	34	35	35	35	36	36	36	38	40
Scotland	45	53	58	70	71	71	71	71	71	71	72	72
Ireland												
North	22	23	23	25	29	12	12	12	12	12	17	18
South	77	80	80	76	75							
Universities	5	6	9	9	12	12	12					
Total	658	658	658	670	707	615	640	625	630	635	650	659
Change[c]		83	34	87	34	46	13	24	6	14	21	18

Notes:
[a] Key to dates: U – the 'unreformed house' pre-1832; IN – the Initial Review, reported 1947; R1 – the First Periodical Review, reported 1954; R2 – The Second Periodical Review, reported 1969 (but implemented 1970); R3 – the Third Periodic Review, reported 1983; R4 – the Fourth Periodic Review, reported 1995.
[b] Key to regions: NE – Northeast; NW – Northwest (incl. Merseyside); YH – Yorkshire and Humberside; EM – East Midlands; WM – West Midlands; E – Eastern; GL – Greater London; SE-Southeast; SW – Southwest; Ireland North – the Irish Counties of Antrim, Armagh, Derry, Down, Fermanagh and Tyrone; South – the remaining Counties of Ireland (now forming the Republic of Ireland).
[c] The measure of change is the sum of the gains and losses, divided by two (to the nearest integer).

into line with the distribution of population. From then on, most of the changes (save the additional seats for Wales and Northern Ireland) have been fine-tuning exercises, ensuring that the geography of representation was in line with the changing distribution of population as London decanted population into its hinterland, whereas within each region, as noted above, the details of individual constituency boundaries have been redrawn to ensure a close approximation to the equality of electorates requirement.

Figure 4.6 *The current government regions (1998)*

Conclusion

In its introductory booklet produced for the Fourth Periodic Review, the Boundary Commission for England summarised its situation in the following terms (Parliamentary Boundary Commission for England, 1991, 33, #8):

> Essentially, the Commission are required to recommend constituencies following local government boundaries and having electorates close to the electoral quota, but with discretion to recommend otherwise in order to find an acceptable distribution. In practice, in one area the Commission may feel able to allow the requirement of rule 5, for electorates to be as near the electoral quota as practicable, to be given effect whereas, in another area, other factors such as the requirement of rule 4, to respect county and London borough boundaries, or the existence of strong local ties, may prevent this. Elsewhere a compromise solution may be found. These subjective decisions are difficult, but the Commission reach their independent and impartial conclusions on the basis of all the information available to them.

The necessity for such subjectivity is clear from the ambiguity of the rules, yet its result is a potential (and often realised) lack of consistency, both between Commissions and within one Commission (across both time and space).

Despite that, however, we have demonstrated in this chapter that over the period since the Commissions were established at the end of the Second World War there has been a major shift in the outcome of their work – there was very much less variation in the size of constituencies after the Fourth Periodic Review than had been the case heretofore. In considerable part this has been facilitated by changes to the country's local government structure, notably in the 1970s, which have removed many of the constraints imposed by the requirement to produce a constituency map as far as possible coherent with aspects of the local government template, but it has been enhanced by the increased willingness of at least two of the Commissions (England and Scotland) to promote equality of electorates so as to counter the in-built tendency for the number of seats to increase.

The mathematic basis for representation has increased in importance relative to the organic in the production of Parliamentary constituencies within the United Kingdom. This is a somewhat surprising outcome in some ways, given the increased participation of the political parties in the procedures applied by the Commissions, for whom electoral equality is only important if it suits their particular interests (as in the *Foot et al.* case launched by members of the Labour party in 1982). The Commissions set the agenda for the Local Inquiries with their provisional recommendations, however, so that although for the parties consistency of treatment is only of importance where it suits their particular purpose – as illustrated here with reference to the application of the harmonic mean rounding rule by the English Commission at the Fourth Periodic Review, and by the decline in equality between the Commissions' provisional and final recommendations as the result of the cases pressed on Assistant Commissioners at the Local Inquiries – nevertheless they are very substantially influenced by the Commissions' work, which they try to modify in most cases rather than substantially change.

This last point is one we have touched on only briefly in this chapter, which has largely focused on statistical material relating to the outcome of each of the five reviews conducted by the Commissions. Thus we turn to a detailed analysis of the procedures applied during the Fourth Review, and of the actors involved, in the next chapters.

Notes

1 The first two were called Periodical Reviews, whereas the Third and Fourth were called Periodic Reviews!

2 Because the Scottish Commission is only required to 'have regard to' the boundaries of local government areas, its members stressed to us that as a consequence the concept of a 'theoretical entitlement' has less validity there, and is nothing more than a guideline.

3 Though less than the number held in 1917 (see p. 51).

4 This interpretation was supported by an article which appeared in the *Essex County Standard* for 12 May 1978 which quoted a Boundary Commission spokesman that 'if the last boundary changes in 1969 are anything to go by, the present recommendations will go through substantially', which led Colchester residents to believe that the recommended 'doughnut' would be implemented and that writtten representations were unnecessary.

5 The evidence provided on behalf of Colchester Borough Council (by then with a Liberal Democrat majority) was that no comparable town had been subjected to the 'sandwich' solution: Bath, Cambridge, Carlisle, Chester, Chesterfield, Crawley, Darlington, Eastbourne, Exeter, Gillingham, Gloucester, Grimsby, Harrogate, Hastings, Hove, Ipswich, Lincoln, Watford, Worcester and York were all cited as towns of a similar size where either a 'full doughnut' had been recommended or a small number of wards had been detached. Furthermore, a 'sandwich' had been provisionally recommended for Bedford, but after the Local Inquiry the final recommendation was for a 'doughnut'.

6 Rule 6 was not mentioned in the report.

7 And called that, even though Tam Dalyell – still a doughty opponent of devolution – was by then MP for Linlithgow.

8 Intriguingly, when Morrison introduced the 1944 Act to the House of Commons he presented it as being 'a scheme of redistribution based on two main principles, first that each vote should, as far as possible, command an equal share of the representation in the House of Commons, and, second, that the number of Members of the House should remain, substantially, as it was' (*Hansard*, vol. 396, 10 February 1944, cols. 1555–6): the issue of constituency boundaries coinciding, as far as practicable, with 'the boundaries of administrative areas' was an inferior criterion.

9 As Figure 4.5 shows, Brent was the only London Borough entitled to an additional seat under the harmonic mean rounding-up rule which was not paired with a neighbouring borough; the issue for the four others (Bexley, Hammersmith, Kingston and Lambeth) was resolved by pairing it with a neighbour where the harmonic mean did not apply.

10 In a small number of cases this has involved dividing individual constituencies

between regions according to the proportions of their electors living there. Each region was allocated a fractional entitlement of the constituency, and the final totals were rounded to the nearest integer. There was a very small number of changes between the dates shown in the tables (ten in all): all but one of these involved the abolition of 'corrupt boroughs' in the nineteenth century; the tenth was the creation of a second constituency in Milton Keynes in 1990.

Part II

The Boundary Commissions' Fourth Periodic Review

5

Setting the agenda

The Fourth Periodic Review of Parliamentary Constituencies within the United Kingdom formally commenced with publication in February 1991 of the statutory notice of the English Commission's intention to begin work and ended with the presentation to Parliament of the report of the Northern Ireland Commission in October 1995. Although the work of the four Commissions was in the public eye for some four and a half years, the work of the Commissioners themselves and that of the Secretariats, the civil servants who provide their administrative support, extended over a longer period of time. In this chapter we concentrate on the work which took place out of the public eye and upon the people who did it. Who are the Commissioners and how are they appointed; what is the relationship between them and the civil servants; and what, if any, political input is there 'behind the scenes'? In short, how was the agenda set for the Fourth Review?

In answering these and subsequent questions we have relied partly on documentary sources and partly upon interviews with those involved in the process. In addition to the published reports of the four Commissions we refer to other publications, such as the English Commission's booklet *The Review of Parliamentary Constituencies* (Parliamentary Boundary Commission for England, 1991) and its leaflet entitled *The Procedure at Local Inquiries* (reprinted as Appendix F of Boundary Commission for England, 1995b), plus the *News Releases* and *Newsletters* produced by the Commissions and the Assistant Commissioners' reports on the Local Inquiries. We have also been given full access to the Commissions' Minutes. Wherever possible we have referred to this range of documentary sources when describing what took place. Our understanding of the Review has also been assisted immensely by interviews with those who helped to formulate the recommendations – members of the English, Scottish and Welsh Commissions and their Secretariats, the Secretary of the Northern Ireland Commission and 60 of the 72 Assistant Commissioners who presided over the Local Inquiries – plus several of those responsible for the responses from the political parties. With the exception of the last-named, all interviews were conducted on the basis that statements made were non-attributable.

The Commissioners

The four Commissions have a similar structure and the nature of their membership is laid down in statute (the *Parliamentary Constituencies Act, 1986:* the current structures were first set out in the *House of Commons (Redistribution of
Seats) Act 1958* – see Box 3.4). The Chairman of each is the Speaker of the House
of Commons although, as already discussed, she does not attend their meetings
and, as far as their day-to-day operation is concerned, has a largely symbolic role.
The Deputy Chairman of each is a High Court Judge, appointed by the head of
the judiciary in the relevant country. He has the assistance of two other Commissioners: in England, one is appointed by the Home Secretary, the other by the
Secretary of State for the Environment;[1] in Wales, one is appointed by the Home
Secretary, the other by the Secretary of State for Wales; while in Scotland and
Northern Ireland, both are appointed by the Secretary of State for the relevant
country. Meetings of the Commissions are also attended by assessors, again identified in statute, whose expertise is considered relevant to redistricting: in England, Scotland and Wales, by the Registrar General and the Director General of
the Ordnance Survey (in practice this was generally their nominees); while in
Northern Ireland the Commissioner of Valuation and the Chief Electoral Officer
replace the involvement of the Ordnance Survey.[2]

Given the political backgrounds of those making the majority of appointments,
the general acceptance of the Commissioners' neutrality is notable. During the
Fourth Review, the replacement of the Roman Catholic Deputy Chairman of the
Northern Ireland Commission, the late Mr Justice Higgins, by a Protestant, Mr
Justice Pringle, shortly before publication of the Commission's provisional recommendations inevitably occasioned comment. The timing was coincidental,
however, as the retiring Deputy Chairman was leaving in anticipation of his
appointment as a Lord Justice of Appeal, and subsequent events gave no credence
to suggestions that the Commission's recommendations were affected by the
change. (For a fuller discussion see Rossiter, Johnston and Pattie, 1998.) On the
other hand, his appointment was seen as consistent with the approach of the then
Secretary of State for Northern Ireland, Sir Patrick Mayhew; similarly the fact
that one of the members of the English Commission during the 1980s, Judge
Newey, had previously been prominent within the Conservative party is unlikely
to have escaped the notice of the Conservative minister responsible for his
appointment.[3]

The procedures followed when selecting Commissioners are little understood,
even by the Commissions themselves. The evidence of those appearing before
the Home Affairs Committee in 1986 indicated a variable approach to vetting,
while the comments of the Deputy Chairman (DC) of the English Commission
suggested an almost casual approach to his appointment:

> David Winnick MP: You said earlier – and I am sure we accept this entirely on
>   both sides of the Committee – that you are non-political. As I say, this is entirely
>   accepted. Again, without wishing to be misunderstood, when members are

appointed to the Commission is it known whether the people concerned have had any political involvement in the past? Is that a bar – on future political activities?

Sir Kenneth Jones DC, BCW: I can only answer for my part. The most careful inquiries were made as far as I can see, to ensure that I had *no* political past, even going back to the days when I was at University, I think.

Sir Raymond Walton DC, BCE: May I say that as far as *I* was concerned, I was hauled in by the Vice Chancellor, the head of my division, and told, "You're the youngest judge. This job has come up. Would you like to take it?", and I took it.

Judge Newey BCE[4]   I understand that before anyone is appointed the name is circulated to each political party, and their comments are requested.

Sir Raymond Walton: That happens now, but did not happen when I was appointed.

In 1987 Sir Raymond Walton was succeeded as Deputy Chairman of the English Commission by Sir John Knox and his early experience suggested that the procedures for appointment remained unsatisfactory. In 1989 the Home Secretary announced the appointment of two new members of the English Commission but as the minutes of the next Commission meeting record:

> The Deputy Chairman had not been consulted about the changes to the membership of the Commission. He had been concerned that two experienced Commissioners had been replaced at the same time when he was still comparatively inexperienced in the work of the Commission. He had therefore written to the Home Secretary to question the practice that the Deputy Chairman should not be consulted about the membership of the Commission. The Home Secretary had agreed that Deputy Chairmen would be consulted in future. (BCE Minutes, 1989/1, 1)[5]

Three Commissioners were appointed between 1989 and the end of the Review: two became Deputy Chairmen – Mr Justice Pill in Wales (1993) supervised nearly all the Review and Mr Justice Pringle in Northern Ireland (1993) supervised the majority – while the third, Dr Charles Glennie (1994), was the most interested and committed of the assessors and as such had already played a significant role. The remaining twelve were appointed at various times before that, with two (Mr Murray McLaggan (1980) in Wales and Mr Patrick Duffy (1978) in Northern Ireland) having also been Commissioners during the Third Review.

All Deputy Chairmen were High Court Judges (including Lord Davidson (1985), Chairman of the Scottish Law Commission since 1988), which ensured that considerable legal experience was available within the Commissions, as did the appointment of other experienced lawyers (Mr McLaggan in Wales and Miss Sheila Cameron QC (1989) in England, the first female appointed to any Commission – the Hon. Lady Cosgrove was appointed Deputy Chairman of the Scottish Commission in 1997). The other members of these Commissions (Mr Peter Davey (1989) in Wales and Mr David Macklin (1989) in England) have backgrounds in local government, as does Mr Duffy in Northern Ireland; a similar input to the Scottish Commission was provided by Professor Urlan Wannop (1983), now an academic but previously a senior planner with Strathclyde Regional Council, and the late Mr Adam Napier (1985), who was a local authority Director of Administration. The remaining Commissioner, Mr David Clement (1990) in Northern Ireland, had experience within the civil service.

As is evident from the background of their members, the Commissions contain a wealth of legal experience and almost as much knowledge of local government. None of those appointed became a Commissioner specifically because of his or her familiarity with redistricting however; only Miss Cameron had previously acted as an Assistant Commissioner and only Messrs McLaggan and Duffy had experience of the Third Review.[6] Furthermore, Commissioners are appointed on a part-time basis and, until the changes introduced by the 1992 *Boundary Commissions Act*, all were unpaid. The workload varies considerably – at the height of the Review the English Commission was meeting weekly, but for most of the time it was monthly, while in the years leading up to 1991 there was an average of just three a year[7] – and the amount of time spent inevitably differs between Commissioners. The demands are not inconsiderable, however, as the following extract from the English Commission's Minutes reveals:

> The Commissioners agreed that, rather than keeping a log of the time spent on Commission work, they would prefer if possible to be remunerated on a flat rate based on average times, i.e. three days preparing for each meeting, one day attending the meeting and half a day clearing Draft News Releases after the meeting (BCE Minutes, 1992/7, 2.6)[8]

In these circumstances – eminent but busy Commissioners with little previous knowledge of the subject faced with a variable workload requiring almost full-time consideration at certain peak times – there was an obvious need for reliable administrative support. This was provided by a series of Secretariats, separate ones for Scotland and Northern Ireland, but a joint body servicing the English and Welsh Commissions. In much the same way as the Commissioners were inexperienced, however, so were the civil servants. At the end of the Third Review the English and Welsh Commissions maintained a joint Secretariat of around six in London; in Scotland the Secretary alone provided support and he transferred most of his attention to other Scottish Office duties (he estimated that only five per cent of his time was spent on Commission business);[9] and the Northern Ireland Commission dispensed with a Secretary altogether for five years. Consequently the Fourth Review really was something of a novelty to most of those who took part. Although they had plenty of advance notice, when faced with the difficult decisions which inevitably arose they had no personal experience to fall back on. In those circumstances a sound preparation was vital. The way in which each Commission approached that task forms the subject of the next section.

Initial policy discussions and decisions

England

The 1986 *Parliamentary Constituencies Act* confirmed the ten to fifteen year interval between the receipt of reports introduced in 1958 and the English Commission, aware that its previous report had been seven years in preparation, started to consider future timings in 1986; it began formal preparations for the Fourth Review in 1988. Its Secretariat had estimated that a minimum of four and a half years would be required for the review itself, but was also aware that the Local Government Boundary Commission for England (LGBCE) was not due to complete its mandatory review of local government boundaries until 1992 (Boundary Commission for England, 1995a, 1); in the event the LGBCE's work was delayed and some local government boundary changes were not implemented in time for the Boundary Commission for England to take them into account. In the circumstances a decision to commence the Periodic Review shortly after publication of the new electoral registers in February 1991, but with consideration of areas timed to meet the progress of the LGBCE, was adopted as the most appropriate solution.

In the meantime, the Commission and its Secretariat had over two years. A first step was a meeting in October 1988 between its Secretary and his counterparts in Scotland and Northern Ireland 'to discuss possible changes in procedures which would not require amending legislation' (BCE Minutes, 1988/2, 2). Although this served a useful purpose in establishing lines of communication at Secretariat level, it seems to have had little influence on the Commission. Of the 24 suggestions in the resulting joint paper, no fewer than 14 were rejected, with the proposal that the four Commissions should adopt a consistent approach receiving a notably unsympathetic response: the subsequent Minutes reported that 'it was not clear whether the suggestion was that (a) all four Commissions should work identically or (b) that one could differ provided its own actions were consistent' (BCE Minutes, 1989/1, 5) – the Commission rejected the first and felt certain that the second already applied. However that meeting approved the Secretary's suggestion that the Commission 'embark upon a comprehensive review of policy' (BCE Minutes, 1989/1, 5) and its next four meetings received papers covering most of the policy issues which were to arise during the course of the Review.

Three major issues – the number of seats, minimum change and London Borough boundaries – were identified as particularly important (BCE Minutes, 1989/1, 5). The Commission 'agreed that Rule 1 was the predominant rule' and considered that the addition of ten or more seats 'would arguably contravene' it (BCE Minutes, 1989/2, 4). This influenced its discussion of London which concluded that, despite the opinion of the Home Office legal advisor that the Commission 'would risk judicial review if they crossed London borough boundaries to any extent … [nevertheless] … they would be prepared to consider the crossing [of the boundaries] of boroughs containing constituencies with excessive electoral disparities' (BCE Minutes, 1989/2, 4). And conscious of the degree of change which resulted from aligning constituency boundaries with the new local government template at the previous Review, the Commission decided to 'return to a minimum change policy' (BCE Minutes, 1990/1, 4.3).

These discussions, in particular the ascription of predominance to Rule 1, undoubtedly set the tone for the English Commission's conduct of the Review. They were followed at further meetings by consideration of tabled papers on the types of information to be used by the Secretariat when drafting schemes (BCE Minutes, 1990/3, 4.6) and on the range of constituency electorates: on the latter, the Commission agreed to set 'flexible guidelines' while aiming for electorates within 5,000 of the quota with a maximum range of 15,000 (BCE Minutes, 1991/1, 5.1). By 1991, and having completed its policy considerations, the Commission was ready to announce the commencement of the Review and a statutory notice was published in the *London Gazette* on 21 February, the same day as the Home Secretary informed the House of Commons in reply to a Parliamentary question. The Fourth Periodic Review of English Parliamentary constituencies had begun.

Although the Review was formally under way, the Commission's consideration of policy was not yet complete. The next significant step was discussion of a paper on apportionment and the 'Walton' factor (i.e. the harmonic mean) at its June 1991 meeting. As already discussed (see Chapter 4, p. 184), there is a conflict between Rules 1 and 5 which revolves around the question of apportionment on the basis of theoretical entitlements. Having decided that Rule 1 was paramount, the Commission could have devised a policy which favoured the removal or non-creation of seats in areas with marginal entitlements. It was reluctant to adopt a hard and fast rule, however, instead requesting that the Secretariat prepare schemes 'both rounding up and rounding down the number of seats' and concluding that it would 'have to consider all the options and treat each case on its merits' (BCE Minutes, 1991/3, 5.4), although the Commission advised the Secretariat that for counties with large theoretical entitlements (the example cited was Avon, entitled to 10.48 seats) 'only one viable scheme rounding up the number of seats need be produced' (# 5.2). The Commission was clear that it wanted to limit the growth of Parliament, but its aversion to the rigid application of policy was genuine.[10]

The Secretariat could now set to work preparing schemes for the Commission's approval. Issues were bound to arise during those preparations and also during the subsequent Local Inquiries, but national policy guidelines were in place. One other dimension of policy was fundamental to the Commission's overall strategy, however, although it did not arise for another two years.

Having mooted the idea of crossing London Borough boundaries as long ago as 1988 and confirmed its willingness to do so in 1989, the Commission only returned to consider the question three years later (BCE Minutes, 1988/2, 6; 1989/2, 4; 1992/7, 4.2). During autumn 1992 both the Conservative and Labour parties had contacted the Secretariat about future arrangements for the capital and the Commission agreed that 'the Secretaries would write to them requesting submission of their thoughts on London' (BCE Minutes, 1992/5, 10.4). Those thoughts, together with a paper produced by the Secretariat, were considered at the final meeting of 1992. The Commission reaffirmed its intention to cross boundaries in order to avoid excessive disparities, before responding specifically to a total of eleven individual points made by the parties and agreeing with the Secretariat's proposal 'that any borough, the average electorate of which differed from the electoral quota by more than 12,500 should be paired'. The Minutes do not reveal any discussion of why that specific figure was chosen, but it was broadly consistent with the national numerical guidelines without leading to wholesale crossing of Borough boundaries. The Commission did recognise that disparities exceeding 12,500 had already been approved for some Counties (BCE Minutes, 1992/7, 4.2.3) and was also aware that constituencies in London Boroughs that were not paired would also inevitably exceed that guideline. In selecting nine Boroughs the Commission went significantly further than the five suggested in an academic paper (Rossiter, Johnston and Pattie, 1992), of which it was aware (BCE Minutes, 1992/7, 4.2.6), and than the two only which would have resulted if it had followed its earlier inclination to define excessive electoral disparities in London as 'electorates more than 25 per cent away from the electoral quota' (BCE Minutes, 1989/2, 17).

Of comparable significance was the Commission's response to the sixth of the eleven points, in which it confirmed that neighbouring Boroughs were eligible for consideration as pairs even if their own average deviation would thereby increase. (The Minute records that the Commissioners would 'not commit themselves to avoid pairing boroughs where to do so would make the average deviation of the pair from the electoral quota worse than the average deviation of one of the individual boroughs: they might wish to pair a borough having a very large average deviation with a borough having a low average deviation if this would greatly reduce the large deviation but only slightly worsen the low deviation'; BCE Minutes, 1992/7, 4.2.2.) Yet when the Commission published its proposals for North London, the decision not to pair Islington (thereby making it the only one of the nine Boroughs exceeding the 12,500 guideline not to be paired) was justified in the relevant *News Release* (1 January 1993) primarily by reference to the satisfactory electorates in neighbouring constituencies. The contrast between the *News Release* and the Commission's earlier response to the political parties is evident, and the criterion subsequently listed in the Commission's report (that a neighbour should not be drawn into pairing if it would adversely affect its own disparity; Boundary Commission for England, 1995, #3.11) is not based on any discussion which appears in the Commission's contemporary Minutes and was to add to the Conservative Party's misgivings about the redistricting of the capital. This contrast is further exemplified by the Commission's treatment of the Boroughs of Redbridge and Waltham Forest. When the guidelines were drawn up it was agreed not to pair Boroughs 'if the joint [theoretical entitlement, or TE] ... would lead to an allocation of seats greater than the sum of the seats allocated to the boroughs individually, in order to give effect to rule 1' (BCE Minutes, 1992/7, 4.2.2; this is repeated in Boundary Commission for England, 1995a, #3.11), but when those two Boroughs were considered, and despite the understanding that 'reviewed individually, the boroughs would each be allocated two seats as their TEs were 2.38 and 2.399' (BCE Minutes, 1993/8, 4.43), nevertheless five seats were allocated. Fortunately for the Commission, by the time that its *News Release* was issued it had been provided with updated electorate figures which showed that Redbridge's TE was 2.42, entitling it to 3 under the 'Walton' (harmonic mean) rule.

The Commission also discussed how best to treat the Metropolitan Districts at its December 1992 meeting (see p. 108 above). It confirmed that 'as there is no mention of metropolitan district boundaries in rule 4, seats would be allocated to each metropolitan county on the basis of the county's TE'. It was also agreed that crossing the District boundaries would be considered only if it would result 'either in the county receiving its correct allocation of seats or in the removal of excessive disparities in the electorates' (BCE Minutes, 1992/7, 4.1.1). Using that guideline, the Commission asked the Secretariat to draw up schemes for seventeen different pairings (BCE Minutes, 1992/7, 4/1; 1993/2, 8) and when considering a possible scheme for Kirklees and Wakefield 'decided that as a matter of principle they would not be prepared to cross a joint boundary more than was necessary' (BCE Minutes, 1993/7, 3.7). Equivalent consideration was not given to crossing County boundaries, however, since these are covered by Rule 4, but when considering schemes for Shropshire two options were discussed which crossed the County boundary with Hereford & Worcester (BCE Minutes, 1992/4, 8.3.3); one of the Secretaries pointed out that the Commission had not earlier considered crossing Cumbria's boundaries, however, and the Commission decided not to proceed with the scheme.

Scotland

The 'number of seats' issue also figured prominently in the Scottish Commission's early considerations. The smaller number of constituencies in Scotland meant that preparations could be left later than in England and only one meeting was held in 1990 and two in 1991. At the last of those the Commission confirmed its intention to commence its Review in 1992, and early that year the Secretary tabled a paper on the allocation of Parliamentary constituencies to Regions and Island Areas,[11] pointing out that 'the Secretariat could not start to formulate proposals until the Commission had reached a view on the number of seats proposed for the individual regions' (BCS Minutes, 28 April 1992, 5).[12] This immediately raised the question of Scotland's total allocation and only after extensive discussions spanning three meetings, at which the possibility of a reduction to 71 seats was given serious consideration, was it agreed to plan on the basis of maintaining the existing national total. The Commission's final report states that 'we did not consider that we would be justified in reverting to 71 seats' (Boundary Commission for Scotland, 1995, 13), but gives no hint as to the serious consideration which was given to the possibility of proposing a reduction in Scotland's representation. The Deputy Chairman was especially concerned about this, emphasising the need to 'address the difficulties inherent in the relationship between rules 1(1) and 1(2)' (BCS Minutes, 5 November 1991, 2; the rules refer to the minimum number of seats for Scotland and the desired maximum for Great Britain); he expressed 'concern about the widening gap between the electoral quotas for Scotland and England' and stated his unwillingness 'to subscribe to any document which committed the Commission, come-what-may, to 72 seats' (BCS Minutes, 25 June 1992, 6).

This decision inevitably meant either that Regional boundaries would need to be crossed or that two Regions would receive fewer seats than their theoretical entitlement (Strathclyde was set to lose a seat whereas Grampian, Lothian and Tayside should all have gained one) and the Secretary 'enquired whether the Commission wished to give the Secretariat any guidance on the generality of crossing boundaries'. The conclusion, that members 'were strongly in favour of keeping this option open', was followed at the Commission's next meeting by a discussion of possible amalgamations of Regions, with two options particularly favoured (grouping Borders with Lothian and Tayside with either Central or Fife; BCS Minutes, 8 October 1992, 4). Although the Commission requested the Secretariat to proceed with proposals for Regions in isolation, the logic of its decisions suggested that these would never be implemented, and in March 1993 it agreed the publication of a 'Statement indicating 72 constituencies in Scotland at conclusion of Fourth General Review' (reproduced in Boundary Commission for Scotland, 1995, Appendix D) and announcing its decision:

> to explore the possibility of grouping regions together in order to provide a means of achieving a total number of constituencies not greater than 72 in circumstances whereby the number of seats allocated to any amalgamated area is not less than that which the electorate of the area justifies.

In effect, the Commission was announcing its intention to cross Regional boundaries.

Although the total number of seats and their apportionment tended to dominate the Commission's discussions of policy, another more practical concern also required considerable thought. Practice at the Third Periodic Review had been to use Regional Electoral Divisions (REDs) and where necessary their subdivisions, District wards, as the building blocks from which to assemble constituencies. However, while new REDs were likely to be in place by 1993, it soon became clear that revised ward boundaries were not, which posed particular problems in Strathclyde, where 104 REDs with an average electorate of around 17,000 had to be allocated between 32 seats. (The Commission had expressed concerns about the timetable for reviewing local government electoral arrangements as early as 1991 – BCS Minutes, 8 January 1991, 2 – as well as noting that proposals for local government reform might make the new wards and REDs obsolete; see the full discussion in Boundary Commission for Scotland, 1995, Chapters 1 and 2.) The new REDs were implemented in 1993 and contested in 1994 before being

abolished following the local government reform which replaced the Regions by
unitary authorities. Despite the drawbacks, it was accepted quite early on 'that
there would be many problems for the Commission if it drew its own boundaries'
(BCS Minutes, 28 April 1992, 4: there is no requirement to use wards as building blocks and the Commission did split Glasgow wards at earlier Reviews, but
without a standard building block the Commission would have great difficulties,
not least in evaluating alternative plans suggested by interested parties in response
to its provisional recommendations). In the interests of consistency it decided in
April 1992 to use the new REDs throughout the country (BCS Minutes, 28 April
1992, 4), and this was announced in the *Explanatory Memorandum* published in
March 1993 (reproduced in Boundary Commission for Scotland, 1995, Appendix C). The reasonableness of this policy and its consequential implications for
the application of the other Rules were subsequently challenged by petition, but
in the opinion of Lord Weir in his judgement on petitions by Philip Roy Gallie
MP *et al.* and by Renfrew West and Inverclyde Conservative & Unionist Association *et al.* for judicial review of the Commission's decisions on this matter;[13]

> I consider that in adopting their approach the Commission did not fetter their dis-
> cretion. Indeed, as senior counsel for the Commission put it, the deliberate selec-
> tion of regional electoral divisions as the basic method was itself an exercise of
> discretion in the performance of their duty under Section 3(1) of the Act.

Wales

Changes to local government boundaries were even more dominant during the
early stages of the Welsh Review. As with Scotland, the government had
announced its intention to introduce legislation for a new unitary system of local
government, but whereas the Scottish Commission decided that it could not defer
a 1992 commencement,[14] the Welsh Commission, faced with a significantly
smaller task, 'agreed that their primary aim for the moment was to avoid the
absurdity of submitting a report just before re-organisation took place and at a
time when the decision on re-organisation had been known for some time' (BCW
Minutes, 1991/3, 6.6).[15] This was further complicated by the draft *Boundary Commissions Bill 1992*, tabled at the Commission's next meeting, which required the
Commission to submit its report by 31 December 1994 *and* to use local government boundaries as existing on 1 June 1994 (BCW Minutes, 1992/1, 7.3). With
no certainty as to when changes to the latter would be enacted (Royal Assent was
eventually granted on 5 July 1994) the Commission was in the unenviable position of attempting to prepare for a Review on uncertain boundaries. The issue
dominated its meetings during the remainder of 1992 and for most of 1993 until
it could wait no longer and announced on 4 November 1993 its intention to commence the Review on existing County boundaries. In coming to this decision, the
crucial factor appears to have been legal advice received that although late submission of a report would not invalidate its contents, the Commission was 'bound

to take steps now to attempt to comply with the statutory duty [to submit the report by 31 December 1994] and to commence the review' (text of a News Release of 9 November 1993 announcing the start of the Review – reproduced in Boundary Commission for Wales, 1995 Appendix D; the issue is set out in the Introduction to that report).

The delays caused by these uncertainties, coupled with the interregnum preceding the appointment of a new Deputy Chairman, arguably affected the Commission's subsequent actions. Mr Justice Anthony Evans presided over his last meeting on 22 July 1992, a year before his successor's first meeting; there was only one meeting during the interim, when it was indicated that the Review should start in February 1993 (though this was never implemented; BCW Minutes, 1993/1, 4.1). Attention was diverted from consideration of policy and increasing time constraints bolstered previously held arguments for adopting an uncontroversial approach to the Review (it was felt that the previous Review had been 'controversial' and hopes were expressed that this one would be 'less radical'; BCW Minutes, 1991/2, 6.4): the possibility of a total "no change" option, 'giving precedence to rule 7 over the others', was seriously considered, and only abandoned when legal advice was received that it would be an improper application of that Rule (BCW Minutes of meeting with political parties, 10 November 1993, 4.1). As early as 1991 it had been agreed that the country's total allocation was 'a major policy decision' and that a total of 40 seats 'might conflict with rule 1. … which is the primary rule governing the work of the Commission' (BCW Minutes, 1991/1, 5.1.3), yet it wasn't until November 1993 that the Commission returned to the issue. At that meeting, despite agreement that the allocation of 'still more seats. … would be unwelcome and would have to be fully justified', it also agreed to 'avoid crossing county boundaries if at all possible' (BCW Minutes, 1993/5, 6.2); even so there was ambiguity in the Commission's discussion of schemes for Clwyd and Gwynedd as members are reported being 'unsure whether it was right to join the two counties in order to restrict the total number of seats allocated' (BCW Minutes, 1993/7, 10.3). It is clear that such an approach had fundamental implications for 'the primary rule' and the failure to devote more time to its consideration is surprising. It seems fair to conclude that there was a general lack of guidance to the Secretariat from the Commission: the Secretary's suggestion to the Commission 'that certain issues would need to be discussed at a policy meeting' (BCW Minutes, 1993/3, 3.1) came after the incoming Deputy Chairman's first meeting at which he had been informed that schemes for the entire country had already been prepared (BCW Minutes, 1993/2, 3.5).

Northern Ireland

The Northern Ireland Commission is faced with the smallest task in terms of volume, though not in terms of the potential for controversy. Again the number of seats was a major issue with Rule 1(4) imposing a presumption in favour of 17 seats, but with discretion for either 16 or 18 (see Chapter 4, pp. 105–7). Before it announced the Review on 19 March 1993, the Commission sought legal opinion from Senior Crown Counsel as to the correct interpretation of that Rule and concluded, on the basis of that advice, 'that they would be justified in recommending a number of constituencies other than 17 only to reduce or alleviate difficulties experienced in applying the Rules on the basis of 17 constituencies' (Boundary Commission for Northern Ireland, 1995, 3). The implications of this advice, both for the existing pattern of constituencies and for the other Rules, appear not to have received much attention and the Commission's Minutes reveal no thoroughgoing discussion of policy issues before the Secretariat began drawing up schemes. Indeed, although the Commission reported to Parliament that it had 'constructed a set of principles on which to base ... decisions' (Boundary Commission for Northern Ireland, 1995, 3) not all of these were in place at the onset of the Review and there is no reference at all in the Commission's Minutes to the 7 per cent tolerance around the electoral quota which is set out as one of those principles in the final report.

Party meetings with the Commissions

Thus far we have considered the Commissions' deliberations in isolation, but there is an established tradition of meetings with political parties at an early stage of any Review. The original impetus for this came from the Vivian Report, which suggested that each Commission should meet 'to hear any representations from the Chief or National Officers of the principal Party organisations with respect to the provisional proposals', in the somewhat unrealistic hope that 'such an arrangement might be of advantage by withdrawing from the local hearings any representations arising out of Party interests' (Vivian Committee, 1942, #111). This recommendation was repeated by the 1944 Speaker's Conference (recommendation 20), but was not embodied in legislation. Although the Commissions' Initial Reports contain no reference to any such meetings, the widespread dissatisfaction over the conduct of the First Periodical Review produced renewed demands for greater consultation, particularly during the 1958 debates on the *House of Commons (Redistribution of Seats) Bill*. The Commissions' general response was that while it would be inappropriate to discuss individual recommendations, meetings with the parties to exchange views on general matters of policy and interpretation would be useful. However there are some significant differences between the Commissions in the way they have undertaken that task.

The English Commission has been the most informative about the meetings. Two were held, on 26 April 1991 and 12 March 1993, and the Minutes of both are included in the Commission's report (Boundary Commission for England, 1995b, Appendix D). The first covered a range of topics, and although it agreed to give sympathetic consideration to several of the points raised, 'the Commission would not give any guarantees of rigid application of policy nor agree to any course of action which would fetter their discretion'. The Commission's Minutes do not record any subsequent discussion of the meeting and there is no evidence to suggest that its policy was influenced in any significant way by the parties' comments.

The second was convened primarily to discuss the Review of London. Subsequent to their formulation of policy on pairing at the end of 1992 the Commission wrote to the parties outlining its intended approach and offering them a meeting 'if they so wished' (BCE Minutes, 1992/7, 4.2). The Conservatives, particularly concerned with both the arithmetic guidelines for pairing (they favoured a figure of 10,000, which would have involved four more Boroughs than finally recommended) and the way in which the Commission had allocated each London Borough to one of seven groups for administrative purposes (fearing that would influence the chances of pairing), were particularly keen that a meeting should take place. But apart from persuading the Commission to alter the composition of the seven groups, something which they had already shown a willingness to do, the meeting changed nothing. (Again, there is no evidence in the Commission's Minutes that the parties' comments were subsequently discussed, and the Commission's guidelines relating to London were not subsequently changed.)

The reports of the Scottish and Welsh Commissions make only passing reference to their meetings, describing them as 'most helpful' and 'very useful' respectively (Boundary Commission for Scotland, 1995, #23; Boundary Commission for Wales, 1995, #30). No formal minutes of the three Scottish meetings were taken, though in each case a brief note was prepared. The timing of the first in May 1993, after the Commission had decided and published its main policy principles and after provisional recommendations had been published for sixteen seats and decisions taken on a further seven, reveals much about the Commission's thinking. In the words of an earlier Minute, the purpose of a meeting would be to discuss 'the overall approach to the review which the Commission *had* adopted and the reasons for this' (our emphasis; BCS Minutes, 8 October 1992, 6.1); the parties were entitled to an explanation, not to prior consultation.

The Welsh Commission adopted a rather different attitude. It held two meetings with the parties within the space of a fortnight in November 1993, both of which had the potential to alter the Commission's thinking. As discussed above, the Commission gave serious consideration to a "no change" option and the minutes of its October meeting report it as being 'anxious to find out the reaction of the political parties to proceeding on these lines' (BCW Minutes, 1993/4, 3.3). Accordingly a meeting was arranged for 10 November. However during the intervening fortnight legal advice was obtained which suggested that such a course of action would constitute an 'improper use' of Rule 7 and instead of helping to mould the Commission's policy, the parties left sympathising with its predicament (BCW Minutes of meeting with representatives of Parliamentary political parties, 10 November, 1993, 4.1). The Commission's willingness to listen was also evident at the second meeting, at which the entitlement of Powys and the parties' varying views on the entitlement of Gwynedd and of the advisability of crossing its boundary with Clwyd were discussed (BCW Minutes, 1993/6, 1.2). Although these views were not referred to in subsequent discussions, the Commission was aware of them when making its decisions, and the possibility that the parties' input influenced the provisional recommendations cannot be ruled out.

In the case of Northern Ireland, that input was undoubtedly greater. First, although the declared intention of the meetings was to discuss 'broad issues of policy', the Northern Ireland Commission also considered it useful 'to get a feel for the political parties' views on changes they might foresee in the framework of constituencies' (BCNI Minutes, 10 March 1993, 4; Boundary Commission for Northern Ireland, 1995, 5). Second, whereas the other Commissions held joint meetings with all parties, this was not considered feasible in Northern Ireland, as a result of which the Commission held six separate meetings, including more than one where specific proposals were tabled. (The tabling of proposals is not mentioned in the Commission's Minutes, but was related to us in our interviews with party representatives.) Third, the Commission subsequently considered a paper summarising these discussions in which it was suggested that advocates of 18 constituencies 'did not forcibly press the case' and that proposals to extend Belfast's constituencies outwards 'in an even, radial fashion' had been unpopular (BCNI Minutes, 30 June 1993, 4). The dividing line between policy and the formulation of individual proposals may not always be clear, particularly when as few as 17 constituencies are under consideration, but there can be little doubt that the Commission laid itself open to charges of political influence both by the timing of the meetings and by their content.

Preparation of the provisional recommendations

England and Wales

The English and Welsh Commissions share the same Secretariat (based in London) and the management of both Reviews was conducted by three senior officers: the Secretary, Bob McLeod,[16] and two Senior Executive Officers, Terry Bergin and Bob Farrance, all civil servants employed within the Office of Population Censuses and Surveys (OPCS). After the introduction of the 1992 Act they received additional assistance from David Ridout, another Senior Executive Officer seconded from the Home Office, who performed the role of Acting Secretary when McLeod was unavailable. However these individuals did not have the primary task of drawing up potential schemes, a job which was assigned to teams of three (a Higher Executive Officer, an Executive Officer and a Clerk), again mainly drawn from the staff of OPCS. Each member of these teams was personally interviewed before appointment by the Secretary, with membership of a political party a bar to appointment. None had any previous experience of redistricting and most had to learn 'on the job', though extensive use was made of the papers from the Third Periodic Review, supplemented by training talks given by the Secretary.[17]

At the formal commencement of the Review there were five teams, but when it became clear that the 1992 Act necessitated additional resources, McLeod approached OPCS for advice on how this might best be achieved. As a result it was agreed to increase the number of teams from five to nine, and at the height of the Review a total of 33 was employed, falling to 20 by September 1994 and 10 by April 1995. Most of the extra staff came from OPCS, though civil servants were seconded from the Home Office and some casual staff were also employed. (Recruitment does not seem to have been easy, and problems obtaining staff at Executive and Administrative Officer grades were reported in October 1992; BCE Minutes, 1992/5, 2.1.) Throughout the Review there was considerable flexibility within this overall structure – some teams would be given an extra member, individuals would move between teams to help with a particularly difficult area, and those dealing with Wales for a time subsequently returned to consider areas in England.

In our interviews with team members it became clear that there was no set approach to the task of devising a set of possible schemes. There was no attempt to prejudge the number of options which would be presented to the Commissions, and the Commission itself, though agreeing that three or four schemes would generally be sufficient, was aware that 'it was difficult to specify an ideal number of schemes for a Review area because it depended on the circumstances of each' (BCE Minutes, 1990/3, 5.1). In the English and Welsh Shire Counties an average of four schemes was produced, sometimes with additional variations, but the number ranged between two and eight. (Two only were discussed for East Sussex, Northamptonshire, Northumberland and Nottinghamshire, whereas for Hampshire the Commission was presented with eight.) In unpaired London Boroughs and Metropolitan Districts the number was generally lower, reflecting the fact that the average total electorate was smaller and the average ward electorate larger. In these areas no more than three schemes were ever presented, sometimes only one, and on several occasions no alternative was offered to the status quo. (These were Brent, Enfield, Hackney, Haringey, Harrow, Merton, St Helens, Sutton and Wirral; only one scheme was tabled for Barking & Dagenham and for Havering, and for Hillingdon, Hounslow and Islington the Commission was presented with only one alternative to the status quo.) More schemes were considered when pairing was an option, but in no pair did the total number exceed six. Some evidence suggests that as the teams became more familiar both with their task and with the probable reactions of the Commissions, the number of options offered tended to decline, but throughout there was an emphasis on flexibility, judging each case on its merits. One member of the Secretariat summarised the approach as follows:

> There was never a set number of options. There would generally be a minimum change scheme which would be less concerned with numbers, a scheme which produced much closer equality of electorates, plus a variable number of other schemes. Whenever looking at an area we would first consider those bits which could stay as they are, or at least where minimal change was needed. This was reinforced by our experience during the review which emphasised people's dislike of change.

The emphasis on minimum change had the dual advantage of making life simpler and according with both the Rules and the Commissions' earlier guidance. Where change was necessary teams could also refer to the guidelines on acceptable variation around the quota,[18] but the rest was largely at their discretion. It was rare for team members to have any first-hand knowledge of the area under consideration, although those who did found it valuable and several of the recommendations to the Commission for London constituencies contained quite detailed justifications based on local knowledge. In most cases, local information was derived from the *Municipal Journal* (for topography) together with local authority Structure Plans and OPCS population projections. Maps were a primary source, revealing not only physical barriers but also settlement patterns and lines of communication. *Census Monitors* were used once they became available (though it was stressed that this was primarily for demographic rather than for socio-economic information) and several emphasised the importance of the Inquiry Reports from the Third Review, both as a source of information and in highlighting opportunities for remedying perceived inadequacies in the existing pattern of seats. In response to our suggestion that shape might have played an important part in their deliberations, few were particularly conscious of it as a factor, though one team member put it that 'clearly an odd-looking constituency was not desirable'.

For most of the Review the mechanics of redistribution differed little, if at all, from earlier Reviews. Possible schemes were produced manually, working on an Ordnance Survey base map with overlays of ward and existing constituency boundaries. Teams would consider various options, testing the advantages of moving ward x from seat y to seat z, looking at the implications of creating a new constituency in different parts of a County or Borough, and so on, but all possibilities were assessed by eye. However, as early as 1988 the Secretariat had begun to investigate the possibility of an easy-to-use Geographical Information System (GIS) to help with this process, and in the spring of 1990 a Senior Executive Officer was seconded from the Information Technology Division of OPCS to oversee the evaluation of a system for implementation by the end of 1991. ESRI won the contract (to provide a SUN UNIX Sparc system running ARC/INFO and OS Boundary Line), but the project was beset by a series of problems and it wasn't until March 1993 that teams were able to use it; it was not employed at all in Wales, and in England only for the preparation of schemes for Greater London, Merseyside, West Yorkshire, Buckinghamshire, Essex, Lancashire and Surrey. It was never intended that it would be an intelligent 'decision-making' package; rather the software offered a 'what if' approach, redrawing boundaries and recalculating electorates, ranges, etc.[19] The teams gave it a guarded welcome (its speed was praised, but its ease of use and aspects of its mapping were not), but its late introduction and limited functionality meant that the 'traditional' way of devising schemes was not significantly altered during the Fourth Review.

One other aspect of the Secretariat's work, that of ensuring consistency, is also worthy of comment. With up to nine teams operating at any one time and relatively flexible guidelines, it was inevitable that the schemes presented to the Commission depended to some degree on which team was responsible; this applied chiefly in England, however, as just two teams were employed in the work for Wales.[20] In order to minimise variability of approach, oversight of the teams was divided between Farrance and Bergin, with the former given the main responsibility for ensuring consistency. To that end the two Senior Executive Officers were 'continually bouncing papers backwards and forwards', in an attempt to ensure that all schemes would be acceptable to the Commission. This role also extended to another important aspect of the Secretariat's work, preparing the written material which accompanied the Commission's recommendations. Ultimate responsibility for these documents resides with the Commission, but the team responsible for devising schemes for a particular area also prepared the *News Releases*, including in particular the 'reasons' for the provisional recommendations. After some early difficulties these *News Releases* undoubtedly became less variable, though the occasional gremlin was always liable to appear, as in the references to future growth that accompanied the Oxfordshire provisional recommendations (see below).

Scotland

Consistency was less of an issue in Scotland where the scale of the task required far fewer personnel. The Secretariat to the Scottish Commission at no time consisted of more than five members, all permanent staff employed within the Scottish Office. The Secretary, David Jeffrey, spent approximately half his time on the Review and the remainder on other Scottish Office duties. The others operated in two teams each headed by a Higher Executive Officer reporting directly to Jeffrey but working very closely together and with common support staff. There was no overlap of personnel from the Third Review and no formal training, just an introduction from the Secretary. As in England and Wales, previous Commission papers proved useful, but in our interviews it was stressed that the new teams established their own methods of working and that they did not feel bound by approaches adopted in earlier Reviews.

The number of options presented to the Commission varied more than in England and Wales, with the Commission on the one hand being invited to accept the Secretariat's sole proposal for Grampian but on the other being offered at least 17/18 different schemes for Strathclyde, including at least four for Glasgow and thirteen for the rest of the Region. (It is not possible to be precise because the BCS Minutes do not identify the number of options tabled in all cases.) As in England, the use of information technology promised more than it delivered: a PC-based system for 'what-ifs', building on Census work from the General Register Office, did not include natural features in its mapping and was not extensively used; and the unavailability of digitised mapping for the new REDs meant that plans to use a computer-based algorithm to devise schemes which minimised the range of constituency electorates was abandoned. The possibility of using an algorithm designed by Prof. Stan Openshaw of the University of Leeds 'as a preliminary to formulating constituency boundaries' was suggested by one Commissioner (Prof. Urlan Wannop: BCS Minutes, 7 January 1993, 6.3), though when interviewed after completion of the Review he expressed doubts as to how useful it would have been.[21]

Northern Ireland

The Northern Ireland Secretariat was the smallest of the four, comprising the Secretary, John Fisher, a Senior Research Officer, an office manager and Fisher's personal secretary. Fisher set up separate offices from the Northern Ireland Office and contracted out to the private sector those aspects which had no security implications. He put out to tender for a Geographical Information System (GIS) and, unlike the other Secretariats, was successful in securing the timely delivery of what he described as a 'very simple but very reliable' system from the Ordnance Survey of Northern Ireland which developed and based the GIS at its headquarters in Belfast. (The system is described in Chapter 3 of the Commission's report – Boundary Commission for Northern Ireland, 1995 – and in greater detail in a professional journal – Boundary Commission for Northern Ireland, 1994.) This permitted the evaluation of a far larger number of possible schemes (32 are referred to in the Commission's minutes alone), though the fact that no set of provisional recommendations was more altered after publication than that for Northern Ireland confirms that the usefulness of any system is constrained by its input.

Commission consideration of Provisional Recommendations

England

The next stage in the process was for the Commissions to consider the schemes produced by the Secretariats. In England this took place over a period of two years commencing in July 1991. The first four groups of Counties were considered at successive meetings between July 1991 and January 1992, followed by the fifth group in July 1992. At this point the Commission had covered 20 of the 39 Shire Counties, but little over a quarter of the English electorate. There then followed an intensive period of seven months, starting in November 1992, during which the Commission met a total of eleven times, with the formulation of provisional recommendations on all but one agenda. Although the pressures placed upon the Commission members by this volume of work were considerable, reaching a peak in the spring of 1993 when provisional recommendations for a total of 192 seats were approved at meetings on successive Fridays, the workload was cleared and the final set of provisional recommendations was approved at the Commission's June 1993 meeting. (Those for Essex, Lancashire, West Midlands, West Yorkshire and all twelve South London Boroughs were approved at the first two of those meetings, covering 113 constituencies, 21 per cent of the English total.) In November 1992 the Commission had 'agreed that future agendas should be tailored so that no meeting should last more beyond a maximum of 7 hours and that priority should be given to papers that precede the publication of recommendations or inquiry notices' (BCE Minutes, 1992/6, 4.3), However, the Minutes of the next meeting record that 'there was still too much business on the agenda for one meeting' and that 'due to pressure of work, the Secretariat had not dispatched any of the papers until one week before the meeting and there had been insufficient time for the Commission to read all the papers and prepare for the meeting' (BCE Minutes, 1992/7, 2.8). When McLeod warned the Commission at its next meeting that 'particularly heavy workloads could be expected and that clearing the work, especially that concerning the selection of provisional recommendations, was crucial to the deadline of 31 December 1994 being met' (BCE Minutes, 1993/1, 10.2) the Commission agreed to hold three further meetings in April, May and June of that year.

How did the Commission choose between the various schemes on offer, how significant was its own independent contribution and which factors were particularly important in determining its choices? The mechanics of the process were reasonably straightforward. Before each meeting at which schemes were to be discussed, each Commissioner received a paper giving background information on the area under consideration, together with the schemes identified by the Secretariat; these papers followed an agreed general format, with information on topography and future population growth, 'reasons why other attempted distributions were unsuitable' and, wherever possible, the Commission 'would welcome a recommendation from the Secretariat as to the scheme they preferred together with the reasons for that choice' (BCE Minutes, 1990/3, 5). At the meeting the team responsible for drawing up the schemes would attend and a brief presentation would be made. The Commission would then proceed to discuss the schemes, asking the Secretariat for its advice where necessary, before arriving at its conclusion. (An initial intention to have a workstation at meetings to assist Commission deliberations – BCE Minutes, 1991/6, 2.1 – was abandoned.) Only once, when considering Lancashire, were the members unable to come to a decision on the basis of the Secretariat's presentation, and the team involved left the meeting for a few hours before returning with modified schemes, developed using the recently available GIS, one of which was adopted by the Commission.[22] Lancashire also provided the only instance where a vote was required in order to determine which scheme to adopt: the Commission's minutes record that 'after further discussion it was agreed by a majority, that 15 seats should be allocated instead of 16' (BCE Minutes, 1993/7, 3.47).

Given the amount of effort devoted by the Secretariat to investigating the various possibilities, it should come as little surprise to find that in most Counties and London Boroughs the Commission was content to adopt one of the suggested schemes. It is true that the Commission decided to make modifications to the chosen scheme in two London Boroughs and in over a third of English Counties, but – other than name changes – these were generally very minor alterations affecting just one or two wards; they impacted on just one in ten of the provisionally recommended constituencies, and fewer than one in every 250 electors. Only in Lancashire and the Isle of Wight were all of the Secretariat's schemes rejected, and in both cases this reflected the importance placed by the Commission on Rule 1. Thus in Lancashire, four of the Secretariat's five schemes were for 16 seats, while in the Isle of Wight the Commission 'instructed the Secretaries to publish provisional recommendations for no change' (BCE Minutes, 1991/6, 6.4.2) even though all four schemes presented allocated two seats to the County. (This is the only case in the Minutes where the word *Instructed* was used in the discussion of provisional recommendations, which may be significant. The decision to allocate only one seat was taken because the Commission 'felt that future growth in the electorate of the Isle of Wight may not be as high as the remainder of England and if two seats were allocated, this would mean the creation of two seats with electorates well below the EQ [electoral quota], rather than one seat above the EQ': BCE Minutes, 1991/6, 6.4.2.)

The factors influencing the Commission in its consideration of the various schemes cast considerable light upon the members' thinking. Predictably the Minutes of those discussions place great emphasis both on reducing inequalities in electorates and on restricting change in order to minimise the breaking of local ties. Both factors were mentioned in a majority of discussions, though significantly the avoidance of disruption tended to receive greater stress. More of a surprise is the emphasis that the Commission placed on the 'shapeliness' of potential constituencies. Fully half of the discussions produced minuted references to the significance of shape, and particularly to the perceived inadequacies of seats with 'awkward' shapes, as with Bromley where one of the three schemes tabled 'was not favoured due to the very poor shape of Seat 1 and was not considered further' (BCE Minutes, 1993/6, 6.2.10), and the decision to place the ward of Boughton Moncholsea in the Maidstone constituency 'to give the seat a better shape' (BCE Minutes, 1993/1, 4.1.4). The Rules and the Commission's report, together with its *News Releases* and booklet, all recognise that shape is a factor, but from our reading of the Minutes we have little doubt that it exerted far more influence over the Commission than any of these sources would suggest. That influence was certainly not improper, but there is inadequate recognition of its powerful, often psychological, impact: it may not have been the decisive factor in the choice of scheme in many instances but it certainly made an important contribution to decisions, as in the transfer of Pendlebury ward from Eccles to Salford because 'it would cause least disruption and produce better shaped ... seats' (BCE Minutes, 1993/4, 4.9).

No other factors came close to these three in frequency, but there are several strands worth emphasising. The importance of following District boundaries and of avoiding the fragmentation of Districts was minuted in around a quarter of discussions, as was the undesirability of splitting towns between seats, of detaching one or two wards from an urban core, and of splitting a town from its rural hinterland. Next in terms of frequency came considerations of future growth, minuted in around one in six discussions, geographical barriers (one in ten) and lines of communication (one in twelve). Clearly it is important not to confuse incidence with importance; although the minutes give a very full account of what the Commission discussed, they do not provide a definitive statement of what proved critical in the final decisions. However on those occasions when the Commission amended one of the proposed schemes, the specific reasons for those changes were recorded, and these tend to confirm the general impression. There were twenty such instances, with thirty stated reasons, which were, in descending order of frequency: non-specific local ties (9), minimising inequalities (9), avoiding the division of towns (3), shape (2), district boundaries (2), total number of seats (2), physical barriers (2) and future growth (1).

Wales

Whereas England's provisional recommendations took some two years to finalise, those for Wales were agreed within a week. The Welsh Commission met on 26 and 30 November 1993 and had little difficulty arriving at a consensus. All but eleven of the existing seats were to remain unaltered; apart from Clwyd and Dyfed Counties, both of which were to receive an additional seat, just one ward and 1,489 electors were to transfer. (That transfer, involving one Monmouth Borough ward, was suggested by a Commissioner not to reduce inequalities but as one of two proposed changes to Monmouth constituency which made 'geographical sense'; BCW Minutes, 1993/6, 6.1.) The Commission's approach is well illustrated by the full minutes of its discussion of Mid Glamorgan (BCW Minutes, 1993/6, 7.1):

> The Commission agreed that Mid Glamorgan would retain seven seats. Having considered the four schemes presented by the Secretariat, the Commission considered that the arguments for recommending no changes to the existing seats are well set out in the schemes paper. Although the disparity between seats is high at 14,938, it was decided that the topography of the county and the need to keep long established communities together meant that the existing seats should be retained without any changes.

The emphasis upon minimising change and upon community ties took clear precedence over 'the numbers game' as far as the Welsh Commission was concerned. The 'high' yet clearly acceptable disparity in Mid Glamorgan was matched by one in Gwent referred to as 'only 10,141', although a scheme for Dyfed (which was allocated an additional constituency) was rejected because the disparity of 9,240 was considered 'unacceptable' (BCW Minutes, 1993/7, 7.3). The Welsh Commission was also more explicit in its references to local ties, expressing them as accepted facts rather than matters of opinion to be tested locally; for example, it recorded that 'to recommend that south Ceredigion be joined to north Pembrokeshire would be contentious as the two areas had little in common; any division of Ceredigion would be unpopular' (BCW Minutes, 1993/7, 7.3).

Scotland

Consideration of the Scottish Commission's approach is limited by the brief reporting of their discussions in the minutes. Beginning with the Islands Areas at the start of the year, proposals for all but Strathclyde Region had been finalised by the Commission's meeting in July 1993, followed by Glasgow and the rest of Strathclyde at two meetings in October. Only in Strathclyde and Lothian did the Commission make (slight) modifications to their identified best of the Secretariat's schemes[23] and only when discussing possible schemes for Highland Region does there seem to have been any difficulty in achieving consensus: the Minutes of that meeting record a 'lengthy' discussion, with one member suggesting that 'the public would see the current review as an opportunity to achieve greater electoral parity' whereas the Deputy Chairman stressed 'the practical problems for Members of Parliament of serving their constituencies' (BCS Minutes, 1 April 1993, 5.1). Differences of opinion such as this were a feature of all Commissions, but one respect in which the Scottish Commission differed from its counterparts was the pro-active role taken by a Commission member in formulating possible schemes. When considering both Tayside and Glasgow, Prof. Wannop presented his own proposal and on both occasions his colleagues were persuaded of its merits, though in Tayside it was not implemented because of the decision to pair with Central Region, while in Glasgow it 'happened to produce a result in conformity with one of the options offered by the Secretariat' (BCS Minutes, 7 October 1993, 5).[24]

Northern Ireland

The Northern Ireland Commission spent the longest time reviewing options. Between 25 March and 22 October 1993 the Commission held thirteen meetings, all of which featured presentations of possible schemes for the province. This represented an important contrast with the approach adopted by their counterparts, where at most two meetings were devoted to consideration of any one area. In Northern Ireland the consideration of specifics tended to inform policy, not vice versa. Thus the decision to impose a limit on deviations from the quota was taken at the eighth meeting, that to maintain rather than increase Northern Ireland's allocation at the twelfth, and that to reduce the number of seats in Belfast at the last. As with the other Commissions, the process was led by the Secretariat and the scheme eventually adopted reflected many of the concerns of the other Commissions: shape, numbers and the undesirability of splitting local government districts. Attention was paid to the views of the political parties, however, and in one discussion 'attention was drawn to the further letter received from Sir James Kilfedder MP, containing recommendations with respect to the North Down constituency which were illustrated in this scheme' (BCNI Minutes, 30 June 1993, 6).[25]

Conclusion

Several conclusions emerge from this consideration of the work leading up to the publication of the four Commissions' provisional recommendations. Perhaps the most striking relates to the variability of approach adopted. At various times all four Commissions identified the total number of seats as the primary issue. In Scotland and, initially, Northern Ireland (where the total is in any case firmly capped and the Commission's flexibility is small), the pressure for growth was resisted by a clear policy decision that Rule 1 was not only primary but also paramount. In England, Rule 1 provided the framework but was not allowed to dominate, while in Wales, despite fine words, it was observed only in the breach. Nor was it just in relation to Rule 1 that the Commissions differed. Far greater emphasis was placed on Rule 7 in the policy reviews in England than in Scotland, whereas special geographical considerations held more sway in Wales than elsewhere, as did the sanctity of local government boundaries. In Wales and Northern Ireland the political parties were given the opportunity to influence the Commission before it published its recommendations, whereas in Scotland a very different approach was adopted. Whatever one's views of the differing interpretations (and it is possible to sympathise with all of them), electors in all four countries return representatives to the same Parliament and it cannot be considered satisfactory that so little effort was made to reconcile these differences.

In addition to variability between Commissions, there was also variability within. The most serious problem appears to have been the patchiness of the policy reviews. Only the English Commission came close to carrying out a thorough examination of all the relevant policy issues, and even that had shortcomings. Most noteworthy was the failure of the other Commissions to discuss, in advance, indicative figures regarding permissible deviations from the electoral quota, a vital aspect of any redistricting exercise.[26] Instead each appears to have become preoccupied with one or two salient issues and to have neglected the wider picture. In this regard it is probably no coincidence that the English Commission faces numerically by far the largest task, spent far longer than its counterparts on preparatory work, and started preparing far earlier; familiarity with the issues and the resources which could be devoted to a policy review, particularly within the Secretariat, were significantly greater. However, had the review of policy been accorded sufficient priority, the necessary resources were available to all Commissions. Given that many of the subsequent criticisms of the Commissions concerned matters of policy, there can be little doubt that greater attention to this aspect would have significantly improved overall perceptions of the Fourth Review.

This leads on to our third and final observation, one which relates to the somewhat unsatisfactory nature of the Commissioner's role. Being a Commissioner is a part-time responsibility and most have demanding jobs elsewhere in public life; indeed all four Deputy Chairmen, by definition, exercise an important judicial function. While we are in no doubt that the Commissioners took their role very seriously, the comments particularly of the members of the English Commission strongly suggest that the demands of the job were disproportionate to the time available in which to do it. For most Commissioners the Review was not their primary interest and as a result considerable reliance was placed upon the Secretariats. All four Commissions were fortunate in having estimable Secretaries, but it would be wrong to under-estimate the difficulties facing the Secretariats themselves. The periodic nature of the process means that most of the experience built up over the course of the previous review is lost and training for new staff was inadequate. The shortcomings of the policy reviews added to these difficulties, but they in turn highlight the rather uncertain relationship between Commissioners and Secretariat; while the former were ultimately responsible for the policy they played a lesser role than might have been expected in its formulation.

Difficulties and shortcomings notwithstanding, the four Commissions had now published their provisional recommendations. Their decisions thus far had set the agenda for the Fourth Review but the rest of the electorate had yet to have its say. After the process of public consultation was over the Commissions would have to consider their response, but for now attention switched to the consultation itself. How was it conducted, who took part, what did they say and did it make any difference? It is to these questions that we now turn.

Notes

1   All but one of the Commissioners and four of the Assistant Commissioners (AC) who acted during the Fourth Review were male, hence the use of 'he'.

2   With the exception of the Registrar General for Scotland, these assessors appear to have played only a very small part in the Commissions' deliberations, with very few mentions of them appearing in the Commissions' Minutes. The Welsh Commission in particular seems to have managed largely without their contributions; the two assessors sent a total of seventeen apologies to the twelve meetings of the Commission during 1993 and 1994.

3   Judge Newey's entry in *Who's Who* both prior to and during the time of his appointment includes reference to his position as Chairman of Sevenoaks & District Conservative Association, 1965–1968.

4   For reasons that we are unable to understand, Judge Newey is referred to in the evidence as a 'Referee' although he was a full member of the Boundary Commission for England (BCE) until 1988.

5   In references to Boundary Commission for England (BCE) Minutes, 1988/2 refers to the year and the meeting in that year, and the subsequent number to the paragraph.

6   The latest (1997) two appointees as members of the Boundary Commission for England both served as Assistant Commissioners during the Fourth Periodic Review.

7   Although the legislation requires the Commissions to keep boundaries 'under continuous review', that responsibility is mainly confined to reviews of the boundaries of constituencies used for elections to the European Parliament and minor realignments of constituency boundaries to follow changes in local government wards; the creation of a new seat for Milton Keynes in 1990 is the sole major exception to this (see Chapter 3, pp. 121–4). In November 1997 the government introduced its *European Parliamentary Elections Bill* which proposes that future elections to that Parliament should use the party list system in multi-member constituencies. If this is passed, the Boundary Commissions will no longer have to undertake the first of their two interim responsibilities, since the multi-member constituencies are to comprise groups of whole

counties in England and both Scotland and Wales are to be single constituencies (Northern Ireland already is for this purpose).

8 Other meetings confirm the pressures that the English Commissioners were under:

> The Deputy Chairman stated that it would significantly impair his availability to do the normal work of a High Court Judge if he had to attend Commission meetings every fortnight. Miss Cameron added that she was not able to guarantee attendance every fortnight, because of the commitments of her practice (BCE, Minutes, 1992/3, 9.4).

> The Commission confirmed that it would not be possible for them to deal with all of the work set down for each meeting. It was not a question of the number of items to be dealt with, but the vast amount of reading that the Commission members would have to undertake prior to each meeting and the limited period available to them to do this between the meetings. (BCE, Minutes, 1994/6, 1.2)

9 There was a change of Secretary between the Third and Fourth Reviews, so none of the Secretaries during the Fourth Review had any experience of a previous Review.

10 In this, it was undoubtedly influenced by the need to avoid charges of what is termed 'Wednesbury unreasonableness' (Rawlings, 1988, 57). In situations in which the final decision-making power lies with Parliament, as with the recommendations of the Boundary Commissions, then according to the House of Lords judgement in the case of *Associated Picture Houses vs.Wednesbury Corporation* (1 KB 223, CA, 1948) it is not appropriate for the Courts to review a Ministerial decision unless the body which advised the Minister (a Boundary Commission in our example) can be shown to have misconstrued the rules under which it operates. Thus, if a Commission has operated its discretion properly within the rules, its procedures and recommendations cannot be subject to judicial review, only Parliamentary scrutiny; see Jowell and Lester (1987).

11 The Islands Areas comprise three unitary authorities: Orkney Islands Area; Shetland Islands Area; and Western Isles Islands Area.

12 The Boundary Commission for Scotland Meetings (BCS) are minuted using a continuous numbering sequence until 1 April 1993, and from then on are dated only. We give only the dates in our references.

13 The quote is from pp. 32–3 of Lord Weir's unpublished opinion. He appears to have been impressed by the Commission's arguments for using the new REDs (as given in its final report, which was in draft form at that stage), which stressed the practical difficulties involved in ignoring local government electoral arrangements (pp. 31–2). Although the REDs were abolished soon after, the new District wards did nest within them and, wherever possible, were used in the electoral arrangements for the new unitary authorities.

14 The Scottish Commission also noted that it was in 'a happier position than its counterparts elsewhere in that it was required only to have "regard" to boundaries of local authority areas' (BCS Minutes, 25 June 1992, 3).

15 The Boundary Commission for Wales (BCW) used the same minuting conventions as its English counterpart: Minutes for Northern Ireland (BCNI) are dated only.

16 Although McLeod officially shared the secretarial role with a civil servant within the Home Office, they were 'joint secretaries' in name only and the day-to-day running of the Secretariat was entirely his responsibility. Both attended the Commission's meetings, but the input of the latter was minimal and neither here nor in Scotland or Northern Ireland (where there is just one Secretary located within the Scottish / Northern Ireland Office) did we find any evidence of what might be termed 'departmental involvement' in the affairs of the Commissions.

17 Although McLeod had no previous experience of Periodic Reviews, the paper that he published in 1989 with his predecessor, Geoff Barnes, indicates that there was far from a 'clean break' between the two administrations (Barnes and McLeod, 1989).

18 This refers to England at least. Interestingly, no member of the secretariat there referred to those guidelines in discussions with us. Several stated that there were no numeric guidelines, and another said that he would generally consider electorates outside the 60,000-80,000 range unacceptable 'without a good reason'. Most stressed that they were involved in a balancing exercise, and that a very large or small electorate may be acceptable because of other compensating considerations (as in York) and that after a while they 'got a feel' for what would be acceptable to the Commission.

19 The issue of using computers had been raised after the Third Periodic Review, with the plaintiffs in the *Foot et al.* case arguing their merits. The then Secretary of the English Commission explored their potential but concluded, in a published paper, that although his consultations suggested that they would be valuable for the production of European Assembly constituencies (for which size is the dominant criterion), for Periodic Reviews they would neither reduce the length of time involved or offer any advantages in the decision-making process since 'the selection in ... each area requires the Commission to make many subjective decisions' (Barnes, 1987, 138): on the potential for using computers see Johnston, Openshaw, Rhind and Rossiter (1984).

20 As an illustration of the different approaches, one team leader told us that he would not have adopted the approach to pairing Metropolitan Districts used by another team working on Greater Manchester.

21 Prof. Openshaw subsequently informed us that he did some work on Lothian Region only.

22 One member of the relevant team told us that 'it simply would not have been possible' to go back to the Commission with modified proposals on the same day without the GIS.

23 One Minute did record, however, that discussion of the eight tabled options for Borders and Lothian was hampered by the absence of maps in advance of the meeting, resulting in reservations 'that it was hard to visualise all options and that it would have been preferable to have more time to look at them' (BCS Minutes, 6 May 1993, #5).

24 The English Commision's Minutes suggest that the Deputy Chairman initiated discussion of a possible alternative scheme for Oxford (BCE Minutes, 1991/5, 7.2) and the Chief Electoral Officer presented an alternative scheme to the Northern Ireland Commission (BCNI Minutes, 27 August 1993, 8). Neither appears to have been fully thought-out, and neither was adopted.

25 For a detailed discussion of this point see Rossiter, Johnston and Pattie (1998).

26 Or at least to minute such discussions: there may have been discussions, but they have not been formally recorded.

6

The process of
public consultation

Public consultation is an integral part of redistricting in Britain. Once a Commission has decided upon a set of provisional recommendations for an area it is required to embark upon a process which allows interested organisations and individuals the opportunity to influence those recommendations before they are made final. That process includes provision for written and oral representations, the latter through the medium of a Local Inquiry, and allows a Commission to modify its recommendations in the light of the representations received. Where a Commission proposes no change and the only representations are in support, no Inquiry is necessary and consultation can be completed within two months. Where proposed change is significant and contested it can require more than one Inquiry, more than one set of modified proposals, and extend over the best part of three years. During the Fourth Periodic Review in England, for example, the whole process took only 54 days in Northumberland but in Devon the provisional recommendations were published on 17 October 1991 and the Commission's final recommendations were not announced until 10 August 1994 (a total of 1,028 days).[1]

Statements and publications issued by all four Commissions recognise and welcome the involvement of the public in this process. The most explicit statements on the issue appear in the English Commission's booklet *The Review of Parliamentary Constituencies* (Parliamentary Boundary Commission for England, 1991), which states (31, #1):

> one of the principal and most persistent problems encountered by the Commission during their reviews is the difficulty in obtaining a reasonable level of participation by interested bodies and the electorate-at-large in the public debate on the Commission's proposals

and continues (32, #4):

> The Commission therefore wish to stress very strongly that any person or organisation interested in the provisional recommendations for their area (especially local authorities and political parties) should always exercise their statutory right and make written representations to the Commission, whether for or against the provi-

sional recommendations. Moreover, they are urged to attend, or send a representative to, any Local Inquiry held in their area to put forward their views on the provisional recommendations.

The potential for public opinion to influence the Assistant Commissioner is emphasised (28, #19):

> He may recommend that the Commission's proposals be accepted intact or with alterations. Or he may recommend that a counter proposal be adopted, with or without modifications, provided that it conforms to the rules and it appears to him to command greater support locally than the Commission's proposals.

And the experience of individual Assistant Commissioners confirms its importance:

> So far as I can see the Parliamentary Constituencies Act 1986, and in particular the Rules for Redistribution of Seats set out in Schedule 2 thereto, do not at any point say in terms that public opinion is to be a crucial factor, or even a factor, in a Boundary Commission's deliberations and decisions. However, section 5(2) of the Act … does say that 'the Commission shall take into consideration any representations duly made'. Moreover, the whole procedure for local inquiries, as provided for in section 6, is clearly designed to provide a Boundary Commission with an indication of local views and opinions, and it would therefore, I think, be contrary to the spirit of the Act as a whole to suppose that it excludes expressions of public opinion as a factor to be taken into account. (Inquiry Report, Borders and Lothian Regions, #15)

These paragraphs reveal the emphasis which is placed on public consultation, yet at the same time highlight a fundamental paradox. Low levels of participation by the 'electorate-at-large' are 'a problem', but the nature of the problem is not explained. Why should the rational elector, without a political axe to grind, care about constituency boundaries? True, from a purely selfish utilitarian point of view, an elector maximises his or her electoral influence by minimising the electorate of a constituency and by maximising its marginality. However, unsurprisingly, the submissions of very few electors proceed on this basis and the Commission would hardly welcome any that did. Instead the vast majority of genuinely apolitical submissions are from electors wishing to associate with, or distance themselves from, other geographically defined groups of electors. These submissions are considered further below, but two aspects are worth emphasising: many representations, though not themselves political, are triggered by publicity instigated by people and organisations with political motives; and many fail to adduce relevant arguments and/or labour under misapprehensions regarding the consequences of the Commissions' recommendations.

From a different point of view the problem is clearer. Elections are at the heart of democracy and Parliamentary constituencies are an integral part of the electoral process, hence low levels of public participation in their delineation is a weakness in democracy itself. Furthermore, insofar as a healthy democracy emphasises opportunities for the public to participate in public affairs, then in the words of John Stuart Mill (1861, quoted in Williams, 1993, 234), 'any participation, even in the smallest public function, is useful'. However, as several authors have pointed out, this viewpoint has never dominated in British political culture (Wright, 1994, 106):

> The British tradition was a governing tradition, and its citizens (properly, subjects) were not required or expected, wars always excepted, to exert themselves in strenuous civic activity.

The particular emphasis on the contributions of political parties and (largely politically controlled) local authorities in the English Commission's booklet constitutes an unmistakable echo of that tradition. In short, we have a system in which the role of public consultation is somewhat confused and in which the tension between the public good (undefined) and partisan interest, though unacknowledged, is never far from the surface.

This lack of clarity reflects, in part, Parliament's unwillingness to address the role of public consultation. There is no necessary correspondence between the volume of legislation and its significance, but the 400 words accorded to all aspects of consultation in the *Parliamentary Constituencies Act 1986* contrast with the over 5,000 words prescribing procedures to be followed at planning inquiries (i.e. *The Town & Country Planning (Inquiries Procedure) Rules 1992*). Apart from the addition of three subsections in 1958 to which we return later, the wording of those parts dealing with notices and Local Inquiries is identical to that of the *House of Commons (Redistribution of Seats) Act 1944* which established the Commissions. When considering that legislation, Parliament at no stage addressed the question of consultation, but instead rubber-stamped the relevant recommendations of the Speaker's Conference, themselves based largely on those of the Vivian Committee. There appears to have been no serious public discussion of the issues involved, and the wording of the Vivian Committee's recommendation suggests that consultation was not accorded a very high priority:[2]

> At a suitable stage, public notice of proposals provisionally framed would need to be given; *and it will probably be thought necessary* that local hearings should be arranged to enable representations or suggestions to be made respecting the provisional lay-out of any adjusted constituencies (Vivian Committee, 1942, #110;, emphasis added)

The only occasion on which Parliament became seriously exercised over this question was 1954, during its consideration of the Commissions' First Periodical Reports. During those debates there were repeated criticisms, particularly of the English Commission, for failing to respond adequately to representations and for refusing to hold more Local Inquiries. Parliament subsequently amended the procedures for calling Local Inquiries (in Section 4 of the 1958 Act (Box 3.4, it is now Section 6 of the 1986 Act (Box 6.1)) so that it was no longer solely at a Commission's discretion whether a Local Inquiry was held, but neither the 1954 nor the 1958 debates contained a discussion of the purposes or functions of consultation. Instead the succession of MPs making irate claims about the lack of reflection of the public's wishes in Commissions' recommendations after each Review seems to have been motivated primarily by the failure to allow politi-

Box 6.1 *The stipulations regarding public consultation in the* Parliamentary Constituencies Act 1986

5 (2) Where a Boundary Commission have provisionally determined to make recommendations affecting any constituency, they shall publish in at least one newspaper circulating in the constituency a notice stating –
   (a) the effect of the proposed recommendations and (except in a case where they propose to recommend that no alteration be made in respect of the constituency) that a copy of the recommendations is open to inspection at a specified place within the constituency, and
   (b) that representations with respect to the proposed recommendations may be made to the Commission within one month after publication of the notice; and the Commission shall take into consideration any representations duly made in accordance with any such notice.
   (3) Where a Boundary Commission revise any proposed recommendations after publishing a notice of them under subsection (2) above, the Commission shall comply again with that subsection in relation to the revised recommendations, as if no earlier notice had been published.
6 (1) A Boundary Commission may, if they think fit, cause a local inquiry to be held in respect of any constituency or constituencies.
   (2) Where, on the publication of the notice under section 5(2) above of a recommendation of a Boundary Commission for the alteration of any constituencies, the Commission receive any representation objecting to the proposed recommendation from an interested authority or from a body of electors numbering one hundred or more, the Commission shall not make the recommendation unless, since the publication of the notice, a local inquiry has been held in respect of the constituencies.
   (3) Where a local inquiry was held in respect of the constituencies before the publication of the notice mentioned in subsection (2) above, that subsection shall not apply if the Commission, after considering the matters discussed at the local inquiry, the nature of the representations received on the publication of the notice and any other relevant circumstances, are of opinion that a further local inquiry would not be justified.
   (4) In subsection (2) above, 'interested authority' and 'elector' respectively mean, in relation to any recommendation, a local authority whose area is wholly or partly comprised in the constituencies affected by the recommendation, and a parliamentary elector for any of those constituencies; and for this purpose 'local authority' means –
   (a) in England and Wales, the council of a county, London borough or district,
   (b) in Scotland,, the council of a region, islands area or district, and
   (c) in Northern Ireland, the council of a district.

cians to have their own say and gain their ends, rather than by any wider concern for the rights of the ordinary citizen.

Ensuing years have seen Parliament less willing to legislate or even to discuss redistricting. Criticisms, particularly of the Local Inquiries, recur (as illustrated by Merlyn Rees' contribution to the Home Affairs Committee in 1986), but Parliament shows neither the will to change nor even much interest in considering it. Having failed to articulate the scope of public consultation in the original legislation, it has left both interpretation and implementation largely in the hands of the Commissions. The ways in which the Commissions have exercised that role form the subject of the next two chapters.

The written representation

Once a Commission has decided upon its initial proposals for an area it is required to publish, in at least one newspaper circulating in each constituency in that area, a notice setting out those proposals and a statement inviting written representations within one month of the notice's publication. Unless the proposals are for no change, the Commission must also publish a list of places where they may be inspected, typically local authority offices and public libraries, and these copies are generally accompanied by a reasonably detailed map. In addition to fulfilling these statutory obligations, all four Commissions issue *News Releases* summarising and explaining the proposals, the statutory framework and the process of public consultation and sent copies to all interested parties (MPs, local authorities, political parties) as well as to the news media; more detailed *Newsletters* were also published and circulated to interested parties.

If, in the light of the representations received, a Local Inquiry is convened, and if, on examining the report of that Inquiry, a Commission decides to modify its proposals, then the above process is repeated. This can happen more than once, either because a second Inquiry is held, or because a Commission modifies its recommendations again in the light of further written representations. Although neither course of action is common, there were instances of both during the Fourth Review. Only when a Commission declares its intention to make a recommendation final is the scope for making written representations exhausted.

In their most recent reports the four Commissions indicated that they received a total of some 45,000 written representations and petitions, with the latter containing in excess of 80,000 signatures. Far more people and organisations wrote letters than appeared at the Local Inquiries and the Boundary Commission for England (1995a, 11) indicated that this form of public participation increased eight-fold compared with the previous Review. However, writing letters to Commissions about Parliamentary boundaries is very much a minority pursuit. For every elector who wrote or signed a petition, over 400 did not. Even amongst those electors for whom the provisional recommendations meant a change of constituency, fewer than one in a hundred put pen to paper. What motivated this minority to take action? Who were they, what did they write, and how influential were they?

Before each Inquiry the Commissions published a list of those making representations on their initial proposals. We have analysed those lists, assigning each representation to one of six categories according to its source (Table 6.1). The numeric dominance of the contributions of individual members of the public is clear, providing almost three-quarters of the 22,000 representations received by the Commissions at this stage; indeed if the 40,000 signatures on petitions are included, then over 90 per cent of those expressing some form of opinion on the Commissions' provisional recommendations were individuals without any stated affiliation. Although these figures show that the public provided by far the greatest volume of responses to the Commissions' proposals, that is not to say that the majority of these representations were apolitical. In the County of Avon, for example, thirteen of the eighteen letters sent by individuals at this stage supported the Labour party's counter-proposal for seats in Bristol (see Chapter 8) and, while there is no reason to believe that the sentiments expressed were other than genuine, the similarities between the letters are clear. To emphasise the point, as a result of the Commission accepting Labour's counter-proposal it received almost 600 representations from individuals objecting to the revised recommendations, including 451 photocopies of five different letters produced by the Conservative party and over one hundred others which began with a similar form of words.

Table 6.1 *The sources of representations and counter-proposals to the Boundary Commissions' Fourth Periodic Reviews (percentages of total)*

Source	Representation	Counter-proposals
Political parties	11	38
MPs and MEPs	2	5
Councillors	5	8
Local authorities	6	26
Voluntary organisations	3	3
Individuals	73	20

Although the vast majority of representations from individuals were politically inspired, that still leaves a significant minority which were not. A number were well argued, reasonable letters from individuals emphasising historic links and local ties. Others were less positive, stressing the writer's dissimilarity from others who the Commission proposes should share the same constituency.[3] This aspect was emphasised particularly by rural area residents who feared association with neighbouring towns and cities. In Avon, for example, three wrote to object to the proposal to extend the Bath constituency to include neighbouring rural parishes. The first referred to 'repeated efforts … [by] the City of Bath to swallow up small rural neighbours thereby depriving them of their independence and individuality' (Representation #8); the second referred to the need to be represented by those 'who understand and have experience of rural problems' (#70); and the third concluded that:

> Towns do not understand the needs of the country dweller and because they have rather more clout because of their greater numbers, could prevail in any argument affecting this village (#71).

Whatever the merits of these arguments, it was in relation to the tension between town and country that the non-partisan views of (one section of) the public rang true.

By contrast, only a small minority of representations contained alternative proposals for the Commissions to consider. This is reflected in the Commissions' lists of representations prepared for the Local Inquiries, which in addition to identifying the source of the letter also highlight those which contained counter-proposals. Just over 400 original counter-proposals are identified, comprising approximately 2 per cent of all representations received at this stage (Table 6.1).

There is a very clear contrast between the role of individuals on the one hand and politicians and local authorities on the other. Whereas representations from the former outnumbered the latter by around 3:1 overall, if attention is restricted to those containing an original counter-proposal, the ratio was almost 1:4. Individuals make a significant contribution to the process of public consultation in terms of volume, but politicians (especially their parties) and local authorities take the lead in putting forward alternative schemes for the Commissions to consider.

What do these representations and counter-proposals achieve? Do they make any difference? The standard *News Release* which accompanies the Commissions' initial recommendations stresses the importance of the written representation. Not only are electors and organisations invited to write, they are also encouraged, in the Boundary Commission for England's words:[4]

> to say whether they approve of, or object to, the Commission's proposals and to give their reasons for their approval or objection. In particular, objectors are advised to say what they propose in place of the Commission's recommendations and should note that an objection accompanied by a counter-proposal is likely to carry more weight than a simple statement of objection.

Despite these exhortations, from the purely self-interested viewpoint of the potential correspondent it may not be obvious why the advice should be followed. When, in 1958, Parliament abolished the absolute discretion of the Commissions to convene Local Inquiries (see p. 96), it significantly altered the status of the written representation. Prior to that date such Inquiries were the exception, and so it made sense to put together a persuasive case in writing if the Commission was to be convinced of the need to modify its recommendations. Since 1958, faced with a Commission's initial proposals, a simple council resolution or a petition signed by a hundred people guarantees a Local Inquiry. In neither case is it necessary to justify the representation – 'we object' is sufficient. Insofar as the

Local Inquiry has become the arena for persuasion, the prior written representation has largely become just a means to that end.

Our interviews with both the Commissioners and the Assistant Commissioners lend some support to this proposition. The former rely primarily upon the Inquiry reports to inform them of local opinion; on the relatively few occasions on which they overturned an Assistant Commissioner's recommendation, it was never because of what somebody wrote prior to the Inquiry. Similarly, although all Assistant Commissioners read the written representations prior to the Inquiry, the majority of those we interviewed attached greater weight to what they heard,[5] and we have identified only one instance of a modification proposed by letter before an Inquiry being adopted by an Assistant Commissioner without supporting oral evidence.[6] Furthermore, it might be argued that although the benefits of a well-argued letter may be questionable, the effort involved in its drafting is not. Nor should the possible pitfalls of well-crafted written representations be overlooked. There is only a one month period for their receipt and this can create considerable difficulties for those wishing to consult before making a submission. A political party wanting to adopt a common position has little time to inform members, digest their responses, persuade the recalcitrants and compose a well-reasoned submission. A local authority wanting to canvass the views of other authorities, perhaps including town and parish councils, but aware that its status in instigating Local Inquiries necessitates a timely response, may feel unable to engage in consultation. Although the Commissions are aware of this problem and adopt a flexible position over 'late' submissions, the letter of the law militates against the production of considered submissions within the prescribed time period, as all four Commissions noted in their reports.[7] Furthermore the detailed representation often produces hostages to fortune and in the case of a political party can alert opponents to its plans. Several months elapse between the closing date for representations and the Local Inquiry, during which time much can change. Control of a local authority may pass from one party to another; those who were not consulted or failed to respond may disagree with conclusions reached in the written representation. An organisation (or individual) which puts one case by letter and another at the Inquiry may gain marks for flexibility but lose more for credibility.

Although legislation has rendered the persuasive letter unnecessary, unrealistic time scales prevent many organisations from effective consultation, and Local Inquiries have a much stronger influence on Assistant Commissioners, the written representation nevertheless continues to serve an extremely important function. When a Commission decides to hold a Local Inquiry, it publishes a notice and arranges for copies of the representations to be deposited in the same public places as the original notice of its provisional recommendations. The Commissions also send a copy of the notice and a summary of the representations direct to all those who made written representations and to all other interested parties. This is a critical part of the process of public consultation because it 'enables all interested parties to be given advance notice of the issues likely to be raised at the Inquiry' (Parliamentary Boundary Commission for England 1991, *The Pro-*

cedure at Public Inquiries). Together with the Commission's own provisional recommendations, these counter-proposals help to set the agenda for the Inquiry.

There is nothing to prevent a counter-proposal from being introduced for the
first time at an Inquiry, but its late introduction is likely to hinder its chances of
adoption, as the Boundary Commission for England pointed out in its second
Newsletter (Winter, 1992):

> Where the public have not had an opportunity to consider counter-proposals in
> advance … . the Assistant Commissioner may not be able to gauge the extent of
> support, if any, that exists for them. An otherwise good submission may lose much
> of its weight and the Assistant Commissioner may feel unable to recommend that
> counter-proposal to the Commission. It is in the interests of those making repre-
> sentations that counter-proposals are received by the Commission as early as pos-
> sible, if not within the one month representation period then shortly thereafter.

Several Assistant Commissioners confirmed that this was the case. Commenting
upon the receipt of a major counter-proposal on the opening day of the Cumbria
Inquiry in his report, for example, the Assistant Commissioner noted that (Inquiry
Report, Cumbria, #4):

> It is obvious that the tardiness of [these] proposals would do nothing to enhance
> them and would substantially reduce the opportunity to adduce the evidence nec-
> essary to their justification.

It is not impossible for a counter-proposal which has received no prior publicity
to succeed, but the fact that 95 per cent of the changes adopted by the English
Commission had been received within the statutory one month period (Boundary Commission for England, 1995a, 287, #6.26) strengthens the argument for
submitting well-argued representations well before the Inquiry, thereby contributing both to its effectiveness and to the wider process of public consultation.

The Local Inquiry: an overview

The Local Inquiry is the focus of public involvement in the process of redistricting in the United Kingdom. Written representations play important roles both
in triggering Inquiries and in setting their agenda, and they can help to alter a
Commission's mind after the Inquiry has finished (something we consider further in the next chapter), but the function of the former and the infrequency of
the latter merely serve to emphasise the importance of the Local Inquiry to the
redistricting process.

Even where the statutory criteria are not met, but there is some evidence of
objection to the provisional recommendations, it has become standard practice
for a Local Inquiry to be held. As a result, only twelve of the one hundred major
local government areas were unaffected by Local Inquiries during the course of
the Fourth Review,[8] with a total of 89 Inquiries considering 606 of the 658 provisionally recommended constituencies. (The Inquiries covered 87 separate areas,

with second Inquiries for parts of Devon and Hampshire; some London Boroughs and Scottish Regions had joint Inquiries, and most of those held in the Metropolitan Counties covered one or more of the constituent Districts only.) The Second Review saw Inquiries into 530 provisionally recommended seats, rising to 632 in the Third Review (only eleven constituencies, all in England and all but four in London, were not the subject of an Inquiry) and then 606 in the Fourth. What was once an occasional luxury has now become commonplace.

The relevant legislation says very little about the conduct or purpose of Inquiries. Although we have argued that this is partly the consequence of a lack of interest on the part of Parliament, it also reflects the long-established role of Public Inquiries in British administrative law. Commencing in the nineteenth century, these have 'arisen piecemeal, largely unplanned, to meet particular needs in particular circumstances' (Wraith and Lamb, 1971, 353). In a variety of areas of public life they have provided a forum for checking that administrative power is fairly and reasonably exercised, based on the legal principles of natural justice, namely that proceedings must be conducted without bias and in such a way that each party involved is given an adequate hearing on each contested issue. 'A very British institution, both in the literal sense that they are not to be found elsewhere, and in the wider sense that they reflect English history and tradition' (Wraith and Lamb, 1971, 352), all Public Inquiries share two basic functions – 'the collection of information and the resolution of conflict' (Wraith and Lamb, 1971, 303). Or, as the English Commission puts it in the context of Parliamentary redistricting in its document on *The Procedure at Local Inquiries* (Boundary Commission for England, 1992, 5-6), they are there to:
(a) ascertain relevant local information and opinion;
(b) hear criticism of or support for the Commission's provisional recommendations;
(c) receive any counter proposals; and
(d) enable everyone attending who wishes to comment on any of these matters to do so.

Preparation for the Inquiry follows a common pattern. Once a Commission has decided that one is to be held, it chooses a convenient public place within the area under review, typically a local authority council chamber, and appoints an independent lawyer to act as Assistant Commissioner. It then publicises the Inquiry by publishing a notice in local papers and issuing a press release to the news media. A statement setting out the reasons for the provisional recommendations is prepared copies of which, and of the representations received by the Commission, are placed on deposit at various places, such as libraries and council offices. A copy of the statement, together with a summary of representations, is also sent direct to all those who made representations, to local authorities and to the political parties. In the ensuing weeks the Commission's Secretariat continues to make the necessary administrative preparations and sends the Assistant Commissioner any further representations which arrive right up to the date of the Inquiry. The Assistant Commissioner is briefed by the Secretariat, in the case of

England and Wales by letter, in the case of Scotland and Northern Ireland by a personal visit from the Commission's Secretary. The typical Assistant Commissioner spends several days reading through the brief and the representations and attempts to familiarise himself with the area by inspecting the relevant maps and, in rare cases, by a personal visit.[9]

At the opening of the Inquiry the Assistant Commissioner can be faced with an audience of anything from a dozen to several hundred. He is assisted by verbatim reporters, there to produce a transcript of the proceedings. The Commission itself, however, is not represented, although (Parliamentary Boundary Commission for England, 1991, 27, #16):

> a member of their secretariat may be present to act as an observer and to assist with the mechanics of the inquiry. The Commission do not seek to defend their proposals and consider that to do so may give the wrong impression that the Commission are unwilling or reluctant to alter what are their provisional recommendations.[10]

The Assistant Commissioner normally welcomes the audience and provides a brief background to the proceedings before drawing attention to the Commission's statement explaining its provisional recommendations. (The Assistant Commissioner at some of the early English Inquiries read out the statement, but this was dispensed with on the Secretariat's advice: BCE Minutes, 1992/4, 4.1.) It is then general practice for an adjournment to be called, during which time those who wish to speak are invited to put their names (and sponsor, if appearing on behalf of an organisation) on a list so that the Assistant Commissioner can draw up an order of speakers. Anybody wishing to propose a comprehensive counter-proposal is urged to emphasise the fact at this stage, so that others can be given as much notice as possible. In many cases, speakers indicate that they are available at certain times only, which means that the Assistant Commissioner's agenda can lack coherence, especially in a large area: some Inquiries are forced to move from topic to topic quasi-randomly according to the availability of witnesses, though in our interviews with Assistant Commissioners we found very few for whom this had been a problem.

The Inquiry proper then commences and continues for as long as the Assistant Commissioner considers necessary, including evening sessions when requested.[11] The eventual duration varies considerably depending upon the number of constituencies under consideration and the degree of change proposed; the shortest during the Fourth Review was completed in little over an hour, the longest took eight days. The evidence is primarily oral, though written representations are accepted and those appearing are generally asked to ensure that copies of their submission are available for distribution to those present. Political parties typically present their evidence by calling a series of witnesses and they and local authorities may be represented by counsel.

Although proceedings differ from those of the courtroom, the dominance and nature of the political and administrative interests inevitably introduces a degree of formality. While the Commission might hope that Inquiries can be seen as 'informal affairs' (Parliamentary Boundary Commission for England, 1991, 27, #16) that is a relative judgement; Inquiries certainly do not have the informality of a public meeting. After each person has spoken, there is usually an opportunity for questions to be asked, but the precise format is at the Assistant Commissioner's discretion.

Although there is no such thing as the 'typical' Inquiry, it is important to emphasise that all are indeed 'local' (i.e. refer to a defined area only). Their terms of reference stipulate that they consider the proposals of a Commission relating to the area covered by one or more existing Parliamentary constituencies. Because Rule 4 emphasises the importance to be attached to local authority boundaries, most Inquiries discuss possible changes to constituencies within a County, a Region or a London Borough: Rule 4 is not absolute, however, and the English and Scottish Commissions convened joint Inquiries to consider neighbouring authorities for the first time during the Fourth Review, whereas more than one was held for a part of the area only in five of the six the English Metropolitan Counties; the five Inquiries held in Northern Ireland referred to *ad hoc* groups of adjacent constituencies. Participants may refer to proposals in other areas or draw wider comparisons, but the focus of discussion is invariably local. As a consequence discussion generally proceeds without reference to, and in many cases in ignorance of, proposals and/or final recommendations for elsewhere in the country.

When the Inquiry is over, the Assistant Commissioner prepares to write the report, perhaps first visiting areas which were discussed at the Inquiry, both to clarify understanding of the issues involved and to assess the validity of the arguments presented. A copy of the verbatim transcript of the proceedings is provided, which can be reviewed alongside the written representations. The report for the Commission summarises the evidence and contains recommendations. The Commission stresses that the Assistant Commissioner (Parliamentary Boundary Commission for England, 1991, 28, #20):

> is fully entitled in that report to comment on any representation or submission, or on the Commission's proposals, or on any other proposals. He may recommend that the Commission's proposals be accepted intact or with alterations. Or he may recommend that a counter proposal be adopted, with or without modifications, provided that it conforms to the rules and it appears to him to command greater support locally than the Commission's proposals.

The completed report is sent to the Commission whose Secretariat checks it for accuracy – requests for alteration to spellings and numerical calculations are not infrequent – before presenting it to the Commission for consideration.

The contents of the Inquiry reports and the Commissions' reaction to them largely determine the contents of the Commissions' final reports. As we discuss in Chapter 7, Commissions do sometimes disagree with an Assistant Commissioner's recommendations and they occasionally modify recommendations in the light of subsequent written representations, but these are uncommon events. The Assistant Commissioner is extremely influential and the major participants at the

Inquiries know that it is essential to present a well-argued and well-supported case. In the second half of this chapter we consider the approach of those who dominate the Inquiries – the political parties and the local authorities. But first we concentrate on those entrusted with their conduct, the Assistant Commissioners.

The Assistant Commissioners

The 72 Assistant Commissioners who conducted Local Inquiries during the Fourth Review were continuing a long tradition in British redistricting. As discussed in Chapter 2, equal numbers of barristers and army officers were appointed to advise the 1867 Commission and although involvement of the military was dispensed with in 1917, barristers have acted as Assistant Commissioners at every subsequent review.[12] Indeed, all Assistant Commissioners now come from the legal profession though the way in which they are selected varies from country to country, as do their characteristics and the way in which they are briefed.

Selection

England
The selection of Assistant Commissioners is an informal process. In England the Deputy Chairman of the Commission sent a letter to all Heads of Chambers in the summer of 1990 inviting them to suggest the names of 'senior barristers in your Chambers who might be prepared to accept appointment'.[13] Other than seniority, the only criterion laid down in the letter was that candidates 'should not, of course, have taken any active part in politics, whether as a candidate or otherwise, within the last ten years'. At the same time the Commission obtained a list from the Lord Chancellor's Department of those solicitors who were also Recorders or Assistant Recorders (BCE Minutes, 1990/2, 3.3), though ultimately no solicitor was appointed to conduct an Inquiry. As a result of the invitation the Commission received 330 nominations, from whom were excluded the junior (those called to the Bar within the last 12 years), the elderly (those who might reach 65 during the course of the Review) and those who admitted recent political activity. The two Commissioners with legal experience then whittled the list down to around a hundred, giving priority to senior eligible members of Chambers and maintaining a balance between London and 'the provinces' (BCE Minutes, 1991/7; several Assistant Commissioners have more than one professional address, but we calculated that 34 of the 55 who conducted inquiries could reasonably be described as London-based.)

Having finalised its list the Commission sent it to the Home Office early in 1991, for consideration prior to the Secretary of State issuing warrants of appointment. The Home Office then sent letters to all nominees asking for confirmation that they were still willing to stand and that they had not taken an active part in politics.[14] It appears that this was the Home Office's only involvement in 'vetting' Assistant Commissioners, though when appointing the first twenty the Home Secretary stated that he was only making an interim list because he considered that too few women had been nominated (BCE Minutes, 1993/11, 8.4; the final total of women Assistant Commissioners in England was four). A second group was appointed in August 1992, bringing the total to 75. The allocation of Assistant Commissioners to individual Inquiries was carried out by the Secretariat, following guidelines produced by the Commission, the most notable of which were that the more senior members of the panel should cover what were perceived as being the more 'difficult' areas and that the individual should neither live in, nor be particularly well acquainted with, the area under consideration. Table 6.2 (which relates to all four Commissions) shows that there was a clear tendency for the more senior lawyers to be appointed to the longer Inquiries and the Commission's minutes contain several references to both aspects: the Secretariat's original selection for Manchester and Trafford was altered, for example, because the Inquiry 'was likely to be a difficult one and should therefore be conducted by a Queen's Counsel' (BCE Minutes, 1993/11, 4.1); and another was removed because one of the Commissioners 'understood that he resided' within the area under review (BCE Minutes, 1993/11, 5.3.). By the end of the Review, 55 Assistant Commissioners had conducted an English Inquiry, most dealing with one, but seven handling two and four dealing with three.

Table 6.2 *Seniority of Assistant Commissioners and length of Inquiries*

Length of Inquiry (days)	Not QC, not Recorder	Not QC, but Recorder	QC, not Recorder	QC and Recorder
1	12	4	1	1
2	13	8	2	8
3+	4	4	5	8

Wales

Selection of Assistant Commissioners elsewhere proceeded in a somewhat different fashion. In Wales, the previous Deputy Chairman, in consultation with the Leader of the Welsh Circuit, drew up a list of 17 barristers which formed the basis for the panel appointed by the Home Secretary; the Commission's criteria were those adopted by the English Commission plus emphases on judicial experience, Welsh speakers, and women (BCW Minutes, 1992/1, 2.2). Not all were Welsh, and only four of those chosen spoke Welsh (BCW Minutes, 1994/2, 6.2: no women were appointed), but all were known to the Deputy Chairman who personally selected seven from the list and allocated them to Counties primarily on the basis of availability and the ability to speak Welsh.

Northern Ireland

In Northern Ireland, five barristers and eleven solicitors were nominated by the Bar Council and Law Society of whom three and two respectively conducted

Local Inquiries. Allocation to individual Inquiries was again influenced by avail-ability, but it is also clear that there was considerable pressure from Nationalists and the Irish government; whether or not that pressure had any effect, it was prob-ably not coincidence that the two Roman Catholic Assistant Commissioners dealt with those areas with the highest concentration of Roman Catholics, and vice versa (see Rossiter, Johnston and Pattie, 1998).

Scotland

The procedure for appointing Assistant Commissioners in Scotland bears little resemblance to that operated by the other Commissions. Instead of choosing from a panel which is itself a subset of the wider community of barristers and solici-tors, the Scottish Commission followed previous practice by requesting the Sec-retary of State to appoint the Sheriff Principal, the senior member of the Scottish judiciary within the area concerned, who must reside within the Sheriffdom. (There was an exception in Dumfries & Galloway where the Sheriff Principal was about to retire, and a Sheriff from Hamilton was appointed in his stead.) Apart from saving money (whereas barristers and solicitors are paid as Assistant Commissioners, Sheriffs have to fulfil this responsibility as part of their normal duties) this practice ensures that Assistant Commissioners in Scotland have judi-cial experience and personal knowledge of the area under consideration. On the other hand, it does make the vetting of potential candidates a more sensitive issue and the Commission's minutes record extended correspondence between the Commission and Sheriff Principal Nicholson (on behalf of his colleagues) regard-ing the political associations of potential Assistant Commissioners. Both appear to have adopted a firm line, the Sheriffs stressing the objectivity and impartial-ity inherent in their role and the Commissions stressing that although it doubted neither, 'there were those who, however unjustified, would be inclined to see the appointment of Assistant Commissioners in political terms' and refusing to con-sider those 'who are or have been actively involved in politics' (BCS Minutes, 1 July 1993, 2.1). Fortunately, no Sheriff Principal appears to have met the Com-mission's criterion for exclusion and the appointments passed off without further difficulty.[15]

Characteristics

Having chronicled their method of appointment, we now turn to the character-istics of the 72 individuals who conducted Local Inquiries during the Fourth Review. Is there such a thing as the typical Assistant Commissioner? The first and most obvious observation is that all Assistant Commissioners were lawyers and consequently exhibited most of the characteristics associated with that pro-fession: they are highly educated, self evidently middle class and predominantly male (on the profession more generally, see Abel, 1988). These and certain other characteristics are accentuated by the age and experience requirements stipulated by the English and Welsh Commissions: in England these ruled out candidates born before 1933 or called to the Bar after 1979 and, as no Assistant Commissioner was younger than 22 when called, effectively limited applicants to those born between 1933 and 1957 and called between 1955 and 1979.[16] However, Table 6.3 shows that the generational effect was even more pronounced in practice, with the vast majority born in the 1940s and called to the Bar around 1970. The Commissions' preference for those with experience is also reflected in the number of Silks (Queen's Counsel who are senior barristers) and/or Recorders (part-time judges who sit for a minimum of twenty days per annum) who were appointed: among the 62 English and Welsh Assistant Commissioners, there were 23 QCs and 32 Recorders compared to a Bar average for both of roughly one in ten. The five Northern Ireland Assistant Commissioners were slightly younger than their counterparts in England and Wales, but the average age of the five Scots was 57, reflecting their seniority within that country's legal system.

Table 6.3 *Year of birth and year of call to the Bar: Assistant Commissioners in England and Wales at the Fourth Review*

Year of birth	Number	Year of call	Number
Pre 1937	4	Pre 1959	5
1938–42	9	1960–64	7
1943–47	17	1965–69	22
1948–52	8	1970–74	21
1953–57	1	1975–79	6
Unknown	23	Unknown	1

Sources: *Havers' Companion to the Bar; Who's Who.*

The combination of the characteristics of the profession and the policies of the Commissions produced 72 Assistant Commissioners with a distinctive profile. All were white and middle-class, only four were female and only two were younger than 40. Except for the Sheriffs and the law lecturer, all were self-employed and capable of commanding sizeable fees in their professional capacity. Of those for whom educational background information is available, the majority went to private secondary schools, over 90 per cent have a university degree, and fully 60 per cent are Oxbridge graduates.[17] As a group they have many of the characteristics associated with the archetypal Conservative voter and it would be naive to assume that they represent a balanced cross-section of electoral opinion.[18] Only rarely in our 60 interviews were we aware of an overt political bias in an Assistant Commissioner, however (and they balanced each other out), and the overwhelming impression from those encounters, from reading the Inquiry transcripts and reports, and also from our interviews with the political parties, is one of solid impartiality.

Briefing

A notable characteristic of the Assistant Commissioners who conducted Inquiries during the Fourth Review was their lack of experience of the Commissions' work. Asked about their reasons for agreeing to become an Assistant Commissioner, the vast majority said that it seemed to offer an interesting challenge, with several emphasising tradition, obligation, civic duty and the honour of playing a significant part in the democratic process. One said that:

> It had interesting aspects – some law, some geography – and it contributed to the democratic process. It was something worthwhile. And it was interesting to organise and run a meeting. Certainly not for the money.

Very few did it on the basis of a clear understanding of the nature of the job. Only four had previously conducted an Inquiry for a Commission, while another four mentioned that they had acted as counsel for a political party or local authority at an earlier Review. Of the remainder (52), only a quarter (13) felt that they knew more about the process than the average layman (many of these referring to conversations with current or former members of the Commission or Assistant Commissioners), while seven claimed total ignorance of the Commissions and their works prior to receiving the letter of invitation. The majority were aware of the Commissions' *raison d'être*, but not of their *modus operandi* and the following comments were typical:

> I had the knowledge of an educated layman. I knew it existed but not how it worked.

> I understood their broad function – that they made boundary changes and that there were local inquiries – but nothing of the rules or mechanics.

> I knew that it existed by statute; that it included the Speaker and a High Court Judge; and that it conducted periodic reviews. But I didn't know much about the statutory rules and nothing about the process of public consultation.

> I knew in general terms that their task was to keep constituency electorates roughly equal and that there was a legal framework for their operations.

> I had a rough idea that they met every 10 years or so to reconsider constituency boundaries, but I had no prior knowledge of the legislation or the rules.

> I had the knowledge of a reasonably well-informed person, namely their statutory responsibility to review constituency boundaries.

Against this background it was clearly important that Assistant Commissioners were well briefed as to their role and responsibilities. In England and Wales briefing was done by post; in Scotland and Northern Ireland this was supplemented by a personal visit from the Commission's Secretary. A typical brief sent out by the English Commission comprised around 4,000 words of general advice relating to the conduct of the Inquiry, the rules to be observed and advice on Commission policy, together with a comparable (though variable) amount of information specific to the area under consideration. To this were annexed over a dozen documents, including a copy of the relevant legislation, copies of statutory notices and *News Releases*, the Commission's pamphlet on the procedure at Local Inquiries, a ward map, electoral statistics for the area under consideration, theoretical entitlements for all English Counties, a copy of a 'model' report from this Review together with the relevant Inquiry report from the previous Review (where applicable) and, of course, copies of all representations.

Most of the information specific to the area under consideration was of a factual nature and most of the guidance on policy and practice could be found in the Commission's booklet published to accompany the Review (Parliamentary Boundary Commission for England, 1991). There were, however, some noteworthy variations. In listing the Commission's objectives, the wording of guidance on the total number of seats, the crossing of local government boundaries, conformity with the electoral quota and the advisability of minimising change was much as in the Rules. To this was added a fifth objective, namely that recommendations should:

> create constituencies of a suitable size and shape to take account of
> (i)   the convenience of electors and their representatives;
> (ii) the local affinities; and
> (iii) transport facilities and lines of communication.

In elevating this to a specific objective alongside those embodied within Rules 1, 4, 5 and 7, the English Commission gave this aspect significantly greater weight than did its published booklet. Another notable difference concerned advice relating to urban and rural areas. In its booklet the Commission merely states that 'the juxtaposition of rural and urban areas' is 'automatically' taken into account in formulating provisional recommendations (Parliamentary Boundary Commission for England, 1991, 21, #16). In its briefing note, however, it was stated that one of the six principles[19] which govern the Commission's proposals is that:

> the Commission should not seek to differentiate between the representation of rural and urban areas, save as necessitated by special geographical considerations.

The lack of clarity in this guidance left Assistant Commissioners to decide for themselves what weight to give to evidence relating to the differences between town and country. In the light of their training it was also rather surprising that the briefing contained no mention of relevant case law, notably *Foot et al.* (see p. 113 above).[20] The guidance also changed over time, though this was generally reflected in the Commission's regular *Newsletters*, in particular regarding the recommended treatment of growth and the submission of late counter-proposals. The other significant change was the decision to include 'a copy of a good report to future ACs as an example of good practice' (BCE, Minutes, 1992/6, 4.5), a change which was widely welcomed by those Assistant Commissioners who benefited.

As part of our interviews with Assistant Commissioners, we asked how they rated the briefing provided by the Commissions. Few (six) complained about the overall standard, with the remainder equally divided between those for whom the briefs were 'sufficient', 'satisfactory' or 'adequate' and those using more positive words. The overall impression, however, was that this was an area where the Commission could have done better or, as one Assistant Commissioner put it:

> As a barrister you're used to working from inadequate briefs and anything half-decent is greeted with open arms. I got sufficient papers and I found the guidance helpful but not overly so.

Almost a quarter of all Assistant Commissioners (13) found it necessary to contact the Commission for additional briefing prior to the Inquiry, with shortcomings in the quality of mapping a particular concern. In the words of one:

> I'm very keen on maps and there I was disappointed – the maps weren't of sufficient detail to allow me to identify many of the points made in submissions. I do think the brief could have been better there.

Others only became aware of shortcomings in the briefing when they came to the Inquiry. One of those conducting an Inquiry at which the crossing of London Borough boundaries became an issue complained:

> I had to decide the meaning and significance of Rule 4 ... but say my interpretation had been wrong or differed from the Commission ... I did have the feeling that I shouldn't have to be puzzling this out, that this was really a matter for the Commission. I think they could have produced clearer guidance in the light of the problems they might have expected to arise.

And another who took a different view on the interpretation of theoretical entitlements from that of the Commission noted:

> Nowhere was it stated that it was the Commission's policy strictly to apply entitlements, with no preparedness to depart from that. That was certainly not clear to me in advance and I would contrast the Commission's News Release with my previous advice. At the end of the day this is essentially a matter of policy and approach for the Commission – but insofar as there is policy and practice the Commission needs to make it clearer if they won't depart from it.

For most, however, the nature of the Inquiry meant that such issues did not arise.

The typical Assistant Commissioner spent between two and three days prior to the Inquiry working through the brief, though there was considerable variation: some spent as little as half a day, while five prepared for a week and one for even longer. Most of this time was spent reading the written submissions and studying maps, and most also referred to the relevant statutes. Only eight specifically mentioned reading the *Foot et al.* case and when asked about their interpretation of the rules, references to the *Foot et al.* judgement were rare. As noted previously, the English Commission did not include an explicit reference to the case in its briefing, and one Assistant Commissioner who had found the case particularly helpful pointedly remarked that he had established its relevance despite rather than because of the Commission.

A minority of Assistant Commissioners (10) also visited the area in advance of the Inquiry. As noted previously, the English Commission preferred Assistant

Commissioners to be 'outsiders', though almost a third of the English Assistant Commissioners we interviewed claimed more than a passing acquaintance with their areas, mainly through family ties or planning inquiries. Those who carried out preliminary visits generally found them helpful. As one said:

> I always viewed the area beforehand especially if there was an important ward – I generally drive but often walk. I feel it's essential to view so that I know what people are talking about. I have to be able to try to listen intelligently.

For others it formed part of the initial testing of the written submissions, as the following Assistant Commissioner noted:

> I visited the ward in question on the day before the Inquiry, a visit I found curiously instructive in the light of the submissions, especially the lack of any crossing point between that ward and its neighbour to the east.

Assistant Commissioners in Scotland (because of the nature of Sheriffdoms) but also in Wales and Northern Ireland (because of the size of the countries and the Commissions' appointment policies), were generally more familiar with their areas, but a number still paid preliminary visits. Indeed a Northern Ireland political party suggested to us that an Assistant Commissioner there carried out his own assessment of the strength of local community ties by visiting the area before the Inquiry, unannounced, and asking the opinions of people on the street.

Given the differences in policy between Commissions and in experience and practice between Assistant Commissioners, we asked interviewees whether they felt familiarity or otherwise with the area under consideration had been an advantage or disadvantage. More thought their background was an advantage than vice versa, regardless of that background!

	Familiar	Unfamiliar
Advantage	16	16
Disadvantage	0	7
Neither/Mixed	7	14

The following comments reveal the range of opinions expressed:

> The public perception is important. I came as a total stranger with no preconceptions, with a totally open mind, and that must be an advantage.

> The bits I knew I found it was definitely an advantage, most definitely. Having done the local plan I knew the villages, the industries, the transport links. I didn't act on my own knowledge in the absence of evidence, but I used my knowledge to inform my questions.

> Being a stranger was a disadvantage. I would have found it a hell of a lot easier to do an area I knew. I don't have a very good memory for names and remembering the place names made it much harder work.

> I don't think it makes a jot of difference really. I'm a professional lawyer and I look to the issues.

It is clear that there was no consensus, but it is also notable that no Assistant Commissioner who knew an area felt that to have been a disadvantage, whereas a significant number who didn't did feel that. The English Commission's policy of asking for those without local connections has attractions, but a significant number of those appointed actually had some local knowledge, while others found their ignorance a disadvantage. From the viewpoint of the Assistant Commissioners at least, this aspect of the English Commission's appointment policy was not without its drawbacks.

The briefing note provided by the English Commission also covered the conduct of the Inquiries, but with a very light touch – for example 'the discretion whether or not to allow cross-examination rests with you' and 'the detailed conduct of an Inquiry is left to your discretion' – and this gave rise to some different concerns. Over half (30) of the English Assistant Commissioners had no judicial experience, and while many of these had experience of public inquiries, often through their involvement in local government law, for several this was their first experience of one. Some regretted the absence of any personal contact with Commission staff prior to the Inquiry (whereas most of the Assistant Commissioners in Scotland and especially Northern Ireland went out of their way to praise the face-to-face briefing they received) and a few suggested that the Commission should organise some form of training for those without previous experience. Several Recorders said that they would not have liked to undertake the exercise when still an 'ordinary' barrister; and the candid comments of two Assistant Commissioners, both QCs and Recorders, suggested that the task may have been more formidable than many were willing to concede:

> There was no advice on how Assistant Commissioners in practice run hearings – no information at all. Fortunately the clerk at my first Inquiry, a very experienced and shrewd lady from the Commission, was very good.

> When I received the briefing from the Commission I thought it was sufficient, though I probably felt slightly at sea at the start of the Inquiry, not entirely confident.

This was not the majority viewpoint, however; most were content that the training and experience of their profession ensured that they were well suited to perform the role of Assistant Commissioner or, as one of them put it:

> Open fairness is what you're looking for. We're experienced in conducting or taking part in such procedures and hence we're ideal candidates. We know how to keep order, impose a timetable, how to organise, how to interpret, and if necessary do all of this politely but firmly. We are used to a position of authority and the whole process is quasi-legal in any case.

In Chapter 7 we consider how this experience was applied to the particular issues of redistricting, but now we turn to consider how others were preparing for the Inquiry. Who came along to the Inquiries, what were their motives, and how did they prepare their case?

The participants

At each Inquiry those present were requested to sign an attendance list and, although a few Assistant Commissioners noted that more people were present than had signed, these lists give a good indication of the numbers present. After making allowance for possible under-enumeration, we estimate that attendance averaged around fifty, but with a considerable range. At one extreme only around a dozen attended the Inquiries in Fife and Wolverhampton, whereas some three hundred packed into the Scottish College of Textiles in Galashiels on the opening day of the Inquiry into the Commission's provisional recommendations for the Borders. The majority of the latter were members of the public who came to observe rather than to participate (just 42 gave evidence there) but public interest on this scale was uncommon. The majority of attendees came to participate, with an average of over 30 people making oral contributions.

We have categorised those who participated in the Inquiries in the same way that we analysed the source of written representations (Table 6.4). The predominance of politicians and administrators is evident. Almost three-quarters of all appearances were made by these groups, and while some councillors and a larger number of local authorities adopted an independent, non-partisan position, this is more than offset by the fact that most individuals and representatives of voluntary organisations appeared as witnesses for or with the active encouragement of the political parties. Indeed the predominance of the parties is more marked than Table 6.4 suggests. We have analysed a sample of the transcripts of the 89 Inquiries to establish how much of the evidence presented to the Assistant Commissioners came from these six sources (Table 6.5). This shows that the political parties spent proportionally longer on their submissions than any other group. When allowance is made for the fact that most individuals, organisations and local authorities gave evidence in support of, or consistent with, that of the political parties, we estimate that between 80 and 90 per cent of the evidence at Local Inquiries could reasonably be described as essentially partisan in nature.

Table 6.4 *Classification of those who participated in the Local Inquiries, compared with those who made written representations (percentages of totals)*

	Participants	Written representations
Political parties	23	(11)
MPs and MEPs	9	(2)
Councillors	20	(5)
Local authorities	20	(6)
Voluntary organisations	6	(3)
Individuals	22	(73)

Table 6.5 *Classification of those who participated in the Local Inquiries, compared with the amount of time they took at the Inquiry (percentages of totals)*

	Time	Participants
Political parties	29	(23)
MPs and MEPs	11	(9)
Councillors	20	(20)
Local authorities	21	(20)
Voluntary organisations	5	(6)
Individuals	14	(22)

In Chapter 7 we consider the arguments put forward by those appearing at the Inquiries and assess the impact they had upon the Assistant Commissioners. Given the clear domination exercised by the political parties and local authorities, however, it is important to look in some detail at the way in which they prepared for the Inquiries.

The Political Parties

All Western democracies depend upon competition between political parties, and few electoral systems place greater emphasis upon the primacy of party than the United Kingdom's. Election to Parliament is virtually impossible without the backing of a party machine and it is the popularity of parties rather than of individual MPs and candidates which largely determines changes in vote share between elections. While representatives of single-member constituencies may have more to gain (or lose) from boundary changes than their counterparts in multi-member electoral divisions employing some form of proportional representation, this merely serves to emphasise the role of their party, without whose support and (hopefully) expertise their prospects of election may be damaged. And the parties themselves, aware of the spatial variability in the distribution of their support, have every incentive to promote those boundaries which are most efficient in converting votes into seats.

The interest of political parties in the redistribution process is clear, therefore, but its realisation poses difficulties. On the whole these are not difficulties of opportunity. Political parties are allowed to make submissions to the Commissions and to propose alternative boundaries. Although not disbarred by law from making those submissions on naked partisan grounds, it is and always has been understood that the Commissions will not entertain such arguments. It does not require a huge degree of sophistication, however, to dress them in non-partisan clothing, citing arguments in support of partisan causes which accord with the relevant rules. Most participants in the process are aware of this fact and it does not, per se, invalidate the case made. If a scheme of constituencies invented for partisan ends better satisfies the Rules than one which was not, then it is a superior scheme regardless of its author's motives.

A more important issue is the availability of resources and expertise. Preparing for a Review, monitoring proposals, preparing counter-proposals, liaising with MPs, regional and local branches, and presenting cases at Inquiries, all take time and money. A national party aspiring to government could easily justify the employment of a senior party official full time for the duration of a Review, together with the services of others as and when required. By affecting the outcome in a dozen marginal seats, well within the bounds of possibility as we shall see, a party can achieve benefits equivalent to those of a one-per-cent swing in national vote share. Yet while they are happy to devote millions of pounds to advertising budgets designed to achieve the latter, none has devoted comparable resources to the former. The problem, in other words, is one of perception. The resources are available, but few have realised the importance of allocating a significant share to redistribution. It is a perception which seems unlikely to survive the Fourth Review.

One relatively intractable problem for most parties in this context is organisation. Before a party can hope to persuade others of the benefits of a particular set of proposals, it must first persuade its own members. Yet all proposals produce winners and losers; every extra vote in seat x takes one away from y. It is no small task to convince members in the latter that the greater good demands their acquiescence. Many are suspicious of central direction or cajoling; most will be unfamiliar with the whole redistribution process and instinctively suspicious of change; others will have genuine objections to proposed new associations; and a few will be quite happy to use the process to settle scores with neighbouring associations or MPs. Nor is internal persuasion always sufficient. The most effective cases are those which demonstrate a degree of external support, and the more genuinely independent it is, the better. None of this is easy. However the degree to which a party is successful has a direct effect on the chances of its proposals being accepted.

Labour

The Labour Party was widely credited as having made the most effective and influential contribution to the Fourth Review. *The Times* (5 June 1995) claimed that Labour's 'determined, nationally coordinated campaign' had resulted in a victory in the 'battle of the boundaries', while Butler and McLean (1996a, 16) describe Labour's contribution as 'the most organized, the most ruthless, and the most professional' of the major parties. Yet although the outcome was generally viewed as a triumph, it was not the result of a clearly thought out strategy emanating from the top of the party. Rather it was bottom-up, the story of an individual identifying a problem (and a personal opportunity), gradually persuading colleagues and, following a fourth successive election defeat, enlisting the support of a determined and disciplined party to ensure that Labour made a more effective contribution to the process than it did at the Third Periodic Review (see Chapter 8).

The individual in question was David Gardner, formerly employed in the South West Regional Office of the Labour Party, who after the 1987 election began to take an interest in the possible effects of the next boundary Review. Part of Labour's strategy was to give some national responsibility to regional officers, and following discussions with Joyce Gould, Labour's Director of Organisation, Gardner was asked to carry out further work on both redistricting and electoral registration. This provided the basis for his *Parameters Report*, a preliminary area-by-area assessment of threats and opportunities which was presented to the party's National Executive Committee (NEC) in November 1989. This meeting identified five core objectives which were to underpin the party's boundaries strategy:

- To maximise the number of winnable seats. Before 1992 this comprised seats with a Conservative majority under 15 per cent, reducing to 9 per cent after the 1992 election, in both cases sufficient to ensure an overall Labour majority;
- To achieve the maximum possible consensus amongst Members of Parliament (including MEPs), constituency parties and other Labour groups;
- To identify objective arguments in support of proposals which met the statutory criteria and which were capable of commanding public support;
- To encourage a positive approach to the exercise throughout the party; and
- To achieve the best starting point, by encouraging electoral registration campaigns and by resisting unfavourable changes to local government boundaries.

A *Boundaries Strategy Group* (BSG) was established, chaired (successively) by Frank Dobson, Jack Cunningham, Margaret Beckett and John Prescott, all of whom held Shadow Cabinet posts under Neil Kinnock (party leader 1983–92) and John Smith (1992–94) and were members of Tony Blair's first Cabinet (1997–). A programme of regional briefing meetings was instituted for Labour MPs and local authority representatives, designed to engender a positive attitude and prepare the ground for consensus. These meetings were coupled with detailed discussions of the *Parameters Report* with regional officers, together with a special training day and resource pack for regional and organising staff. Meanwhile, targeted registration campaigns in Merseyside, South Yorkshire, West Yorkshire and Glasgow in 1990 and 1991 increased their theoretical entitlements above the relevant thresholds, thereby safeguarding four Labour seats, and attempts were made to counter any proposed local government boundary changes that would be unfavourable to Labour.

The foundations of the strategy in place, Gardner turned his attention to individual Review areas. The first step was the preparation of an *Options Paper* for each area, containing ward maps of the main potential schemes together with an analysis of their probable electoral consequences based upon ward-level estimates of support for each party.[21] This was followed by a consensus meeting, to which all the relevant party units and elected representatives were invited and which included a presentation of the party's strategy, followed by detailed consideration of the *Options Paper*. The vast majority of these meetings achieved the desired aim, but where necessary one or more further meetings were held. Having reached a consensus, a letter supporting the chosen scheme was circulated throughout the party directly following publication of the Commission's provisional recommendations for that area, with local parties requested to mobilise support from community groups and individuals. Before the Local Inquiry a further meeting was held to consider the best tactical approach to adopt and at the Inquiry itself this was supplemented by the provision of a full proof of evidence, by witness statements and by the cross-examination of opponents, generally under the guidance of either a barrister (many of whom donated their services free of charge) or Gardner himself (who performed the role at 17 Inquiries).

The early Inquiries were encouraging, with strong cases presented in Avon, Devon and Wiltshire, but it was not all plain sailing, with local disputes in Berkshire and an absence of witnesses in Northamptonshire. By this time, however, more significant changes were taking place within the party which were to raise the profile of the entire undertaking. The General Election defeat in April 1992 further concentrated the party's collective mind, and brought the BSG under the chairmanship of Margaret Beckett. She adopted a more pro-active role than her predecessors and in December 1992 a *Boundaries Task Force* was established to assist with implementation of the strategy determined by the BSG. From working roughly half-time on boundaries, Gardner was given full-time responsibility for convening the *Task Force*, assisted at various times by five other party officials who between them provided an additional full-time equivalent. The additional resources devoted to the Review allowed the party to keep abreast of the increased workload during 1993, when the majority of Inquiries took place, though even those resources were 'overstretched' in the latter stages, notably in late 1993 when the Lancashire Inquiry was being held. The established procedure of consensus meetings was continued, reaching a total of 66 by the end of the Review (56 in England, seven in Scotland and three in Wales), and more staff were available to monitor representations and competing counter-proposals. The first few months of the *Task Force*'s life were also a critical time in preparing for the Review of London, coinciding as they did with the correspondence between the Commission and the political parties on appropriate groupings of London Boroughs.

What conclusions can be drawn about Labour's approach? First, it would be wrong to under-estimate the role of Gardner in the process. He was primarily responsible for raising the profile of the Review within the party and, with the assistance of Gould, whose contacts with senior figures were invaluable, bringing it to the NEC's attention. Not only did he recognise the Review's significance, he was also largely instrumental in devising and implementing the strategy which helped to ensure the effectiveness of Labour's contribution. Second, the involvement of all levels of the party at an early stage proved invaluable. Although the internal structures of the Labour Party are more conducive to a degree of centralised control than those of its opponents, in themselves they are not sufficient. The party's regional offices played a pivotal role in ensuring that the overall strategy was disseminated, while the consensus meetings increased awareness of the need for an over-arching plan for each Review area. Third, the party's self-discipline was particularly marked and undoubtedly assisted in the presentation of the consensus case. Only three Labour MPs (Don Dixon, John Gilbert and Martin Redmond) and one Labour council (South Tyneside) argued against the consensus view at a Local Inquiry, and only in Berkshire was internal dissension (from the Wokingham constituency Labour party) serious. This was due in part to the party's desire to win, evident in nearly everything it did after its 1992 defeat; in part to what Gardner describes as 'a clear political commitment from the very top to our objectives', exemplified by the several meetings with MPs from difficult areas chaired by Margaret Beckett, some of whom also met the party leader on the issue; and in part to the usual political processes of pressure and manipulation (Jack Cunningham dealt with difficult local authorities, such as Stoke, and the Chief Whip – who was on the BSG – with recalcitrant MPs).

Conservative

The Times' judgement that the Conservative party had lost the 'battle of the boundaries' was widely shared within the party. In the debate on the draft Parliamentary Constituencies Order, Peter Luff MP said that the party had 'missed a trick' (*Hansard*, vol. 261, 14 June 1995, col. 834) and John Carlisle, MP for Luton North, touched on dissatisfaction within the party when observing (col. 848) that:

> Blind loyalty to my leader, to the chairman of the party and certainly to my political following … . prevents me from saying what I should perhaps say, and what some people have said to me, regarding the way in which Conservative central office has handled the whole affair.

Insofar as it failed, to what extent was the party its own worst enemy?

The Conservatives approached the Review with a degree of optimism. On the basis of the 1987 General Election results, Rob Hayward, MP for Kingswood and one of the few in the party with an interest in psephology in general and redistricting in particular, had calculated that the Review could be worth a net extra twenty seats to the party. It was generally accepted that the Conservatives had benefited from previous redistributions and that there was nothing obviously different about the forthcoming one, so the figure of twenty gained a degree of popular currency in the party. This encouraged a degree of complacency, and while David Gardner was busy laying the foundations for Labour's campaign, Conservative Central Office was quiescent. Chris Patten, Party Chairman from 1990 until 1992, failed to prepare the party for the exercise, and Paul Gribble, the member of staff within Central Office with 'responsibility' for the Review, exercised a purely administrative role. (Compare Gribble's minuted contribution to the English Commission's 1991 meeting with political parties to that of Gardner for the Labour party: Boundary Commission for England, 1995b, 114–116.) The party in general, and Central Office in particular, were preoccupied with the forthcoming general election and insofar as the work of the Boundary Commissions was discussed, conversations largely centred on the need to ensure that the new seats were in place for a 1996 election and hence on the proposed *Boundary Commissions Bill 1992,* for which Hayward was a prime mover.

The 1992 election victory encouraged the complacency within the party, even though Hayward revised his estimates downwards, suggesting that the Review might produce a net gain of only twelve seats to the Tories (who had a Parlia-

mentary majority of 21). Hayward and Patten both lost their seats, leaving the former without a job and the party with a new Chairman, Norman Fowler. He allocated responsibility for overseeing the Review to Dame Angela Rumbold, one of
the Deputy Chairmen, but it was only one of her responsibilities and she was given
no budget and little in the way of backing. Meanwhile Hayward was approached
by two backbench MPs concerned at possible boundary changes, who offered to
pay him to represent them. Feeling that it was more sensible for him to act for the
party as a whole, Hayward offered Rumbold his services, and with the help of Ken
Hind, a barrister and another casualty of the 1992 election, he took responsibility
for co-ordinating the party's submissions at the Local Inquiries.

When he started, in the summer of 1992, Hayward thought his involvement would
be short-term and no attempt was made to plan strategically for the remainder of the
Review. He had no office, no access to computer facilities, did his own typing at
home and, initially at least, worked free of charge. The first of a series of occasional
meetings was arranged with Rumbold and regional directors of the party in an
attempt to inject a degree of structure into the party's responses, and he produced a
leaflet which was distributed to Conservative Constituency Associations to raise
awareness of the Review and of its implications for the party. At this stage the party
was still unaware of the efficiency of the Labour Party operation, but this changed
when Hayward attended the Hampshire Inquiry in September. The discovery that
Labour had done a great deal of work behind the scenes, with Labour-controlled
Southampton City Council 'selling' its counter-proposal to neighbouring non-Labour
local authorities in advance, horrified Hayward who returned to London that night
and 'raised hell'. In his view it was not too late for the party to recover the situation, but despite sympathetic words, the warning signs were ignored.[22]

Before the next set of Inquiries towards the end of the year, Hayward visited
the Counties in question, generally for meetings convened by the area chairman
and agent, and attended by group leaders from local authorities, constituency association chairmen and agents. At these he explained the nature of the process and
attempted to establish support for a counter-proposal where the provisional recommendations appeared unsuitable. This was an advance on earlier practice, but
it still fell far short of Labour's consensus meetings in terms both of preparation
and inclusivity. A more fundamental stumbling block, however, was the attitude
of the Party Chairman, who was preoccupied with the financial crisis facing Central Office and unwilling to provide additional resources to support an effective
response. Furthermore, he showed little interest in the process, calling his first
meeting with Hayward as late as June 1993 and then only in response to a request
for a briefing by the Prime Minister.

By then the situation was beyond recovery. Another former MP and barrister,
Ernle Money, represented the party at a number of Inquiries, but Hind had secured
alternative employment and Hayward was nominated as the party's candidate for
the Christchurch by-election. He was to play no further part in the Review, and
nobody with his expertise and reputation was available to replace him. Morale in
the party, on a downward trajectory since Black Wednesday in September 1992

(when the UK was forced out of the European Exchange Rate Mechanism and interest rates were changed three times in a single day; see Butler and Kavanagh, 1997), had reached a new low. The stage of the Review which required the greatest central co-ordination, with the publication of provisional recommendations for 192 seats in just three weeks, could hardly have come at a worse time. The remaining months were characterised by the same mixture of relative disinterest at the top of Central Office and lack of expertise in many of the areas, to which were added the worried voices of an increasing number of Conservative MPs. Huge efforts were made in several areas, but either through lack of preparation or internal disagreements, very few were successful. Rumbold, with some assistance within Central Office, continued to do the best she could, ensuring that 'some very determined and well-thought out leadership and advice' was disseminated within the National Union of Conservative Associations. But, she lamented, according to *The Times* (5 July 1995), 'unlike the Labour Party we cannot impose anything. We simply can't tell them what to do, whereas the Labour Party enforced its view right from the beginning'.

A good example of the Conservatives' disarray comes from Dame Angela's own constituency. The London Borough of Merton comprised two constituencies prior to the review – Mitcham and Morden (with a 1991 electorate of 61,063) and Wimbledon (60,633). Not surprisingly, the Commission's provisional recommendation was for no change (apart from slight realignment of boundaries to reflect local government boundary changes). The local Conservative party in Mitcham and Morden (Dame Angela's seat) contested this, however, arguing that one of its wards (Colliers Wood) should be transferred to Wimbledon, with another (Cannon Hill) transferred in the other direction (Figure 6.1). Mitcham and Morden was a very marginal seat, with a Conservative lead over Labour of only 3.4 percentage points at the 1992 general election; Wimbledon, on the other hand, had a Tory majority then of 29.7 points. The Mitcham and Morden Association sought to bolster their candidate's chances of re-election without, it expected, seriously denting those of Wimbledon's incumbent, by transferring a strongly Conservative ward from Wimbledon in return for a much more marginal one. Their grounds were that this would create a constituency that, in effect, reconstituted the former Borough of Merton. But the Wimbledon Association was not aware of this proposal until it was later made public, and its representation to the Commission endorsed the 'no change' provisional recommendation. By the time of the Local Inquiry, however, the two Associations were, in the Assistant Commissioner's words, 'of a mind' regarding the proposed change – which was opposed by Labour, which wanted to keep Mitcham and Morden as marginal as possible. The Assistant Commissioner 'considered the case for retaining Colliers Wood in Mitcham and Morden to be little short of overwhelming' (Boundary Commission for England, 1995a, 66, #9), however, noting that the proposal would 'not produce the desired result … to re-unite Morden' (#10). The provisional recommendations were upheld – and the Conservatives lost both seats to Labour at the 1997 general election.

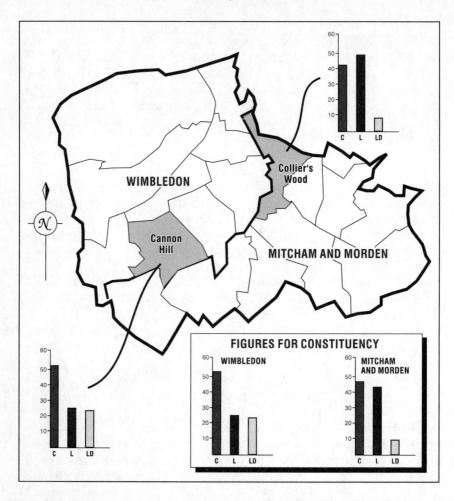

Figure 6.1 *The wards whose constituency allocation was contested in provisional recommendations for the London Borough of Merton at the Fourth Periodic Review, indicating the estimated 1992 voting for the three main parties in the recommended constituencies and the contest wards*
Source: based on the Ordnance Survey map with the permission of The Controller of Her Majesty's Stationery Office © Crown Copyright

To what extent does complacency explain the result of the 'battle of the boundaries'? It is undoubtedly true that the internal structures of the Labour Party are more conducive to central control than those of its opponents. Conservative Constituency Associations are autonomous bodies, financially independent of Central Office, which many of them view with considerable suspicion. It would be a mistake, however, to assume that the Labour Party was in a position to *impose* its plans on reluctant members. There were indeed areas where constituency parties or MPs or local authorities did not toe the party line and there was nothing David Gardner could do to stop them. A large part of Labour's success was in *persuading* the party to adopt a common approach and thereby reducing the rebels to insignificant numbers. This was undoubtedly helped by the party's collective psychological condition, but it also depended, critically, upon foresight and planning, elements which were almost entirely lacking in the Conservative Party's approach. The failures of successive Conservative Party Chairmen to recognise the Review's significance and to provide adequate resources to those willing and able to help were self-imposed handicaps which owed nothing to party structures *per se*. Furthermore, the government's own legislative programme added to the party's difficulties. The work of the Local Government Commission in England (see below) heightened tensions between town and country, making it difficult to generate support for the inclusion of Conservative-inclined rural areas in otherwise urban seats; and the rushed timetable created by the *Boundary Commissions Act 1992*, coupled with local government reorganisation in Scotland, left regional electoral divisions as the smallest available building blocks there with adverse implications for Conservative prospects in seats such as Ayr and Stirling.

The conclusion must be that the Conservative Party could and should have done better. It was undoubtedly hampered by low morale and the financial independence of the constituency associations which encourages parochialism. Nevertheless it failed to plan, it failed to allocate sufficient resources, and it was hindered by its own legislative programme. From a party machine that was once hailed as the greatest in the western world, it was a singularly unconvincing performance.

Other parties

Of the other political parties that participated in the Fourth Review, involvement was, unsurprisingly, dominated by those with current Parliamentary representation. There were occasional written representations and isolated Inquiry appearances by representatives of the Green Party and the Liberal Party, but neither of these had any form of central advice or co-ordination. In England the domination of the procedures by Conservative and Labour was challenged only by the Liberal Democrats, joined in Scotland and Wales by the SNP and Plaid Cymru respectively, whereas in Northern Ireland eight parties sought to influence the composition of just eighteen seats.

Redistricting poses particular difficulties for the *Liberal Democrats*. The party is a long-standing opponent of the first-past-the-post system of elections, of which Periodic Reviews are an indispensable part, and hence many members view the process with a certain distaste. This is sometimes exacerbated by its emphasis upon 'grass-roots' politics and the importance of communities, many of which are inevitably divided by the process of boundary drawing. The party receives far less income than Labour or the Conservatives and, together with its federal structure, this results in a relatively small central headquarters at Cowley Street, London, encourages devolved decision-making and hinders central co-ordination. Furthermore whereas both Conservative and Labour appeal differentially to social classes which exhibit a significant degree of residential segregation, Liberal Democrat support is more evenly distributed, making the redistricting process less important to the party's prospects.

For all these reasons the Liberal Democrats could have been expected to adopt a lower profile than their opponents, but there was still scope for a significant input from Cowley Street. Much as in Conservative Central Office, however, the Review was accorded a low priority. The party's Chief Executive, Graham Elson, had initial responsibility for monitoring it, but apart from representing the party at meetings with the Commission, at which his input was minimal, he seems to have taken little notice of the Review. Certainly the party's response to the English Commission's early recommendations, covering its areas of greatest strength in south-west and central southern England, was unimpressive. It was also at this stage that it missed its clearest opportunity, that of requesting an Inquiry into the provisional recommendation not to allocate additional representation to the Isle of Wight until some twenty months after the due date for representations (Boundary Commission for England, 1995, 219).

After the 1992 General Election responsibility was transferred from Elson to Chris Rennard, the party's Director of Campaigns and Elections, who as David Alton's agent at the time of the Third Review had first-hand experience of the Commission's procedures and of how to achieve a successful outcome. (Alton's Edge Hill seat was recommended for abolition, and the then Liberal party successfully argued for a new seat – Mossley Hill – which Alton won in 1983, 1987 and 1992; it had the oddest shape of any urban constituency in the UK; see Figure 6.2.)[23] He commissioned a short paper from David Rossiter, a sympathetic academic observer of the process, containing advice on how to make submissions, and this was distributed to local parties. In the latter part of 1992 Rennard also asked Rossiter to prepare an analysis of possible changes in London and the Metropolitan Counties, and there was talk of instituting a routine whereby regional parties and constituencies were alerted to possibilities in advance of the Commissions' proposals. This was not realised, however, as preparations for impending by-elections in Newbury and Christchurch began to dominate his attentions and for the remainder of the Review Rennard maintained only a watching brief. He brought proposed changes to the attention of individual MPs, but whereas some were grateful for advice, as in the Scottish Borders, others such as David Alton and Liz Lynne chose to adopt their own approach. (Alton's Liverpool Mossley Hill seat was abolished, despite much local protest, and he retired from Parliament in 1997; Lynne's Rochdale seat was considerably changed, and she lost it to Labour then.) Rennard worked closely with some regional organisers, notably in the North West, but the vast majority of submissions were the work of local parties without any input from Cowley Street; in contrast to Labour and the Conservatives, the party was never represented by counsel. Towards the end of 1993 he pressed the English Commission to reconsider its decision on the Isle of Wight, but without success, and as the Review entered its closing stages his involvement reduced further.

It is difficult to argue with Rennard's assessment of priorities. Liberal Democrat success has always been dependent far more upon campaigning effort than upon constituency composition and the results of the 1997 general election confirmed the importance to the party of its target seats initiative, which he coordinated. Whereas Labour and Conservative strategists could generally be sure of the balance of party advantage from a particular set of boundaries, this was much less certain for the Liberal Democrats. To divert resources from an already under-resourced central team would not have made sense. Nevertheless regional offices could have been more fully involved in the process (as happened, belatedly, when Cowley Street passed responsibility for co-ordinating the party's response to the Commission's proposals for London to the London region of the party) , and the party's initial lack of preparation almost certainly affected Parliamentary representation in the south of England. While redistricting will never be as important for the Liberal Democrats as for their major rivals, the party was almost always reacting to events. Scarce resources do not preclude an effective strategy, indeed they make it more important, and the failure to make strategic plans in advance of the Review was Cowley Street's major failing.

For the two Nationalist parties the Review was a relatively low-key affair. In Wales this was mainly a reflection of the Review itself, which involved very few recommended changes to existing boundaries. *Plaid Cymru's* Chief Executive, Karl Davies, took personal responsibility for the conduct of the party's response, representing it at meetings with the Commission and appearing for it at some of the Local Inquiries. (The exception to this was in Dyfed, where different, albeit similar, proposals were submitted by different party branches.) The party's strategy emphasised the importance of 'rural weighting', citing Rule 6, with its emphasis upon the size, shape and accessibility of constituencies. This made obvious sense given the concentration of its electoral support in the Welsh-speaking rural parts of North and West Wales and provided the basis for the party's case at the three Inquiries where it made significant contributions. It met with mixed results, maintaining the status quo in Gwynedd, home to three of its four MPs, but failing to produce favourable changes in Clwyd and Dyfed. Although the outcomes tell us little – the cards were stacked strongly in the party's favour in the former and against it in the latter – at least its contributions show that the party was alive to the Review and able to marshal and present an informed response.

Redistricting poses rather different problems for the *Scottish National Party (SNP)*. Its support shows neither the class base of Labour and the Conservatives nor the cultural foundation of Plaid Cymru. The rewards (and perils) of boundary changes are more elusive and, much like the Liberal Democrats, the party's response reflected this. SNP Director of Organisation, Allison Hunter, represented the party at its meetings with the Commission and there were internal discussions of the Commission's proposals 'at very senior level'. National advice was available, but implementation was intended to take place locally, led by local constituency officers, prospective candidates, councillors or MPs. The party encouraged constituency associations to meet on an area basis to discuss the Com-

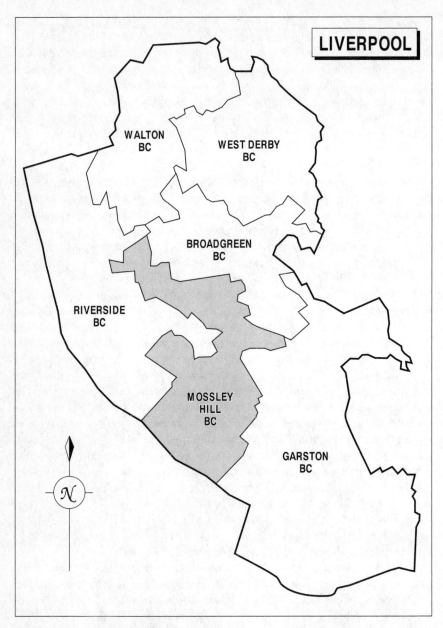

Figure 6.2 *The oddly-shaped Mossley Hill constituency in the Boundary Commission's final recommendations for Liverpool at the Third Periodic Review*
Source: based on the Ordnance survey map with the permission of The Controller of Her Majesty's Stationery Office © Crown Copyright

mission's proposals and to reach a position which all could support, but its own assessment of the response was that it was 'patchy'. In fact it was worse. Only two Inquiries witnessed a co-ordinated SNP response, significantly both areas with SNP MPs (Grampian and the joint Inquiry for Central and Tayside), and its limited success was achieved with the support of its political opponents. Elsewhere little or no interest was shown in the Review, even in Regions such as Highland and Dumfries & Galloway which contained realistic target seats for the party. Although the SNP suffered no major reverses, it signally failed to mobilise the local members upon whose involvement its strategy depended. While it is extremely doubtful whether effective implementation of the strategy would have reaped rewards in terms of Parliamentary representation, as an exercise in member participation it could hardly be described as a success.

A total of eight political parties in *Northern Ireland* participated in the Fourth Review, of which five made a significant impact. As the largest, the *Ulster Unionist Party* was able to devote the greatest resources. A 'high-powered committee containing the party's better minds' was established to co-ordinate reaction to the provisional recommendations and local branches were instructed to await a central response. Apart from local difficulties in South Belfast (which seat was proposed to be abolished by the Commission) the party line prevailed and the Commission was generally supported as having produced proposals which were 'logical and workable'. The *Democratic Unionist Party*, while maintaining its original contention that an eighteenth seat should be created, was not too unhappy with the Commission's proposals. Peter Robinson MP, the party's Deputy Leader, co-ordinated the response and represented the party at two Inquiries, while the party's other MPs and its Secretary presented submissions at the remainder. Apart from the allocation of four wards, the *Alliance Party* was delighted with the provisional recommendations. Believing that the proposed constituency of Castlereagh and Newtownards was 'as near an Alliance gerrymander as you could get', the party had little difficulty in agreeing a common approach, but the lack of support away from Belfast's periphery resulted in its Secretary having to represent it at the Newry Inquiry and in no presence at all in Omagh.

The provisional recommendations were greeted with dismay by Nationalists, but the response of the two Nationalist parties was very different. To its opponents at least, the initial response of the *SDLP* was seen variously as 'disorganised' and 'shambolic'. There was heated debate within the party as it attempted to formulate a coherent overall solution, but by the time of the Inquiries the situation had improved somewhat and in Omagh and, more particularly, Newry an effective case was presented with the assistance of paid barristers. There were widespread suspicions that the party had been 'bailed out by Dublin' (it was a matter of public record that the Irish government had pressed for changes to the Commission's provisional recommendations and it had close connections with some of those appearing at Inquiries in the SDLP interest; Rossiter, Johnston and Pattie, 1998). But the response was still patchy, for whatever reason: the lower profile at the Belfast Inquiry was notable, while the lone Councillor appearing at Newtownards was only willing to address issues in one of the four seats under consideration. *Sinn Fein*, by contrast, adopted a centralised approach, setting up a four-member committee which took soundings from its supporters and produced a comprehensive counter-proposal for the entire province. The party was represented at each Inquiry (including at Newtownards, where its representatives entered and left under police protection); by far its most effective contribution was in Belfast where its success in mobilising support from community groups in and beyond the city's western boundary helped to persuade the Assistant Commissioner to recommend a Belfast West constituency which crossed that boundary.

The Local Authorities

After the political interests, the next most important players at the Inquiries were the local authorities. In discussing their contribution it is important to draw a distinction between what might be termed 'minor' and 'major' authorities. The former comprise town, parish and community councils and are to be found primarily (though not exclusively) outside the major metropolitan areas. Numerically they constitute by far the majority of local authorities (over 95 per cent), but they are not 'interested authorities' under the terms of the *Parliamentary Constituencies Act*. Most of their members, particularly in the smaller councils, secure election without a party label and most only have the services of a clerk. The latter, by contrast, are specifically identified in the Act and thus have a special status. They are responsible for the conduct of elections, host the vast majority of Inquiries, and can call upon the services of professionally-qualified officers with local knowledge. What they share with their 'minor' authority counterparts, however, is the credibility which comes from having been chosen to represent the interests of electors in their area. In short, local authorities are the only bodies which can claim both a democratic mandate and an independent interest in the outcome. In the remainder of this chapter we consider the ways in which they exercised this status.

Minor Authorities

Because they are not 'interested' authorities under the terms of the Act, minor authorities cannot trigger an Inquiry on their own; nor were they notified individually of the Commissions' proposals. Following a complaint from a local authority in Dorset about the lack of publicity, the English Commission:

> agreed that we request from the National Association of Local Councils the addresses of their County Associations in order that we could send copies of news releases for them to circulate to town and parish councils (BCE Minutes, 1993/2, 4.9),

though as two-thirds of the provisional recommendations for Shire England had already been published, this could only have a limited impact. In a few cases District Councils canvassed their views; otherwise they will have learned about the Commissions' proposals in the same way as ordinary members of the public, though any party political connections amongst their members will have helped. In the circumstances, it is perhaps surprising that minor authorities were responsible for almost a thousand written representations, around 4 per cent of the total received by the Commissions in response to their provisional recommendations and equivalent to seven in every ten received from all local government sources.

Reflecting the rural bias in their distribution, submissions in respect of the Shire Counties were more numerous (notably the 57 received in Essex and 46 in Devon) but it is also worth noting, for example, that one town and nine parish councils commented on the Commission's proposals for the Metropolitan Borough of Doncaster. Most submissions were relatively brief – fewer than 30 councils were identified by the Commissions as putting forward a counter-proposal – and in the light of their written responses it is not surprising to find that they played a relatively limited role in the Local Inquiries. Just over one hundred representatives of town, parish and community councils attended them, and whereas it was not uncommon for major authorities to be represented by more than one person, this was very rare for minor authorities. Outside the major metropolitan areas the vast majority of Inquiries had contributions from at least one minor authority but, as with the written representations, these tended to be brief and particular. Few authorities were represented by their clerk or other paid officer; rather it tended to be an elected councillor, typically the chairman, who spoke on the council's behalf and there were many instances of councillors with dual membership of District and parish councils speaking on behalf of the latter.

Two aspects tended to be stressed (and often linked) in their contributions: the maintenance of the status quo and the relationship between town and country. From the viewpoint of an individual parish or community, the disruptive effect of the 'numbers game' was almost invariably seen as unwelcome and most minor authorities were reluctant to address the wider issues. Most saw their role as preserving the status quo and, because they were only interested in defending the perceived interests of their own community, were understandably unwilling to propose alternative solutions which would affect others. Proposals which would result in the division of a minor authority between constituencies were a particular cause of concern (because of their size, this tended to impact primarily upon towns, though several larger rural parishes were also affected) and a dozen minor authorities emphasised this point at an Inquiry.

References to long-standing ties with neighbouring areas were a recurring theme, sometimes to other parishes but more usually to historic towns such as Bury St Edmunds, Chester and Salisbury, which act as a focus for surrounding villages. An interesting contrast emerges, however, when the town or city is seen as less attractive, often with assumed predatory intentions (for example, larger cities such as Brighton, Hull and Plymouth, industrial towns such as Mansfield and Scunthorpe and new towns such as Bracknell, Harlow, Redditch and Telford). In some cases there were mixed messages (as with reactions to proposals to extend the boundaries of both Darlington and Lincoln), but on balance it was the clear preference of rural parishes (in the ratio of approximately 3:1) to keep their distance from their urban neighbours. This had implications for the political parties, particularly for the Conservatives who stood to benefit from the incorporation of rural wards in primarily urban constituencies.

Major Authorities

At the time of the Fourth Review there was a total of 539 major authorities in the United Kingdom. There were significant differences between them in both size and function; from the higher-tier Strathclyde Regional Council with an electorate of 1.7 million to the lower-tier district of Radnorshire with fewer than 20,000; and amongst the unitary authorities from the city of Birmingham with over 700,000 electors to the district of Moyle in Northern Ireland with barely 10,000. Apart from size and the consequent level of resources at their disposal, the other factor which differentiated them from the minor authorities was their responsibility to represent more than one spatially discrete interest. Most of the major authorities covered areas with differing viewpoints and this inevitably affected both the way in which they made their decisions and the approach they brought to the issue.

Although the more powerful contributions came from the major authorities, two factors tended to influence the presentation and interpretation of their case. Of these the more significant was partisan self-interest. At the time of the Fourth Review the Labour Party was in a particularly strong position, controlling 34 per cent of all major authorities and 57 per cent of those with unitary status (Table 6.6). Compared with previous Reviews, the rise of the Liberal Democrats in local government had resulted in a significantly higher proportion of councils on which no party had overall control, but nevertheless 59 per cent of authorities (and a higher proportion of the larger ones) were under majority political party control. In such circumstances the impartiality of many authorities' response was, understandably, unlikely to be accepted without question.

Another complicating factor in most parts of Britain was the concurrent Review of local government. In 1992 the Government announced its intention to implement a new structure of unitary authorities in both Scotland and Wales and to review the existing two-tier arrangement in 'Shire' England with a presumption in favour of a unitary outcome. As a result the disposition of Parliamentary boundaries became linked in the eyes of many with those of local government, an association which the Commissions tried their best to dispel; the English, Scottish and Welsh Commissions used the same form of words in their *News Releases* to stress the independence of the two processes, stressing that their recommendations 'do not affect the structure or arrangements of local government or the services they provide'. Nevertheless the English Commission noted that the coincidence 'created a good deal of confusion amongst electors' (Boundary Commission for England, 1995a, 287), confusion which was occasionally exacerbated in Scotland by the statements of government ministers.[24] It also coloured the approach of a number of local authorities, more anxious than usual to minimise fragmentation of their authority between constituencies and thereby to emphasise its identity.

Table 6.6 *Political control of major local authorities at the time of the Fourth Review*

	C	L	LD	SNP	I	NOC	ALL
London Boroughs	11	14	3	–	–	4	32
Metropolitan Boroughs	1	25	–	–	–	10	36
English Shire Counties	6	8	1	–	–	24	39
English Shire Districts	78	76	23	–	23	96	296
Welsh Counties	–	5	–	–	1	2	8
Welsh County Districts	1	19	–	–	12	5	37
Scottish Regions	–	4	–	–	2	3	9
Scottish Districts	3	23	1	1	21	7	56
Total	100	174	28	1	59	151	513

Note: control has been determined at the time of the Inquiry or, where no Inquiry was held, at the date of the publication of provisional recommendations. Isles of Scilly and City of London are excluded as are authorities in N. Ireland.
Key to parties: C – Conservative; L – Labour; LD – Liberal Democrat; SNP – Scottish National Party; I – Independent; NOC – no overall control

Against this background we can investigate the role of major authorities by tabulating their response to the Commissions' provisional recommendations. Their overall response rate was 71 per cent (Table 6.7), with over 150 authorities choosing not to express an opinion. In many cases, however, this was because the Commission was proposing to leave constituency boundaries unaltered within that authority's area and if we analyse just those authorities where change was proposed (the 304 councils in the second block of Table 6.7), the response rate rises to 88 per cent. Only in Northern Ireland was the response rate significantly lower, reflecting and arguably reinforcing the generally lower level of public involvement in the process there.

Table 6.7 *Responses by major local authorities to the Boundary Commissions' provisional recommendations*

	All			Areas with Change		
	N	R	% R	N	R	%R
London Boroughs	32	20	63	23	19	83
Metropolitan Boroughs	36	29	81	28	28	100
English Shire Counties	39	31	79	35	31	89
English Shire districts	297	228	77	161	143	89
Welsh Counties	8	6	75	3	3	100
Welsh County Districts	36	20	56	7	7	100
Scottish Regions	9	7	78	8	7	88
Scottish Districts	56	35	63	27	25	93
Northern Ireland	26	7	27	12	5	42
Total	539	383	71	304	268	88

Key: N – number of authorities; R – number of responses; %R – percentage of authorities which responded

This high level of participation was repeated at the Local Inquiries, where the overall attendance rate of major authorities was 75 per cent (this figure excludes the 41 authorities which could not appear because the uncontentious nature of the Commissions' proposals meant that no Inquiry was necessary). Although a number of authorities 'dropped out' at this stage, choosing to rely on their written representation, several became involved for the first time, either because of difficulties agreeing a position earlier or because they had become aware of a counter-proposal which might affect electors in their area. Altogether we estimate that just over 90 per cent of those authorities with a direct interest in the outcome attended the relevant Local Inquiry.

What of those which didn't? Why did they choose to forego their right to influence events? And how did these authorities which attended view their role at the Inquiry? How was their response determined and presented? And in particular, what was the political input? To investigate these questions, we sent a brief questionnaire to the Chief Executives of 300 authorities, all of which were affected by the Commissions' provisional recommendations or by a subsequent counter-proposal. We received replies from 132, a 44 per cent response rate, and we are satisfied that they provide a reasonable cross-section of local authority viewpoints.[25] Together with the evidence of the Inquiry reports they provide a sound basis on which to assess the significance of the local authority input to the Fourth Review.

Some authorities stayed away because, as already noted, they chose to rely upon their earlier written representation. For many of these the decision not to attend seems to have been an uncomplicated reflection of the priority afforded to the exercise by the authority or of its confidence in others (typically a neighbouring or higher-tier authority) to reflect its concerns. Elsewhere as the following responses confirm, it was decided that a corporate view was inappropriate, or should not be pressed at the Inquiry, leaving elected members to make their own submissions if they wished:

> My Council did not submit direct representations regarding the Commission's proposals. The matter was regarded as the subject of party politics and was left to the party and the public to respond to the proposals.

> At the time the Council was considering this, there was a Conservative majority of one and in the circumstances there was a consensus amongst Members that it would be inappropriate for the majority party to impose its views as the Council's views, given that the core issues were essentially ones of party political electoral advantage or disadvantage.

In a few cases, the absence of local authority input reflected a change in political control between the lodging of a written representation and the holding of the Local Inquiry. West Sussex County Council, for example, put forward a detailed counter-proposal in the early part of 1993, but when the Conservatives lost control in the May elections, Liberal Democrat and Labour members on the new Council made it clear that they were not willing to run with the original scheme and no officer appeared at the Inquiry. (Interestingly none of the Inquiry Reports for the five English Shire Counties where the Conservatives lost control after publication of the provisional recommendations – Cambridgeshire, Kent, Suffolk, and East and West Sussex – refers to any input from the County Councils.) Elsewhere it reflected the inability of the various political groups to agree a common position. As another respondent explained:

> The Council as a body was in some difficulty. Although initially it was hoped to reach some consensus on a view to be put forward at the Inquiry, none of the political parties could agree between themselves on the preferred course of action and it soon became clear that there was little likelihood of the Council being able to put forward proposals which everyone would agree.

This response came not from a 'hung' authority but from one with a large Conservative majority and is symptomatic of an important difference in approach between those authorities with an overall Labour majority and those without. Among the latter there were several notable examples of absence, in particular of the London Borough of Tower Hamlets (Liberal Democrat controlled) where the Assistant Commissioner was moved to comment that it was:

> doubly unfortunate that (despite my causing an invitation to be sent to the Borough) Tower Hamlets declined to send a representative to the Inquiry (Inquiry Report, 9)

and of Trafford Borough Council (Conservative controlled) where the provisional recommendations breached the Borough boundary in two places and where the belated efforts of Winston Churchill MP failed to save a Tory seat.

It is important to stress, however, that the absentees formed a small minority. Most authorities did attend and many made a significant contribution. We asked our respondents to estimate how long they spent preparing their submission and to indicate the seniority of the officers involved. Differences in management structure between authorities make comparisons difficult, but significant input from senior officers (typically the Chief Executive, Head of Legal Services and/or Chief Electoral Registration Officer) was common. The level of response was, understandably, related to the perceived impact of the proposals, with a significant proportion, particularly of non-metropolitan authorities, adopting a low profile: some 40 per cent of those authorities spent two days or less preparing their responses, with one reporting that the submission was drafted in about 30 minutes by a third-tier officer, and was vetted by the Borough Secretary and Clerk in another 30 minutes, with no external expertise. One-third of authorities spent in excess of ten person days preparing their case and one in six employed counsel to present it, with a marked tendency for the unitary authorities to adopt a particularly high profile. (Among the unitary authorities, 82 per cent spent ten days or more and 55 per cent employed counsel. In part this reflects size – unitary authorities are generally large – but also that many of them are Labour-controlled.) The seriousness with which many authorities approached the Inquiry is clear from some of the responses:

The officers involved were at a senior level and included the Director of Planning and Economic Development, the Chief Executive, the Director of Legal Services and the Divisional Manager, General and Electoral Services Division. It is estimated that the equivalent of 40 officer days, mostly at senior level, were used in preparation and research connected with the Council's submission. The Director of Planning and Economic Development attended the Inquiry to give evidence and the Council also employed a barrister for the three days of the Inquiry.

Initially about 4–5 person weeks were spent preparing alternative schemes to be considered by the council, followed by a protracted period of consultation to establish the consortium, develop the case and prepare the evidence. This second period effectively took up the time of one officer for three months with an additional significant input from the electoral officer and a senior lawyer amounting to around 2–3 person weeks. Expert witnesses were used in preparing the evidence and the consortium engaged a barrister for the Inquiry.

Counsel were engaged to draft and present the Council's evidence as was one main expert witness with considerable experience of public inquiries. Total costs were approximately £35,000 for counsel and £4,000 for the expert witness, along with uncosted officer time.

Given the lack of guidance in the relevant legislation, we asked each of the 119 attending authorities how it viewed its role at the Inquiry and what it hoped to achieve by presenting evidence. In particular we were interested to establish how many saw their role as informative rather than persuasive and, amongst the latter, how many emphasised the interests of the authority rather than those of its electors. We were aware, of course, that these options are not mutually exclusive, but we were keen to see where the emphasis was placed.

As far as the information/persuasion continuum was concerned, few eschewed persuasion altogether. Six authorities appear to have attended out of a sense of duty, or with a 'watching brief', without any intention of influencing the outcome; two others stressed their desire to inform, as the following respondent explained:

We did not get worked up about our role. Our aim was to be as helpful as possible by providing electorate projections.

The remainder emphasised persuasion. The sole stated aim of over one-third of respondents was to achieve their desired outcome and the following response was typical of many: 'Quite simply, to get the Commission's initial recommendation changed'. The majority, however, set their aim in context:

The Council viewed itself as the body in possession of the key facts about the area and therefore in a position to state whether proposals met the statutory criteria.

The information and knowledge about the County and its inhabitants which is gathered in the course of providing services, together with the direct local personal knowledge of elected councillors puts the County Council in a unique position to measure any proposals for change against the statutory criteria.

As well as looking to secure the outcome it was supporting, officers in preparing the Council's case recognised the importance of the Local Authority being seen to take a non-political and objective stance by emphasising the principles upon which the Commission had to operate and highlighting how those principles should be applied to local circumstances.

> Individuals and groups tend to have a high level of local knowledge but little understanding of the rules. Their proposals tend to be discounted because of their implications outside the constituency, which they do not consider. Because of its expertise a district council can consider both.

In elaborating upon their approach, many respondents referred to the authority's democratic credentials:

> The council is the only democratically elected body in the borough and saw itself as having a key role in representing local opinion.

> I personally feel our role was crucial because the local council is unique in being the only democratically elected body in the area. The council represents the voice of the borough and its residents. As such it has the authority to act as an advocate and should be given due weight and attention.

Some emphasised the role of the authority in representing the interests of local communities and the views of local residents:

> There were concerns among officials of the Council about the proposals and their relationship to coherent communities. The objective of appearing at the Inquiry was to present a balanced view and to secure boundaries that were more easily recognisable and related to distinct communities.

> The principal intention was to represent local views.

> The authority's role at the Inquiry was to represent the majority view of the residents of the two areas affected as established by a survey of local public opinion.

> The Authority conducted a postal ballot of electors living in the ward concerned and saw its role as representing their overwhelming majority view.

In the majority of cases, however, attention tended to concentrate upon the interests of the authority *per se*. Sometimes this was couched in general terms or reflected the administrative convenience of the council:

> To achieve a workable outcome – district council staff are the only people involved in the whole process who have ever run an election!

> The council's main concern was to avoid the borough being split between two Parliamentary constituencies. It was felt to be administratively difficult to have to deal with two different MPs, possibly of different political persuasions.

> There was a strong feeling that, if it was to be divided, the District should be a substantial part of two constituencies rather than having almost all its area in one constituency with a small part in another. In this way, it was hoped that two MPs would represent the views of the District.

More usually it reflected boundary issues, particularly where the Review coincided with local government reorganisation:

> There was concern here (and it seems elsewhere) that the pattern set by the Parliamentary Review could shape any local government review.

> The general aim of the Council's submission was to create a new constituency whose boundaries would be co-terminous with those of the authority.

> It was an opportunity to emphasise the authority's identity.

> The Council saw the Review as a potential threat to its retention as a viable unit of local government and considerable emphasis was place on the retention of its southern boundary as a Parliamentary boundary.

> The Review took place during the recent review of local government. This authority took the view that it wanted to be a unitary authority based on its existing boundaries and it was felt that [aspects of the provisional recommendations] detracted from the sense of place/identity that it was trying to establish.

> The most important factor was the impending review of local government boundaries.

A few respondents expressed doubts as to the proper role of local authorities and questioned whether it could be disentangled from electoral advantage:

> All electoral division exercises seem to me to run like a game played to artificial rules with the proponents vying with each other to think of all the reasons they can to support their particular point of view excepting the one true reason, which it is not done to mention, namely party political advantage.

> The question inevitably arises – "Of what real concern is the matter to local government?" The answer is not, from an officer's (but not necessarily local politician's) view, at all clear.

> Other than the local governance argument and the role of the Acting Returning Officer, I am not convinced of the merits of local authority involvement in the process.

There were nine cases, however, in which the respondents indicated that differences between elected members caused problems for the officers in presenting the authority's agreed case. Some expressed the problems in general terms:

> The key issue was electoral advantage/disadvantage and it is difficult to find a ground on which the local authority can comment from a 'civic' standpoint regardless of party political considerations.

> The process will often place officers in an invidious position in relation to one political party or another. Clear guidance on the criteria to be used to assess the various options is some help, but clear guidance on the role of local authorities and their officers might also have some value.

Others were more specific. One reported that:

> During the Inquiry the City Secretary was challenged as to his objectivity when he was thought to be critical of an element in the Conservatives' scheme. The answer

which he gave was quite simply that the City Council was Labour controlled and that the majority view was therefore the City Council view.

Another indicated the discomfort an officer may feel in such a situation:

> The submission was determined solely by the controlling Labour group. The Assistant Chief Executive who was instructed to present the Council's case did not feel comfortable in that role and my personal view is that it should have been made by a local politician.

In some authorities, a Council officer was required to present a partisan case because no member of the relevant party was available to present evidence. Where the officer was presenting an authority's agreed position, this was sometimes the cause of conflict:

> Several leading members of the Opposition were representing alternative views on behalf of their constituency parties and used the opportunity to attack their own Chief Executive.

> I was 'accused' of pushing the Labour administration's case by the Conservatives. They did not appreciate that as an officer I was advocating the City Council's determined policy on the issue.

To investigate issues of political influence in greater detail we asked each authority how much political guidance was exercised in determining its response, whether there were differences between various groups on the authority and how those were managed. A clear distinction emerged between those authorities with an overall Labour majority and the remainder. We received replies from 43 Labour-controlled authorities which were represented at an Inquiry and all confirmed that there had been a significant political input to the authority's submission. In seven cases the Labour view had been supported by other parties on the Council (including two Scottish Councils where it contravened the 'national' party line), but in the remainder the authority viewpoint was determined by the Labour group without the support of its political opponents. The way in which this was implemented varied from authority to authority. In one London Borough there seems to have been a genuine, though ultimately unsuccessful, attempt to achieve consensus:

> The Council felt that due to the political sensitivity of the draft proposals, it should aim to achieve cross–party support. It therefore kept all the Party Groups informed of the work being undertaken by officers. In practice, however, the Majority Group was more involved in determining the direction of the Council's response with the (main) Opposition Group keeping a 'watching brief'. The Minority Party did not support the Council's initiative and did not give officers its view on the Council's response other than its formal opposition.

In another the initial response was drafted by the officers and subsequently formally adopted by members:

> As officers working for the Council, we assumed the primary role of assessing the Commission's proposals for the City, considering alternatives and proposing the

best technical option. In doing so, we were following a model which had been adopted for earlier boundary Reviews. No other approach was seriously considered. Our proposal was accepted by the Majority Group and we presented our proposal to the Inquiry.

In the majority of Labour authorities, however, the response was politically driven, typically by majority outvoting minority, and the comments of several respondents confirm the partisan nature of the process:

> A majority group [Labour] working party was established with responsibility for determining strategy. Its prime interest was to secure an outcome which best served the group's political interests. No members of other groups were involved in the detail of the case.

> The submission was determined by the Council, in practice by the controlling [Labour] group. This has been the custom over many years.

> The process was entirely politically driven. The submission was determined solely by the controlling Labour group.

> The Council Leader gave to my Chief Officer, the City Secretary, a small map showing the boundaries which they wanted. He was then commissioned to work up the best case he could put together to support those boundaries. Politically speaking, there was much at stake from this boundary Review and the City Council, being a strongly and traditionally Labour–controlled Authority, was anxious to ensure that its scheme was chosen. It seemed natural that it should invest whatever resources were necessary in terms of research and presentation to ensure this.

The importance of partisan considerations is particularly clear in the response of three authorities where intervention by the Labour Party resulted in modification of a previously agreed position:

> The Council's initial response was determined by the Policy and Resources Committee. Each of the three groups put forward representations and that of the majority group was taken forward. The decision to appear at the Inquiry was taken in the context of a decision to alter the original representations. The reason for this decision was that the District Labour Party had decided that the authority's response had to be amended to accord with that which was being put forward on behalf of the regional Labour Party and which was to be reflected in the response of all Labour authorities in the county.

> The Council hoped to achieve an adjustment to the boundary of the proposed constituency incorporating the authority's area and detailed evidence to justify this change was prepared. The suggested adjustment was, however, withdrawn on the instruction of the Council Leader, just as it was about to be presented at the Inquiry, following a request from the regional party hierarchy.

> At the initial meeting of the Policy Committee, there was unanimous support for the Commission's provisional recommendations. Two weeks later, at the Council meeting which would confirm the Committee's decision, out of the blue a Majority Group amendment was tabled to write to the Commission proposing an amendment. There had been no consultation with or indeed even notification of officers

that this change was going to be proposed and I believe that it resulted from an instruction issued centrally by the Labour Party. The matter was then an issue of considerable political debate and eventually became Council policy on a vote.

Taken together, these responses paint a very clear picture of political direction behind the approach of the large majority of Labour-controlled authorities. This is entirely consistent with our earlier discussion of the Labour Party's strategy and contrasts with the response of its political opponents. That is not to say that Conservatives and Liberal Democrats did not also use their control of local authorities to further their partisan ends. Several respondents confirmed that political direction was not the sole preserve of the Labour Party:

It was viewed as a very political issue by the then Conservative majority and was solely a decision of that majority. Officer involvement was restricted to providing factual information, with the interpretation of that information and presentation very much in the hands of the Leader of the Council.

There was strong member involvement in the process, by the [Liberal Democrat] Leader of the Council personally.

The authority's role was to give the majority party yet another voice. My suspicions are that the counter-proposal was arrived at through negotiation by constituency chairmen of the local Tory party branches on a golf course. I was presented with the proposal and asked to produce/argue a statistical case to support it as being more representative of 'local interest'. I was not asked what arrangements I could argue best.

Three factors rendered these two parties' control of local authorities less effective, however. First the authorities concerned tended to be smaller, typically English Shire Districts, unable to speak for all of the County or to call upon the resources and expertise of larger urban authorities. Second, the other parties didn't exhibit the same degree of ruthlessness as Labour in pushing their own agenda – almost half of the 32 responding authorities in question (10 of the 24 Conservative and three of the eight Liberal Democrat) adopted a cross-party approach, or presented more than one option to the Commission. And, third, several Conservative authorities saw their efforts hampered by the actions of other Conservatives, as the following respondents explained:

The majority political group wanted to oppose any Labour Party–led proposals (which had clearly been made for assumed electoral advantages) and to resist a move from a neighbouring Conservative authority to transfer a Conservative ward to the adjoining constituency.

This Council's representations were very much the work of the majority party's (Conservative) leadership who felt most strongly that the proposals affecting the district were a recipe for confusion amongst the electorate. Members of all political parties supported the approach of the majority party. The main difficulty for the Leader of this Council in presenting our case at the Inquiry was due to the fact that every other Conservative constituency party in the county supported the Commission's proposals.

The importance of political control in influencing the position of local authori-

ties is emphasised by consideration of the 44 remaining respondents, those councils where no one political group had an overall majority. Three-quarters of these
adopted a consensus view (including six councils controlled by Independents),
six submitted alternative options reflecting the views of different groups within
the council, and in only five was the response the result of two groups outvoting
another. As the following respondents explained, where the circumstances were
right it was possible for councils to reach agreement over a common approach:

> The process followed that established within the District for many similar policy
> issues. This calls for officers to submit impartial reports with options for consider-
> ation to enable members to make final decisions. Inevitably there were differences
> of opinion between individual councillors. However, my recollection is that no polit-
> ical group took a formal line which was followed by its members.

> A small sub-committee comprising a leading representative from every political
> group on the Council was set up to give 'detailed instructions'. This body had one
> meeting; however, I communicated with its members quite frequently by telephone
> and letter and managed to achieve an ongoing consensus of views. None of the lead-
> ing members from any side saw this as essentially a party political exercise.

> Officers were instructed to prepare alternative proposals for consideration by the
> General Purposes Committee. The Independent councillors did not operate as a
> group but supported whichever of the six options they regarded a being in the 'best
> interests' of their electors.

It is important to stress, however, that part of the price of reaching consensus was
that several authorities were obliged to play a relatively minor role in proceedings, leaving the more contentious elements to the political parties. This was a
particularly important aspect of the Review in Shire England, where only 38 per
cent of counties had overall majority party control at the time of the Inquiry (the
average for the other types of authority was 61 per cent):

> The County Council is not controlled by a single political group. The three major
> groups on the Council appreciated that their party interests were not likely to coin-
> cide and none of them sought to use the County Council to project that viewpoint.
> As a result the County Council's evidence was minimal and peripheral.

It also resulted in occasional difficulties where a submission was a less than happy
compromise between opposing interests:

> The matter was dealt with entirely formally through Committee and ultimately the
> Full Council. This tends to be the case in this authority, which has had no overall
> control for some years, especially with issues on which there is (or is expected to
> be) no unanimity of view. The Council's corporate view in the end comprised ele-
> ments of views from two political parties which left certain questions unanswered.

> Even where local authorities were not pursuing a partisan agenda, it is difficult to escape
> the conclusion that political considerations play a key part in understanding their
> response.

Conclusion

In this chapter we have considered certain aspects of the process of public consultation: the role of written representations and of the Local Inquiry; the characteristics of the Assistant Commissioners and the way in which they are chosen and briefed; and the dominance of the political imperative in the process, either directly through the parties or indirectly through local authorities. It is the dominance of partisan motives in an ostensibly non-partisan process which has led many to question the value of Local Inquiries. Butler and McLean (1996a, 30) describe them as 'farcical and expensive' and there is widespread acceptance that much of the evidence placed before the Inquiries is presented purely in the furtherance of electoral ends. Assistant Commissioners are generally aware of this; of our sixty interviewees, only seven felt that there was not a significant underlying political agenda (and several of these conducted the relatively few Inquiries where this assessment was probably correct). Very few felt that this posed any difficulties, however, as the following comments reveal:

> It was glaringly obvious. They decided which constituencies they wanted and then cast around for arguments to support them.

> I think it's not difficult. That's the benefit of an open Inquiry. You can judge it, you can tell, you can sniff out the humbug. You can hear people hissing and get a good feeling of what really is the case.

> It's instinctive – you can tell whether a point is valid.

> You ask a judge the same question! I regret to say I approached the evidence of all the witnesses called with a pinch of salt – not just the overtly partisan, but also those whose evidence was being used for partisan ends. In the end it's fairly straightforward – you look at the arguments and the responses when they're tested by opposing counsel. You get a feel for whether they're exaggerating. You also get the benefit of the few ordinary people who came. I barely intervened. The evidence of the political parties was being adequately tested. If not I would have intervened.

> The first thing an Assistant Commissioner must do is to acknowledge that it's happening, that there will be people there with a political agenda. As soon as it's acknowledged, the problem's solved.

> It would be very naive to assume that they were all there to help satisfy the statutory criteria. If I move a ward I have no idea what effect it will have on the political parties – all I can do is assume that if they want me to do it, it will help them, which doesn't mean I shouldn't do it, nor does it mean I should.

> It's not a problem at all. Is there substance to the argument – if so I don't give a toss whether it comes from a political party. They do represent a body of opinion and I had no overtly political submissions.

> One would only need a GCSE in carpentry to enable one to work it out, often because the other parties start shouting and when cross-examined the reasons become more and more pathetic. I suppose there may be circumstances in which

an Assistant Commissioner could be hoodwinked. You have to look at the quality of the evidence.

In the end you could generally tell. There are usually a few little facts that come out. You get a real flavour by hearing lots of people talking about their territory – that's the value of an oral Inquiry.

You start off with a presumption of scepticism. Labour did a quite remarkably good job, but however well it's done you still view it with the maximum possible suspicion.

During the course of the Inquiry you draw people out, ask them to explain, and so on. All in all it's much more easily detectable than I think they believe it is.

It's fairly easy, it's what lawyers do all the time. Set a thief to catch a thief.

I find that my total ignorance of the areas and of their political complexion is a great help. I simply assess the validity of the arguments. To be honest you've got enough to think about without trying to judge why people are saying what they are saying. It's the facts that you have to decide.

This last point was echoed by Assistant Commissioner after Assistant Commissioner and was admirably summed up in the report of the Norfolk Inquiry:

Each side accused the other of supporting particular schemes for political advantage, while vehemently denying any such motives on their own part. It will always be the case that groups of people with common interests will tend to favour outcomes which are to their advantage. This fact ensures lively debate and, in this particular case, has enabled a wide variety of possibilities to be examined. It would clearly be quite wrong for the Commission to be influenced by political considerations; I have put such considerations from my mind. However, a proposal may have merit, whatever its source. I have considered each proposal on its merits and in accordance with the Rules. (Inquiry Report, #4.1)

We return later to consider the extent to which the process of public consultation did produce a partisan effect in the revised constituencies, but first we must take a closer look at the arguments which were presented at the Inquiries. If Assistant Commissioners considered the proposals on their merits, how did they evaluate them? Which factors were uppermost in their minds in arriving at a decision? Was there a consistent interpretation of the Rules, both between the Commissions and their Assistants, and between the Assistant Commissioners themselves? It is to these questions that we now turn.

Notes

1 This contrasts with the situation in 1917, when the entire process for England and Wales was completed within six months, although then the Commission was not required to re-consult on its revised recommendations.
2 Rawlings (1987, 328) has observed that the Local Inquiry procedures have 'never been

the subject of analysis'; there are 'no statutory rules of procedure and considerable discretion is afforded to the (ad hoc) assistant commisioners' whose advice is much respected by the Commissions.

3 Few went as far as the Devon fireman and his partner who were contemplating moving house to be nearer his place of work, but who would be 'very much swayed' by any decision to include the fire station in a constituency which included wards from Plymouth (Devon representation, #50).

4 This wording was common to the *News Releases* from the English, Scottish and Welsh Commissions (the Welsh Commission's documents all appeared in English and Welsh). The Northern Ireland Commission merely invited representations; the Welsh Commission also requested that 'those who are content with, or at least do not object to, the Commission's provisional recommendations, should make known to the Commission their support or lack of objection'.

5 About one-third were unwilling to identify a priority between written and oral representations, but among the remainder those preferring the latter outnumbered the former by 5:1. One Assistant Commissioner commented that he gave 'comparatively little weight to the written submissions because the debate had moved on'. More typical, however, was another's observation that 'a written submission is, in the nature of things, untested. If I am dubious about its merits, then it's difficult to be convinced'.

6 This occurred in Cumbria. The Commission's Minutes (BCE Minutes, 1992/7, 7.1.5) record that 'The AC noted, however, that part of the Conservative counter-proposal advocating the transfer of the Silloth and Waver wards ... from Penrith and the Border [constituency] had also been proposed in a letter from the Labour Party and had not been objected to at the inquiry. The reasons for this proposal were that the geographical size of Penrith and the Border would be reduced and there were ties between the two wards and Workington. The AC had therefore recommended the inclusion of Silloth and Waver wards in the Workington seat. The Commission decided to accept his recommendation'.

7 The Boundary Commission for England (1995a, 286, #6.25) recommended that the period for representations be doubled to two months, for example.

8 There were 45 English, 8 Welsh and 6 Northern Irish Counties at the time of the Fourth Periodic Review, plus 32 London Boroughs and 9 Scottish Regions. There were also three Islands Areas in Scotland but, apart from an attempt to combine the Western Isles with Skye during the Second Periodical Review (Boundary Commission for Scotland, 1969, p.7 #12,) their representation has been unchanged since the current system was introduced.

9 One in six of the Assistant Commissionrs we interviewed (see p. 243).

10 However, 'members of the Secretariat often speak to the press (and MPs) at Inquiries'. Despite advice from Home Office Inspectors that the Secretariat should not give such interviews and that only staff in the most junior executive grade should attend Inquiries, this was strongly opposed by Bob McLeod, and he was supported by the Commission (BCE Minutes, 1992/5, 5.2).

11 Commissions generally book a venue and an Assistant Commissioner for longer than the Inquiry is expected to take, but on a few occasions the AC had to hurry because the booking was running out or he/she had other business to attend to.

12 The 1867 Report states that two Assistant Commissioners were appointed for each area 'namely a Barrister-at-Law and an officer of the Royal Artillery or Royal Engineers, in order to secure a combination of the special professional qualities required

for receiving and weighing evidence, and for inspecting and describing existing and proposed boundaries' (Boundary Commission, 1868, i).

13 The quote is from a letter from Sir John Knox to all Heads of Chambers, dated 31 July 1990. Several Assistant Commissioners made comments to us regarding the apparent informality of the procedure and more than one found the system casual:

> There was a round robin letter, the Head of Chambers isn't interested and says 'do you fancy it?'. Having seen the list of names I must say, personally, I wondered why some of them are on the list. I've been blooded in public service and hence qualify as one of the great and the good, but I'm not happy about the way it's done. If it were a PR exercise, writing to all Chambers is fine, but this actually means something, it's a fundamental part of our democracy, and I don't think it should be treated quite so casually.

14 Failures in the vetting procedure caused the Commission considerable embarrassment. One individual who was on the list submitted to the Home Office replied to the subsequent letter confirming that he had been politically active in several capacities, including as an SDP Councillor and as an (unsuccessful) Parliamentary candidate in 1983. He was not appointed, but the Commission mistakenly invited him to conduct the Shropshire Local Inquiry; it was only after the Inquiry was completed and his report submitted that the Commission realised that he did not have a warrant of appointment, necessitating a second Inquiry under a properly appointed Assistant Commissioner. Two other barristers invited to conduct Inquiries were also replaced beforehand, one because she declared her membership of a political party, the other because he 'had been found to be an active County Councillor' (BCE Minutes, 1992/4, 7.3). It is also noteworthy that the Assistant Commissioner who conducted the Birmingham Local Inquiry was appointed to conduct an Inquiry into proposals for European Parliament constituencies in South West England in 1997, but withdrew shortly beforehand when he discovered 'that a local political organisation, of which he is a member, had made a representation to the Commission' (BCE *News Release*, 3 July 1997).

15 Nevertheless, the same minute (BCS Minutes, 1 July 1993, 2.1) refers explicitly to one Sheriff 'whose past political affiliations prevented him from consideration'.

16 When Assistant Commissioners were appointed in 1990/1, the Commission expected the Review to continue until 1997 so the Assistant Commissioner born in 1929 and called in 1953 appears to have slipped through the net! There is a certain irony in the fact that most of the Commissioners themselves were born before 1930.

17 The data quoted here are taken from *Who's Who* and *Havers' Companion to the Bar*.

18 Increasingly, candidates to become magistrates are asked to indicate their usual voting behaviour on the application form, so that a balance can be maintained within their ranks (Rosenberg, 1994).

19 The others were that there should be no prior consultation with interested parties; that district boundaries should be taken into account where possible; that wards should not be divided; that constituencies should not have detached parts; and that an MP's workload should not be taken into account other than as a corollary of Rules 5 and 6.

20 Interestingly, Barnes and McLeod (1989) – Secretaries to the English Commission at the Third and Fourth Periodic Reviews respectively – did not mention the case in the historical section of their article on redistributions.

21 These estimates were based on local election results, which caused Gardner difficulties in many rural areas lacking a history of Labour candidature for local Councils. He was not alone in facing such difficulties; because general election returns are not published in disaggregated form, all parties are forced to make their calculations in a

state of greater or lesser ignorance as to how electors cast their Parliamentary votes at ward level. Gardner's approach was similar (though not identical) to that conventionally used in equivalent academic studies (e.g. Rallings and Thrasher, 1995), though alternative approaches are available which in part avoid this difficulty. These approaches are discussed in Chapter 8.

22 Dame Angela Rumbold has pointed out to us that the Hampshire Inquiry coincided with 'Black Wednesday' and its aftermath, when the corner-stone of the Conservative government's economic policy was shattered.

23 The Commission noted in its Fourth Review that 'Mossley Hill was not only eccentrically shaped, but that it was heterogeneous' – with no reference to the basis of the latter claim, which if it refers to social composition is outside the Commission's brief. It also noted that Mossley Hill's central location within Liverpool 'facilitated the relocation of its wards to other seats' (Boundary Commission for England, 1995a, 97, #35).

24 The Scottish Commission's provisional recommendations for Borders and Lothian, for example, were twice cited by Ministers in support of government proposals for local government reorganisation in the area (Secretary of State for Scotland, *Hansard*, vol. 228, 8 July 1993, col. 479; Minister for Local Government, *Hansard*, vol. 230, 27 October 1993, col. 815), support which, in the opinion of the Assistant Commissioner who conducted the Local Inquiry there, resulted in a 'temporal conjunction of separate, though not wholly dissimilar, proposals [which] had been unfortunate' (Inquiry Report, 6).

25 The response rate was slightly higher from local authorities in England (48 per cent) than the other three countries.

7

From provisional
to final recommendations

There can be little doubt that the Local Inquiries are influential in determining the final shape of Parliamentary constituencies. A few simple statistics confirm their importance. Following public consultation the Commissions confirmed their provisional recommendations for 382 seats but recommended changes to the other 276. However, many of those provisional recommendations were for no change to existing constituencies (including 52 which were not the subject of a Local Inquiry) or for minor alterations consequential upon local government boundary changes. If attention is confined to the 468 provisionally recommended constituencies in which a Commission was proposing substantive change, then just 200 emerged unaltered following the Local Inquiries compared with 268 which were amended, including 38 where the existing boundaries of a seat were reinstated. And whereas the provisional recommendations would have resulted in six million electors moving to another seat, the final recommendations moved just over five million.[1]

It is clear from these figures that 'the public' can indeed influence constituency boundaries, but on their own they cannot explain *how* this is achieved. We have seen that the political parties and local authorities are the main advocates of change to the Commissions' provisional recommendations, but we have still to examine the way in which they presented their arguments and assess the ways in which Assistant Commissioners responded. The fact that a million fewer electors were 'moved' as a result of the Inquiries might suggest that Assistant Commissioners were more influenced by the need to minimise change than were the Commissions themselves, but to be sure we need to examine the Inquiries in some detail. Nor is that the end of the process. Once an Inquiry Report has been written it is sent to the Commission which may or may not choose to implement its recommendations. This in turn is followed by a second opportunity for written representations, again with the possibility of further change. We consider the Commissions' response and the impact of further written representations towards the end of the chapter. First, however, we draw on the Inquiry Reports and our interviews with Assistant Commissioners to examine their work against the framework of the Rules for Redistribution, beginning with Rule 1.

The number of seats (Rule 1)

General acceptance of the Commissions' use of theoretical entitlements to determine the appropriate level of Parliamentary representation for an area has ensured over the years that this does not become a controversial issue at most Inquiries. Nevertheless, as the Assistant Commissioner who conducted the Inquiry into the London Boroughs of Lambeth and Southwark pointed out, 'proposals to reduce the number of Parliamentary seats in a given area are inherently unlikely to be popular in that area' (Inquiry Report, Lambeth & Southwark, #3.4) and changes in Commission policy ensured that this became a more prominent issue than at previous reviews. In order to limit any further increase in the number of seats the English Commission adopted a more parsimonious implementation of theoretical entitlements and chose to cross London Borough boundaries (Boundary Commission for England, 1995a, 7), while the Scottish Commission achieved a similar result by pairing Regions (Boundary Commission for Scotland, 1995, 167–9). These changes were inevitably challenged, supported in many cases by reference to well documented deficiencies in the electoral register. As a result, the question of apportionment became an issue in around a quarter of all Inquiries.

The commonest cause for complaint was that the Commission's provisional recommendations involved the loss of an MP. The London Boroughs of Bromley and Croydon, for example, while recognising that their theoretical entitlements (3.34 and 3.42 respectively) indicated otherwise, both objected to the reduction in representation. Five other London Inquiry reports refer to similar objections, but in each case the issue became entangled with opposition to the crossing of Borough boundaries (itself a reflection of the English Commission's desire to 'save' seats and considered more fully below). Elsewhere the Liberal Democrat Group on Liverpool City Council objected to the loss of the city's sixth MP despite the city's entitlement having fallen to 5.10,[2] and in Lancashire the Conservative Party in particular argued strongly for the retention of a sixteenth seat despite a reduced entitlement of 15.44. In all these cases, however, either the Commission's allocation was in line with the area's theoretical entitlement or the provisional recommendations could be justified by reference to its revised policy on the crossing of London Borough boundaries. And in all it was supported by the Assistant Commissioner, though in the case of Lancashire, as the Inquiry Report makes clear, this was by no means a foregone conclusion (Inquiry Report, Lancashire, #3.4, 3.10):

> having regard to Rules 5, 6 and 7 and to the evidence of a recent increase in the electorate, in my opinion it is theoretically open to the Commission to recommend either 15 or 16 seats for this county. ... It is with considerable reluctance that I am driven to conclude that an allocation of 16 seats to this county is neither practicable nor viable.

Another Inquiry at which the possible reduction of seats became an issue, but for very different reasons, was Birmingham (Theoretical Entitlement – TE – 10.64). Here it was the Assistant Commissioner himself who proposed the reduction: he was unhappy with 'the gross disparity between constituency electorates that would exist' under the eleven-seat scheme proposed by the Commission (a level of disparity which could be avoided with a ten-seat scheme; see Chapter 5), though when he 'invited views to be expressed as to why there should be 11 rather than 10 constituencies ... all those who expressed views were against the concept of 10 seats' (Inquiry Report, Birmingham, #63). As discussed below, the Commission seems to have been totally unprepared for this suggestion and whilst acknowledging that 'his scheme complied more closely with Rule 5' (Boundary Commission for England, 1995a, 119), concluded that 'for the sake of consistency we felt obliged to allocate 11 seats.' (Boundary Commission for England, 1995a, 121)

The willingness of this particular Assistant Commissioner to question the Commission's policy contrasts with that of the Sheriff Principal who conducted the Inquiry in the Highland Region of Scotland (TE 2.88). He was presented with arguments by a 'significant number of witnesses', including local authorities and MPs, that a fourth seat should be allocated to the Region, but concluded (Inquiry Report, Highland Region, 4):

> Whether or not the Highlands should have a fourth MP is an issue which goes beyond the scope of this inquiry and which would entail balancing the interests of that region with those of the rest of Scotland.

Whatever the merits of the case (while clearly entitled to three seats in arithmetic terms, Highland Region contains by far the largest constituencies by area in the United Kingdom and was allocated three seats at the Third Review under Rule 6 when its TE was 2.54) it is unclear why the issue of apportionment was considered *ultra vires* and the Commission did not address the issue in its consideration of the Inquiry Report (Boundary Commission for Scotland, 1995, 110–11).

In other parts of the country experiencing growth, the debate was somewhat different. The provisional recommendations for a total of 23 Counties or Regions proposed an increase in representation, increases which were generally welcomed. Only in Staffordshire (TE 11.62), where South Staffordshire District Council in particular objected to the disruptive effects of the extra seat, in Hereford & Worcester (TE 7.59), where Peter Luff, the Conservative MP for Worcester, argued for the retention of seven seats thereby allowing no change to his constituency, and in Cheshire (TE 10.69), where similar arguments were presented by Conservative interests in relation to Macclesfield, was there any evidence of significant opposition. The English Commission, however, did not recommend an extra seat in five Counties – Avon (TE 10.48), Derbyshire (TE 10.49), the Isle of Wight (TE 1.47), Norfolk (TE 8.48) and Warwickshire (TE 5.46) – which were entitled to one under Rule 5 (i.e. they applied the arithmetic mean rather than the harmonic mean). Yet at only two of those Inquiries – Avon and Norfolk – was the question even discussed. Why was this? A variety of contributory factors can be cited. In the case of Avon, the Isle of Wight and Norfolk, the Commission's *News Releases* did not make it clear that the County was entitled to an extra seat based on a strict application of Rule 5: the Commission changed the wording of its *News Releases* as a response to criticism at the Norfolk Inquiry (see Chapter 5). In Derbyshire, Norfolk and Warwickshire an extra seat would have resulted in greater fragmentation of Districts between constituencies (as it would in the Isle of Wight, where the possibility of being joined with part of Hampshire was an additional deterrent). Only the Labour Party in Norfolk and (belatedly) the Liberal Democrats in the Isle of Wight decided that the potential gain from an extra seat was worth the effort and risks associated with its promotion.[3] And in all five cases the disruptive effect of change acted as a powerful disincentive.

So what of the two Inquiries where it was discussed? The principal proponents of an extra seat at the Avon Inquiry were two local authorities (Wansdyke District Council and Charlcombe Parish Council) and two academics. In addition to arguments relating to Rule 5, it was pointed out that an 11-seat solution would permit a far closer match between District and constituency boundaries, but they were unable to enlist the support of any other major authorities, all of which supported the allocation of ten seats, as did the three main political parties. In coming to his conclusion not to allocate an additional seat the Assistant Commissioner was assisted 'to a significant extent' (Inquiry Report, Avon, #23) by statistical information provided by Avon County Council which set out to demonstrate that projected growth in the County was modest (though by 1997 the TE had risen to 10.59), by the lack of general support for an extra seat and by the fact that 'the retention of 10 seats would provide continuity without the need for a wholesale redrawing of boundaries' (#24).

At the Norfolk Inquiry the case for an extra seat was argued by the Labour Party and by a consortium of three local authorities (Norwich City and Great Yarmouth Borough, both Labour-controlled, and Conservative-controlled Broadland District Council), supported again, amongst others, by two academics. Much of the debate again centred on Rule 5, but an extra seat was also advocated in order to create a seat covering the Broads, to allow for anticipated development and to enhance community ties. As with Avon, the Assistant Commissioner rejected these arguments. But whereas his colleague had accepted the significance of Rule 5, had taken population projections into account and had played down the advantages of a close match between District and constituency boundaries, this Assistant Commissioner 'reject[ed] the argument that argument that Norfolk is prima facie entitled to 9 seats' (Inquiry Report, Norfolk, #1.8), was unimpressed with the evidence on future population growth 'because predictions are often confounded' (#4.2) and found the greater departure between District and constituency boundaries a disadvantage.[4] The common factor was the degree of change with the Assistant Commissioner concluding that 'the need would have to be very great to justify the upheaval involved' (#4.11).

What conclusions can be drawn from the way in which the issue of apportionment was handled at the Local Inquiries? The first point to make is that in each case the final recommendation was for the same number of seats as the provisional. Only in Lancashire and Birmingham was the Assistant Commissioner convinced of the desirability of a different allocation, but in the former he concluded that it was not feasible and in the latter he was overruled by the Commission. There are examples from earlier reviews of extra seats being allocated as a result of an Assistant Commissioner's recommendations (see Chapter 5), but this is an area in which the Commission wields enormous influence by virtue of setting the agenda.

Second, there is an important distinction between Inquiries where the issue is a reduced number of seats and those where it relates to a possible increase. The former are primarily an urban phenomenon and, given the English Commission's readiness to cross Metropolitan District boundaries and its new-found willingness to do the same in London Boroughs, these apportionment problems have very largely been converted into boundary issues. Only in Lancashire was the question fully aired, though the Brent and Croydon Inquiries had similar potential.[5] The latter, by contrast, are primarily to be found in Shire England. Here the Commission has largely neutralised the apportionment debate by placing increased emphasis on Rule 7. This approach secured the unequivocal backing of the Assistant Commissioners in Avon and Norfolk, thereby emphasising the difficulties facing anybody arguing for fundamental change to the existing pattern of seats, a theme we return to below.

Third, the nature of those putting forward arguments on these points tended to be different from the usual participants. It is noticeable, for example, that of the political parties it was the Liberal Democrats who were responsible for the greatest number of challenges to the Commission, the majority of them naive. It is also noteworthy that academics were involved in the more significant debates. In part this is because of the interest taken by one individual, Iain McLean, in the issue (he appeared at the Avon Inquiry, and as a witness at the Norfolk and Southwark Inquiries), but it also reflects the fact that apportionment is one of the least straightforward aspects of redistricting.

In addition, an extra seat was allocated in Northern Ireland despite no Assistant Commissioner having explicitly advocated it. Indeed four of the five Inquiries barely touched upon the issue. As the Assistant Commissioner who conducted the Newry Inquiry commented (Boundary Commission for Northern Ireland, 1995, 139):

> The question of whether there should be 17 or 18 Parliamentary seats for Northern Ireland was not canvassed in any detail at the inquiry. ... Therefore, I have not considered that issue and it would have been difficult for me to do so given that I am dealing with only three constituencies in any event.

The exception was the Inquiry held in Belfast, where the provisional recommendations involved the abolition of one of the city's four seats. While making it clear that he did 'not regard it as part of my task to advise on what the total number of seats in Northern Ireland should be' (Boundary Commission for Northern Ireland, 1995, 70), the Assistant Commissioner adopted a far more pro-active role than most of his colleagues, specifically asking each of the political parties for their views on the possibility of eighteen seats. Indeed when Peter Robinson,

MP for Belfast East and spokesman for the DUP, did not proceed with the party's written representation (which had argued for precisely that), the Assistant Commissioner specifically invited him 'to make a submission in relation to 18 seats, and what would happen in Belfast if there were 18 seats' (Inquiry Transcript, 84). In his report he recommended the retention of four Belfast seats, each extending beyond the city boundary in a radial fashion (possible because Rule 4 as it applies to Northern Ireland does not provide a local government template within which seats can be defined and Inquiries limited), and each containing fewer electors than the smallest of the three provisionally recommended seats. On the basis of these recommendations the Commission felt bound to abandon its plans for three Belfast seats and with it any realistic prospect of retaining 17 seats overall. Paradoxically this sole example of a change in apportionment came about with a minimum of political or public pressure.

Local government boundaries (Rule 4)

Rule 4 of the Rules for Redistribution sets out the local government template within which constituencies are to be created. It places a presumption against crossing Borough boundaries in London and County boundaries in the rest of England and Wales; requires the Scottish Commission to have 'regard' to the boundaries of local authority areas; and leaves the Northern Ireland Commission without any template at all. The last-named Commission must not, however, split local authority wards. In addition to the Rules, government advice given in 1972 encourages the English and Welsh Commissions to minimise the crossing of District boundaries and, though not required to by Rule 4, they and the Scottish Commission have adopted the invariable practice of not splitting wards.

To what extent are local government boundaries a source of contention at Local Inquiries? In answering this it is important to distinguish between the requirements of Rule 4 and the Commissions' practice. Few Inquiries become embroiled in disputes over the 'correct' interpretation of Rule 4, but when it occurs it tends to assume considerable significance. On the other hand, the integrity of one or more Districts is an issue at most Inquiries outside the English Metropolitan Counties and a surprisingly large number of Inquiries are presented with requests for the splitting of wards. Rarely, however, do these generate the same level of debate. We deal with each in turn.

Rule 4 issues

London was the major focus for challenges to provisional recommendations which involved the crossing of those local authority boundaries mentioned in Rule 4. The Commission's provisional recommendations involved pairing a total of fourteen Boroughs, and it was not long before a variety of alternative or additional pairings was proposed; only the Boroughs of Barnet and Sutton escaped suggestions from some quarter that they be paired. Most of these alternative proposals came in written form from individuals, but faced with the unpromising text of the Commission's subsequent *News Releases* (which, while conceding that alternative pairings 'cannot be ruled out for consideration', proceeded to list four demanding conditions which, by implication, would need to be satisfied),[6] it is not surprising that few were followed up at the relevant Inquiries. Nevertheless significant parts of the Inquiries in Bromley, Croydon and Merton were spent considering counter-proposals which would have breached the Borough boundary. None was successful, each encountering considerable resistance from within the Borough and leading all three Assistant Commissioners to reject them.

The Commission's own proposals for cross-Borough constituencies were considered at a total of six Local Inquiries (the proposals for Ealing, Hammersmith & Fulham, Kensington & Chelsea and the City of Westminster being heard together). In three cases there was general acceptance of the Commission's proposals: according to the Assistant Commissioner for Bexley and Greenwich 'the overwhelming response has been to accept the principle of pairing the two boroughs' (Inquiry Report, Bexley & Greenwich, #6); in Newham and Tower Hamlets no 'substantial oral submission' opposed the Commission's proposals (Inquiry Report, Newham & Tower Hamlets, #12); while in Redbridge and Waltham Forest the Assistant Commissioner reported that 'the case for the pairing of the boroughs and the loss of one seat is overwhelming, and was rightly accepted by all but one person during the inquiry itself' (Inquiry Report, Redbridge & Waltham Forest, #2.03).

Opposition was confined to Kingston and Richmond, where the local authorities both proposed pairing Kingston with Surrey (with Richmond suggesting a cross-border seat comprising wards from Kingston and Merton as an alternative); to Lambeth and Southwark, where a formidable legal challenge was mounted against the very principle of crossing Borough boundaries; and to the Inquiry held in Chelsea, where the principle was largely accepted, but where the choice of appropriate pairings was bitterly contested. Despite all these efforts, at Inquiries which collectively lasted twelve days, all three Assistant Commissioners accepted the principles underlying the Commission's proposals.

In the case of Kingston, the Assistant Commissioner concluded that the Borough had 'simply failed to identify and explain, or support by evidence the alleged community of interest' with neighbouring wards in Surrey (Inquiry Report, Kingston & Richmond, #E10), nor had it tested opinion within those wards or dealt with the resulting knock-on effects. While the 'Merton option' had some advantages, these were insufficient to outweigh the Commission's proposals 'which cause the least inconvenience or disruption' (Inquiry Report, Kingston & Richmond, #J6).[7] The Assistant Commissioner who conducted the Ealing Inquiry stressed the advantages of the provisional recommendations in terms of clearly defined boundaries and majority local support (Inquiry Report, Ealing *et al.*, #4.8.8), concluding that it also offered 'the best solution to the problem of over-representation within the entirety of the Inquiry area' (Inquiry Report, Ealing *et al.*, #4.8.13).

The Assistant Commissioner who conducted the Southwark Inquiry rejected the proposition that the Commission had acted unlawfully in framing its provisional recommendations. His reasons are set out in considerable detail in the Inquiry Report (they cover eighteen pages) but in essence he concluded that the Commission 'has very significantly more freedom of action than any of the various legal submissions was prepared to contemplate' (Inquiry Report, Lambeth & Southwark, #4.3; the arguments and his conclusion are summarised in Boundary Commission for England, 1995a, 61). While emphasising that 'it is important to differentiate between the legal argument and the factual Inquiry which also has to be undertaken' (Inquiry Report, Lambeth & Southwark, #3.1), he also found himself agreeing with the thrust of the Commission's provisional recommendations, concluding that there was 'an excessive disparity between the electorate of Norwood and the electoral quota … [which] cannot practicably be addressed without crossing the boundary between Lambeth and Southwark' (Inquiry Report, Lambeth & Southwark, #6.14) and describing the view that an MP could not satisfactorily represent two Boroughs as one with which he was 'wholly out of sympathy' (#6.1).

Taken together this constitutes further persuasive evidence of the important agenda-setting role of the provisional recommendations. All 14 Boroughs proposed for pairing were paired; each was paired with the Borough recommended by the Commission; no alternative pairing proved acceptable. Those arguing against pairing where such was proposed by the Commission faced the difficult (as we have seen) task of defending significantly larger disparities; those arguing for a different choice of partner had to produce an acceptable solution with a neighbouring, quite possibly unpaired, Borough; while those promoting pairing *de novo* were faced with the same task, but in duplicate.

It should come as little surprise, therefore, that the Commission emerged almost unscathed from this first experience of boundary-crossing in the capital. For several of the Assistant Commissioners, however, it was not a particularly satisfactory experience. We interviewed nine who came up against a significant cross-boundary issue involving a London Borough and most expressed reservations as to the procedure:

> I don't think the system provides for crossing alternative Borough boundaries in a fair way. I was conscious I would be trespassing into other areas. If there's an answer, I suppose the Commission must take greater responsibility. It certainly brought home how good a rule it is to stick to Boroughs and Counties.

> There was great potential for a problem – I could have caused untold difficulties in the neighbouring Borough, for example, and if satisfied by a case I would have had no hesitation in recommending it. I don't know the correct solution to the London Borough issue, but it is a problem.

> In the end it didn't arise but if I had been convinced by an alternative pairing I don't quite know how it would have been resolved unless you hold a further Inquiry covering the combined area.

If I'd thought that a cross-border seat was desirable, there wasn't a proper procedure to deal with that. The Commission could well have received conflicting reports,
which is unsatisfactory in a way. Indeed it's very difficult to assess the arguments
for crossing a Borough boundary without examining the internal allocation within
both Boroughs. Hence I suspect that Assistant Commissioners start off with an
unwillingness to cross the boundary – it would be a brave Assistant Commissioner
who would recommend a cross-border seat.

I had to decide the meaning and significance of rule 4 and I decided that my understanding of the rules was the right one and that there was no need for me to consider the issues as they affected the neighbouring Borough. But say my interpretation
had been wrong or differed from the other Assistant Commissioner or from the
Commission, or say there had been an overwhelming case for a bit of my area to
be added to his. In that case it could be said that the Commission's brief was not
satisfactory. I did have the feeling that I shouldn't have to be puzzling this out, that
this was really a matter for the Commission, not for an Assistant Commissioner
whose remit is only to consider one area. I think they could have produced clearer
guidance in the light of the problems they might have expected to arise.

The comparable experience in Scotland was even less satisfactory. The Scottish
version of Rule 4 requires the Commission to 'have regard' to all local authority
boundaries, though during the Third Review it viewed Regions as equivalent to
English Counties and treated District boundaries in the same way as the English
and Welsh Commissions. The latter policy was repeated during this Review and
was generally supported by Assistant Commissioners; at the Grampian Inquiry,
for example, Gordon District Council's claim that its boundaries were of equivalent status to those of an English County was rejected by the Assistant Commissioner who pointed out that the differences in wording of Rule 4 'call for a different
approach' (Inquiry Report, Grampian, 12). In seeking to ensure that the total number of seats in Scotland did not rise above 72, however, the Commission changed
its policy towards Regional boundaries and proposed new constituencies straddling the border between Central and Tayside and between Borders and Lothian.
The Inquiry held in Perth saw some opposition to the principle of a cross-border
seat, primarily from the District Councils of Clackmannan and of Perth and Kin-
ross, but other local authorities together with all the political interests were persuaded, as was the Assistant Commissioner, who concluded that the provisional
recommendations 'would in general produce electorates nearer in size to the electoral quota' (Inquiry Report, Central & Tayside, 4).

The other Inquiry, by contrast, saw 'very substantial and widespread opposition
to the Commission's recommendations' to cross the Regional boundary (Inquiry
Report, Borders & Lothian, #13), opposition which the Assistant Commissioner
found persuasive(#44,#49–50):

Nowhere, apart from the brief reference at the end of paragraph 6 [of the Commission's written statement], can I find any indication at all that the Commission
had any regard to the boundaries of local authority areas when determining con-

stituency boundaries, nor can I find any convincing explanation for a departure from the requirements of Rule 4 … In 1983, the Commission … was at pains to respect local authority boundaries whereas now the emphasis appears to be on achieving electoral parity at the expense of such boundaries. … One might reasonably expect to find some explanation and justification for the change of view. Unfortunately, no such explanation or justification appears in the statement prepared for this inquiry.

Accordingly he recommended that the two Borders constituencies remain unaltered, while accepting that one could be extended to include an electoral division within Midlothian 'if it were thought to be necessary to make some adjustments in order to reduce or remove excessive disparities' (#92). As discussed below, the Commission rejected much of the Assistant Commissioner's analysis, though it did adopt his alternative proposals. This was the one example of an Inquiry resulting in changes to a Commission's proposals to elevate Rule 5 above Rule 4. Furthermore it was helped by the very clear physical and social identity of the Borders Region; by strong public opposition effectively harnessed by local authorities and Members of Parliament; and by the Commission's own failure to provide reasoned justification for its approach. It was the exception which proves the rule.

The other examples of Rule 4 issues can be dealt with briefly. A few participants advocated proposals which would cross designated boundaries, but apart from the cases discussed above, the only significant attempts related to the border between Lancashire and Merseyside, and to that between Powys and Clwyd. The former was inspired by dissatisfaction with the proposal to link parts of Sefton with neighbouring Knowsley. This gave birth to the Lydiate and Maghull Parliamentary Action Group (LAMPAG) which advocated the creation of a seat joining two wards in Sefton with neighbouring wards in West Lancashire, supported by a petition with some 8,000 signatures. Showing that the strength of public opinion is not always an advantage, the Assistant Commissioner commented on the 'antipathy, prejudice even in some cases' of those from Sefton who objected to links with neighbouring Knowsley (Inquiry Report, Knowsley & Sefton, #30) and was also critical, to varying degrees, of the failure of those advocating a cross-border seat to attend the Lancashire Inquiry. In finding that 'a sufficiently compelling case' for breaching the County boundary had not been made out (Inquiry Report, Knowsley & Sefton, #33), he rejected the counter-proposal.

At the Powys Inquiry, Montgomeryshire District Council argued for the inclusion of three communities from Clwyd totalling 1,272 electors in the proposed Montgomery constituency. The communities in question were to be transferred from Clwyd to Powys as part of the *Local Government (Wales) Bill* and the Assistant Commissioner recommended the change because 'Parliamentary constituencies should as far as possible coincide with local government boundaries' (Inquiry Report, Powys, 12). In rejecting his recommendation the Commission relied primarily upon the correct interpretation of relevant boundaries as laid down in the *Boundary Commissions Act 1992* (see Box 3.7), but also pointed out that 'the proposal had not been discussed at the inquiry held earlier in Clwyd' (Boundary Commission for Wales, 1995, #149). This is yet further confirmation of the importance of the geographical terms of reference of the Local Inquiry and of the practical obstacles to promoting alternative cross-border constituencies.

District boundaries

District boundaries are not recognised in the Rules, but in the English Metropolitan Counties they play an important role in providing the template within which apportionment takes place.[8] Of the 36 Metropolitan Districts, 15 were treated singly in the provisional recommendations and 16 in pairs, while all five Boroughs within Tyne and Wear included one or more cross-Borough seats. With just one exception, this structure was reflected in the organisation of Inquiries: 9 of the 15 'singles' had their own Inquiry, as did six of the eight pairs, whereas Tyne and Wear was covered in one Inquiry. In Greater Manchester, however, counter-proposals received in relation to Stockport and the provisionally recommended pairings of Bury and Rochdale, and Oldham and Tameside, led the Commission to hold one Inquiry covering all five Boroughs. What role did District boundaries play in these Inquiries and did any changes affecting cross-border seats result?

Four of the nine Metropolitan Districts which had their own Inquiry were the subject of written cross-border proposals, but only in Liverpool were these arguments developed in oral form. There, the Liberal Democrats argued for the pairing of the City with Knowsley, but the Assistant Commissioner appointed to conduct both this and the neighbouring Inquiry rejected this 'for the principal reason that I found that there was little support locally for this counter proposal' (Inquiry Report, Liverpool, #36). Alternative partners were also proposed for most of the Boroughs featured in the six 'paired' Inquiries, but only for Knowsley was this actively pursued at the Inquiry and only the pairing of Barnsley with Doncaster attracted significant opposition in principle. At the latter Inquiry the Assistant Commissioner was presented with evidence that 'there was no community of interest between "Doncastrians" and "Barnsleyites" and that a member representing such a constituency could not properly represent the disparate interests' (Inquiry Report, Barnsley & Doncaster, #7.4). He concluded, however, that 'In the ultimate and by reason of the substantial discrepancy [between the largest and smallest electorates in the joint Boroughs] … I was unpersuaded that the local ties were of sufficient weight' (#7.7).

The other two Inquiries, each covering five Districts, offered greater potential for discussing the merits of cross-Borough constituencies. In Tyne and Wear, the Commission proposed retention of the existing cross-border seat of Tyne Bridge and the creation of three others (see Figure 4.2). Support for the Commission's approach came from the Conservative and Labour parties and four of the five local authorities and in the absence of any viable alternative the Assistant Commissioner approved the composition of all four seats. In the eastern part of Greater Manchester, the Third Review had produced two cross-border seats, one joining

Oldham with Rochdale, the other linking Stockport with Tameside. At this Review the Commission provisionally recommended leaving Stockport unpaired and instead linking Rochdale with Bury and Oldham with Tameside (see Figure 4.3). Several counter-proposals were presented by political parties, local authorities and individuals, variously involving one, two and three cross-Borough seats and discussion of the disadvantages of such constituencies formed a critical part of the Inquiry. MPs referred to the increased workload and to difficulties if the two Boroughs had a different interest, while local authorities referred to administrative difficulties both in organising elections and liaising with MPs. Arguments of this type tended to be used wherever neighbouring areas were linked, whether they be London Boroughs, Scottish Regions, Metropolitan Boroughs or even Shire Districts. Generally speaking, they cut little ice. While recognising that the evidence of inconvenience was 'essentially accurate', the Assistant Commissioner felt that the difficulties 'might have been somewhat over-stated' (Inquiry Report, Bury, Oldham, Rochdale, Stockport & Tameside, #5.59) and concluded that 'they are not such as to justify so great a departure from Rule 5' (#7.4).

In the Shire Counties of England and Wales and in Northern Ireland, District boundaries are not recognised in the Rules, nor do they provide a template for the convening of Inquiries. Government guidance confers upon them the same status as their Metropolitan equivalents, however, and the three Commissions have generally attempted to minimise their crossing; indeed for all practical purposes they can be considered equivalent to Scottish District boundaries (to which the Scottish Commission must 'have regard' under Rule 4). Despite the fact that the median nonmetropolitan District electorate (just over 70,000) is very close to the electoral quota (particularly in England), the practical difficulties in matching constituency and District boundaries are significant; even amongst those Districts in the 60,000–80,000 range, the majority were divided between constituencies (see Figure 4.1).

Nevertheless slightly over half of the nonmetropolitan Inquiries witnessed attempts to reduce the number of divisions, particularly by the Districts themselves and especially in the larger Counties where the number of permutations was greater. Where a local authority merely attempted to minimise division of its own territory between constituencies, this generally tended to shift the problem elsewhere, and the more effective local authority submissions came where common ground was established, though even these were not always successful. For example, agreement amongst the councils of Beverley, Boothferry and Holderness to a counter-proposal designed to reduce the number of cross-border seats in Humberside from six to four was rejected by the Assistant Commissioner. While acknowledging the significance of District boundaries, he concluded that allegiances to older administrative units held greater sway, 'with those to the north [of the River Ouse] retaining their loyalties to the old East Riding of Yorkshire and those to the south feeling ties to the West Riding and Lincolnshire' (Inquiry Report, Humberside, #6.2).

In the two largest Shire Counties, however, consortia of local authorities were successful in persuading Assistant Commissioners to adopt a framework based on District council boundaries. In Essex, six councils of various political persuasions proposed the division of the County into six groups of adjacent Districts, each entitled to a number of seats whose average electorate was near to the electoral quota and largely coterminous with existing groupings of constituencies. Stressing that Districts constitute 'readily identifiable and familiar entities', he reported that he was 'particularly impressed' by this approach which resulted in 'significant advantages over the Commission's provisional recommendations which would result in considerable fragmentation of Districts and disruption of existing constituencies' (Inquiry Report, Essex, #3.2; see also Figure 4.5). In Hampshire the lead was taken by one authority, the City of Southampton, but it was assiduous in enlisting the support of four other councils of various political hues together with a number of associations and individuals. In listing the advantages of the counter-proposal, the Assistant Commissioner laid great stress on the fact that 'it takes into account district boundaries to a greater extent than the Commission's proposal' (Inquiry Report, Hampshire, #32) and on the Assistant Commissioner's advice the counter-proposal was incorporated in the final recommendations.

Local authorities played the major part in these counter-proposals, but political parties also used the argument when it suited their interests. There was a noteworthy difference, however, in the degree to which Conservative and Labour schemes attempted to follow District boundaries, with the latter significantly more likely to minimise the number of cross-border constituencies. Whereas the Commission's provisional recommendations for Shire England, Scotland and Wales would have resulted in 192 seats including electors from more than one District, the Conservatives actually proposed a total of 196, while Labour's proposals were for just 176. These net totals disguise a mixture of proposed increases and reductions in individual Counties; although the Labour Party advocated less boundary crossing in thirteen Counties, for example, its proposals would have created more cross-Borough seats in seven. Nevertheless the difference in approach between the two parties is interesting and is consistent with the Conservatives' greater emphasis on numerical considerations discussed below.

In Northern Ireland the picture was more confused. Although the four main areas of controversy identified by the Commission all involved local government boundaries (Boundary Commission for Northern Ireland, 1995, 13), in the case of Belfast the council expressed no view on the matter while the proposal to create a Newry & Mourne constituency incorporating the whole of Newry & Mourne Local Government District (LGD) was actively opposed by the local authority. In both areas there were extenuating circumstances – the boundary of Belfast LGD bears little relation to the boundary of the built-up area, while Newry & Mourne LGD comprises almost equal parts of the far longer-established Counties of Armagh and Down – but as elsewhere political considerations also played their part. Indeed of all the Local Inquiries held during the Fourth Review that

in Newry featured the most sustained attack upon the motives of a local authority with Unionists contrasting the attitude of Newry & Mourne with that of neighbouring Down LGD (also with a Nationalist majority) which argued strongly that
it should not be divided.

How did Assistant Commissioners respond to these arguments? On the basis
of our interviews and their reports, they seem to have been content with the Commission's advice that constituency and District boundaries should coincide 'as
much as practicable' (Parliamentary Boundary Commission for England, 1991,
21). Inevitably there were differences of emphasis between individuals, with those
stressing the numerical aspects of redistricting generally (and to a degree,
inevitably) more willing to recommend cross-District seats. Thus the Assistant
Commissioner who conducted the Inquiry in East Sussex, while 'mindful' of the
guidance given to and by the Commission, laid emphasis on the fact that 'making borough/district boundaries co-terminous with Parliamentary boundaries is
not one of the statutory Rules' (Inquiry Report, East Sussex, #3.6). However his
counterpart in Suffolk concluded that 'it really is not satisfactory to have the Central Suffolk constituency of such a size and shape that it covers part of four separate District Councils' (Inquiry Report, Suffolk, #19.2) and the Assistant
Commissioner in charge of the Nottinghamshire Inquiry observed that: 'If it is at
all practicable the boundaries of constituencies should be coterminous with local
government boundaries. This is not only because of convenience but also because
the local government boundary often reflects the local ties which exist in the local-
ity' (Inquiry Report, Nottinghamshire, #9.8).

As their reports show, several Assistant Commissioners were able to recommend greater coincidence between Parliamentary and District boundaries. Including the cases of Essex and Hampshire, a total of 21 Assistant Commissioners
were presented with counter-proposals which would have reduced the number of
cross-District seats, nine of whom made recommendations which incorporated a
reduction. Although four of their colleagues recommended an increase the net
effect was to reduce the number of cross-District seats in Shire England, Scotland, Wales and Northern Ireland from the provisionally recommended 204 to
198. This was only a modest decrease and in most cases it was other arguments,
notably those relating to local ties and minimum change, which Assistant Commissioners cited when explaining their recommendations; indeed where the two
conflicted (as in Belfast and Newry) local government boundaries usually came
out worse. A counter-proposal which follows District boundaries is better than
one which doesn't, *ceteris paribus*, but only in the few instances mentioned was
it a persuasive factor.

Wards and other 'internal' boundaries

All four Commissions have consistently adopted a policy of not including a ward
partly in one constituency and partly in another, though only in the case of Northern Ireland is it a statutory requirement (Rule 4(1)(c); Box 3.6). The policy was

repeated in the various *News Releases, Newsletters* and other publications issued during the Fourth Review, but still this did not prevent several individuals and organisations pressing for the division of wards. Over twenty Inquiries witnessed such attempts with a remarkably high proportion (almost half) coming from one political party, the Liberal Democrats. Given the clear lead indicated by the Commissions it is not surprising to find the near universal rejection of such arguments as exemplified by the Assistant Commissioner who conducted the Inquiry in Tyne and Wear (Inquiry Report, Tyne and Wear, #4.1.5):

> A number of speakers representing Liberal Democrat interests criticised the use by the Commission of the ward as the smallest 'building block'. It was suggested that problems might often be solved by using polling districts to facilitate the splitting of wards. I concede that this solution can sometimes be attractive, notably where a ward itself contains diversities of interest. I considered the solution at length but concluded that it would be a practice fraught with potential difficulties and a dangerous precedent.

Only one Assistant Commissioner demurred. Faced with strong opposition to the crossing of the boundary between the London Boroughs of Lambeth and Southwark and the consequent cross-Borough seat, the Assistant Commissioner in question recommended splitting two of its wards so as to better reflect local ties (Inquiry Report, Lambeth & Southwark, #6.14):

> In my view the divisions I have proposed would be an improvement on the provisional recommendations and I leave it to the Commission to weigh whether they appear to offer a sufficient advantage to be worthy of adoption.

The Commission was not convinced and the wards remained intact.

Wards are the smallest building blocks used by the Commissions, but they are not the only electoral divisions in existence. In Northern Ireland the introduction of proportional representation for local authority elections resulted in the creation of District Electoral Areas (DEAs), combinations of wards which are used for electing local councillors. In preparing its provisional recommendations the Northern Ireland Commission made explicit efforts to respect DEA boundaries but few of those making representations accorded them equivalent status. As the Assistant Commissioner for Belfast stated (Inquiry Report, Belfast, #30):

> While it might be preferable for DEAs to be kept within the same constituencies as far as possible, I do not see this as a significant factor. ... No strong submission was made which suggested that the existing split in DEAs has caused significant problems or that splits in the future might do so.

In Shire England and in Wales the two-tier system of local government results in the need for County Council electoral divisions and the case for observing their boundaries was made at around one in five Inquiries. This tended to be a very minor issue, however, and although the Assistant Commissioner for Surrey was 'influenced by the desirability, if reasonably possible, of avoiding the splitting of county divisions' (Inquiry Report, Surrey, 35), none of his colleagues mentioned it as a factor influencing their decisions.

Scotland also had a two-tier system at the time of the Fourth Review, with councillors elected to the higher tier representing Regional Electoral Divisions (REDs). The Scottish Commission decided to use recently revised REDs rather than pre-existing (and soon to be obsolete) wards as their building blocks but, as discussed in Chapter 5, this led to serious problems. Many REDs were large (the average RED in Strathclyde had over 17,000 electors) and their boundaries frequently divided recognisable communities.[9] As a result five of the seven Inquiries saw calls for the division of REDs. The response of Assistant Commissioners was much more divided than that of their English counterparts. In three cases the request was dismissed, but in Strathclyde the Assistant Commissioner decided to 'respectfully invite the Commission to consider … making an exception to their general policy' (Inquiry Report, Strathclyde, #11.27) in both Kyle & Carrick and in Inverclyde; while in Fife, where the splitting of an RED in order to permit the retention of Steelend (246 electors) in the same constituency as its neighbour, Saline, was the sole issue at the Inquiry, the Assistant Commissioner concluded that 'the numbers involved are so small and the evidence so compelling that an exception should be made in this case' (Inquiry Report, Fife, 3). The Commission, while recognising the strength of feeling in all three areas, stuck to its policy, a policy which was subsequently recognised as reasonable on application for judicial review (see Chapter 5).

Electoral equality (Rule 5)

The minimisation of inequalities in constituency electorates lies at the very root of redistricting. Apart from a small number of instances when a Commission proposed very minor changes to align constituency and local government boundaries, the need to reduce departures from the national quota was given as the main reason wherever a Commission was proposing change.

This does not mean that all Inquiries were called as a result of changes proposed by the Commissions. Nine Inquiries took place in areas where the Commission was content with existing arrangements. In all but three of these, proponents of change relied partly on the numerical superiority of their proposals: the Conservative Party in Merton and St Helens (whose proposals would have reduced disparities between the largest and smallest seats from 970 to 134 and from 3,358 to 1,034 respectively); the Labour Party in Wolverhampton and South Glamorgan (from 11,120 to 8,542 and from 9,967 to 8,364 respectively); the Liberal Democrats in Somerset (from 7,999 to 4,587); and Aberconwy Borough Council in Gwynedd (from 21,603 to 10,994). None was successful. The respective Assistant Commissioners in the first four Inquiries found the reductions to be 'not at all significant' (Inquiry Report, Merton, #7.3), 'fairly modest' (Inquiry Report, St Helens, #14.5), 'not … any important improvement in arithmetical terms' (Inquiry Report, Wolverhampton, #8.1) and 'a worthless piece of "tinkering"' (Inquiry Report, South Glamorgan, #3.2). The Assistant Commissioner who held the Somerset Inquiry concluded that the proposal 'cannot be justified numerically' (*sic*; Inquiry Report, Somerset, 25) while the conclusions of his colleague in Gwynedd made no reference to the possible halving of the disparity!

Numerical arguments were singularly unsuccessful at these Inquiries, but what of the remainder (78 out of the total of 87) where the Commission itself was proposing change? Did those appearing here argue for less variability, and if so, were they more successful? We have analysed all counter-proposals presented at these Inquiries and have calculated both the range and the standard deviation of the electorates proposed. On either measure it is clear that relatively few counter-proposals would have resulted in lower variation than those of the Commission. On average around one in four of the other schemes presented at Inquiries could be described as superior in terms of Rule 5, although in many cases the advantage was insubstantial and relatively few proponents relied primarily upon this aspect of their scheme. Nevertheless, we have identified around two dozen well-argued counter-proposals presented at Local Inquiries which involved a four-figure reduction in the overall disparity. Several of these had local authority involvement: at the Inquiries in Avon and Norfolk, authorities argued for schemes which better accorded with Rule 5 as part of their alternative interpretations on apportionment; in Strathclyde, Kyle & Carrick District Council together with the Conservative Party proposed the splitting of Regional Electoral Divisions in order to reduce the 14,000 disparity between neighbouring constituencies; and in Humberside, Boothferry Borough Council and three neighbouring authorities put forward a counter-proposal which would have halved the range provisionally recommended by the Commission. Only in Strathclyde was the Assistant Commissioner persuaded, but despite his 'respectful invitation' to the Commission to consider making an exception to their general policy, the provisional recommendations were confirmed.

Political parties were hardly more successful. The Conservatives placed most emphasis on the numerical aspect, putting forward a total of nine counter-proposals which would have reduced overall disparities. None was accepted; indeed in six of the nine the Assistant Commissioner chose an alternative scheme which actually increased the disparity over that provisionally recommended by the Commission. In Coventry, for example, where the provisional recommendations involved a range of 4,504, a counter-proposal from the Labour Party was chosen because (Inquiry Report, Coventry, #13):

> The disparity between the highest and lowest constituency of 5619 is in my view acceptable. I recognise that the Conservative Federation's counter-proposal achieves a better mathematical result [1436], but in my view it gives insufficient weight to local ties.

Even the party's counter-proposal for North Yorkshire, which would have reduced the disparity from 14,840 as proposed by the Commission to just 5,814, was rejected by the Assistant Commissioner despite 'the significant improvement in electoral figures that the Conservatives' proposals achieve' (Inquiry Report, North Yorkshire, #25).

The other parties had only marginally greater success. Both Labour and the Liberal Democrats put forward four such schemes and each 'won' one. The Labour Party counter-proposal for the London Boroughs of Redbridge and Waltham Forest (supported by the latter authority) was accepted *in toto* by the Assistant Commissioner. It involved a disparity of 4,298 against 8,792 provisionally recommended, but both the Conservatives (supported by Redbridge Borough) and the Liberal Democrats put forward counter-proposals which would also have reduced the disparity. The Assistant Commissioner made it clear that Rule 5 played little part in his decision, concluding that 'in terms of size and comparability of the numbers of electors in each proposed seat, there was little to choose between the options' (Inquiry Report, Redbridge & Waltham Forest, #8.01).

The North West Liberal Democrats' successful scheme was for the four Greater Manchester Boroughs of Oldham, Rochdale, Stockport and Tameside. Its provisions resulted in a disparity of 9,416 against 15,356 under the Commission's provisional recommendations, and 15,871 and 16,068 under the counter-proposals of the Conservative and Labour Parties respectively. This caused the Assistant Commissioner to observe that 'the most serious criticisms of the [Labour Party] scheme, in my opinion, concern the size of the constituencies which it would create' (Inquiry Report, Bury, Oldham, Rochdale, Stockport & Tameside, #6.35), whereas the Liberal Democrats' option 'significantly improves upon the provisional recommendations. I regard this as a strong argument in favour of the scheme' (#6.14). Although he recommended minor modifications to the scheme, this was the one example from the Fourth Review of a significant counter-proposal succeeding primarily because of the numerical improvements it produced.

If counter-proposals involving closer adherence to the electoral quota than those proposed by the Commission were the exception, and if those which were put forward had so little success, what of those who argued for greater disparities? Does it follow that Assistant Commissioners were relatively relaxed about recommending schemes which involved greater variation about the electoral quota than those provisionally recommended by the Commission? On this question the answer is less clear-cut. While it is true that a majority of the Inquiry reports recommended an alternative arrangement of constituencies with a larger range of electorates (46 of the 87 reports to be precise), almost as many did not. In addition to the Inquiries in Birmingham, Redbridge & Waltham Forest and Greater Manchester discussed above, another nine reports advocated minor reductions in inequality, while the remainder produced no change. Furthermore, of the 46 increases, half were less than 2,000 and only five (Oxfordshire, Wiltshire, Borders & Lothian, Dumfries & Galloway and Highland) exceeded 5,000.

These figures suggest that the majority of Assistant Commissioners could be persuaded to increase disparities, but only by a relatively modest amount. To what extent is this impression borne out by what they say in their reports? Several referred to the legal precedent established by the *Foot et al.* case (Inquiry Report, Lincolnshire, #5.1-5.2):

During the course of the enquiry it was suggested that the Commission's duty was to equalise the voting numbers in each constituency so far as they could without inflicting bruising damage on affiliations or District council boundaries. It was suggested that numbers were the prime factor. Several of those who appeared at the enquiry spoke about 'the numbers game' as if that was what the review was all about. I think that one has to look at what Lord Donaldson said in R[egina] v Boundary Commission for England, ex parte Foot and others to appreciate the true relevance of numbers . ... There are other factors as well as numbers which are important.

The Sheriff Principal who conducted the Borders Inquiry used the same line of reasoning to question the Scottish Commission's own approach: (Inquiry Report, Borders & Lothian, #47-8):

I am unable to read these sentences [from the Commission's statement of reasons] as being anything other than the clearest possible indication that, in carrying out its current review of constituencies in Lothian and Borders Regions, the Commission decided to give primacy, above all other considerations, to the requirements of Rule 5. Such an approach is, of course, at odds with the approach as set out in the opinion of the Master of the Rolls in the *Foot* case and at odds with the Rules themselves as they were explained in that case. ... In my opinion, and with all respect to the Commission, the approach to this review, as revealed in the Commission's statement, is inconsistent with the requirements of the Rules to an extent which would justify a complete reconsideration of the provisional recommendations in respect of [these] constituencies.

Others adopted a different interpretation, placing far more weight on the principle of 'one vote, one value' as for example in:

It is clear that in general the requirement of rule 5 that a constituency electorate shall be as near the electoral quota as is practicable is to take priority over the inevitable problems to which changing constituency boundaries will give rise. In other words, the rules provide that the principle that each vote should carry the same weight throughout the country so far as is possible is to be regarded as more important than the principle that each separate community should form part of one constituency. (Inquiry Report, Surrey, p.26)

and

In my opinion Rule 5 concerning the convergence of electorates to the electoral quota is a very important provision. The reason for it was made clear in the evidence put before the Court in the Foot case namely the principle of equal representation for all electors required by the modern system of Parliamentary representation. (Inquiry Report, East Sussex, #5.8)[10]

This division of opinion was reflected in our interviews with Assistant Commissioners. We asked each where the balance lay between the need to reduce electoral inequalities and the need to minimise change. Just under half of the respondents exhibited a clear preference for one over the other with ten emphasising the organic and thirteen the mathematic. Amongst the former group the following comments were typical:

> I decided that Rule 7 was overriding in the sense that you don't start with a clean sheet.

> Numerical inequality always has to yield to the maintenance of stability in terms of clear community ties.

> If the existing pattern can be sensibly retained, it should be done. People get used to it and 'if it ain't broke don't fix it'.

As well as being slightly more numerous, the 'egalitarians' tended to hold their viewpoint more strongly:

> I thought it was important to minimise inequalities; I would play the numbers game more firmly than the Commission.

> I felt the balance lay, as far as possible, in having seats of an equal size. That must be the main consideration. The Commission subsequently moved a ward to satisfy local demands, but I wouldn't have done that.

> In general my impression was that electoral equality was a high priority and that the avoidance of change was comparatively much less so. In the provisional recommendations I thought that the avoidance of change was acting as a heavy restraint. I recommended more change and I was fascinated that this led the Commission to go on to propose a further change, which I thought was ideal.

> I tend to think that equality is the priority. You then see whether that produces unacceptable change, not the other way round.

The majority (37), however, were unwilling to identify priority, either questioning the validity of the question or emphasising the need for flexibility:

> I don't believe there's necessarily a tension there. They're not necessarily incompatible. Once you change the total number of seats, you're bound to have major change and the numbers are bound to take on a greater importance. With the same number of seats, the approach would be very different.

> I'm not going to say, because I can't [if it is] unrelated to a specific context. It all depends on the circumstances.

> I decided on the merits of the case. There was no fixed formula. The Rules give you that flexibility, that latitude.

> They're on a level and that's what it's all about.

From these comments it is clear that there was no such thing as a common approach. Most Assistant Commissioners were pragmatists and the same person could come to very different conclusions when faced with different circumstances. For example, the Assistant Commissioner who rejected a counter-proposal in Durham because 'in my opinion the electoral disparities involved in the Conservative proposals [8,081 compared with 2,981 in the provisional recommendations and 2,746 as recommended by the Assistant Commissioner] cannot be justified' (Inquiry Report, Durham, #25), was prepared to approve a range of 13,578 in Cumbria (the same as that recommended by the Commission). There are two possible

explanations for this phenomenon. On the one hand it may be that the circumstances of Cumbria demanded a figure some four to five times higher than Durham
and both the Commission and the Assistant Commissioner came to the same conclusion. On the other it could be that the Assistant Commissioner was heavily
influenced by the size of the range in the provisional recommendations and felt
constrained to adopt a comparable figure. There is no way of testing this of course,
but the fact that several of the Commissions' more surprising recommendations
remained unaltered – Gloucestershire (range 13,605) and Shropshire (range
14,858), for example – suggests that the lead could be extremely influential.

We have already noted that few Assistant Commissioners recommended disparities significantly greater than those provisionally recommended by the Commission and as part of our interviews we asked Assistant Commissioners what
they regarded as an 'excessive disparity' (the phrase used in Rule 5) and how
they formed that view. Most were reluctant to give a figure, the majority again
emphasising the importance of circumstance:

> I didn't have a figure as to what was an excessive disparity because you have to
> consider it in the light of other factors; it's only excessive if it's wrong *in context*.
> It seems to me that the legislation is specifically designed to ensure flexibility.

> I think it's virtually impossible to answer – it depends on the circumstances.

> I would adopt a fairly pragmatic approach. From looking at my recommendations
> I obviously thought 6–7 per cent above or below was OK, which isn't to say that I
> wouldn't go along with a bigger range in a particular case.

The provisional recommendations constituted the most obvious standard against
which to assess counter-proposals, while in London, as one Assistant Commissioner
pointed out, the Commission's guideline for pairing Boroughs was very influential:

> To a large extent that judgement is pre-empted by the Commission. They decided
> to pair London Boroughs on the basis of a 12,500 disparity and hence they chose
> the interpretation, not I.

Assistant Commissioners also had other ways of making this judgement:

> The parameters for disparity emerge, for example from the Commission's News
> Releases. Having said that when I looked at some of the News Releases I was sur-
> prised at the proposed disparities.

> I am content with the view of the Court of Appeal. I might begin to feel uncom-
> fortable with disparities over 10,000, but even then some cases write their own
> result.

> I found the previous reports I was sent very helpful there. I also had a very helpful
> assistant from the Commission who gave me advice 'off the record'.

> I tried to get a sense of what's acceptable by looking at the previous recommenda-
> tions in the Borough and from the model report for Wiltshire. In the end I didn't
> need to worry. In a sense it's like a sausage, you can't necessarily define it but you
> can surely recognise it.

Where does this discussion leave us in understanding the significance of the 'numbers game'? It is clear that few participants rely upon the minimisation of electoral inequality when presenting counter-proposals and those who do have little success. We have found only one example from the Fourth Review of a significant counter-proposal succeeding primarily because of the numerical improvements it produced; if the Commission has not found an acceptable way of further reducing inequalities it is unlikely that anybody else will be able to persuade Assistant Commissioners to do so. If a counter-proposal is to succeed, however, it should not ignore the arithmetic parameters embodied in the provisional recommendations. While a modest increase in the overall disparity will generally prove acceptable, there are few examples of significant escalations. The Labour Party was well aware of this. Although it was far readier than the Conservatives to propose greater disparities (at 48 Inquiries compared to 30 for the Conservatives), most of the proposed increases were under 3,000. Some Assistant Commissioners maintain strong views as to the relative priority between minimising electoral inequalities and minimising change, but most approach the exercise pragmatically.

Indeed this is probably the most important aspect of the 'numbers game'. In much the same way as the Commissions effectively determined apportionment decisions when they published their provisional recommendations, so they set a clear lead with respect to electoral inequality. The majority of Inquiries certainly resulted in greater disparities than provisionally recommended but, as Chapter 4 clearly demonstrates, the Commissions have succeeded in progressively reducing the degree of inequality in constituency electorates. Participants and Assistant Commissioners alike have taken their lead from the Commissions; Inquiries may lessen the impact but Rule 5 has already set the agenda.

Special geographical considerations (Rule 6)

Rule 6 permits a Commission to depart from the strict application of Rules 4 and 5 'if special geographical considerations, including in particular the size, shape and accessibility of a constituency, appear to them to render a departure desirable'. The Rule has been used sparingly over the years and it was only explicitly invoked in four areas at the Fourth Review: to justify the low electorate of Copeland and the high electorate of the Isle of Wight, and to justify the allocation of four seats to Gwynedd and three seats to the Scottish Islands areas. The English Commission in particular has been careful to discourage references to it, stressing in the *Review of Parliamentary Constituencies* that it 'seldom' applies to England. While this has not prevented all four Commissions including references to size, shape or accessibility in statements explaining their provisional recommendations, most Assistant Commissioners seem to have accepted that these are reflections of the Commissions' general discretionary powers (Inquiry Report, Bury et al, #2.4):[11]

> While I recognise the relevance of geographic features to the more general ques-
> tion as to how the area should best be divided within the scope afforded by the
> statutory provisions, it does not seem to me that the area contains any *special* geo-
> graphical considerations.

Just as the Commissions made sparing use of reference to Rule 6, so did those
who appeared at the Inquiries; nevertheless over a dozen Inquiry reports mention
it explicitly. Its applicability was most apparent in relation to the Highlands Region,
as the Assistant Commissioner pointed out (Inquiry Report, Highlands, 8):

> Its area is huge, its population small and unevenly distributed and its road system
> of variable quality. From an MP's point of view it is a long way from London. In
> my opinion, in the Highlands Rule 6 entitles the Commission to take a fairly lib-
> eral view of Rule 5.

As if to emphasise its limited role, however, the same Assistant Commissioner
rejected a proposal in nearby Grampian Region to reduce the size of a provisionally recommended seat (Inquiry Report, Grampian, 14–15):

> The justification for this proposal is the 'geographical size and nature' of the pro-
> posed … constituency, which I take to be a reference to Rule 6. I find no great merit
> in that submission. The proposed Deeside and the Howes constituency is certainly
> large and rural in nature, but neither the present nor the former MP, nor indeed Kin-
> cardine and Deeside District Council, suggested that its size, shape and accessibil-
> ity would pose any significant problem.

On the other hand the Assistant Commissioner who conducted the Inquiry in
Dumfries & Galloway rejected the Scottish Commission's proposal to extend the
seat of Galloway & Upper Nithsdale largely because of the size of the proposed
seat. Similarly in a couple of English Inquiries (Humberside and Sefton) Assistant Commissioners accepted that Rule 6 might be considered relevant, though
in neither case was it sufficient on its own to influence their recommendations.

Attempts to extend interpretation of the rule beyond size, shape and accessibility met with little success. At the Hereford & Worcester Inquiry the representative
of Ledbury Town Council argued that the Malvern Hills not only formed a physical barrier, 'more than that they also represent a philosophical, psychological and
demographic division and have done so since before the establishment of the county
system by the Saxons before the Norman invasion' (Inquiry Report, Hereford &
Worcester, #10.5). While accepting the significance of the Hills, the Assistant Commissioner concluded that Rule 6 did not come into play. Similarly the Assistant
Commissioner who conducted the Inquiry into the City of Westminster was unimpressed by attempts to extend the rule's scope (Inquiry Report, Ealing *et al.*, #1.5):

> I was invited to treat as special geographical considerations (1) the presence in the
> City of Westminster of a large population of foreign residents ineligible to vote but
> in need of Parliamentary representation, and (2) the unique position of Westmin-
> ster at the heart of the capital City giving it a political importance disproportionate
> to the number of its voters … I rejected that invitation. I concluded that the con-

siderations envisaged by Rule 6 were of a more limited nature as the examples given in the rule tend to confirm.

Just once was an Assistant Commissioner convinced to accept a wider interpretation. Faced with what he considered persuasive evidence that the electorate of the London Borough of Tower Hamlets was likely to grow significantly in the coming years, the Assistant Commissioner concluded (Inquiry Report, Tower Hamlets, #20):

> With some hesitation … I am prepared to proceed on the assumption that I can and must, as a matter of law, take into consideration the evidence of population growth which was placed before me. It seems to me that it is at least arguable that an unusual rate of population growth is a factor falling within the meaning of the term (in Rule 6 of the Rules) 'special geographical considerations'.

In the end it had no effect upon his recommendations, however, as even taking projected growth into account he felt unable to allocate two whole seats to the Borough. This was not the only example of an Assistant Commissioner being urged to take account of future growth (as noted in Chapter 5, until it issued its Winter 1992 *Newsletter* the English Commission had itself seemed uncertain of the proper weight to accord it) but it was the only case of a significant difference of opinion between Commission and Assistant Commissioner and the only time that it was interpreted in the context of Rule 6.

It will be clear from this discussion that Rule 6 had little effect upon the Fourth Review, but that does not mean that size, shape and accessibility were unimportant. As far as size was concerned, the English Commission's briefing was that there should be no attempt 'to differentiate between the representation of rural and urban areas, save as necessitated by special geographical considerations' and this approach was generally accepted by Assistant Commissioners. There was the occasional exception, however, as with the Assistant Commissioner appointed to conduct the second Devon Inquiry (Report of the Second Devon Inquiry, #3.3):

> If there is to be a numerical imbalance within a particular county between the electoral populations of particular constituencies, it is generally desirable to ensure that the more confined urban area has if practicable a larger electoral roll than its contiguous neighbour, with its more scattered electorate.

Considerations of accessibility tended to be covered under Rule 7 ('inconvenience' and 'local ties'), but as we have seen in Chapter 5 the shape of constituencies tended to be a topic which exercised the Commissions whatever size the seat. This is consistent with research undertaken at the time of the Third Review (Johnston and Rossiter, 1981) which found that 'shapely' solutions were more likely to be chosen than 'unshapely' ones but an examination of the Inquiry transcripts reveals that the question of shape was little discussed. Around a third of Inquiry reports mention shape, but this was mostly in passing; insofar as it was considered the comments of the following two Assistant Commissioners are indicative of the typical approach:

> The shape of the two constituencies would be unfortunate. … I concluded that this disadvantage was more apparent than actual and carried with it no significant practical consequences. (Inquiry Report, Havering, #10.6)

and

> Appearance is not everything, of course, and I note that the shape of a constituency is mentioned in the rules only in relation to special geographical considerations which are not present here. (Inquiry Report, Dudley & Sandwell, #21)

That this view was not universal is shown by the comments of another Assistant Commissioner who, faced with a request to vary a constituency boundary in order to minimise fragmentation of County Council electoral divisions, commented (Inquiry Report, Northamptonshire, p.14):

> No evidence of any particular confusion on the part of an actual voter was produced and, even if it existed, I consider the shape and compactness of the proposed constituencies to be an overrriding factor.

There were other references to shape – 'pleasing' in Sheffield, 'unsatisfactory' in St Helens, 'peculiar' in Nottinghamshire, 'rather amazing' in Lincolnshire, 'extraordinary' in Highland, and 'very unnatural' in Omagh, for example – but as our interviews confirmed, it was never a critical factor in an Assistant Commissioner's recommendations.

Minimising change and respecting local ties (Rule 7)

The need to minimise disruption to the existing pattern of constituencies is embodied in what has come to be known as Rule 7 (Box 3.6), which requires Commissions to 'take account so far as they reasonably can of the inconveniences attendant on alterations of constituencies … and of any local ties which would be broken by such alterations'. This can justifiably be read as a general exhortation against change, but the specific references to inconvenience and to broken ties also suggest a more particular requirement. Assistant Commissioners, in other words, may reasonably apply four tests relating to Rule 7: (1) does a counter-proposal involve the 'transfer' of fewer electors than under the Commission's provisional recommendations or under any competing plan?;[12] (2) is there any evidence that inconvenience would result from change?; (3) is there evidence of ties which would be broken?'[13] and (4) how do these correspond to 'communities of interest'.

In the introductory remarks to this chapter it was pointed out that the effect of the Inquiries was to reduce the total numbers of electors 'transferred' to a new constituency from six to five million. This is a sizeable difference and came about as the result of many decisions by many Assistant Commissioners. An analysis of the 87 areas which had an Inquiry shows that in 53 the Assistant Commissioner's recommendations involved the transfer of fewer electors than provisionally recommended by the Commissions, compared with just ten where the converse was true. Apart from Birmingham (where the additional change proposed by the Assistant Commissioner was inextricably linked with his views on apportionment) the largest increase suggested was in Bedfordshire, where the Assistant Commissioner's recommendations resulted in the transfer of 26.6 per cent of the electorate compared with the 22.0 per cent proposed by the Commission. Set against that, a dozen Assistant Commissioners were able to recommend changes to the provisional recommendations which resulted a reduction in 'disruption' of 5 per cent or more. There can be no doubt, therefore, that the effect of the Local Inquiries was to reduce change.

To a considerable extent this can be seen as a response to the arguments presented at those Inquiries. As part of our investigation, we have examined each major counter-proposal to see whether it would have resulted in more or less change than embodied within the provisional recommendations. This analysis shows that around 55 per cent of counter-proposals involved the transfer of fewer electors, with the Conservatives favouring less change more often than Labour. Counter-proposals are not the whole story, however: most representations are of a more limited nature, relating to individual wards or groups of wards. Here the predominance of those arguing for the status quo is more marked. Indeed, the vast majority of those individuals without a stated political affiliation who attended the Inquiries did so specifically to argue for the retention of existing arrangements. It is clear, therefore, that the weight of evidence was opposed to change, but on its own this does not explain the response. In particular, it does not show whether Assistant Commissioners were persuaded by general arguments against change or by particular arguments relating to ties and inconvenience. In order to distinguish between them it is necessary to look in more detail at what they said in their reports, supplemented where necessary with evidence from our interviews.

The lack of appetite for change amongst Assistant Commissioners is most clearly exhibited in the nine Inquiries where the Commission had provisionally recommended retention of the status quo. In eight of these cases counter-proposals were dismissed, whether they came from the Conservatives in Merton (which would have involved the transfer of 11 per cent of the electorate), St Helens (31 per cent) and West Glamorgan (23 per cent); from Labour in Somerset (4 per cent), South Glamorgan (1 per cent), Wirral (10 per cent) and Wolverhampton (5 per cent); or from a local authority in Gwynedd (25 per cent). Only in Powys (1 per cent) did the Assistant Commissioner recommend a counter-proposal and that had more to do with his (incorrect) interpretation of Rule 4 than it had to do with the merits of change. It is noteworthy that none of the eight reports specifically referred to the numbers of electors transferred. Perhaps this is not too surprising: when a Commission proposes no change, any counter-proposal must involve more. Where a Commission is also proposing change, however, one might expect Assistant Commissioners to attempt to assess the relative degrees of disruption involved in the various proposals. Several Inquiries were presented with figures showing the number of electors who would be transferred under rival schemes. There can be difficulties with these calculations, especially where an extra seat is created or an existing one abolished. They are not insuperable, however, and when parties can arrive at an agreed set of figures, as the Conservative and Labour parties did at the East Sussex Inquiry, they can prove helpful to an Assistant Commissioner (Inquiry Report, East Sussex, #3.6):

> It will be for the Boundary Commission for England to decide what weight they should attach to such figures. Given the circumstances of East Sussex, I am prepared to accept that an exercise such as this may be used as a proxy for the extent of change and that the exercise demonstrates that the Labour Party's proposals give rise to significantly greater change than those of the Commission.

It is notable, however, that relatively few reports contain comments such as these. Whereas the vast majority contain discussions of disparities between electorates, measurement of change is much less common. This does not mean, of course, that Assistant Commissioners were oblivious to the volume of change. Most recognised the desirability of minimising it and, as their recommendations show, few were prepared to propose more. Nevertheless a significant number of Assistant Commissioners made recommendations in the absence of objective information as to how many electors were affected by the various options. In part this probably reflects the lack of confidence amongst a surprising number of Assistant Commissioners with matters statistical (as evidenced by the significant number of reports which had to be amended for arithmetic errors and as confirmed by our own interviews). More importantly, however, it reflects the approach embodied within the Rules themselves. Whereas Rule 5 invites, even demands, a statistical interpretation, Rule 7 does not. References to inconvenience and to ties can justifiably be interpreted as requiring a qualitative rather than a quantitative approach. Accustomed in their professional lives to dealing with the former rather than the latter, the only statistical interpretations of Rule 7 came from those who were presented with such evidence. Although most Assistant Commissioners had a good idea as to the relative levels of disruption involved in competing plans, for an explanation of how they came to their decisions we must turn from numeric interpretations of change and look elsewhere.

It is possible to argue (and many at the Inquiries did) that the two specific elements identified within Rule 7, namely inconvenience and the breaking of local ties, are inextricably linked. When local ties are broken, so the argument goes, inconvenience inevitably results. In the absence of guidance from the Commissions (the booklet on T*he Review of Parliamentary Constituencies,* for example, gives no help on the interpretation of either phrase; Parliamentary Boundary Commission for England, 1991), the attraction of such arguments is obvious. If an organisation is opposed to the separation of two areas, all it has to do is produce evidence of links between them and it has satisfied not only 7(b) but also 7(a). When we asked Assistant Commissioners for their views, very few were sympathetic to this approach:

> I suppose around 98 per cent of the electorate couldn't care a twopenny hoot which constituency they're in. A lot wouldn't recognise as real the evidence of ties, but it's a necessary concomitant of the system. And how much peoples' lives are really affected – I don't frankly believe it makes much difference.

> I had plenty of evidence, but either local ties just weren't there or were such as to have no effect on the establishment of electoral boundaries. Things like where were the nearest shops – just because people like to shop in the town hardly means that they need to be in the same seat – the arguments become rather ridiculous really.

> Most extreme was the vicar who seemed to believe that it would be a problem for his congregation to attend a church outside their constituency or to cross a constituency boundary in order to shop. This seemed to me a particularly absurd example, but there were plenty more.

Rather a distinction tended to be drawn between the two. Local ties were typically considered in the context of 'community identity', something we deal with in greater detail below, while inconvenience was treated in a more literal sense. This had two important implications. First, more was expected of those who sought to demonstrate inconvenience. A witness could describe a whole range of ties between areas x and y, all of which might be indicative of 'community identity', but as the Assistant Commissioners quoted above point out, very few of them would be affected by changes to constituency boundaries. Second, and resulting from the first, the question of inconvenience was an issue for far fewer Assistant Commissioners. Less evidence made explicit reference to inconvenience and much of it could be readily dismissed. Whereas virtually every report discusses the significance of local ties, far less space is devoted to discussions of inconvenience.

That said, we must now consider the response of those Assistant Commissioners who were presented with such arguments. An important distinction to draw at the outset relates to the person(s) suffering the inconvenience. The convenience of Members of Parliament received short shrift. The briefing sent to Assistant Commissioners by the English Commission stressed that an MP's workload was not a factor to be taken into account when determining boundaries and this was largely accepted by Assistant Commissioners. The issue was given its fullest airing at the Inquiry into the London Boroughs of Lambeth and Southwark, where the Assistant Commissioner concluded (Inquiry Report, Lambeth & Southwark, #6.17):

> Whilst I accept that a member will need to build up personal contacts in order to become an effective lobbyist and I can also accept that it will be more time-consuming to have to build them up with (say) the housing departments of two London Borough organisations, I do not accept that this cannot reasonably be done by an averagely energetic member. Furthermore insofar as the member conducts correspondence with a particular department it surely matters not whether all the letters go to or are received from one borough or whether there is a split between two boroughs.

The convenience of local authorities, for example with regard to electoral administration, was viewed in similar terms. The message was clear: those elected or employed to govern must be prepared to accept any extra inconvenience as part of the job.

Electors, however, were a different matter and two factors were considered particularly important. The first of these related to communications, a consideration stressed by several Assistant Commissioners in their conversations with us:

> It is important that electors who wish to play a part in the democratic process in their constituency are able to move to other parts of the constituency, whether at times of elections or otherwise.

> The ability to get to a public meeting is important when many are reliant upon public transport.

> It's significant if the argument relates to transport, going to an MP's surgery, especially where a constituency is in danger of becoming impossibly big to get round.

> You're thinking of transport, especially roads, and the difficulties for a political organisation especially in bad weather trying to get to meetings in other parts of a constituency.

Arguments such as these were not universally accepted: the Assistant Commissioner who conducted the Cheshire Inquiry, for example, felt that it was 'self-evident that given the existence of a road and some means of transport, there is no difficulty crossing boundaries' (Inquiry Report, Cheshire, #2.8), but this was the exception that proved the rule. Less common, but also mentioned by more than one Assistant Commissioner, was the question of newspaper circulation. In Warwickshire, for example, the Commission's provisional recommendations involved the transfer of two wards from Rugby & Kenilworth to Nuneaton, but evidence was produced to show that Nuneaton newspapers did not circulate in the two wards and the Assistant Commissioner concluded that inconvenience would result from electors being 'deprived of news of activities of their MP' (Inquiry Report, Warwickshire, #3.2).

The second element of inconvenience identified by a number of Assistant Commissioners was what might be (and often was) termed 'confusion'. Sometimes this arose in areas which had experienced a change in constituency during the Third Review. The Assistant Commissioner who conducted the Ealing Inquiry, for example (Inquiry Report, Ealing *et al.*, #3.1.15):

> felt sympathy with the view expressed by the Chairman of Pitshanger Conservatives who said that the proposal to return Pitshanger to Ealing North made her feel 'like a ping-pong ball'

while his counterpart who conducted the first Hampshire Inquiry, commenting on proposals to exchange one Southampton City ward for another (First Inquiry Report, Hampshire, #20):

> accept[ed] the force of the argument that it would be unsatisfactory to have this 'in-out' problem at every Review.

In both cases, however, other factors proved more influential. Indeed, areas which had experienced recent change were seen by some Assistant Commissioners as more suitable for disruption, not less (Inquiry Report, Newham and Tower Hamlets, #69):

> Newham South only came into existence as a Parliamentary seat in 1983 as a result
> of the last General Review. ... If any constituency has to be wholly destroyed or
> split, it does seem to me that Newham South is the obvious candidate .

Of greater significance were those situations in which identifiable communities
would be split, as the Assistant Commissioner who presided over the Buckinghamshire Inquiry pointed out (Inquiry Report, Buckinghamshire, #8.3):

> I have no hesitation in concluding that the proposal to split Aylesbury Town in the
> manner suggested would be greeted with profound dismay by the majority of the
> local electorate, for whom a lost sense of constituency "identity" would be exacerbated by a real confusion in relation to who would be their proper Parliamentary
> representative.

Where the community in question was already experiencing difficulties, the
inconvenience was seen as even more compelling, as in:

> The history of this 1970s estate has been consistent with the unhappy accounts of
> similar estates which are regularly in the news. Tackling crime and providing relief
> from the grim appearance of the estate have been the aims of the police and of many
> others who are in positions of leadership in the community. It was persuasively
> argued that the fulfilment of these already daunting tasks would be far more difficult if the community (or what is sought to be made into a community) is split in
> the manner suggested. ... I was satisfied that the suggested change if implemented
> would seriously hamper the efforts of those who now work for improvements on
> this estate. In my view such difficulties as may derive from people on the estate
> having to look to two sets of three councillors are small compared with those which
> would derive from the estate being represented by two Members of Parliament.
> (Inquiry Report, Merton, #7.6.1)

> Mr Tom Pendry MP, who has represented the Stalybridge and Hyde constituency for
> 23 years, told me that the problems of the estate, with its poor housing stock and
> high levels of youth unemployment, produce a considerable part of his workload as
> an MP and that it was the sort of area where a split between constituencies would
> cause confusion among the residents. He also told me of the great efforts which had
> been made to build up community spirit in the estate; and urged upon me that any
> disruption would be a great mistake. No-one suggested that his evidence did not paint
> the true picture and I entirely accept it. (Inquiry Report, Tameside *et al.*, #5.52)

> I was satisfied that the process of democratic integration, so important to the successful development of a multi-racial society, could itself be harmed if these two
> areas, already manifestly disadvantaged compared to the more prosperous residential areas of Bedford, were in Parliamentary terms to be put asunder. (Inquiry Report,
> Bedfordshire, #3.5)

> Of the two wards, I have no doubt that generally, Bassett is the more resilient and
> has the greater strength to deal with the inconveniences, and will in fact, be better
> placed to protect its long-standing relationship with Southampton. Coxford is not

so homogeneous, has more problems and of the two wards is the more likely to be the most adversely affected. (Second Inquiry Report, Hampshire, #14)

It is clear from these statements that a number of Assistant Commissioners were persuaded that disruptions to the existing pattern of constituencies would produce inconvenience for electors. Although the numbers were not great and the areas of concern were often limited to one or two wards, in several Inquiries these were decisive considerations. The burden of proof was not insignificant and some Assistant Commissioners reacted with scepticism, but if a convincing case could be made it was generally possible to accommodate it. The willingness of some Assistant Commissioners to distinguish between the ability of different categories of electors to withstand inconvenience also introduces the possibility of a partisan effect to the Rule's operation. In each of the four examples quoted above the Labour Party stood to gain from the Assistant Commissioner's acceptance of the argument, and while there is no simple equation between Rule 7(b) and Labour Party interest, it will generally be easier for Labour to produce witnesses willing to attest to inconvenience in such areas than it will be for other parties. This in turn raises another question. If these Assistant Commissioners were persuaded that differences between groups of electors produce variable resistance to inconvenience, were they and their colleagues also persuaded that differences of this or another kind also generate ties of differing strengths? It is to the question of local ties that we now turn.

Local ties

Local Inquiries are invariably dominated by consideration of local ties. When a Commission draws up its provisional recommendations for an area it does so largely in ignorance of local affinities. The area's theoretical entitlement is a matter of record, as are the numbers of electors and the boundaries of local government areas; even the accessibility of constituencies will be largely obvious. Objectors can suggest alternatives, but the Commission has drawn up its recommendations with full knowledge of information pertaining to Rules 1–6. Local ties are another matter. Maps can help it to avoid the worst mistakes, as can reports of previous Inquiries, but as far as Rule 7(b) is concerned there can be no substitute for local knowledge. Given that the Commission's recommendations have been drawn up without that knowledge, that aspect is inevitably vulnerable to most criticism and hence to most debate. But that is not the end of the matter. For whereas Rules 1–6 deal with what might be termed objective considerations, local ties are frequently subjective. Indeed if Inquiry transcripts are to be believed there can be few more subjective matters; time after time we read of one person's link acting as another person's barrier, which inevitably leads to yet more discussion. Many of these differences of opinion are perfectly genuine, but others are not, which brings us to the third reason for the dominance of local ties. Because they are subjective and because those deciding upon their merits generally have little or no independent knowledge, local ties offer the perfect opportunity to disguise partisan motives in statutory clothing. Local authority officers, councillors, MPs, even 'ordinary' members of the public can be encouraged, cajoled or persuaded to stress a particular interpretation of 'ties', only rarely involving dishonesty, more typically involving the application of a 'gloss' or 'spin'.

So what are the ties which are relied upon by those presenting evidence to the Inquiries? We have analysed each Inquiry report and have come up with the following list of factors cited as evidence of local ties. They are, in no particular order:

> Newspapers; magistrates courts; police stations; bus services; train services; tube services; Training and Enterprise Councils; shopping centres; public libraries; Chambers of Commerce; school catchment areas; 'local feeling'; architectural coherence; postcodes; church congregations; historical traditions; housing offices; types of employment; levels of unemployment; pensioners; housing estates; Travel to Work Areas; historical administrative boundaries; local authority administrative divisions; community associations; 'mental maps'; parish (church) boundaries; University halls of residence; telephone codes; public transport; voluntary groups; whole towns; continuity of development; shared parish councils; 'tradition'; ownership of council estates; district centres; family ties; the student population; cleansing services; hotel and restaurant facilities; housebound library service; tennis clubs; swimming baths; water authority areas; Scouts areas; Guides areas; British Legion areas; mining tradition; shipbuilding tradition; regimental recruiting patterns; 'The Arts'; dialect; local landowners; slum clearance areas; numbers of households without cars; historic battles; sports centres; cheaper telephone charges; distance from cities; ward names in business names; place names on signposts; National Park; use of beaches; fishing industry; New Forest perambulation; patterns of rehousing; golf courses; deanery boundaries; cycle ways; police divisional boundaries; Rotary club; Round Table; fire stations; cemeteries; rifle clubs; cattle markets; tax offices; landscapes; Petty Sessional Divisions; electricity and gas showrooms; the flax trade; family planning centres; Citizens Advice Bureaux; MPs' surgeries; companies which built villages; pubs; the Domesday Book; coastal erosion; motorways; visibility of cathedral spires; TV stations; Welsh language; where people 'look to'; soil surveys; rugby; river basins; EC regions; NFU areas; Development Corporations; the 1745 Rising; the Green Belt; fish houses (*sic*); city centres; sewerage; hospitals; tourism; the Orange Order.

Because this list is based on Inquiry reports it does not include all the arguments which will have been deployed. A longer list could be created by analysing each of the Inquiry transcripts, but the effect would be to place even more emphasis on the bizarre and off-beat. A better flavour of the typical representation on local ties is found by considering just one or two presentations. Almost any transcript could have been chosen, but we have selected that from the Strathclyde Inquiry for 12 May 1994. On that day the Assistant Commissioner heard evidence relating to the Scottish Commission's proposal to transfer some 11,000 electors from Ayr to the neighbouring constituency of Carrick, Cumnock & Doon Valley. Opposition to the proposal came from the Conservative Party, from Conservative-controlled Kyle & Carrick District Council, from Alloway & Doonfoot Community Council and from individuals with no declared political affiliation. The strongest objection was to the removal of Alloway (though Kyle & Carrick District Council also argued against the exclusion of nearby Holmston), and a series of witnesses gave evidence on both sides of the argument. Here we reproduce edited extracts from the statements of two of those who argued for the status quo, beginning with the Head of Planning for Kyle & Carrick District Council (Transcript of Strathclyde Inquiry, 416–24):

> The first issue I've identified as transportation ... there are four main roads out of Alloway that take traffic in a northerly direction towards Ayr ... Residents of Alloway or Holmston wishing to travel by train, whether to work or for social purposes would need to go to Ayr railway station ... The local bus services connect Alloway and Holmston with Ayr ... there used to be a tram system connecting Ayr with Alloway ... most if not all of those wishing to use a taxi will use services operating out of Ayr. Turning now to education, there is no formal nursery school provision in Alloway or Holmston. The nearest provision is in Ayr ... There is no Roman Catholic primary school in either area. These children are dependent on Ayr for their schooling ... There is no school provision for pupils with learning difficulties in Alloway or Holmston. There are two such facilities available in Ayr ... In relation to shopping there are no supermarkets or large comparison goods shops within Alloway or Holmston. Residents of both areas will do some if not most of their shopping in Ayr ... There are no banks, building societies, travel agencies, insurance offices, solicitors offices, estate agents or travel agencies based in Alloway. All such facilities are available in Ayr. Turning to industry and employment ... the residents rely if working locally to a large extent on Ayr to meet these local needs. Furthermore the local job centre is in Ayr. In relation to leisure and recreation Alloway and Holmston ... have no swimming pools, cinema or theatre. The nearest facilities are in Ayr ... Alloway area itself houses Ayr Cricket Club, Ayr Hockey Club and Ayr Rugby Club. These facilities provide the focus ... for the whole of Ayr. Alloway also contains two of the largest public parks ... these serve a much wider community than Alloway including the Ayr area. They contain not only recreational facilities, garden walkways and a pets corner but also two 18 hole golf courses. The proposed constituency boundary would divide ... both the golf courses ... In relation to housing there are few Local Authority or public sector houses in Alloway. The needs of that part of the community ... will be met from Ayr. On the other hand, Alloway contains a large number of upper market or more expensive houses ... to serve the needs of the town of Ayr. In relation to urban form ... both Holmston and Alloway are a continuation of residential uses and especially in Holmston there is no distinguishing break except the River Ayr to the north. In my view both areas form an integral part of the town of Ayr itself ... Turning to certain miscellaneous matters ... the residents of Alloway and Holmston ... are likely to use the nearest veterinary services which are in Ayr. Persons resident in Alloway or Holmston wishing to use the services of funeral directors – the same point applies there. The proposal will in fact split Ayr Cemetery.'

The second witness, Mr James Brodie, appeared on his own account (Transcript of Strathclyde Inquiry, 500–2):

I am an honest to goodness resident of Alloway, and there are very many others who live in this very highly popular and prized part of Kyle which apparently everyone wants! I've one or two very brief observations to make. They are more of a personal nature. I should like to point out that for the past 40 years I have resided in the town of Ayr. During that period I have stayed in different parts of the town ... and latterly in the Alloway area. Although each area inevitably displayed its own features and characteristics there was never any doubt in our minds that we were still resident within the town of Ayr, and it made not one whit of a difference to all the social, personal and cultural associations we have formed in the district, in the town, over the years ... [Alloway] always will be an integral part of Ayr. Virtually all organisations, associations, societies, churches embrace members from these areas ... In my opinion it would be a nonsense ... to hive off what is an integral part of a cohesive community unit and transfer it within a constituency with which there is little inter-related community rapport. This could only result in two Members of Parliament serving different areas of virtually the same community, and thus producing a mishmash of responsibility and a hotch potch of responsibility and a hotch potch too tragic to behold.

It will be clear from these extracts that the task facing Assistant Commissioners in relation to local ties is not straightforward. Neither individual makes explicit reference to any inconvenience which electors would experience from boundary changes, nor is evidence adduced to show what practical effect the breaking of ties would have. On the other hand each, in his own way, offers powerful confirmation of the community of interest which exists between Alloway and Ayr. The Assistant Commissioner who conducted the Inquiry did not recommend retention of Alloway in the Ayr constituency, but only because of the Scottish Commission's policy of using Regional Electoral Divisions as building blocks. As far as Rule 7 was concerned he was persuaded that Alloway's proper place was in the same constituency as Ayr, referring specifically to 'the local ties which, in the view of the electors from Alloway who have made representations, would be broken by the provisional recommendations' (Inquiry Report, Strathclyde, #11.27). Later in the same report he refers to the importance of 'reflecting current local ties and community of interest', an approach which he was convinced 'would enjoy a considerable measure of support' (#13.12). This interpretation of Rule 7 goes beyond what is literally required, but it is undoubtedly what most participants at the Inquiries expect. Given the dominance of such issues and in the absence of clear guidance from the Commissions,[14] it will be important to determine whether this was the typical response or whether Assistant Commissioners were divided in their approach to Rule 7.

We can begin to answer this question by looking for examples of Assistant Commissioners who adopted what might be called a literal interpretation of the breaking of local ties. Few made explicit reference to the issue, but for the Assistant Commissioner who conducted the Wolverhampton Inquiry, this was clearly the correct approach (Inquiry Report, Wolverhampton, #7.2.2):

Many if not all counter proponents appeared to be under the impression that the best way to develop or support their case was to show what local ties would be recognised and fortified by the proposed alteration, and did not see it as necessary to give close attention to whether there were ties which might be broken.

His interpretation was reflected in his assessment of the evidence placed before him (#7.2.3):

> Every area of course has local ties with its neighbours, often particularly obvious in an urban context. It did not appear to me to be of materiality that many Blakenhall residents resorted to the Penn Road shops and library, nor especially relevant that many Penn residents took or sent their children to an important school in Blakenhall ward or used its sports or other community facilities.

Several other Assistant Commissioners adopted a similar approach, as exemplified by the following comment from the report of the Berkshire Inquiry (Inquiry Report, Berkshire, #7.12):

> It may be that in the perception of Foxborough residents their ward is linked with Slough constituency, but wards on constituency boundaries do change from one constituency to another, and such changes are usually absorbed by Local Inhabitants without causing any serious or lasting damage to local ties. I have no doubt that this will be the case so far as Foxborough ward is concerned.[15]

Observations such as these were not typical, however, and several reports contain a clear indication that all local ties were of interest to their authors, not just those that would be broken. The Assistant Commissioner for Dudley and Sandwell was the most explicit (Inquiry Report, Dudley & Sandwell, #20):

> I do not think the rules should be interpreted narrowly. The phrase 'alterations of constituencies' must refer to any or all of the constituencies made on the Review, including those to neighbouring ones, so it would in my view be wrong to place undue weight on the fact that the two wards are at present not in the same seat.

Others emphasised discretion rather than the wording of the rule, but the effect was the same (Inquiry Report, Bury et al, #2.5):

> I observe that the statute directs attention specifically to the consequences of alterations though no doubt in the exercise of the Commission's general discretion as to how, subject to the statutory requirements, the area in question should be divided, all inconveniences and local ties generally can properly come into account.

For most Assistant Commissioners the point at issue was not the breaking of ties *per se*, but rather what their existence said about communities of interest. Their approach was perhaps best captured by the Assistant Commissioner who conducted the Sheffield Inquiry (#5.3):

> There was a great deal of discussion regarding local ties, and, on occasion, perhaps misapprehension of the effect that any changes to the composition of constituencies could have. Shopping habits, the choice of a doctor's surgery, or indeed, the availability of schools are generally not directly related to Parliamentary boundaries. However, the sense of belonging to a particular community is an important feature of many people's lives, and any change which is perceived to undermine those ties must be balanced by a very real need for it to occur.

Inquiry reports are full of comments from Assistant Commissioners who adopted this point of view. Not all were expressed in the same terms, but there can be little doubt that the majority of Assistant Commissioners approached the issue in a similar way:

> I was struck by the number of different groups which in their own ways pointed out that the community ties of Avondale lay with the north Kensington wards. Two points in particular struck me as compelling. First, many Golborne families were re-housed in Avondale in the 1970s, and secondly these two wards between them contain the largest Moroccan community in England. (Inquiry Report, Ealing *et al.*, #3.3.7)[16]

> The evidence in respect of Wythenshawe's development as a planned area and its struggle and ultimate achievement of a strong sense of community with ties between the wards which make it up appeared to me to be clear and compelling. Witness after witness spoke in one way or another of the local ties which existed. (Inquiry Report, Manchester & Trafford, #15)

> The Inquiry received evidence to support their close ties in all areas of the community; both young and old were at pains to show people's loyalty to Wigan wanting to be brought up in Wigan and remain living and working there and finally dying there. (Inquiry Report, Salford & Wigan, 11)

> Although it may not be uniformly felt throughout the area, I have no doubt that there is a sense of identity on the coastal strip; a sense that it is a definable area with a community of interest within the County. (Inquiry Report, Tyne & Wear, #6.3.15)

> There are areas of the city which undoubtedly have an identity (although it may be impossible to define the extent of such areas in a way that everyone would agree upon) and it is advantageous if constituencies are formed having regard to these. (Inquiry Report, Birmingham, #29)

> There are very strong ties with other villages of a similar type in the Sherwood constituency. These villages are or were mining villages and the links between them are both historical and psychological going back in particular to the sinking of the pits in the 1920s and the immigration of miners from the north of England. (Inquiry Report, Nottinghamshire, #18.4)

Most of the comments in the previous paragraph are taken from the reports of Inquiries into English Metropolitan Counties and there is no doubt that arguments relating to local ties were most vigorously argued (and accepted) in predominantly urban areas. But Assistant Commissioners still needed firm evidence of links if they were to be persuaded; merely demonstrating that two places were similar was not sufficient:

> Census data suggest social similarities and community of interest between electors of different wards. This must have some weight. But ... there is no reason why a diverse population cannot nevertheless form a true community. (Inquiry Report, Redbridge & Waltham Forest, #7.02)

> I am in no way to engage in social engineering ... nor should I, in my opinion, seek to bring together areas of, for example, high unemployment merely on the grounds of that level of employment. (Inquiry Report, Leeds, #1.5)

> I heard a good deal of evidence from professional witnesses in the Town Planning
> or associated fields. They produced voluminous material to point out similarities or,
> as the case may be, differences between wards under consideration. Similarities may
> denote 'ties', but they do not necessarily do so. I thought that the more authentic
> voices who spoke or wrote of local 'ties' and indeed of the wishes of communities,
> were the local residents, and particularly those who were demonstrably apolitical.
> To them I paid the greatest heed. (Inquiry Report, Ealing *et al.*, #1.8)

When it came to the Shire Counties, however, there was an important difference.
While there were still plenty of references to local ties, these repeatedly became
subsumed within the wider issue of town versus country. In towns and cities from
Stirling in the north to Brighton in the south, from Plymouth in the west to Ipswich
in the east, proposals or counter-proposals to include free-standing communities
within primarily urban seats met with fierce resistance. In some places, such as
Bedford, Colchester, Lincoln and York, the argument became one of doughnut versus sandwich: whether to maintain (or create) one predominantly urban and one
predominantly rural seat, or whether to divide the urban area down the middle,
attaching rural wards to each part (see Chapter 4). Although these became the
more celebrated cases, they constituted the tip of the iceberg. Over thirty battles
took place to determine the most appropriate boundary for primarily urban seats,
with community after community asserting its independence from and unwillingness to be 'taken over' by its larger neighbour. Tensions were heightened by concurrent Local Government Reviews, as the text of a petition presented in evidence
at the Shropshire Inquiry demonstrates (Inquiry Report, Shropshire, #6.3.3)

> Bridgnorth and District Labour Party is recommending that Broseley should be
> moved into the Wrekin Parliamentary Boundary. This could well mean that when
> local government reorganisation is looked at next year Broseley could find itself
> becoming part of Telford with all that this entails, i.e. Poll Tax increases in the
> Region (at present) of £200, higher council house rents, higher car and insurance
> premiums and plummeting property prices. The inquiry is on December 14th. If
> you are against Broseley going into Wrekin PLEASE SIGN THIS PETITION AND
> MAKE YOUR VOICE HEARD BEFORE IT IS TOO LATE.

The Assistant Commissioner who conducted the Avon Inquiry was not alone in
noting the connection (Inquiry Report, Avon, #5):

> I gained the distinct impression that a number of individuals and organisations were
> looking at the Commission's proposals more in terms of local government bound-
> aries and issues instead of in terms of the best practicable arrangements for Parlia-
> mentary constituencies within the rules.

In many cases the battle assumed partisan overtones with the Labour Party frequently
on the side of those wanting to keep town and country apart (thereby improving their
chances in the urban seats) and the Conservatives arguing for fusion. (As with most
of these issues, however, there was no simple relationship, and in Shropshire the
Labour Party was hoping to create two winnable seats based on Telford which necessitated the inclusion of a number of outlying wards including Broseley.) This cre-

ated particular difficulties for the Tories who repeatedly found themselves at log-gerheads with their own supporters; indeed Rob Hayward identified the tensions between town and country, exacerbated by the prospect of local government reorganisation, as one of the major factors undermining Conservative efforts during the Fourth Review. However, it would be wrong to view this solely as a party political battle. It is certainly the case that the political parties harnessed these tensions when it suited them but, as discussed in Chapter 6, this was the issue above all others where the voice of the politically unattached (if not always disinterested) was at its most convincing.

So how did Assistant Commissioners respond? A few were unimpressed. The Assistant Commissioner who conducted the Kent Inquiry dismissed the Labour Party's counter-proposal for Gravesham because it 'distinguishes avowedly between the representation of rural and urban areas' (Inquiry Report, Kent, #22). In adopting this viewpoint he could justifiably cite the English Commission's briefing that there should be no attempt 'to differentiate between the representation of rural and urban areas', but few of his colleagues appear to have adopted this interpretation as the following statements testify:

> The electors in a rural area have a general community of interest which is less likely to be shared with those whose main focus of attention is concentrated on urban problems. (Inquiry Report, Bedfordshire, #5.3)

> Ideally one would prefer to see one MP representing a rural area and vice versa. (First Inquiry Report, Devon, 45)

> A charming village such as Hurworth has, in my view, little in common with the urban character of Darlington, and much in common with the other rural wards. (Inquiry Report, Durham, #25)

> Blackpool is a distinct urban area and its residents have little community of interest or links with the essentially rural wards of the Fylde. (Inquiry Report, Lancashire, #12.5)

> Country dwellers will naturally use City services and seek work there, especially now that services and employment opportunities are increasingly centralised. This does not make them City dwellers or mean that their electoral identity should be merged with that of the City. (Inquiry Report, Norfolk, #4.4)

> It makes sense to have purely coastal constituencies. Shoreham, Worthing, Little-hampton, Bognor and the small places between them have more in common with each other, I find, than they have with the rural hinterland. (Inquiry Report, West Sussex, #12)

We are now in a position to draw some conclusions regarding the significance of Rule 7 in the light of the four tests identified at the beginning of this section. The overall weight of evidence is clear. Assistant Commissioners generally accepted that minimisation of change was important, though few attempted to quantify it. Those seeking to persuade them of the benefit of maintaining existing configurations stood a far greater chance of success than those who began with a 'clean slate'. Relatively little evidence of inconvenience was presented, whether that related to accessibility or to confusion. When it was, however, Assistant Commissioners were ready to respond. Similarly, very few representations sought to show *how* ties would be broken by changes to constituency boundaries. This was not a significant problem for most Assistant Commissioners, who typically adopted a pragmatic approach. Responding particularly to evidence of ties amongst less affluent communities and to those in rural areas anxious to maintain independence from their urban neighbours, they showed a willingness to recognise such links provided they were compatible with the electoral arithmetic. For most practical purposes Rule 7 was interpreted as an exhortation to recognise 'communities of interest' and as such it largely dominated the Inquiries.

The Commissions' response

The Inquiry reports inevitably carry considerable weight, but a Commission does not have to accept an Assistant Commissioner's recommendations. Each report must be digested and a reasoned response prepared, summarising the issues identified at the Inquiry and explaining how the Commission intends to proceed.

England

The fullest account of the process appears in the minutes of the English Commission. From these it is clear that each Inquiry Report, together with the verbatim transcript and copies of the written representations, was sent to Commission members in advance of their meetings and detailed consideration of the Reports and recommendations took place at those meetings. The Commission's satisfaction with what they read is reflected in their final report, which notes that 'the Local Inquiries conducted on our behalf and the reports submitted to us by Assistant Commissioners were of a consistently high standard' (Boundary Commission for England, 1995a, #2.45). Few were able to match the following accolade (BCE Minutes, 1994/12, 3.44):

> The Commission agreed that the AC had produced a thorough, well reasoned, well written, and excellent report. After a lengthy discussion, they fully agreed with all his recommendations (except for one name) and with all his reasons for those recommendations.

Nevertheless of the thirty occasions on which the Minutes record comments on the standard of a report, only one was uncomplimentary: this was recorded as containing 'a number of errors which could not go uncorrected' and that 'well argued and presented counter-proposals had been rejected by the AC without any indication as to what his reasons for doing so were', leading to an overall judgement of 'very poor' (BCE Minutes, 1992/6, 4.4). This was in stark contrast to phrases such as 'comprehensive, conscientious and helpful', 'very full and well considered', 'very concise and well argued', and 'full and fair' which were typical of the Commissioners' response to what they received from the Assistant Commissioners.

It would be wrong to assume, however, that the Commission agreed with everything in the Inquiry reports, and the Commissioners expressed the view that their own reading of the representations, submissions and transcripts, which constituted a 'different approach to their predecessors', 'had a considerable influence on their decisions on ACs' recommendations, numbers of which they decided to modify or reject' (BCE Minutes, 1994/16, 4.12). Well over a third of the Commission's discussions contain references to disagreements either with the reasoning or the recommendations of Assistant Commissioners and several important strands emerge.

Potentially most serious were disagreements over interpretation of the Rules. There were several notable examples, with the two most important relating to the issue of apportionment. Early *News Releases* for Avon and the Isle of Wight failed to indicate that each County warranted an additional seat, according to the theoretical entitlements, than was being provisionally recommended; the opening paragraph for the Isle of Wight was particularly misleading, stating that the entitlement was 1.47 seats and so the island should 'therefore' continue to form one constituency. The harmonic mean issue (see p. 184) was referred to in the Assistant Commissioner's brief (BCE Minutes, 1992/2, 7.3) but no reference to it was made in the Assistant Commissioner's opening statement to the Avon Local Inquiry and the Commission 'accepted the criticism expressed ... [there] that their proposals had lacked sufficient detail as to the reasons for rejecting 11 seats' and agreed that it 'should have stated clearly that a strict application of Rule 5 required an allocation of 11 seats and should then have given a full explanation of their reasons for rejecting such an allocation' (BCE Minutes, 1992/5, 4.5). The issue reappeared when the final report was being drafted and the Deputy Chairman 're-opened the question of the justification for not allocating an extra, eleventh, seat in the county' (BCE Minutes, 1993/3, 5.1).

In response to such early criticisms, the Commission's statement of reasons for its provisional recommendations for Norfolk justified its decision to maintain the County's allocation of eight seats in some detail. It is somewhat ironic, therefore, that the report of the Assistant Commissioner responsible for the Norfolk Inquiry (#1.6-1.8) did not reflect this line, concluding that the Commission was operating a policy of rounding about the arithmetic mean and that Norfolk was not *prima facie* entitled to an additional seat. The Commission distanced itself from these remarks, with some justification (BCE Minutes, 1993/8, 5.3 and *News Release* of 8 July 1993), but the Assistant Commissioner's emphasis upon the flexibility in the rules cited in the *Foot* judgement rather than upon the concept of theoretical entitlements constituted an important substantive difference in interpretation.

This theme recurred in the City of Birmingham Inquiry report. The Commission had recommended that the City's theoretical entitlement of 10.64 be reflected in the allocation of 11 seats. The Assistant Commissioner noted, however, that by allocating ten seats rather than 11 it would be possible to reduce variations in electorates within the City and also ensure that individual constituency electorates conform more closely to the electoral quota, as required by Rule 5. The Commission was sufficiently surprised by this finding to ask 'whether a mathematical explanation of this phenomenon could be provided' (BCE Minutes, 1994/6, 2.6), but it nevertheless had little hesitation in rejecting the proposal for 10 seats and in confirming the provisional recommendations. A mathematical justification was provided at a subsequent meeting, by the OPCS observer, Mr Craig, who recommended that 'disparity should continue to be used as the main numerical guide to the suitability of constituency electorates' (BCE Minutes, 1994/8, 1.3), which sustained the Assistant Commissioner's case. But after further discussion, the Commission decided that 'the situation in the City was a quirk and ... decided not to allow it to deflect them from their normal practice' (BCE Minutes, 1994/8, 1.5); the eventual justification for the decision in the final report relies on that part of Rule 7 which states that 'it shall not be the duty of a Boundary Commission to aim at giving full effect in all circumstances to the above Rules' (Boundary Commission for England, 1995a, 119). Intriguingly, although at the meeting at which the Commission discussed the Birmingham report it decided that it was 'legitimate to look at the average electorate for the City as a whole rather than individual seats' (BCE Minutes, 1994/6, 2.7), eight days later it agreed with the Assistant Commissioner who conducted the Lambeth & Southwark Local Inquiry that 'it was necessary to look at individual seats, rather than the borough, when considering Rules 4(1)(a) and 5, as each referred to "constituency"' (BCE Minutes, 1994/8, 2.14).

The Commission's failure, even at this late stage, to defer a decision pending a more detailed consideration of the Assistant Commissioner's report (arguing that to allocate only 10 seats 'would be extremely unpopular locally, and would lead to Birmingham being under-represented in Parliament'; BCE Minutes, 1994/6, 2.7), and the willingness to rely upon arguments which would have been (and were) dismissed in other circumstances, must be considered unsatisfactory. Decisions on other Metropolitan Districts and several London Boroughs almost certainly resulted in similarly-perceived, unpopular under-representation, and the stress on the theoretical entitlement for Birmingham sits uneasily alongside its Autumn 1993 *Newsletter* statement that 'in Metropolitan areas the Commission allocate to the county and not necessarily to the borough'. In this case, it seems that well-reasoned questioning of one of the fundamental bases of the Commission's operational approach was given insufficient consideration.

There were two other occasions on which the Commission disagreed with an Assistant Commissioner over the interpretation of the Rules. On one, the Assistant Commissioner argued for a broad interpretation of Rule 7(b) to include the failure to join wards which had ties, even though those wards were already in different constituencies (and indeed in different Boroughs; Dudley and Sandwell). On the other it was suggested that possible future growth in the London Borough of Tower Hamlets was a special geographical consideration as laid down in Rule 6. Unsurprisingly the Commission was not convinced by either interpretation, though the question of growth had caused the Commission some difficulties at an earlier stage of the Review. The published reasons for the provisional recommendations in Oxfordshire included reference to the need 'to allow for the planned development in the county', despite the fact that their own booklet stated that they 'do not base their recommendations on forecast or projected electorates' (Parliamentary Boundary Commission for England, 1991, 20). This approach was challenged at the Inquiry, supported by the Assistant Commissioner, and when discussing the Inquiry Report the Commission conceded 'that they had placed too much emphasis on growth' in their published reasons (BCE Minutes,1992/5, 4.12). Although the Commission clarified its position in its Winter 1992 *Newsletter*, there was at least one further interpretation of growth which did not meet with its approval: the report on the Lancashire Inquiry referred to growth in the County's theoretical entitlement since 1991, but the Commission 'disagreed with the AC's view that in relation to the number of seats to be allocated, growth should not be disregarded' (BCE Minutes, 1994/10, 2.12).

The remaining disagreements with Assistant Commissioners took a variety of forms. In some the Commission disagreed with the assessment of evidence. For example, it noted the absence of any reference in the Coventry Inquiry report to the 'conflicting' evidence about ties in the east of the city (BCE Minutes, 1994/6, 2.31); although it agreed that four Exmoor wards should stay in Taunton, it 'did not agree that the evidence was overwhelming' (BCE Minutes, 1992/5, 3.1); and it noted that the Assistant Commissioner's conclusion that there was no opposition to the Commission's proposals for the Bessacarr area of Doncaster 'was not correct' (BCE Minutes, 1993/14, 5.41). On other occasions it disagreed with the recommendations: the suggested division of wards in Lambeth and Southwark was rejected as contrary to the Commission's 'oft stated position' (BCE Minutes, 1994/8, 2.29); the suggested transfer of two wards in Buckinghamshire was rejected because 'no one at the inquiry had suggested it' (BCE Minutes, 1994/11, 3.99); as were proposals for parts of Devon which the Commission felt 'would undoubtedly cause a storm of protest' (BCE Minutes, 1994/3, 4.6; on this occasion the Commission felt that if it accepted the advice, it would 'feel bound to hold a third inquiry ... to debate the AC's untested ideas' – 4.5). Elsewhere it disagreed with the reasoning: the City of Southampton ward of Bassett rather than nearby Coxford was transferred from Southampton Test constituency to Romsey, though not because it was 'better able to withstand the impact of its broken ties' (BCE Minutes, 1993/14, 3.7); and the suggestions that Luton's electorate was affected by under-registration and that the incidence of mortgage repossessions and the distribution of ethnic minorities provided 'a useful check on the approach which I have adopted' (Inquiry Report, Bedfordshire, #10.3) caused the Commission to observe that they 'did not wish to associate themselves with the above quoted reasons even as a useful check' (BCE Minutes, 1993/4, 6.7).

Despite these differences, it is important to reiterate the general approval with which the reports of the Assistant Commissioners were greeted. The commonest reaction of the Commission was to accept their recommendations in full; only nineteen of the seventy sets of recommendations were modified, and in seven of these the change related solely to the name of one or more constituencies. Three of the remaining cases – Birmingham, Dudley/Sandwell and Lambeth/Southwark – revolved around interpretation of the Rules or Commission policy, as already noted, leaving nine instances where the Commission's assessment of the evidence resulted in modifications to the Assistant Commissioner's recommendations (for Bexley/Greenwich, Bromley, Buckinghamshire, Devon (twice), Hertfordshire, Norfolk, Staffordshire, and West Sussex). On the whole these modifications were of a minor nature, reflecting either straightforward disagreements as to the evidence relating to local ties, or a differing assessment as to the appropriate balance between local ties and equalising electorates, with considerations of shape an occasional contributory factor. (The Commission allowed greater variations in electorates than recommended by the Assistant Commissioner in Norfolk and Staffordshire, but considered the recommended variations for West Sussex too great.) Only in Devon, where the Commission adopted a counter-proposal for major changes in the City of Plymouth despite the Assistant Commissioner's support (after the first Inquiry) for the provisional recommendations, were the differences fundamental, although the Commission did give very close consideration to counter-proposals for both West Sussex and the Spen Valley area of West Yorkshire (BCE Minutes, 1994/2, 3.4 and 1994/9, 3.88).

Wales

Each of the other Commissions also found it necessary to modify certain of their Assistant Commissioners' recommendations, though the circumstances of each were very different. In Wales the sole modification affected Powys, where the Assistant Commissioner supported a proposal to include three communities from Clwyd in the Montgomeryshire constituency. This change would have resulted in constituency boundaries which followed those of the new unitary authorities, but would have been in contravention of the requirement to follow existing County boundaries and was proposed without any consideration of the knock-on effects in Clwyd. Otherwise the Commission appears to have had no difficulty in accepting Assistant Commissioners' recommendations, all of whose reports were dealt with at the same meeting (BCW Minutes, 1994/3, 6).

Scotland

The approach of the Scottish Commission was significantly different from its English and Welsh counterparts. It too was appreciative of the work of the Assistant Commissioners, thanking them for 'the careful and constructive way in which they conducted the inquiries, and for the full and informative reports' (Boundary Commission for Scotland, 1995, 10, #20) and there was minuted agreement 'that unless there was a serious flaw in the report, the Commission should accept the recommendations made by an Assistant Commissioner' (BCS Minutes, 10 February 1994, 5). The clear impression created by reading their minutes, however, is of a Commission far readier to question Assistant Commissioners' recommendations than were its counterparts, and also of a Commission more attached to its provisional recommendations, as illustrated by the Minute noting that 'it was pleasing to note that a great deal of the Commission's initial proposals [for Strathclyde] had proved broadly acceptable' (BCS Minutes, 7 July 1994, 7). Its questioning of Assistant Commissioners' advice took two main forms: the 'reopening' of major issues which had been discussed at length at the Inquiry and which had been the subject of clear recommendations; and the unwillingness to accept an Assistant Commissioner's support for maintenance of the status quo. The Commission also rejected the advice from two Assistant Commissioners to divide a Regional Electoral Division – one in Fife and the other in Strathclyde.

There are two clear examples of the 'reopening' tendency. The first relates to the Central Region Electoral Division of Airthrey, which the Assistant Commissioner recommended be transferred from Stirling to the neighbouring constituency of Ochil. Although the Commission's own minutes described this as 'a clear recommendation which could not be seriously challenged' (BCS Minutes, 10 Febnruary 1994, 5), the Commission gave lengthy consideration to just that possibility, with notable differences of emphasis between individual members, but then accepted it. In fairness to the Commission, the Assistant Commissioner had stated that the arguments were finely balanced but this was not the case in Dumfries & Galloway for which, despite agreement that the Assistant Commissioner's report 'was well founded' (BCS Minutes, 4 November1993, 4.1) and with his conclusion that a Conservative counter-proposal was untenable, the Deputy Chairman raised the possibility of adopting the latter and it was only 'after lengthy discussion' (BCS Minutes, 4 November 1993, 4.3) that the Assistant Commissioner's recommendations were accepted. We are in no doubt that this treatment of Assistant Commissioners' recommendations marks a significant difference between the Scottish and the other Commissions.

The Scottish Commission also had important disagreements with two Assistant Commissioners regarding the weight to be placed on preservation of the status quo. In both Borders and Highland Regions the Commission proposed major changes to constituency boundaries, including alterations to Caithness & Sutherland and to the two Borders constituencies, which were not accepted by the Assistant Commissioners. In the latter case, the Assistant Commissioner's report contained a damning indictment of the Commission's provisional recommendations, including a critique of its interpretation of the Rules which found little favour with the Commission. (This is summarised in Boundary Commission for Scotland, 1995, 33–4, #29-32, where the Commission records that it 'respectfully differed from his conclusion that our proposals would be at odds with the ... opinion of the Master of the Rolls in the *Foot et al.* case ... We believe that there is a significant difference between Scotland and England which is accommodated by the Rules'.) The Commission rejected both Assistant Commissioners' support for the status quo and adopted their alternative recommendations instead. As the English Commission had shown over Birmingham, where a major question of policy was at issue an Assistant Commissioner was unable to alter a Commission's approach. (The Commission also 'queried the Assistant Commissioner's comments that it was beyond his powers to recommend an additional seat to the Highland region' – BCS Minutes, 7 July 1994, 5; the Assistant Commissioner was incorrect, but if he had offered such advice it would probably not have been favourably received – Boundary Commission for Scotland, 1995, 102, #3.)

Northern Ireland

In Northern Ireland the content of the Inquiry reports was bound to create difficulties. Only one of the five Assistant Commissioners supported the provisional recommendations in full and the Commission's proposals for Belfast and the southern seats were comprehensively rejected. Despite this rebuff, the Minutes of the meeting which received the reports reveal no hint of disappointment; as the Commission's own Report notes, 'the Assistant Commissioners had the benefit of relevant local information and opinion and the Commission were anxious to respect their views and their recommendations wherever practicable' (Boundary Commission for Northern Ireland, 1995, 16). With the minimum of delay the Commission set about producing a solution consistent with the Inquiry reports (bearing in mind that the absence of a local government template meant that each set of recommendations produced knock-on effects elsewhere) and within weeks of receipt of the final report 'the Deputy Chairman proposed that one way to give practical effect to the recommendations would be to create 18 constituencies with four in Belfast' (BCNI Minutes, 27 October 1994, 5). A month later it had come up with revised recommendations which implemented the Assistant Commissioner's recommendations for Belfast in full while at the same time honouring the spirit of the other four reports (for further details see Rossiter, Johnston and Pattie, 1998).

Post-Inquiry written representations

After considering an Assistant Commissioner's report, the Commission publishes a notice announcing either the confirmation of its provisional recommendations or the publication of modified proposals. In the former case the process of public consultation is complete and the Commission will generally not discuss that area again other than to approve the passages which are to go into the final report. In the latter, interested parties have a further opportunity to comment on the modified proposals and the Commission must consider those comments. Although the Commissions did not publish lists of representations received in response to revised and/or modified proposals, the preponderance of individuals then was even more marked, reflecting in large part high profile disputes in a small number of areas: almost 10,000 of the 23,000 representations received at this stage came from electors in Trafford objecting to the Commission's revised recommendations for their Borough, and in particular their impact on the seat held by Winston Churchill MP (which was to be abolished). It is important to stress that representations submitted at this stage have a different status from those presented earlier. On a statutory level, whereas an objection from an interested local authority or from a large enough number of interested electors is sufficient to require a first Local Inquiry, that is not the case at this stage (under Section 6, Subsection 3 of the 1986 Act). On the other hand, whereas an earlier objection would not of itself convince a Commission to alter its recommendations – an Inquiry would be held first – the opportunity now exists to persuade the Commission directly.

These considerations naturally affect the Commissions' approach. Their *News Releases* after the Inquiries placed far less emphasis on inviting further representations; indeed they offered no direct advice regarding representations submitted at this stage. The potential objector was left to draw inferences from the Commission's hope (Parliamentary Boundary Commission for England, 1991, 29, #22):

> that first inquiries will be full and complete and that only exceptionally therefore will it be necessary to hold a second inquiry to obtain more information or ascertain local opinion on aspects which were not aired previously.

The Commissions were true to their word. Second Inquiries were only held in Devon and Hampshire, in both cases because proposals which 'had not been discussed at the first Inquiry … appeared to offer alternative and possibly more acceptable solutions' (Boundary Commission for England, 1995a, #6.17). Although this was true, it was also true in a number of other areas considered by the Commissions. Despite the English Commission's statements to the contrary (as in its 'stress that the statutory deadline for submission of their report had not influenced them in their decision not to hold a second Inquiry'; BCE Minutes, 1994/20, 3.22), our reading of the evidence suggests that the incidence of second Inquiries owed more to pressures of time introduced by the *Boundary Commissions Act 1992* than to the merits of individual cases. Both of the Second Inquiries held concerned constituencies which were among the first hundred to be reviewed. The contrast with the final decision from all four Commissions, that of the Northern Ireland Commission not to hold an Inquiry into the decision to allocate an additional eighteenth seat after all of the Local Inquiries had been reported, despite its inevitable knock-on effects, is clear. (The English Commission did make provisional arrangements in 1994 to schedule a second Inquiry into the London Boroughs of Greenwich and Bexley – BCE Minutes, 1994/13, 3.64 – but when it had discussed the representations received on its modified proposals it decided not to and made them final – BCE Minutes, 1994/20, 3.22.)

Although Second Inquiries were rare, this does not mean that written representations about revised recommendations had little effect. In addition to the second Inquiries, 16 of the other 67 sets of revised recommendations published by the Commissions were subsequently modified as a direct result of written evidence, although half of these only involved names. (The recommendations for

Leicestershire and Norfolk were also modified, to reflect minor changes in local government boundaries, but in neither case did this stimulate representations.) The Commissions are relatively relaxed about modifying the names of constituencies, however, because there are no rules to be observed and there are no knock-on effects on other constituencies; local feeling is likely to be a particularly useful guide and a Commission can emphasise its consultative credentials by responding to local wishes on this issue.[17] When the Lord Lieutenant of Aberdeenshire advised the Scottish Commission that the appropriate name for one of their recommended constituencies was West Aberdeenshire & Kincardine, and not vice versa, the decision to accede to his wishes did not result in significant disagreement![18]Nevertheless there were eight areas where a Second Inquiry was not deemed necessary but in which a substantive change to constituency boundaries took place.[19] Several characteristics recur in the majority of these cases: a single ward only was involved; new evidence was produced; the revised recommendations broke particular local ties which had been preserved in the original proposals; and the response was considerable in volume with little or no division of opinion. Also, in half the cases there had been little discussion of the particular area at the Local Inquiry. No single factor nor combination of factors distinguishes these cases from the unsuccessful ones, however, and for each successful appeal it is possible to find an unsuccessful one with remarkably similar characteristics.[20] In short, we have been unable to identify a consistent approach in the Commissions' treatment of these representations.

Consistency will always prove difficult to achieve, but although the English Commission stated in the Conclusion to its report that 'consistency of treatment is a prime objective of the Commission but the nature of the task sometimes leads to results which create an appearance of inconsistency' (Boundary Commission for England, 1995a, 284, #6.6) two cases where it published modified recommendations for London Boroughs suggest that it did not always accord it the priority it deserved. In Greenwich, the Commission adopted a counter-proposal from the Borough Council to transfer a total of seven wards because 'we acknowledged that it had raised a good point not previously considered' (Boundary Commission for England, 1995a, 25), while in Southwark it agreed to transfer the ward of Bellenden because 'there was now sufficient new evidence to justify altering our recommendations' (Boundary Commission for England, 1995a, 63). The latter decision took the form of a further modified recommendation. The Assistant Commissioner's first preference was to split a ward (which the Commission rejected), failing which he accepted the boundaries of the provisionally recommended seats; the earlier revision and modification had only concerned constituency names. The most suitable arrangements of constituency boundaries in Greenwich and Southwark is obviously an open question and it may well be that the final recommendations observe Rule 7 more closely than the alternatives. However, there can be no doubt that the Commission operated a different practice in these Boroughs from that employed elsewhere. In dissenting from the majority view at the Commission meeting which approved the modifications in

Greenwich, one of the Commissioners complained of a lack of consistency, pointing out that the counter-proposal 'should have been made at the Local Inquiry' and that 'late counter-proposals in other areas had been rejected for these reasons' (BCE Minutes, 1994/15, 3.10).[21] Although there is no evidence of misgivings at the meeting which agreed to Bellenden's transfer, that decision is surely more remarkable in that the only changes on which the Commission was consulting concerned constituency names.

So what is the impact of post-Inquiry representations? Had we been writing this at the end of October 1994 we would have had no hesitation in concluding that they made little difference in the Fourth Review. A couple of Second Inquiries were triggered early on, several names had been changed and a handful of wards had been re-assigned; otherwise the Commissions had largely adhered to their revised recommendations. The changes in Greenwich and Southwark put a different complexion on matters, however. In both cases an active campaign resulted in significant changes both in terms of electors moved and in terms of political advantage (in Labour's favour). It may be coincidental that the Second Inquiries (in Devon and Hampshire) came at the start of the Review, and that Greenwich and Southwark came at the end, under the pressure to meet the new deadline set by the *Boundary Commissions Act 1992*, but we think not. But for that Act the Commissions would have faced far fewer time pressures and we suspect that they would have made greater use of second Inquiries (as suggested by the English Commission's provisional arrangements for one in Greenwich). Certainly the experience of implementing significant changes solely on the basis of written representations does not appear desirable and a return to the practice of earlier Commissions, which eschewed such an approach, would seem advisable.

Conclusions

We can now address questions raised earlier as to the significance of public consultation in British redistricting. In numeric terms the numbers of electors affected is impressive: as noted previously, one million fewer electors 'changed seats' as a result of the Inquiries and almost as many were 'moved' to a different seat. However, these figures have to be seen in the context of others, notably a total UK electorate of over 40 million and over 4 million transferred in line with the Commissions' provisional recommendations. It is clear, in other words, that the Commissions set the agenda. Not only do the majority of their initial recommendations become final, but the way in which they are promulgated and the parameters within which they are set exert a powerful influence over those seeking to change them. Even the scope of the Inquiries themselves encourages certain types of response, notably with the pairing of London Boroughs. The Commissions have the first word and it is extremely influential.

It follows that few of those appearing at the Inquiries challenged the Commissions' overall approach. Most were aware that the best chance of success is to go along with their interpretation of Rules 1 to 6. There were challenges, on apportionment, on the significance of local government boundaries, on appropriate levels of disparity, even on the meaning of special geographical considerations. Occasionally they succeeded, but the examples are few and far between. That does not mean that the Commissions' provisional recommendations acted as a straitjacket. Most participants were aware that some of the parameters can be stretched, but only some. What it does mean, however, is that those parameters which have been least clearly defined, those relating to Rule 7, became the focus of the Inquiries.

This, in turn, has predictable consequences. The thrust of Rule 7, as confirmed by its origins, is that change should be minimised, but its wording is unhelpful. Taken literally it demands evidence of inconvenience or of the breaking of ties which would result from a proposed alteration to constituency boundaries. Neither is tangible and neither, by definition, can be shown to have happened already. Unable to provide suitable proof, those appearing at the Inquiries have largely re-interpreted it, downplaying the convenience element and stressing all manner of links between neighbouring areas, very few of which would be in the slightest affected by changes to constituency boundaries. In the absence of any clear expression of the role of public opinion in the redistricting process, Rule 7 has in some senses come to embody it, either by explicit reference to 'what people want' or, by inference, from discussions of patterns of association. Its use is generally consistent with minimum disruption – after all (and ironically) there is very little evidence of dissatisfaction with constituencies once they have been established – but specific statutory justification is lacking.

This places Assistant Commissioners in a predicament. As lawyers one might expect them to reject much of the evidence placed before them as irrelevant. By and large they do not. Rather they adopt what most of them would be happy to characterise as a 'commonsense' approach, acceding to local requests whenever possible. In this respect it is important to understand how most, if not all, Assistant Commissioners view their task. Typically, appointment is considered both an honour and a challenge. Most are unfamiliar with the area and the process of 'discovering' it and (some of) its inhabitants frequently produces an empathetic response. In the circumstances most are anxious to do what they can to satisfy the wishes expressed at the Inquiry which is, after all, both public and local. In the absence of specific advice to the contrary, and with briefing which encourages them to take account of local affinities, the average Assistant Commissioner simply uses his discretion and responds as best he can within those parameters which *have* been laid down by the Commission.

If, as we have argued, Assistant Commissioners respond to the weight of evidence relating to 'communities of interest', what implications does that have for the process? Because such matters are subjective and because only an infinitesimal proportion of the electorate participates in the Local Inquiries, we are in no doubt that it lays the Inquiry process open to manipulation. This is not a novel suggestion. Political parties, local authorities, Commissioners and Assistant Commissioners are all well aware that partisan self-interest is behind the majority of evidence produced at Local Inquiries. For most Assistant Commissioners, however, this was not a matter of concern. In our interviews we were told repeatedly that just because an argument was inspired by partisan motives that didn't make it a bad argument. As far as it goes, that analysis is clearly correct. The difficulty comes when the other side of the argument is not presented or is presented less effectively. If one party is better organised than another, better for whatever reason at enlisting support, the balance is affected. And because Assistant Commissioners have no local knowledge of their own (in England at least) they have no independent evidence base.

The analysis of partisan advantage which we present in Chapter 8 supports this thesis, but we also have the evidence of our interviews. Several Assistant Commissioners were prepared to accept that they had probably been hoodwinked by the parties and several others were unsure. But perhaps the most persuasive evidence came from an Assistant Commissioner who 'got it right'. At one Inquiry in the north of England, debate focused on the most appropriate destination of a dozen wards, a relatively modest Inquiry by most standards. In order to remedy an imbalance in electorates, the English Commission had provisionally recommended the transfer of one ward between neighbouring seats, but a counter-proposal from a political party advocated an alternative arrangement which would have resulted in two wards being included within the same constituency. At the Inquiry the Assistant Commissioner was presented with persuasive evidence of the links which existed between the two wards, evidence which was sufficient to convince him to accept the counter-proposal subject to his site visit. When he paid that visit, however, he found that 'one was a bijou Barratt estate, the other was an area where every door had its own CRO number. And there was no physical link between them!': as a result he changed his mind.

In one sense this is reassuring, but when one considers that a significant number of Assistant Commissioners paid no site visit, that several told us that they were reluctant to overlook the evidence of witnesses on the basis of their own cursory inspection, and that few will have been able to visit all the areas at issue, it is clear that the scope for manipulation is significant. These fears are heightened by subsequent comments made by the same Assistant Commissioner when asked how he assessed the reliability of the evidence about local ties:

> In the end you could generally tell. There are usually a few little facts that come out. You get a real flavour by hearing lots of people talking about their territory – that's the value of an oral Inquiry. I made it clear, I hope, in my opening remarks that I was aware of hidden agendas. Basically I ignored the subtext – the reason doesn't disqualify the argument.

This book does not seek to prescribe remedies for the faults of the existing system, even less does it seek to question the judgement of those appointed to implement it. But it can highlight areas of concern and we finish this chapter by observing that without a routine arithmetic interpretation of the volume of change and without a far stricter interpretation of inconvenience and the breaking of local ties, the process of Local Inquiries will remain open to hijack by those with partisan motives.

Notes

1 The electors who 'move' from an existing seat are those who are not on the register in the existing seat's 'successor', defined as the new seat which contains the largest number of the existing seat's electors.

2 As previously noted the accuracy of the electoral register became an issue at most of these Inquiries. While acknowledging the basis for these concerns, the Commission adopted a firm line, pointing out 'that in determining the number of seats to recommend for the area, they are bound by the statutory definition of electorates and do not have the power to substitute any other criterion' (*Newsletter*, July 1993, reproduced in Boundary Commission for England, 1995b, 123–4), guidance which all Assistant Commissioners were happy to follow.

3 The background to the latter is discussed in Chapter 6 and in Boundary Commission for England (1995a, 219–20). Warwick and Leamington Constituency Labour Party made a written representation arguing for an extra seat in Warwickshire, but, intriguingly, this was withdrawn by letter on the eve of the inquiry (Inquiry Report, #1.8). Whether the parties, and in particular the Conservatives who held 23 of the 34 seats in these counties, were correct in their assessment is an interesting question.

4 The Commission dissociated itself from the Assistant Commissioner's remarks about entitlements (see p. 317). As was the case in Avon the theoretical entitlement continued to grow and by 1997 had reached 8.60.

5 Although a Liberal Democrat councillor in the London Borough of Brent (TE 2.47) argued for the Borough having just two seats the local authority, MPs and the other political parties had no wish to encourage this debate. The only other case we can find of a party arguing for reduced representation also came from the Liberal Democrats, whose representatives at the Tyne & Wear Local Inquiry (TE 12.66) proposed just twelve seats for the County, five to the north of the Tyne and seven to the south.

6 The four conditions were that: '(a) any such proposals would need to deal with the whole of the combined area and any other area affected by the proposals; (b) the Commission would need to be convinced that the disruption caused would be outweighed by the advantages gained; (c) any proposals which included crossing the boundaries between London Boroughs, other than those paired by the Commission, would need to be argued at all the relevant Local Inquiries; and (d) any such counter-proposal would carry less weight if all interested parties on both sides of the London Borough boundary had not been notified of the counter-proposal by its author before the Local Inquiries'.

7 It is interesting to note that whereas he accepted a submission that crossing London borough boundaries was no more significant than crossing the boundary between Kingston and Surrey (Inquiry Report, Kingston and Surrey, #F3), his counterpart who conducted the Surrey inquiry stated that he considered the former to be 'less of a breach of rule 4' (Inquiry Report, Kingston and Surrey, 13). This was not the only example of a differences in interpretation affecting London boroughs. The Assistant

Commissioner for Bexley and Greenwich was of the opinion that 'once one overlapping seat has been created ... there is then reasonable equality in the size of the seats, and rule 5 does not therefore sanction the creation of a second overlapping seat' (Inquiry Report, Bexley and Greenwich #20) whereas the Assistant Commissioner for Redbridge and Waltham Forest considered the creation of two cross-border seats 'inevitable ... if proper account is taken of the local ties in the area' (Inquiry Report, Redbridge and Waltham Forest, #9.03). In adopting the latter's recommendations the Commission took care to point out that it relied upon 'the further discretion given to us by Rule 7' (Boundary Commission for England, 1995a, 72).

8 The Boundary Commission for England (1995a, 285, #6.15) stressed that although District boundaries are not mentioned in the rules 'we have tried to achieve coterminous boundaries to recognise local convenience and ties. It has frequently not been possible'.

9 Indeed in its Report the Scottish Commission felt moved to recommend that 'some consideration should be given to reviewing the statutory basis on which the LGBCS [Local Government Boundary Commission for Scotland] carries out this part of its remit so that the Commission may make recommendations which include a greater sensitivity to local community considerations, at a marginal cost to parity of electorate' (Boundary Commission for Scotland, 1995, 15).

10 The same Assistant Commissioner was also strongly opposed to attempts to justify smaller electorates in urban seats because of alleged under-registration: 'It was suggested to me that in consequence of a desire to avoid (or, maybe, evade) liability to Community Charge or "Poll Tax" potential electors had failed to include their names on the electoral register. In my judgement, no credible evidence was presented to me to support the proposition in the case of East Sussex. However, even if evidence had been available I do not consider that I can go behind the clear words of the definition of the "electorate". If individuals, whether deliberately or by ignorance or oversight, have failed to have their names included in the electoral register it is not for me or for the Commission to provide a remedy. I have, therefore, not allowed such arguments to influence my judgment.' (Inquiry Report, East Sussex, #2.3). While few others used such trenchant language, the approach was universal.

11 The English Commission, in its Spring 1993 *Newsletter*, reiterated its view as to the limited applicability of Rule 6 while confirming that it does take into consideration 'the effect of geographical features which have influenced the location of settlements, their subsequent development or demise, and the building of routes of communication'.

12 The number of electors moved between constituencies seems a reasonable measure of 'minimising disturbance', which is the shorthand reference to Rule 7 frequently employed by the Commissions.

13 The Boundary Commission for England (1995a, 10, #2.41) stresses that the rule 'relates to the breaking of ties by new proposals rather than the restoration of ties allegedly broken on a previous occasion'.

14 Though those with keen eyes may have noticed reference in the English Commission's Winter 1992 *Newsletter* to school catchment areas and travel to work areas as factors which 'may influence choices between various possible schemes which comply with the rules' (Boundary Commission for England, 1995b, 120).

15 This issue was reopened in 1998 when the commission conducted an interim review. The boundaries between Berkshire, Buckinghamshire and Surrey were altered on 1 April 1995, and provisionally recommended consequential changes to constituency

boundaries to make the two sets coincident involved moving 1,149 electors from the Beaconsfield constituency (in Buckinghamshire) to Windsor (in Berkshire), which would also receive 1,350 electors from Spelthorne (Surrey). The areas being added to Berkshire were creating a new ward of Colnbrook and Poyle in the Unitary Authority of Slough (which took effect from 1 April 1998), but the Commission argued in its *News Release* (dated 18 February 1998) that it would not be possible to include the new ward in the Slough Parliamentary constituency (although 'there may be some merit in creating a constituency that would be coterminous with the new unitary authority of Slough') because this could only be achieved if the Foxborough ward was moved from Windsor to Slough (otherwise the new constituency would not have had an exclave). This, the Commission felt, 'would be more than the minimum required to being the constituency boundaries back into alignment with altered local government boundaries and that such a change would create an unacceptable disparity between the adjoining constituencies of Slough and Windsor, which would be best considered at a general review'. (The provisionally recommended electorate for Windsor was 72,549. Without both the new ward and Foxborough, it would be approximately 65,000. Slough's electorate was 69,000 in 1994 and so would rise to c. 76,500.)

16 References to the need to keep ethnic minority areas intact occurred at around a dozen Inquiries though, as the Assistant Commissioner who conducted the Birmingham Inquiry pointed out, 'whether it is right to create constituencies on the basis of the ethnic make-up of the population is a matter on which different views can be held' (Inquiry Report, Birmingham, #53). These remarks about the Moroccan community were criticised in subsequent written representations because Moroccan nationals are not eligible to vote in British elections (Boundary Commission for England, 1995a, 46–47).

17 Mortimore (1992, 164-7) has a section on names, which he claims 'despite its triviality, has always been a contentious part of the boundary drawing process'. In 1885, discussion of constituency names was 'the lengthiest portion of an eighteen night debate in committee and no small part of the subsequent report stage'. Now that Local Inquiries are held in most areas, however, Mortimore considers that 'there is at least adequate opportunity for the Commissioners to be warned which are the sillier of their proposals before they publish their final report'.

18 Changes to constituency names were very rarely contested at the Local Inquiries, and most were made on the basis of written representations. One of the few exceptions referred to Corby, which the Conservatives wanted renamed as Rockingham Forest.

19 They refereed to: the town of Alness in the Highland Region; the wards of Willingdon in East Sussex, Moulsham Lodge in Essex, Ulceby in South Humberside, Bellenden in Lambeth, and Bramley in Surrey; several rural wards near the towns of Bourne and Sleaford in Lincolnshire; and several wards in the London Boroughs of Bexley and Greenwich.

20 For example, the Commission refused to transfer Charterlands ward (electorate 1,515) from South West Devon to Totnes, despite a petition containing 1,323 signatures, because it would have increased the range of electorates in Devon from 11,073 to 12,588 (BCE Minutes, 1994/13, 1.5, 1.6, 1.13); yet on the basis of fewer than three dozen representations it agreed to transfer Bramley ward (electorate 2,531) from South West Surrey to Guildford, increasing that county's disparity from 11,203 to 12,075 Boundary Commission for England, 1995a, 269–70).

21 The associated decision to publish modified recommendations for the neighbouring constituencies of Bexleyheath & Crayford and Erith & Thamesmead 'in order to have the benefit of further representations before deciding on their final recommendations, but contrary to the Commissioners' initial views' (BCE Minutes, 1994/15, 3.19-20) also suggests inconsistency.

8

Electoral consequences

In a first-past-the-post electoral system, the outcome of an election depends not just on the numbers of vote cast, but also on the relationship between votes and seats (Taagepera and Shugart, 1989; Farrell, 1997). In the two-party politics (Conservative and Labour) of the 1950s and 1960s, British election results followed the so-called 'cube law'. This described the tendency of the first-past-the-post system to 'exaggerate' the majority, in Parliamentary seats, of the party with the largest share of the vote: the ratio of seats won by the most popular party to seats won by the second party was equal to the ratio of the cubes of the two-party vote won by each party.[1] Winners got more seats than they were 'entitled' to on a proportional basis, and losers get fewer. Since about 1970, partisan dealignment and growing support for other parties (primarily the Liberals in the 1970s, the Alliance in the 1980s, and the Liberal Democrats in the 1990s, but also the Scottish and Welsh Nationalists) weakened the exaggerating effects for the two major parties, turning the cube law for the joint Conservative and Labour share of votes and seats into first a 'square law' and subsequently rough proportionality (in terms of the two-party shares of votes and seats) between them (Johnston, Pattie and Fieldhouse, 1994; Curtice, 1995).

The system continues to discriminate heavily against smaller parties, most dramatically at the 1983 election when the Liberal-SDP Alliance ran Labour a very close race for second place in terms of the vote (getting 25.4 per cent to Labour's 27.6 per cent), but fell far short in terms of seats won (23 to Labour's 209). Arguably, that failure to make a 'breakthrough' in terms of its Parliamentary representation in 1983 (and hence to challenge Labour for the position of official opposition) contributed to the Alliance's decline (Crewe and King, 1995). The reason for this inequity in electoral outcome lies, in large part, in the link between the geography of party support and the geography of Parliamentary constituencies (Johnston, 1985; Johnston, Pattie and Allsopp, 1988). The Alliance vote was spread fairly evenly throughout the country, gaining between 20 and 30 per cent of the vote in most constituencies. However, that is rarely enough to win a seat in a winner-takes-all contest. The geography of Labour support, by contrast, was very uneven. In some areas, the party did very badly indeed (Labour lost its deposit in 119 seats in 1983, more than at any previous election contested by the party since 1918; Butler and Butler, 1994). In others (primarily in the inner cities and the old industrial areas of the north), it did extremely well, winning by large majorities. The concentration of Labour support in particular areas meant the party had a large reserve of rock solid safe seats it could rely on winning, even in its worst years. But for the Alliance parties, their reasonable performance in most places left them short of sufficient votes to win in more than a few specific places.

Furthermore, the precise definition of the boundaries of a constituency can affect which party will win there. The inclusion or exclusion of a Labour-voting ward, for instance, might make the difference between a constituency being safe or marginal for that party. Twice since 1945 this has had consequences not only for individual seats but also for the outcome of the entire election. In the 1951 election, Labour won the largest share of the vote (48.8 per cent, compared to the Conservatives' 48.0 per cent) but the vagaries of the election system meant that the Conservatives' vote was spread more efficiently, and they had a comfortable majority of seats in Parliament (321 to Labour's 295), winning the election despite (just) losing the vote. The tables were reversed at the February 1974 election: Labour emerged as the largest single party with 301 seats to the Conservatives' 297, even though Labour's share of the vote (38.0 per cent) was smaller than the Conservatives' (38.8 per cent).

Not surprisingly, therefore, each political party has a vested interest in trying to ensure that, when constituencies are changed, the new boundaries benefit it and disadvantage its opponents as much as possible. As we saw in Chapters 6–7, the political parties try to influence the outcome of the boundary review process, but what are the electoral consequences of a review?

Partisan redistricting and gerrymandering

In order to advance their own careers, professional politicians need to be sure of their election and subsequent re-election to Parliament. Standing in a safe seat is better, clearly, than in a marginal. But few, if any, politicians enter Parliament solely to become MPs: most, perhaps all, also believe in and want to advance the ideology and policies of their party. The only real way of achieving that (especially in an adversarial political system such as Britain's) is for their party to win sufficient seats to form the government.

In large part, that is achieved through the normal electoral process. Parties put their cases to the electorate through their campaigns, in the hope of: mobilising their committed supporters to turn out and vote for the party in large numbers; winning over uncommitted floating voters; persuading supporters of other parties to defect; and gaining votes from those who had either previously abstained or been unqualified to vote. But simply winning the largest number of votes does not necessarily guarantee that a party will form the government, especially in very close electoral competitions. In such circumstances, the precise definition of Parliamentary constituencies can mean the difference between victory and defeat, both for individual candidates and for parties. Parties have an interest, therefore, in trying to affect the redistricting process.

Where parties are able to influence constituency boundaries directly, there is a risk that gerrymandering will take place. Successful gerrymandering requires two things. First, political parties need some say in redistricting. Classic gerrymanders take place in systems where redistricting is highly politicised and (especially) the government (and hence the governing party) has full control over the allocation of seats. The greater the degree of non-partisanship in redistricting, the more difficult it is for the parties to engineer successful gerrymanders.

Second, deliberate gerrymandering requires detailed local knowledge of the electoral geography of an area, at a more intimate scale than that of the Parliamentary constituency. There are many different ways of amalgamating localities into seats, and each will have somewhat different electoral consequences (an example of the modifiable area unit problem; see Openshaw and Taylor, 1979; Openshaw, 1984). Consider the following hypothetical example. A Parliamentary constituency comprises nine local government wards and each has the same electorate (Figure 8.1a). Party A wins all the votes in five of the local government wards (clustered in the north and west of the constituency) while party B wins all the votes in four wards in the south and east. Because of population growth, the constituency needs to be split into three new ones with equal sized electorates, so each of the new constituencies should comprise three contiguous local government wards. This can be achieved in ten different ways: we look at two here. Solution 1 employs a simple division of the constituency into three new seats running north-south (Figure 8.1b). Solution 2 is slightly more complex, with one north-south oriented seat, and two east-west seats (Figure 8.1c). Both solutions meet the basic requirement: they both create three new, equally-sized seats out of the original one. There is little to choose between them in terms of the rules under which the redistricting has taken place.[2] The partisan effects are quite different, however. Under Solution 1, Party A (the largest in the area, with 55.6 per cent of the votes cast) wins two out of the three new seats. However, Solution 2 effectively pens a large proportion of Party A's voters into just one new seat, in the north-west: Party A wins that seat outright. However, the other two wards supporting Party A are each placed in a different new seat, neither of which now contains enough Party A voters to elect an MP from that party. Party B now commands a majority of votes in these two new seats, therefore, and manages to win two out of the three new constituencies despite having only 44.4 per cent of the local vote.

To take a more concrete example, at the time of Britain's Fourth Periodic Review the City of Sheffield contained 29 local government wards and was entitled to six Parliamentary seats. There was a very large number of possible combinations of the 29 wards into six seats. Even applying reasonable constraints (that only adjoining wards could be in the same seat, and that the electorate in each seat should be

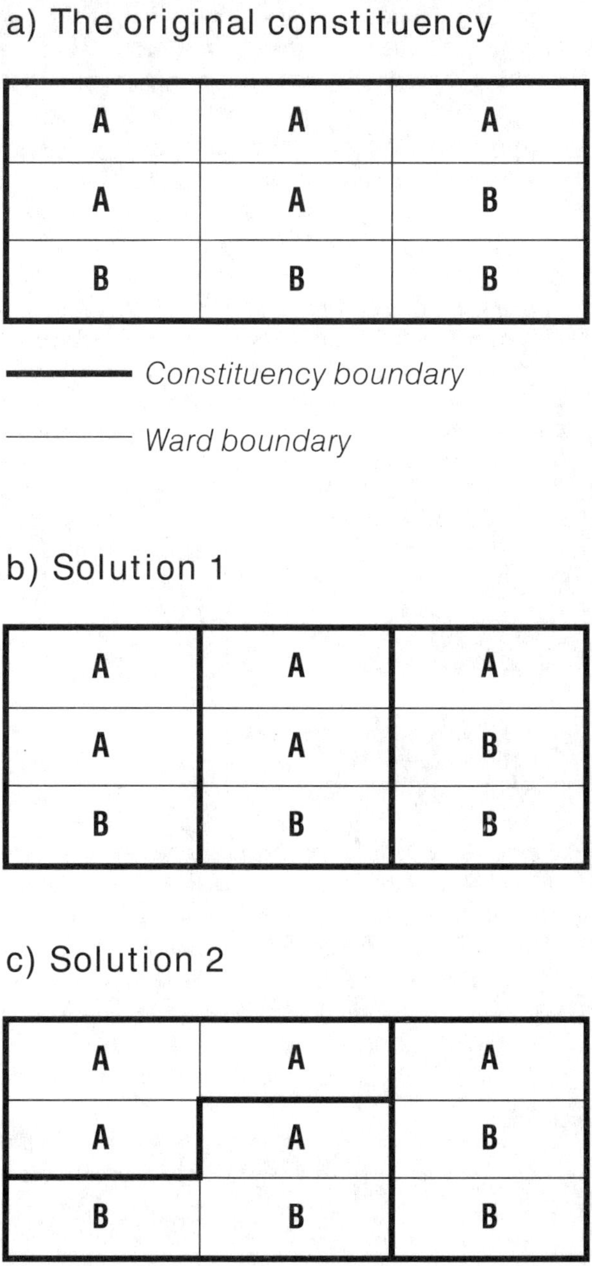

a) The original constituency

A	A	A
A	A	B
B	B	B

──────── Constituency boundary

──────── Ward boundary

b) Solution 1

A	A	A
A	A	B
B	B	B

c) Solution 2

A	A	A
A	A	B
B	B	B

Figure 8.1 *A hypothetical example of the partisan impacts of redrawing constituency boundaries.*

no more than 8 per cent away from the average electorate), there were still 1,515 different ways of arriving at Sheffield's Parliamentary entitlement (Johnston, Pattie and Rossiter, 1992, 1074).[3] Furthermore, using estimates from 1992 local election results for each ward, if people voted in the same way at a Parliamentary election as they did at that recent local government contest, there could be substantial differences in the outcome of Parliamentary elections, depending on which set of six constituencies was adopted (Table 8.1); there were, for example, 64 ways of drawing the boundaries to give the Conservatives one constituency, Labour three and the Liberal Democrats two. (At the 1992 election, Labour won five of the six Sheffield seats, the Conservatives won one, and the Liberal Democrats none; five years later, Labour again won five, with the other going to the Liberal Democrats.)

Table 8.1 *Simulating the electoral implications of the Fourth Periodic Review –* *Sheffield, 1992: the number of solutions to the constituency-drawing process by the* *number of seats likely to be won by each party*

Distribution of Seats			
Conservative	*Labour*	*Liberal Democrat*	*Number of solutions*
1	3	2	64
2	3	1	376
0	4	2	14
1	4	1	1,054
0	5	1	7

Source: Johnston, Pattie and Rossiter, 1992, 1074

Gerrymandering is not simply about parties trying to create as many safe seats for themselves as possible. There are wider tactical issues. First-past-the-post elections tend to 'waste' votes in two ways. Where a party loses, every vote for it is 'wasted' since none played a part in electing an MP. But equally, where a party wins, every vote in excess of the minimum required for a majority is wasted too, since they were surplus to requirement. The secret of a good gerrymandering strategy, therefore, is to waste as few of one's own votes as possible (while still ensuring that one's own seats do not become too marginal for comfort), while also wasting as many of ones opponent's votes as possible. The strategy for minimising the wastage of one's own votes is obvious: try to draw the boundaries to bring areas with more of one's own supporters into marginal seats. Removing areas containing as many as possible of one's opponents' supporters from marginals also helps. Ironically, maximising the wastage of one's opponents' votes can also be done very effectively by ensuring that one's opponents are bound to win a few very safe seats, but by huge majorities. This can be achieved by drawing the boundaries of the seats in question so as to capture as many of one's opponents supporters as possible (a 'packed' gerrymander: this is the strategy followed by Party B to win two out of three seats in Figure 8.1c above).

Partisan redistricting in Britain

Gerrymandering was part of the political scene in nineteenth century Britain (see Chapter 2). But it has been much harder in the second half of the twentieth century for British parties to guarantee the partisan outcomes of redistricting. Neither the political parties nor the government plays a key part in the formal process of redistricting: the job is left to the Boundary Commissions and to the neutral civil servants who staff their Secretariats. The Boundary Commissions are scrupulously impartial in their deliberations, and pay no attention whatever to the political consequences of their decisions. (To do so would not only go beyond their legal powers but would also deeply undermine both the civil service's tradition of impartiality and trust in the fairness of the process.) Furthermore, Parliament is unable to alter the final recommendations made by the Commissions: they must be accepted or rejected wholesale by MPs. (The Government, however, in the shape of the relevant Secretary of State, can make alterations, a power which Home Secretary James Callaghan tried to exercise in 1969; see Chapter 3.)

British boundary reviews are not impartial, however, and have partisan effects which arise from two main sources. First there are 'unintended partisan effects': no set of electoral boundaries, no matter how impartially arrived at, is neutral in its political effects. Second, there are 'intended partisan effects'. While the parties play no formal role in the review process, they, like any citizen or group, have the right to make representations to the Commissions and can put their case at Local Inquiries (see Chapter 7). If they make their case well, they can win revisions in the Commissions' recommendations.

Unintended partisan effects

Unintended partisan effects can be specific to particular areas. The Periodic Reviews are often accompanied by discussions about the relative merits of 'doughnuts' and 'sandwiches' (see Chapter 4). By and large, towns and inner urban areas tend to favour Labour whereas rural areas and suburbs tend to be Conservative, so that a 'doughnut' can create a safe Labour seat in the 'hole', surrounded by safe Conservative territory in the 'dough' whereas 'sandwiches' are more likely to create politically more mixed constituencies: the balance of power would depend upon the relative contributions of the different areas to the new seats. In the 1980s, the Carlisle and Penrith and the Borders constituencies made a classic 'doughnut', with the compact, industrial, urban and Labour-voting Carlisle seat entirely surrounded by the much larger, rural, and Conservative Penrith and the Borders (the Fourth Review 'breached' the doughnut, but the seats still come very close to the 'ideal'). Norwich, meanwhile, divided into Norwich North and Norwich South, is close to an archetypal 'sandwich'.

On a more general scale, and arguably more important in terms of the overall outcome of elections, is the partisan effect of population change within Britain. Throughout the twentieth century, suburbanisation (and, since the 1960s, counterurbanisation, as more people quit the cities altogether; Champion, 1989) resulted in population decline in the major cities. Furthermore, inter-regional migration has meant that while populations have declined in many parts of northern Britain (especially in the older industrial areas), they have grown in the south-east. Both processes have implications for electoral redistricting, since they create pressure to reduce the number in areas suffering population decline, and to increase the number of seats in growth areas. Failure to do so would mean growing disparities in electorates, with voters in inner city and northern urban areas becoming over-represented in Parliament, relative to suburbanites and southerners.

The law governing constituency reviews effectively prevents reductions in the numbers of Scottish, Welsh and Northern Irish MPs, even though all three experienced slower population growth than England throughout much of the twentieth century. Indeed, albeit for somewhat different reasons, each of these countries has seen its Parliamentary representation increase somewhat over the post-war period (Chapter 4). The impact of population migration is felt most keenly, therefore, in England. The number of seats in southern regions of England (especially in the south east) has grown at each Review while the number in the north of the country has declined relatively (Table 4.15). At any single Review, these inter-regional changes in the numbers of seats are relatively small for a particular region but over longer time periods the cumulative effect can be substantial: in 1945, the South East region (excluding Greater London) returned 53 MPs; in 1997, it returned 83, for example, whereas the equivalent figures for the North West of England were 88 in 1945 and 76 in 1997.

The unintended partisan consequences of population change are broadly predictable. The areas experiencing population growth – the suburbs, rural areas, and the south east – tend to be predominantly Conservative-voting, and the declining areas tend to be Labour-supporting. More seats in the south will mean more Conservative MPs, *ceteris paribus*, and fewer seats in the north will mean fewer Labour MPs. Furthermore, since Labour's inner-city strongholds are in general losing population, there is pressure on the Boundary Commissions to reduce the number of inner urban seats, and, to some extent, to amalgamate them with more suburban areas, threatening Labour's majorities. A likely outcome of any redistricting exercise, therefore, is more Conservative and fewer Labour seats (see below for estimates of the size of that partisan advantage at the Third and Fourth Reviews). Equally, the more time that passes between a Review and an election, the greater the unintended partisan advantage for Labour, as its (declining) strongholds retain more representation than they are entitled to. Elections fought in old constituencies, therefore, give Labour an advantage, whereas those fought in new seats tend to favour the Conservatives (if anything, they redress the balance).

The electoral registers listing all eligible voters living in each constituency form the basis for the Commissions' decisions. But the registers themselves also produce some unintended partisan biases. Since reviews take place on old electoral registers (even the most recent register is several months out of date, given the time-lag between collation and publication), areas with rapidly growing populations (and hence normally Conservative areas) are always at something of a disadvantage relative to declining (and Labour-voting) areas. At the same time, however, there is evidence of sizeable under-registration in some areas, especially after the early 1990s as some (especially younger and poorer) people in inner-city areas tried to avoid a new local government tax by not registering their votes (Smith, 1993; Butler, Adonis and Travers, 1994; Smith and McLean, 1994; Pattie, Dorling, Johnston and Rossiter, 1996). To the extent that under-registration is particularly prevalent in inner-city areas, it works against Labour's interests during Boundary Reviews.

Labour, meanwhile, benefits from the protected status of Scotland and Wales. Both countries return a large majority of Labour MPs (though as recently as the 1950s this was not true of Scotland), and both are over-represented in Parliament, relative to their electorates. The 'Celtic preference' in terms of Parliamentary seats has the unintended partisan impact of boosting Labour's representation in the Commons. The size of that boost is not large: at the Fourth Review, for instance, the Celtic preference 'saved' around 13 Labour seats which would have been lost had the Commissions applied equal electorates throughout the UK (Rossiter, Johnston and Pattie, 1997c). The Celtic preference, therefore, to some extent limits the electoral damage Labour suffers as a consequence of redistricting. This is an unintended partisan outcome of the interaction between the rules, impartially applied, under which the Boundary Commissions operate, and the underlying geography of the vote.

Intended partisan effects

As a consequence of the potential for unintended partisan effects, the Conservatives tend to see boundary reviews as an opportunity, while the Labour party sees them as a threat (though as will be discussed below, the two parties' experiences of the Fourth Review may have led to a partial reappraisal). However, the partisan impacts of any given boundary revision cannot be read off automatically from a consideration of which regions gain and which lose seats. Much depends upon the precise details of where the boundaries fall. Political parties will try, therefore, to influence the eventual outcomes in some fashion. Since they have no direct control over the Boundary Commissions' deliberations, any attempt must be indirect. Five main routes are open to political parties: (1) controlling the timing of the implementation of a Review; (2) controlling the local government framework within which the Reviews take place; (3) taking part in Local Inquiries into proposed revisions during a Review; (4) influencing the number of registered electors in an area; and (5) seeking judicial review. The first two strategies are open primarily to the party which forms the national government; the others are open to all parties.

Strategy 1: Control of timing and implementation
Once the Boundary Commissions' final recommendations come before Parliament, there is no further scope for detailed changes: since 1958, Parliament must accept

or reject them *in toto* although, as noted earlier (Chapter 3), this is because of the practice adopted by Secretaries of State rather than any legislative requirement. There is, however, scope for either speeding through or for delaying implementation. The legislation concerning Reviews is weak and ambiguous on how quickly the government should act once a Commission's Final Report has been submitted. The *Parliamentary Constituencies Act 1986* stipulates a clear timetable for a Commission's submission of its Report (Clause 3.2: 'not less than ten or more than fifteen years from the date of the submission of their last report', subsequently shortened by the *Boundary Commissions Act 1992* to between eight and twelve years). No such stricture applies to the Secretary of State to whom the Report is submitted, however. The 1986 Act only requires that: '[a]s soon as may be after a Boundary Commission have submitted a report to the Secretary of State under this Act, he shall lay the report before Parliament' (Clause 3.5). Clearly, there is wide scope for interpretation over how soon 'as soon as may be' is. Labour, as the party most likely to be adversely affected by the Review process, has on two occasions sought to delay the implementation of a Review until after an upcoming election, allowing the party one more run in old seats (see Chapter 3 for details). On both occasions, in 1969 (when in government) and 1982 (when in opposition), the party feared that it would fare less well in the new seats than in the old.

The Second Review in the late 1960s was the first change in seats since 1955, and large discrepancies in constituency size had developed in the interim. Labour gained an electoral advantage from this, as many of its MPs were elected from small, declining urban constituencies. The Review was an object of concern within the party, as it would inevitably lead to fewer inner city seats (and so fewer Labour MPs): 'in England it will lose us fifteen to seventeen seats' (Crossman, 1978, 516). As the party of government at the time, Labour had something of an advantage. Through its ability to control Parliamentary business, and through the ambiguity in the governing legislation over how quickly a Report should be laid before Parliament, it had a large degree of influence over when the recommendations would be placed before Parliament. It used this power as a delaying tactic and the new boundaries were not implemented until after the 1970 General Election (Johnston, 1979, 102–4). Ironically, Labour lost the election anyway, despite the expectation that it would win.

Labour also attempted to delay the implementation of the Third Review. This time, however, the party was in opposition and so was unable to make use of the levers of government. Instead, several leading Labour members, including the then party leader, Michael Foot, took their case to the courts using the judicial review procedures discussed below (Johnston, 1983). The politicians' case (discussed in Chapter 3) was that the Commissions had failed to apply properly the statutory rules under which they work, specifically by failing to implement the 'equal electorates' rule, since large disparities existed between constituency electorates, even within the same County. Labour's claim was rejected, by both the High Court and the Court of Appeal, in time to allow the new boundaries to be adopted for use in the 1983 election.

For the Conservatives, the opposite has on occasion applied, and whereas Labour has often been concerned to slow down the process, the Conservatives have generally been keen to speed things along. The incoming Conservative government led by Edward Heath soon enacted the Second Review which Labour had delayed, for instance. The Fourth Review provides another example in which the party's expectation of an electoral benefit seems likely to have resulted in a decision to move towards rapid implementation (in the event it was an exaggerated expectation, for reasons discussed below). The *Boundary Commissions Act 1992* (discussed in more detail in Chapter 3) was introduced by the Conservative government while the Fourth Review was in progress. The Review had started in February 1991, and was originally due to be completed by January 1998. The 1992 Act shortened considerably the time available for the Commissions to do their work, requiring them to make their final reports by 31 December 1994; in the event, all but one missed the deadline. The government's stated rationale for speeding up the process was twofold. First, population movement was becoming more rapid, necessitating faster and more frequent reviews. Second, the Third Review, instituted in 1983, had been based on very dated local electorate data (1976 in England, 1978 in Scotland and Northern Ireland, 1981 in Wales). As a result, had the 1997 election been fought on the boundaries introduced by the Third Review, the seats would have been based on electorates up to twenty years old.

There was also almost certainly a political dimension to the decision, however. The Conservative government had unexpectedly been re-elected in 1992, but with a much reduced majority (down from 102 seats in 1987 to just 21 in 1992). Given the closeness of the result, the government was understandably concerned to maximise its chances of another re-election. Boundary Reviews were generally advantageous to the Conservatives, and a new Review was under way. Some initial estimates, including those made by Rob Hayward (see p. 251), suggested that, based on their 1987 election performance, the Conservatives stood to gain an extra 20 seats as a result of the Review, even if no votes changed hands. For a government with a slim majority, this held obvious attractions.

Unfortunately the next general election would have to be held by mid-1997 at the latest, several months before the Boundary Commissions were due to report. By bringing the report date forward by three years, however, the government ensured that the new boundaries would be in place by 1997 at the latest (and could potentially be in place some time before then, if the government had to go to the country earlier than anticipated). If the Review process had gone as anticipated, therefore, the Conservatives would have gained an advantage before polling had begun but, as we show below, things did not work out quite as well for the party as anticipated (see also Chapter 6).

Strategy 2: Control of the local government framework
A second strategy is to control the institutional framework within which the Review takes place. Political parties cannot directly determine the boundaries of Britain's Parliamentary seats, but government does control the local government

map. And since the rules by which the Boundary Commissions work require that they follow local authority boundaries as far as possible, there is scope for government to set some of the parameters within which the Commissions work. As we have seen, the changing local government map formed part of Labour's rationale for delaying the Second Periodical Review.

The detailed issues which arise were made clear in Richard Crossman's candid diaries of his period of office as Minister of Housing (1964–66), when local government was one of his responsibilities. He records that in 1964 he was faced with decisions whether to implement recommendations of the Local Government Boundary Commission regarding Borough boundaries. He 'realized that this is one of my most important responsibilities … as a Labour politician these are for me not merely decisions about the boundaries of *local authorities* but decisions which will influence the boundaries of *constituencies*. The reason for that is simple: constituency boundaries are drawn broadly in conformity with the boundaries of county boroughs … [so that] every time, as Minister in charge of local government boundaries, I alter a county borough boundary I may affect the fate of the MP sitting for this borough' (Crossman, 1975, 64–65). A colleague had told him that two Labour seats in Leicester would be under threat if the proposed changes were implemented, and 'I also discovered that in Coventry there were risks involved, but that I could by a minor amendment make practically sure that Coventry remains our way' (Crossman represented a Coventry constituency). He recognised that this was 'a little improper' but decided to go ahead with them, recording that they were his personal decisions, that 'not even the Prime Minister can influence me' and (Crossman, 1975, 88):

> My colleagues know this and this gives me an odd detached power in dealing with them. After all I can make or mar George Brown at Belper, Bert Bowden in Leicester, Bill Wilson in Coventry, Ted Short in Newcastle; each of them now knows that as Minister for Housing the decision I make may be life or death for them in terms of representation at Westminster.

Nearly two years later, reflecting on his time in that office, he recorded that no decision about local government boundaries was taken 'without the Parliamentary repercussions being fully considered and without my trying to shield the Labour position … All the way through I think I managed to combine a sound local government policy with an extremely shrewd defence of Labour's Parliamentary interests' (Crossman, 1975, 621).

Redrawing local government boundaries is not undertaken on a regular or even a frequent basis. It is a major and complex task in its own right and is expensive and disruptive to local services. The local government system set up in England and Wales in 1888 lasted almost unchanged until 1963, when the Greater London County was formed. The next major change, establishing the local government units within which the Third and Fourth Periodic Reviews occurred, took place in 1974. More recently, local government was again extensively reorganised in the mid-1990s, though this was not complete in time to influence the work of the Fourth Periodic Review (Johnston and Pattie, 1996b).

The local government review implemented in 1974 had partisan consequences for the Parliamentary boundary review process (Johnston, 1982). The process was begun in the 1960s by the Redcliffe-Maud and Wheatley Royal Commissions. However, the schemes eventually adopted were modified significantly by the Conservative government elected in 1970 (Dearlove, 1979; Dunleavy, 1980; Honey, 1981). Crucially, the government watered down proposals in England for major city-region authorities which would have brought large rural hinterlands into the same authorities as the main cities (as was the case in Scotland, where the new Strathclyde Region encompassed the Greater Glasgow area, Dunbartonshire, Renfrewshire, Bute, Lanarkshire, Ayrshire and Argyll). The Metropolitan Counties introduced in England were not as extensive as the city-regions proposed by the Royal Commissions.

As far as the work of the Parliamentary Boundary Commission for England was concerned, the creation of the Metropolitan Counties in 1974 created the very real potential for 'packed gerrymanders' in the big cities (Dunleavy, 1980; Johnston, 1982, 465). Because the county boundaries were in most cases drawn close to the urban boundaries (relative to the original proposals made by the Redcliffe-Maude Commission), and because Labour's vote was concentrated in the major urban areas, Labour would be almost guaranteed to win a large proportion of the Metropolitan seats, but with very large majorities. Conservative hegemony in the Shire Counties would not be threatened by the diluting effect of Labour-voting urban areas contributing to new seats.

Manipulating the local government framework is a crude strategy, however. It alters the parameters within which the Commissions work, but does not affect the detail of where constituency boundaries are drawn within each major local government area. And it is that detail which can be crucial in determining the partisan impacts of a Boundary Review. Furthermore, the districts making up the Metropolitan Counties themselves varied in terms of how closely they followed the urban areas. Some were more tightly defined around urban areas than were others. Since it was the Metropolitan Districts which the Boundary Commission for England worked with during the Third Review, there were variations in the extent to which Labour held on to seats in the main cities. In Greater Manchester, for instance, the Third Review would have resulted in Labour losing several seats to the Conservatives, largely as a result of the boundaries of Bolton Metropolitan District.

A further aspect of the local government framework which could be manipulated for electoral gain concerns the system of local election wards which form the building-blocks for the construction of Parliamentary constituencies. Wards are delineated by the relevant Local Government (Boundary) Commission, in consultation with local interests which on occasion may seek a set of wards which favour their Parliamentary as well as local interests. An example of this occurred at the time of the Third Periodic Review in England. The London Borough of Harrow had three constituencies after the Second Review, but its entitlement was likely to fall: its theoretical entitlement on 1976 electoral data was 2.32 seats and the Commission therefore recommended two constituencies only. The Borough had been rewarded in 1976–77, into 21 wards, on the assumption that it would continue to be entitled to three constituencies, which the Assistant Commissioner who conducted the Local Inquiry noted was 'expressly designed to provide approximately equal constituencies' (Boundary Commission for England, 1983, 27, #123). Because only two were allocated, there was a disparity of some 7,000 electors between the two provisionally recommended constituencies and as a consequence the Assistant Commissioner:

> recommended that Harrow should be allowed to retain three constituencies and that the counter-proposals submitted at the inquiry for the adjustment of constituency boundaries to realign with the new ward boundaries should be adopted.

The Commission decided, however, that 'exceptional treatment was not justified on the grounds that consideration of electoral arrangements for the purpose of local government had imported erroneous assumptions about future representation at Westminster' (Boundary Commission for England, 1983, 28, #124).[4]

Strategy 3: Evidence to Local Inquiries
The most frequently used method by which the political parties seek to influence the outcome of Parliamentary Boundary Reviews is through the Local Inquiry process. At the Fourth Review, the political parties were among the most assiduous bodies making representations to the Commissions concerning the provisional recommendations: in every county or region where the recommendations were challenged, at least some of those challenges came direct from one or more parties (Chapter 6). As part of such a challenge, a party may present its own proposals, which it may then have to defend should a Local Inquiry be called. There is no guarantee of success there: much depends on the persuasiveness of the case, compared to the arguments of other groups. Furthermore, the parties (or for that matter, any other group or individual) are not permitted to make a case for change based on the potential partisan impacts of any given set of proposals for new seats. Indeed, to make an explicitly partisan argument in any submission to the Commissions would automatically render it inadmissible: the Commissions are scrupulous in maintaining their impartiality.

The rules by which the Boundary Commissions work provide a number of means by which a well-prepared party can present its case. If the Commission's provisional recommendation is not to a party's best advantage, it can, for instance, put forward a recommendation of its own, arguing that its proposals are designed to produce smaller deviations from the electoral quota than those proposals put forward by the Commission. More commonly, parties will present proposals based on either minimising disruption to existing arrangements, or on maintaining local ties. If a local community group can be found to lend weight to a 'local ties' argument, so much the better. This was the case in part of Bristol, for example, where the parties disagreed over whether Lockleaze or Westbury-on-Trym should be moved from Bristol Northwest constituency to Bristol West (Figure 8.2). West-

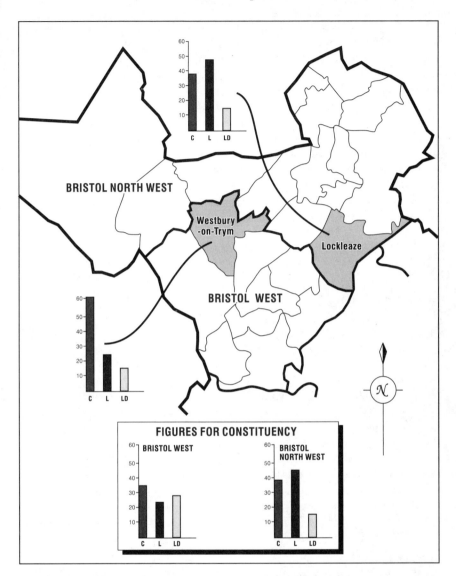

Figure 8.2 *The wards whose constituency allocation was contested in the provisional recommendations for the Bristol Northwest and Bristol West constituencies at the Fourth Periodic Review, indicating the estimated 1992 voting for the three main parties in the recommended constituencies and the contested wards.*
Source: based on the Ordnance Survey map with the permission of the Controller of Her Majesty's Stationery Office © Crown Copyright

bury is a very strong Conservative ward, whereas Labour has the edge in Lock-leaze. The Commission proposed moving Lockleaze into Bristol West, but Labour wanted to keep it in Bristol Northwest (one of the most marginal seats won by the Conservatives in 1992), which it had much greater hopes of winning; Labour sug-gested moving Westbury instead.

Apart from the political parties, twelve individuals made written representa-tions about this aspect of the proposals for Avon; all opposed the recommended move of Lockleaze (with half of them recommending that Westbury be moved instead), as did the Lockleaze Community Association. At the Local Inquiry 19 people spoke on this issue. Those speaking either for or as members of the Labour Party pressed for Westbury to be moved, stressing its links with Stoke Bishop ward (to its immediate southwest) and arguing that Lockleaze's main links are with other wards recommended to remain in Bristol Northwest: the representa-tive of Bristol City Council supported the latter case, whereas the representative of Avon County Council supported both. The Conservative counter-argument was that Westbury-on-Trym acts as the main service centre for northwest Bristol and so its ward should be in the Northwest constituency, whereas Lockleaze is a 'city ward': the Liberal Democrats' spokespersons accepted the evidence of links between Westbury and Stoke Bishop on the one hand and Lockleaze and Hor-field (to its west) on the other, and argued that each pair should be in the same constituency. (Figure 8.2 shows that the Liberal Democrats were estimated as the second-placed party in Bristol West – for details on the estimation procedure, see below – but in a poor third place in Bristol Northwest.) The Labour case was accepted, and the revised recommendations placed Westbury in Bristol West. In response, the Commission received 662 representations arguing for a return to the provisional recommendations, which included 451 *pro formas* (produced by the Conservatives) and 150 individual letters – the majority of which had the same opening (pro-Conservative) lines. Against them were 42 representations commending the revised recommendations (including one from a member of the Bristol Northwest Conservative Association, dissociating herself from its actions!). Clearly the Conservative strategy here failed – not least because not a single representation was received supporting the provisional recommendations after their initial publication plus a poor performance at the Inquiry. (Labour mobilised comparatively little 'grassroots support' there and the later written rep-resentations indicate that there was much potential pro-Conservative support in the local community, but it wasn't galvanised into action soon enough.)[5]

For a party to take part effectively in the Local Inquiry process requires a great deal of intra-party co-ordination and co-operation. A particular proposal might help the party in one constituency (by making the seat safer, for instance) but it might also mean concomitant changes elsewhere in the County which disadvan-tage it and help its rivals. Without some co-ordination, there will be a temptation for each constituency party to follow its own interests, even if this is to the detri-ment of the party's wider interest. That co-ordination can be difficult to achieve, requiring not only a well-planned strategy on the part of the national party but also co-operation among constituency and regional organisations; political parties, as fallible organisations, will not always accomplish this. Furthermore, even if a party makes a strong case at an Inquiry, that effort can be nullified by a variety of possibilities beyond its control: rival parties might make equally convincing representations, as might non-party groups (including local authorities, citizen groups, and so on) also, and the Assistant Commissioner chairing the Inquiry might fail to see the merits of their case. There are no guarantees in the Local Inquiry process.

Strategy 4: Electoral registration
The fact that each area's theoretical entitlement to seats is based on the number of registered electors on the Review's enumeration date raises the possibility of a fourth strategy: influencing the composition of the electoral register prior to the announcement of a Review. A party might wish to maximise the number of seats in areas where it is strong, and minimise the number in areas where it is weak. It can help achieve this by encouraging more people to register to vote in its strongholds: if the strategy is successful, there will be a case for rounding entitlements up in strongholds, and rounding them down in other areas.

The scope for such a strategy emerges from the *ad hoc* nature of the electoral registration process in Britain, where all eligible adults are required by law to register to vote but responsibility for registration is largely devolved to local authorities, among which there are wide variations in practice. Some are assiduous in finding and registering new voters (both 18-year-olds and people moving into the area): others are not. At the other end of the process, people leave the electoral register for a number of reasons, moving house or death being the main ones. If a previously registered individual fails to return a registration form, some authorities assume that he or she is no longer eligible in that area and will remove the name from the register: other local authorities assume that he or she has simply failed to return a form, and will leave the name on the register.

None of this would matter if over- and under-registration were random, in terms of both their geographies and of the individuals affected, but they are not. Recent research suggests that under-registration is a particular problem in the inner cities (especially Inner London, where rapid population turnover means many miss the registration deadlines as a result of moving house at the 'wrong time'), and among younger, poorer voters, especially those in ethnic minorities (Smith, 1993). Furthermore, one of the side-effects of the so-called poll tax, introduced to pay for local government in the late 1980s, was to discourage many (again mainly young, poorer inner city residents) from registering to vote (Smith and McLean, 1994; Pattie, Dorling, Johnston and Rossiter, 1996). Since people in these groups are more likely to be Labour voters (if they vote at all) than to support another party, there is a partisan dimension to registration. Under-registration is likely to result in slightly lower theoretical entitlements in Labour-supporting areas than elsewhere – and hence in fewer Labour seats. Part of Labour's strategy for the Fourth Review was therefore to run target registration campaigns in several of its key strongholds, raising their theoretical entitlements sufficiently to safeguard four seats (see Chapter 6).

The issue of under-registration was also raised by participants in some Local Inquiries, although by this stage it was too late. Theoretical entitlements had already been calculated and the Commission was unwilling and unable to reopen the issue.

Strategy 5: Judicial review

A final strategy open to the parties is to challenge the Boundary Commissions' decisions through judicial review. This was the route followed (unsuccessfully) by Manchester Conservatives in 1954 regarding the number of seats target adopted by the Boundary Commission for England during its Second Periodical Review (see Chapter 3, p. 94) and again by four senior members of the Labour party in 1982, in this case focusing on inter-constituency variations in electorates (p. 113). Petitions for judicial review of an administrative decision by such as a Boundary Commission rely on claims that a Commission has failed to follow the rules adequately and hence has misdirected itself. Given the ambiguity of the rules, however, there is wide scope for discretion on the part of a Commission and in both of the cases referred to here the relevant courts determined that the claim was not sustained. The 1982 judgements led Rawlings (1988, 61) to conclude that:

> the scope of discretionary powers which have been allocated [by the 1982 judgements] renders it unlikely in the extreme that a court will feel able to hold either that the rules ('guidelines') have been misconstrued such as to justify judicial intervention, or that the discretionary powers have been used unreasonably in the *Wednesbury* sense.[6]

Despite this, a further attempt to use judicial review to counter a Commission's final recommendations was brought in Scotland in November 1994 by the Conservative MP for Ayr (Philip Gallie), Ayr Conservative and Unionist Association, Renfrewshire Conservative Association and several other party members. Their case was that by using Regional Electoral Divisions (REDs) rather than wards as building blocks, the Scottish Commission had placed the community of Alloway in a constituency other than that with which it had most of its ties, and that in so doing the Commission had created greater inter-constituency variations in electorate than would otherwise have been the case.[7] (The Conservatives won Ayr with a majority of only 85 in 1992. Rallings and Thrasher (1995) estimated that the new constituency would have a Labour majority of 1,895, which the petitioners hoped to overturn by having Alloway's 4,547 electors returned to that constituency. The Commission's proposed Ayr constituency had 55,307 voters whereas Carrick, Cumnock and Doon Valley, in which Alloway ward had been placed, had 67,001: Carrick, Cumnock and Doon Valley was a safe Labour seat.) The Assistant Commissioner who held the Strathclyde Local Inquiry had guardedly supported their argument that Alloway ward should be detached from its

RED, but his advice was rejected by the Commission on the grounds that 'We considered ... that it was of fundamental importance that our policy of using regional electoral divisions as the building blocks for the formation of constituencies should be carried out consistently across the country as a whole' (Boundary Commission for Scotland, 1995, 142, #44; see also Chapter 5, p. 309). In his opinion on the petition, Lord Weir set out the general situation regarding judicial review very clearly:

> The power of the Court in judicial review is limited to examining cases where it is alleged that an administrative body, such as the Commission, failed to act in accordance with the law, whether by acting beyond their powers, by failing to have regard to the statutory rules by which they were bound, by failing to follow in a regular and proper way the procedure prescribed, or by reaching a decision which no reasonable body could possibly have reached.

His examination of the Rules for Redistribution led to the conclusion that these 'confer flexibility and a wide discretion' with the Commission:

> left to exercise their judgement in the light of the circumstances prevailing. They cannot ignore the rules but, keeping them in mind, they have to exercise their judgement weighing up various competing and no doubt at times irreconcilable considerations.

He then restated the concept of '*Wednesbury* unreasonableness', equating that with 'irrationality' in:

> a decision which is so outrageous in its defiance of logic or of accepted moral standards that no sensible person who had applied his mind to the question to be decided could have arrived at it.

In those terms it is almost impossible to believe that a petition for judicial review would ever succeed, because Lord Weir's opinion was that 'I might agree or disagree with the workings of the Boundary Commission, but can only intervene where there has been shown by them such a degree of irrationality that it amounts to a defiance of logic'![18]

Measuring the partisan impacts

Two questions emerge from the above discussion: what are the partisan impacts (whether intended or unintended) of redistricting; and how successful were the political parties in making their cases through the Inquiry process? We answer these questions with regard to the Third and (especially) the Fourth Periodic Reviews.

Some constituencies are unaffected by the review process (203 at the Fourth Review; see Table 4.10): their boundaries remain the same. Any changes in the partisan loyalties of these seats cannot be due to the Review, therefore. Instead, they will be a consequence of other sorts of change – to the demographic profile of the constituency, for instance, to the state of the local economy, perhaps, or to general shifts in the standing of the parties – all of which would occur whether or not a Review takes place. The majority of seats are affected to some extent by the Review, however, and adding or subtracting (or both) particular areas and their resident voters to or from a constituency can have an obvious partisan impact.

The first election fought in the new constituencies is not necessarily a good guide to that partisan impact. Local voting intentions change between elections, irrespective of boundary reviews. The partisan outcome of that first election will, therefore, conflate both the effects of any boundary review and the effects of changing party popularity. To see the effects of a review, we need to look at one particular election (thus controlling for inter-election shifts in party popularity). The task is to produce two sets of results for that election (on the assumption that all electors would have acted the same way): one set comprises the results in the old seats, the other the results in the new. Following both the Third and Fourth Reviews, the media commissioned estimates of what the results of the last election fought in the old seats (1979 and 1992 respectively) would have been had the contest been fought in the new seats (BBC/ITN, 1983; Rallings and Thrasher, 1995). The value of using the last pre-Review election is that estimates of the results of that contest had it been fought in the new constituencies provide a benchmark against which to compare the results of the first election fought in the new seats. Unfortunately, under British electoral law votes cast at general elections are not published for any unit smaller than Parliamentary constituencies so that we cannot make a direct comparison between the two by adding up the actual results in smaller electoral units which constitute the old and new seats and so an indirect method is needed.

Ideally, to describe the partisan effects of redistricting we need estimates of the constituency results of the last election held in the pre-Review seats, had that contest been fought in the new seats. Furthermore, they should allow us to see the partisan impacts of the Review at three stages in the process. First, what are the partisan impacts of the provisional recommendations put forward by the Boundary Commission? Since these recommendations are made by the Commissions alone and solely with regard to the rules governing redistricting, they are free from party attempts to influence the outcome of the process. They suggest the unintended partisan impacts of redistricting. Second, at the public consultation stage, if each party was to achieve all of its requested changes to the provisional proposals (in other words, if each party achieved the 'best case' scenario in its own proposals), what would be the partisan outcomes? Third, at the end of the process, once the Commissions have taken on board the reports of the Assistant Commissioners (influenced, to a greater or lesser extent, by the cases the parties put at Local Inquiry), the final recommendations give an idea of the intended partisan impacts of the process. Which parties managed to effect changes to their advantage, or defend gains already manifest in the preliminary proposals, and which parties lost out?

Estimating the effects for the Third and Fourth Reviews in Great Britain

The approach adopted in analyses of the Third and Fourth Periodic Reviews by those commissioned by the media employs local government election results at the ward level as indicators of the state of the parties (BBC/ITN, 1983; Rallings and Thrasher, 1995; Rallings, Thrasher and Denver, 1996). Because of differences between voting and party competition in local and national elections, some adjustments are necessary (for discussions of the extent to which local elections are guides to national voting, see Newton, 1976, Chapter 2; Curtice and Payne, 1991; Rallings and Thrasher, 1993). These estimates have only been published for the Final Recommendations, however.

We have adopted an alternative strategy, using the results of the last general election preceding the boundary change. The method relies on the well-established research finding that the level of support each party gets in a constituency is related to the socio-economic characteristics of its population. The Conservatives, for instance, do better in middle-class areas, in affluent areas, and in areas with high proportions of owner-occupiers, and worst in working-class districts, areas which are less affluent, and places with a high proportion of people who rent their home from the local authority (there is an extensive literature on this; see, for instance, Crewe and Payne, 1976; Johnston, Pattie and Allsopp, 1988). Furthermore, party support in each constituency is affected by how much effort the party puts into the local campaign, and how much its rivals put in too. The more intense a party's campaign in a constituency, the better it does there, and the worse its rivals do: the more effort its rivals put in, the worse it does (Whiteley and Seyd, 1994; Denver and Hands, 1997; Johnston, 1987; Pattie, Whiteley, Johnston and Seyd, 1994; Pattie, Johnston and Fieldhouse, 1995). Finally, there are long-standing regional differences in party support, over and above the effects of variations in socio-economic conditions or local campaign efforts. By and large, the Conservatives tend to do best in the south of the country, in suburbs, and in rural areas: Labour does best in northern, industrial urban centres; and the Liberal Democrats have developed regional concentrations of support in the South-West and in parts of rural Scotland (Curtice and Steed, 1982; Johnston and Pattie, 1993; Pattie *et al.*, 1997).

Multivariate regression models describing a party's share of the constituency vote can be constructed for any given election, therefore, employing socio-economic data from the Census, data on campaign spending (a surrogate for campaign activity) and information on the location of each constituency.[9] A regression model can be used to predict a party's share of the vote in each constituency, for any given set of values of the original socio-economic, campaigning or regional variables comprising the equation. By carrying out regression analyses of the constituency vote shares of each of the main parties at the last election prior to a boundary change, we derive the relationship between vote, socio-economic conditions, campaigning and region for that contest.

Because Census data are available for local government wards and wards nest into Parliamentary constituencies, it is possible to reconstruct the socio-economic profile of the new constituencies, which can be assigned to particular regions. By substituting the socio-economic and regional data for the new constituencies into the equations derived for the last contest fought in the old boundaries, it is possible to replay that contest, as though it had been fought in the new seats, enabling us not only to assign winners to the new seats, but to say how well or badly each party would have done in each seat. The estimate of the partisan impact of redistricting is therefore consistent with voting at an actual general election (for details of the method used, see Rossiter, Johnston and Pattie, 1997a).

The Third Review

This method has been applied to the 1979 election, the last before the implementation of the Third Review, for Great Britain only. The first step was to construct regression models of the major parties' constituency vote shares at the 1979 election. The data comprised the actual results of the 1979 election in each constituency, socio-economic variables from the 1981 Census, information on campaign spending by each party in each seat, and variables indicating which region each seat was in. For our purposes, an important aspect of each equation was how well it described the vote for each party.[10] All three equations had high R-squares; around 90 per cent of the variation in both the Conservative and Labour votes in 1979, and almost 70 per cent of the variation in the Liberal vote, is captured by our equations.

Having derived these equations describing the socio-economic correlates of the vote in 1979, the process was reversed to work out, for any given set of socio-economic conditions, what the vote for each party should have been within the new geography. By substituting into each equation the socio-economic profiles of the new constituencies created in the Third Review, we estimated what the 1979 vote shares of the three main parties would have been in each constituency had those seats been in operation then rather than in 1983. By comparing these 'predicted' results to the actual results of the contest fought in the 'old' seats, we obtain an idea of the partisan effects of the Third Review.[11]

This process gives best estimates of how the 1979 election would have turned out had it been fought in those new seats (Table 8.2). The Third Review increased the size of Parliament, and the number of Scottish, Welsh and English MPs rose from 623 to 633. Party prospects were altered by both changes to existing seats and new opportunities in the additional seats. Had the 1979 election been fought in Third Review constituencies, the Conservatives would have won an extra 21 seats (making them the main beneficiary not only of the changes but also of the additional seats). Labour, meanwhile, would have lost 9 MPs and the Liberals would have lost three. All this without any votes changing.[12]

Just looking at winners and losers in terms of the number of seats each party could expect to win tells only part of the story. As time passes between Reviews, the Conservatives are increasingly disadvantaged by the constituency framework, since declining populations in the inner urban areas compared to the suburbs means it takes fewer voters to elect a Labour MP than a Conservative. Insofar as a Review redresses the balance between inner urban and suburban constituencies, it is almost bound to benefit the Conservatives. A simple way of seeing this is to compare the proportion of seats won by a party to its proportion of all votes. One consequence of first-past-the-post as an electoral system is that it tends to exaggerate the Parliamentary representation of the winning party, relative to its share of the vote, and to disadvantage smaller parties. But this inherent electoral system bias will interact with partisan biases introduced by the geography and age of the constituency boundaries. Other things being equal, for instance, we would expect that if the Conservatives won an election fought in old seats, they should receive a smaller winner's advantage than they would have had the election been fought in revised seats (since old seats tend to produce a relatively pro-Labour bias by preserving constituencies in inner city areas). How big was that winners' advantage in 1979, and how would it have been affected by the Third Review?

Table 8.2 *The partisan effects of the Third Periodic Review: re-running the 1979 election using the Census method showing the number of seats that would have been won by each party (percentage of seats in brackets)*

	Conservative		Labour		Liberal		Nationalists	
Actual result	338	(54.3)	269	(43.2)	12	(1.9)	4	(0.6)
Third review seats	359	(56.7)	260	(41.1)	9	(1.4)	5	(0.8)

The easiest way of investigating this is to subtract the percentage of the vote going to a party from the percentage of seats won in the Commons. No difference indicates that a party's share of MPs is in line with its share of the vote. A party whose difference is positive benefits from the electoral system; one whose difference is negative is under-represented relative to its vote. Not surprisingly, the Conservatives, as the winners of the 1979 election, were the main beneficiaries of the electoral system in that year: their share of Parliamentary seats was almost 9 percentage points ahead of their share of the vote (Table 8.3; we have excluded Northern Ireland from the calculations). As a large party with concentrations of support in particular areas, Labour also benefited, though to a lesser extent: its share of MPs was 5 percentage points higher than its share of the vote. The main losers were the Liberals, whose share of MPs trailed 12 percentage points behind their share of the vote. The nationalist parties were disadvantaged too, though to a lesser extent. Their share of MPs was only 1.5 percentage points smaller than their share of the vote: in particular, the concentration of Welsh nationalist support in certain areas helped Plaid Cymru win MPs.

Had the 1979 election been fought in the constituencies introduced by the Third Review, however, the Conservatives' advantage would have been even greater: they would have won 11 percentage points more MPs than their share of the vote 'entitled' them to, compared to the 9 percentage point advantage they

actually enjoyed (Table 8.3). Labour, meanwhile, would have lost some of its
(smaller) advantage: the difference between its share of MPs and share of the
vote would have fallen from the 5 percentage point advantage it actually enjoyed
to a 3 percentage point advantage. The impacts on the smaller parties – the Liberals and the Nationalists – would have been smaller; both would have remained
disadvantaged by the electoral system in 1979, and to roughly the same extent as
they in fact were.

Table 8.3 *Deviations from proportionality, 1979*

	Conservative	Labour	Liberal	Nationalists
Vote per cent, 1979	45.4	38.2	14.3	2.1
Per cent of seats won				
Actual 1979 result	54.3	43.2	1.9	0.6
1979 result in 1983 seats	56.7	41.1	1.4	0.8
Deviation from proportionality				
Actual 1979 deviation	8.9	5.0	–12.4	–1.5
1979 deviation in 1983 seats	11.3	2.9	–12.9	–1.3

How did the Third Review enhance the Conservatives' electoral advantage
while diminishing, but not removing, Labour's? Under a single-member constituency plurality system, bias is introduced through the interaction between the
geography of Parliamentary constituencies and the geography of support for each
party. A party wishing to exploit the system to its advantage needs to win the
maximum number of seats possible on the minimum number of votes; for
instance, in 1979, it took 40,406 votes to elect one Conservative MP, and 42,870
to elect one Labour member, but 392,165 votes were needed to elect a Liberal.
This very large discrepancy (to the Liberals' disadvantage) at the level of the
electoral system as a whole is replicated in individual seats. Achieving equality
of electorates between constituencies is only one of the Boundary Commissions'
goals, and can be superseded by other rules (Chapter 3). The substantial variations in constituency size which result, even after Reviews, can help create bias
if they coincide with the geography of support for particular parties. A party which
does well predominantly in smaller seats needs to gain fewer votes to win there
than a party which does well predominantly in larger seats and so will find it easier to 'convert' votes into MPs. Variations in the effective size of constituency
electorates can be a source of bias, therefore.

There are several causes of variations in the size of constituencies, each of
which can act as a component contributing to electoral bias. By decomposing the
total electoral bias into its component parts, therefore, and by looking at how a
Boundary Review affects them, we get a clearer picture of the electoral impacts
of that Review. One 'seat size' effect arises because of the different seat quotas

in operation for each of the constituent parts of the United Kingdom. Because of guaranteed levels of representation for both countries, Scottish and Welsh seats are, as we have seen (Chapter 4), smaller on average than those in England. Therefore parties which do well in Scotland and Wales gain an advantage relative to parties which do well in England. Furthermore, constituencies vary substantially in size within each country too. And as people migrate over time, the discrepancies in constituency size tend to increase between Reviews, producing a separate 'constituency size' effect.

A third source of bias relates to the efficiency (or otherwise) of a party's geography of the vote. Ideally, a party would like to have a distribution which meant it had just enough votes in each constituency to beat its rivals there. Too few votes to win means that those votes are wasted: they have not contributed to electing an MP, since winning 49 per cent of the constituency vote is worthless if your only rival wins 51 per cent. Too large a winning majority is also 'bad news', however (though it is likely to be welcomed by the individual MP!), since the 'surplus' votes over and above the minimum needed to win are also wasted. In a two-party contest, a party only needs to win 51 per cent of the vote to win the seat. If a party gets 70 per cent of the vote, the extra 19 per cent is surplus to requirement there: it might be better for the party if a means could be found to shift the constituency boundaries in such a way as to put that 'surplus' vote into another constituency where its candidate was facing a closer contest. Neither distribution of votes is 'efficient': in the first example, votes are spread too thinly to win many seats, whereas in the second they are too concentrated, leading to very safe results in some seats but large surpluses of votes there, and potential 'vote drought' in other seats. However, a party which wins 51 per cent of the votes in every seat in a two party contest will win them all – a highly efficient geography of the vote for that party (and an extremely inefficient one for its rival!). In reality, of course, few parties will want to win by so small a majority: the geography of the vote in this case is highly efficient, but it is also highly vulnerable to a small swing away from the winning party.

All three of the above sources of bias can be affected by a Boundary Review. Allocating more seats to England ameliorates the 'national quota' bias; moving closer to equal electorates ameliorates the 'seat size' bias; and changing constituency boundaries can affect the 'vote efficiency' bias – for good or ill. These are not the only sources of bias in an electoral system, however. The number of votes a party needs to win a seat can also be affected by turnout in the constituency (parties which do well in areas with low turnout need fewer votes in total to win there than parties which do well in areas with high turnout). It can also be affected by the strength of support for minor parties in the constituency (the more votes a minor party gets in a constituency, the fewer votes one of the main parties needs to get to win there – so long as the minor party does not win!). Finally, minor party success, by depriving major parties of a win, can also be a source of bias – major parties which come second to a minor party in a seat might argue that they would have won there, had it not been for the minor party intervention. The latter three components of bias are less likely to be affected by the activities of the Boundary Commissions.

To work out the size of each of these bias components and the Third Review's impact on them, we analyse the actual 1979 election result and our estimates of the result in each seat if that election had been fought in the Third Review constituencies, using a method first outlined by Brookes (1960; see also Rossiter, Johnston and Pattie 1997b).[13] Brookes' definition of electoral bias concentrates on the constituency geography of the vote for the two major parties. Bias is measured by calculating the additional number of seats one major party would have won at an election had it gained the same share of the vote as the other major party, assuming a uniform national swing between the major parties and no change in either the votes won by the minor parties or abstentions. If there is no electoral bias (at least as far as the major parties are concerned), then the two parties should win the same number of seats for the same share of the vote. The greater the bias in favour of one party rather than the other, however, the greater the former party's would-be representation relative to the latter, had they won the same share of the vote. Defining bias in this way means that, by assuming a level playing field in terms of share of the vote, we can differentiate between the political situation at any given election (which party is popular with the electorate at a given point in time and which not), and the underlying biases inherent in the constituency system.

The bias can then be broken down into its constituent components (Table 8.4).[14] Looking first at electoral bias in the seats actually used in 1979, we see that although Labour lost the election, it was the party which gained most, other things being equal, from the electoral system. Had there been a uniform swing from Conservative to Labour sufficiently large to give both parties the same share of the vote in 1979 (and had the other parties performed as they actually did), Labour would have won a total of 26 more seats than the Conservatives. Labour's electoral strength in Scotland and Wales, where constituencies tend to be smaller than in England, was worth eight seats to the party (the national quota). And because Labour was strong in the inner cities, where constituencies were also small (and had, in general, become smaller since the Second Review), it was the main beneficiary from intra-national variations in constituency size too; this was worth 31 extra seats to the party. By lowering the effective threshold of votes needed for victory, abstention (highest in Labour's strongholds) also worked in the party's favour (worth an extra 12 seats). But the Conservatives gained most (about twenty seats, *ceteris paribus*) from small party votes (the main small party challenge, from the Liberals, was strongest in Conservative seats, lowering the latter party's effective vote threshold for victory). Advantages to Labour and Conservative from minor party victories and efficiency respectively were small and self-cancelling, however.

Had the 1979 general election been fought in the seats introduced in 1983 by the Third Review, however, Labour would have lost its overall advantage. Again assuming equal shares of the vote for Labour and the Conservatives in 1979,

Labour would have gained slightly through the national quotas bias (Scotland and Wales both gained seats in the Review) and also through the effect of minor party victories (in each case, the new seats would have created a bias worth two extra seats for Labour). But these small gains would have been heavily offset by the reduction in inequalities between electorates as large and small seats were squeezed towards the quotas. A pro-Labour bias of 31 seats in the actual election as a result of intra-national variations in constituency size would have been reduced to an advantage of just four. Furthermore, the new seats would have enhanced the Conservatives' advantage gained from minor party votes and the efficiency of their vote distribution across constituencies. Overall, therefore, the Third Review would have removed the bias Labour gained in 1979 in the old constituencies and replaced it with a pro-Conservative bias. The Third Review confirmed the received wisdom about redistributions, therefore: old seats were biased in Labour's favour, and the new ones were biased to the Conservatives' advantage.

Table 8.4 *Electoral bias and the Third Review: decomposing the bias components, 1979 (assuming Conservative and Labour had equal vote shares)*

	1979 result	*1979 result in Third Review seats*
National Quotas	8	10
Intra-national variations	31	4
Abstentions	12	12
Minor party votes	−20	−22
Minor party victories	1	3
Efficiency	−1	−8
Total	26	−6

Note: a positive value indicates a bias towards Labour; a negative value indicates a bias towards Conservative. Total bias does not equal the sum of the individual elements because of interactions between them.

The Fourth Review: party influences

Discussion of the partisan effects of the Third Review concentrated on the change between the *status quo ante* and the position after the Review. This implicitly ignored the internal dynamics of the Review process itself, which goes through several stages: the publication of provisional recommendations for the new constituencies in each area; public consultation and (if necessary) a Local Inquiry; revision, where needed, of the provisional recommendations (with the possibility of a further round of consultation); and publication of final recommendations. The Commissions' provisional recommendations may differ, both in detail and in partisan impacts, from their final recommendations which define the new seats.

And between the publication of the provisional recommendations and the implementation of the final recommendations, the political parties may put forward
proposals via the Inquiry process, with obvious partisan intent. At any given stage,
there will be potential winners and losers. A party may do well out of the preliminary proposals, but fail to defend those advantages at a Local Inquiry, and so
lose out, relatively speaking, in the final recommendations. Equally, a party disadvantaged by the preliminary proposals may successfully improve its position
via its representations at Inquiries, and hence do relatively well in the final recommendations. Comparing the final result with the situation before the Review
started misses this. The Conservatives were the 'winners' in the Third Review.
But they would have gained some seats in any case, because of the nature of
Britain's changing population geography. Did they gain as many seats as they
might have hoped? Did the other parties do as badly as they might have feared?

Much depends on what each party does by way of making representations to the
Commissions, in terms of both the intrinsic merits of its own proposals and their
merits relative to proposals put forward by other parties, by other organisations, and
by members of the public. The dynamics of the Review process vary from area to
area depending on, for instance, the strategies adopted by each party and the effectiveness of their arguments. One way of investigating the changing partisan impacts
of the Review process as it progresses is not only to compare the start and end points
of the process but also to look at the partisan consequences of the provisional recommendations, and of the preferred solutions for each of the main parties, as revealed
by the proposals they put to the Commissions via the Local Inquiries. There is, of
course, a wider issue concerning how well, or badly, each party did in identifying
its 'best interest' solution in any given area (see Chapter 6). In the following discussion, we concentrate upon what the parties actually put forward.

For the Fourth Review, we have estimated the partisan impacts of not only the
Commissions' provisional and final recommendations but also the proposals put forward by each of the major parties. By applying the method outlined above for estimating the partisan outcomes of a Review, using data from the 1991 Census, it is
possible to re-run the 1992 election in each of five possible sets of seats: the Boundary Commissions' provisional recommendations; the seats suggested by each of the
three main parties; and the Commissions' final recommendations (for details, see
Rossiter, Johnston and Pattie, 1997a). By doing so, we obtain some indication of not
only the unintended partisan impacts of the Fourth Review (as indicated by the provisional recommendations) but also of each party's attempts to influence the Review
to its own partisan advantage (intended partisan effects), plus the partisan effects of
the final outcome. The regression equations provide a very good fit to the data,
accounting for 92 per cent and 94 per cent of the variation respectively in the Conservative and Labour vote shares, and 77 per cent of the Liberal Democrat vote share.

Applying the equations to each, we have calculated the partisan implications of:
the Commissions' provisional recommendations; the three sets of proposals put forward by the Conservatives, Labour and the Liberal Democrats (reconstructed from
the case put by each party at each Local Inquiry); and the Commissions' final rec-

ommendations which informed the actual boundary revisions (Table 8.5). Comparing the actual results of the 1992 election with the results as they would have been had the election been fought on the seats finally recommended by the Fourth Review, the Conservatives once again emerged as overall 'winners' (they would have won an extra 16 seats), while Labour ('losing' six seats) and the Liberal Democrats ('losing' two seats) would have been worse off in terms of Parliamentary representation. To that extent, the complacency which marked the Conservatives' early approach to the Fourth Review was understandable.

Table 8.5 *The partisan effects of the Fourth Review: re-running the 1992 election using the Census method showing the number of seats that would have been won by each party (percentage of seats in brackets)*

	Conservative		Labour		Liberal Democrat		Nationalists	
Actual result	335	(52.9)	271	(42.8)	20	(3.2)	7	(1.1)
Provisional recommendations	357	(55.7)	260	(40.6)	17	(2.7)	7	(1.1)
Conservative proposals	366	(57.0)	252	(39.3)	17	(2.6)	7	(1.1)
Labour proposals	339	(52.7)	280	(43.5)	17	(2.6)	7	(1.1)
Liberal Democrat proposals	357	(55.7)	259	(40.4)	18	(2.8)	7	(1.1)
Final recommendations	351	(54.8)	265	(41.3)	18	(2.8)	7	(1.1)

But if we take as our baseline not the actual 1992 election result, but the result as it would have been had the election been fought in the seats proposed in the Commissions' provisional recommendations for the Fourth Review, the picture is somewhat different. Under the provisional recommendations, the Conservatives could have expected to win 357 seats in 1992 (22 more than they actually won). But had the election been fought in the seats eventually adopted as a result of the Fourth Review, they would have won 351, 16 more than they actually won but 6 fewer than the provisional recommendations would have given them! The outcome of the Fourth Review was good for the Conservatives, but not as good as it might have been had no changes been made to the provisional recommendations. Labour, meanwhile, would have fared even worse under the provisional than under the final recommendations: it would have lost 11 MPs as a consequence of the former, compared to 'only' six as a result of the latter proposals. The Liberal Democrats, too, had reason not to be too gloomy about the eventual outcome of the Fourth Review: had the provisional recommendations been in operation in 1992, they would have had three fewer MPs than they actually obtained, a large slice out of only 20 MPs. But had the election been fought in the final recommendation seats, they would have clawed back one of the three, losing only two.

Why was the eventual outcome of the Fourth Review worse for the Conservatives than the unintended partisan implications of the provisional recommendations might have led them to expect (even though the party was the gainer overall), and better for Labour and the Liberal Democrats (even though they were, in absolute terms, losers)? The answer lies in part in the parties' efforts to influence the Commissions through the Review process. As discussed in Chapter 6, Labour, worried about the potential damage to its electoral prospects, was prepared for the Fourth Review in a way it had not been for previous exercises. It took the public consultation process very seriously from the outset, presenting its cases effectively up and down the country. The Conservatives, by contrast, were complacent, at least initially, and allowed Labour to steal a march, whereas the Liberal Democrats were too poorly resourced to fight a nationally co-ordinated campaign on anything approaching the scale adopted by the two bigger parties. Furthermore, both the Conservatives and the Liberal Democrats suffered the effects of grass roots independence, finding it hard to establish and enforce decisions regarding which might be in the interests of the national but not the local party. Labour, by contrast, was tightly disciplined, and generally 'on message' with regards the Fourth Boundary Review.

We have estimated the partisan implications of each of the main parties' proposals; each was in its own favour. The Conservatives' plans would have won the party 366 MPs in 1992, 15 more than they would have won from the final recommendations, whereas Labour would have lost even more than either it actually did or than it would have as a result of the provisional recommendations: the Conservatives' proposals allowed it only 252 MPs. Labour, meanwhile, put together a set of proposals which would have increased the party's Parliamentary representation in 1992 by 9, to 280 MPs, while limiting the Conservatives' almost irresistible rise to only four extra MPs: Labour would still have lost the 1992 election, but the Conservatives' Parliamentary majority would have been even more precarious than it was. For the Liberal Democrats, the problem was somewhat different. As a relatively small party, both in terms of vote share and in terms of resources, they were fighting something of a rearguard action. But their own proposals would have improved the party's standing in 1992 by a single MP relative to the provisional recommendations, at Labour's net expense. What is striking, however, is that while all parties would have gained had their own proposals been adopted in 1992, Labour would have gained most.

As with the Third Review, there were notable variations in terms of how each party fared during the Fourth Review (Table 8.6). As we would expect under first-past-the-post, the Conservatives once again enjoyed a large winners' advantage in 1992. In the real election, their share of seats was about 9.5 percentage points higher than their share of the vote. Almost every one of the alternative scenarios we evaluated for seats in 1992 would have increased the Conservatives' winners' advantage. Not surprisingly, their own proposals would have made the largest difference, increasing their percentage point lead on MPs to votes to 13.6 per cent. Tellingly, however, under Labour's proposals, that winners' advantage would have been limited to 9.3 percentage points, about the same level as the party actually achieved. While the final recommendations were better for the Conservatives, they still provided the smallest winners' advantage (11.4 percentage points) of any of the proposals for change apart from Labour's plans.

Table 8.6 *Deviations from proportionality, 1992*

	Conservative	Labour	Liberal Democrat	Nationalists
Vote per cent, 1992	43.4	35.6	18.5	2.4
Per cent of seats won:				
Actual 1992 result	52.9	42.8	3.2	1.1
Provisional recommendations	55.7	40.6	2.7	1.1
Conservative proposals	57.0	39.3	2.6	1.1
Labour proposals	52.7	43.5	2.6	1.1
Lib Dem proposals	55.7	40.4	2.6	1.1
Final recommendations	54.8	41.3	2.8	1.1
Deviations from proportionality:				
Actual 1992 deviations	9.5	7.2	−15.3	−1.3
Provisional deviations	12.3	5.0	−15.8	−1.3
Conservative deviations	13.6	3.7	−15.9	−1.3
Labour deviations	9.3	7.9	−15.9	−1.3
Lib Dem deviations	12.3	4.8	−15.7	−1.3
Final deviations	11.4	5.7	−15.7	−1.3

As in 1979, Labour in 1992 benefited from the electoral system even though it lost the election; the party's share of MPs was 7.2 percentage points higher than its share of the vote. But redrawing the constituency boundaries would, under most scenarios, have reduced (though not removed) Labour's over-representation. The worst scenario for Labour was full adoption of the Conservatives' proposals, which would have reduced its deviation from proportionality to 3.7 percentage points (compared to 5 percentage points under the provisional recommendations). Labour's own proposals would have, uniquely, improved the party's ability to benefit from first-past-the-post, raising its deviation from proportionality to 7.9 percentage points. The final recommendations, while worse for the party than the actual result, were better than it could have hoped for had the provisional recommendations been approved without challenge, or had either the Conservative or the Liberal Democrat proposals been adopted.

The Liberal Democrats remained massively disadvantaged by the electoral system, even under their own proposals. Their share of MPs in 1992 fell far short of their share of the national vote, no matter which set of seats was considered. Their deviation from proportionality in 1992 was consistently between −15.3 percentage points (the actual result) and −15.9 percentage points (under both the Conservatives' and Labour's proposals). Given the adverse impact of first-past-the-post on third parties generally, they faced an almost insurmountably large uphill struggle and it is little surprise that they failed to make the climb.

We can again use Brookes' method to decompose the electoral bias in 1992 into its component parts (Table 8.7). The picture from the actual election results in 1992 is similar to that for the actual results in 1979. Labour gained an advantage from its strength in Scotland and Wales: had Labour and the Conservatives gained the same share of the vote in 1992, Labour would have had an advantage of 12 seats over the Conservatives as a result of this bias. An even more substantial advantage of 29 seats would have accrued to the party as a result of intra-national variations in constituency size: the 1992 election, like the 1979 contest, was fought in old constituencies, and Labour's inner city constituencies had lost population, meaning the party needed fewer votes there to return MPs. Abstentions and minor party victories once again worked to Labour's advantage, and to the Conservatives' disadvantage, while the Conservatives gained from minor party votes and from the efficiency of their geography of the vote (the latter was worth seven seats to the Conservatives, had the two major parties been neck and neck in vote share). But the overall bias in the electoral system worked to Labour's advantage: on equal vote shares with the Conservatives, Labour would have won the 1992 election, with 38 more seats than its main rival.

Table 8.7 *Electoral bias and the Fourth Review: decomposing the bias components, 1992 (assuming Conservative and Labour had equal vote shares)*

	1992 result	1992 result in Fourth Review seats
National Quotas	12	13
Intra-national variations	29	4
Abstentions	19	21
Minor party votes	−30	−30
Minor party victories	20	18
Efficiency	−7	0
Total	38	21

Note: a positive value indicates a bias towards Labour; a negative value indicates a bias towards Conservative. Total bias does not equal the sum of the individual elements because of interactions between them.

The Fourth Review diminished this pro-Labour bias, but did not remove it. Had the 1992 election been fought in the seats introduced for the 1997 election and had the two parties won the same share of the vote, there would have been a smaller, but still appreciable 21 seat advantage for Labour. Most of the decline in the pro-Labour bias can be ascribed to the impact of the Boundary Review on creating greater equality in electorates: the bias produced by intra-national variations in seat size would have been much smaller, at only four seats for Labour. Few other components of bias would have been substantially altered. The next largest change, working in Labour's favour, would have been the disappearance of the Conservatives 'efficiency' bias.

The contrast between the Third and Fourth Reviews is instructive, not least in that the former would have removed a pro-Labour bias in 1979 whereas the latter would not have done so in 1992 (compare Tables 8.4 and 8.7). In general, the changes in the bias components as a consequence of each Review were in the same direction, albeit starting from larger pro-Labour biases in most cases in 1992, especially with minor party victories. The major difference between the two Reviews was in the changes in the efficiency bias, however. Whereas the Third Review enhanced a small pro-Conservative bias, the Fourth Review actually removed it. There would have been no advantage to the Conservatives in 1992 from the interaction of the geography of their vote with the geography of the new constituencies. This is entirely consistent with the view that Labour was more effective in its representations to the Commissions during the Fourth Review than were the Conservatives and, further, that Labour had learned from its experience with past Reviews.

The partisan impact of the Local Inquiries

Our analysis of the partisan impacts of the Fourth Review suggests that Labour, while a net loser, did well in limiting the damage, while the Conservatives, although net gainers, did badly in that they should have done better. Labour seems to have been better at challenging proposals which were against its interests, and at promoting proposals which were to its advantage, than were the Conservatives. But comparing the net partisan implications of the provisional recommendations, the parties' alternatives, and the final recommendations, may be misleading as a guide to how effective each party was during the Local Inquiries; for instance, Labour's 'success' might have been the result not of the adoption of its proposals by the Commissions but rather from the implementation of yet other sets of boundaries, which happened to work to Labour's relative advantage too.

Who, then, 'won' the Inquiries? We have answered this in two ways. First, how many of the finally recommended constituencies were the same as those proposed by the main parties? Table 8.8 shows the number of successes secured by each party broken down by the location of the seat: thus 'Con' indicates that a finally recommended seat had exactly the same boundaries as those proposed by the Conservatives alone, 'Con LD' indicates that the seat's composition of wards was proposed by both Conservative and Liberal Democrats, and so on. If the seat was not recommended by any party, then a check has been made to determine which party's proposed seat shared most electors with the finally recommended seat and these appear as 'con', 'lab', 'ld'. The table includes the many cases where parties approved of the provisional recommendations: the Liberal Democrats' failure to comment in many areas has inevitably depressed their figures.

Second, which party's scheme for each Inquiry area was most similar to that finally recommended? To test this we have matched each of the seats proposed by a party with the most similar seat finally recommended by the Commission and summed the total electorate common to both. Only if a party actively pursued an entire scheme has this been included in the table (this significantly reduces the number of Liberal Democrat schemes eligible for consideration) This was done for all three parties, and Table 8.9 shows the number of wins secured by each party where victory was secured by achieving the highest electorate in common with the final recommendations.

Table 8.8 *Who 'won' the Fourth Review Local Inquiries? Proposer of finally recommended seat, by seat type*

	Seat type (number of seats)				
Proposer	*Greater London*	*Metropolitan Counties*	*Shire Counties*	*Wales & Scotland*	*Total*
Con	3	11	58	2	74
Con LD	0	8	19	4	31
Con Lab	12	16	44	34	106
Con Lab LD	5	26	67	29	127
LD	0	9	13	2	24
Lab	19	20	63	17	119
Lab LD	5	16	9	11	41
con	8	0	32	1	41
lab	3	2	13	2	20
ld	1	1	3	1	6
Total	56	109	321	103	589

Note: there was no Local Inquiry for 52 seats.

Table 8.9 *Who 'won' the Fourth Review Local Inquiries? Proposer of scheme most similar to finally recommended seat, by seat type*

	Seat Type (number of schemes)				
Victor	*Greater London*	*Metropolitan Counties*	*Shire Counties*	*Wales & Scotland*	*Total*
Conservative	4	5	19	3	31
Labour	8	10	15	7	40
Lib Dem	0	1	2	0	3
Total	12	16	36	10	74

Note: there was no major party disagreement over eight schemes.

It is clear from these tables that Labour did indeed win the Inquiries. So why did they not secure a significant partisan advantage (the final recommendations gave them five seats more than the provisional recommendations)? A clue lies in the breakdown of success by type of area. Labour won overwhelmingly in London, the Metropolitan Counties, Scotland and Wales, whereas the Conservatives won in Shire England (though by a much smaller margin). Yet it was in these latter areas that Labour most needed to win. Whether success is defined in terms of maximising the number of Labour seats or in minimising the number of safe Conservative seats (a 1992 majority of greater than 9 per cent), most of the targets lay in the Shire Counties (Table 8.10). In some respects this is confirmed by an analysis of the areas in which, according to our estimates, Labour was hoping to increase the number of Labour seats and/or minimise the number of safe Conservative seats. Although Labour hoped to make progress in all types of seat, its hope of reducing the number of safe Conservative seats was largely confined to the English Shires (Table 8.11). Labour's achievement did not match these hopes, however. It was able to achieve a net increase the number of Labour seats outside Shire England, but it only got rid of a net total of one safe Tory seat throughout Great Britain (Table 8.12).

Table 8.10 *1992 result, by seat type*

| | Seat type (number of seats) | | | | |
Result	Greater London	Metropolitan Counties	Shire Counties	Wales & Scotland	Total
Safe Conservative	33	15	200	7	255
Conservative	6	13	32	10	61
Labour	26	84	65	68	243
Lib Dem	1	2	4	9	16
Nationalist	0	0	0	7	7
Total	66	114	301	101	582

Note: there was no Local Inquiry for 52 seats.

Table 8.11 *Labour boundary targets, by seat type*

| | Seat type (change in number of seats) | | | | |
Target Net change	Greater London	Metropolitan Counties	Shire Counties	Wales & Scotland	Total
Safe Conservative	0	−1	−9	0	−10
Conservative	−2	−8	+5	−3	−8
Labour	+3	+9	+5	+3	+20
Lib Dem/Nationalist	0	0	0	0	0

Table 8.12 *Actual boundary changes, by seat type*

| | Seat type | | | | |
Actual Net change	Greater London	Metropolitan Counties	Shire Counties	Wales & Scotland	Total
Safe Conservative	0	0	−1	0	−1
Conservative	−1	−3	+1	−2	−5
Labour	+1	+3	0	+1	+5
Lib Dem/Nationalist	0	0	0	+1	+1

Our conclusion is that Labour was able to win a large number of Inquiries, especially in the Metropolitan areas where it had the help of local authorities and community links and where, because of the smaller number of options, outright 'victory' was easier to achieve. It will also generally be easier to achieve significant partisan effects in urban areas where residential segregation involves larger blocks of electors. However there were very few safe Conservative seats in those areas in the first place, so the scope for minimising their number, David Gardner's stated primary aim (see p. 249), was small. In the English Shires, however, there were far more options, residential segregation is on a smaller spatial scale and fewer of the local authorities were under Labour control: hence the chances of getting a whole scheme adopted were small. As soon as part of its strategy began to unravel, the consequences were unpredictable, and as a result Labour gained no significant partisan advantage between the provisional and final recommendations there.

An example of the complexities and imponderables facing Labour's campaign in the Shire Local Inquiries can be found in Shropshire. The Commission proposed 'to allocate an extra, fifth, seat to take account of growth in the Wrekin District' and 'decided that the proposed Telford seat would contain as much of the New Town area as possible' (*News Release*, Sepember 1992). This was supported by the Conservatives as Labour support would be concentrated in the new Telford seat (we estimate Labour's majority in 1992 would have been 14 per cent), with the redrawn Wrekin seat having a Conservative majority of approximately 11 per cent: the net effect would have been to create an extra Conservative seat. Labour sought to counter this by creating a sandwich with seats of Wrekin North (Conservative majority 4 per cent) and Wrekin South (Labour majority 6 per cent), thereby maintaining a Labour seat but rendering the other seat winnable for Labour in Gardner's terms. To that end it argued for changes to the Provisional Recommendations affecting thirteen wards (supported by Labour-controlled Wrekin District Council insofar as the Wrekin seats were concerned).

In terms of the Commission's proposed boundary within the built-up area, Labour argued that it cut across established community ties and that a preferable solution would be to use the M54 as the constituency boundary, moving four wards compared to the Provisional Recommendations. The Assistant Commissioner accepted these arguments as 'essentially well-founded: I find that the motorway did to a considerable extent divide communities which are already distinct' (Inquiry Report, Shropshire, #6.1.4), and concluded:

> Accordingly if the issues could be considered in isolation I would recommend the inclusion of these four wards in the Wrekin rather than the Telford constituency. Although opinion was far from unanimous this would accord with the views of the majority of the electorate of those wards. (#6.1.6)

In other words Labour had 'won' the urban part of the argument. However its counter-proposal also involved changes to nine extra-urban wards. On four of them the Assistant Commissioner 'heard comparatively little evidence' (#6.2.5), but regarding Broseley he heard a great deal (see Chapter 7) and concluded that 'in my judgment Broseley is both geographically separated from Telford by the river and is fundamentally different in character' (#6.3.5). The counter-proposal for the four remaining wards was opposed by the Conservatives, by three District Councils and by all of the parish councils affected, and 'the overwhelming majority of the written representations opposed the counter-proposal and no elector in any of the four wards spoke in support of it at the inquiry' (#6.4.2) The Assistant Commissioner's summary was that 'In my judgment the objections to the transfer of these wards is very strong. I am satisfied that such a transfer would be wholly contrary to the wishes of the electorate' (#6.4.3), and he concluded that 'The central issue, as it appears to me, is whether the advantages of a preferable boundary between the Wrekin and Telford constituencies outweigh the disadvantages. In my judgment they do not' (#8.1). Thus while Labour had again succeeded in marshalling evidence relating to local urban ties, it was unable to match this with support for those parts of its case affecting extra-urban wards and as a result its counter-proposal was rejected.

Gardner does not claim to have reduced the number of safe Conservative seats. His claim in his *Boundaries Report* is that he converted 10 provisionally recommended Conservative seats (on a 1992 election basis, note) to Labour. On our figures, this seems an overstatement – we agree that six of them (Carlisle, Sale, Dewsbury, Leyton & Wanstead, Bristol North West and Southampton Test) became Labour and add two more (Coventry South and Stirling) to the list. However we do not agree with the other four and we think he 'lost' three provisionally recommended Labour seats (Blackpool South, Middlesbrough South & Cleveland East, and Southampton Itchen), making a net gain of five not ten.

So was it all a waste of time? There were some real and significant changes in particular areas. In Manchester/Trafford, for example, Labour was able to concentrate Conservative support in one seat, whereas in Wakefield/Kirklees it was able to spread its own support more effectively. In Sheffield Conservative and Labour together overturned the provisional recommendations which were supported by the Liberal Democrats and in the Borders the Liberal Democrats undoubtedly 'saved' a seat; in Colchester, their support (through a local government consortium; Chapter 6) of a 'doughnut' for the town seat made it winnable for both Labour and the Liberal Democrats. Labour had its successes in Shire England, too, especially in or around urban areas, for instance Bedford, Carlisle, and Welwyn Hatfield; the Conservatives also had successes in such areas, but these were primarily successful defences against Labour schemes. The clear impression is of a well-organised Labour Party securing partisan advantage in the areas where it was already strong; and of a disorganised Conservative Party managing to resist a Labour advance, which was always going to be difficult to achieve, in the Shires.

Conclusions

No system of electoral redistricting can be entirely non-partisan in its consequences, even when the redistricting process is carried out by independent and politically neutral Commissions. Changing constituency boundaries necessarily changes the results of elections, even if the partisan impacts are unintended and accidental side-effects. In Great Britain, redistrictings generally favour the Conservatives, as they tend to increase representation in the south and the suburbs (areas of Conservative strength) at the expense of the inner cities and the north (areas of Labour strength).

There is nothing sinister in this. It is an inevitable result of long-term trends in Britain's population geography: not redistricting at all would produce equal but opposite unintended partisan impacts, since areas of population decline would gradually become more and more over-represented relative to areas of population growth. Since the declining areas are Labour-voting, Labour would benefit electorally from a failure to redistrict. Whether boundaries change or not, therefore, there are political consequences. The need for regular boundary reviews in Britain therefore creates opportunities and risks for the parties, especially for the Conservatives and Labour.

As a result, the parties would be either remarkably self-sacrificing or remarkably naive if they allowed the Review process to take place without trying to influence the results to their advantage. The Boundary Commissions are politically non-partisan and will not entertain overtly partisan approaches and proposals, but there are several avenues open to parties by which they can try to exert influence over the process. We have discussed five: controlling the timing of Reviews (delaying them for Labour, hastening them for the Conservatives); changing the local government framework within which the Review process takes place; challenging the Commissions' proposals through the public consultation process (which the parties have open access to, just as does any organisation or individual); electoral registration; and judicial review.

Of these, only the Inquiry process gives the parties a chance to put forward partisan proposals. The rules governing the Commissions' workings provide a range of possible and ostensibly non-partisan (and hence admissible) grounds for challenging any given set of proposed boundaries. Most partisan proposals can be justified in non-partisan terms which accord with those rules, and parties use this loophole to introduce a partisan dimension to the Review. There is an inbuilt counterweight, however, in that all parties can do so. In any Inquiry, the proposals made by one party can be challenged by another, which can in its turn put forward its own proposals, challengeable in their turn, and so on. Much depends on the relative balance of the arguments put forward, and on the evaluation of these arguments by the Assistant Commissioner.

The Fourth Review provides an instructive case study. It was widely expected to result in significant electoral advantages for the Conservatives whereas Labour was expected to lose out. In both cases, however, how the party approached the Review, and especially the Local Inquiry stage, was crucial to the eventual partisan outcome. Overall, Labour's highly organised approach paid off. It lost out as a result of the Fourth Review, just as it had from the Third Review, but it managed to contain the damage, thereby limiting its losses. The Conservatives, despite the fact that they were the eventual and overall winners (again, just as they had been at the previous Review), suffered for their initial complacency: they could have done considerably better. The Liberal Democrats and the Nationalists, meanwhile, were relative side-shows in the process. As small parties, they started from weak positions in terms of their representation, and they found it almost impossible to use the Fourth Review to improve their lot; they were too small, their support was too dispersed, and their resources and organisation were not sufficient for a national effort on the scale necessary.

The partisan effect of a Review depends partly on Britain's changing social geography, therefore. But that social geography does not determine the outcome. There is an immense number of different ways of skinning the 'redistricting cat'. Virtually any proposal for a set of constituencies can be challenged, with many equally good or bad alternative sets of proposals. Political parties, acting in their own self-interests, can make quite legitimate use of the Review process to lobby for proposals which fit their own partisan needs. That they do so is hardly surprising. The intriguing issue is the extent to which each party is effective in pushing its case. As the Fourth Review clearly shows, there is nothing inevitable about the partisan outcome.

Notes

1 The cube law was first described by James Parker Smith in his evidence to the 1908–1910 Royal Commission on the electoral system, and was 'rediscovered' by David Butler in the late 1940s (Kendall and Stuart, 1950; Butler, 1953). Formally, in a two-party political system, the cube law can be stated as:

$$\frac{S_i/(1-S_i)}{(V_i/(1-V_i))^3} = 1$$

Where:

S_i is the proportion of seats won by party i;
V_i is the proportion of votes won by party i;
$(1-S_i)$ is the proportion of seats won by the other party; and
$(1-V_i)$ is the proportion of votes won by the other party.

Where more than two parties contest elections, the cube law may still hold, but it is limited to the two-party vote and seat shares of the two main parties.
2 Though application of Rule 6 (Box 3.6) might lead a Commission to disregard possible constituencies which were physically too large, inaccessible, or oddly shaped.
3 If the size constraint is relaxed somewhat to allow each seat to vary in electorate by up to 11 per cent from the average, the number of possible solutions is even larger, at around 15,000!
4 It is not entirely clear from the Commission's report that this situation (which Mortimore, 1992, terms the 'Harrow paradox') reflected a deliberate attempt to gain an additional seat for Harrow or simply the result of a mis-calculation. The Assistant Commissioner reported that 'if the present proposals had been foreseen, different adjustments would have been made' (Boundary Commission for England, 1983, 27,

#122), which implies the latter interpretation. However, the case was made in concert with one that Harrow should retain three constituencies because of its above-average proportions of elderly residents and of Commonwealth immigrants, which are clearly outside the rules: Mortimore (1992, 99), however, says that 'there is no particular reason to suppose that it was deliberately planned with malice aforethought'.

5 The Avon Inquiry was one of the first to be held, and clearly illustrates the Conservative party's complacency at that time (see Chapter 6).

6 On 'Wednesbury reasonableness', see Chapter 5, Note 10.

7 The first part of the case was further advanced by noting that after local government reorganisation in 1994 Alloway would be in a separate unitary authority with Ayr. It was currently separated from Ayr by the allocation of its RED to an adjacent constituency, with which the other wards in the RED indeed had closer ties.

8 Interestingly, the Commission indicated to Lord Weir that they wished him to come to a decision on the facts of the petition rather than on the reasonableness of the procedure, and he found for it on those grounds too. In his opinion the choice of REDs as building blocks was a valid exercise of the Commission's discretion, and not an unreasonable means of constraining itself and so preventing it applying the rules properly (notably Rule 5 regarding electoral equality). Furthermore, when it reviewed the Assistant Commissioner's advice and decided to be consistent in using REDs throughout Scotland it was again properly exercising its discretionary power.

9 All Census data were made available through the auspices of the Economic and Social Research Council and are Crown copyright.

10 See Rossiter, Johnston and Pattie (1997a), in which we use two measures: R^2, and the standard error.

11 There is a problem, however, in the use of our measure of party campaigning at the real contest. Because party spending (our surrogate) is only reported for the entire (original) constituency, it is not possible to disaggregate the campaign data to the ward level directly and reaggregate it into the new constituencies. However, we have estimated what the effects of 1979 campaign spending would have been had the election been fought in the 'new' seats (for details, see Rossiter, Johnston and Pattie, 1997a).

12 Our estimates of the partisan consequences of the Third Review are very similar to those derived by the Press Association team using local election results (BBC/ITN, 1983).

13 An alternative approach is outlined in Grofman, Koetzle and Brunell (1997). We have modified Brookes' method slightly, in line with suggestions made by Mortimore (1992).

14 For the algebra, see Rossiter, Johnston and Pattie (1997b); Johnston (1977).

9

MPs and their seats

The previous chapter looked at the partisan consequences of the Boundary Review process. Under first-past-the-post arrangements, changing the constituency framework will change the political complexion of Parliament, even if each party wins the same number of votes overall. Some parties' Parliamentary representation will grow, while others will decline. In general, the Conservative party has benefited most from British redistrictings but at the Fourth Review Labour, while losing out, did not do as badly as expected, due to its co-ordinated strategy.

There are clear implications from this for the political parties, which were explored in Chaper 8. Not surprisingly, since parties form governments, much attention has been given to how they are affected by a Review, and to how they try to influence its outcomes. Rather less attention has been given to how individual representatives, the Members of Parliament, are affected by the Review process, and how they react to it. Yet MPs' political futures, careers and even livelihoods can be altered at a stroke by a change to their constituency. In this chapter, therefore, we turn to the individual MPs.

Boundary Reviews and the careers of Members of Parliament

Making a career in British politics can be a long slog. In the great majority of cases, much time and effort is spent between joining a party and winning the nomination to stand as a candidate in a winnable seat (Norris and Lovenduski, 1995). Once elected to Parliament another, often long, struggle to rise within the party hierarchy begins (Riddell, 1996).

At the same time, MPs have to retain the continued support of their constituents. Without a seat in the Commons, a politician is virtually unable to become Prime Minister, for instance.[1] Many senior politicians have had their careers delayed, or even thwarted, through the loss of their Parliamentary seat. Tony Benn was a major figure in the Labour party prior to the 1983 election, for example, and played an important part in that party's swing to the left. He came very close to becoming Deputy Leader in 1981, and was a possible contender for the leadership. But he lost his seat in 1983, removing him from Parliament for a crucial year, until the Chesterfield by-election. During that time, Benn's influence within the party waned. His situation is discussed in more detail below.

More recently, a number of MPs who had been mentioned as possible future leaders of the Conservative party saw their chances frustrated when they lost their seats. On the left of the party, Chris Patten lost Bath in 1992,[2] and Secretary of State for Defence Michael Portillo, on the party's right, lost Enfield Southgate in one of the most dramatic turn-rounds of the 1997 election. Other potential Conservative leaders who lost their seats in 1997 included Foreign Secretary Malcolm Rifkind (Edinburgh Pentlands), Scottish Secretary Michael Forsyth (Stirling), and President of the Board of Trade Ian Lang (Galloway and Upper Nithsdale). All were more senior and better known than the man who eventually replaced John Major as party leader following the 1997 defeat, William Hague (a very young Secretary of State for Wales – his first Cabinet post – in the previous government). Hague would probably not have stood for the leadership, let alone won, had the field included the 'big guns' who could not stand as they were out of Parliament.

But how might MPs hold on to their seats? Individuals have limited direct control over their fates, which are tied up with their parties' fortunes. Much depends on the basic level of support established by the extent of partisan identification and by the political cleavages within the electorate (Butler and Stokes 1969; Heath *et al.*, 1985, 1989; Johnston, Pattie and Allsopp, 1988). Furthermore, to the extent that a government is able to deliver prosperity, it can win or retain support, though if it delivers recession, it will probably lose it (Sanders, 1996; Pattie and Johnston, 1995). Individual MPs cannot bring much influence to bear in these areas at all and their scope to build substantial personal followings in their seats is limited, therefore.

It is limited, but is not non-existent. A diligent MP will have worked hard in his or her constituents' interests, dealing with problems, lending support to local causes, attending local events and so on. This can help an MP build a constituency personal support base (Cain *et al.*, 1984; Wood and Norton, 1992). Furthermore, MPs who take a principled stand on an issue of particular salience to the public in their constituency might find their local support enhanced (Pattie, Fieldhouse and Johnston, 1994). Although these effects are small when compared to the standing of an MP's party, they may make the difference between retaining and losing a seat in the event of a close election contest.

In addition, MPs can mobilise local support through constituency election campaigns. The electoral studies orthodoxy has been that local campaigns have been superseded in the post-war period by the growth of the national campaign, fought on television, the radio and in the national press (Kavanagh, 1995; Scammell, 1995). However, the local campaign is far from dead. Votes can still be won or lost in a constituency battle through the efficacy or otherwise of the local campaign (Pattie, Johnston and Fieldhouse, 1995; Denver and Hands, 1997). Mounting an effective local campaign requires resources, commitment, party members, planning, and often a long-term outlook, for a campaign which starts *ex nihilo* during the formal election campaign may be too little, too late. Rather, what is required is a constant low-key campaign which can run between elections, to be stoked up in intensity as the contest approaches.

Of course, not all MPs are equally vulnerable to electoral competition. Many represent safe seats, where there is no serious risk that they will lose. Ambitious politicians might try to win the nomination for one of their party's safer seats so that having been freed from the threat of losing their seats at the next election, they are in a better position to concentrate on their Parliamentary careers. It is no accident, for instance, that most recent Prime Ministers have represented safe seats.[3]

That said, by no means all MPs representing safe seats will rise to the top: many are backbenchers throughout their (long) careers. Also, many high fliers do not start their careers in safe seats, and may have to spend periods outside the Commons when they lose their seats. They can, of course, use these periods to try to gain a safe seat nomination, for instance at a by-election (though by-elections can be problematic for governing party candidates, even when held in supposedly safe seats; see Norris, 1990; Cook and Ramsden, 1997). Yet other high fliers will spend much of their careers in marginals (as with Michael Forsyth in Stirling), or will see their seat become marginal over time (as with Chris Patten in Bath). There is a constant threat for these MPs that they will lose their seat at some point in the future. By and large, safe seats are reassuring for politicians and their careers, while marginals are risky and threatening.

MPs rely on their constituency support, therefore, and can take measures to protect and nurture it. The Boundary Review process cuts across those measures. The period of the Review can be one of worry and uncertainty, even if the eventual outcome is to leave the seat unchanged. Safe seats can become marginal if the Commissioners recommend that key wards be removed to another seat, or that wards of a different political hue be moved into the constituency from a neighbouring seat (as exemplified with Bristol Northwest; Figure 8.2). MPs in marginals, faced with the same situation, might find they are left with a seat which they are likely to lose although those with hopes of government office might take a wider view and think of the consequences of the Review for their party's representation and its chances of forming an administration. If the Review is bad for their party, it might also be bad for their careers in Parliament, irrespective of its impact on their own seat: no truly ambitious politician is likely to settle happily for life on the opposition benches.

A Review can also be a time of opportunity and possibility, however. MPs in marginals can find their constituencies made safer by boundary changes and some whose existing seats are destroyed or substantially adversely changed by a Review might seek the nomination for one of the new seats which most Reviews create. Equally, irrespective of changes to their own seat, their party's prospects might be improved, increasing its chance of forming a future government and hence their chance of promotion.

But there is a sense in which any change is unsettling, whether or not the seat becomes safer as a result. Efforts made by an MP to build up his or her local profile through efforts on behalf of constituents, or through local campaigning, can be weakened or even undone by boundary changes. The new seat may include a substantial number of new voters who do not know the MP, having come from another constituency, who have not been contacted by him or her, and who have not built up any particular judgement on the MP's individual worth. Furthermore, the more a seat is changed, the more disruption there is likely to be to the local party structure there. This may have adverse consequences for the MP's ability to mount effective local campaigns in the immediate future, especially if the ward parties which had provided the most active and experienced campaigners in the past have been transferred to a new seat.

MPs' responses to the threats and opportunities of the Boundary Review process will depend on their evaluations of the impacts on their own ambitions, on their abilities to wage campaigns, and on their parties nationally. Their responses are likely to fall into one of three types: exit, voice or loyalty (Hirschman, 1970). Loyalty occurs when the individual decides to accept the new circumstances without demur. Exit, on the other hand, occurs when the individual so objects to the new circumstances that the only recourse is to leave and go elsewhere, where the circumstances do not hold. Voice is an intermediate position, where the individual objects to the new circumstances, but, rather than avoiding them by leaving, decides to stay and object, hoping by doing so to change the circumstances.

The loyalty option during a Boundary Review might arise from a variety of different scenarios. Most obviously, loyalty would come into play where an MP's seat was either little changed or changed for the better, from the Member's point of view. In those circumstances, there is little point in following an exit strategy and, other things being equal, a voice strategy need not be considered. But loyalty might also be invoked if the MP is acting as a partisan altruist – willing to accept adverse changes to his or her own seat if that is deemed to be in the best interests of the party as a whole.

In some circumstances, an exit strategy might be called for instead. An MP might decide that, due to boundary changes, his or her seat is no longer a safe prospect, and rather than face the uncertainty of fighting an election which might be lost, seek nomination for a different, safer seat elsewhere. During the 1992 Parliament, for instance, the Conservative MP Peter Thurnham tried to move from his marginal seat (Bolton North East) to a safer one (Westmorland and Lonsdale). When he was not selected for the latter, he adopted a different exit strategy, defecting from the Conservatives to the Liberal Democrats. Alternatively, an exit-minded MP might decide to leave Parliament altogether and retire from national politics rather than face the effort of rebuilding support in a much changed seat: Dudley Fishburn, Conservative MP for Kensington before the Fourth Periodic Review, chose this option, as did David Alton, Liberal Democrat MP for Liverpool, Mossley Hill. (Kensington was to be split in half between two seats, and

Mossley Hill was split three ways, with the largest component of the previous seat being only 40 per cent of the total.) Finally, some MPs might have an exit strategy forced upon them. Some will have seen their former seat change so much that there is virtually nothing left of it in a meaningful sense. In those circumstances, they are forced to leave. Equally, a local party might take the opportunity offered by the adoption of new constituencies to get rid of an unpopular MP, arguing that, as the seat has changed, there is no longer a debt of loyalty to the sitting member as there is no longer, technically, a sitting member! Exit can also be 'encouraged' by the actions of the national party. After the Fourth Review, for instance, where a seat had been changed very substantially (defined as a change involving 20 per cent or more of the electorate), Conservative Central Office advised the local Conservative Association to hold an open selection process to find a new candidate (although, because local Conservative Associations are formally independent of the national party, this could not be enforced; Ball, 1994). MPs in this position will also have to use an exit strategy, either to seek reselection elsewhere, or to retire.

Finally, many MPs will be reluctant either to leave a seat they may have represented for many years or to accept quietly the changes proposed by the Boundary Commissions. For them, the appropriate strategy is voice. Just like any other concerned individual, MPs can make representations to the Commissions following the provisional recommendations, and they can put their case at any Local Inquiry held in their areas. They can, of course, appear as representatives of their party but they can also appear on their own behalf, even where this conflicts with wider party interests. The object of a voice strategy for an individual MP is to try and head off potentially adverse changes to his or her constituency by pointing to flaws in existing proposals for change, where these are against the MP's interests, supporting proposals where they are, and perhaps even making new proposals, in an attempt to persuade the Assistant Commissioner running the Inquiry to recommend in their favour.

The voice strategy need not be limited to MPs who face a threat as a result of the provisional recommendations, however. Even MPs who are happy with their lot under the provisional recommendations and who might be persuaded into a loyalty strategy may opt for voice instead. This might arise if a rival candidate or party tables a counter-proposal which will harm the sitting MP's interests. The voice strategy would then be to argue the wisdom of the provisional recommendations and the folly of the counter-proposal. Even where no formal counter-proposal is known to an MP, he or she might still decide to exercise the voice option to head off the possibility. Finally, it is also possible that an MP will decide to exercise the voice option against proposals put forward by his or her own party, where these are felt to be in the interests of the party as a whole but at the cost of the individual MP. It will, however, be a brave or determined MP who will do so, since flying in the face of one's own party is rarely a good means of gaining preferment within it.

Voice strategies: MPs and the Fourth Review

Voice is a popular strategy among MPs who were frequent participants in Local Inquiries at the Fourth Review (Table 6.4). However, while the above discussion lays out the risks and opportunities facing MPs as a result of a Boundary Review, and some of the strategies open to them, it does not tell us what they actually do to influence a Review. Nor does it tell us how MPs employing a voice strategy co-ordinate their efforts with those of their parties. Do they act as local party representatives, taking advice from the national party and following it? Or do they act as freelances, consulting no one but themselves and perhaps their local supporters? What sorts of activities do they undertake? Is an appearance at the Local Inquiry the sum of their efforts, or are they involved in wider campaigns? In this section, we consider these questions through the analysis of a survey of all MPs conducted in the immediate aftermath of the Fourth Review. All sitting MPs were approached, and 304 (mainly backbenchers) replied, a response rate of 47 per cent. Clearly, there is some risk of bias here but, insofar as we have been able to check, the sample seems to be a good cross-section of backbench opinion. There were, for instance, no significant differences in party affiliation between respondents and non-respondents, suggesting that no major Parliamentary party is over- or under-represented. There were, however (and inevitably), only a few responses from MPs in the Liberal Democrat party, the SNP, Plaid Cymru and the Northern Ireland parties; these have not been separately identified by subsequent analyses, which focus on Conservative and Labour Members.

Individual MPs are liable to differ in the extent to which they adopt a voice strategy, and some will not adopt it at all. Furthermore, they are likely to differ in the extent to which they co-ordinate their efforts with other MPs or with their party as a whole. On a priori grounds, we might expect inter-party variations between MPs. As has been shown in earlier chapters, Labour's approach to the Fourth Review was highly centralised and disciplined, so Labour MPs are likely to have consulted widely within their party and not to have 'freelanced' when it came to the Local Inquiry. The Conservatives, meanwhile, suffered from both a lack of central co-ordination and the independence of local party organisations and individual Conservative MPs should have been much more likely to go their own way and less likely to consult. Similarly, MPs whose seats were threatened with large scale disruption as a result of the Fourth Review should have been more likely to exercise the voice strategy, and more likely to seek advice in doing so, than MPs whose seats were little affected (though, as we argue above, there is a rationale for even those MPs not directly affected by the Review to make their case).

Seeking advice

The issues raised by a Boundary Review are complex. For individual MPs, deciding whether and how to respond to the Commissions' provisional recommendations is not a simple process. As shown in the previous chapter, a very large number of possible outcomes can be designed for even quite small areas. Some will be better for the individual MP than others, but how is he or she to identify the best? Furthermore, some outcomes, through their effects on other seats, will be better for the MP's party (and hence for his or her career) than others – but again, how to decide which is which? Not only that, but what best serves the MP's self-interest may conflict with the wider party interest. How is a compromise to be reached (and, indeed, can one be reached) between these competing claims?

The nature of the response required from an MP also varies. Many factors are involved. For instance, how should the proposals be approached? Are they basically good for the MP, making the seat safer, or bad, making it more vulnerable? In the former case, any response might well be supportive, trying to ensure that the Commission kept to its provisional recommendations. In the latter, the imperative would be to try to ensure changes which would make the seat safer again. If the decision was to try to win changes in the boundaries of the seat, how might this best be achieved? Which areas should be included in the seat, which excluded, and what should be the grounds for arguing the desired case? From a wider perspective, what would be in the best interests of the party overall, rather than simply of an individual MP? In some cases, for instance, the party might feel that it was necessary to sacrifice one seat locally (or to allow it to become more vulnerable than it had been previously, even though it remains winnable) in order to increase its chances of securing two others. Add to this the ambiguity of the law governing the Review process, the wide potential range of arguments which could be used in making a case, the likelihood that other parties will make their own proposals regarding the seat (which are unlikely to aid the sitting MP), and the possibility that other, non-party groups will become involved, and it is hardly surprising that MPs seek advice when faced by recommendations for new seats.

But to whom did they turn? Our evidence from the Fourth Review provides some clues (Table 9.1). Not surprisingly, MPs talked to those of their supporters closest at hand and with the greatest degree of local knowledge. Once the provisional recommendations for their area had been published, the overwhelming majority of MPs (94 per cent) consulted their constituency party and there were no real differences between MPs from different parties in their tendency to do so. This is to be expected. MPs' main local contacts are usually through their constituency parties, which know the area and which can help provide information on 'local ties' arguments which might be put in front of the Assistant Commissioner at any Local Inquiry. In any case, the constituency party stands to be affected by change almost as much as the MP. Altering the constituency boundaries can lead to substantial changes in membership, as some ward organisations are removed from the constituency and others join it. Just as an MP might face losing the seat, so the local party might face dismemberment, which might create animosity in a new constituency between party members drawn from different old constituency parties. Furthermore, local parties are important contributors to election campaigning, of both resources and campaign workers. The disruption of local party organisations entailed by changing constituency boundaries could have an adverse (though as yet unknown) impact upon local campaigning potential. For all these reasons, then, we expected that MPs would consult closely with their local parties over anything which might threaten the boundaries of their seat.

Table 9.1 *MPs' consultation over the Boundary Commission's Fourth Periodic Review, by political party (percentages of respondents)*

	All MPs	Conservative	Labour
Did you consult with your local party?			
Yes	94	93	95
No	6	7	5
N*	286	134	125
Did you consult with your national party?			
Yes	76	66	88
No	24	34	12
N*	273	124	123
Did you consult with other MPs from your county?			
Yes	80	80	88
No	20	20	12
N*	274	132	117
Did you consult with any of the local authorities within your constituency?			
Yes	57	37	78
No	43	63	22
N*	267	127	115
Total respondents	304	140	133

Note: *number responding to the question.

Source: survey of MPs

Equally, an MP should consult more widely, both to compare notes and to develop strategies, not least because there could be knock-on effects for him or her from proposed changes to the Commission's recommendations in other seats, as well as for other MPs as a result of changes in his or her seat, not to mention the overall concern about the implication of the Review for representation of the MP's own party. Consulting with the national party is, of course, likely to be a two-way process. In ideal circumstances, the individual MP will want advice on making the best of his or her own seat: the national party will wish to ensure, as far as possible, that no individual acts as a maverick to the detriment of the party's overall prospects. Talking to the national party may well be as much about co-ordinating efforts as about improving individual prospects.

MPs were less likely to consult more widely, although most did seek some form of wider consultation: 80 per cent reported consulting other MPs in their County, London Borough, or Scottish Region (as the Commissions' provisional recommendations are published separately for each County, London Borough and Scottish Region, MPs from each local authority area will all be affected at the same time), while 76 per cent discussed the Review with their national party organisations. But whereas there were no real inter-party differences in MPs' propensity to consult their local parties, there were differences in the extent to which they sought wider advice. Labour MPs were by far the most likely to seek advice from their national party and other local MPs (88 per cent reported doing so). Conservative MPs were somewhat less likely to consult other MPs (80 per cent did so), and markedly less likely to consult with Conservative Central Office (only 66 per cent of them did so).

These results reflect the major parties' very different approaches to the Fourth Review, described in Chapter 6. Labour's highly centralised strategy necessitated a great deal of consultation between MPs and various levels of the party organisation. The party ran a highly centralised and controlled national campaign to ensure that all Labour representations to the Boundary Commission and to Local Inquiries were co-ordinated and designed to maximise the party's electoral benefit. Party headquarters were aided in this by Labour's strong party structure and, almost certainly, by the more general modernisation process of the late 1980s and 1990s which had taken power within the party back from activists to the leadership (Shaw, 1994). Labour, to a remarkable degree, 'sang from the same hymn sheet', with positive consequences for the party, in terms of minimising the damage (see Chapters 5 and 7).

The Conservatives' early but ultimately misplaced confidence about the Review meant the party was less effective than Labour in using Local Inquiries. Furthermore, Conservative efforts to create a co-ordinated response were hampered by the formal independence of its constituency associations. Many saw attempts by Conservative Central Office to co-ordinate the party's response to the Review as unwanted outside interference, and they resisted it.

Other MPs and national parties do not exhaust the range of extra-constituency bodies MPs sought advice from, though they were among the most important. Fewer MPs consulted their local authorities over the Commission's proposals than consulted their national parties (only 57 per cent reported doing so). At first sight, this is surprising, not least because local authorities are important 'players' in the Inquiry process (Chapter 6) and if they make negative representations to a Boundary Commission concerning its recommendations, an Inquiry must be held. As a consequence, local authorities were almost invariably represented at Local Inquiries: they were important witnesses in their own rights. They have an interest in maintaining effective links with the area's Parliamentary representatives (and, for instance, in the case of English District authorities in County areas, in avoiding as far as possible having constituencies which overlap several Districts). Furthermore, although many authorities give non-political evidence, it is possible for a party in control of a local authority to use that evidence to advance the partisan interest in an attempt to avoid having the evidence seen as partisan. We expected close links between MPs and local authorities in discussions over boundary changes, therefore, in terms of both groups' interest in the nature of local representation and of MPs' interests in getting sympathetic support from major public bodies, where possible.

The reason for the apparent shortfall in MPs' consultations with local councils becomes apparent when we look at how MPs from each party acted. Conservative MPs were by far the least likely to get in touch with their local authorities: just over a third reported doing so. Labour MPs, meanwhile, were much more likely to contact their local authorities; a large majority, around 80 per cent, did so. This must be seen in the context of trends in local authority elections during the 1990s. The Conservatives fared very badly, losing control of many councils, even in the normally true-blue Home Counties. Conservative MPs looking for politically sympathetic local authorities to consult in the mid-1990s were relatively unlikely to find one in their area, whereas Labour MPs could do so relatively easily. It was not necessarily an antipathy towards local authorities which explains Conservative MPs' failure to consult them but rather a lack of opportunity. When the Fourth Review took place, the party did not have the local government resources to draw on. Had the Conservatives' local government base not eroded so rapidly in the 1990s, it would have been more surprising had their MPs not sought advice and help there (see Chapter 6).

The other factor which played a part in determining whether MPs sought advice, and who from, was the extent to which they felt that their seat had been affected by the Commission's proposals (Table 9.2). We asked MPs to assess whether the provisional recommendations for their constituency had left it unchanged, slightly changed, substantially changed, or had eliminated it entirely (the analyses reported here combine those who said their seat had changed substantially and those who said it had been eliminated): 24 per cent reported no change; 34 per cent reported slight change; and 41 per cent said their seat had been affected more substantially. Not surprisingly, the more an MP felt his or her seat had been changed, the more likely he or she was to consult another group. The only variation from this was consultations with local authorities: MPs whose seat changed substantially were most likely to consult their local council, and MPs whose seat did not change were the least likely to do so, but the differences were not statistically significant.

There was clearly an element of 'if it ain't broke, don't fix it'! What is remarkable, however, is the extent to which MPs did consult. Even among those whose own seat was not changed, 80 per cent still consulted their local party, 67 per cent consulted their national party, 63 per cent talked to other local MPs, and 50 per cent consulted their local authorities. This may reflect a range of factors. The Boundary Reviews represent a considerable unsettling factor for MPs. Some may have needed reassurance, and sought consultation even when they were not affected. Others, whose seats remained unchanged by the provisional recommendations, may have felt unhappy with the existing boundaries of their constituencies (perhaps because they were marginal), and harboured hopes that the Commission would give them a safer seat. Finally, insofar as MPs and parties were taking the wider view, even those whose seats were not affected by the provisional recommendations might find that alternative proposals put in place by their party to serve its wider interests locally would have an effect on them if successfully argued at Local Inquiry. Labour's nationally co-ordinated campaign especially made this latter scenario quite possible. Most MPs know the geography of their own seats – including the geography of party support within the seat – reasonably well, but their knowledge of the area beyond their constituency may be much less complete: by providing the 'big picture', Labour gave its MPs and candidates that wider knowledge.

Table 9.2 *MPs' consultation over the Boundary Commission's Fourth Periodic Review, by extent to which seat was altered by provisional recommendations (percentages of respondents)*

| | All | Unchanged | When the provisional recommendations were published, was your constituency: | |
			Slightly Changed	Substantially Changed/Eliminated
Did you consult with your local party?				
Yes	94	81	97	98
No	6	19	3	2
N*	286	63	100	123
Did you consult with your national party?				
Yes	76	67	72	83
No	24	33	28	17
N*	273	61	98	114
Did you consult with other MPs from your county?				
Yes	80	63	82	87
No	20	37	18	13
N*	274	60	97	117
Did you consult with any of the local authorities within your constituency?				
Yes	57	50	57	59
No	43	50	43	41
N*	267	58	94	115
Total respondents	304	74	104	126

Note:*numbers responding to the question.
Source: survey of MPs

Taking steps

Having consulted on the impact and implications of the Boundary Commissions' proposals, MPs had to decide how to respond (to exercise their voice strategy). Part of the strategy was to create an impression that their views had wide support in the constituency. Over three-quarters encouraged either their local party or other groups to write to the Commission, either supporting or opposing the recommendations (Table 9.3; the majority of representations were opposed to the recommendations). Labour MPs were the most diligent in encouraging people to make representations (87 per cent said they did so: possibly another mark of Labour's professional approach). Conservative MPs were rather less likely to encourage people to write, but a large number (71 per cent) did.

Table 9.3 *Organising representations to the Boundary Commissions, by political party (percentages of respondents)*

	All MPs	Conservative	Labour
Did you encourage your local party, or other individuals or organisations, to make written representations to the Commission?			
Yes	78	71	87
No	22	29	13
N*	289	136	125
Did you take any other actions to try and influence the outcome of the Commission's work?			
Yes	58	54	62
No	42	46	38
N*	278	133	117
Total respondents	304	140	133

Note: *numbers responding to the question.

Source: survey of MPs

Fewer MPs reported doing anything beyond taking consultations or encouraging others to write. Just under 60 per cent reported taking further action, and there were no significant differences between the parties in the probability that their MPs did. Among those who took some further action, by far the most common response was to give evidence to the Local Inquiries: 86 per cent of those who took further action did so, and Labour MPs taking further action were more likely to than were Conservatives (97 per cent compared to 73 per cent). In addition, 20 per cent reported some sort of co-ordinated effort with their local party. No other activities were undertaken by more than a tiny handful of MPs, though one or two had written to the local press, addressed local meetings, claimed to have met the Commission, or had urged a Local Inquiry (Michael Forsyth MP, for instance, approached the Scottish Commission). Three MPs reported that they had appointed legal counsel to act on their behalf.

MPs whose seats changed substantially were rather more likely to get involved in further action of some kind, or to encourage others to do so, than were those whose seats did not change much (Table 9.4). The greater the threatened change to the seat, the more likely an MP was to get involved in some response to the Commission. MPs' own accounts suggest important differences in whether, or how, they used 'voice' strategies in their approach to the Fourth Review, therefore. For those who did exercise the voice option, the formal channels offered by the Boundary Commissions, primarily written responses to the provisional recommendations and participation at Local Inquiries, were by far the most important vehicle for representations. But the extent to which MPs exercised the voice strategy and sought wider advice in doing so, and the range of individuals and institutions from whom they sought advice, depended on two things: how much they felt their existing seat was affected by the Review, and which party they represented.

Table 9.4 *Organising representations to the Boundary Commissions, by extent to which seat was altered by provisional recommendations (percentages of respondents)*

		When the provisional recommendations were published, was your constituency		
	All	*Unchanged*	*Slightly Changed*	*Substantially Changed/Eliminated*
Did you encourage your local party, or other individuals or organisations, to make written representations to the Commission?				
Yes	78	63	77	87
No	22	37	23	13
N*	289	65	100	124
Did you take any other actions to try and influence the outcome of the Commission's work?				
Yes	58	41	57	68
No	42	59	43	32
N*	278	63	95	120
Total respondents	304	74	104	126

Note: * numbers responding to the question.
Source: survey of MPs

Voice strategies can be applied at quite late stages of the Review process. MPs (like other groups and individuals) can and do make representations regarding the Commissions' revised recommendations. During the Fourth Review, for example, Winston Churchill MP was sufficiently unhappy with the revised recommendations for his Davyhulme seat to organise a constituents' petition to the English Commission: as a means of making the Commission change its recommendation further, the strategy was unsuccessful. On occasion, representations at this stage can pay off, however, as in the case of the proposals for Lambeth and Southwark (see Chapter 7).

Almost the last opportunity MPs have to exercise a voice strategy arises when the Commissions' final recommendations are placed before Parliament by the relevant Secretary of State and debated. At this stage, MPs can do nothing to effect detailed changes: all they can do is raise general issues, express their approval or disapproval, and (if they dislike the changes) hope that Parliament does not adopt the recommendations, though this is very rare: on the only occasion Parliament has done so, in 1969, it was a result of Government, not backbench, pressure (see Chapter 3). A voice strategy at this late stage is a very long shot indeed.

The Boundary Commission for England's Fourth Periodic Review was debated by the Commons on 14 June 1995. Not counting front benchers, 27 MPs took part: 16 Conservatives, 10 Labour, and 1 Liberal Democrat. Of those, about a quarter had not been affected at all by the Review (roughly in line with the proportion of all MPs unaffected). Conservative participants were on average slightly more likely to have been affected than other speakers, but the difference was not statistically significant. Few raised concerns about their own seats. Sir Teddy Taylor, for instance, worried over the new name given to his constituency; Winston Churchill complained about the failure of the Commission to re-examine its proposals for his seat; and Peter Luff discussed doughnuts and sandwiches at some length in the context of his Worcester constituency. But in general, the debate ranged over broader issues – equality of electorates, the treatment of Scotland, the effects of electoral registration, and so on. The Commons chamber was not (ironically) a good arena for a voice strategy.[4]

Exercising the exit strategy: moving seats, the 'chicken run' and retirement

Some MPs exercise only voice or loyalty strategies in their reactions to a Boundary Review. Others follow an exit strategy, either moving to another constituency or retiring from Parliament altogether (both, of course, with effect from the first election consequent on the completion of a Review). The most likely reason for doing so as a result of boundary changes would be that the seat has become harder to defend, or even likely to be lost as a result of the change: a move to a better prospect protects career, while an opportune retirement ahead of an expected election defeat preserves dignity.

Moving seats

An exit strategy could be an MP's last resort. A great deal has been invested in the constituency he or she has fought, won and (for most) held. That investment includes the time and effort put into campaigning, the incumbency advantages built up through constituency work, the advantages of familiarity and local knowledge, and perhaps even the cost of buying a home in the constituency. In addition, though less tangible, MPs considering moving seats must consider the risk of gaining a reputation as carpetbaggers. Local branches of their party, and local voters too, might react badly to the idea of being 'used' by someone more interested in advancing their career than in defending their local record in their original seat.

Even so, MPs faced with boundary changes that make their seat marginal or worse have a difficult choice between moving and staying put, even at the risk of ending (no matter how temporarily) their Commons career. Bristol was an area where the Third Review effected some important changes. Tony Benn had represented Bristol South East for 33 years, but his seat could either become much harder to win or even cease to exist as a result of the Review. He was faced with a dilemma. Should he stay in Bristol, fight and probably lose, or move to a safer seat (Benn, 1992). His predicament was particularly acute. He was the leader of the left in the party, and had a real chance of taking the party leadership after the upcoming election – but only if he remained in the Commons – and he had also built up long-term commitments and loyalties to his Bristol constituency. In addition, and politically potentially more embarrassing, he had berated Labour MPs who had defected to the SDP in 1981 for not resigning from Parliament and precipitating by-elections, to allow their constituents the chance to express their view of the decision (Crewe and King, 1995): had he left Bristol to fight elsewhere, he could equally have been accused of failing to face the people who had voted for him in 1979.

His initial resolution, recorded in his diary on the 29 November 1981, was 'to fight for my [Bristol South East] constituency to the bitter end'. He recognised, however, that the decision might be taken out of his hands by the Boundary Commission: 'but if it was abolished I would be eligible for the short list for either of the new constituencies' emerging from his old seat (Benn, 1992, 176). He intended to 'go down with the ship' (2 April 1982; Benn, 1992, 203), despite warnings from local party activists that he should look for a seat elsewhere as 'there is no hope of winning in Bristol once the boundaries change'. By 13 November 1982, however, he was wavering: 'it has become clear to me that I should leave', partly because of his doubts over being selected as a candidate in any of the new Bristol seats, partly because of his concerns about his political future (Benn, 1992 254). A month later, he was approached to consider standing for the new Livingston seat in central Scotland, an offer he took seriously (partly because, as a totally new seat, there was no incumbent Labour candidate to worry about unseating; Benn, 1992, 260).

The defining moment for Benn came at the Bermondsey by-election. Peter Tatchell, Labour's candidate in a normally safe Labour seat, had been at the centre of a media furore concerning his far left politics, his sexuality, and the extent of leadership support for his candidacy, and had been under pressure to stand down for a more moderate candidate. Tatchell did not stand down and Labour lost badly, to the Liberal/SDP Alliance. Benn's diary entry for 24 February 1983

(Benn, 1992, 276) records his reaction:

> Poor old Peter Tatchell, who has been massacred by the press, only got 7,600 votes, but he came out of [the by-election] with considerable courage and dignity ... I resolved there and then ... not to desert Bristol and that, when I go to Scotland on Saturday for a meeting I will make a statement saying I couldn't accept nomination for Livingston.

He did leave himself a small escape route, however, telling the Livingston Labour party that he would stand for their nomination if he failed to win nomination for any of the new Bristol seats (26 February 1983; Benn, 1992, 276). He was selected for Bristol East, fighting and losing it at the 1983 General Election. He re-entered the Commons a year later (after winning a by-election at Chesterfield), but his career was damaged and arguably never recovered. He was probably the most prominent victim of the Third Review. Had he not been absent from the Commons in the immediate aftermath of the 1983 election, he could have contested the Labour party leadership, and at the very least acted as a rallying point for the Parliamentary left. In the event, however, he was ineligible to stand. The leadership contest was won by Neil Kinnock, who went on to shift the party from its leftward trajectory and away from 'Bennism'.

Other MPs faced with similar dilemmas come to different decisions. Another hopeful for the Livingston nomination in 1983 was Robin Cook, then a relatively unknown Labour MP for Edinburgh Central, another seat threatened by the Third Review. Cook did move, and won Livingston at the 1983 election; he was appointed Foreign Secretary when Labour won the 1997 general election.

Not all moves arising ostensibly from boundary revisions are with the intention of moving to a safer seat, however. In 1970, another politician who later became a major figure in his party and a challenger for its leadership took the opportunity of a Boundary Review to change seats. Michael Heseltine had represented Tavistock in Devon, a safe Conservative constituency, since 1966. In 1970, it was largely absorbed by the new West Devon seat and Heseltine took the opportunity to move to another safe Conservative seat, Henley in Oxfordshire. In his case, the Review created an opportunity for a move he wished to make anyway, rather than forcing him to consider an unpalatable uprooting to save his career. Heseltine's Parliamentary ambitions and his business interests in London made the relatively remote Tavistock seat inconvenient (Crick, 1997, 164). Furthermore, his flamboyance caused concern among some of the more traditional members of his local Conservative Association. Had he stayed in Devon, the risk would have come from his own party members (there is no guarantee that he would have been retained as candidate for the new West Devon seat): better to move closer to London.

Moving carries its own risks, and there is no guarantee that the new seat will be a better prospect. But there is nothing new in MPs moving to safer seats, as shown in the 1950s in the career of another rising politician, Tony Crosland. The First Review seriously affected his South Gloucestershire seat. Machinations by his mentor, the former Labour Chancellor Hugh Dalton, failed to free the nomination for West Gloucestershire (Pimlott, 1985, 621) and he sought a safer seat, eventually winning the nomination for Southampton Test. Ironically, in the ensuing 1955 general election he lost heavily, though he could have won had he fought in South Gloucestershire (Riddell, 1996, 110). Crosland remained outside the Commons until 1957, when he won Grimsby at a by-election.[5]

Crosland did rise through his party, despite the miscalculation. So did Ian Sproat, one-time Conservative MP for Aberdeen South (Riddell, 1996, 110–1). He had already begun to rise up the ministerial ladder in the Conservative government when the Third Review made his seat more marginal. He promptly left, taking the nomination for the supposedly safer Roxburgh and Berwickshire seat. At the following election, the Conservatives held Aberdeen South, but Sproat lost in Roxburgh. He remained out of the Commons until 1992, when he was elected for Harwich; he became a junior Minister in John Major's government, but was defeated at the 1997 election.

The 'chicken run'

The 'chicken run' is not a new phenomenon, as Mortimore (1992) has shown. Over the period covered by the Commissions' Initial Reports and the first three Periodic Reviews, he identified 71 English MPs who moved seats between elections, all but four of them after a redistribution (the largest number was in 1950 when 41 moved). In addition, there were 31 cases of contests between two sitting MPs, all but two of which occurred after redistributions (with 15 of them at the 1950 election after the Initial Reports were implemented). Of those MPs whose seats were abolished in 1950, 18 retired, 17 fought a constituency formed partly from their old seat, and a further 17 contested another seat elsewhere in England. After the subsequent reviews, much larger proportions fought in constituencies formed at least in part from their old seats.[6] The changes in 1950 were clearly the most extensive, and there was considerable mobility among not only MPs whose seats were abolished but also those whose seats remained in place, albeit perhaps altered. Of the 451 MPs whose seats were not abolished, 41 retired and 32 moved: according to Mortimore (1992, 63) 'there were opportunistic shifts of territory … [that] played their part in numerous illustrious careers … among those unnecessarily on the move were Harold Wilson, Roy Jenkins and Ray Gunter'.

During the Fourth Review, MPs' decisions about whether to stay in their seats or move became a political issue in its own right, especially for Conservatives. Most MPs stayed put, fighting their old constituencies (where these had not changed) or the seat which formed the bulk of their old constituencies, some even when they knew it was not to their advantage to do so. But 16 Conservative MPs, many well-known, decided to move seats, as the Boundary Review had made their existing constituency much less winnable (particularly in the context of a prospective Labour landslide). Their decisions were widely reported and taken by some as indicating that, despite public pronouncements, they were pessimistic about the Conservative government's re-election chances and concerned with saving their own Parliamentary careers come what may. For the press, and for Labour, these MPs, by moving seats, were engaged in a 'chicken run' (Table 9.5).

Table 9.5 *The 'Chicken Run': Conservative MPs moving seats as a result of the Fourth Review*

| MP | 1992 and 'Successor' Seats | |
	Pre-move seat	Successor seat
MP moving to either a neighbouring seat or one containing part of their previous seat		
Stephen Dorrell	Loughborough	Charnwood
David Evenett	Erith & Crayford	Bexleyheath & Crayford
Peter Lilley	St Albans	Harpenden
Peter Luff	Worcester	Mid Worcestershire
Brian Mawhinney	Peterborough	North West Cambridgeshire
Andrew Rowe	Mid Kent	Faversham & Mid Kent
Nicholas Soames	Crawley	Mid Sussex
MP moving to a non-neighbouring seat		
David Amess	Basildon	Southend West
James Arbuthnott	Wanstead & Woodford	Hampshire North East
Sir Paul Beresford	Croydon Central	Mole Valley
Peter Bottomley	Eltham	Worthing West
Eric Forth	Mid Worcestershire	Bromley & Chislehurst
Nick Hawkins	Blackpool South	Surrey Heath
Norman Lamont	Kingston upon Thames	Harrogate & Knaresborough
John Watts	Slough	Reading East
Sir George Young	Ealing Acton	Hampshire North West

All of the 'chicken run' MPs would have lost in 1997 had they remained in the new constituency taking the largest share of their former seat. But 1997 was an unusually large landslide defeat for the Conservatives and many of their MPs who did not move lost too. Equally, all of the 'runners' were originally members for seats which had been altered to some extent at the Fourth Review, for most of whom the move paid off. Only three were defeated in their new seats: John Watts (who moved from Slough to nearby Reading East), David Evenett (Erith and Crayford to Bexleyheath and Crayford) and former Chancellor Norman Lamont (Kingston upon Thames to Harrogate & Knaresborough).

Beyond that, their experiences were quite diverse. Some accused of taking part in the chicken run could claim to represent part of their old constituency, although almost invariably it was a relatively small part subsumed within a larger and more Conservative area. Party Chairman Brian Mawhinney MP fell into this group, moving to Cambridgeshire North West, which included about a third of the electorate from his former Peterborough seat. So did Stephen Dorrell, Peter Lilley,

Peter Luff, David Evenett and Andrew Rowe. Nicholas Soames, meanwhile, moved from Crawley to Mid Sussex (which neighboured his old seat). Others, however, moved greater distances. David Amess' narrow victory in Basildon was one of the defining moments of the 1992 election, an early indication that the Conservatives would win. He spent much of the subsequent Parliament praising his constituency, often in extravagant terms, yet he left it and crossed the County to fight Southend West in 1997.[7]

Whereas some 'runners' were voluntary, others were forced into it. James Arbuthnott, Paul Beresford, Eric Forth and Norman Lamont all failed to secure the nomination in any of the successor seats into which their former constituency had been split so all had little choice but to move. Norman Lamont, in particular, was forced into a tour of seats, seeking nomination in each. Despite the media interest, however, there is no evidence to suggest that the Fourth Review generated more moves than the Third. Rather the opposite: whereas nine Conservative MPs moved to entirely new seats in 1997, for example, 13 did so in 1983 (Criddle, 1997, 187).

Retiring

Moving seats is not the only exit strategy open to MPs: some retire from the Commons altogether. A number retire before each general election, some because they have tired of political life, some because they have realised that they have few prospects for promotion, and some because they feel too old to continue. Changes in the constituency boundaries might precipitate the decision on whether to continue in Parliament. For some MPs, a Boundary Review may well be the last straw: starting again and building up a new support base in a new constituency may prove too unattractive a prospect, so the number of MPs retiring should be higher at elections fought after Boundary Reviews than at elections where the constituencies have not changed.

Some high profile MPs cited the Fourth Review as a reason for standing down. David Alton, Liberal Democrat MP for Liverpool Mossley Hill, was particularly aggrieved; his seat had been changed by the Third Review (see Chapter 6) and was changed again by the Fourth. Other retiring MPs were also affected. Of the 72 Conservatives retiring at the 1997 election, six were from seats changed substantially by the Commissions, and seven of Labour's 38 retirements were also in part a consequence of the Review (they are listed in Criddle, 1997). But the Boundary Review seems to have played only a small part in the decisions of those MPs who retired. In our survey, conducted a year before the 1997 General Election, MPs were asked whether they had considered retiring at the next election, and, if they had, whether the recently completed Boundary Review had influenced them. Only 4 per cent said that they intended to retire at the upcoming election and that the boundary changes had been a factor in that decision.

It is possible that MPs who responded did not wish to discuss their potential retirement or the reasons for it, and those intending to retire might have been less likely to complete the questionnaire and so under-represented in the sample. Furthermore, looking at one election in isolation does not provide a good basis on which to judge whether Boundary Reviews affect retirements: we need information from a number of elections, some affected by Reviews and some not. Data are available on the number of MPs retiring at each election from 1945 to 1997 (in Norris and Lovenduski, 1995 and *The Times Guide to the House of Commons*). Of these, six (1945, 1950, 1955, February 1974, 1983, 1997) were fought in constituencies which had been changed substantially since the previous contest because of Boundary Reviews and nine (1951, 1959, 1964, 1966, 1970, October 1974, 1979, 1987 and 1992) were fought on essentially the same map as the previous election.

On average, 67 MPs retired at each election over the period: the average number at elections fought after Boundary Reviews was 80, while for elections fought in unchanged seats it was 58. More MPs retire at elections following boundary changes than at those where no change has taken place. But there is wide variation in the number of retirements at any particular contest, as indicated by the large standard deviations (31 for elections following boundary changes; 26 for elections fought in unchanged seats), introducing doubt as to whether the apparent difference in the average number of retirements between elections fought in new and in old seats is sufficiently large to suggest that the two sorts of contest are distinct in terms of their impacts on MPs' decisions to stand down. This was tested formally using regression analysis which sought to explain the number of MPs retiring at each election (Table 9.6). The first explanatory variable, indicating whether an election followed a Boundary Review, was coded 1 when the election was fought in changed seats, and 0 when it was not. The coefficient can be interpreted as the difference in the number of retirements between boundary change elections and non-change elections. Retirement from the Commons is not affected by one factor only, however. Perhaps the most obvious influence is demographic: as time goes on between elections, more MPs will decide that they are becoming too old to remain in Parliament. Under the British system, the timing of an election is normally under the control of the incumbent government so that the lifetime of individual Parliaments varies greatly. The 1992 Parliament went almost to its maximum possible five-year term whereas the Parliament elected in February 1974 lasted only a few months but the Parliament elected in 1935 lasted till 1945, because of the emergency conditions of the Second World War. Other things being equal, it makes sense to expect that more MPs will retire following long Parliaments than after short ones. This may have a confounding impact on any influence of boundary changes on retirement. To take this into account, a second explanatory variable was included in the regression equation, measuring the duration in months of the Parliament preceding each election between 1945 and 1997.[8] As expected, the longer the life of a Parliament, the larger the number of MPs who retired. On average, for every extra month a Parliament continued, one more MP retired at its end. The life span of a Parliament was a good predictor of the number of retirements at the next election. When the length of each

Parliament was controlled for, there was no significant relationship between boundary changes and retirements. In the aggregate, therefore, changing constituency boundaries does not seem to have encouraged MPs to take the most drastic exit strategy in any greater numbers than we would normally expect.[9]

Table 9.6 *Retiring from the Commons, 1945–97: regression analyses*

Dependent variable: Number of MPs retiring at the end of a Parliament	
Independent variables	
Boundary change?	1.6
Duration of Parliament (months)	1.0*
Constant	16.9
R^2	74.9

* significant at the 0.01 level

Evaluating the review process: MPs' wider views

The chapter so far has discussed how MPs reacted to the Review process as 'consumers' of the new constituencies. While they are not directly involved in the deliberations of the Boundary Commissions, however, have no greater right to present their views concerning their own seats to the Commissions than any other citizen, have no guarantee that the Commissions will act on their proposals, and can only accept or reject the final recommendations *en masse* once they come before Parliament, MPs are, in an important sense, also 'producers' of the Boundary Review. As legislators, they are involved in setting the rules under which the Commissions operate. If the rules are to be changed, MPs make the decisions. This puts them in an unusual position: as consumers of the rules, their livelihoods and careers can be affected by Boundary Reviews; as producers, they can use their experience of Reviews to change the primary legislation. An important question concerning MPs' evaluations of the rules under which the Review took place, as opposed to the situation in their own seat, therefore, is what MPs thought of the Boundary Review process once it was over.

Two dimensions are considered here. The first is pragmatic: how happy were MPs with their new seats? The second involves a rather deeper set of issues: what did MPs think of the rules and procedures by which the Review was carried out? To answer them, we turn once again to our survey of MPs following the Fourth Review.

Satisfaction?

Were MPs satisfied with the outcome? Redistricting is more important to them than it is to the public (only relatively a few members of the public were more than peripherally aware that the Fourth Review was taking place, or had any knowledge about its outcomes). Did they feel well served by the process?

We asked MPs whether the final recommendations for their seat differed from the provisional recommendations, and, if the recommendations did differ, whether they were more or less satisfied with the outcome. Just under half reported that the final recommendations differed from the provisional ones, and a clear majority (67 per cent) were more satisfied with the final than with the initial recommendations. Clearly, there must be winners and losers if changes are made to the initial recommendations as a result of Local Inquiries. What is striking is the clear partisan dimension to that balance of winners and losers (Table 9.7). 84 per cent of the Labour MPs felt that the final recommendations were an improvement over the initial ones. It is worth stressing again Labour's professional approach to the Local Inquiries; where recommendations were changed, the party was often able to promote successful alterations which advantaged its sitting MPs. Labour MPs' relative happiness with the final outcome (and the Conservatives' relative unhappiness) is also at least as much to do with MPs' state of mind as with the actual results. Labour members had expected to lose many seats when the Review started: in the end, they did not lose as many as they had feared. Conservative MPs had hoped for many gains: they did not make as many as they had anticipated. By contrast, Conservative MPs were much less sanguine about changes to the provisional recommendations. Almost as many were less satisfied with the final constituencies, compared to the initial recommendations, as were more satisfied. The implication is that the Conservatives were systematically underperforming in the Inquiry process – and knew it.

Table 9.7 *Satisfaction with the outcome of the final recommendations, by political party (percentages of respondents)*

	All MPs	Conservative	Labour
(If the final recommendations were different from the provisional) Were you more or less satisfied with the outcome?			
More satisfied	67	49	84
Less satisfied	30	45	16
Neither	3	6	0
N*	141	71	57

Note: * numbers responding to the question.
Source: survey of MPs

Evaluating the rules

Moving away from immediate concerns about particular seats, we also asked the MPs about the rules under which the Commissions acted. They were presented with summaries of the six main rules, and were invited to indicate which they thought was the most important, and which the second most important. Almost all (94 per cent) did so (Table 9.8: because some MPs did not specify a single 'first preference' but ranked two or more rules as 'joint first', the percentages of MPs' 'first preferences' sum to more than 100). The answers to this question cannot be interpreted as a 'popularity poll' for the rules. Nor do they indicate which rules MPs think work well. Rather, they suggest how much emphasis MPs think should be placed upon each rule in the Boundary Commissions' deliberations.

There was no dominant single rule that MPs felt the Boundary Commissions should follow; none commanded overwhelming majority support as a first choice. Two were each chosen as first preference by around a third, however. There was widespread support for equality of constituency electorates (Rule 5), chosen as first preference by 37 per cent of the sample (a further 18 per cent ranked it as their second preference). But it was run a close second by the provision that the Commission should take local ties into account (Rule 7), supported as first preference by 32 per cent of MPs (with 24 per cent indicating it as their second choice). There was a clear split, therefore, between those who felt that constituencies should be drawn up to ensure that each vote has equal weight (just over half of all MPs ranked this first or second), and those who felt that the primary role of the constituency system is to represent local communities (again, just over half ranked this first or second: the overlap is due to some MPs choosing one as first choice, and the other as second).

Few other rules had anything remotely approaching this level of support from MPs. Only the stricture that the size of the Commons should not increase (Rule 1) came anywhere close, with just over a third of MPs giving that option as their first or second choice (20 per cent put it first, and a further 14 per cent put it second). The least paramount in MPs' minds was the 'special geographical considerations' rule (Rule 6): only 16 per cent named it as first or second preference, and only 6 per cent placed it first.

Conservative and Labour politicians differed in their first preferences. Virtually equal proportions from the two parties placed electoral equality at the head of their list of priorities. But Conservative MPs were much more likely to place limiting the size of the Commons at the top of their priorities than were Labour MPs (30 per cent compared to 12 per cent). Labour MPs, meanwhile, were more likely to choose the maintenance of local ties as a top priority (35 per cent did so) than were Conservative MPs (27 per cent).

Overall, virtually the same proportion of MPs (38 per cent) placed maintaining the status quo (the fundamental feature of Rule 7) at the top of their list of preferences as had done so for equality of electorates (Rule 5: 37 per cent). Conservative MPs were more likely to favour electoral equality than maintaining the status quo (39 per cent against 31 per cent) but Labour MPs were somewhat keener on preserving existing constituencies as far as possible than on achieving equality of electorates. (42 per cent of Labour MPs placed minimising disruption at the head of their list of priorities, for example, compared to 38 per cent who plumped for electoral equality.)

Table 9.8 *MPs' preferences between the rules governing the Boundary Reviews, by political party (percentages of respondents)*

	All MPs	Conservative	Labour
Rule 1: The number of seats in the House of Commons should not increase			
First preference	20	30	12
Second preference	14	20	8
Rule 4: Constituencies should not overlap County or London Borough boundaries			
First preference	12	11	14
Second preference	12	11	14
Rule 5: The electorate of each constituency should be as close to the national quota as practicable			
First preference	37	39	38
Second preference	18	20	17
Rule 6: The Commission may depart from the preceding two criteria where 'special geographical considerations' apply			
First preference	6	5	7
Second preference	10	10	10
Rule 7: The Commission shall take into account the inconveniences that may be caused by changes to constituency boundaries			
First preference	8	6	10
Second preference	17	15	18
Rule 7: The Commission shall take into account any local ties which would be broken by changes to constituency boundaries			
First preference	32	27	35
Second preference	24	20	28
Rule 7: Both parts combined			
First preference	39	31	42
Second preference	16	11	21
N*	286	132	126

Note: * numbers responding to the question.
Source: survey of MPs

These party differences in the priority given to different rules reflect the circumstances within which the parties operate. It is arguable that moving closer to equality of electorates benefits the Conservatives, for instance, since it increases the pressure on Commissions to redraw small and declining inner city and Scottish seats, both of which return many Labour MPs (as demonstrated in Chapter 8). Labour, meanwhile, would benefit from preserving its strongholds as far as possible. That said, the inter-party differences are not overwhelming, and all major parties have substantial internal differences of opinion on which rules to prioritise within their Parliamentary ranks.

The politicians were also invited to suggest whether they thought the current approach to Boundary Reviews in the UK was the most appropriate (75 per cent did so), and, if they did not, what changes they would like to see in the rules. Only 21 per cent specified changes to the current arrangements, and just four measures received the support of more than 10 per cent of those who wanted to see some change to the rules. A reduction in the size of the Commons was favoured by 27 per cent (the Commons is one of the largest elected assemblies in the West). Under the current regulations, Northern Ireland, Wales and especially Scotland have more seats than their electorates would entitle them to if a UK-wide quota was adhered to, and that advantage is enshrined in Rule 1. Just over a quarter of those who wanted to change the rules (26 per cent) wanted this 'Celtic preference' (Rawlings, 1988) to be removed, restoring parity of treatment between the constituent parts of Britain. A further 15 per cent raised the desirability of greater equalisation of electorates, independent of the Celtic preference.

This drive towards greater equalisation nationally runs against the desire, expressed by 23 per cent of those who wanted change, to maintain or strengthen the provisions for preserving local ties in revised constituencies, however. The divide between 'equalisers' and 'localists' identified above in terms of MPs' preferences between the existing rules is unlikely to disappear in any future debates about reform of the legislation, therefore.

Impacts on local party organisation

The final area where a Boundary Review might affect MPs (or, indeed, a non-incumbent candidate) is in the ability of their local party organisation to campaign. Changes to seats disrupt local constituency parties, potentially affecting fund-raising, party membership, and so on. To what extent did MPs see this as a problem? Our survey cannot answer this but data are available from the British Representation Study 1997, a survey of candidates (some MPs, some not) conducted in the run-up to the 1997 election.[10] Our analyses of these data concentrate on the responses of Conservative, Labour and Liberal Democrat candidates.

The survey explored four areas in which the Boundary Review might have had an effect on candidates and their local party organisation: their ability to win the local nomination, raise money for campaigns, recruit activists, and create an effective local party organisation. Candidates were also asked for their views on the impact of the Review on voter turnout (Table 9.9). Few candidates thought the Review had any bearing on the ease (or otherwise) with which they won the party nomination: 83 per cent felt it made no difference. But rather fewer were indifferent to the potential impact of the Review on local party organisation. On all the questions, a majority felt the Review made no difference, but the size of that majority varied substantially: 72 per cent thought it had made no difference to local fundraising, while 17 per cent felt this had become harder as a result of the Review, compared to 11 per cent who felt it had become easier. Only 64 per cent thought the Review had made no difference to their ability to recruit activists for the local campaign, and once again the weight of opinion among those who felt there was some difference was towards a negative effect: 20 per cent felt it had become harder to recruit activists as a result of the Review, compared to 15 per cent who felt it had become easier. The story was similar for views of the impact on their ability to create an effective party organisation in the constituency (61 per cent saw no effect, 24 per cent thought it had become harder and 14 per cent thought it easier), and on turnout (63 per cent seeing no difference, compared to 21 per cent who thought it had become harder to encourage turnout, and 15 per cent who thought it had become easier). Among those candidates who thought the Fourth Review had some impact on their local party organisation, therefore, more thought that impact had been adverse than thought it had been benign. But the majority on all occasions thought the Review had no effect on party organisation.

Table 9.9 *Election candidates' perceptions of the impact of the Fourth Review (percentages of respondents)*

	Winning nomination	Raising money	Recruiting activists	Creating effective organisation	Voter turnout
Far harder	0.9	2.9	3.2	3.4	3.2
Somewhat harder	6.4	14.1	17.1	21.2	18.3
No difference	83.0	72.2	64.4	61.0	63.3
Somewhat easier	7.6	10.1	14.7	13.0	13.9
Far easier	2.0	0.7	0.7	1.5	1.4
N*	884	887	887	888	886

Note: * numbers responding to the question.
Source: British Representation Survey, 1997

Conclusions

Boundary Reviews are unsettling events in MPs' already unpredictable careers. Both as individual professional politicians and as members of parties with hopes of forming and participating in governments, they inevitably are concerned by any development which might alter the safety or marginality of their constituency, or affect the outcome of an election for their party. As (arguably) the group of people with most to gain or lose as a consequence of boundary changes, therefore, it is unsurprising that they take a keen interest in the Review process as it affects their interests.

As discussed in this chapter, however, MPs' responses to the Review process vary greatly, depending on a range of factors including: how much the individual MP is affected by a Commission's proposals; the extent to which his or her party takes a hand; whether or not (especially in seats which have changed greatly) the local party wishes to continue with the same candidate as before; and so on. Some MPs are happy with (or unaffected by) the Review, and remain quiet; others lobby the Commissions. Some stay in their seats, while others look for better prospects elsewhere, or even retire from politics altogether (though, as we have seen, there is no systematic variation in total retirement rates between elections fought in new and old seats).

Not surprisingly, also, MPs (and candidates) have views on the Review process, in terms both of particular effects on politics, and of the general underlying principles and rules. There is very little direct evidence of what the general public thinks about Reviews, but it seems likely that few electors are either aware or really care about them: MPs and political activists are in a small minority.

Notes

1 By convention, most twentieth century Prime Ministers since the Marquis of Salisbury have been drawn from the Commons, though Sir Alec-Douglas Home was still a peer when he succeeded Harold Macmillan in 1963.

2 Ironically he was Party Chairman at the time, responsible for the campaign which led to the unexpected re-election of the Conservative government.

3 At least at the time that they held them: Margaret Thatcher's successor in Finchley had a majority of 6,388 in 1992, and Rallings and Thrasher (1995) estimated that his lead in the new Finchley seat (60 per cent of which came from his old constituency and 40 per cent from the equally safe Hendon South) would have been 12,474 in 1992: he lost it in 1997.

4 The recommendations of the Northern Ireland Commission were debated in the First Standing Committee on Statutory Instruments on 31 October 1995, for 39 minutes. The proceedings were dominated by the only Ulster MP present – Clifford Forsythe (Ulster Unionist, Antrim South) – who stressed that he was not opposed to the recommendations, but raised the issue of whether the Commission had been influenced by the government of the Irish Republic: the Minister of State, Michael Ancram, in response stressed the Commission's independence (for more details, see Rossiter, Johnston and Pattie, 1998). They were then briefly discussed in the House of Lords (*Hansard House of Lords*, vol. 566, 3 January 1995, cols. 1537–40). The main contribution was from Lord Fitt, formerly an SDLP MP, who rehearsed his 1977 argument (see Chapter 3) that Northern Ireland's representation should have been retained as 12 and who claimed that 'there were very highly political motives behind the recommendations of the Boundary Commission' in its Fourth Review. As in the House of Commons Standing Committee, however, the question that the recommendations be approved was agreed without a formal vote.

5 There is a further irony here: arguably, losing in Southampton Test actually helped Crosland's career. While out of Parliament, he published *The Future of Socialism*, the book that established him as perhaps the major thinker on the revisionist wing of the party. According to a biography of the Labour leader at the time, Hugh Gaitskell, 'Crosland had ill-advisedly abandoned his South Gloucestershire seat for what Dalton and others felt to be a better bet in Southampton, and ended up losing': Gaitskell was then instrumental in getting Crosland the nomination for Grimsby (Brivati, 1997, 239). Interestingly, the Southampton Test seat was later won by Bryan Gould, who contested the Labour leadership in 1992 after losing that seat and moving to a safer one in Dagenham.

6 The figures for the elections were: 1955 – 3 retired, 4 fought constituencies based in part on their old seats, and 2 moved elsewhere; 1974 (February) – 6,16, and 6; and 1983 – 16, 11 and 6.

7 Rallings and Thrasher (1995) estimated that if the 1992 election had been fought in the new constituencies Basildon's Conservative majority would have been 2,646 whereas Southend West's would have been 11,902. Amess won in Southend and his successor lost in Basildon.

8 All analyses were repeated omitting the unusually long 1935–1945 Parliament, to see if this contest biased the results in any way: it did not.

9 We have also found that not only Conservative MPs who were retiring but also those whose constituencies had been unchanged were more likely to vote against the government on the implementation of the Nolan Committee's recommendations regarding constraints on MPs external earnings (Johnston, Pattie and Rossiter, 1996).

10 We are grateful to Dr Pippa Norris for generously allowing us access to the British Representation Study data. She is not responsible for the conclusions we draw here. The survey contacted 999 candidates for the 1997 election: 178 were incumbent MPs, and 821 were non-incumbent challengers.

Conclusions

In this book we have traced the emergence of the redistribution process currently employed in the United Kingdom, evaluated the outcome of the five Reviews conducted since 1944 against the criteria set out in the Rules for Redistribution, and reported on our detailed research into the conduct of the latest of those Reviews.

Much of our attention has focused on the period since 1944, when the initial *House of Commons (Redistribution of Seats) Act* established the principle that redistricting should be undertaken by independent, politically neutral Commissions, staffed by civil servants who operate entirely outwith the party political process. The Commissions' *bona fides* have only rarely been queried, and they and their staffs have won widespread respect. Their work is not immune from the political process, however, because Parliament not only writes the rules within which they operate but also occasionally changes these when it is politically desirable – as illustrated by the alterations to the length of the prescribed period between Reviews detailed in Chapter 3.

From our many findings regarding the Commissions' work recorded in the previous chapters, three major conclusions stand out:

1 The principle of electoral equality has come to dominate the outcome of the Periodic Reviews.
2 The Rules are ambiguous and unclear, and so invite inconsistency in treatment.
3 The Commissions' procedures, which are very largely determined by Parliament, are immensely time- and resource-consuming, largely because of the public consultation processes.

First, *the principle of electoral equality has come to dominate the outcome of the Periodic Reviews.* The great majority of constituencies are now within 10 per cent of the relevant electoral quota – using the qualifying date figures on registration. This shift occurred gradually through the nineteenth and twentieth centuries, but gained momentum after 1944 and especially after 1970. The local government reforms enacted by the Conservative government of 1970–74 provided the main impetus for the emphasis on equality that now characterises the Commissions' work; not only was the number of local government units very substantially reduced, thereby significantly weakening the constraint of fitting constituencies into the local government template, but in addition the requirement to do that was reduced by removal of the need to pay heed to local government District boundaries (through consequential amendments included in the Local Government Acts rather than primary legislation regarding redistribution).[1] There is no evidence that this shift resulted from a deliberate policy decision by the Commissions in the light of those changes, but removal of the constraints provided by a complex map of local government areas ensured that equality of electorates became more important in the procedures and outcomes.

This accelerating trend towards the primacy of electoral equality as a determinant of the Boundary Commissions' policies largely occurred after Parliament amended the legislation in 1958 to emphasise criteria other than constituency size. To MPs, electoral equality was less important than community ties and the disruptions to their organisations (plus their chances of re-election) generated by changed constituency boundaries. These further criteria were added to the Act, the importance of electoral equality was downgraded by a reordering of the Rules, and the Court of Appeal judgement on the *Foot et al.* case some 25 years later suggested that the new criteria were mandatory whereas the others were guidelines only. And yet the Commissions apparently focused increasingly on the criterion which MPs wanted to downgrade. In part this was because of the later changes to the country's local government structures and consequential amendments to the Rules for Redistribution discussed above, but in part it was because the Commissions became more skilled at achieving electoral equality while not ignoring the other criteria. They are very cognisant of the disruptions which change can engender, and seek to minimise them. In many cases community ties are local issues that are beyond the purview of a Commission sitting in London, Cardiff, Edinburgh or Belfast, however, and are therefore more likely to be the focus of interested parties' representations to Local Inquiries. Thus the Commissions produce provisional recommendations within the local government template that meet the electoral equality requirement, and activists try to have these modified to serve their particular (usually electoral) interests. The changes which they succeed in getting usually reduce the degree of equality somewhat, compared to the provisional recommendations, but the Commissions have set the agenda and the modifications are almost invariably at the margins only.

The second general conclusion is one that other commentators have also reached: *the Rules are ambiguous and unclear, and so invite inconsistency in treatment* – between Commissions at particular Reviews, between Reviews by the same Commission, and even within a Commission at an individual Review (especially that with the largest task, the English). This has led Rawlings (1988, 61) to claim that 'the edifice of Parliamentary government in Britain appears to rest upon somewhat insubstantial foundations' and McLean and Mortimore (1992, 304) to argue that 'the English Commission has not consistently followed any one formula' for allocating seats to local government areas, with its entire procedure suggesting a 'failure to understand (let alone deal with) the issue of fair apportionment' (McLean and Mortimer, 1992, 307). Butler (1992, 6), who has studied the work of the Commissions for almost fifty years, sees them operating 'under strict but confusing statutory rules' and concludes that 'the commission processes could be greatly improved both by altering their terms of reference and by adding to their staffing and administrative facilities' (Butler, 1992, 11); indeed in his opinion (Butler, 1992, 7):

> Britain may have pioneered the commission approach to redistricting, but it no longer provides the best example. All the other major democracies once ruled from the United Kingdom have single-member districts, and all now use impartial commissions for redistributing seats, following the UK model but often improving on it.

Our analyses confirm and extend all of these conclusions – as does the experience of at least one of the civil servants most intimately involved in operating the Rules, Bob McLeod, who was Secretary to the English and Welsh Commissions throughout the Fourth Review (McLeod, 1996b).[2]

Not only are the Rules ambiguous and likely to produce inconsistent outcomes but the Commissions' work is not subject to scrutiny, let alone appeal, other than in Parliament, where the recommendations of the later Reviews received much less attention than those of the first three (in 1947, 1954 and 1969). Each of the four Periodic Reviews has stimulated litigation by parties claiming that the Commissions have not properly conducted their task, in one case (*Foot et al.* in 1982) with regard to a Commission's entire work, but all have failed even though in some the complaint has been shown valid (as with the *Gateshead* case in 1982). This is because the Commissions do not implement their recommendations, unlike their counterparts in Australia, Canada and New Zealand, but only make recommendations to Parliament, which is sovereign. Judicial review of the work of administrative bodies such as the Boundary Commissions is difficult to sustain unless very clear evidence can be adduced that they have acted unreasonably within their terms of reference, which is extremely difficult given the ambiguity of the Rules for Redistribution, as shown in the judgements in the *Foot et al.* case (p. 113) and Lord Weir's later interpretation of unreasonable (p. 208). Furthermore, the courts have commented on that ambiguity and, at least in the *Foot at al.* case, added to it by their interpretations.

Our third general conclusion relates to *the Commissions' procedures, very largely determined by Parliament, which are immensely time- and resource-consuming, largely because of the public consultation processes.*[3] Our interview with one English MP (whose seat 'disappeared' after the Fourth Review) produced strong criticisms of those processes. When asked how well he thought the Commission had done its job in his area, he responded:

> Although I was unhappy with the conclusions, I have no complaints about the way they performed their role. I certainly can't complain that we were short-changed given the lengthy and elaborate inquiry. However, the process is far too elaborate

> ... we have this enormous and elaborate Commission and Inquiry structure all about
> so little. Only in public life would you get that.

And then, in response to a question regarding the Assistant Commissioner who
conducted the Local Inquiry:

> I attended parts of the Inquiry and he was absolutely fine. To criticise him would
> be a bit like complaining that the second violin was out of tune as the Titanic sank.
> It was typical English law – desperately polite, wonderfully open. But what is this
> all about – it's impeccable but wrong.

A major reason why the public consultation process was inflated in the Fourth
Review is that the parties, especially Labour, have become skilled at exploiting
it to their own ends (p. 366; see also Johnston *et al.*, 1998). They have learnt how
to manipulate the process, and although much of the detailed argument about constituency boundaries at Local Inquiries may only have a marginal impact on a
party's electoral prospects there, such impacts – when summed across 80 or more
Inquiries – can be quite substantial across the whole country (although the benefits to individual parties tend to balance out, so that none makes a very substantial overall gain). Our findings show that the parties were much more
successful in achieving modifications to the provisional recommendations in areas
where they were dominant politically, thus exaggerating the spatial polarisation
of representation which characterises British election results.

These three general conclusions point to the need for a radical rethink of the
redistribution process in the UK. The 1986 discussion in the Home Affairs Committee demonstrated political unwillingness to grasp the difficult problem of Scottish and Welsh over-representation (something that has become even more
pressing since 1997 with the decision to proceed with limited devolution to those
two countries), and the government's response to the Committee's suggestions
regarding limits to the continued growth of the House of Commons was inadequate (see p. 118): it even failed to introduce the requested amendment to extend
the period for making written representations from one month to two!

If such a rethink were to be embarked upon, many important items would be
on the agenda of whichever body was entrusted with the task, including:

1 the size of the House of Commons;
2 the relative representation of England, Scotland, Wales and Northern Ireland;
3 the need for unambiguous Rules for Redistribution;
4 the nature, if any, of the public consultation process;
5 synchronisation of the work on local government and Parliamentary boundaries; and
6 the independence of the Boundary Commissions – should they only recommend to Parliament or should they have the power to implement new constituencies?

A number of these raise constitutional issues of much greater import than just
how Parliamentary constituencies are to be defined; all demand urgent consideration by any reforming government.

Such a reforming government was elected in 1997, and within nine months of taking office had moved on a number of issues relevant to this book's subject matter. Its enacted proposals for devolution to Scotland and Wales included electoral systems different from that used for elections to Westminster, for example; it introduced a further proportional system for elections of Members of the European Parliament; and it appointed a Commission which would recommend a more proportional alternative to the system currently used for elections to the House of Commons, to be placed before the electorate in a referendum (though not necessarily with government backing for the proposed change).[4] In all of the debates about electoral reform, however, strong arguments are made for retaining the important link between MPs and defined territorial constituencies (see, for example, the two reports produced for the Labour party from a working party chaired by Lord Plant; Plant 1991, 1993). But virtually every electoral system requires constituencies – either single- or multi-member: a procedure is thus needed for regularly redefining them, as a response to changes in the size and distribution of the population (or registered electorate).

A Boundary Commission or its equivalent is fundamental to the good order of a country's electoral system if it has a constituency base, therefore. Geography is an inevitable component of that good order (as we illustrated in Johnston, Pattie and Rossiter, 1998a): drawing-up constituencies involves respecting geography, and at the same time creates geography – which acts as a template for future political activity. Rules for this geographical work are needed; if the United Kingdom is to have new electoral systems, rules will have to be constructed *de novo*, but even if it is not, the current rules desperately need substantial redrafting (Johnston, Pattie and Rossiter, 1998b, 1998c).

The *House of Commons (Redistribution of Seats) Act 1944* established important principles for redistricting in the United Kingdom: the four independent Boundary Commissions conducting regular reviews to a set timetable; the Rules for Redistribution; and the process of public consultation. These were modified and extended by subsequent Acts, not least those reforming local government in the 1970s which substantially altered the constituency-definition process 'by the back door'. They now need to be overhauled, if not entirely replaced; they may have served the country well over much of the last fifty years, but no longer do so. Constitutional reform occupies an important place on the contemporary political agenda, and implementation of many issues regarding human and civil rights means that the nature and form of political representation must once again take centre stage in British political debate, irrespective of whether that involves changing the electoral system.

Notes

1 As noted in Chapter 4, Ministerial advice was that this should be attempted, but it was no longer a legal requirement.
2 In 1975, the Home Office defended the status quo strongly, in response to a paper (Rowley, 1975a, 20) which criticised the application of the Rules for Redistribution, espe-

cially those referring to equality and to community ties, in the Second Periodical Review as 'both conflicting and contradictory'. A response from a Minister of State at the Home Office, Lord Harris, which Rowley published (Rowley 1975b, 280) claimed that: (1) 'the criteria of equality and preservation of local ties may often be mutually conflicting, but it is the task of the Commissions to reconcile such conflicts in the light of local representations'; (2) that other criteria are also important, though perhaps varying 'from time to time', but to include them in the Rules would imply that they had to be constantly reviewed; and (3) 'The existing rules go as far as is practicable to enable the Commissions to balance the conflicting elements in this difficult work'.

3 The Boundary Commission for England records (1995b, 155) that its Fourth Review cost an estimated £4,953,000 for the period 1990–91 to 1994–95.

4 Its proposals for a Northern Ireland Assembly in April 1998 incorporated a further electoral system, one which usually produces results close to proportional representation from multi-member constituencies.

References

Abel, R. L. (1988) *The Legal Profession in England and Wales*, Blackwell, Oxford.

Balinski, M. and Young H.P. (1982) *Fair Representation: Meeting the Ideal of One Man, One Vote*, New Haven CT, Yale University Press.

Ball, S. (1994) Local Conservatism and the evolution of the party organisation, in A. Seldon and S. Ball (eds) *Conservative Century: The Conservative Party Since 1900*, Oxford, Oxford University Press.

Barnes, G. P. (1987) The use of computers in redistributing constituencies, *Electoral Studies*, 6, 133–8.

Barnes, G. P. and McLeod, R. (1989) The criteria for revising constituency boundaries, *Population Trends*, 57, 30–4.

BBC/ITN (1983) *The BBC/ITN Guide to the New Parliamentary Constituencies*, Chichester, Parliamentary Research Services.

Benn, T. (1992) *The End of an Era: Diaries, 1980-1990*, London, Hutchinson.

Birch, A. H. (1971) *Representation*, London, Pall Mall Press.

Blackburn, R. (1995) *The Electoral System in Britain*, London, Macmillan.

Blake, R. (1960) *Disraeli*, London, Macmillan.

Boundary Commission (1868) *Report of the Boundary Commissioners for England and Wales*, London, HMSO.

Boundary Commission (England & Wales) (1917) *Report of the Boundary Commission (England & Wales) Volume I*, Cd. 8756, London, HMSO.

Boundary Commission (Ireland) (1917) *Report of the Boundary Commission (Ireland)*, Cd. 8758, London, HMSO.

Boundary Commission (Scotland) (1917) *Report of the Boundary Commission (Scotland)*, Cd. 8759, London, HMSO.

Boundary Commission for England (1945) *Report in Regard to the Division of the Abnormally Large Constituencies*, Cmd. 6621, London, HMSO.

Boundary Commission for England (1947) *Initial Report of the Boundary Commission for England*, Cmd. 7260, London, HMSO.

Boundary Commission for England (1954) *First Periodical Report*, Cmd. 9311, London, HMSO.

Boundary Commission for England (1969) *Second Periodical Report*, Cmnd. 4084, London, HMSO.

Boundary Commission for England (1983) *Third Periodic Report*, Cmnd. 8797-I, London, HMSO.

Boundary Commission for England (1990) *Report with Respect to the Areas Comprised in the County Constituencies of Buckingham and Milton Keynes*, Cm. 298, London, HMSO.

Boundary Commission for England (1992) *The Procedure at Local Inquiries*, London, Boundary Commission for England.

Boundary Commission for England (1995a) *Fourth Periodic Report*, Cm. 433-i, London, HMSO.

Boundary Commission for England (1995b) *Fourth Periodic Report: Volume Two Appendices*, Cm. 433-ii, London, HMSO.

Boundary Commission for England and Wales (1885) *Report: Part 1 Counties*, Cd. 4287, London, HMSO.

Boundary Commission for Northern Ireland (1947) *Initial Report of the Boundary Commission for Northern Ireland,* Cmd. 7231, London, HMSO.

Boundary Commission for Northern Ireland (1954) *First Periodical Report*, Cmd. 9314, London, HMSO.

Boundary Commission for Northern Ireland (1969) *Second Periodical Report*, Cmnd. 4087, Belfast, HMSO.

Boundary Commission for Northern Ireland (1982) *Third Periodic Report* , Cmnd. 8753, London, HMSO.

Boundary Commission for Northern Ireland (1994) GIS and democracy: redrawing Northern Ireland's electoral boundaries, *GIS Europe*, 3, December.

Boundary Commission for Northern Ireland (1995) *Fourth Periodic Report* , Cm. 2949, London, HMSO.

Boundary Commission for Scotland (1947) *Initial Report of the Boundary Commission for Scotland*, Cmd. 7270, Edinburgh, HMSO.

Boundary Commission for Scotland (1954) *First Periodical Report*, Cmnd. 9312, Edinburgh, HMSO.

Boundary Commission for Scotland (1969) *Second Periodical Report*, Cmnd. 4085, Edinburgh, HMSO.

Boundary Commission for Scotland (1983) *Third Periodic Report*, Cmnd. 8794, Edinburgh, HMSO.

Boundary Commission for Scotland (1995) *Fourth Periodic Report*, Cm. 2726, Edinburgh, HMSO.

Boundary Commission for Wales (1947) *Initial Report of the Boundary Commission for Wales*, Cmd. 7274, London, HMSO.

Boundary Commission for Wales (1954) *First Periodical Report*, Cmd. 9313, London, HMSO.

Boundary Commission for Wales (1969) *Second Periodical Report*, Cmnd. 4086, Cardiff, HMSO.

Boundary Commission for Wales (1983) *Third Periodic Report*, Cmnd. 8798, London, HMSO.

Boundary Commission for Wales (1995) *Fourth Periodic Report*, Cm.195, London, HMSO.

Bradford, S. (1996) *Disraeli*, London, Phoenix.

Brivati, B. (1997) *Hugh Gaitskell*, London, Richard Cohen Books.

Brock, M. (1973) *The Great Reform Act*, London, Hutchinson University Press.

Brookes, R. H. (1960) The analysis of distorted representation in two-party single member elections, *Political Science*, 12, 158–67.

Brown, G. (1972) *In My Way*, London, Penguin Books.

Budge, I. and O'Leary, C. (1973) *Belfast: Approach to Crisis – A Study of Belfast Politics, 1613–1970*, London, Macmillan.

Butler, D. (1953) *The British Electoral System 1918–1951*, Oxford, Clarendon Press.

Butler, D. (1955) The redistribution of seats, *Public Administration*, 33, 125–47.

Butler, D. (1963) *The Electoral System in Britain since 1918*, Oxford, Clarendon Press.

Butler, D. (1992) The redrawing of Parliamentary boundaries in Britain, *Journal of Behavioural and Social Sciences* (Tokyo), 37, 5–12.

Butler, D., Adonis, A. and Travers, T. (1994) *Failure in British Government: The Politics of the Poll Tax*, Oxford, Oxford University Press.

Butler, D. and Butler, G. (1994) *British Political Facts 1900–1994*, London, Macmillan.

Butler, D. and Kavanagh, D. (1992) *The British General Election of 1992*, London, Macmillan.

Butler, D. and Kavanagh, D. (1997) *The British General Election of 1997*, London, Macmillan.

Butler, D. and McLean, I. (1996a) The redrawing of Parliamentary boundaries in Britain, in I. McLean and D. Butler (eds) *Fixing the Boundaries: Defining and Redefining Single-Member Electoral Districts*, Aldershot, Dartmouth, 1–38.

Butler, D. and McLean, I. (1996b) Afterword, in I. McLean and D. Butler (eds), *Fixing the Boundaries: Defining and Redefining Single-Member Electoral Districts*, Aldershot, Dartmouth, 271–2.

Butler, D. and Stokes, D. (1969) *Political Change in Britain: The Evolution of Party Choice*, London, Penguin Books.

Cain, B. E., Ferejohn, J. A. and Fiorina, M. P. (1984) The constituency service bias of the personal vote for US representatives and British Members of Parliament, *American Political Science Review*, 78, 110–25.

Callaghan, J. (1987) *Time and Chance*, London, Collins.

Campbell, A., Converse, P. E., Miller, W. E. and Stokes, D. E. (eds) (1956) *Elections and the Political Order*, New York, John Wiley.

Cannadine, D. (1996) *The Decline and Fall of the British Aristocracy*, London, Macmillan.

Chadwick, M. E. J. (1976) The role of redistribution in the making of the Third Reform Act, *The Historical Journal*, 19, 665–83.

Champion, A. G. (1989) *Counterurbanisation: The Changing Pace and Nature of Population Deconcentration*, London, Edward Arnold.

Chisholm, M. (1995) Some lessons from the review of local government in England, *Regional Studies*, 29, 563–9.

Congressional Quarterly (1994) Constitutional doubt is thrown on bizarre-shaped districts, *Current American Government, Spring 1994 Guide*, Washington DC, Congressional Quarterly.

Cook, C. and Ramsden, P. (1997) *By-Elections in British Politics*, London, UCL Press.

Cowling, M. (1967) *1867: Disraeli, Gladstone and Revolution*, Cambridge, Cambridge University Press.

Craig, F. W. S. (1969) *British Parliamentary Election Results 1918-1949*, Glasgow, Political Reference Publications.

Craig, F. W. S. (1971) *British Parliamentary Election Results 1950–1970*, Chichester, Political Reference Publications.

Craig, F. W. S. (1984a) *British Parliamentary Election Results 1974–1983*, Chichester, Political Reference Publications.

Craig, F. W. S. (1984b) *Britain Votes 3: British Parliamentary Election Results 1983*, Chichester, Political Reference Publications.

Craig, F. W. S. (1988) *Britain Votes 4: British Parliamentary Election Results 1987*, Chichester, Political Reference Publications.

Craig, F. W. S. (1989) *British Electoral Facts 1832–1987* (5th edn), Aldershot, Gower.

Crewe, I. and Fox, A. (1984) *British Parliamentary Constituencies: A Statistical Compendium*, London, Faber and Faber.

Crewe, I. and King, A. (1995) *SDP: The Birth, Life and Death of the Social Democratic Party*, Oxford, Oxford University Press.

Crewe, I. and Payne, C. (1976) Another game with nature: an ecological regression model of the British two-party vote ratio in 1970, *British Journal of Political Science*, 6, 43–81.

Crick, M. (1997) *Michael Heseltine: A Biography*, London, Hamish Hamilton.

Criddle, B. (1997) MPs and candidates, in Butler, D. and Kavanagh, D., *The British General Election of 1997*, London, Macmillan.

Crossman, R. (1975) *The Diaries of a Cabinet Minister. Volume One: Minister of Housing 1964–1966*, London, Hamish Hamilton and Jonathan Cape.

Crossman, R. (1976) *The Diaries of a Cabinet Minister. Volume Two: Lord President of the Council and Leader of the House of Commons 1966-1968*, London, Hamish Hamilton and Jonathan Cape.

Crossman, R. (1978) *The Diaries of a Cabinet Minister. Volume Three: Secretary of State for Social Services 1968–1970*, London, Hamish Hamilton and Jonathan Cape.

Curtice, J. (1995) The British electoral system: fixture without foundation, in D. Kavanagh (ed.) *Electoral Politics*, Oxford, Clarendon Press.

Curtice, J. and Payne, C. (1991) Local elections as national referendums in Great Britain, *Electoral Studies*, 10, 3–17.

Curtice, J. and Steed, M. (1982) Electoral choice and the production of government, *British Journal of Political Science*, 12, 249–98.

Dearlove, J. (1979) *The Reorganisation of British Local Government: Old Orthodoxies and a Political Perspective*, Cambridge, Cambridge University Press.

Denver, D. T. and Hands, G. (1997) *Modern Constituency Electioneering: Local Campaigning in the 1992 General Election*, London, Frank Cass.

Dunleavy, P. (1980) *Urban Political Analysis*, London, Macmillan.

Farrell, D. (1997) *Comparing Electoral Systems*, London, Prentice Hall.

Forrest, B. (1997) Regionalism in election district jurisprudence, *Urban Geography*, 17, 572-678.

French, F-J. (1978) Submission to *Mr. Speaker's Conference on Electoral Law*, 70-iii, Session 1977–78, 25–36, London, HMSO.

Gay, O. (1992) *The Parliamentary Boundary Commissions and the Boundary Commissions Bill*, Research Note 92/61, London, House of Commons Library Research Division.

Government Reply (1988) *Redistribution of Seats*, Cmnd. 308, London, HMSO.

Grofman, B., Koetzle, W. and Brunell, T. (1997) An integrated perspective on the three sources of partisan bias: malapportionment, turnout differences, and the geographic distribution of party vote shares, *Electoral Studies*, 16, 457–70.

Gudgin, G. and Taylor, P. J. (1979) *The Spatial Organization of Elections*, London, Pion.

Hanham, H. J. (1978) *Elections and Party Management: Politics in the Time of Disraeli and Gladstone*, Brighton, Harvester.

Hayes, W. A. (1987) *The Background and Passage of the Third Reform Act*, London, Garland.

Heath, A., Jowell, R. and Curtice, J. (1985) *How Britain Votes*, Oxford, Pergamon.

Heath, A., Jowell, R. and Curtice, J. (1989) *Understanding Political Change*, Oxford, Pergamon.

Hirschmann, A. O. (1970) *Exit, Voice and Loyalty: Responses to Decline in Firms, Organisations and States*, Cambridge MA, Harvard University Press.

Home Affairs Committee (1986–87) *Redistribution of Seats*, London, HMSO.

Honey, R. (1981) Alternative approaches to local government change, in A. D. Burnett and P. J. Taylor (eds) *Political Studies from Spatial Perspectives: Anglo-American Essays on Political Geography*, London, Wiley.

IDEA (1997) *The International IDEA Handbook of Electoral System Design*, Stockholm, International Institute for Democracy and Electoral Assistance.

Jenkins, R. (1965) *Dilke: A Victorian Tragedy*, London, Collins.

Jenkins, R. (1995) *Gladstone*, London, Macmillan.

Johnston, R. J. (1977) Spatial structure, plurality systems and electoral bias, *The Canadian Geographer*, 20, 310–28.

Johnston, R. J. (1979), *Political, Electoral and Spatial Systems*, Oxford, Oxford University Press.

Johnston, R. J. (1982) Redistricting by independent commissions: a perspective from Britain, *Annals of the Association of American Geographers*, 72, 457–70.

Johnston, R. J. (1983) A reapportionment revolution that failed, *Political Geography Quarterly*, 2, 309–17.

Johnston, R. J. (1985) *The Geography of English Politics: The 1983 General Election*, London, Croom Helm.

Johnston, R. J. (1987) *Money and Votes: Constituency Campaign Spending and Election Results*, London, Croom Helm.

Johnston, R. J., Openshaw, S., Rhind, D. W. and Rossiter, D. J. (1984) Spatial scientists and representative democracy: the role of information-processing technology in the design of Parliamentary and other constituencies, *Environment and Planning C: Government and Policy*, 2, 57–66.

Johnston, R. J. and Pattie, C. J. (1993) Where the Tories lost and won: geographical variations in voting at the 1992 British General Election, *Parliamentary Affairs*, 46, 192–202.

Johnston, R. J. and Pattie, C. J. (1996a) Intra-local conflict, public opinion and local government restructuring in England, 1993-1995, *Geoforum*, 27, 97–114.

Johnston, R. J. and Pattie, C. J. (1996b) Local government in local governance: the 1994–1995 restructuring of local government in England, *International Journal of Urban and Regional Research*, 20, 671–96.

Johnston, R. J. and Pattie, C. J. (1996c) Great Britain: new local government structures, *Geography Review*, 9:5, 27–33.

Johnston, R. J., Pattie, C. J. and Allsopp, J. G. (1988), *A Nation Dividing? The Electoral Map of Great Britain 1979–1987*, London, Longman.

Johnston, R. J., Pattie, C. J. and Fieldhouse, E. A. (1994) The geography of voting and representation: regions and the declining importance of the cube law, in A. Heath, R. Jowell and J. Curtice (eds) *Labour's Last Chance? The 1992 Election and Beyond*, Aldershot, Dartmouth, 255–74.

Johnston, R. J., Pattie, C. J. and Rossiter, D. J. (1992) Redistricting revisited: The Parliamentary Boundary Commission for England at work again, *Environment and Planning*

A, 24, 1071–5.

Johnston, R. J., Pattie, C. J. and Rossiter, D. J. (1996) Sleaze, constituency and dissent: voting on Nolan in the House of Commons, *Area,* 29, 20–33.

Johnston, R. J., Pattie, C. J. and Rossiter, D. J. (1998a) Can we ever get rid of geography? Observations on the possible use of STV in United Kingdom general elections, *Representation,* 35, 63–9.

Johnston, R. J., Pattie, C. J. and Rossiter, D. J. (1998b) Electoral reform: establishing principles of constituency definition, *Renewal,* 6, 42–54.

Johnston, R. J., Pattie, C. J. and Rossiter, D. J. (1998c) Electoral reform, constituencies and Boundary Commissions in the UK: Defining constituencies for proportional representation electoral systems, *Renewal,* 6 (3), 72–81.

Johnston, R. J., Pattie, C. J., Rossiter, D. J., Dorling, D., MacAllister, I. and Tunstall, H. (1998) Anatomy of a Labour landslide: the constituency system and the 1997 general election, *Parliamentary Affairs,* 51, 131–48.

Johnston, R. J. and Rossiter, D. J. (1981) Shape and the definition of Parliamentary consitituencies, *Urban Studies,* 18, 219–23.

Johnston, R. J. and Rossiter, D. J. (1982), Constituency building, political representation and electoral bias in urban England, in D. T. Herbert and R. J. Johnston (eds) *Geography and the Urban Environment Volume 5,* Chichester, John Wiley, 113–56.

Johnston, R. J. and Rossiter, D. J. (1983) The definition of Parliamentary constituencies in Great Britain: a computer-based information system, *Journal of the Operational Research Society,* 34, 1079–84.

Johnston, R. J., Rossiter, D. J. and Pattie, C. J. (1996a) How well did they do? The Boundary Commissions at the Third and Fourth Periodical Reviews, in I. McLean and D. Butler (eds) *Fixing the Boundaries: Defining and Redefining Single-Member Electoral Districts,* Aldershot, Dartmouth, 39–86.

Johnston, R. J., Rossiter, D. J. and Pattie, C. J. (1996b) A change in the rules and a change in the outcomes? An evaluation of the work of the Boundary Commission for England in its Third and Fourth Periodic Reviews, *Environment and Planning C: Government and Policy,* 14, 325–50.

Johnston, R. J., Rossiter, D. J. and Pattie, C. J. (1997) The organic or the arithmetic: independent Commissions and the redrawing of the UK's administrative maps, *Regional Studies,* 31, 337–49.

Jones, A. (1972) *The Politics of Reform 1884,* Cambridge, Cambridge University Press.

Jowell, J. and Lester, A. (1987) Beyond Wednesbury: substantive principles of administrative law, *Public Law 1987,* 368–82.

Kavanagh, D. (1995) *Election Campaigning: The New Marketing of Politics,* Oxford, Blackwell.

Kendall, M. G. and Stuart, A. (1950) The law of cubic proportion in election results, *British Journal of Sociology,* 1, 183–96.

Leonard, D. and Natkiel, R. (1987) *The Economist World Atlas of Elections,* London, Hodder & Stoughton.

Lipset, S. M. and Rokkan, S. E. (1967) Cleavage structures, party systems and voter alignments: an introduction, in S. M. Lipset and S. E. Rokkan (eds) *Party Systems and Voter Alignments,* New York, The Free Press, 3–64.

Local Government Board (1905) *Redistribution of Seats: Memorandum by the President of the Local Government Board.,* Cmnd. 2602, London, HMSO.

Local Government Board (1906) *Redistribution of Seats,* London, HMSO.

McLean, I. (1995) Are Scotland and Wales over-represented in the House of Commons?, *The Political Quarterly*, 66, 250–68.

McLean, I. and Mortimore, R. (1992) Apportionment and the Boundary Commission for England, *Electoral Studies*, 11, 293–309.

McLeod, R. (1996a) The Fourth Periodical Review in its context: how the Boundary Commissions for England and Wales approached their task, in I. McLean and D. Butler (eds) *Fixing the Boundaries: Defining and Redefining Single-Member Electoral Districts*, Aldershot, Dartmouth, 87–96.

McLeod, R. (1996b) Distribution of constituencies: the Commissions' attitude to the ratchet effect, in I. McLean and D. Butler (eds) *Fixing the Boundaries: Defining and Redefining Single-Member Electoral Districts*, Aldershot, Dartmouth, 97–118.

Mill, J. S. (1861) *Considerations on Representative Government*, reprinted in 1912, Oxford, Oxford University Press.

Morris, H. L. (1921) *Parliamentary Franchise Reform in England from 1885 to 1918*, New York, Columbia University Press; reprinted in 1969, New York, Ams Press.

Mortimore, R. (1992) *The constituency structure and the Boundary Commission: the rules for the redistribution of seats and their effect on the British electoral system 1950–1987*, D.Phil. thesis, University of Oxford.

Newton, K. (1976) *Second City Politics: Democratic Processes and Decision-Making in Birmingham*, Oxford, Oxford University Press.

Norris, P. (1990) *British By-elections: The Volatile Electorate*, Oxford, Clarendon Press.

Norris, P. and Lovenduski, J. (1995) *Political Recruitment*, Cambridge, Cambridge University Press.

Openshaw, S. (1984) *The Modifiable Area Unit Problem*, Concepts and Techniques in Modern Geography 38, Norwich, Geo Books.

Openshaw, S. and Taylor, P. J. (1979) A million or so correlation coefficients: three experiments on the modifiable area unit problem, in R. J. Bennett, N. J. Thrift and N. Wrigley (eds) *Statistical Applications in the Spatial Sciences*, London, Pion.

Parliamentary Boundary Commission for England (1991) *The Review of Parliamentary Constituencies*, London, Boundary Commission for England.

Parliamentary Representation (1831) *Instructions,* Accounts and Papers, Vol. 36, O39.

Pattie, C. J., Dorling, D., Johnston, R. J. and Rossiter, D. J. (1996) Electoral registration, population mobility and the democratic franchise: the geography of postal votes, overseas voters and missing voters in Great Britain, I*nternational Journal of Population Geography*, 2, 239–59.

Pattie, C. J., Fieldhouse, E. A. and Johnston, R. J. (1994) The price of conscience: the electoral correlates of free votes and rebellions in the British House of Commons, 1987–1992, *British Journal of Political Science*, 24, 359–80.

Pattie, C. J. and Johnston, R. J. (1995) It's not like that round here: region, economic evaluations and voting at the 1992 British General Election, *European Journal of Political Research*, 28, 1–32.

Pattie, C. J., Johnston, R. J., Dorling, D., Rossiter, D. J., Tunstall, H. and MacAllister, I. (1997) New Labour, new geography? The electoral geography of the 1997 British General Election, *Area*, 29, 253–9.

Pattie, C. J., Johnston, R. J. and Fieldhouse, E. A. (1995) Winning the local vote: the effectiveness of constituency campaign spending in Great Britain, *American Political Science Review*, 89, 969–83.

Pattie, C. J., Whiteley, P. F., Johnston, R. J. and Seyd, P. (1994) Measuring local campaign effects: Labour party constituency campaigning at the 1987 General Election, *Political Studies*, 42, 469–79.

Philbin, J. H. (1965) *Parliamentary Representation, 1832, in England and Wales*, New Haven CT, Published Privately.

Pimlott, B. (1985) *Hugh Dalton*, London, Jonathan Cape.

Plant, Lord (1991) *The Plant Report: A Working Party on Electoral Reform*, London, The Guardian.

Plant, Lord (1993) *Report of the Working Party on Electoral Systems*, London, The Labour Party.

Pugh, M. (1978) *Electoral Reform in War and Peace 1906–1918*, London, Routledge & Kegan Paul.

Rallings, C. and Thrasher, M. (1993a) Exploring uniformity and variability in local electoral outcomes: some evidence from English local elections 1985–1991, *Electoral Studies*, 12, 366–84.

Rallings, C. and Thrasher, M. (1993b) *Britain Votes 5: British Parliamentary Election Results 1992*, Aldershot, Dartmouth.

Rallings, C. and Thrasher, M. (1994) The Parliamentary Boundary Commissions: rules, interpretations and politics, *Parliamentary Affairs*, 47, 387–404.

Rallings, C. and Thrasher, M. (1995) *Media Guide to the New Parliamentary Constituencies*, Plymouth, Local Government Chronicle Elections Centre for BBC/ITN/PANews/SkyNews.

Rallings, C., Thrasher, M. and Denver, D. T. (1996) The electoral impact of the new Parliamentary constituency boundaries, in I. McLean and D. Butler (eds), *Fixing The Boundaries: Defining and Redefining Single-Member Electoral Districts*, Aldershot, Dartmouth.

Rawlings, H. F. (1987) The redistribution of Parliamentary seats, *Public Law 1987*, 324–328.

Rawlings, H. F. (1988), *Law and the Electoral Process*, London, Sweet & Maxwell.

Reeve, A. and Ware, A. (1992) *Electoral Systems: A Comparative and Theoretical Introduction*, London, Routledge.

Riddell, P. (1996) *Honest Opportunism: or How We Get the Politicians We Deserve*, 2nd ed, London, Indigo.

Rosenberg, J. (1994) *The Search for Justice*, London, Hodder & Stoughton.

Rossiter, D. J., Johnston, R. J. and Pattie, C. J. (1992) Redistricting London: the issues and likely political effects, *Environment and Planning* A, 24, 1221–30.

Rossiter, D. J., Johnston, R. J. and Pattie, C. J. (1996) Reforming the Act and the procedures, in I. McLean and D. Butler (eds) *Fixing the Boundaries: Defining and Redefining Single-Member Electoral Districts*, Aldershot, Dartmouth, 251–70.

Rossiter, D. J., Johnston, R. J. and Pattie, C. J. (1997a) Estimating the partisan impact of redistricting in Great Britain, *British Journal of Political Science*, 27, 319–31.

Rossiter, D. J., Johnston, R. J. and Pattie, C. J. (1997b) Redistricting and electoral bias in Great Britain, *British Journal of Political Science*, 27, 466–72.

Rossiter, D. J., Johnston, R. J. and Pattie, C. J. (1997c) The evolution and partisan impact of Scottish and Welsh over-representation in the redrawing of British Parliamentary constituencies, *Regional and Federal Studies*, 7, 49–65.

Rossiter, D. J., Johnston, R. J. and Pattie, C. J. (1998) The partisan impacts of non-partisan redistricting: Northern Ireland 1993–1995, *Transactions, Institute of British Geographers*, NS24, 455–80.

Rowley, G. (1975a) The redistribution of Parliamentary seats in the United Kingdom: themes and opinions, *Area*, 7, 15–21.

Rowley, G. (1975b) Parliamentary seat redistribution elaborated, *Area*, 7, 279–81.

Royal Commission on the Constitution (1973) *Volume I Report*, Cmnd. 5460, London, HMSO.

Salisbury, Lord (1884) The value of redistribution: a note on electoral statistics, *The National Review*, 4, 145–62.

Sanders, D. (1996) Economic performance, management competence and the outcome of the next General Election, *Political Studies*, 44, 227–38.

Scammell, M. (1995) *Designer Politics: How Elections Are Won*, London, Macmillan.

Seymour, C. (1915) *Electoral Reform in England and Wales: The Development and Operation of the Parliamentary Franchise 1832-1885*, New Haven CT, Yale University Press; reprinted by David & Charles, Newton Abbot, 1970.

Shaw, E. (1994) *The Labour Party since 1979: Crisis and Transformation*, London, Routledge.

Shepherd, R. (1997) *Enoch Powell: A Biography*, London, Pimlico.

Smith, F. B. (1966) *The Making of the Second Reform Bill*, Cambridge, Cambridge University Press.

Smith, J. and McLean, I. (1994) The poll tax and the electoral register, in A. Heath, R. Jowell and J. Curtice (eds) *Labour's Last Chance? The 1992 Election and Beyond*, Aldershot, Dartmouth.

Smith, S. (1993) *Electoral Registration in 1991*, London, OPCS.

Speaker (1944) Conference on Electoral Reform and Redistribution of Seats: Letter from Mr. Speaker to the Prime Minister, Cmnd. 6534, London, HMSO.

Speaker (1978) *Conference on Electoral Law*, Cmnd. 7110, London, HMSO.

Speaker's Conference (1977) *Mr. Speaker's Conference on Electoral Law: Minutes of Evidence*, Cmnd. 70–ii, London, HMSO.

Steed, M. (1969) Callaghan's gerrymandering, *New Society*, 26 June 1969, 996–7.

Taagepera, R. and Shugart, M. S. (1989) *Seats and Votes: The Effects and Determinants of Electoral Systems*, New Haven CT, Yale University Press.

Taylor, P. J. and Johnston, R. J. (1979) *Geography of Elections*, London, Penguin Books.

Vivian Committee (1942) *Report of the Committee on Electoral Machinery*, Cmnd. 6408, London, HMSO.

Waller, R. J. (1983) The 1983 Boundary Commission: policies and effects, *Electoral Studies*, 2, 195–206.

Westminster Communications Group (1993) *Who Gains? Analysing the Political Implications of the 1994 Boundary Commission Review*, London, Westminster Communications Group.

Whiteley, P. F. and Seyd, P. (1994) Local party campaigning and electoral mobilisation in Britain, *The Journal of Politics*, 56, 242–52.

Williams, G. (ed.) (1993) *John Stuart Mill: Utilitarianism, On Liberty, Considerations on Representative Government*, London, The Everyman Library.

Wilson, H. (1974) *The Labour Government 1964–1970: A Personal Record*, London, Penguin Books.

Wood, P. and Norton, P. (1992) Do candidates matter? Constituency-specific changes for incumbent MPs, 1983–1987, *Political Studies*, 40, 227–38.

Wraith, R. E. and Lamb, G. B. (1971) *Public Inquiries as an Instrument of Government*, London, Allen & Unwin.

Wright, T. (1994) *Citizens and Subjects*, London, Routledge.

Index